sociology

a critical introduction

SUPPLEMENTARY MATERIAL

Study Guide
0-17-604916-9

Instructor's Manual
0-17-604919-3

Test Bank
0-17-605561-4

Computerized Test Bank
0-17-605562-2

sociology

a critical introduction

karen l. anderson

york university

Nelson Canada

I(T)P An International Thomson Publishing Company

Toronto • Albany • Bonn • Boston • Cincinnati • Detroit • London • Madrid • Melbourne
Mexico City • New York • Pacific Grove • Paris • San Francisco • Singapore • Tokyo • Washington

I(T)P™
International Thomson Publishing
The ITP logo is a trademark under licence

© Nelson Canada
A division of Thomson Canada Limited, 1996

Published in 1996 by
Nelson Canada
A division of Thomson Canada Limited
1120 Birchmount Road
Scarborough, Ontario M1K 5G4

Canadian Cataloguing in Publication Data

Anderson, Karen L.
    Sociology : a critical introduction

Includes bibliographical references and index.
ISBN 0-17-603539-7

1. Sociology.   I. Title.

HM51.A54   1995   301   C95-931797-X

Acquisitions Editor	Charlotte Forbes
Senior Editor	Rosalyn Steiner
Senior Production Coordinator	Carol Tong
Managing Editor	Margot Hanis
Art Director	Liz Harasymczuk
Cover Design	Stuart Knox
Interior Design	Katharine Lapins
Cover Photograph	© Maria Taglienti/The Image Bank
Senior Composition Analyst	Suzanne Peden
Input Operator	Elaine Andrews

Printed and bound in Canada

1 2 3 4 5 (BBM) 99 98 97 96 95

CONTENTS

∎∎∎

PREFACE

■■■

Although I have provided students with a review of what constitutes the discipline of sociology—its founders, its theoretical and methodological perspectives, its various "fields" of inquiry—I have another, quite different objective in writing this introduction to sociology. The objective foremost on my agenda has been to provide students with the tools they will need to become critical thinkers. I believe critical thinking skills are a requirement for all sociologists. Any introduction to the discipline should also introduce beginners to those skills.

For my part, it has been a challenge to meet these two objectives: to provide students with a foundational repertoire of what constitutes the discipline while, at the same time, to provide them with the tools to assess critically the very things to which they are being introduced. How does one give students a sense of the historical and contemporary iterations of the discipline, and provide them with the tools to assess each statement, theory, and method they are being presented with?

In trying to accomplish this task, I have drawn on a wide range of writings by sociologists and nonsociologists alike. Many of the examples I have used to illustrate points throughout the various chapters have been drawn from historical as well as cross-cultural events, contexts, and experiences. I have deliberately done so to provide students with a sense of the rich variety of experience available, and to underscore the ways in which those experiences are shaped and constructed by the social world in which people live at any given time.

The message I hope to convey throughout this textbook is "nothing about human behaviour is inevitable," and, in the same vein, "the future is yet to be invented." I hope that my approach to introducing sociology to beginning students will provide them with some of the tools they need to become more active participants in their own learning. That is my ultimate objective.

ACKNOWLEDGMENTS
∎∎∎

This book could not have been written without the help of many people, and I would like to thank them here. One person in particular, Gary Woodill, deserves special thanks. Gary read and commented on each draft of the manuscript and assisted in the writing of three chapters—Chapter 9 on research methods, Chapter 17 on disability, and Chapter 20 on social relations in cyberspace. His help and support greatly contributed to the final shape that this book has taken.

That I undertook to write this introduction to sociology at all is due to the encouragement of Jim Rozsa, then college representative for Nelson Canada. Jim listened to me express my concerns about the failure of most introductory sociology texts to provide students with tools for making their own critical analyses of society, and then suggested I write a textbook of my own. Charlotte Forbes, acquisition editor, was there from the beginning and offered much needed encouragement. Maryrose O'Neill worked with me during a crucial, formative part of this project. I want to thank her for her enthusiasm; I could not have asked for a better developmental editor. Rosalyn Steiner's task of copy editing was carried out with humour and grace, making one of my least favoured chores much more palatable. The manuscript of this work was reviewed at various stages of its development by a great number of my peers across Canada, and I wish to thank those who shared their insights and their constructive criticism. Among them are Dawn Currie, University of British Columbia; Susan Edwards, Laurentian University; Charles Gordon, Carleton University; John Goyder, University of Waterloo; Roberta Hamilton, Queen's University; Colm Kelly, St. Thomas University; Graham Knight, McMaster University; and Keith Preston, University of British Columbia.

As I point out repeatedly in the text, sociology is a social construction influenced by the history, culture, class, and gender of a given sociologist. This book is no exception, for which I take full responsibility.

part 1

I begin this introduction to sociology with a close look at what constitutes knowledge about the world we live in and how a critical stance toward knowledge production might be applied to the study of society. The entirety of this book, in fact, constitutes an extended explication of the proposition that all knowledge, all understanding, is based on our experiences and invariably reflects some point of view. But the "constructedness" of knowledge is, for the most part, invisible. As we live our daily lives, few of us recognize that our world view (the way we understand everything that we experience in the world) is not "natural" or common to all human beings. Our own world view makes such good sense to us because everything we see through it appears to be a perfectly reasonable reflection of "the way things really are."

Many chapters in this book take either a historical or crosscultural perspective in presenting content about a specific topic. This is deliberately done in order to point out the extent to which the knowledge constructs we use to interpret our everyday world are ordinarily invisible to us and vary across place, time, and culture. The historical and crosscultural examples I have chosen are intended to illustrate how different people, in different societies or historical periods, have held varying views on all aspects of human social behaviour. Not only are wildly different views possible, but the sense of logic that is used to construct and support those views differs from the ones most Westerners are familiar with today.

By asking you to consider both crosscultural and historical examples, I wish to give you a basis from which to develop an appreciation of the social, cultural, and historical specificity of your present way of understanding your own and others' behaviours. I also hope to provide you with a way of understanding that the knowledge you now have about the social world you live in, including knowledge about all forms of social interaction and social practices, is neither inevitable nor shared by everyone.

SOCIOLOGY—AN INTRODUCTION
■ ■ ■

CHAPTER 1

SOCIOLOGY: STUDYING CHANGE AND UNCERTAINTY

CHAPTER OPENING QUESTIONS

- What does it mean to say that knowledge is "socially constructed" or "socially produced"?

- What value does critical thinking bring to everyday life?

- If "taken-for-granted" understandings serve us so well in our daily lives, why would we want to question them or subject them to critical scrutiny?

- How do historical and crosscultural perspectives help us question our taken-for-granted knowledge?

If we could use just two words to describe the social climate we live in today, those two words would have to be "change" and "uncertainty." In the last decade or so, we have seen the enormous growth in computer-based technology and information processing. The generation of "artificial intelligence" systems is no longer astonishing but rather appears to be commonplace. Moreover, the political map of the world has changed recently with the demise of many communist states in Eastern Europe, including the break up of the former Soviet Union and the reunification of East and West Germany.

All of this change and uncertainty might lead us to believe that we are living in unique and turbulent times. But concern about social, economic, political, cultural, religious, and personal changes has played a major role in the life experiences of most people living in industrialized, Western societies at least since the end of the eighteenth century. The discipline of sociology, which is the subject matter of this book, emerged between the French Revolution (1789) and the end of the First World War (1918), both as part of and as a response to those changes.

At the end of the eighteenth century, most Europeans and North Americans had no formal education and lived in largely rural, isolated areas. On both continents, the majority was without any organizational affiliation; few unions or professional organizations and few mass-based political parties

A crowded London street in 1872. Sociology emerged as an academic discipline at at time when thinkers tried to make sense of the rapid and disruptive changes that were taking place in society.

existed. Except to collect taxes, form an army, or prosecute criminals, state governments mostly ignored their citizens.

By the beginning of the twentieth century, just over a century later, enormous social, political, and economic changes were taking place. Mass education was introduced on both continents. Rural peasants became urban labourers, and distinctions between individuals based solely on birth were replaced by the ideals of popular democracy: equality before the law and equality in rights. Individuals were joining unions or trade organizations. Increasingly, they were being closely supervised in most aspects of their lives by government and non-government agencies alike (Ashley and Orenstein 1990, 1–2). Within less than 150 years, both Europeans and North Americans went from living in societies with weak central governments, where remnants of feudalism still permeated their daily lives, to living in modern, bureaucratically organized nation states. Figure 1-1 illustrates some of the important changes that have occurred in Western societies since the end of the eighteenth century.

Sociology emerged as an academic discipline because of the attempts of several social thinkers to make sense of these extraordinary changes. **Sociology** can be defined broadly as the study of all human social experience, whether that experience is a chance encounter between two individuals, the outcome of the activities of some highly structured social group, or the result of a worldwide social phenomenon. In its broadest application, sociology is an interpretation of, or commentary on, the social experiences that sociologists share with members of the wider society.

As we will see in Chapter 12, early sociologists identified many social problems that arose out of the Industrial Revolution. Alienation, loneliness, social disorganization, secularization and the decline of religious values and practices, inequalities, class conflict, and societal conflict in general were all cited as problems directly produced by the rapid social upheaval that accompanied the Industrial Revolution.

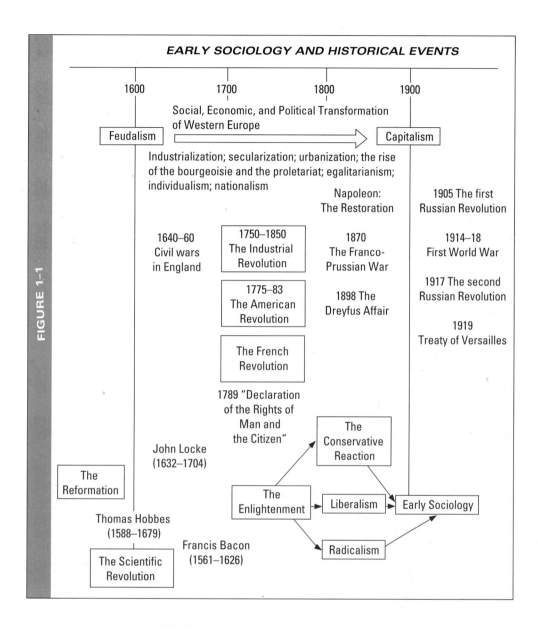

FIGURE 1-1

EARLY SOCIOLOGY AND HISTORICAL EVENTS

Today, sociologists continue to be concerned with many of the same issues that occupied the attention of the founders of the discipline.

WHAT DO SOCIOLOGISTS STUDY?

Sociologists study everything from such seemingly personal matters as love, sexual preferences, organization of family life and child-care practices, to large-scale social issues such as the way in which nation states govern their citizens and the globalizing effects of international financial capital. A sociologist is "intensively, endlessly, shamelessly" interested in "the infinite riches of human conduct." Nothing is "too sacred" or "too distasteful" or "too commonplace" and mundane for investigation (Berger 1963).

Sociologists often make a distinction between **macrolevel** and **microlevel** orientations in sociological analyses. Microlevel orientations focus on individuals and their interrelations, especially on the face-to-face interactions that occur between individuals in specific social settings. For example, a sociologist with a microlevel orientation might be interested in how racism or prejudice is expressed between two or more social actors. That sociologist might also study how poverty affects the lives of individuals.

By contrast, a sociologist with a macrolevel orientation studies and interprets large-scale social phenomena that affect society as a whole. A sociologist interested in macrolevel issues might look at the ways in which racism and prejudice are institutionalized in society today. Or the focus might be on the rise and development of capitalism and the effects this form of social organization has had on the creation of a class of impoverished and/or unemployed persons.

Few if any sociologists would claim to be expert in all aspects of human social interaction in all possible settings. Rather, sociologists tend to specialize in one or more fields of study. A recent undergraduate calendar from a large Ontario university indicates a wide range of fields of study in sociology, including course offerings in the following areas: urban life, education, gender relations, deviance, the family, ethnicity and race, religion, work and occupations, health and illness, social class, social change, and social movements. As well, some sociologists specialize in devising theories of society, while others specialize in refining the methods by which social research is carried out. This is by no means a complete list of everything that makes up the discipline of sociology. But it does give some indication of the wide variety of fields that sociologists might study.

Sociologists study everything from individual relationships to issues such as the consequences of the breakup of the Soviet Union.

THE SOCIAL CONSTRUCTIONIST PERSPECTIVE

While there is much that separates sociologists in terms of theoretical perspective and substantive research interests, contemporary sociologists do share the common conviction that all human interactions and activities are shaped by social experience. Most sociologists start from the premise that the people they study have already been "socialized" into or shaped by a particular culture and society. They adopt a **social constructionist perspective:** human experiences are socially constructed; those experiences are social accomplishments or artifices. Some sociologists go even further to argue that, because experience is the product of social interaction, all interpretations of, or knowledge about, those experiences are open to questions and challenges (Bauman 1992, 87).

Seen from this perspective, sociology as a discipline is both conservative and potentially subversive. On the one hand, sociologists are concerned with defining and describing human existence as it is experienced in a given society at a particular point of time. On the other hand, many sociologists recognize that whatever members of a given society experience, those experiences are socially constructed or contingent and are therefore capable of being challenged and changed.

FIGURE 1-2

THE TWO FACES OF SOCIOLOGY

Conservative	Subversive
Sociology defines and describes human existence as it is experienced in a given society.	Sociology recognizes that how we experience and understand our lives is socially constructed. Because of this, all understandings and ways of living in the world are capable of being challenged and changed.

CRITICAL THINKING

In keeping with the conservative and subversive nature of the discipline, I have two objectives in writing this book. The first is conservative: to introduce beginning sociology students to the discipline of sociology. Who are the most influential sociologists in the past and today? What are the major theoretical perspectives on, or approaches to, the study of human social interaction? What kinds of social interaction and social issues do sociologists study? What insights into the human condition can such a study provide? These and other similar issues are addressed throughout this text.

My second objective is to introduce students to **critical thinking.** This objective has much more to do with the subversive side of sociology. It is shaped by my conviction that learning should lead to a change or transformation of consciousness. Because sociologists accept that the reality we experience on a day-to-day basis is not inevitable, natural, or universal, but rather is a product of social life, sociology is a discipline in which it is possible (even mandatory) to cultivate a reflective or critical state of mind. I call this reflective state of mind the capacity for critical thinking.

Critical thinking is the ability to reflect upon yourself, your social world, and the beliefs you hold about that world, and to report on what you find. As a critical thinker you must set aside the premise that the "real" world you (and other members of your community) inhabit contains the same elements and is experienced in the same way as the "real" world of other communities. The emphasis I place on critical thinking means that rather than focusing on communicating a body of knowledge to you, I have focused on helping you develop critical-thinking skills that you can apply outside the classroom. While this text certainly contains information that can be learned, I have shifted the focus from the information itself to helping you acquire the tools necessary to understand how information and knowledge about the world we live in is produced. An important part of understanding how social knowledge is created is realizing that social practices and the ideas and understanding we hold about them are never produced "once and forever," but rather are moving, fluid, and transforming (Vygotsky 1978). Moreover, because all knowledge is ultimately aimed at another person, it is primarily a means of establishing social relations. I believe that knowledge is always in the process of being constructed and communicated.

Becoming a critical thinker can help you take fresh approaches to familiar, taken-for-granted beliefs and understandings. It allows you to cast your explanatory net widely. Yet there are shortcomings and pitfalls to be aware of. By its very nature, all of critical thinking produces tentative and temporary solutions and explanations. Here lies both its greatest strength and weakness. Taking a critical perspective and engaging in critical thinking can be a liberating experience. It can also be marked by an all-dissolving destructiveness (Bauman 1992, viii). In becoming critical thinkers, we come face to face with Dostoyevsky's warning that if there is no God, everything is permissible. Émile Durkheim, one of the nineteenth-century founders of sociology, secularized Dostoyevsky's warning by replacing "God" with "society." For Durkheim, if the controlling grip of widely accepted societal customs, beliefs, and values were to be undermined, then the entire moral order of society would collapse (ibid., xvii).

In the face of these dire predictions, why then do we not just leave well enough alone and drop the concern about critical thinking? Along with Zygmut Bauman, I am convinced that our age requires that we not only recognize the right of others to be different from ourselves, but also that we enter into friendly conversations with them. The kinds of societal changes that we have experienced in the late twentieth century make it necessary for us to be able to accept that there are different, but equivalent, ways of producing knowledge about the world. To engage in such conversations with others is an ethical and moral choice that I am convinced must be made. Critical thinking provides an intellectual orientation that supports open exchanges with "others."

Throughout this text, therefore, I deliberately convey the understanding that knowledge is not obviously either right or wrong, that questions don't always have a single valid response, and that authority figures do not necessarily have the best answers or the best ways of discerning an answer. At the same time, however, I have taken care to point out that not all views are equal, not all answers are either useful or worthwhile, and not all positions should be equally accommodated. I do take a strong stand against racism, sexism, and homophobia. But I hope that you develop the realization that the views you hold are only some among many and that an attitude of curiosity toward other views is basic to your own intellectual growth.

EXPLORING TAKEN-FOR-GRANTED BELIEFS

As a discipline, sociology upholds the proposition that human interaction is socially based and systematically organized. This proposition is potentially useful to all of us because it supports critical thinking about our own lives and the society we live in, as well as about other societies distinct from our own. But sociological findings arrived at via critical thinking often disturb and even challenge the everyday or **taken-for-granted** beliefs that most members of Western society share about themselves and the world they inhabit. Taken-for-granted beliefs and assumptions are based on immediate experiences and are rarely, if ever, reflected upon or reasoned out. The ancient Greeks called these shared beliefs, customs, and traditions *nomi* or laws. Norms constitute the foundational traditions and values of a given society or culture. These may be written or unwritten. They are primal beliefs and understandings shared by the society's members concerning right and wrong. Ideas based on critical thinking and those based on taken-for-granted beliefs are compared in Table 1-1.

INDIVIDUALISM

For most Westerners, individualism, defined as the right of each societal member to be satisfied, serves as a kind of lens through which most other beliefs are evaluated. This taken-for-granted belief in individualism operates in much the same way as a mathematical theorem: it acts as a rule that substitutes for direct evidence. Thus, in Western societies, individualism is not a proposition that must be supported by evidence and proofs; it is something most people consider to be self-evidently true. Yet, critically motivated research into the concept suggests that this was not always the case. Contrary to everyday understandings, individualism has not always been universally understood as a natural and therefore highly desirable state of human affairs.

When we consider the writings of sixteenth- and seventeenth-century social theorists such as Thomas Hobbes, John Locke, and Machiavelli, all of whom contributed to the development of our concept of individualism, and we compare their work to that of authors from antiquity, we begin to understand the problematic origins of our modern understanding of this concept. Hobbes, Locke, and Machiavelli were among the first Western writers to argue in favour of individualism. But they did so in explicit opposition to the writings of philosophers of classical antiquity, whose ideas up to that point had dominated Western philosophy. Today, propositions about individualism that Hobbes, Locke, and Machiavelli all favoured have become part of our taken-for-granted frame of reference and no longer appear in need of defence. Thus a concept that was once hotly contested has become part of our belief system. If we take the time to inquire into the

11

	TAKEN-FOR-GRANTED BELIEFS	CRITICAL THINKING
TABLE 1-1	1. Such beliefs are based on shared values, norms, customs, and traditions in a given society.	1. Critical thinking calls into question the shared values, norms, customs, and traditions of a given society.
	These primal beliefs are basic and beyond questioning.	All beliefs can and should be questioned.
	2. Shared values, norms, customs, and traditions are rarely, if ever, reasoned out or reflected upon.	2. The social world and the individual's relation to it are reflected upon.
	3. Ideas, social practices, and customs are viewed as foundational, firmly established, and slow to change.	3. Ideas, social practices, and customs are seen as fluid and transforming.
	4. They result in definitive solutions and explanations.	4. Critical thinking produces tentative and temporary solutions and explanations.
	5. These provide an intellectual orientation that sees "others" as different from, and less desirable than "insiders."	5. Critical thinking provides an orientation that supports open exchange with others.
	6. These beliefs are based on the premise that the social world and everything in it is "naturally occurring."	6. Critical thinking is based on the premise that all knowledge is a social product.

history of other examples of our society's most cherished taken-for-granted beliefs and understandings, a new and potentially critical standpoint from which to question them emerges. Often, taking a fresh viewpoint, such as one provided by a historical or a cross-cultural perspective, allows us to begin thinking in new ways about the everyday beliefs and norms that we use to make sense of our lives.

RACIAL PREJUDICE

Canadians pride themselves on their tolerance and lack of prejudice. But we do not need to look very far into our history to find examples of taken-for-granted understandings that have led to discriminatory and prejudicial treatment. Some segments of the population have been classified as undesirable and thus as unwanted or undeserving outsiders. The treatment of Native peoples in Canada is a familiar example. Less familiar, perhaps, is the example of non-European immigrants to Canada. As Figure 1-3 shows, until the

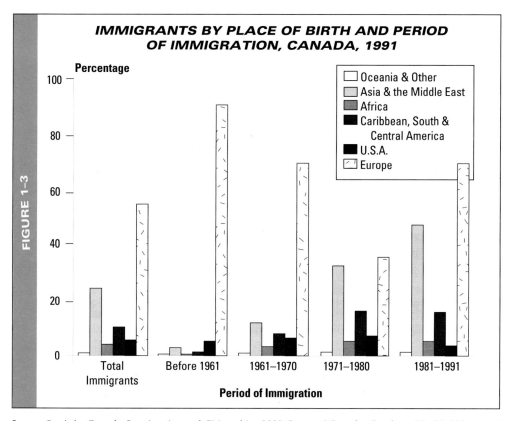

FIGURE 1-3

Source: Statistics Canada, Immigration and Citizenship. *1991 Census of Canada, Catalogue No. 93–316.*

1960s, Europeans made up well over 90 percent of all immigrants to Canada. This fell to 64 percent between 1961 and 1970 and to 36 percent between 1971 and 1980. Between 1981 and 1991 less than 25 percent of those immigrating to Canada were Europeans.

While well over 90 percent of persons immigrating to Canada during the late nineteenth- and early-twentieth centuries were European, the Canadian government also promoted the immigration of a relatively small number of Asian labourers. These men, mostly Chinese, worked on the construction of the transcontinental railway. But the arrival of even a few Chinese-born labourers disturbed many European-born citizens.

The decision to bring in Chinese workers to build the rail lines in British Columbia was made by Prime Minister Sir John A. Macdonald, over the emphatic opposition of the people of that province. To make his decision more acceptable, Macdonald conceded that Chinese immigrants would reside in British Columbia only temporarily. In the debates of the House of Commons, Macdonald reassured Canadians that they need have "...no fear of a permanent degradation of the country by a mongrel race" (Debates 1883, 1905). Concern about the "non-assimilating race," as these immigrants were called, was widespread among Canadians. For example, in a submission made to the Royal Commission on Chinese Immigration, 1885, members of organized labour maintained:

13

Chinese labourers, brought to Canada in the late nineteenth century to build the railway, were subjected to government discrimination policies.

They [the Chinese] are thus fitted to become all too dangerous competitors in the labour market, while their docile servility, the natural outcome of centuries of grinding poverty and humble submission to a most oppressive system of government renders them doubly dangerous as the willing tools whereby grasping and tyrannical employers grind down all labour to the lowest living point.

While today these views are not tolerated in public statements, nonetheless private sentiments similar to these continue to form part of the taken-for-granted understanding of a number of Canadians. For example, in Canada in 1993, a turbaned Sikh was prevented from entering a Legion Hall in Surrey, British Columbia, to celebrate a commemorative service. The stated reason for refusing to admit the man was that he was wearing a head covering, something that is explicitly prohibited by Legion rules. Legion members are expected to enter Legion premises with bare heads as a means of showing honour to the Queen and to those who have fallen in war. But practising Sikhs, who fought alongside Canadian soldiers in the Second World War, must wear their turbans as a sign of religious commitment.

In the ensuing debate over the refusal to allow turbaned Sikhs to enter Legion premises, some disturbing evidence emerged. Members of the same Legions who had voted against allowing their turban-wearing comrades into the Hall had no problem with other members wearing more Westernized headgear, such as baseball caps.

Often, then, taken-for-granted understandings are prejudicial and reflect deeply felt fears and biases harboured by some (or most) members of society against "others." These others might even be members of the same society but are considered to be sufficiently different from, or inferior to, the real insiders to warrant differential treatment. Or the others might be members of another society who are perceived as undesirable or as a threat to that society's quality of life. Taking a critical approach allows us to reveal what those prejudices are.

WARFARE

One widely held, taken-for-granted understanding of warfare is that aggression is part of human nature (i.e., the urge to be aggressive is part of our genetic makeup, and so acts of human aggression are, in fact, instinctual). From this perspective, warfare is simply an outlet for the natural, genetically programmed aggression that all men (and, to a lesser extent, women) have. Taken-for-granted thinking would thus have us believe that biologically based human aggression, and the need to find an outlet for that aggression, is a perfectly reasonable explanation for the actions of the American and former Soviet governments in their race to build up nuclear arsenals. Once we begin thinking critically and make some crosscultural and historical comparisons, we quickly discover that while most human societies have engaged in some kind of warfare, it is only within the second half of the twentieth century that certain societies have developed the technical capacity to annihilate the entire population of the planet.

If we cannot attribute the fighting of wars and the preparation for fighting those wars directly to genetically programmed human aggressiveness, how might we critically explain the defence spending of the United States and the former Soviet Union in the second half of the twentieth century? While it has become clear that the risks of a nuclear confrontation in the next few years between the Americans and the Russians have become quite remote,

In an army of conscripts, an ordinary man must be persuaded to kill. For the vast majority, killing has to be taught.

American military strategists and those in the various nations that formerly made up the Soviet Union continue to find reasons to maintain high levels of military spending. Commenting on this state of affairs, Dr. Helen Caldicott, the Australian physician who has devoted her life to studying and speaking about the horrors of nuclear war, writes: "Ours is a world of nuclear giants and ethical infants. We know more about war than we do about peace. We know more about killing than we do about living" (1984, 31). Caldicott's appraisal of the policies of the United States and the former Soviet Union is chilling, and her challenge to our common-sense understanding about warfare appears to be borne out by a great deal of evidence.

Even though individual soldiers might be able to give vent to feelings of aggression on the battlefield, the actual mounting and carrying out of a battle has little to do with aggressive "instincts." Anyone who has participated in boot-camp training knows that soldiers must be trained to kill. The new recruits' attitudes toward indiscriminate killing has to be greatly altered before they are ready to go into battle. As Canadian war historian Gwynne Dyer has noted:

> The business of armies, at the end, is killing, and so a crucial part of training people to be soldiers is teaching them to ignore the limits they normally place on the actual use of violence, so that in the right circumstances against the "enemy," they will go all the way and actually kill him. For the vast majority of people, killing has to be taught—though there are exceptions. There is such a thing as a "natural soldier"; the kind of man who derives his greatest satisfaction from male companionship, from excitement, and from the conquering of physical and psychological obstacles. He doesn't necessarily want to kill people as such, but he will have no objections if it occurs within a moral framework which gives him a justification—like war—and if it is the price of gaining admission to the kind of environment he craves....But armies are not full of such men. They are so rare that they form only a modest fraction even of small professional armies, mostly congregating in the commando-type paid forces. In large conscript armies they virtually disappear beneath the weight of numbers of more ordinary men. And it is those ordinary men, who do not like combat at all, that the armies must persuade to kill (1985).

NOTIONS OF LOVE

Some of the most deeply rooted taken-for-granted beliefs held by North Americans concern their personal experiences. Consider the following proposition: Romantic love is a natural, possibly instinctual part of the human makeup. It is found in all societies, and throughout all of human history.

But is this the case? Certainly, most North Americans and Europeans expect to fall in love at least once in their lives. They also expect to subsequently set up house with their loved one and to find emotional and sexual satisfaction with that person. While most North Americans are privately sceptical that love will last forever, most nevertheless tend to hold strongly to the conviction that falling in love is a natural and universal experience. Yet the experience of falling in love and the expectations that go with it are not as widespread as most North Americans believe. In many societies, decisions about when and whom to marry are rarely left up to the individuals involved, who often have very little say in the matter. In countries such as India, marriage is considered too important to be left to the whims of the individual. The majority of marriages in that country are arranged by parents and other relatives. Romantic love, while recognized, is considered a temporary infatuation and a barrier to a happy marriage.

Even in Western cultures, romantic love has not always been experienced as it is today. Two movements concerning love—courtly love and romanticism—have influenced our present-day practices. According to Ann Swidler (1980), the cultural ideal of courtly love in

Styles of love and marriage change over time; in the fourteenth century, noble marriages were formal contracts validated by religion and embraced by society.

Western societies can be traced back to the twelfth century. Heralded by the troubadours of the time, this tradition was begun in medieval France, linked to the courage of the knight in his quest for moral heroism and for the love of his chosen lady. The practice of courtly love was complex and focused not on the actual relationship, but on a complicated, mutual idealization between two people who rarely had any contact with each other. Unlike the Church's conception of love, which it challenged, courtly love promoted the ideal that, under certain highly codified circumstances, sexual love between a man and a woman was well worth striving for. Moreover, sexual love between a man and a woman could be ennobling for both (and not degrading as the Church insisted).

But the expression of that ideal love was encumbered by an elaborate system of ethical and aesthetic rules connected with ideals of courtesy and courtship and decidedly not with marriage. It was a widely accepted belief that one could never love a marriage partner. Instead love was an intense, passionate relationship, a holy unity between one man and one woman who never married and who rarely had any contact. In the ideal situation, a gallant knight performed heroic deeds to win and keep the love of his lady to whom he rendered years of faithful service. At the same time, this gallant knight was most likely married (as the lady herself usually was), had several children, and numerous sexual affairs. Although sexual contact between the two was permitted in some geographical areas of Europe, the relationship often went unconsummated, guided by rules of decorum and the pursuit of ideal, not sexual, love (Hendrick and Hendrick 1992, 38–39).

Around the late eighteenth century a new movement emerged called romanticism. With it came an emphasis on the feeling of love, as opposed to the emphasis on correct and decorous behaviour, which had characterized courtly love. Sexual love also emerged as a state that all men and women, regardless of class origin, could strive for. According to I. Singer, romantic love in this period came to mean

...oneness with an alter ego, one's other self, a man or woman who would make up one's deficiencies, respond to one's deepest inclinations, and serve as possibly the only person with whom one could communicate fully. If the world were properly attuned to the value of love, this would be the person one married, establishing a bond that was permanent as well as ecstatically consummatory. The sexual bond would participate in a social order constructed out of loving relationships that united all people to one another and mankind to nature as a whole (1987, 4).

17

During the Victorian era, from the second or third decade of the nineteenth century to the early part of the twentieth century, a progressive devaluation of the worth of women took place. Men became paid wage workers, and women, confined to the home, were considered weak and in great need of men's protection and economic support. Women were also thought to be of a delicate constitution with minds not quite able to stand up to the rigours of a great deal of education. Women became the weaker sex—nurturing, tender, made solely for childbearing and rearing.

Extensive changes in the ideals of love resulted from this devaluation of women. One ideal to emerge was that women were, by virtue of their delicate natures, disinclined toward sex. Their role was to resist prior to marriage and then after marriage to succumb to the sexual advances of their husbands. Men, on the other hand, were viewed as being charged with sexuality. Their role was to take the lead, to woo their intended, and to persuade her to submit. Summing up love in the Victorian era, Hendrick and Hendrick write:

> It is perhaps difficult for us to imagine today the limits within which couples lived in the Victorian era, with respect to their sexuality and feelings of love they experienced for each other. It appears that in addition to the hardness of life in simply earning a living there was poverty of the spirit in terms of people's ability to communicate their most intimate desires and needs to each other....These conditions of the Victorian era, the disjunction between communication about love and sex and the ongoing natural desires of men and women, set the conditions for the creation of sexual dysfunctions and disorders of love and desire that opened the twentieth century (1992, 42–43).

By about 1880, romantic love had become even more romantic; the common view of love was that it was a strong magnet pulling together two people who were "just made for each other." The customs of courtship had become quite formal. Young women and men of good breeding, meaning of middle- or upper-class backgrounds, were not to speak to each other until formal introductions had been made (Waller 1951). Once that happened, the mother of the young lady was then at liberty to invite the young gentleman to call on her daughter. Later the young lady herself could extend an invitation (Bailey 1988). In this era, most courtship took place in the home of the young woman, and sexual restraint was important. In spite of this, sex and marriage were strongly connected and sexual fulfilment in marriage was the ideal. As well, outside of the genteel parlours of the middle and upper classes, a great deal of sexual behaviour that did not meet the cultural ideals was already happening.

According to American sociologist L.M. Terman, who published his findings in 1938, while 87 percent of women born before 1890 were virgins at marriage, only 30 percent of those born after 1910, and prior to publication of his study, "waited until marriage." By the first decade of the twentieth century, a virtuous woman was one who had sex only with the man she was going to marry (Cate and Lloyd 1992, 22). By 1920, dating, the main focus of the North American courtship system, was in place. Dating—the informal, unchaperoned interaction between a couple with no specific commitment to each other—followed rules established by local peer groups. The rise of dating has been

Elizabeth Taylor and Fernando Lamas in The Girl Who Had Everything *typified the 1950s ideals of romance and courtship.*

attributed to a variety of cultural phenomena and events, including the creation of adolescence as a distinct period in the life cycle, the rise of mass culture, the emancipation of women, widespread ownership of cars, motion pictures, and the decline of the community as a means of social control.

Dating meant spending money, and this in turn shifted the locus of power out of the hands of the young woman and her mother and into the hands of the young man himself. With the introduction of dating as the courtship ritual of preference, a young woman (or her mother) could no longer expect to be able to invite a young man to call on her in the family's front parlour (Bailey 1988). Ideally, dating led to a steady relationship between a man and woman, with the women still expected to exercise sexual control and the man expected to pay for all expenses. At the same time romantic love remained the only basis on which to marry. Mate selection, in popular ideology at least, continued to rest on the presence of a mysterious attraction felt between two people destined to spend their lives together.

Although the particulars involved in the rating and dating system of the first half of the twentieth century have changed as we approach the twenty-first century, the cultural ideal that love is the most important factor in mate selection continues to be

In the film Sleepless in Seattle, *Tom Hanks, Meg Ryan, and Ross Malinger reflect the romantic ideals of the 1990s.*

emphasized. Coontz (1988) has pointed out that the importance of love in mate selection has even increased during this century. According to her, "The degree of emotional satisfaction…demanded from husband-wife…relations in the twentieth century would have astounded previous generations" (356).

Today, popular literature, including a plethora of articles in women's magazines, emphasizes "finding and keeping a man," often through the use of what might euphemistically be called the "wiles of femininity" (Cate and Lloyd 1992, 31). According to them (1992), "The vision of the perfect relationship now emphasizes the importance of balancing togetherness and individuality, other-orientation and self-fulfillment, and communicating openly while protecting the partner's feelings" (31). Meanwhile, the ever-present threat of AIDS has caused a rethinking of the free-love ideals promoted by the hippie generation of the 1960s. A strong cultural emphasis is re-emerging on chastity and lifelong monogamous relations between a couple who are forever in love with each other.

By exercising our critical-thinking facilities to trace out the wildly different ways that love in its various courtly and romantic guises has been expressed and experienced over the past eight centuries, we can gain a new perspective on our own "romantic" experiences today. Instead of being a natural outcome of the human condition, romantic love appears to be a socially constructed and culturally mitigated experience. As difficult as it might be to accept, the way we fall in love, the emotions we feel, the person we choose to be the object of our affection (and desire), and even the ways we choose to express our most intimate feelings are all socially mediated and shaped.

■ ■ ■

SUMMARY

Since its inception at the end of the eighteenth century during the Industrial Revolution, the discipline of sociology has focused on explaining and interpreting the changes and uncertainty that have been a consistent part of the lives of Western Europeans and North Americans. Sociologists today continue to be concerned with many of the same issues that occupied the attention of the founders of the discipline, such as rapid social changes, economic inequalities, and feelings of separation from one's fellow men and women. But sociologists also study a wide variety of other topics—everything from interpersonal issues, such as love and sexual preference, to large-scale social concerns about the causes of poverty or the globalization of the economy.

In this chapter I introduced critical thinking as a powerful tool for sociological analysis. I have contrasted a taken-for-granted understanding of human social interaction with understandings that are possible using a critical-thinking approach. I have promoted critical thinking throughout this chapter as a way of questioning how we know what we know, and why we accept certain kinds of knowledge to be more valid than other kinds. I have compared what I called taken-for-granted explanations or opinions with ones arrived at through critical thinking. I argued that taken-for-granted explanations and understandings are informed by the traditions, beliefs, and customs (norms) that dominate in a given society or culture. These understandings are shared by most members of a society or culture and are used as the basis for making sense out of day-to-day existence. They inform the members of a given society about what is true and what is false; what is right and what is wrong. They colour how everything is seen and understood.

I suggested that the task of critical thinking applied to sociological inquiry is to explore present and past conditions of human experience. If we apply critical thinking to sociological inquiry, we are immediately faced with the task of both questioning and challenging taken-for-granted understandings and envisaging creative and alternative futures for our society that are potentially more inclusive and equitable.

■ ■ ■

FOR DISCUSSION

1. What do sociologists study?

2. What skills does critical thinking involve?

3. What are some of the assumptions that underlie most Westerners' taken-for-granted understanding of their social world?

4. Are Canadians fundamentally prejudiced and bigoted? Or are they among the least prejudiced people in the world? Explain.

5. How central is the ideal of romantic love to the lives of most Canadians?

21

2

THINKING SOCIOLOGICALLY, THINKING CRITICALLY

In English, the word *critical* comes from the Greek root *krinein*, meaning "to estimate the value of something." Thus, a critic is someone who judges, appreciates, or estimates the value of something: a critical thinker is a critic of thought. He or she applies norms and standards to intellectual products in order to judge their value. Critical thinking is not negative or destructive thinking. Rather it is "thought evaluating other thought" (Johnson in Talaska 1992, 75). Put another way, critical thinking can be defined as "reasonable reflective thinking focused on deciding what to believe or do" (ibid., 6). It involves the ability to assess statements about the world with an attitude of reflective scepticism in order to produce new statements and understandings.

CRITICAL THINKING IN HISTORICAL PERSPECTIVE

In one sense critical thinking or reasoning is the same for all times and places. It is certainly not an invention of late-twentieth-century social sciences. Ancient Greek philosophers, medieval theologians, and postmodern theorists examined and challenged the established beliefs of their times. But critical thinking also differs from society to society and even from one historical period to another within a given society because the established beliefs that are being questioned change.

For the ancient Greeks, critical thinking meant actively questioning the beliefs that were commonly held by members of different city-states. In place of these nonphilosophical beliefs, the early Greek philosophers sought out universal truths that were independent of any untested assumptions or opinions. This search for universal truths, they believed, was the highest activity to which any human could aspire. It afforded knowledge-seekers ultimate answers to questions that were traditionally, but inadequately, answered by *nomi*. Greek philosophers, beginning with Aristotle, looked for universal knowledge of the nature or "essence" of all things. They believed knowledge could be very precise and thus applicable to all similar cases.

Early-modern philosophers, in their turn, questioned the authority of the Greek philosophers. In doing so, they cast doubt on a conceptual system that had been used for over two thousand years. They claimed that Aristotle and his followers based their thinking on erroneous principles and because of this produced uncertain work with no practical results. For seventeenth-century philosophers like René Descartes, reasoning had to produce absolute certainty, which could be achieved only if it was freed from opinion and if thinkers followed a universal method that had no presuppositions as its basis. Descartes was convinced that scientific inquiry was that universal method. While the ancient Greeks used their critical thinking skills for the philosophical attainment of happiness for the good of all human beings, early-modern philosophers strived for ideals of survival and comfort. They restricted themselves to discovering what could be tested by the new scientific method of inquiry (Talaska 1992, 257–64).

Over the past half-century, philosophers and social scientists have been able to show that all traditions in philosophy and science operate on the basis of systems of pre-established and unexamined assumptions. Not only our moral and political beliefs and laws, but also our scientifically achieved and therefore supposedly "objective" truths are actually part of a world view composed of traditional values, beliefs, and ways of thinking. So-called objective scientists think about the world and everything in it, often without examining the basic assumptions and ideas of their particular traditions of thought.

This insight has led some thinkers to ask whether the human mind discovers or constructs reality. According to many contemporary philosophers and social scientists, the way we make sense of our world is dependent both on the empirical evidence we gather and on the socially constructed and culturally specific sense we make out of that evidence. For example, when Native peoples first arrived in what is now central Canada, they "discovered" rather than "constructed" what we call the St Lawrence River. Similarly, when European explorers arrived, they also "discovered" rather than "constructed" the existence of that same river.

But Native peoples and European settlers "constructed" what the purpose of the St Lawrence River should be in very different ways. For most Native peoples, the St Lawrence was a source of food and a means of transportation. For Europeans, the river also became a place to dump unwanted waste products. These different culturally and socially constructed understandings about the purpose of the St Lawrence River have had

23

significant consequences. The way in which we construct our ideas about individualism or the way we perceive and treat others who seem racially different are further examples of how our understanding of the world is socially constructed.

C. WRIGHT MILLS AND THE SOCIOLOGICAL IMAGINATION

One of the foremost critical thinkers in the discipline of sociology has been the American sociologist C. Wright Mills (1916–1962). Mills coined the phrase "sociological imagination" to describe what he considered to be the ideal attribute of a critical sociologist. He was particularly concerned with the relationship between the individual and society, and he developed this concept to facilitate an understanding of that relationship. In his book *The Sociological Imagination* (1959), Mills argued that to think critically means to cultivate a "sociological imagination" and to use that "imagination" to help break away from routine, day-to-day understandings of social situations.

In the following excerpt, Mills states what it might mean to use a critical sociological imagination as a tool for thinking critically about our own lives and the social forces that shape them:

Dorothea Lange's 1930s photo of a dispossessed mother and her children. Upheavals like the Great Depression impact the lives of individuals and place them within the context of larger social processes.

When a society becomes industrialized, a peasant becomes a worker; a feudal lord is liquidated or becomes a businessman. When classes rise or fall, a man is employed or unemployed; when the rate of investment goes up or down, a man takes new heart or goes broke. When wars happen, an insurance salesman becomes a rocket launcher; a store clerk, a radar man; a wife lives alone; a child grows up without a father. Neither the life of an individual nor the history of a society can be understood without understanding both.

Yet men do not usually define the troubles they endure in terms of historical change and institutional contradiction. The well-being they enjoy, they do not usually impute to the big ups and downs of the society in which they live. Seldom aware of the intricate connections between the patterns of their own lives and the course of world history, ordinary men do not usually know what this connection means for the kind of men they are becoming and for the kinds of history-making in which they might take part. They do not possess the quality of mind essential to grasp the interplay of men and society, of biography and history, of self and world…. (3–5).

The objective of using a sociological imagination is to produce an understanding of, or knowledge about, human experience that both recognizes the individual's experiences and places those experiences in a larger context. Mills further suggested that the sociological imagination is particularly useful in times of great social disruption when the relationship between the individual and society is in conflict. For example, during the Great Depression of the 1930s, which followed the stock market crash of 1929, about 25 percent of the American labour force was unemployed. Instead of turning to taken-for-granted understandings about job loss and personal responsibility, and therefore blaming themselves for not being able to find a job, many people came to understand that their own personal troubles were, in fact, public issues.

Mills went so far as to argue that sociology should never be some sterile and inconsequential enterprise, detached from the daily experiences of all people. Rather, sociology should be a vital undertaking—one that allows everyone to become engaged in understanding and changing the social world in which he or she lives. In this way, Mills hoped, a critical and sociologically aware populace would be able to transform its society, making it more equitable for all members.

When Mills suggested that the "individual can understand his own experience and gauge his own fate only by locating himself within his society," he made a very important point, one that is among the most significant insights of contemporary social inquiry. But in his writing, and indeed in most of the writing done by sociologists until the late 1970s, women are almost totally absent. When women were to be included, as probably was the case with Mills, it was sufficient to leave that inclusion implicit and to use the terms "his" or "he" to refer to both men and women. With the rise of feminist scholarship in academia, however, this usage is no longer acceptable.

When we think critically, we must always consider the concepts and shared understandings that inform our approach to the very thing we want to study. For example, if we want to study gender relations in Canada today, we must first examine the taken-for-granted understandings that most members of Canadian society share about gender. It is only then that we can begin to analyze critically gender and to propose new ways of dealing with either issue.

OBJECTIVE KNOWLEDGE AND THE SOCIOLOGICAL IMAGINATION

Mills's concept of a sociological imagination focuses on the interplay between our common social history and the kind of critical thinking we must employ if we are to reveal and transform our culturally and historically acquired beliefs and understandings. But just what is required to produce knowledge about the social world we live in using our sociological imaginations? For most of us, the use of our imaginations seems to contradict everything we have been taught about neutrality, rational thought, and objective, dispassionate observation.

To many, rational, scientific inquiry and imagination are diametrically opposed. Scientific inquiry produces true knowledge of events and things, while imagination results in fantasy and fiction. While science is an undertaking that produces real, material benefits, imagination is ethereal and nonconcrete.

Now, modern scientific inquiry can hardly be criticized for lack of results or for producing useless categories of knowledge. Indeed, modern natural sciences are compelling precisely because they have been able to exercise a certain mastery over nature. In spite of all of the recent criticisms of the natural sciences, North Americans and Europeans continue, for the most part, to be enthralled by the promises science holds.

The taken-for-granted view of science in North America is that science is a means—the best and only true means—of gaining **objective knowledge** about the world around us. If we wish to produce true (i.e., objective knowledge as opposed to fiction or fanciful knowledge, or knowledge based on superstitions and misguided beliefs), we must use scientific methods for collecting and interpreting information.

The proponents of this taken-for-granted understanding of science often refuse to give careful attention to how scientific researchers are actually locked into a specific kind of relationship with whatever it is that they are researching. Their taken-for-granted understanding is that scientists can be objective because they can become independent of the very world they are studying. However, what scientists seek to discover is intimately connected to whatever *world view* and assumptions they bring to their investigation. As many theorists have pointed out, objectivity, based on the radical separation of observer and observed, is an impossibility. "Human beings," says moral philosopher Mary Midgley, "direct their enquiries to things that strike them as important." As humans we ask questions that matter to us. What matters, says Midgely, is "what brings things together, what shows a pattern, what tends to make sense of the whole" (1992, 65).

Once we realize this, we see that any object of scientific study may actually be viewed from many different perspectives or standpoints. Moreover, the same object can be interpreted through a wide range of **value systems**. When we understand that knowledge is relative rather than absolute, we can also see that knowledge is a set of claims that are socially constructed. What gets constituted as true knowledge ultimately depends on the researcher and on the social and cultural conditions in which the researcher operates.

I want to turn, once again, to the example of love discussed in Chapter 1. For thirteenth-century European nobility, love was an emotion appropriately shared between a high-born knight and his chosen lady. It could be expressed through acts of daring and bravery committed by the knight in the name of his lady, whom he could never hope to marry.

For late twentieth-century Westerners, however, true love is something to be experienced by everyone, regardless of social class. It is considered the only true feeling on which a marriage can be founded. The recent confession by Prince Charles that he never loved his wife, Princess Diana, makes him a cad in the eyes of many people today and justifies to them Diana's rather erratic behaviour over the last several years. But if we were living in the thirteenth century, Prince Charles's extramarital activities would hardly be cause for public concern. Indeed, his seeming obsession with a woman not his wife would be considered normal behaviour. And Princess Diana would most likely have her own devoted champion—someone who would openly express his undying devotion to her; someone decidedly not her husband.

Critical thinking calls into question the taken-for-granted understanding of a dichotomy between "true" knowledge and imagination. If we really want to understand how we go about producing knowledge about the world we inhabit, we must pay serious attention to the **myths, metaphors,** and cultural images underlying the official interpretations of truth available to us in this society (Midgley 1992). A critical approach to knowledge abandons the search for universal measures of truth or authority. Instead, critical-thinking sociologists will look for diverse ways of understanding the same set of events.

The nineteenth-century German philosopher Wilhelm Dilthey (1833–1911) has noted that the subject matter of all the human sciences, including sociology, are mental objects different from the physical objects that form the subject matter of the natural sciences. Knowledge produced by social scientists is an understanding of the shared meaning given to social behaviour rather than simple observation of social behaviour.

We gain self-knowledge, Dilthey maintained, through a circuitous route of understanding, which is historical and always refers back to the larger social group of which we are members. Our personal knowledge about life is always shaped by the beliefs and values

To understand a culture, attention must be paid to its myths and metaphors. Cars in the early years of the twentieth century personified the dreams of the North American man.

Cars in the 1950s were an important feature of the emerging suburban family model. Advertisements like these sent emotionally charged messages and images.

that emerge out of the social groups to which we belong. Assertions about the passage of life, judgments of value, rules of conduct, definitions of goals and what is good all are products of social life. Our minds, Dilthey tells us, can understand only what they have created.

The arguments of Mills and Dilthey about the relationship of the individual to society are underscored by the work of other contemporary philosophers. In his analysis of the historical structure of understanding, Hans-Georg Gadamer has shown that we cannot understand things unless we approach them from a point of view that is consistent with our own mental history (1986, 220–34). This means that there is no neutral point from which we can understand things with absolutely no presuppositions to guide our thought.

Gadamer's findings also echo in the work of the German philosopher Edmund Husserl, who has shown that all experience and understanding of experience is developed out of the communal system of meanings that underlies everyday life. Husserl calls this entire communal system of meanings the "lifeworld." There are significant differences between taken-for-granted understandings and critical ones. The former are based on unexamined assumptions about the "lifeworld" and all that it contains, while critical ones bring all assumptions forward for examination (Husserl 1970, 285).

CHARACTERISTICS OF A CRITICAL THINKER

Basic assumptions about what can be known, and how it can be known, separate taken-for-granted thinkers from those who use critical thinking. People who believe that all knowledge comes from authoritative sources usually believe that any solution to a problem comes directly from that authority, too. Taken-for-granted thinkers accept that there is a strong correlation between what they personally believe to be true, what an accepted authority has told them is true, and what is actually true. In the minds of taken-for-granted thinkers, most problems can have only one correct answer, one ultimately justified by reference to some authority: "It's in the textbook so it has to be true," or "If my minister says that homosexuality is a sin, it must be so."

By contrast, critical thinkers question epistemological assumptions (assumptions about knowledge) and recognize that all knowledge is contextual and subjective. It is filtered through personal perceptions. A critical thinker constructs knowledge on the basis of what appears to be the most reasonable assessment of the existing evidence. He or she is willing to re-evaluate conclusions when new evidence, perspectives, or tools of inquiry become available (King and Kitchener 1994, 15).

Richard Paul (1990) has identified several characteristics of a critical thinker today. Among the characteristics he identifies are the following:

1. **Independence of Mind.** *The disposition and commitment to autonomous thinking, thinking for oneself.* Most of the beliefs we hold today were acquired when we were very young and tended to form beliefs merely because we wanted to believe something, or because we were rewarded by significant adults in our lives for doing so. To develop as

critical-thinking adults, we must now learn to question what has been presented to us as "the truth." We must learn to judge for ourselves who or what constitutes a legitimate, justified authority, and who or what is not legitimate.

2. **Intellectual Curiosity**. *The disposition to wonder about the world*. Critical thinkers must be curious about the world they live in. They must seek to explain apparent discrepancies in that world, as well as to wonder about how they became who they are. A critical thinker must be perplexed about how we deceive ourselves, and about how we fail to perceive our contradictions and inconsistencies while we seemingly know so much about ourselves.

3. **Intellectual Courage**. *The willingness to evaluate all ideas, beliefs, or viewpoints fairly*. Critical thinkers must have the courage to recognize that even their most deeply held convictions and beliefs may be questioned. They also must have the courage to address the possibility that some seemingly absurd or even dangerous ideas may be justified. Often critical thinkers will go against taken-for-granted opinion. Pressure to conform can sometimes be great, and penalties for not conforming can be severe. Intellectual courage is called for if a critical thinker is to reassess all that he or she has been taught to believe.

4. **Intellectual Humility.** *Awareness of the limits of one's knowledge*. Critical thinkers must be sensitive to the biases and limitations of their points of view. They should strive for insight into the foundations of their own beliefs.

Individuals acquire knowledge through experience.

5. **Intellectual Empathy.** *Consciousness of the need to put oneself in the place of others in order to understand them.* A critical thinker must be able to construct the viewpoint and reasoning of others. A critical thinker is willing to remember the occasions on which he or she was wrong and can imagine the possibility of misunderstanding someone in a current situation.

6. **Intellectual Perseverance.** *The willingness to pursue intellectual insights and truths in spite of difficulties, obstacles, and frustrations.* A critical thinker is prepared to struggle with confusion and unsettled questions over a long period of time with a view to achieving a deeper understanding or insight.

Aristotle once wrote, "The unexamined life is not worth living." Perhaps the most simply stated justification for becoming a critical thinker is to be able to expand one's horizons. Critical thinking also allows one to become actively engaged with life rather than merely reacting to what is presented.

Constructing a critical sociological analysis of an event, or social institution, or practice is a creative undertaking that involves bringing together information from a variety of different sources.

THINKING CRITICALLY ABOUT THE CRIMINAL JUSTICE SYSTEM[1]

For many Canadians, crime is the result of the actions of individual wrong-doers. The general perception is that once caught all wrong-doers are treated equally before the law. But critical sociologists have shown that race, social class, or gender can make a difference to the rights of the accused or the sentence of the convicted. Inequalities of power and social position based on race, class, and gender affect not just who commits crimes, but how the criminal justice system responds to them.

One area of particular interest to critical-thinking sociologists is "corporate crime." Corporate crime is usually defined as a "crime" committed by one or more corporate officials in their pursuit of organizational goals—usually profits. Sociologists have remarked on the seeming lack of effort displayed by the Canadian state to prosecute corporate executives whose companies have broken laws. Nor does the Canadian criminal justice system seem to be overly concerned that the social costs of corporate crimes exceed those of crimes committed by individuals.

In analyzing corporate crime in Canada, critical-thinking sociologists usually start out by making a careful empirical study of who commits corporate crimes and how they are treated within the Canadian justice system. Rather than accept the taken-for-granted understanding of what society claims should be true, they try to establish what the situation really is like. To do this they often begin by looking for discrepancies between what society generally claims to be the case and what their research tells them is actually the case.

---

1   This section is based on Samuelson (1994).

For example, most critical-thinking criminologists who have studied the Canadian criminal justice system agree that the economic costs to society of "corporate crimes" far exceed those of "street crimes." By searching out comparative data on crime rates, criminologists have been able to estimate that while the average economic loss for a street crime such as robbery or burglary is between $700 and $900, the average loss for a corporate crime is in the neighbourhood of $8000 (Cullen, Maakestadt, and Cavender 1987).

Yet when corporate offenders are prosecuted and convicted, their sentences seem disproportionately light. Critical-thinking sociologists believe they have evidence indicating that the criminal justice system is not blind to social class differences, but that it treats upper- and middle-class offenders more leniently than it does those who hold less powerful positions in society.

In Canada, one person is murdered approximately every 12 hours, and everyone agrees that homicide is a serious criminal act. But almost every six hours, a Canadian worker dies from an preventible employment condition: between 1985 and 1987 on-the-job fatalities averaged about 907 per year (Reasons, Ross, and Patterson 1991). Statistics gathered in 1986 show occupational hazards to be the third-leading cause of death in Canada, preceded only by heart disease and cancer (ibid.). Yet these deaths are not considered homicide, and corporate executives usually go unprosecuted.

Many critical-thinking criminologists have expressed the opinion that disregard for health and safety standards on the part of corporate executives, combined with lax governmental control and a lack of will on the part of authorities to prosecute corporate offenders, is at the root of many job-related deaths (McMullan 1992; Snider 1993, Reasons, Ross, and Patterson 1991). Even when charges have been laid and fines levied, corporate officials are more likely to pay more for a suit than for the death of a worker (Samuelson 1994, 131).

By citing discrepancies between what is generally claimed about the criminal justice system and what is actually the case, sociologists are in a position to challenge the claimed objectivity of the criminal justice system. Decisions reached in the Canadian courts are often influenced by such supposedly noncriminal considerations as a person's race, social class, and gender.

Criminologists have found wide differences in the ways in which poor offenders are sentenced in the Canadian courts, compared to their middle- and upper-class counterparts. August Brannigan has shown that poor defendants are more likely to be found guilty than wealthy ones. Representation by a privately retained lawyer rather than a legal aid one seems to strongly influence the outcome of many cases. Brannigan found that, while 51 percent of those pleading not guilty with private lawyers were exonerated, only 31 percent of those pleading not guilty with legal aid lawyers were acquitted (1984, 106).

Race is another factor that strongly influences an individual's treatment before the courts. Native people made up less than 3 percent of the Canadian population in 1991, but constituted 11 percent of the federal inmate population. In provincial correctional institutions in Western Canada, Native people made up 44 percent of inmates in

31

Violence in our society is perceived as pervasive. Three officers apprehend two youths suspected of possessing guns. A desk sergeant later said he thought the weapons were pellet guns.

Manitoba, 66 percent in Saskatchewan, and 88 percent in the Northwest Territories (Task Force on Aboriginal People 1988, 5). Native women not only enter the criminal justice system with more frequency than both non-Native women and Native men, they also enter the system very early in their lives. A study published by the Ontario Native Women's Association (La Prairie 1987, 104) found that 37 percent of Native women interviewed in Ontario provincial correction centres were under 20 years of age. Seventy percent of these women had been arrested for the first time before they were 18 years old.

In the face of these statistics, critical-thinking criminologists ask what kinds of offences Native peoples are being convicted of compared with non-Natives. One 1991 study of the Alberta justice system found that while 20.9 percent of Native offenders were sentenced for Liquor Control Act violations, only 5.5 percent of non-Native offenders were similarly convicted (Alberta 1991). Another study done two decades earlier for the whole of Western Canada tells the same story. Native people are frequently incarcerated for being in default of payment of fines for minor, frequently alcohol-related convictions. Researchers studying female inmates in Saskatchewan's Pine Grove Correctional Centre found that almost two-thirds of them were sentenced for either drinking and driving, or for nonpayment of fines (Daubney 1988: 22).

Given these and other findings, critical-thinking sociologists ask if patterns of differential convictions and sentencing might not be the result of prejudice and discrimination on the part of Canadian society in general, and criminal justice system personnel in particular. Based on research carried out in Regina, Geoffrey York reports that while "30 percent of the Indians arrested for drunkenness were charged and sent to court...only 11 percent of non-Natives arrested for drunkenness were charged" (1990, 148).

Once in court, however, there appears to be little difference in the kinds of sentences handed down to Native, as compared with non-Native, offenders (Verdun-Jones and Muirhead 1982, 275). However, there are substantial differences between Native and non-Native convicts when it comes time for parole. The report of the Task Force on Aboriginal Peoples in Federal Corrections (1988) shows that 42 percent of non-Native offenders were granted full parole, but only about 18 percent of Native offenders were similarly treated. Another study, done in Alberta, indicates that while 54 percent of non-Native federal offenders had been released on full parole, only 31.6 percent of Native offenders were released. In Canada, Native offenders consistently serve a greater portion of their sentences than do non-Native offenders.

Sociologists are interested in determining how personal biography intersects with large-scale social structures and events. In looking at the differential treatment that Native and non-Natives receive in the Canadian criminal justice system, critical-thinking criminologists note that a central factor influencing treatment is not so much overt individual racism as it is **systemic racism** (Stevens 1991). La Prairie (1987), for example, has noted that parole is often made conditional on a number of factors, including employment prospects, available social support, and the conditions in the community where the potential parolee is to be released. The courts invariably find that social and economic conditions in which many Native people live are substandard and do not qualify them to meet the court's (class-based) criteria for early parole.

Critical-thinking sociologists have been able to show that systemic discrimination exists in the Canadian justice system against Canadians who are unable to meet middle-class standards of employment, and whose conditions of living do not meet court expectations. But racist attitudes toward nonwhites clearly exist outside the court system. For example, the problem of racism among police officers has emerged as a volatile issue in the last several decades. In September 1979, Toronto City Council passed a vote of non-confidence in the Metro Toronto Police Commission after a series of killings of members of minority groups by officers (Brannigan 1984, 58). More recently, police killings of blacks and Native people in Western Canada and in Toronto have exacerbated an already tense situation.

As a result, critical-thinking sociologists frequently offer new and potentially utopian solutions to the pressing social issues they encounter. They often identify openings for, as well as barriers to, progressive change. Some critical-thinking sociologists feel that Canadian society must move toward implementing criminal justice policies and programs run by Native peoples themselves. Such programs, they argue, should include on-reserve policing as well as healing and sentencing circles headed by elders of the community, in place of the existing adversarial trial system and prison terms. They argue that the band-aid solutions currently being pursued ignore systemic racism and stand little chance of achieving success.

THE VALUE OF CRITICAL THINKING TO SOCIOLOGICAL INQUIRY

Before I end this chapter on critical thinking and sociology, two final points need to be further clarified. First, in drawing a distinction between critical sociological and taken-for-granted understandings, I am not making the claim that a critical sociological understanding is more valuable than a taken-for-granted one because the former is disinterested, objective, or value-free while the latter is subjective and value-laden. There is no such thing as a neutral, value-free point of view. What is valuable about a critical sociological approach is that it often challenges or comes into conflict with taken-for-granted understandings. Second, by challenging taken-for-granted explanations, critical-thinking sociologists promote objectives of openness, justice, and democracy. Sociologists who operate in the tradition of C. Wright Mills are concerned with the restructuring of society for the benefit of all and not just in sociological research for its own sake.

We live in a society that encourages liberal, egalitarian ideals and that promises enlightenment and prosperity for all. Yet it frequently does not deliver on its promises. The treatment of Native people by the Canadian criminal justice system is just one case in point. Critical thinking can help us to arrive at new and more equitable solutions to pressing social issues.

■ ■ ■

SUMMARY

In this chapter we have seen that the objective of critical thinking in sociology is to explore the present and past conditions of human experience with a view to questioning and challenging taken-for-granted understandings and to constructing imaginative conceptions of possible futures. We learned that C. Wright Mills coined the phrase sociological imagination to describe what he considered to be the ideal quality of critical thinking in sociological inquiry. To think critically and sociologically, for Mills, means to cultivate powers of imagination, and to use those powers to help break away from routine day-to-day understandings of social issues and problems.

The objective of using a critical sociological imagination, then, is to produce an understanding of, or knowledge about, human experience that both recognizes the individual's experiences and places them in the context of larger-scale social processes.

■ ■ ■

FOR DISCUSSION

1. In what ways does critical thinking for the ancient Greeks differ from critical thinking in the late twentieth century?

2. In what ways does critical thinking today challenge the kind of critical thinking done by seventeenth-century philosophers such as René Descartes?

3. How might a sociological imagination be applied to the analysis of poverty in Canada?

4. What is the difference between "objective" or "scientific" knowledge and knowledge produced through critical inquiry?

5. Is being able to expand one's horizons a reasonable or defensible justification for becoming a critical thinker?

part 2

Sociologists, like all other scientists, endeavour to produce knowledge about the world around them. Although the assumed wisdom in the sciences has been that scientists "discover" reality, that position has recently been challenged by critical thinkers. The position of these thinkers is that, although we may perceive that the order of whatever we are studying existed prior to our arrival, in fact we actually impose that order ourselves.

But if what we are doing actually as social scientists is imputing order and meaning to events or actions, it becomes crucial to understand clearly how we distinguish one set of events and actions from another. It is equally important to understand how we recognize and attribute significance to patterns of relationships that we find among different events and social actions.

In Part 2 we explore the use of categories and concepts in sociological analysis. Learning about the discipline of sociology involves learning to think sociologically. We all make sense of the world we live in by using taken-for-granted categories and concepts that we have acquired as members of a given society. We use those categories and concepts to discern and make sense of all patterns of social relations. When we think sociologically, however, we replace taken-for-granted concepts and instead use concepts and categories that are part of the tools of sociological inquiry. These afford a different perspective on social relations than is the case when we employ concepts from day-to-day living.

To become sociologists, we must learn to make sense of the world in new ways. This involves acknowledging that common-sense ways of thinking about the world are neither "natural" nor common to everyone. Some of the most commonly used concepts in sociology include "social structure," "social change," "society," "culture," "socialization," "inequality," and "difference." These act as shorthand descriptions of complex social phenomena. By drawing our attention to the existence of underlying structures, rules, social practices, and processes, including laws, beliefs, and values, sociological concepts allow us to take new and often revealing perspectives on everyday social events and social relationships.

THE PRODUCTION OF SOCIOLOGICAL KNOWLEDGE

■ ■ ■

3

CATEGORIES, CONCEPTS, AND THE PRODUCTION OF SOCIOLOGICAL KNOWLEDGE

CHAPTER OPENING QUESTIONS

- What do we gain by questioning the categories we use to order our world?

- In what ways do our taken-for-granted concepts and conceptual systems shape our understandings of the social world?

- How do sociological concepts serve as tools that help us to understand our social world?

For introductory sociology students, sociological concepts are largely unfamiliar ways of categorizing or ordering the world and of speaking about it. As with other systems of knowledge, certain central concepts and principles have to be learned. In order to make sense of any social world, sociologists employ different concepts that allow them to categorize aspects of human experiences and to give those experiences a particular ordering.

Consider this example. Why can we say that two men resemble each other more closely than a man and a woman even if the man and woman live in the same household or hold the same kind of job? Why, even, are the **categories** "man" and "woman" valid ones for Western thinkers? Are the categories that we use in our everyday lives ones that are shared by all humans, regardless of time, place, and culture? In short, what are the criteria of similarity, analogy, and identity that we use on a day-to-day basis? Can we expect those criteria to be universally valid?

Certainly the distinctions we make between one class of things or events and another are the result of the application of certain criteria. We all believe we "know" the difference between men and women; aristocrats and peasants; whites, blacks, and Asians; punk-rock musicians and opera singers; the working, middle, and upper classes.

Ways of categorizing

We do hold very strong beliefs about categories and conceptual systems and their meaning; after all, this is the way we make sense of the world on a day-to-day basis. It is a difficult undertaking indeed to be a critical thinker and question those categories and concepts. To do so means that we must also question the way we make sense of the world and be willing to consider that the categories and concepts we use, and the meanings we impose on the world as a result, are not natural or common to everyone. Coming to this understanding is part of exercising a critical, sociological imagination.

It is not an easy task to give credence to the point of view that "our conceptual system is dependent on, and intimately linked to, our physical and cultural experiences" (Lakoff 1987, 112–13) when this flies in the face of our taken-for-granted beliefs. A couple of examples, drawn from non-Western societies, will help us understand the social and cultural specificity both of the categories and concepts we use and of the resulting knowledge we produce about our world. Consider the following two examples, one drawn from the playful fantasies of Argentinean author Jorge L. Borges and the other from the life experiences and practices of the Dyribal of Australia.

BORGES'S CATEGORIES

In 1966, Latin American writer Borges published a novel, *Other Inquisitions,* in which he invented "an ancient Chinese encyclopedia" entitled the *Celestial Emporium of Benevolent Knowledge.* Referring to this imaginary encyclopedia's system for classifying animals, Borges tells us that it is written that animals are divided into:

(a) those that belong to the Emperor,

(b) embalmed ones,

(c) those that are trained,

(d) suckling pigs,

(e) mermaids,

(f) fabulous ones,

(h) those that are included in this classification,

(i) those that tremble as if mad,

(j) innumerable ones,

(k) those drawn with a very fine camel's hair brush,

(l) others,

(m) those that have just broken a flower vase,

(n) those that resemble flies from a distance (Borges 1966, 108).

In his book *The Order of Things: An Archaeology of the Human Sciences* (1970), the French philosopher and historian Michel Foucault tells of "laughing and laughing" at this passage, which shattered "all the familiar landmarks of my thought—*our* thought." In wondering about the "exotic charm of another system of thought," the limitations of his own system of thought became clear: it was simply impossible, using familiar, Western categories, to comprehend the ordering of animals given by that "certain Chinese encyclopedia."

But what, exactly, was Foucault's problem? It was not, as he himself tells us, that he was unable to assign a precise meaning to each of the categories. Each category, by itself, makes perfect sense to a Western thinker. Categories such as stray dogs and suckling pigs have a precise meaning and content and in themselves pose no problem. What is strange, what does pose a problem, however, is the fact that the different categories are linked to each of the others *in a series*. To Foucault, and to most Westerners, that linking is completely incongruous and inappropriate. Where could the fabulous ones, innumerable, having just broken the flower vase, stray dogs, and suckling pigs ever meet except in Borges's fanciful list?

While Borges's classification of animals is pure fantasy, it does give us a sense of the kinds of impressions that many Westerners have of non-Western languages and cultures: they are impenetrable, irrational, illogical. It also gives us a sense of the culturally specific nature of both language and knowledge. In doing so, it helps us to question our own language, culture, and knowledge systems. To understand others as well as ourselves, we do need to exercise our critical faculties. And to exercise our critical faculties means to step outside the familiar and the everyday. By trying to understand Borges's Chinese encyclopedia, Foucault was able to gain an important insight into his own way of thinking. He was able to understand the arbitrariness of all systems of classification, including his own.

CATEGORIES OF THE DYRIBAL

A second example of the classification of things in ways not immediately understandable to Westerners can be found in linguist R.M.W. Dixon's work with traditional Dyribal, an aboriginal language of Australia (Lakoff 1987).

There are four words in the Dyribal language, *bayi*, *balan*, *balam*, and *bala*, which are used by speakers to classify everything in their universe. Every time a Dyribal speaker uses any noun, that noun must be preceded by some variant of one of the four classifying words. Nouns in the Dyribal universe are distributed among the four categories as follows:

1. *Bayi*: men, kangaroos, possums, bats, most snakes, most fishes, some birds, most insects, the moon, storms, rainbows, boomerangs, some spears, etc.

2. *Balan*: women, bandicoots, dogs, platypus, enchidna, some snakes, some fishes, most birds, fireflies, scorpions, crickets, the hairy may grub, anything connected with water or fire, sun and stars, shields, some spears, some trees, etc.

3. *Balam*: all edible fruit and the plants that bear them, tubers, ferns, honey, cigarettes, wine, cake.

4. *Bala*: parts of the body, meat, bees, wind, yamsticks, some spears, most trees, grass, mud stones, noises and language (92–93).

Intrigued with this distribution, Dixon set out to learn why the four categories would make perfect sense to any traditional Dyribal speaker (ibid., 93). What Dixon found was a basic schema that operated in most cases, except when some specialized principle took precedence. Dixon proposed this basic schema:

1. *Bayi*: (human) males; animals

2. *Balan*: (human) females; water; fire; fighting

3. *Balam*: nonflesh food

4. *Bala*: everything not in the other classes

Let's consider the category *Bayi*. Men, as human males, fit the category. So do kangaroos, possums, bats, most snakes, most fishes, some birds, and most insects as animals (Lakoff, 93). Most birds, however, are believed to be the spirits of dead human females, so they are in class *Balan* (Lakoff, 94).

In the category *Balan*, we have of course women as human females. Crickets are also in this category because, in myth, crickets are old ladies. In myth the moon and the sun are husband and wife, so the moon is in category *Bayi* with other husbands, while the sun is in category *Balan*, with other wives. Although most fish are in category *Bayi*, two types of fish, the stone fish and the gar fish, are harmful and are thus in category *Balan* along with two stinging trees and a stinging nettle vine. All other trees, vines, bushes, and grasses with no edible parts are in category *Bala* (Lakoff, 94–95).

Dixon's achievement in figuring out the sense of Dyribal language has remarkable implications for Westerners. As George Lakoff points out, Dixon "has shown that what might look superficially, to the Western eye, as a fantastic classification out of Borges, is from the perspective of the people doing the classifying a relatively regular and principled way to classify things."

The significance of Dixon's discovery parallels that of Foucault's understanding of the significance of categories and systems of classification. All systems of classification devised by humans are nonuniversal in that they are not immediately apparent to those who have not learned how to use them. At the same time, each particular system of classification has its own inherent logic. Most people rarely consider the extent to which the system of categorization that their language and cultural experiences provide is anything but natural. Dyribal speakers no more think of why women, fire, and other dangerous things belong in the same category than do most English speakers think about why inanimate objects are without gender, or most French and Spanish speakers think about why, in their language, inanimate objects are either masculine or feminine. In this respect each and every system of categorization is usually invisible to its users.

SOCIOLOGICAL CONCEPTS

Loosely defined, a **concept** is any general or abstract representation. Time, space, chair, man, woman, white, black are all concepts in that they are generic or class terms that refer to a category of things with a specific set of characteristics. When we learn a concept, we learn the rules that allow us to distinguish that concept from all other related concepts. We learn rules that allow us to place a thing, action, or event in a category along with other similar things, actions, or events. For example, when we learn the concept "chair," we are able to distinguish the category of things labelled "chair" from other general categories of things labelled "stool," "couch," "chaise longue," and so forth. When we learn the concept "war," we learn to distinguish between the categories of events "war" and other events such as "battle," "skirmish," "fight," and "attack."

Sociologists also use concepts to distinguish one class of things from another and to define specific properties of whatever it is they are studying. For example, in his work on personal taste, French sociologist Pierre Bourdieu employed the concepts of "social class," "society," "difference," "change," and "reproduction," among others, to explain differences in something as seemingly individual as taste. We will discuss Bourdieu's work in more detail in Chapter 14. Here I want to emphasize that Bourdieu, like all other sociologists, used sociological concepts whose meanings have been carefully defined and constructed in order to engage in a critical assessment of aspects of human behaviour.

The sociological concepts Bourdieu employed in his study permitted him to develop an assessment of how and why the tastes of individual members of society might differ from person to person. He was able to demonstrate that a close connection exists between an individual's social class and social position and his or her personal tastes in such things as music, food, and home decor. Bourdieu's use of such concepts as "class" and "society" allowed him to explore the relationship between individual taste and class position in ways that would have been unavailable to him if he had relied on everyday, taken-for-granted concepts.

By investigating the close connection between social class and tastes in entertainment, we can expand our sociological understanding.

Concepts shape how we perceive and how we understand the world we live in. We use them as a part of our everyday lives to help us know how to distinguish people from each other, categorize them, and relate to them, as well as to determine how other people can be expected to relate to us.

CONCEPTUAL SYSTEMS AS METAPHORS IN EVERYDAY LIFE

Single concepts do not stand alone. Rather, they are organized into conceptual systems that define our everyday reality, even though we are largely unaware of them. On a day-to-day basis, we simply think and act more or less automatically, without stopping to reflect. George Lakoff and Mark Johnson have pointed out very convincingly that most of the conceptual systems we use are metaphorical. But just what do they mean by this?

In *Metaphors We Live By* (1980), they show how we tend to view all new situations as examples of something else that is more familiar to us. By becoming aware of the constructed nature of all knowledge, we are able to identify the dominant metaphors that help to shape our everyday, taken-for-granted understandings. We are also able to observe the consequences of changing the dominant metaphors that shape our view of the social world. For example, the dominant metaphor for understanding what goes on in a classroom is the workplace. In the classroom, as in the workplace, certain tasks are accomplished in exchange for some reward—for instance, good grades. Common terms used include homework, classroom management, teacher or student accountability.

But suppose we change the metaphor to something else, say to that of a consulting service. Now instead of an agenda of tasks set by the teacher for the students, the teacher becomes a consultant and the students become clients who want help accomplishing some task. Teachers and students become potential sources of insight, assistance, and information.

Another example is the concept of *time*. To get some idea of how metaphorical expressions in everyday language can provide insight into the nature of concepts that structure our daily activities, consider the metaphorical concept "time is money." In colloquial conversation, Lakoff and Johnson (1980) have noted that the following phrases often appear:

- You're *wasting* my time.

- This gadget will *save* you hours.

- I don't *have* the time to *give* you.

- How do you *spend* your time these days?

- That flat tire *cost* me an hour.

- You're *running out* of time.

- You need to *budget* your time.

- Is that *worth your while*?

- He's living on *borrowed* time.

In our society time is considered to be a valuable commodity: in many ways time *is* money. We are paid wages by the hour or by the day; we pay our telephone bills for monthly services, our hotel bills for each night's stay; we pay monthly interest on our loans; we repay our debt to society, if convicted of a crime, by "doing time" (Lakoff and Johnson 1980, 8).

The metaphor time is money fits within a conceptual system in which it makes sense to equate time with money. But can you imagine a conceptual system in which time is not tied to money; where the metaphor time is money would make no sense? That conceptual system would have to be found in a culture where wage labour was not a part of almost everyone's experience, where people supported themselves, and each other, in ways other than by working for a weekly or monthly salary. In short, one would have to imagine a society without commodity production and exchange, without wage labour: a society based on exchanges between people of a more personal and specific nature.

FOUNDATIONAL CONCEPTS OF SOCIOLOGY AS METAPHORS

The foundational concepts of sociology are metaphorical in the same sense that "time is money" is metaphorical. Sociological concepts, like the concepts we use on a daily basis and out of which we form our taken-for-granted understandings, draw heavily on the cultural context in which they appear and are used. What sets sociological concepts apart from everyday, common-sense ones is that they are deliberately constructed as tools to help sociologists reflect on the meaning and significance of the social world we live in. Some of the most commonly used concepts in sociology include society, social structure, social reproduction, social status, social roles, and social change. These concepts act as shorthand descriptors for complex social phenomena.

SOCIETY

One very general definition of sociology is that it is the systematic study of people living together in organized groups. **Society** is that broad grouping of people who live together and who have developed, through interacting with one another, common interests, institutions, and collective activities. Society is that "which links individuals to one another everywhere, whatever that may be" (Frisby and Sayers 1986, 120).

The concept of society has a long tradition in Western thought. Over two thousand years ago, the Greek philosopher Plato reflected on the possibility of an ideal and just political system in his *Republic*. His student, Aristotle, carried on that tradition of reflection in his works *Ethics* and *Politics*. For Aristotle, the concepts of association, community, and society were not separate and were covered by the common term *koinonia*. The *Shorter Oxford English Dictionary* gives 1531 as the date for the first usage of the word society in its modern form, meaning "association with one's fellow men" (Frisby and Sayers 1986, 7). But it wasn't until the late nineteenth century that Émile Durkheim set out to establish the discipline of sociology as a science with its own object of study—society.

Durkheim contended that society is something that exists in and of itself. He believed that it could be studied objectively, in the same way that any other phenomenon of nature could be studied. He contrasted human society with animal society. In all animal societies, Durkheim argued, each individual animal is governed from within, by instincts. Human societies are a completely different phenomenon. In human societies, "certain ways of acting are imposed, or at least suggested *from outside* the individual and are added on to his own nature" (Lukes 1985, 248).

It is important to note that for Durkheim, society is a concrete object made up of an association of individuals. For him, society is not something abstract but is something that has a real existence and therefore can be treated as a material object. He also argued that, as an object, society is always more than just the sum of its individual parts. To explain what he meant, he used the metaphor of a chemical synthesis, such as that which produces bronze or water. Consider the example of bronze, which is an amalgam of copper, tin, and lead. The hardness of bronze, as Durkheim points out, is not due to the properties of any one of its three components. Instead "it arises from the mixing of them," in the same way the liquidity of water does not result from the properties of either hydrogen or oxygen, but from "the complex substance which they form by coming together" (ibid., 39).

While the validity of Durkheim's concept of society is contested by some sociologists, it continues to be used. The concept is far removed from the everyday, taken-for-granted understandings of society. At the very least, Durkheim has provided us with a rationale for studying society as an entity in its own right.

SOCIAL STRUCTURE

A basic premise of sociological inquiry is that all human societies, regardless of time, culture, or geographical location, are characterized by some discernable structure. Whatever social situation human beings find themselves in—from making love to making war; from taking an aerobics class to running a halfway house for probationary prisoners—the social interactions that occur among individuals are neither random nor unique to the participants.

The discipline of sociology is founded on the premise that human social interaction is ordered and patterned; in other words, it is structured, although the exact nature of that structure may not be immediately apparent to either the participants or an observer. It is this premise that makes sociology as the study of human existence possible. As the insights of C. Wright Mills have shown in the previous chapter, to study human behaviour from a sociological perspective is to become aware of the social forces or structures that affect our personal lives.

Sociologists often use the concept of **social structure** to refer to the fact that human social interaction is regularized, ordered, predictable, and relatively stable over time. Our entire lives take place within social structures that define and limit the choices we can make. Like the concept of society, the concept of social structure implies that some concrete entity exists, provides relative stability, and is independent of the individuals whose lives are regulated by a specific set or pattern of social interaction.

Norms, Folkways, and Mores

We all go about our daily lives knowing more or less what to expect from most social interactions. True, there are those occasions where we find ourselves neither knowing what to expect from others nor what is expected by others of us. A very formal dinner, for example, where the cutlery arranged on either side of the plate seems endless, might present certain problems. Which fork to begin with? Which knife to use for the fish, the fruit, and the main course? Which glass to drink which wine for which course? And just how do I get the edible part of the snail out of the shell?

Even on the most awkward social occasion, when we feel ill at ease and confused, we do know that there is an order to things, a set of rules that govern social interaction. Our task is to learn what those rules or **social norms** are. Social norms can be *prescriptive*, in that they tell us what we must do, or they can be *proscriptive*, and tell us what is forbidden. Together, proscriptive and prescriptive social norms make up the rules that guide our behaviour in social settings. If we fail to observe them, we risk making fools of ourselves, or worse. Some norms, of course, are more important than others and carry more severe penalties if they are broken. The American sociologist William Graham Sumner (1907) distinguished between what he called **folkways** and **mores** (pronounced MORE-ays).

Folkways are the everyday norms that have little moral significance and that can be broken on certain occasions without serious consequences. They include conventions that govern dress, table manners, and bodily gestures. For example, there are certain norms or folkways about what is appropriate to wear to university lectures. If a woman shows up to a lecture dressed in a formal evening gown, complete with high heels, gloves, and a corsage, she would attract considerable attention. A man dressed in this fashion would attract even more attention and might be subject to derogatory comments and questioning. But on most university campuses, neither the woman nor the man would be barred from attending class or expelled from the university. While they would have broken a folkway norm, that norm has little moral importance. A person who breaks a folkway norm might be considered ill-mannered, crude, foolish, or socially inept, but not criminal or morally reprehensible.

However, if either our hypothetical man or woman turned up for class wearing just the high heels and the corsage, he or she would have broken a mos (singular of mores), a cultural norm of great conventional significance. In North America, one crucial social mos is that all members of society are expected to appear in public places clothed to conform to certain standards. Other social mores include moral prohibitions against incest, rape, murder, theft, and fraud. Violators of these mores must pay heavy penalties.

SOCIAL REPRODUCTION

While sociologists who study social structure are concerned with the underlying regularities, patterns, and rules of human interaction, they are also concerned with the repetition of, or changes to, those patterns and rules. The concept of social structure is, therefore, closely tied to the companion concepts of **social reproduction** and **social change**. Social reproduction refers to how societies continue over time, while social change refers to the changes that they undergo.

Societies and social structures cannot exist without the social reproduction of patterned human interactions and the rules or norms that govern them. Think of it this way. Every time you leave your home to go to class at university or college, you expect to encounter the same kinds of social interaction that you encountered the previous time you went to class. For example, you reasonably expect that attending school, whether in Victoria, British Columbia, or St John's, Newfoundland, means, in large part, attending classes in your chosen subjects. Moreover, you expect that the classes you attend will be made up of an instructor who gives a lecture, presents a film, or leads a discussion, and of students who listen to the lecture, watch the film, or participate in the discussion. You expect these and similar kinds of things to be repeated from class to class, whether the actual content of any particular class concerns biology, painting, English literature, or sociology.

Your actions as a student are influenced by the social structure, folkways, and mores underlying Canadian educational institutions. You are not the first student to attend lectures, write exams, or graduate with a bachelor of arts degree. Nor did you make up and impose on others the patterns of interaction that occur with regularity in classrooms across this country. In spite of the fact that you are not personally responsible for the

Venus Simultaneous *by Michael Snow. Pattern and order appear to exist within apparent chaos. It is the sociologist's task to uncover that order.*

structure of the postsecondary system in Canada, as a student, you are quite reasonably expected to be able to walk into any classroom and make sense of the kind of social interaction taking place. You might not be able to make such good sense of the actual content of the course, but at least you will know where to sit, what the appropriate signals are to indicate that the class has started, and how to take notes. You also know when the instructor is lecturing, when he or she is answering questions, and what the appropriate signals are to indicate the class is over.

We all have extensive, common-sense knowledge of the structural characteristics of the society in which we live and the norms that we must follow if we are to be successful members of that society. Our own actions are profoundly influenced by our understandings of what those structural characteristics and rules are and how we should relate to them. At one and the same time we both re-create, and to some extent alter, the social structure of which we are a part.

The postsecondary system is part of Canadian society. It is clear to all of us that the current generation of students did not invent this system. Rather, those who constitute this generation of students and professors are confronted with what has already been accomplished by the students and professors who preceded them, just as those who will come after will be confronted by what this generation has done.

While a student from a university in medieval Europe, transported to a late twentieth-century Canadian university or college, would certainly find similarities, he (with few exceptions students then were only males) would also find many striking differences, beginning with the fact that present-day Canadian students actually own books. So social structures are not just reproduced. They are also changed. It seems almost trite to say that the world we live in today is profoundly different from that of two hundred years ago. Changes occur in part because they were planned and desired by people, and in part as unintentional consequences of unforeseen actions and events.

The dissolution of the former Soviet Union is a case in point. While many wanted that dissolution to occur and actively worked to ensure the emergence of separate nation states, few intended that the outcome would involve a precipitous decline in the standard of living, food shortages, and further impoverishment of large numbers of people.

STATUS AND SOCIAL ROLES

Social structures inevitably place constraints on everyday life by establishing regularized and expected patterns of social interaction. The existence of these patterns leads us to the next two concepts that are commonly used by sociologists—**social status and social roles**. Consider this example.

A man and his son are involved in a serious car accident. The man is pronounced dead at the scene, but his son is rushed to a nearby hospital in critical condition. A famous surgeon on staff at the hospital is summoned from a golf game to save the boy's life. Arriving at the hospital, the surgeon takes one look at the boy and says, "Oh my God, I can't operate, get someone else. That's my son!"

How can the surgeon's reaction be explained? If the boy's father died in the car accident, why does the surgeon state, "That's my son!"? A contradiction exists, how ever, only if the assumption is made that the surgeon must be male. If the surgeon is the boy's mother, the contradiction is resolved. As long as we follow traditional expectations about status and social roles, we will not be able to understand the riddle. But once we are able to challenge those expectations, the answer to the riddle becomes perfectly clear.

Social status is the recognized position that a person occupies within society. Every status has a number of different rights, obligations, and expectations attached to it that are widely acknowledged by most members of a given society. In everyday, taken-for-granted usage, the term status often is used synonymously with prestige to refer to high ranking within a social hierarchy. Within Western everyday usage, the status of surgeon has been accorded much prestige, and because most prestigious positions have traditionally been occupied by men, it is not surprising that it is difficult for some people, even today, to expect a woman to occupy such a position.

Status differences are found everywhere. Within a university or college, statuses include student, secretary, professor, dean, and president. Within a church, statuses might include priest, rector, congregant, or bishop. A Western family includes such statuses as mother, father, sister, brother, aunt, uncle, grandparent, and cousin. Within the classroom at a university or college, the statuses of professor and student have well-defined and different duties and obligations attached to them. Similarly, the interaction among family members is defined in terms of, and reflects the differences between, the statuses of mother, father, child, and so on.

A social role is the expected pattern of behaviour that is attached to a particular status. The role of student, for example, involves attending lectures, taking notes, receiving and handing in assignments, and being graded on one's performance in a course. The role of professor involves, among other things, giving lectures or conducting seminars, and devising and marking student exams and assignments.

The term role is borrowed from the language of the theatre. It conveys the understanding that in performing or playing their roles, most people behave according to the dictates of society (society's script). Not only do the roles we play dictate the kinds of actions we might take, they also prescribe appropriate emotions, beliefs, and attitudes to accompany those actions. All roles are social in that they organize our relations with other people. Some aspects of the roles played by students are related to some aspects of the roles played by professors; the roles played by parents are in direct relation to those played by their children. There is usually more than one role attached to each status. Take, for example, your status as student. Do the roles you play as student remain the same regardless of whether you are having coffee with your fellow students, discussing an assignment with your instructor, or having a meeting with the dean of your faculty? In each of these interactions, you act out different roles in the guise of student. The set of roles attached to a status is sometimes given the name **role set.** Because there are different roles attached to each status, there is the possibility that those roles will conflict with each other. **Role conflict** refers to the instances of conflict that occur between two or more different roles in a role set.

SOCIAL CHANGE

In some ways, the concept of social change is all-inclusive. Nothing stays exactly the same over time. Everything is subject to change, whether that change is minuscule, such as the minute-by-minute aging that we all experience, or the gargantuan effects of a collision of a comet with a planet. In the first instance, there is sufficient continuity in our appearance and agility from day to day, and even from month to month, that we remain recognizable to family and friends even if they haven't seen us for several years. In the second case, the change is almost instantaneous, and it is

The discipline of sociology is founded on the premise that human social interaction is ordered. Can you detect any pattern here?

irrevocable. What existed at one instance in time no longer exists in its previously recognized form. To demonstrate that social change has taken place, we need to be able to show the degree to which the social structures have been modified over time.

Social Change and the Treatment of Prisoners

Michel Foucault's work on changes in the treatment of prisoners in France roughly between 1750 and 1850 provides one interesting example of the kind of change that occurred with the decline of feudalism and the rise of industrialized society. He opens his book *Discipline and Punishment: The Birth of the Prison* (1979) with the following description of the execution of a man by the name of Damiens, who had been convicted and condemned to death for regicide in 1757. As Foucault recounts the story,

> on 2 March 1757, Damiens was condemned "to make the *amende honorable* before the main door of the Church of Paris," where he was to be "taken and conveyed in a cart, wearing nothing but a shirt, holding a torch of burning wax weighing two pounds"; then, "in the said cart, to the Place de Grève, where, on a scaffold that will be erected there, the flesh will be torn from his breasts, arms, thighs, and calves with red-hot pincers, his right hand, holding the knife with which he committed the said parricide, burnt with sulphur, and, on those places where the flesh will be torn away, poured molten lead, boiling oil, burning resin, wax and sulphur melted together and then his body drawn and quartered by four horses and his limbs and body consumed by fire, reduced to ashes and his ashes thrown to the winds" (*Pièces originales*, 372–74)....

> "It is said that, though he was always a great swearer, no blasphemy escaped his lips; but the excessive pain made him utter horrible cries, and he often repeated: 'My God, have pity on me! Jesus, help me!'" The spectators were all edified by the solicitude of the parish priest of St. Paul's who despite his great age did not spare himself in offering consolation to the patient" (cited in Foucault 1979, 3).

Less than a century later, Foucault contends, an entirely new "theory of law and crime, a new moral or political justification of the right to punish" was put in place throughout Europe and North America. Old laws and customs were abolished and "modern" codes were planned or drawn up (ibid., 7). Prominent among the changes was the disappearance of torture as a public spectacle.

To illustrate his argument, Foucault asks us to compare the rules for the House of Young Prisoners in Paris, drawn up in the late 1830s, with the description of the punishment of Damiens, not 80 years before. The rules for the House, Foucault contends, provide an example of the way in which the "modern" penal style differs from that of less than a century ago. A sample of those rules follow.

Art. 17. The prisoners' day will begin at six in the morning in winter and at five in summer. They will work for nine hours a day throughout the year. Two hours a day will be devoted to instruction. Work and the day will end at nine o'clock in winter and at eight in summer.

Art. 18. *Rising*. At the first drum-roll, the prisoners must rise and dress in silence, as the supervisor opens the cell doors. At the second drum-roll they must be dressed and make their beds. At the third, they must line up and proceed to the chapel for morning prayer. There is a five-minute interval between each drum-roll.

Art. 20. *Work*. At a quarter to six in the summer, a quarter to seven in winter, the prisoners go down into the courtyard where they must wash their hands and face, and receive their first ration of bread. Immediately afterwards, they form into work-teams and go off to work, which must begin at six in the summer and seven in winter.

Art. 27. At seven o'clock in the summer, at eight in winter, work stops; bread is distributed for the last time in the workshops. For a quarter of an hour one of the prisoners or supervisors reads a passage from some instructive or uplifting work. This is followed by evening prayer.

Art. 28. At half-past seven in summer, half-past eight in winter the prisoners must be back in their cells after the washing of hands and the inspection of clothes in the courtyard; at the first drum-roll, they must undress, and at the second get into bed. The cell doors are closed and the supervisors go the rounds in the corridors, to ensure order and silence (cited in Foucault 1979, 7).

Within a few decades of the brutal public execution of Damiens, not only had torture disappeared as a public spectacle, but punishment itself had also stopped being a spectacle. Chain gangs and public executions ceased, and punishment became "the most hidden part of the penal process." Publicity shifted from punishment to the trial and the sentence. This new approach to crime and punishment held that while it is "ugly to be punishable," there is "no glory in punishing." Those who actually carry out the criminal's sentence, far from being major players in public spectacles, were separated from those who imposed the sentence.

But even more important, instead of the body of the convicted person being punished, concern was focused on the punishment of the convict's mind and soul. The objective of punishment ceased to be the infliction of physical pain on the offender's body. Rather, the objective became to deprive the convicted person of his or her right to liberty or, in some cases, existence. This is the model of treatment of prisoners that we continue to use today.

■ ■ ■

SUMMARY

So far I have reviewed only a very few of the concepts that are used by sociologists to help them construct knowledge about the social world. Sociological concepts share certain qualities with taken-for-granted ones. Both kinds of concepts have the ability to order, organize, and give sense or meaning to the social world. But sociological concepts do more than this. By drawing our attention to the existence of underlying structures, rules, and social practices and processes, including laws, beliefs, social change, and reproduction, sociological concepts afford us a means whereby we can critically assess everyday social events and social relationships.

There are a number of foundational concepts that sociologists use to help them construct knowledge about the social world, such as society, social structure, social role, and status. In large part, learning to think sociologically is learning to use sociological concepts to categorize social actions and social behaviours. In the next chapter, we will examine culture, another of the core concepts of sociology.

■ ■ ■

FOR DISCUSSION

1. To what extent is the conceptual system we use on a daily basis linked to our physical and cultural experiences?

2. In what ways is learning to use sociological concepts similar to learning a new language?

3. What are some of the more common metaphors that underlie day-to-day social relations in Canadian society?

4. In what ways does Durkheim's concept of society differ from the everyday use of the concept?

5. What are some of the proscriptive and prescriptive social norms that operate in Canadian society? Are those norms the same for all members of Canadian society?

6. What kinds of role conflicts might students experience during their university or college careers?

4 CULTURE IN CONTEXT

In 1956 American anthropologist Horace Miner published the results of an ethnographic study of a group of people he called the Nacirema. Miner was particulary interested in the elaborate, strange, and seemingly obsessive daily body rituals these people engaged in. He reported his observations in an article published in the journal *American Anthropologist*, and it is worth quoting from that publication.

> The fundamental belief underlying the whole system appears to be that the human body is ugly and that its natural tendency is to debility and disease. Incarcerated in such a body, man's only hope is to avert these characteristics through the use of the powerful influences of ritual and ceremony. Every household has one or more shrines devoted to this purpose....The focal point of the shrine is a box or chest which is built into the wall. In this chest are kept the many charms and magical potions without which no native believes he could live. These preparations are secured from a variety of specialized practitioners. The most powerful of these are the medicine men, whose assistance must be rewarded with substantial gifts....

> However, the medicine men do not provide the curative potions for their clients, but decide what the ingredients should be and then write them down in an ancient and secret language. This writing is understood only by the medicine men and by the herbalists who, for another gift, provide the required charm.

The Nacirema have an almost pathological horror of and fascination with the mouth, the condition of which is believed to have a supernatural influence on all social relationships. Were it not for the rituals of the mouth, they believe that their teeth would fall out, their gums bleed, their jaws shrink, their friends desert them, and their lovers reject them. They also believe that a strong relationship exists between oral and moral characteristics. For example, there is a ritual ablution of the mouth for children which is supposed to improve their moral fibre.

Daily body ritual performed by everyone includes a mouth-rite. Despite the fact that these people are so punctilious about care of the mouth, this rite involves a practice which strikes the uninitiated stranger as revolting. It was reported to me that the ritual consists of inserting a small bundle of hog hairs into the mouth, along with certain magical powders, and then moving the bundle in a highly formalized series of gestures (Miner 1956, 503–4).

These odd people, of course, are American (Nacirema is American spelt backward). In his article Miner succeeds in making the everyday activities that most North Americans engage in seem strange. He accomplished this by taking an everyday, familiar action, brushing teeth, out of its familiar context. Miner observed tooth brushing as a person might who has no cultural "knowledge" about this daily activity. Indeed, the point of Miner's article is that any activity, including those that we are intimately familiar with, can be made to seem strange and even nonhuman if we interpret it through another "cultural framework."

THE CONCEPT OF CULTURE

Culture is one of the most widely used concepts in sociology. "Culture," writes the British sociologist Raymond Williams in his book *Keywords*, "is one of the two or three most complicated words in the English language" (1976, 76). A large part of the complexity of the word has to do with its history and the meanings that it has come to acquire.

The word culture is most commonly used to designate static and sometimes elitist notions of the highest achievements of civilization. Indeed, in everyday language, the word is used to describe the products of intellectual and artistic activity such as literature, music, theatre, painting, philosophy, and architecture. But as Williams (1976) points out, the term culture has not always been used in this way. The first use of the word culture as a noun was to describe certain processes, including growing and cultivating crops, the breeding and raising of animals, and then only by extension "the active cultivation of the human mind" through such pursuits as art, literature, and religious contemplation. By the eighteenth century, the word culture had taken on the additional meaning of "a distinct whole way of life" that involved all forms of social activity.

During the nineteenth century, the term culture, in the sense of "a distinctive way of life," was adopted by the fledgling discipline of comparative anthropology, and later by

55

sociology. In 1871, for example, the British anthropologist E.B. Tylor published *Primitive Culture*, in which he maintained that

> [c]ulture...taken in its wide ethnographic sense is that complex whole which includes knowledge, belief, art, morals, law, custom, and any other capabilities and habits acquired by man as a member of society. The condition of culture among the various societies of mankind, in so far as it is capable of being investigated on general principles, is a subject apt for the study of laws of human thought and action (1).

Sitting Bull, 1885.

In sociology today, the term culture is used to indicate a complex set of relations between "general human development and a particular way of life" (Williams 1976, 80–81). Culture, declares the British sociologist Paul Willis, is the very material of our daily lives, the bricks and mortar of our most commonplace understandings (1977, 185). Or, as another British sociologist, Stuart Hall, puts it, the concept of culture includes "the actual, grounded terrain of practices, representations, languages and customs of any specific historical society (as well as)...the contradictory forms of 'common sense' that have taken root in and helped to shape popular life" (Hall 1986, 26).

The concept of culture includes all of the social institutions that shape and manage our daily lives; the ways in which we produce and distribute the material goods we need for survival; the ways in which we bring new members into our social world; and the ways in which we exclude others from participation. It includes the sets of logically interrelated symbols and values that we use to determine desirable and undesirable social qualities, as well as all emotionally charged symbols that differentiate the sacred from the profane, the good from the bad. For example, in Hollywood Westerns of the 1950s, the "good guys" always wore light clothing while the "bad guys" were dressed in black. Everyone watching knew the characters' moral status by their clothing.

The concept of culture, then, includes everything that people have, think, and do as members of a society. It refers equally to material goods, ideas, values, beliefs, attitudes, and behaviour patterns. It encompasses such diverse things as marriage customs, music, living arrangements, health care, housing, food, clothing, belief systems, transportation systems, manners, educational practices, child-rearing practices, masculinity and femininity, sexual practices, politics, religion, and economics. Together, these constitute the culture of any given group of people.

CULTURAL VARIATION

There are hundreds of different cultures that have existed or continue to exist in the world today. Moreover, there is great variation among them with regard to traits, values, norms, social practices, and belief systems. Let's consider the cultural institution of marriage. In North America only one kind of marriage is legally recognized—a marriage between a living man and a living woman who do not fall within a prohibited degree of biological relationship. (The degree of prohibition, however, varies from province to province in Canada, and from state to state in the United States).

But among the Nuer of Africa, there are two other "legitimate," although uncommon, forms of marriage. One form, ghost marriage, occurs when the husband of a woman of child-bearing age dies. When a Nuer woman marries, the rights to her unborn children are transferred from her father to her husband's group in exchange for cattle. If her husband dies, the contract is sustained, ideally through the woman's remarriage to some other member of her husband's group. But any children that are born from this second marriage are socially defined as the children of her first husband. Even if the widow never remarries but takes lovers, any children she has are defined as the children of her deceased husband.

A second, even rarer form of legitimate marriage among the Nuer occurs when an older, wealthy woman "marries" a young girl. The older woman finances the marriage in the same way as a man would, by buying the rights to the young woman's offspring with an exchange of cattle. The young woman then takes lovers with whom she has children. These children are socially defined as the children of their mother's "female husband," who in turn is construed as their father (Keesing 1981, 217).

ETHNOCENTRISM

While there is a great deal of cultural diversity in the world, most people have been raised in a single culture. They have never experienced other ways of living and engaging in the world so their own culture, with its attendant values, beliefs, ideas, and ways of behaving, seems the most natural and acceptable means of functioning. In the most general sense of the term, **ethnocentrism** refers to the tendency to interpret everything through the lenses of one's own culture.

This rather broad definition of ethnocentrism, however, tends to mask two problematic tendencies. In the first place, people who are ethnocentric often assume that what is true of their own culture is also true of all other cultures. But more problematic are those who believe that their own ways of behaving, thinking, and acting are natural and desirable and that other ways are less so or even inferior. One good reason for studying cultural diversity, then, is to reduce ethnocentrism.

The inclination to view other cultures as inferior has had a long history in Western societies. Nineteenth-century sociologists and social anthropologists adopted the view that all societies passed through a series of stages of development that ran from savagery, through barbarism, and on to civilization. They believed that most non-Western cultures were stuck at the level of savagery or, at best, barbarism. The choice of the terms savagery, barbarism, and civilization speaks volumes about the regard in which cultures other than Western ones were held. While ethnocentrism is less extreme today, it still exists. An awareness of cultural diversity, with a keen appreciation of the socially constructed nature of our own culture, is an important step toward dealing with ethnocentrism. In concocting his amusing parody of American society, Miner shows us ethnocentrism in action and the strangeness (when looked at through an outsider's eyes) of one of our own most ingrained and innocuous rituals. By making the familiar strange, Miner helps us see just how much we take for granted the cultural practices and customs that structure and give meaning to every aspect of our lives. He also provides an opportunity to question our own ethnocentrism as he highlights the folly of our presumption that our ways of living are self-evidently "natural" and "superior" to those of other cultures.

*CROSSING CULTURAL BARRIERS

To be human is to be a member of a culture in the most general sense of the term. A member of a culture is able to communicate with other members of that culture in ways that are mutually intelligible and acceptable. Ashley and Orenstein write convincingly about what this might mean when they describe the experiences of the cultural anthropologist, Napoleon Chagnon, who lived and studied among the Yanomamo for a number of years. Over a 25-year period, Chagnon spent many years living with the fierce Yanomamo of the Venezuelan rain forest. At first it was clear to the Yanomamo that Chagnon was not a complete human being. There was something terribly wrong with him: he was exceedingly pale, his speech was execrable, he could not provide for himself, and he was hopelessly lacking in practical skills such as finding grubs. Yet, recently, some of the Yanomamo have come to the conclusion that there is hope for Chagnon. After years of study, Chagnon can function a little more effectively; in short, he can communicate with the Yanomamo on their own terms, and thus he has become more human to them. To achieve this status, Chagnon has had to learn to participate within a particular culture. The *test* of whether or not one has learned to communicate with others is the ability to share a meaningful universe with them (Ashley and Orenstein 1990, 37–38).

Sometimes the results of cultural differences and misunderstandings can be quite amusing. For example, while doing field work among the Guajiro Indians living in the northern part of Colombia, an American anthropologist learned that the Guajiro have a custom known as bride price. According to this custom, when a man and woman marry, the family of the husband-to-be is required to pay for his bride with cattle, other goods, or money. This practice upset the anthropologist, who felt that it was an insult to the dignity of women to be bought and sold in such a manner, much like a possession. She confided her feelings to a recent Guajiro bride, and asked the woman if she was offended at being purchased like a cow. The bride asked the anthropologist just how much her own husband had paid for her when they married. Taken aback, the anthropologist proudly announced that her husband had paid nothing for her. Such a practice was not done where she came from. "Oh what a horrible thing," came the reply. "Your husband didn't even give a single cow for you? You must not be worth anything!" (cited in Whiteford and Friedl 1992, 70).

But sometimes the results of cultural differences can be quite painful, as is illustrated by Jean Briggs's description of her time spent living among the Utkuhikhalinmiut of the Canadian Arctic in her book *Never in Anger* (1970). In 1963, Briggs began a 17-month field study of a small group of Utkuhikhalinmiut or Utku (Inuit to southerners) living at the mouth of the Back River, northwest of Hudson Bay. The nearest settlement was 240 kilometres north, in Gjoa Haven, which was then a small mission-and-trading settlement of perhaps 100 Inuit and 4 or 5 whites. At the time of Briggs's study, the Utku were almost self-sufficient.

Utku children doing chores in a small settlement in Gjoa Haven. Jean Briggs lived among the Utku for 17 months, with sometimes humorous and sometimes disastrous results.

When Briggs arrived, she was adopted as a daughter by a couple, Inuttiaq and Allaq, who had four younger daughters. But Briggs could never manage to control her emotions or their expression—she was angry constantly and, unlike her Utku adoptive family, unable to conceal her irritation and to behave in the culturally appropriate mild and noncomplaining fashion. After many attempts to teach her how to behave, the Utku finally resorted to what was, in Briggs's words, the "ultimate sanction against the display of aggression...ostracism."

The differences between my behaviour and that of the Utku could not help but create difficulties, on occasion, for the latter....It was not only the strangeness of my face and tongue that made me different. I was incongruous in other ways as well. I was an adult, yet as ignorant of simple skills as a child. I was a woman, yet I lacked the usual womanly attributes of husband and children; a "daughter," yet independently wealthy and accustomed to organizing my own life....In retrospect, my relationship with the Utku seems to divide approximately into three phases, in which from the Utku point of view I was first a stranger and a curiosity, then a recalcitrant child, and finally a confirmed irritant (225–26).

Briggs's original intention was to study the social relationships of shamans. She reasoned that, because the Utku were so far away from missionary influence, she would find practising shamans among them. But she had been misinformed. The Utku had encountered both Catholic and Anglican missionaries about 30 years before her arrival and were all devout, practising Christians. In the view of the people themselves, their shamans were all "either in hell or in hiding."

A new direction was determined with the Utku when Briggs lost her temper with some southern sports fishers who flew into the island near the Utkus' camp during the summer. Because Briggs was the only bilingual person, she was pressed into service as translator between the Utku and the whites, who wished to borrow two canoes. The outcome was that they could take the canoes. But now the Utku were stranded on their island and were dependent on the sports fishers to come and bring them food, which they themselves could no longer fish for, in exchange for carved toys and trinkets. As Briggs recounts the situation:

> I do not know how strongly the Utku felt about the absence of their canoes and their dependence on the foreign visitors. Perhaps none of the alterations in the daily patterns troubled them as much as they did me. Characteristically, the Utku kept well under control whatever negative feelings they may have had. Gratitude was the feeling they expressed openly.... Nevertheless, a change was clearly evident in the atmosphere of the Utku camp.... Though I have no way of knowing whether the Utkus' feelings coincided in detail with mine, there was evidence that the loan of the canoes was to them, as it was to me, a source of strain (279–80).

The situation came to a head when Briggs was asked to interpret again for another group of sports fishers who had arrived on their shores and who also wanted to borrow the canoes. At first the Utku complied and lent one canoe, which was subsequently returned because it was damaged. When the fishing guide asked for the loan of the good canoe, Briggs reacted:

> I exploded. Unsmilingly and in a cold voice I told the kapluna leader a variety of things that I thought he should know: that if he borrowed the second canoe we would be without a fishing boat, that if this boat also was damaged we would be in a very difficult position....I also pointed out the island where our supplies of tea, sugar, and kerosene were cached and mentioned our inability to reach it except by canoe....I told the guide that the owner of that second canoe did not wish to lend it.

The guide was not unreasonable; he agreed at once that if the owner did not wish to lend his canoe, that was his option: "It's his canoe, after all." Slightly soothed, I turned to Inuttiaq, who stood nearby, expressionless like the other Utku. "Do you want me to tell him you don't want to lend your canoe?" I asked in Eskimo. "He will not borrow it if you say no."

Inuttiaq's expression dismayed me, but I did not know how to read it; I knew only that it registered strong feeling, as did his voice which was unusually loud: "Let him have his will!"

I hoped my voice was calm when I replied to Inuttiaq: "As you like," but I was filled with fury at kapluna and Inuttiaq alike, as well as at myself for having undertaken the futile role of mediator, and my tone was icy when I said to the guide: "He says you can have it." Turning abruptly, I strode back to my tent, went to bed, and wept in silence (284–85).

Brigg's anger and hostility toward the sports fishers was, for the Utku, the final confirmation of her volatility and inability to control her emotions, attributes strongly shunned in Utku culture. For the next three months, Briggs was socially isolated and subtly shunned. Even though her questions had always been considered rude, the Utku had tried to humour her with answers. Now they simply refused to respond. And yet she was still treated with much care by the people she had offended. "I was amazed...that although my company was an anathema, nevertheless people still took care to give me plentiful amounts of the food I liked best, to warn me away from thin ice, and to caution me when my nose began to freeze" (295).

The works of Chagnon, Briggs, and other anthropologists have made it clear that while there are certain similarities between all human cultures—such as symbolic communication (language), conceptualization, and tool making, there is a vast range of differences. Values, norms, and expected behaviour vary extensively among different cultures. Even within a given culture, there may be large variations in how different members live, experience, and behave in such matters as family organization, work ethics, health and illness, or even expression of feelings.

Sociological perspectives on culture

Like everything else that is studied by sociologists, an analysis of culture may be accomplished from a number of different approaches or perspectives. We will briefly consider four different approaches to the analysis of culture: functionalism; structuralism; cultural materialism; sociobiology. While no proponent of any of these perspectives argues that culture does not play a fundamental role in all human activities, there is controversy over whether certain aspects of human behaviour are primarily rooted in social or in genetic causes. The first three of these perspectives are strongly sociological in nature, while the fourth, the sociobiological perspective, takes the point of view that certain kinds of behaviour are genetically transmitted from one generation to the next.

We have come to identify the totem as an easy symbol for Native people of the West Coast, but in fact it holds a precise and important meaning for those who created it.

FUNCTIONALISM

The functionalist approach to understanding culture assumes that whatever aspect of culture we consider—whether it is a marriage ceremony or a way of treating criminals—can be explained by showing how that aspect of culture contributes to the overall stability or survival of the society in which it exists. The work of social anthropologist Bronislaw Malinowski (1954) provides one of the best examples of the functionalist approach to explaining culture.

Malinowski studied a group of people, Trobriand Islanders, living in the South Pacific. When Malinowski lived among them, fish constituted their main food supply, and every aspect of ocean fishing was surrounded by an elaborate system of magic. Malinowski asked why this was so. At first the explanation seemed to be obvious. The Trobriand Islanders use magic because they believe it works to help them catch more fish. But why then, he asked, do the Trobriand Islanders use magic, while other societies do not?

In answering this question, Malinowski noted that ocean fishing is extremely hazardous, and the Trobriand Islanders have no control over either the weather or the locations where fish might be caught. This, he assumed, would make anyone nervous. But that anxiety could be reduced if one believed one had some control over the environment. Magic gives us exactly this feeling, he maintained. Malinowski concluded that whenever people feel insecure or in danger they will use magic. In other societies, where the environment is relatively safe, there is no need for magic. Even the Trobrianders, he noted, did not use magic when they went fishing in a sheltered island lagoon. The lagoon is a reasonably safe environment where finding the right place to fish is quite unproblematic. Therefore there is no need for magic.

Michael Carroll has pointed out how Malinowski's explanation of the use of magic by the Trobrianders fits with the basic assumptions of functionalist analysis. In Malinowski's view, magic contributes to the overall stability of Trobriand society because it reduces people's anxieties about the dangers and uncertainties associated with open ocean fishing (Carroll 1989, 31). In short, magic is functional in Trobriand culture because it gives the Trobrianders the sense that they can do something to control the environment. The sense of security in turn contributes to the overall stability of the society.

STRUCTURALISM

During the 1960s, the work of French anthropologist Claude Lévi-Strauss was widely followed. Lévi-Strauss developed a structuralist approach to culture in which he was concerned with identifying those mental processes that were common to all human beings, regardless of culture, and that shaped human perceptions. While the functionalists saw culture as a pragmatic adaptation to some need confronted by members of a society, Lévi-Strauss viewed culture much more theoretically. He grappled with the question "What makes human beings human?" His answer was that humans, unlike animals, are capable of abstract thought.

This question led him to a second, more complex one: "How do humans acquire the ability to think abstractly?" His reply was that the ability is not innate but learned. He set out to explain how this happened in *Totemism* (1963), where he defined **totemism** as "a belief system in which the members of a social group feel a mystical relationship of some sort with some natural category, usually an animal category." Members of a social group will often express this belief by claiming that they are descended from a given animal, which is their totem.

Malinowski, as a functionalist, contended that totemic animals were those animals that contributed most to the totem members' diet. But later research has shown this to be incorrect. Lévi-Strauss, on the other hand, took the approach that totemism established a one-to-one relationship between a natural category, an animal for example, and a social category, such as a lineage. Relationships that exist among the members of the natural category, Lévi-Strauss maintained, are reflected in the relationships among people making up the social category. Thus in nature, for example, all turtles or bears or foxes constitute separate categories. Members of the turtle clan have special relationships with each other that they do not have with members of the bear or fox clans.

Because we are not born with an innate ability to think about social structures, Lévi-Strauss contended, we must develop that ability by using analogies and by referring to the relationships we observe among things in nature. In short we use natural categories such as animals, or even flowers, as metaphors to help us think about social relationships.

CULTURAL MATERIALISM

During the late 1960s, a strong reaction against the popularity of abstract systems of thought, such as structuralism, appeared. One result was cultural materialism, a perspective on culture that de-emphasized the role of ideas and abstract thought, and saw culture instead as a kind of adaptation that humans make to specific kinds of physical environments.

One of the most prolific proponents of cultural materialism is American anthropologist Marvin Harris. In 1974 Harris wrote about the ban on the killing of sacred cows in India. To a Western observer, the ban on slaughtering cows seems senseless, especially in the face of widespread hunger. For a family to starve to death rather than kill one of the cows wandering the countryside appears to us a tragedy that could be prevented if only more sensible attitudes toward religion were adopted.

63

But Harris argued that the situation would be even more terrible if the Indian farmers started to slaughter their sacred cows. In India, agricultural production is not mechanized and relies on draught animals like oxen for power and on their dung for fertilizer and fuel. Mechanization is not an option in the country: first, there is a lack of funds to purchase the necessary machinery; second, mechanization always leads to a displacement of people from the countryside into the city. But cities in India are already overpopulated and cannot absorb the additional immigration that mechanization would bring. So India retains nonmechanized agriculture.

In addition, Indian farmers have at their disposal about one-third fewer oxen than they need. To get more oxen means there must be more cows. To slaughter the sacred cows for food would only further serve to undermine the already fragile agrarian economy. And the only way to really make sure that such a ban is followed is to make that ban total and religiously inspired, says Harris.

SOCIOBIOLOGY

This perspective on culture is the most controversial. Sociobiologists make two basic assumptions. The first is that predispositions toward certain kinds of behaviours in humans are transmitted genetically, in much the same way as upright posture and large brains. Culture, they argue, is more or less instinctual. The second assumption is that Darwin's theory of evolution is *essentially correct*. On the basis of these two assumptions, sociobiologists conclude that just as we use evolutionary theory to explain the evolution of certain physical traits in human beings, we can use the theory to explain the evolution of some social traits.

Sociobiology is a term taken from the work of American entomologist (insect specialist) E.O. Wilson (1975, 1978). The term sociobiology refers to "the application of biological principles to explain the social activities of all social animals, including human beings" (Giddens 1991, 40). Wilson believes that much of human social activity is rooted in human genetics, and that much of human behaviour is in fact instinctual.

He concludes from his observations that "genes promoting flexibility in social behaviour are strongly selected at the individual level," and that a wide variety of behaviours can exist within any one given society. One possible explanation for this, he notes, is that over the past ten thousand years "man as a whole has been so successful in dominating his environment that almost any kind of culture can succeed for a while, so long as it has a modest degree of internal consistency and does not shut off reproduction altogether" (273).

In direct contrast to Wilson, anthropologists such as Dobzhansky (1962) have argued that "culture is not inherited through genes" but is, rather, "acquired by learning from other human beings."

Instincts

Many species that inhabit this planet are genetically equipped with the ability to deal with the environment in which they live. Members of these species seem to meet their basic needs by "doing what comes naturally," and much of doing what comes naturally is said to be governed by **instincts**. Behaviours or actions are considered instinctual if they are

- relatively complex;

- unlearned, genetically transmitted, innate, inborn;

- species-wide, invariant among members of a species or common to all members of a species;

- manifest full-blown the first time the required level of maturity has been reached and the triggering stimuli are present in the environment;

- present (dependent, of course, on the required triggering stimuli) in a member of any given species even if that member is reared without contact with any other members of the same species (adapted from Knutilla 1993, 25).

While most of us might be ready to concede that, in matters such as the acquisition of language or manners, humans are definitely not guided by instincts, we might also be tempted to maintain that nonetheless there are a limited number of instances in which instincts just might play a role in shaping human behaviour. Common-sense understandings suggest to us that human beings *do* have a limited number of instinctual behaviours. Consider, for example, what happens when you become aware that something or someone is going to hit you. Your immediate reaction is to duck, blink, or in some way try to get out of the way. Consider, too, the behaviour of an infant when presented with a nipple. Isn't her suckling behaviour instinctual, just as is your moving away from potential danger?

The answer is no. There is a great difference between instincts and reflexes, such as pulling a hand away from a hot stove, blinking the eyes if something threatens to enter them, or trying to catch something for support when balance is lost. Reflexes are single, simple responses to perceived danger. Instincts, on the other hand, are complex patterns of behaviour that are genetically preprogrammed and that regulate the activities of members of a given species.

In the same way that reflexes are not instincts, neither are needs. While we are all born with a group of related physical requirements such as sleep, food, drink, elimination, bodily warmth, and possibly sex, these are broad, nonspecific needs that may be fulfilled in a number of ways. There is no set of complex, innate behaviours that accompanies any specific human bodily need. Rather, like everything else in human behaviour, culturally appropriate responses are learned to accommodate those needs.

Many sociologists, anthropologists, and even biologists agree, then, that human beings do not have instincts. They concur that there is no evidence to indicate that all human beings are genetically programmed to react to triggering stimuli in exactly the same way, regardless of their personal histories, social training, and experiences. But this is not the case for members of many other species. All ants, for example, will secrete substances in proportion to the severity of the danger of a given situation to warn their fellow ants of the danger. All bees will respond to a fall in ambient temperature by direct-ing their activities toward repairing their hive. Both ant and bee behaviours are examples of complex patterns that have been genetically predetermined and that are invariably elicited by changes in the environment. These activities occur independently of the voli-tion or control of any one individual ant or bee, who, as part of its genetic makeup, has inherited specific response mechanisms or instincts. All ants and all bees respond to trig-gering stimuli in their environment with exactly the same kind of species-specific complex behaviour.

When it comes to human behaviour, however, it is impossible to find a similar exam-ple of species-specific response to specific triggering stimuli. Certainly there are cultural-ly specific and generally expected responses to specific triggering stimuli. North American children, for example, are expected to say either yes, please or no, thank you, when answering the questions "Would you like some ice cream?" But most social scientists agree that, unlike bees or ants, each human being is born with relatively little, if any, pre-determined behaviour patterns. If the human infant is to survive and become a function-ing member of a society, he or she must *learn* how to communicate with other members of that society in a way that is mutually intelligible.

Because most of human communication is learned, the opportunities for variation in interpreting events and behaviours are almost infinite. The fact that human beings can live together in large social groupings attests to the extent to which sharing a common cul-ture provides us with a shared set of taken-for-granted understandings about our social world and how we must live in it. The importance of learning culture as a means for pro-viding all members of a given society with a shared set of skills and understandings was recognized as early as 1917 by American anthropologist Alfred Kroeber. Kroeber pro-poses the following mental experiment as a way of understanding the difference between the innate, instinctual behaviour of insects and the learned, cultural behaviour of human beings.

> Take a couple of ant eggs of the right sex—unhatched eggs, freshly laid. Blot out every individual and every other egg of the species. Give the pair a little attention as regards warmth, moisture, protection and food. The whole of ant "society," every one of the abil-ities, powers, accomplishments and activities of the species...will be reproduced, and reproduced without diminution, in one generation. But place on a desert island...two or three hundred human infants of the best stock from the highest class of the most civilized nation; furnish them the necessity of incubation and nourishment; leave them in total iso-lation from their kind; and what shall we have?...only a pair or a troop of mutes, without arts, knowledge, fire, without order or religion. Civilization would be blotted out within these confines—not disintegrated, not cut to the quick, but obliterated in one sweep ([1917] 1952, 177–78).

In the same book, Kroeber proposes another mental experiment to illustrate how, at birth, any child is capable of learning any language and acquiring any culture.

Let us take a French baby, born in France of French parents, themselves descended for numerous generations from French-speaking ancestors. Let us, at once after birth, entrust the infant to a mute nurse, with instructions to let no one handle or see her charge, while she travels by the directest [sic] route to the interior heart of China. There she delivers the child to a Chinese couple, who legally adopt it, and rear it as their son. Now suppose that three or ten or thirty years passed. Is it needful to discuss what the growing or grown Frenchman will speak? Not a word of French; pure Chinese, without a trace of accent and with Chinese fluency; and nothing else (29).

Sharing a common culture means that we learn not just a common language but, with that language, a common set of taken-for-granted assumptions about the social world. We use those assumptions as a basis on which we understand, explain, and interpret all our experiences. Although humans lack instincts, sociologists contend that they all have culture, and by having a shared culture, all members of a given society share in common a set of understandings about how and why their world works the way it does.

Some Final Arguments Against Sociobiology

Sociobiology does not just try to account for the contribution of biology and genetics to the evolution of human behaviour. It rests, instead, on a specific view "that natural selection is a virtually omnipotent architect, constructing organisms part by part as the best solutions to problems of life in local environments" (Gould 1981, 16). Applied to humans, sociobiology sees *species* behaviours as adaptations built by forces of natural selection. Forces of natural selection, furthermore, are posited to work only through genetic change. Thus any change in human behaviour is an adaptive change that is the result of genetic modifications. Genetic adaption, in turn, explains specific human behaviours: why some people are aggressive, xenophobic, religious, acquisitive, homosexual, and so on (ibid.).

Gould points out that while humans are indeed animals, they are animals with a difference. Humans have enormous flexibility as a result of an oversized brain. Unlike other animals, they have culture as a nongenetic basis for adaptive behaviours. Gould argues that sociobiologists are fooled because they believe that what are human behaviours are to be found, albeit in rudimentary form, in lower species. In other words, sociobiologists observe human behaviour, describe it, and then look for similar behaviour in lower animals. Once they have found something they can make fit, they then look back at human behaviour and compare it with some animal behaviour that they have decided is equivalent. If the behaviour of the animals is natural, they reason, then the developed form of behaviour in humans is also natural.

Thus, as Gould further points out, sociobiologists will talk about "slave ants, rape in mallard ducks, and adultery in mountain bluebirds" and then argue that if these traits can be found in lower animals, they are also to be found among humans as natural, genetic, and adaptive. Gould is quick to note, however, that none of these behaviours exists outside the human context and that sociobiologists are merely projecting onto animal behaviour interpretations that have no place outside human cultural life. The final assessment of sociobiology, offered by sociologists, is that while sociobiology may have a lot to say about animal social organization and social life, it has little to contribute to our understanding of human social existence.

NATURE AND CULTURE

DIFFERENT APPROACHES TO THE ANALYSIS OF CULTURE	
Theoretical Approach	**Summary Statement**
1. Functionalism	All aspects of a given culture contribute to the overall stability or survival (functioning) of that culture.
2. Structuralism	All culture is based on abstract thought, and ideas are central to establishing cultural practices.
3. Cultural Materialism	Culture is an adaptation that humans make to specific kinds of physical environments.
4. Sociobiology	Genetic inheritance exercises a certain amount of influence over human social behaviour.

TABLE 4-1

If we reject as too simplistic and ultimately unsatisfactory the assumptions of sociobiology concerning genetic inheritance, where do we turn for an explanation of the relationship between nature and nurture, between culture and our biological existence as a species? What is the relationship between our embodiment as a two-legged species with an opposable thumb and a large and labile brain, and the wide variety of human cultures that have existed in human history and currently exist?

Western thinkers have debated for centuries the nature of the interrelationship between culture and nature. Wars have been fought, genocide has been practised, women, blacks, gays, and disabled people have been excluded from full human status all on the basis of arguments that derive in some way from notions about natural or biologically based conditions justifying differential treatment of people. The concepts of nature and culture are not neutral ones in Western thought. They imply moral and political consequences. From racial discrimination to the genocide of Jews during the Second World War, from discriminatory legislation based on ideas of the natural inferiority of women to laws that prohibit gays from marrying (as an unnatural act), Western ideas about what is, and what is not, natural to humans have serious consequences for everyone.

Until recently the two sides of the debate about nature and culture appeared to be totally opposed. On the one side, sociobiologists argue that our social existence can be explained by biological imperatives. On the other side, **cultural determinists** argued that human behaviour is the result of processes that are culturally driven with no biological imperatives.

Recall for a moment E.B. Tylor's definition of culture, which is a good example of a cultural determinist position. As part of this definition, Tylor tells us that culture is "acquired by man as a member of society." This definition implies quite clearly that culture is learned rather than instinctive. We are not born knowing how to be culturally Canadian, how to speak English or French, how to use the public transportation system, or to attend church or school. Rather we learn these and myriad other behaviours, beliefs, and ways of being in the world from other members of our society.

That human beings have culture implies for many anthropologists and sociologists a distinct split, an opposition between culture and nature. Culture is something other than and separate from nature. Indeed many would go so far as to argue that culture is a denial of nature. Recently, however, some social scientists have begun to reject both arguments as too simplistic and to replace them with more complex theories that take into consideration both the independent nature of culture and the fact that all humans are embodied beings.

CULTURAL AND HUMAN EMBODIMENT

Many social scientists now concur that, while much of human behaviour is explicable in terms of cultural processes that are learned, the fact that we are all embodied beings means that certain physical aspects of our existence cannot be ignored. Instead of focusing on the genetic makeup of humans and looking for genetic determinants of cultural practices (as in the case of sociobiology), these social scientists are turning to the material, physiological nature of human embodiment to help them understand the links between nature and nurture.

These researchers and writers believe that the best place to begin an inquiry into human culture is with the relationship between culture and human embodiment. Some have now come to recognize that, as embodied creatures, humans do have bodily needs and a particular physiological configuration. The shape of the human body, its needs and characteristics, continue to be significant in shaping the ways in which we behave socially.

American anthropologist Mary Douglas (1984, 60) has pointed out that, while all humans have the same body, "with the same number of orifices, using the same energies and seeking the same biological satisfactions," each culture is highly selective in the treatment accorded to any one of these themes. Thus, while every human has bodily needs that must be fulfilled, how those needs are fulfilled is purely a matter of culture.

The rules for how bodily needs are fulfilled vary widely from culture to culture. There does not seem to be any human physical condition for which cultural treatment is consistent across the globe. In each culture, some bodily functions or life events are viewed as good, while others are viewed as dangerous or "polluting" (Douglas 1984, 60). We have seen that among North Americans particular attention is paid to a ritualized cleansing of the mouth after eating. Among the Mae Enga of the New Guinea Highlands, ritual cleansing takes place after sexual intercourse to rid the participants of sexual pollution, while the Nyakyusa of Tanzania insist on ritualized washing, seclusion, and fumigations after a funeral to make mourners and burial party members fit once again for social contact.

There are many other instances to choose from. For example, while all humans need to eliminate bodily wastes, where it is done, in what physical position it is done, and even how often it is done is culturally specific. In Western cultures, it is customary to wash the hands after urinating. Among Arab and other Muslim groups, only the left hand—considered the profane hand—is used to clean oneself after elimination. The right hand, considered pure, is used for eating. Men of the Chagga tribe wear anal plugs, claiming to have sealed up their anuses and therefore never needing to defecate (Becker 1973, 32).

Eating is essential for survival. As Margaret Visser writes, although food is an everyday thing, it is never just something to eat. In our treatment of food, we "echo the preferences and principles of our culture." But how we eat, when, where, and even what we eat follow cultural dictates, rules of propriety, and beliefs about what is appropriate food for humans. North Americans, for example, are taught that it is impolite to talk with a full mouth, to eat peas with a knife, or to eat most foods with their hands. The Yurok of California learn to eat with a serious expression on their faces and to think about wealth while they are eating, while the Mundurucz of Brazil will not behave boisterously while eating in case they offend the spirit-mothers of the animals.

> Food choices and presentations are part of every society's tradition and character. An elaborate frozen dessert moulded into the shape of a ruined classical temple can be read as one vivid expression of a society's view of itself and its ideals; so can a round ground hamburger patty between two circular buns. Food shapes us and expresses us even more definitively than our furniture or houses or utensils do (Visser 1986, 12).

The complex and even convoluted relationship between needs, physiological response, and culture is illustrated by the following example. American anthropologist Clyde Kluckhohn tells of an acquaintance in Arizona who took a certain perverse pleasure in causing a cultural response to food. She would frequently serve her luncheon guests sandwiches filled with a light meat that looked and tasted similar to tuna or chicken. After the meal had been served, the hostess would inform her guests that they had lunched on rattlesnake salad sandwiches. Invariably the response of at least one guest would be to vomit (1949, 19).

To further illustrate the extent of diversity both within and between different cultures I want to consider the significance of cultural context for understanding two seemingly invariant biological or bodily experiences—death and memory. It would appear that dying or remembering something are, in and of themselves, purely biological processes. While we may want to concede that different cultures specify different activities or rituals focusing on death or the use of memory, our everyday experience of the world tells us that the actual acts themselves and our understandings of what they are should be fairly constant for all humanity. After all, death and memory are bodily undertakings, biologically based and as such invariant. Or are they?

DEATH AND CULTURE

As Paul Hirst and Penny Woolley have pointed out (1981), while death is inescapable for all human beings, it is not the simple and self-evident occurrence that taken-for-granted understanding might lead us to believe. And the reasons for this complexity are not as self-evident as they may first appear, either. For example, we might want to argue that determining when the exact moment of death has occurred is becoming more and more problematic because of advances in modern medical technology and knowledge. What was not so long ago a simple matter of determining whether or not a person continued to breathe and therefore continued to live has now become less straightforward. Moreover, with new technology it is possible to keep a body alive without there being any brain activity. Thus it is now possible to speak of someone being brain dead while the body remains alive via technological means.

But the problem of defining when death has occurred is not merely a technical one, which can be resolved as we become more technologically proficient. Death is a cultural

A young boy wearing his father's war insignia searches to connect with his name at the Vietnam Memorial in Washington.

issue. Western Christian culture defines death as the opposite of life. There is an instantaneous transformation between one state (life) and the other (death). But as new medical evidence and practices force us to realize, matters are not so simple. Our culture is beginning to think it quite possible that those "deluded primitive cultures" that do not accept the instantaneous transition from life to death might just have a case.

As Hirst and Woolley (1981) point out from the work of Robert Hertz, what is considered death, in fact, varies from culture to culture and depends greatly on social beliefs and categories. In many societies, death is not considered to occur instantaneously but is rather a slow-changing condition. Among the seventeenth-century Huron, a body was buried twice, first in an individual grave and later, when the entire village moved to take up new agricultural land, all individuals who had died between one move and the next were disinterred and buried in a common grave. The period during which a Huron body lay decomposing in an individual grave and its final re-interment in a common grave marked a series of changes in the individual's state of being dead.

Today North Americans usually consider death a private affair. But as little as 150 years ago in Western Europe, the dying often publicly said good-bye to as many of their relatives and acquaintances as possible. Even those who did not know the dying individual, but were in the vicinity, felt free to come and watch the final hours of a stranger's life. In his book *The Hour of Our Death* (1981), French historian Philippe Ariès tells of the public nature of death in Western Europe during the eighteenth and nineteenth centuries, where the dying person was expected to be at the centre of a group of people. Ariès recounts the death of Mme de Montespan (a mistress of) Louis XV of France, who, according to one of her biographers, was "less afraid of dying than she was of dying *alone*." Ariès describes her final moments:

> On May 27, 1707, when she realized that she was about to die, she was no longer afraid. She summoned all her servants, "down to the lowest one," asked their forgiveness, confessed her sins, and presided, as was the custom, over the ceremony of her own death (18–19).

Although by the late eighteenth century French doctors had begun to complain about the unhygienic aspects of having so many people invading the bedrooms of the dying, their complaints went unheeded well into the next century. Quoting from the memoirs of a nineteenth-century French gentlewoman, Mme de La Ferronays, Ariès recounts how she was

> walking in the streets of Ischl during the 1830s when she heard the church bell and learned that the holy sacrament was about to be administered to a young priest whom she knew to be sick. She had not dared to visit him yet, because she had not met him, but the holy sacrament "brought me there *quite naturally* [italics added]. I knelt down by the main entrance along with everyone else, while the priests went by. Then I went upstairs and watched while he received the last sacrament and Extreme Unction" (19).

Even the act of going from a state of health to one of decline and ultimate death is not immune from cultural influences. Hirst and Woolley report on the work of W.B. Cannon, a physiologist who published a paper entitled "Voodoo Death" in 1942. Cannon contends that death can occur as a result of cultural beliefs in which evil spirits, black magic, and cursed objects can do an intended victim irreparable harm. The belief in the efficacy of such things, Cannon argues, is enough to induce a state of fear in a person who thinks himself or herself to be the target of a curse or of the anger of an offended spirit. The fear and terror experienced by individuals while awaiting their anticipated fate is sufficient to induce a change in their physiological state, something equivalent to severe wound shock. The result is a malfunctioning of the circulatory system as the individual's blood pressure drops and he or she falls into a coma. At this point, the victim is beyond the capacity to respond consciously to any intervention and ultimately dies as a result of oxygen starvation to the vital organs. These deaths serve in their turn to reinforce the convictions of others concerning the effectiveness of occult powers and evil spirits (Hirst and Woolley 1981, 26–27).

What these and many other examples illustrate is the complex relationship between death as a biological experience and death as a cultural one. The understanding of what constitutes being dead and even the experience of dying is clearly not universal in all human societies. As with all human experiences, it is mediated both by culture and by the embodied nature of human beings. And like all human experiences, the range of cultural diversity in formulating, shaping, and giving meaning to something that on first examination appears to be a simple and straightforward biological matter is boundless.

MEMORY AND CULTURE

By now it should be clear that, in contrast to everyday, taken-for-granted understandings, what is biological and what is cultural should not be thought of as separate, opposing forces. Memory, for example, is not merely a biologically based, psychological capacity that all humans have, independent of any kind of cultural content. A biologically based facility such as memory is simultaneously dependent on the functioning of the brain and on the culturally specific techniques that the individual has acquired. That which at first appears to be purely biological (memory) and that which at first appears to be strictly culture (technologies to aid memory such as writing and printing) are in fact closely interwoven.

Paul Hirst and Penny Woolley (1981) compare the consequences of the use of the techniques of writing with other techniques used by nonliterate people as an aid to story telling. They also discuss non-Western forms of recording information as well as the effects of printing on memory and language use. While the cultural prejudices of many Westerners have led them to conclude that writing is the best memory device invented by any culture, and as such is essential for any advanced civilization or culture, Hirst and Woolley dispute this view. In so doing, they cite examples that demonstrate the close connection between our biological capacities for memory and the culturally defined techniques or "mnemonics" we use to assist memory.

In nonliterate societies, culture and tradition were learned through storytelling. The storyteller stored and retold information for people.

Writing and Other Mnemonic Techniques

The cultural consequences of writing for human social relations have either been ignored or have been overrated by most cultural theorists. In the first case, writing is treated only as a cultural technique, as a way of recording and representing ideas and symbols. In the second case, writing is heralded as *the* mark of civilization because it makes cultural preservation possible by allowing it to be transmitted in a stable form. The anthropologist V. Gordon Child illustrates this latter approach when he notes that writing represents

an epoch in human progress....The true significance of writing is that it was destined to revolutionize the transmission of human knowledge. By its means a man can immortalize his experience and transmit it directly to contemporaries living far off and to generations yet unborn. It is the first step to raising science above the limits of space and time (Child 1956, 186).

In spite of Child's convictions, writing, as a vehicle for storing information, has had a number of rivals. Sophisticated literatures and cultures don't necessarily have to depend on writing. Nor is the running of highly bureaucratized societies dependent on writing in the proper sense of the world. So-called illiterate or unlettered peoples have been able to produce elaborate oral compositions and stories, and to carry out the complex administration of a state or empire.

For example, Homer's *Iliad,* an indisputable literary masterpiece, was composed before writing. Moreover, it was preserved and retold by countless different storytellers. In explaining the *Iliad*, Albert Lord (1960) argues that Homer composed it not as a set text, but as a tale that could be told with variations. The storyteller learns a repertoire of devices and phrases that are appropriate to certain themes or situations. Rather than recalling a memorized tale, the storyteller draws on these devices and phrases to produce a story as he or she is telling it. Thus, a story exists only as it is performed by a storyteller. Any given story is the property of a collective of storytellers rather than a single author.

In a similar way, we can challenge the idea of the need for written records as a mnemonic device necessary for controlling the resources of large-scale administrations. Drawing on Karl Polanyi's 1966 study, *Dahomey and the Slave Trade*, Hirst and Woolley note that during the eighteenth century, the African kingdom of Dahomey rose to power based on a system of careful controls exercised by the king's administrators in charge of military service and livestock. The administrators levied taxes, took censuses, and were able to prevent local frauds, all by employing an accounting system that used pebbles kept in boxes as tallies.

Printing and Memory

The introduction of printing, which can be defined as "the mechanical reproduction and duplication of writing by means of moveable type," had profound effects on memory and on Western culture in general. Printing transformed techniques of reading, writing, and learning as well as the character of what was read, written, and learned (Hirst and Woolley 1981, 35). Experiments with printing that took place in Europe during the mid-fifteenth century resulted in the invention of the printing press. By the end of the sixteenth century, printing was widespread and most instruction throughout Western Europe was based on the printed word. Estimates made by Febvre and Martin (1976) illustrate the rapid domination of printing. While 20 million books were printed before 1500, somewhere between 150 and 200 million were put into circulation in the century that followed.

But why should the introduction of printing into a culture that already uses writing transform that culture so profoundly? After all, isn't printing just another way of recording what could already be set down with writing? Hirst and Woolley offer a very strong no in response to this question for the following reasons.

First, the labour involved in producing a hand-written manuscript is very different from the labour involved in printing a book. Scribes who produced books engaged in a laborious and time-consuming occupation. They were always struggling with the demand to produce as many books as possible and the need to preserve the integrity of the text from copying errors.

Second, books produced in such a fashion were rare and precious and were often kept locked away. Personal possession of books was restricted to the wealthy. Individuals such as lawyers and scholars, who relied on books for their profession, usually possessed small, specialized libraries.

Third, without printing and therefore without accessibility to large quantities of books, mass education in a preprint culture is almost impossible. Unlike today, our medieval ancestors were not considered uncultured if they were illiterate. A person who could not read in medieval Europe was by no means cut off from popular culture as he or she would be today. While members of the nobility in many European countries were illiterate, they were nonetheless highly cultured and well aware of the written literature, which they could not read themselves.

Fourth, prior to the widespread availability of printed books, university teachers lectured from hand-copied manuscripts. The word lecturer means, literally, "reader of books." Those few who were skilled in reading and writing used those skills in the service of a largely oral culture. As Hirst and Woolley point out, "literacy was not the everyday means of cultured communication." Rather reading and writing skills were ancillary to the spoken language, which dominated medieval culture.

Fifth, the content and style of preprinted stories and poems were closely tied to an oral tradition. Themes were chosen and composed to hold the interest of a listener, not a reader. Writing, then, was undertaken with listeners in mind rather than with readers.

How did the literate but as yet printless cultures of antiquity and the later Middle Ages resolve the problem of sharing complex information in medicine, law, philosophy, and theology? According to Hirst and Woolley's assessment, knowledge systematization and memory training were the answer. But memory techniques also affect the form and content of knowledge itself. In the Middle Ages, analytical and observational knowledge was marked by the dominance of systems of ordered hierarchies of categories. What is significant to note about systems of knowledge until the Middle Ages is that the form of order needed to retain knowledge often restricted growth or change.

There are certain very powerful, conservative tendencies imposed by a knowledge system that is dependent on the memory practices of individuals for recalling, storing, and presenting that knowledge. The tendency is to add new knowledge, which is a much more simple and less demanding task than to restructure what is already known. Rarely could a medieval scholar place one text beside another for cross-referencing or comparison. The development of the kind of critical attitude that many late twentieth-century university teachers think essential for their students to have is possible only when material can be accumulated on a massive scale *and* when different accounts can be consulted by the same person.

■ ■ ■

SUMMARY

Culture is one of the most widely used concepts in sociology. As a concept, it encompasses everything that people have, think, and do as members of a given society. To be a fully functioning member of a culture is to be able to communicate with other members of that culture in ways that are mutually acceptable. There are many different cultures in the world today, with a great deal of diversity between them in social practices, values, norms, and belief systems. One very good reason for studying this diversity is to help reduce ethnocentrism, the tendency to believe that one's own culture is superior to all others.

Sociologists use a number of different perspectives or approaches to study culture. Four of the most prevalent are functionalism, structuralism, cultural materialism, and sociobiology. Each of these perspectives highlights different aspects of culture as central to an understanding of human behaviour. While sociologists who follow either the functionalist, structuralist, or cultural materialist approaches agree that all of human culture is learned, sociobiologists take the point of view that certain aspects of human culture are not learned but are passed on as part of our genetic inheritance.

Although sociobiology has not provided sociologists with the means to understand the relationship between human biological existence and culture, the physical aspects of human existence should not be ignored. Recently sociologists and other social scientists have studied the sociology of the body, focusing on the links between bodily functions and human social behaviour.

■ ■ ■

1. Using Miner's example of brushing teeth, discuss other taken-for-granted aspects of Canadian culture from the point of view of someone unfamiliar with the culture.

2. In what ways is Canadian society ethnocentric?

3. Jean Briggs's work on the Utku suggests that the expression of emotions such as anger are culturally specific. What are the culturally appropriate ways for Canadians to express other emotions, such as happiness, love, fear?

4. Lévi-Strauss suggests that what makes human beings unique is our capacity for abstract thought. In what ways do you agree or disagree with this statement?

5. How useful is a sociobiological perspective to sociological inquiry?

5

HUMAN ORIGINS AND CULTURE

CHAPTER OPENING QUESTIONS

- How and why have our perspectives on human origins changed over the past two centuries?

- What is unique about Darwinian evolutionary theory?

- What is the significance of physical differences between *Homo sapiens* and the other primates?

- How does our contemporary social existence influence the ways we currently understand our origins as a species?

- What are some possible connections between human thinking and human evolution?

One of the challenging issues for critical sociological inquiry is the relationship between the individual, culture, and nature. In pursuing this theme, researchers are often concerned with establishing the fundamental determinants of human behaviour. This issue is frequently raised in research into the history of our species, *Homo sapiens*. **Paleoanthropologists** have long been concerned with the role of genetic inheritance, including physiology and intelligence, in establishing human culture and social behaviour. They have explored the relationship between nature and nurture in their search for an understanding of human evolution. While some regard changes in hominid physiology and intelligence as central to the process of our evolution, others see certain aspects of specifically human social behaviour—monogamous couples, food-sharing families, and social fission and fusion, such as division of family groupings and their recombination into clans—as providing the key.

In this chapter we examine some of the most recent and often contradictory findings in the evolution of our species. In so doing, we will explore the various available ways of explaining the social basis of human existence, including what it means to be human and what distinguishes *Homo sapiens* as a species from our nearest primate relatives.

The many different perspectives on the role of culture in human evolution have produced radically different interpretations; thus this chapter emphasizes the importance of theoretical perspectives in shaping our understanding of human behaviour and human history.

THEORIES ABOUT HUMAN ORIGINS

Biologist Donna Haraway has noted, "Language is the tool of human self-construction, that which cuts us off from the garden of mute and dumb animals and leads us to name things, to force meanings, to create opposition and so to craft human culture" (1991, 81). She goes on to say that "scientific debate about monkeys, apes, and human beings, that is about primates, is a social process of producing stories, important stories that constitute public meanings." Evolutionary biology of the nineteenth and twentieth centuries, she points out, is part of the ongoing public debate about the relationship between politics and society.

All scientific practice and theory, Haraway contends, is embedded in language and the use of metaphors. Because metaphors structure scientific vision, scientific practice is also a storytelling practice. It is a historically specific practice of interpretation and testimony. Looking at the scientific study of human evolution primarily as a storytelling craft, Haraway argues, is particularly appropriate. *Homo sapiens* has emerged in palaeoanthropology as a distinct species in relation to "elaborate narratives about origins, natures, and possibilities" (1989, 4).

From the beginning of the eighteenth century, the notion of the evolution of *Homo sapiens*, what constitutes it as a species, what its origins and its future are, have been built on tales about the duality between nature and culture, animal and human, mind and body. Treating these scientific explanations about human origins and evolution as narratives or stories is not being dismissive. But neither is it being worshipful of nor mystified by scientific knowledge. To question the assumptions that underlie our knowledge about human evolution is part of critical sociological inquiry.

Haraway is not the only writer to note the storylike nature of the debates concerning human evolution. John Durant of Oxford University writes:

> Could it be that like primitive [sic] myths, theories of human evolution reinforce the value-systems of their creators by reflecting historically their image of themselves and of the

Michelangelo's depiction of the creation of Adam. Detail from the Sistine Chapel.

society in which they live?...Time and again ideas about human origins turn out on closer examination to tell us as much about the present as about the past, as much about our own experiences as about those of our remote ancestors (1981, 427).

In his book *Bones of Contention: Controversies in the Search for Human Origins* (1988), paleoanthropologist Roger Lewin tells of how, as a graduate student at Yale in 1979, Misia Landau came to the realization that there existed a strong link between literary traditions and the presentation of ideas concerning evolution by contemporary paleoanthropologists. Drawing on classic folk tales, she learned how the hero myths all followed a basic structure in which the hero enters the scene, is challenged by some adversity, overcomes that adversity through a series of tests, and finally triumphs.

Landau discovered that the same scenario, the same tale, has also been repeatedly used by scientists to describe human evolution in the textbooks she was reading (Lewin 1988, 32). Her reading consistently centred around four main events, which were used by scientists to represent the evolutionary transformation of some sort of primate ancestor into a protohuman. Those events were a shift from the trees to the ground; another shift from walking on all fours to upright posture and bipedalism (walking on two legs); the expansion of the brain, which included the development of intelligence and language; and the emergence of technology and culture, including morals (Lewin 1988, 32–33).

The story that Landau was able to distil from contemporary scientific accounts of human evolution can be summarized as follows:

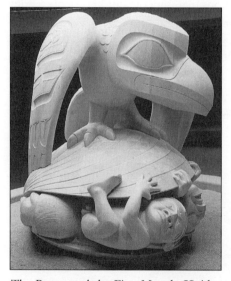

The Raven and the First Men *by Haida artist Bill Reid, 1980. Carved from a laminated block of yellow cedar, the sculpture depicts an episode from a 19th century Haida origin story in a contemporary style.*

Accounts begin with the introduction of the humble hero (an ape, a monkey or a diminutive prosimian) in an initially stable environment; our hero is then expelled from this safety (because of climatic change) and is forced to embark on a hazardous journey during which he must overcome a series of tests (new environmental conditions) and thereby display his work (develop intelligence, bipedalism, etc.); thus endowed our hero develops further advantages (tools...reason...), only to be tested again (the rigors of Ice Age Europe); the ultimate triumph is the achievement of humanity (Lewin 1988, 33–34).

Some paleoanthropologists, however, are aware that their work does more than just objectively describe hominid evolution. As British paleoanthropologist Glynn Isaac remarked at the 1982 centenary commemoration of Darwin's death: "Regardless of how scientists present them, accounts of human origins are read as replacement materials for Genesis. They...do more than cope with curiosity, they have allegorical content, and they convey values, ethics and attitudes" (Lewin 1993, 3). The changes in these stories (theories) are particularly fascinating in that they illustrate the relationship between popular, taken-for-granted beliefs and what eventually become accepted as scientific truths and objectively produced knowledge.

By now it should be clear that deriving true, objective knowledge about human evolution and the relationship between human nature and the development of culture is not simple. The evolution of our species has been explained by many serious scholars in ways that are essentially contradictory. Various explanations about the relationship between human culture, biology, and evolution are strongly influenced by what scientists have believed to be the most salient features of human existence. In what follows we will see how hominid fossils, as well as living animals and human beings, are deemed proper objects for scientific investigation within a historically particular way of constructing both the object of study and the relationship between the scientist and what is to be studied. The answers we reach to questions concerning the origin of human behaviour or influences on the development of human culture depend very much on who is doing the asking and on what is considered to be, at that moment, the most likely and reasonable explanatory route.

As Misia Landau suggests, paleoanthropologists need to examine the myths beneath the stories they tell. In so doing, they need to find new and more workable stories to tell, ones with larger and more complicated plots. "Bolstered by our simplifying theories and archetypes," Landau explains, "we have behaved as though the past were knowable, as though our questions could be answered by fossils, when, in truth, they are answered as they are asked: by humans" (1987, 122).

Landau quotes an aphorism another paleoanthropologist, David Pilbeam, used to end his paper "Current Arguments on Early Man" (1980, 285).

> We do not see things as they are
> We see things as we are.

At the time Pilbeam used the aphorism, he was under the impression that it was a Talmudic quotation. But after an extensive search for the exact reference, he concluded that it came from a Chinese fortune cookie. As Landau concludes:

> This could be a good omen. For depending on how you regard Chinese fortune cookies (or the Talmud, for that matter), maybe we do have the power after all: if not to see things as they are, then to see, within known limits, how we are (1987, 122).

Keep this caution in mind as we a look at some of the perspectives on human evolution that have been proposed over the past two centuries.

PERSPECTIVES ON HUMAN EVOLUTION

Over the last two centuries, ideas about the relative status of human beings and all other animals have changed dramatically. There have been a series of different perspectives on human evolution that have claimed to reveal the "truth" about our species' place in relation to nature and culture. From the medieval concept of the Great Chain of Being to Darwin's evolutionary model and on into present-day formulations by paleoanthropologists, a central concern has been with identifying the single, all-explanatory motor force behind human evolution.

THE GREAT CHAIN OF BEING

The special status of humans among God's creatures was the most widely held understanding about humanity's place in nature throughout Western Europe from the Middle Ages until the mid-nineteenth century. Humans are special, the argument went, because they are given a number of unique capabilities, including transcendent intelligence and moral and spiritual sense. Because of this, they are amply justified in considering themselves superior to the rest of nature. This belief formed the core of a perspective on the world that has been called "The Great Chain of Being" thesis. As biologist Stephen Jay Gould explains:

> In the great chain of being, each organism represents a definite link in a single sequence leading from the lowest amoeba in a drop of water to ever more complex beings culminating in, you guessed it, our own exalted selves....The chain is a static ordering of unchanging, created entities—a set of creatures placed by God in fixed positions of an ascending hierarchy that does not represent time or history, but the eternal order of things. The ideological function of the chain is rooted in its static nature: each creature must be satisfied with its assigned place—the serf in his hovel as well as the lord in his castle—for any attempt to rise will disrupt the universe's established order (1983, 11).

Gould points out the clear connection between the metaphor of a Great Chain of Being in which each creature has its assigned place and the structure of feudal society that served as the model for the thesis. Feudal society in Western Europe was dependent on a static ordering of social positions, from the serfs who lived and toiled on the land, to the lords who commanded the serfs, to the king in his castle, who commanded the loyalty and obedience of the lords. This metaphor can be both a descriptive and an explanatory device because it simultaneously represents the world as it was perceived and as it was supposed to be. Not surprisingly, the proponents of this thesis placed white Europeans at the highest point in the chain linking earth and heaven, just a few steps below the angels. As Charles White, a British physician who defended the thesis, wrote in 1799:

> Ascending the line of gradation, we come at last to the white European; who being most removed from the brute creation, may, on that account, be considered the most beautiful

of the human race....Where except on the bosom of the European woman [can one find] two such plump and snow white hemispheres, tipt with vermilion? (cited in Gould 1983, 20).

White was doing no more than expressing a commonly held opinion, one that is still attractive to people with racist and sexist views. The Great Chain of Being thesis handily offered an explanation for the perceived superiority of the Western European male.

CAROLUS LINNAEUS AND *SYSTEMA NATURAE*

However resonate it was with medieval life, the Great Chain of Being thesis had certain problems in explanatory logic that became increasingly apparent as feudalism crumbled and as new, scientific ways of knowing began to replace older, theologically based ones. Although the Great Chain of Being thesis required that there be a steady, graduated progression throughout the entire natural world, there were certain gaps that could not be accounted for, including the apparent gap between minerals and plants, plants and animals, and (most problematic of all), apes and humans. To compensate, eighteenth- and nineteenth-century scientists claimed that apes were known to walk upright, to carry off human slaves, and even to mate with humans and produce offspring. The "lower races" of humans, by the same token, were held to exhibit apelike qualities. They were considered brutal, savage, and lacking culture and language (Lewin 1993, 4).

This perception of the natural world was encompassed in the work of the Swedish biologist Carolus Linnaeus, who provided modern biology with its classificatory system of animals. In 1735 Linnaeus published *Systema Naturae*, a study of the basis of zoological classification. In this book, he took a significant step away from the Christian assumptions that had dominated thinking about human origins. Instead of placing humans alone at the highest pinnacle, Linnaeus took the radical step of placing them in a taxonomic order of nature along with all other animals.

Linnaeus placed man (whom he labelled *Homo sapiens*) in the taxonomic order of Primates. But at the same time, he was compelled to postulate the existence of two forms of protohumans in the same category as *Homo sapiens*, which he called *Homo troglodytes* and *Homo caudatus*. These two fanciful species of protohumans were intended to fill in the gap between apes and humans. Linnaeus illustrated *Homo troglodytes* as a hairy woman (Haraway 1989, 9). *Homo troglodytes* was reputed to live in forests, to be nocturnal, and to communicate only in hisses, while *Homo caudatus* was fancied as having a tail (Lewin 1993, 5).

With *Homo troglodytes* and *Homo caudatus*, Linnaeus, in fact, created two species that he strongly believed had to exist, even if no one had ever seen them. Does this make Linnaeus a delusional liar? I think not. Placed in context, Linnaeus should be viewed as an honest scientist who saw what his theory led him to believe must be there. As the one who was able not just to rename animals, but to give them their true names, Linnaeus believed his role was to ensure that nature was accurately represented (Haraway 1989, 9). In carrying out his taxonomic work, he claimed that he was a "second Adam," the "eye of God" who could restore the true names and representations that had been lost by the first Adam's sin. European scholars often took information about the peoples of Africa, gleaned from travellers' accounts, as evidence to support their belief in the evolutionary gaps between Europeans and all others.

Linnaeus was one of many scientists of the eighteenth and nineteenth centuries who used the increasing information about Africa to help him fill in and substantiate theories about the place of humanity in relation to the rest of nature. While the notion of the radical separation between humans and animals was being challenged, European scholars struggled to find the means to justify their beliefs that the "white races" were well in front of all others in terms of evolutionary development.

For example, Carl Vogt, a mid-nineteenth-century Geneva scholar, wrote: "The pendulous abdomen of the lower races...shows an approximation to the ape, as do also the want of calves, the flatness of the thighs, the pointing form of the buttocks and the leanness of the upper arm" (1864, 53). Moreover, he noted, "We may be sure that wherever we perceive an approach to the animal type the female is nearer to it than the male. Hence we should discover a greater resemblance of the Negro to apes if we were to take a female as our standard" (ibid.).

CHARLES DARWIN AND THE EVOLUTION OF *HOMO SAPIENS*

In contrast to the static model of the world that came from the Great Chain of Being thesis, nineteenth-century evolutionary theory presented the world as a very different and dynamic place. In this evolutionary model, the world and everything in it is in constant motion. The idea that contemporary forms of animal and plant life were the result of evolution—the transmutation of species by changes to or modifications in ancestral forms—slowly gained ground (Richards 1987, 8). By the early nineteenth century, it was no longer fashionable to hold the Book of Genesis—the first book of the Bible—as a literal account of creation. But naturalists continued to maintain that some supernatural agency, if not a miracle, was responsible for the creation of new species in the course of the history of the earth. If God did not do it directly, He was held to have achieved His goals through creating the "self-designing forces of nature" (Bowler 1986, 1).

By the time Darwin published *The Origin of Species* in 1859, the concept of evolution had become well established and familiar. In many ways, Darwin's work simply built on what had gone before. But in one very significant way his work differed from almost everything else that had been written. Previous thinkers had discussed evolution with the view that it was a *purposive* process in which the hierarchy of organic nature was perfected and completed. It could be accounted for in terms of the divine will of a supernatural power. Darwin, by contrast, contended that evolution was not directed. There was no divinely conceived definitive end, no state of completion and perfection. For Darwin, evolution was simply what happened to all species as the result of the action of natural causes: a process he called natural selection.

Darwin's concept of natural selection, which replaced divine will as the causal force in the evolution of species, was profoundly disturbing to his contemporaries in both religious and intellectual establishments. The notion of natural selection challenged the idea that God had purposefully created all existing categories of species. In place of divine purpose, Darwin proposed that evolution resulted from the operation of indifferent, material laws (Greenwood 1984, 48). This image of evolution as the outcome of a meaningless and brutal struggle for existence threatened the taken-for-granted view of the world and the morality of the time.

The Modern Theory of the Descent of Man. *An evolutionary chart composed in 1876 by Ernest Haeckel, the first German advocate of Darwinism.*

The Origin of Species

Darwin wrote *The Origin of Species* in order to explain how, by natural and nonpurposive processes, all species are subject to transformation and change in their physical characteristics. Moreover, he used this theory of evolution to explain how new species might emerge (Hirst and Woolley 1981, 5–6).

Other thinkers had seen clear-cut differences between members of one species and another, but little if any **variation** within a given species. Darwin, by contrast, saw a range of variation both between species and within a given species. The concept of variation is central to his view of evolution, and he spent much of his life observing and cataloguing those variations. He observed that the physical characteristics of the individual members of any species-population vary in small but significant ways. These differences, moreover, may be inherited by offspring from their parents. Recognizing intra-species variation, then, was the first step in Darwin's argument about nonpurposeful evolution.

The next concept that Darwin introduced was the struggle for life. Darwin adopted the term "survival of the fittest" from the work of Herbert Spencer (1820–1903), a philosopher who was his contemporary and also interested in evolution. Spencer's use of the term, however, implied a kind of moral dimension that was absent in Darwin's work. For Spencer, what was the "fittest" was also understood as the "healthiest and cleanest" and thus the most deserving of survival. Darwin's use of the term, by contrast, implied no notion of moral superiority or any form of justification for fitness. His understanding was that those who were best adapted to existing environmental conditions within a population of varied individuals would most likely survive to pass their characteristics on to their progeny. He wrote:

> Owing to this struggle, variations, however slight and from whatever cause proceeding, if they be in any degree profitable to the individuals of a species, in their infinitely complex relations to other organic beings and to their physical conditions of life, will tend to the preservation of such individuals, and will generally be inherited by the offspring. The offspring also will thus have a better chance of surviving for, of the many individuals of any species which are periodically born, but a small number can survive. I have called this principle...by the term Natural Selection, in order to mark its relation to man's power of selection. But the expression often used by Mr. Herbert Spencer of the Survival of the Fittest is more accurate....([1859] 1958, 17).

The publication of *The Origin of Species* caused much excitement and outrage. It challenged taken-for-granted views about nature with an appeal to a scientific appraisal of facts and to the value of scientific method and rational analysis (Greenwood 1984, 57). The central event in the scandal was the now-famous meeting of the British Association, held at Oxford in 1860, a year after *Origin*'s publication. At that meeting Samuel Wilberforce, then Bishop of Oxford, challenged Thomas Huxley, who was representing Darwin's side in the proceedings, by asking him whether it was through his grandmother or grandfather that he was descended from the apes. The following response by

Huxley was recorded by historian Richard Green, who attended the meeting while an undergraduate at Oxford.

> I asserted—and I repeat—that a man has no reason to be ashamed of having an ape for his grandfather. If there were an ancestor whom I should feel shame in recalling, it would rather be a *man*, a man of restless and versatile intellect, who, not content with an equivocal success in his own sphere of activity, plunges into scientific questions with which he has no real acquaintance, only to obscure them by an aimless rhetoric, and distract the attention of his hearers from the real point at issue by eloquent digressions and skilled appeals to religious prejudice (cited in Himmelfarb 1968, 291).

Today, certainly in universities and colleges across North America, a belief that was radically opposed less than 150 years ago is commonplace. Although some attempts to suppress Darwin's ideas about human evolution continue, most people accept his theories and their application to human evolution.

Heredity, Chromosomes, and Genes

There was, however, at least one immediately obvious problem with Darwin's argument, which he himself recognized. He was unable to explain either the hereditary transmission of characteristics from generation to generation, or what the source of the variation between different individuals within a species-population might be. Originally he thought that inheritance was the result of a type of blending of parental characteristics, but he gave up this view when he realized that blending would quickly eradicate any variation in a species, the very thing he wanted to explain.

Darwin eventually adopted a modified form of **pangenesis** in order to solve his problem. According to the pangenesis view, all organs produce tiny replicas of themselves—called pangens—which find their way into the bloodstream and, via the bloodstream, into the sex cells. When organs are modified by changes in the environment, they produce new replicas or pangens of themselves. These new pangens in turn influence the sex cells, which in turn produce corresponding modifications in the next generation (Hirst and Woolley 1981, 8).

But the beginnings of a much more satisfactory answer to Darwin's problem of determining the mechanisms of inheritance had already been worked out by the Czech monk and amateur botanist Gregor Mendel (1822–1884). Mendel had conducted experiments in breeding with two varieties of common garden peas. He published his results in 1866, read his papers at scientific meetings, and circulated copies of his work to over 120 scientific organizations and universities in Europe and the United States. It was all in vain. His work was virtually ignored and he died in 1884 without any recognition of his worth as an experimental scientist. Even his notes and records disappeared (Birdsell 1972, 43).

In 1900, no less than three researchers, working separately, rediscovered his principles. With their rediscovery, the study of genetics rapidly developed. While Mendel himself knew nothing about genes, chromosomes, or DNA, the laws of heredity that he worked out in 1866 became the foundation for the modern genetic approach to the study of evolution (Zihlman 1982, 32). By 1902 it was suggested that chromosomes might be the units through which traits are passed from one generation to the next. Shortly afterward, the theory of genetic linkage was developed, which stated that traits are transmitted by genes located at different places along the same pair of chromosomes.

The Descent of Man

Darwin barely mentioned human evolution in *The Origin of Species*. The only reference is a few cryptic lines at the end of the book. There he wrote: "In the future I see open fields for far more important researches....Light will be thrown on the origin of man and his history" (449). Darwin did not publish any more on the subject, however, until 1871, when in *The Descent of Man* he elaborated his hypothesis regarding humanity's descent from the apes. He concluded *Descent* with the following:

> The main conclusion here arrived at, and now held by many naturalists who are well competent to form a sound judgement, is that man is descended from some less highly organized form. The grounds upon which this conclusion rests will never be shaken, for the close similarity between man and the lower animals in embryonic development, as well as in innumerable points of structure and constitution, both of high and of the most trifling importance...are facts which cannot be disputed. They have long been known, but until recently they told us nothing with respect to the origin of man. Now when viewed by the light of our knowledge of the whole organic world, their meaning is unmistakable. The great principle of evolution stands up clear and firm, when these groups of facts are considered in connection with others, such as the mutual affinities of the members of the same group, their geographical distribution in past and present times, and their geological succession. It is incredible that all these facts should speak falsely. He who is not content to look like a savage, at the phenomena of nature as disconnected, cannot any longer believe that man is the work of a separate act of creation ([1871] 1981, 601–2).

Darwin's hypotheses that the physical and behavioural gaps between humans and animals are only a matter of degree are quite remarkable, considering the paucity of the fossil records that were available to him at the time.[1] Although by 1872 many serious researchers were convinced of an extended human antiquity, the time frame remained obscure. Today a great deal more fossil evidence is available to paleontologists and paleoanthropologists. Certainly, the theory of evolution has been altered since Darwin's time both as a result of new ideas about genetics and new fossil discoveries. But while the theory has been altered, its essentials remain the same and provide a frame for all the other theories that we will consider in this chapter.

---

1 See Richards (1987, 15–23) for a discussion of the material available to Darwin.

WHO IS RELATED TO WHOM, AND HOW?

In *Descent of Man* Darwin argued that what distinguishes humans from other species is intelligence, manual dexterity, technology, and upright posture. Any ape who possessed even some of these characteristics would have had an advantage over all other ones. Once some group of apes was established on this evolutionary path, it was almost inevitable that *Homo sapiens* would result.

According to paleoanthropologist Roger Lewin, the main challenge to any present-day theory about human evolution is explaining how it was that "an apelike ancestor, equipped with powerful jaws and long, daggerlike canine teeth and able to run at speed on four limbs, became transformed into a slow, bipedal animal whose natural means of defense were at best puny" (1988, 312–13). The answer has changed greatly since Darwin published his seminal work. Before we consider current knowledge about the fossil record as well as past and current interpretations of the motor force behind human evolution, we should consider what present-day paleoanthropologists have to say about similarities and differences between humans and the other primates.

HUMANS AS PRIMATES

Homo sapiens is just one of the 185 living species that make up the order Primates. The classification of living organisms into groups has a long history in Western thought, going back as far as Aristotle's *The Classification of Animals*. The framework that is currently in use is based on the work of Carolus Linnaeus, *Systema Naturae*. Before the publication of *Origin of Species,* the system of classification in use did not reflect evolutionary processes. Moreover, biologists clearly separated *Homo sapiens* from all other mammals. After Darwin's work, however, biologists were able to approach classification of animals with the concept of the evolution of species specifically in mind (Lewin 1993, 36). (see Figure 5-1).

OUR PRIMATE HERITAGE

As Lewin points out, *Homo sapiens*, as a species, has clearly departed from its primate roots. In spite of this, all the characteristics that we think separate us from other primates, including upright posture, greater intelligence, and extreme sociality, are in fact extensions of, rather than departures from, a definition of a primate (1993, 44). But defining just what a primate is has proven a difficult task. According to Robert Martin of the Anthropological Institute in Zurich, primates are "typically arboreal inhabitants of tropical and sub-tropical forest ecosystems." Alison Jolly, an anthropologist at Rockefeller University, notes: "If there is an essence of being primate, it is the progressive evolution of intelligence as a way of life" (1993, 45).

Generally primates are characterized as having hands with opposable thumbs and opposable great toes that afford individuals the ability to grasp. (Humans are the only exception here. The human foot has lost its grasping function and now serves as a base for upright walking). Primate fingers and toes have nails, not claws. Locomotion is either

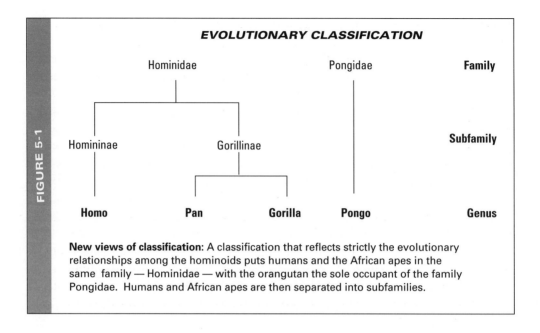

FIGURE 5-1

EVOLUTIONARY CLASSIFICATION

New views of classification: A classification that reflects strictly the evolutionary relationships among the hominoids puts humans and the African apes in the same family — Hominidae — with the orangutan the sole occupant of the family Pongidae. Humans and African apes are then separated into subfamilies.

quadrupedal or brachial (swinging by the arms.) In all cases of locomotion, though, the centre of gravity is near the hind limbs, which means that the body can be held in a vertical position. This fact alone makes the transition to bipedalism in humans less of a dramatic shift than might be imagined.

Vision is accentuated in primates, while the sense of smell (olfaction) is diminished. Eyes in all primates are in the front of the head rather than the sides, making vision more stereoscopic (eyes focus together to send a single image with depth perception to the brain) than in any other mammal. In part because of this focus on vision, primate brains are bigger than in other mammalian orders. Moreover, this encephalization (big brain size) is linked to a series of life-history factors including greater longevity and lower reproductive output. Litters are small (often one), offspring are dependent for long periods of time, age of reproductive maturity is late, and the interval between births is comparatively long.

All of these criteria for membership in the order Primates fit humans. Although by primate standards *Homo sapiens* is mentally well endowed as a species, our generous brain size is easily seen as nothing more than an extension of a primate trait (Lewin 1993, 47).

HOMINID PRECURSORS AND EARLY *HOMO SAPIENS*

The Hominid family originated sometime between 10 and 5 million years ago with the appearance of a single species of bipedal ape. This single species then gave rise to a wide range of descendants, which formed the many separate species that we now group into the two subfamilies of Homininae and Gorillinae. Over time the number of separate species declined until just one was left as the Homininae subfamily's sole representative: *Homo sapiens.* But even two million years ago, no less than three and possibly as many as six different hominid species coexisted in Africa.

Paleontologists have divided these species into two groups: those with relatively small brains and large cheek teeth, and those with relatively large brains and small cheek teeth. The small-brained group has been called australopithecines (members of the genus *Australopithecus*). All members of this group eventually became extinct. The second group of larger-brained species were members of the genus *Homo.* So far only one species, *Homo habilis,* has been formally named from this group, but scholars believe that many others also existed (Lewis 1993, 105).

The crucial questions that have occupied the attention of several generations of paleoanthropologists are how, when, where, and why did a split take place among those primates ancestral to both humans and apes? There is a great deal of controversy about the sequence of events and their interpretation. Social scientists have focused on different factors as being *the* leading explanatory factor in human evolution. Those factors include bipedalism, male-based hunting, female-centred gathering, strategies for controlling sexual relations and reproduction, language, consciousness, and intelligence.

These are the issues that occupy the attention of today's paleoanthropologists. An examination of their arguments and ideas about the causes of human evolution reveals much about the current social, economic, cultural, and moral situation, just as the ideas and beliefs of other theorists, including those who supported the Great Chain of Being thesis, reveal a great deal about past situations.

These different perspectives on human evolution will give us some new points of view about how and why human beings are social creatures and about the ways in which social relations affect the direction of human evolution. They will also illustrate how different theoretical perspectives can produce wildly differing explanations of a single event or phenomenon. Finally, they illustrate, yet again, how important it is to maintain a critical perspective in assessing knowledge and truth.

Bipedalism

The common ancestors of both humans and the great apes were arboreal, that is, they were predominately tree-dwellers. Like all primates, they had prehensile hands and feet—they were capable of grasping objects. Prehensile hands and feet, along with stereoscopic vision, adapted our arboreal ancestors well to living in trees. But at a certain point, some of the common ancestors of humans and apes gained the capacity for upright posture and bipedalism. In short, they evolved to become hominids.

There are various hypotheses (or better, stories) that have been devised to explain "how it was that a tree-dwelling ancestor became a ground-dwelling upright walker" (Washburn 1978, 153). While the stories about how and why our distant ancestors got down out of the trees vary considerably, the benefits of bipedal movement are immediately apparent.

....our hands are freed to carry, make tools, and gesture, our forward facing heads atop a vertical spinal column maximize our range of vision, hands can add another sound channel to the vocal one by clapping, drumming, etc., while the whole posture facilitates incorporation of a range of others (an upright animal may stoop where a bowed one cannot straighten (Richards 1987, 154).

While *Homo sapiens* is not the only primate to walk on two feet—chimpanzees and gibbons do this, too, under certain circumstances—we are the only primate to do so habitually and to move with a striding gait. Because of this, paleoanthropologists have sought explanations for our "humanness" in the origins of bipedalism. Many have argued that bipedalism evolved in order to free the hands. But others have proposed that bipedalism evolved as a result of changes in the distribution of food sources in East Africa during the Late Miocene period. These changes in turn were brought about by extensive climatic changes that included cooling and drying. What had once been an almost continuous tropical forest was fragmented into a mosaic of grasslands and forests. In the more open environments of the Late Miocene period, hominid food sources were greatly reduced in some areas. In order to obtain food, according to this view, our ancestors had to develop a much more energy-efficient mode of travel. The evolution to ground-living hominids was most likely the result of adaptations required for finding food by foraging between patches of tropical forest.

CAUSAL FACTORS IN HUMAN EVOLUTION

Objections to this argument come from Graham Richards (1987) who points out that, while the transformation of forests into savannah grasslands was a significant factor in the development of **bipedalism**, it was not the only one. As our early ancestors got out of the trees, so did the ancestors of present-day baboons. There is no reason to believe that having failed to sustain the leap to complete upright posture, the great apes are simply behind us on the evolutionary track. Rather, the ancestors of the great apes and the ancestors of present-day humans took very different evolutionary routes.

Several other reasons for the development of bipedalism have also been suggested. These include stalking game, reducing the risk of heat stroke, and improved vision. Merker (1984) suggests that the alignment between foot, leg, and associated sensory, postural, and locomotor mechanisms in a human are well designed for the silent stalking of prey without having to expend great amounts of energy on the chase. One considerable problem for mammals living in hot climates is the risk of heat stroke, especially in those mammals with large brains, such as primates, who also lack the large sinus cavities found in most mammals, which help cool the blood supply to the brain. Bipedalism and hair loss help solve this problem. Bipedalism reduces the amount of body surface exposed to the sun. As Wheeler ([1939] 1966) notes, "When the sun is overhead, an upright hominid presents only about 40 percent of the area it would if it was in a quadrupedal position" (94). Naked skin, combined with a layer of subcutaneous fat, aids in the dissipation of heat during the day and provides insulation during cooler nights.

While some paleoanthropologists have focused on species-wide physiological traits such as bipedalism, stereoscopic vision, and opposable thumbs as factors in human evolution, others have focused on what they consider to be sex-specific traits. Some, like Sherwood Washburn, propose "man-the-hunter" scenarios; others like Nancy Makepeace Tanner and Adrienne Zihlman have countered with a vision of "woman the gatherer." Still others argue that permanent female sexual receptivity or, in the case of Owen Lovejoy, a specific reproductive strategy that included monogamous pairing, were primary in bringing about the evolution of *Homo sapiens*.

Left: Hunters in the Snow *by Pieter Bruegel the Elder, 1565.* Right: The Gleaners *by J.-F. Millet, 1857. Separated by almost 300 years and modern in comparison to early* Homo sapiens, *these paintings still depict men as hunters and women as gatherers.*

Man the Hunter?

The change from tree living to ground dwelling involved fundamental dietary changes and changes in the way that food was procured. It also involved changes in tool use, social organization, reproductive strategies, and the size and complexity of the brain. As a result, questions about the dietary habits of our ancestors and especially about the significance of meat in the diet are significant.

Some paleoanthropologists have suggested provisionally that our early hominid ancestors were food-sharing, opportunistic scavenger/hunters. These theorists see behavioural changes specifically in males and, prompted by hunting for meat, as central to the evolution of the genus *Homo*. Proponents of the man-the-hunter scenario include Sherwood Washburn of the University of California at Berkeley and his collaborator, David Hamburg.

In a paper published in 1965, Washburn and Hamburg argue that male aggression is a fundamental adaptive mechanism common to the entire primate order, including human beings. "Order within most primate groups," they asserted, "is maintained by a hierarchy, which depends ultimately on the power of males....Aggressive individuals are essential actors in the social system and competition between groups is necessary for species dispersal and control of local populations" (282).

But human males do not have the fighting anatomy and behaviour shared by other male primates. They lack the daggerlike canines, threat gestures such as chest thumping, and great body differences with females that are common among other primates. *Homo sapiens* are also missing those extra structures such as a mane, which can be used to enhance their threatening aspects (ibid., 36). Instead, Washburn and Hamburg argue, the male members of the genus *Homo* took advantage of their bipedal stance and ability to use tools, along with their relatively large brain size and language capabilities, to establish a hunting way of life that no longer needed to rely on teeth, size, threatening gestures, or impressive body structures. Hominid males relied on handmade weapons and on language as a means of communication. In place of big teeth, they threw knives and hurled insults.

In "The Evolution of Human Behaviour," written in 1958, Washburn and Virginia Avid argue that the introduction of hunting by hominids had important implications for our ancestors. "Hunting," they note, "not only necessitated new activities and new kinds of cooperation but changed the role of the adult male in the group....The very same actions which caused man to be feared by other animals led to more cooperation, food sharing and economic interdependence within the group" (433–34).

Within this perspective, it is clear that male hunting is given pride of place as the motor force behind the eventual evolution of *Homo sapiens* as a species. Although our hominid ancestors lost much of the fearsomeness associated with hunting animals in the process, the selection process as envisioned by Washburn and his collaborators favoured aggressiveness in males and submissive dependence in females to support a whole new and complex way of life.

Woman the Gatherer?

While these assumptions about man the hunter were acceptable in the 1950s and 1960s, by the 1970s they had become increasingly unacceptable, especially to feminist scholars. Up until the rise of second-wave feminism, little or no attention was given to women's role in the evolutionary process. Since then, however, women's roles have been reconsidered, and much of the male-centredness of evolutionary theory as represented in the work of Washburn and his colleagues has been addressed. The work of Nancy Makepeace Tanner and Adrienne Zihlman, both separately and together, serve as examples of feminist interpretations of human evolution that centre the process on women instead of on men. Tanner and Zihlman are well aware that the evolutionary reconstructions developed by different theorists are shaped by, and in turn help to shape, our understandings of contemporary social relationships between men and women. It is their contention that

> ...observers usually begin from their own perspective, and so inadvertently the question usually has been: how did the capacity and propensity for adult Western male behaviours evolve? This viewpoint offers scant preparation for comprehending the wide range of variability in women's roles in non-Western societies or for analyzing the changes in the roles of men and women which are currently occurring in the West (1976, 608).

In their co-authored article, "Women in Evolution, Part 1: Innovation and Selection in Human Origins" (1976), Tanner and Zihlman tell a very different story about human nature and evolution than the one told in the man-the-hunter scenario. Instead of focusing on male-centred aggression and hunting, they focus on female-centred activities of gathering and cooperation. Like Washburn and his collaborators, Tanner and Zihlman are concerned with the reproductive success that new productive strategies might have occasioned. But unlike Washburn and others, Tanner and Zihlman deliberately employ female-centred reasoning. Instead of imagining that biological imperatives lead directly to aggression, hunting, and male dominance, they develop another scenario.

Tanner and Zihlman begin with the objective of understanding human evolution in terms of "processes which shaped our physical, emotional and cognitive characteristics" (1976, 585). Noting that the hunting thesis largely ignores the contributions of the females of the species, Tanner and Zihlman pronounce it deficient as an explanatory device. In the place of hunting they propose "the development of gathering both plant and animal material as a dietary specialization of savannah living" that was "promoted by natural selection of appropriate tool using and bipedal behaviour." They go on to suggest that this pattern "interrelates with the roles of maternal socialization in kin selection and of female choice in sexual selection." It is the connection between "savannah living, technology, diet, social organization, and selective processes" that can best account for the emergence of the human species (586).

Food sharing within social groups of females and their offspring was the result of gathering as a way of procuring adequate food supplies. This happened after our hominid ancestors moved onto the savannah. New technological inventions, including digging sticks, and carrying baskets for food and babies, were related to both the new diet and to the new habits of food sharing among women and their children. As knowledge of edible plants and animals and their distribution became more important, pressures to communicate symbolically mounted. Meanwhile, dangers from predators were met with cunning, not with brawn, so that the need for male dominance and fighting anatomy decreased. Gathering plants and hunting small animals is an unlikely scenario to favour large, aggressive males; thus male dominance ceased to be of importance.

Tanner and Zihlman propose instead social units composed of mothers and their young children. Selection pressures then favoured sociability and cooperation, especially between the two sexes. Females chose to mate more readily with nonthreatening males, and so males learned to interact in a friendly way with others, even strangers. With increased friendliness came a way of life that included small bands, frequent out-breeding, and symbolic communication based on language.

Permanent Female Sexual Receptivity

Tanner and Zihlman (1976) and Tanner (1981) present the kind of sexual relationships that might have existed between our distant ancestors in a very specific way. In their view, males were occasional visitors to the basic social unit of mother and children. In visiting females who were highly selective, the males were constrained to behave in a friendly, helpful manner in order to make themselves sexually attractive. They offered food as a gesture of good will to ingratiate themselves into the group and to gain favour with the sexually active females in the hope of gaining sexual access.

Other paleoanthropologists disagree strongly with Tanner and Zihlman's version of the role of females in human evolution. In Kim Hill's (1993) view , our distant female forebears were not independent food gatherers as suggested by Tanner and Zihlman but were almost totally dependent on meat-hunting males. Far from being independent and in control of their lives, these females were very eager to acquire a share of meat in exchange for sexual favours. As dependants on male largess, our female ancestors learned to prostitute themselves, and those who were sexually available at all times naturally gained more frequent access to meat. Males became big and strong, while females remained weak and dependent. For Hill, the consequence of female dependence on males for food was the development and accentuation of sexual dimorphism.

As a means of giving credence to her story, Hill maintains that females would have been excessively burdened with the responsibilities of child bearing and care giving. This would have led to dependence on males, who were not so burdened, for a great deal of their nutritional intake. Thus a sex-for-meat scenario evolved. The loss of *estrus* (coming into heat) aided females in securing relationships with meat-providing males. As females became permanently sexually receptive, they were able to trade sex for meat on an pay-as-you-go basis, so to speak. All tools, according to Hill, are a male invention, used to enhance foraging and food gathering (as opposed to Tanner's notion that they are a female invention).

In 1981 the physical anthropologist Owen Lovejoy entered the debate. Lovejoy argues that the evolutionary process toward the development of *Homo sapiens* is best explained in terms of reproductive factors. He contends that primates have adopted what he calls a "K-adaptation" reproductive strategy. Following this strategy means that female primates bear relatively few young, who are dependent on adult support for extended periods. As well, primate life span is generally long, and population levels are usually held at a constant level. Lovejoy then envisages a scenario occurring in the Late Miocene period in which our ancestral primates were already long living and relatively intelligent; they established strong social bonds and practised intensive parenting. Together these qualities and practices reduced environmentally induced mortality.

These Late Miocene primates, Lovejoy argues, had reached a kind of reproductive success that they could not exceed except by dramatically altering their behaviour. That change came about with the introduction of monogamous pairing. Lovejoy conjectures that monogamous males provided food *only* to their own mates and offspring and not to the group as a whole. The better a male was at foraging, the better off were his mate and offspring. In turn, a healthy, well-fed female would have an increased reproductive rate and could manage to provide her mate with more and healthier offspring.

Once monogamy was established, Lovejoy argues, bipedalism can be seen as a reproductive advantage, especially for males who did prolonged and extensive carrying in order to provision their mates and offspring. Females, too, would have adapted to bipedalism as a result of the local foraging they did and the necessity of carrying their infants on these expeditions. Tool use would have logically followed.

Lovejoy concludes that such a food-sharing system among a breeding pair and their dependent offspring exerts influences that favour the evolutionary development of some system of communication—such as a protolanguage that is effective and accessible to all group members. The development of such a system of communication hones the social and intellectual skills and abilities of its members. Lovejoy cautions, though, that the level of language skills and social organization among early hominids would have unmistakeably distinguished them from humans. In fact, "they probably represented a mode of life that has no living counterpart" (92).

Man the hunter, woman the gatherer, sex for meat, or K-strategy—which among these is the "true" explanation of human evolution and the rise of culture? As if these are not enough to contend with, scholars have recently added two more scenarios, one focusing on intelligence and consciousness, the other on language and consciousness.

INTELLIGENCE, CONSCIOUSNESS, AND LANGUAGE

The development of the human capacity to think and reason is another important area of investigation that researchers have explored in order to explain the evolution of human culture. For example, the question of what happened to differentiate the large-brained *Homo* lineage from the small-brained *Australopithecus* lineage has been answered by some paleoanthropologists in terms of the evolution of intellectual skills associated with stone tool making and use.

The utilization of stone tools can be seen as both a result of and an impetus to further development of brain capacity of the genus *Homo*. Recently it has been suggested that both *Homo* and *Australopithecus* lineages were equally skilful in making stone tools. What, then, were the selection pressures on mental skills that led to the separation of the two lineages? How did humans come to possess extraordinary powers of creative intelligence as well as consciousness and language? (Lewin 1993, 169).

Over a three-million-year period hominid brain size expanded from around 400 cubic centimetres to 1350 cubic centimetres, the average size of the human brain today. This expansion, moreover, was unique to hominids. The human brain is a very

Prehistoric art from the Lascaux Caves in Dordogne, France. Horse in Style III, about 5 feet tall. With the growth of artistic expression came a vast growth in the evolution of language.

expensive organ: it takes up 2 percent of body weight, but it consumes 18 percent of available energy. Thus any expansion in brain size requires stable sources of high-energy food supplies and minimal threat from predators.

Human infants are born after a 270-day gestation period (comparable to that of the apes). But human newborns have bodies and brains that are twice the size of newborn apes. Like other primates, the brain of the human neonate experiences a period of rapid growth after birth, but with humans the growth continues for 12 months, giving them the equivalent of a 21-month gestation period (9 in the uterus, 12 outside). The argument is that this extended period of development resulted in an extended period of infant care and had a major impact on the social life of our hominid ancestors (Lewin 1993, 170–71).

While the brain size of early *Australopithecines* never increased during the existence of this genus, there was a marked expansion in hominid brain capacity with the genus *Homo. Homo habilis,* who existed between 2.5 million to 1.6 million years ago, had a brain size of about 650 cubic centimetres to 800 cubic centimetres. Archaic *Homo sapiens* (including Neanderthal) brain sizes ranged from between 1110 to over 1400 cubic centimetres, larger than modern *Homo sapiens.* But while it is relatively easy to plot increases in brain size over time, it is not so easy to measure increases in intelligence (Lewin 1993, 171–72). Little cultural evidence is left for paleoanthropologists and archaeologists to work with.

INTELLIGENCE AND CONSCIOUSNESS

As we have discussed, during much of the 1950s and 1960s, paleoanthropologists focused on "man the toolmaker" and then "man the hunter." Emphasis was placed on the males of the species whose mastery of practical skills for living and surviving was seen as the engine force behind the evolution of intelligence and the expansion of the hominid brain. During the 1970s and 1980s, as feminism gained recognition in academia, the focus turned in part to "woman the gatherer." Her social and nurturing ways were emphasized as the guiding force behind hominid evolution. Recently the focus has been on "humans as social animals."

While finding daily food places little demand on the high degree of intelligence that monkeys and apes possess, the management of social relations among the members of a troop is an entirely different matter. Interactions within primate groups are far more complex than those of any other mammal. As Lewin notes, "For a nonhuman primate in the field, learning the distribution and probable time of ripening of food sources is intellectual child's play compared with predicting—and manipulating—the behaviour of other individuals in the group" (173). A new focus has thus emerged around the question of why social interactions among primates are so complex.

Among other mammals, when conflict arises between two individuals, it is almost inevitable that the largest, strongest, and most aggressive will win. Big canines, antlers, tusks, and the like can be deciding factors. But this is not the case among primates. Individual members of a troop of monkeys or apes spend a lot of time cultivating relationships—establishing their own networks of alliances and observing the alliances of others. When a challenge comes from a physically weaker individual, it can result in the defeat of a physically stronger one if enough allies are at hand to assist while the victim's allies are absent. Alexander Harcourt of Cambridge University observes:

> Alliances are far more complex social interactions than are two-animal contests. The information processing abilities required for success are far greater: complexity is geo-metrically, not arithmetically, increased with the addition of further participants in an interaction....In sum, primates are consummate social tacticians (1988, cited in Lewis 1993, 173).

Dorothy Cheney, Robert Seyfarth, and Barbara Smutts (1986) recently conducted a study of social relationships and social cognition among contemporary primates. Cheney and her colleagues were interested in determining if primate behaviour reflects humanlike social cognition and if primates other than humans exhibit creative intelligence. They found many examples that allowed them to conclude that all primates, not just humans, "can predict the consequences of their behaviour for others and they understand enough about the motives of others to be capable of deceit and other subtle forms of manipul-ation."

It is possible that primate intelligence was developed and honed in relation to skills developed for manipulating social interactions and not, as formerly thought, primarily in relation to solving practical problems such as finding and acquiring foodstuffs. But as Lewin has pointed out, there still remains the question "Why have primates found it advantageous to indulge in alliance building and manipulation?" The answer Lewin offers, based on field studies of primates, is that those individuals who are adept at build-ing up alliances are also the most successful in terms of reproduction strategies. Making allies is a step toward securing mating opportunities.

Nicholas Humphrey (1986) of Cambridge University makes another point about social relationships between primate individuals and the evolution of intelligence. Given the complexity that arises in understanding oneself and others in the process of making and using social alliances, conscious awareness of self and others becomes the ultimate tool of the social animal. An individual who is able to look at his own reactions is going to be able to predict more surely how others will react in similar situations. Conscious awareness helps individuals interact more successfully in highly social contexts.

LANGUAGE AND CONSCIOUSNESS

The origins of language, that species-specific quality humans seem most proud of, is vir-tually impossible to assess from the archaeological record. While the first records of inscription date back to the ancient Sumarian civilization about 6000 years ago, this does not begin to mark the origins of language. According to J.T. Laitmann (1983, 20–27), the fossil record indicates that the *Australopithecines* probably had vocal cords similar to living monkeys or apes. The position of their larynx would have made it impossible for them to produce the universal vowel sounds found in human speech. *Homo erectus,* on the other hand, most likely was able to make modified laryngeal sounds. But it was only with the origins of archaic *Homo sapiens*, about 300 000 years ago, that the mechanical potential for the full range of sounds produced by modern humans appeared.

Iain Davidson and William Noble, two Australian archaeologists, argue that spoken language is a very recent development. While all higher primates vocalize and produce a wide range of sounds, sometimes to great effect, those sounds are very different from the structured use of words (syntax) that characterizes human language use. According to Davidson and Noble, language is closely tied with the development of imagery and art (1989, 125–56).

If there is a linkage between the possession of complex language and artistic expression, that linkage is only about 300 000 years old. The earliest abstract artifact found so far has been a carved ox rib from the site of Pech de l'Aze in France (Lewin 1993, 179). Following this earliest example, there exists a growing number of other examples of abstract artifacts dating from Mousterian times, about 150 000 to 40 000 years ago. Examples of engraved bone and ivory as well as deliberate, ritualistic burials indicate an awareness of the abstract. However, artistic expression began to flourish little more than 30 000 years ago. And with the blossoming of artistic expression, social scientists argue, came a quantum jump in the evolution of language (Oakley 1966).

Until recently it had been argued that language evolved as a result of a shift from individualistic subsistence activities of higher primates to cooperative ventures in foraging and (especially) in hunting. These complex subsistence patterns required more and more proficient means of communication, and language was believed to have evolved out of gesturing. Lately, however, a new kind of explanation has emerged, in keeping with new explanations for the evolution of intelligence. These explanations of the origins of language now look to the inner world of thought and image making (180).

According to Maxine Sheets-Johnstone (1990), fundamental human abilities such as bipedality, tool making, engraving, painting, language, and counting have deeply rooted origins in the physical, tactile, and kinesthetic experiences afforded by possessing a hominid body. Certainly speech requires a specific type of physiology. But in accepting human physicality as the sole explanatory factor in the origins of human speech, we are taking for granted the very thing on which the practice of speaking ultimately rests. To be able to speak, says Sheets-Johnstone, individuals must have a concept of themselves as a sound-maker. To count, individuals must have the concept of numbers.

In order to account for the origins of any human practice or belief, Sheets-Johnstone says, we must pay attention to "the standard in terms of which the relevant concepts were forged." In the case of human abilities and practices, it is the living body that serves as a "semantic template." All concepts, she maintains, have either been generated or awakened by the living body in the course of everyday actions such as chewing, urinating, striding, standing, breathing, and so on. Sheets-Johnstone goes on to argue that once everyday actions give rise to basic concepts, those concepts in turn give rise to new possibilities, and thus new ways of living, and finally to the establishment of the revolutionary practices and beliefs that are definitive of hominid evolution.

According to Sheets-Johnstone, there is an "indissoluble bond between hominid thinking and hominid evolution," and that bond is "cemented in the living body" (4). Hominid evolution was shaped, she argues, by hominid thinking. "The cognitive impetus for the cultivation and establishment of those behaviours shaping the development of a hominid style of living originated in bodily concepts entailed in animate form and tactile kinaesthetic experience. Just as without evolution there would be no human thinking, so without thinking there would have been no hominid evolution."

■ ■ ■

SUMMARY

In this chapter I introduced a variety of different perspectives on the motor force behind human evolution. I pointed out that each tells a different story, which passes for scientific knowledge, about the processes and causes leading up to the evolution of our species, *Homo sapiens.*

I examined a number of different views on the emergence of our species, beginning with the Great Chain of Being. This view, popular from medieval times to the nineteenth century, assumed that each creature was assigned a place by God in a hierarchy of all creatures on earth. Humanity in general and white, male Europeans in particular were held to occupy the highest position.

With Darwin's work, however, the focus for the relative position of human beings on earth changed from a premier position to a process of evolution, brought about by the forces of natural selection. During the mid- to late twentieth century, different scenarios emerged purporting to explain human evolution, especially the role of culture in the evolution of *Homo sapiens* as a species. In the 1950s and 1960s, explanations based on a conception of man the hunter, in which aggressive males sought to provision dependant females, were very popular.

This view was challenged in the 1970s by feminists who proposed their own model of woman the gatherer, in which human evolution was guided by cooperative females, not by aggressive males. Other scenarios explored in this chapter include the exchange of female sex for hunted meat provided by males and reproductive strategies that resulted in sexual dimorphism.

Recently, paleoanthropologists and linguists have developed complex understandings of the relationship between human intelligence, consciousness, physical attributes, and language. They have used these understandings in their attempts to explain the relationship between human culture, abstract thought and art, and hominid evolution.

■ ■ ■

FOR DISCUSSION

1. To what extent is all scientific practice and theory influenced by culture, language, and the use of metaphors in constructing explanations?

2. What are the major assumptions of the Great Chain of Being thesis? What relation did these assumptions have to the structure of European feudal society?

3. What was revolutionary about Darwin's notion of natural selection as the causal force in human evolution?

4. A number of different factors have been suggested as being the leading causal factor in human evolution. What are some of those factors? What are their strengths and weaknesses in the role as the motor force behind human evolution?

5. What does each one of the factors noted in question 4 reveal about our current social, moral, and cultural situation today?

6. Which, if any, of the scenarios explaining human evolution discussed in this chapter do you find most reasonable?

6 SOCIALIZATION, ISOLATION, AND HUMAN EXISTENCE

> **CHAPTER OPENING QUESTIONS**
>
> - To what extent is a human being recognizable as such if he or she grows up without human contact and society?
>
> - What can the study of feral children tell us about the relationship between human nature and culture?
>
> - How have different theories of human learning affected our understanding of the socialization process?

In sociology, psychology, and anthropology, the concept of **socialization** refers to the learning process whereby a human infant gradually acquires a cultural fluency, becoming both self-aware and skilled in the ways of the culture in which he or she is being reared. Most sociologists would agree that it is through the process of socialization that a child becomes acquainted with all the values, beliefs, understandings, and rules of his or her society and culture. As the child is socialized, he or she acquires a sense of self, as well as a body of knowledge and a set of skills that equip him or her to live as a member of a given society. Moreover, the socialization of the very young allows for the more general process of **social reproduction** to take place. Through socialization, the structural continuity of society at large is guaranteed over time.

Questions about abandoned or feral children—children who have grown up without the influence of human contact and thus without being socialized—have been raised in the hope of learning about the extent to which human behaviour is the result of socialization or is the product of inherent (and inherited) traits. But just as in the case of debates over human evolution, the various studies that have been made of feral children over the last two centuries tell us at least as much about the beliefs and values held by the people investigating the children as they do about the feral children themselves.

Social thinkers continue to turn to accounts of children raised in virtual isolation in order to gain insights into the relationship between human nature and human culture. Modern studies done of the lives and treatment of abandoned children strongly indicate the importance of early social relationships in forming a person's development as a social being. These studies emphasize the need for sustained, supportive, and caring contact with other human beings if the human child is to grow into a socially adept adult. While these are conclusions reached by social scientists working in the present, they are both different from, and in some respects similar to, the conclusions reached by eighteenth- and nineteenth-century scholars.

For most contemporary sociologists, the essence of humanity is to be found, above all, in the social relationships we have with each other. Human beings are first and foremost social beings. Isolation from established patterns of social interaction, expectations, and practices can have far-reaching consequences for any human being's conduct, especially for his or her ability to exercise already acquired skills, or to practice already established belief systems. It can even have serious consequences for that person's sense of identity.

ISOLATION IN ADULTS

Before I examine what happens when a child grows up in isolation, I want to present two examples of the effects of isolation and deprivation of social interaction on adults. These two examples serve as important counterpoints for the study of feral or abandoned children. In the case of isolated adults, the process of socialization has already been well established and the consequences of isolation are quite different from those experienced by young children. The first example of what happens to adults in isolation comes from the case of the eighteenth-century British sailor Alexander Selkirk. The second example is that of the early twentieth-century Native American Ishi.

While looking for Spanish ships to loot off the coast of Chile, the captain of an English privateer noticed a fire on one of the then-uninhabited Juan Fernandez Islands. The next morning an armed party from the privateer discovered not a Spanish garrison, but a marooned English sailor clad in goatskins. The island's sole occupant was Alexander Selkirk, a 30-year-old Scottish sailor who had marooned himself on the island four years previously after a quarrel with his captain.

As the captain of the privateer that rescued Selkirk from his self-imposed isolation recorded:

> At his first coming on board us, he had so much forgot his language, for want of use, that we could scarce understand him, for he seemed to speak his words by halves. We offered him a dram, but he would not touch it, having drunk nothing but water since his being here (cited in Shattuck 1980, 192).

Selkirk told his rescuers that when he was first marooned, he had been both afraid and melancholic. But after a period of time he had managed to fashion an agreeable life for himself. According to the report of the captain who found him, Selkirk had "tamed some Kids (goats) and to divert himself would now and then sing and dance with them and his Cats." The English novelist Daniel Defoe used Selkirk as partial model for his famous castaway, Robinson Crusoe.

The case of Ishi is more tragic. Ishi's tribe, the Yahi, were exterminated by American settlers. He spent many years completely alone until he was found in 1911, exhausted and starving. In spite of enormous challenges, Ishi managed to continue to keep alive the language, customs, and beliefs of his group. He became a sort of living museum and spent his last years at the University of California's Museum of Anthropology.

Hirst and Woolley (1981) note that personality and social agency are intimately connected. An individual's identity, they argue, is dependent on it being expressed in meaningful ways within sets of social relationships. Any individual, then, acquires an identity and the ability to express that identity in social interaction, which is both the effect and the support of their repertoire of social relationships. Identity and agency, therefore, are dependent on use.

The examples of Alexander Selkirk and Ishi illustrate this point. When he was rescued from his self-imposed isolation, Selkirk could barely communicate with his rescuers, although just four years earlier he had been fluent in his use of language. Although he was able to keep up some kind of social interaction by dancing with his goats and cats, Selkirk had lost some of his facility in communicating with others who shared his social and cultural origins.

Ishi, by contrast, lost his entire society—all those people who shared a common culture with him had been killed. Ishi was then given a new identity as a "living museum" by certain American anthropologists. Unable to be a Yahi, with no others around him to support his identity as a member of that society and culture, Ishi became instead an "informant" to those interested in learning about a society that no longer existed. It was in this new role that he was able to develop an identity as a member of a society (American now instead of Yahi) and secure a living.

While the consequences of isolation in adults can often be severe, once recontacted the isolated individual is easily recognizable as a functioning human being. But what happens to very young children who have spent most of their childhood in isolation? A human child is not born knowing how to act as a member of any given society. What happens when a child grows up in isolation without the benefit of human social interaction and culture?

FERAL CHILDREN

The theme of abandonment is a very old one in Western mythology. For example, the twin brothers Romulus and Remus, legendary founders of Rome, were believed to be feral children. Set adrift on the Tiber River by enemies of their parents, the boys were saved by a she-wolf who suckled them and raised them to adulthood.

We have already studied how scientists began in the eighteenth century to place all living beings into one system of classification. We learned that Linnaeus, in writing his treatise *Systema Naturae* (1735), identified *Homo ferus* or wild men as a separate variety of the human species. Homo ferus was hairy, ran on all fours, and lacked language skills.

Pictured above is Tarzan, a popularized depiction of a feral child. Contrast this with the physical accounts in the text of Peter and Victor.

In contrast, *Homo sapiens* walked upright, spoke, and was hairless. In that same edition of *Systema Naturae*, Linnaeus also identified nine cases of *Loco ferus*, feral children who were known to him.

Linnaeus made his classification of the various kinds of *Homo* or humanlike beings at a point in intellectual history when there was a great deal of interest in distinguishing the natural or unencumbered mind of the "uncivilized" human from the influences of civilization on the human mind. But it was the philosophers and not the scientists who made the question of wild or natural children a central issue in the eighteenth century.

Philosophers such as John Locke had concluded that the human infant was born essentially without ideas and beliefs, but was infinitely capable of being moulded into whatever role he or she was taught by adult caregivers. These philosophers, who were concerned with issues of democracy and the "Rights of Man," wanted to determine whether those rights were natural to the human condition in that they were given and guaranteed by the capacity to reason that all humans were born with, or whether they were something that had to be guaranteed by an external agency, either by the state, or by God. This concern emerged as the politicized aspect of the question "What behaviour is innate, or natural to the human condition, and what behaviour is the result of learning?"

Eighteenth- and nineteenth-century philosophers and social thinkers were fascinated with the issue of feral children precisely because of these questions. They were convinced that, if these children could be made to speak, all might be understood. Twentieth-century writers and thinkers have been equally curious about what children raised in isolation can tell us about the secrets of human existence. A large part of this curiosity is informed by a concern about what is truly natural or biological about human behaviour and what can be attributed to nurture or culture.

While it is unthinkable for any humane person to bring up a child under conditions of isolation, there have been several historical instances of children raised in isolation that have been reported on and studied over the course of the last two centuries. We will examine critically some of these cases in order to explore the significance of early social interaction and cultural learning on the personalities and abilities of human beings and to determine the effects of the investigator's own theoretical perspective on the way in which the behaviour of feral children has been understood.

Peter was discovered in 1724 in the now-German town of Hameln. He was eventually given to England's King George I and Queen Caroline. They in turn gave him to a Dr. Arbuthnot, a friend of Alexander Pope and Jonathan Swift. Victor, also known as the wild boy of Aveyron, had been abandoned at a very early age and was found living alone, in a feral state. He was captured on January 9, 1800, near the village of Saint-Serin in southern France. He was about 12 years old at the time of his capture. Victor became the object of much scientific study, first by Dr. Pinel, and later by Dr. Itard.

Anna, Isabella, and Genie are three cases of extreme isolation, all from the United States. Two of the children, Anna and Isabella, were discovered in the late 1930s, while the third child, Genie, was first seen by a social worker in 1970. In each of these three cases the girls had been given food and shelter by adults but had otherwise been kept in isolation. All three came to the attention of twentieth-century researchers.

PETER AND EIGHTEENTH-CENTURY SCIENTIFIC OBSERVATION

In the late summer of 1724, Jårgen Meyer, a farm worker who was returning from a day's work in the fields, met up with a "naked, brownish, black-haired creature, who was running up and down..." (Singh and Zinng 1939, 182–83). The boy appeared to be about 12 years old and was mute. By showing him two apples in his hand, Meyer was able to entice the boy into the town where he was captured and placed in the Hospital of the Holy Ghost for safekeeping.

Thus incarcerated and under observation, Peter (the name given to him by a gang of street-boys who had helped with his capture) showed no signs of "civility." He either sat on his haunches or waited expectantly on all fours for a chance to escape. He refused to sleep on the bed provided and slept instead on a straw pallet on the floor. He captured birds, tore them apart, and ate the pieces. He did not like to wear clothes or shoes but eventually learned to tolerate them.

107

One of his observers in the hospital had this to say about Peter:

> Because of his wild manners a man was ordered to stay with him in the poor-house, who could watch his actions and projects as well as check his wildness. The man told me that he [Peter] showed great fear of flogging, and when he threatened him with the rod, the boy behaved much more moderately, so that within three days he was much easier to handle, and that it sufficed to merely show him the rod in order to make him obey. Nevertheless, no one can deny that a wild nature is so deeply rooted in him that he always tries to run away (Singh and Zinng 1939, 193).

Fifteen months after his capture, Peter had attracted the attention of members of the German aristocracy. At this time, European aristocrats amused themselves by keeping human "curiosities"—dwarfs, freaks, people of different racial extraction, and feral children—almost as favoured pets. Peter, accordingly, became the "pet" of the royal house of Hanover in 1725. In 1726, when the family became the rulers of England, he was sent, along with the Duke of Hanover, now King George I, to London. George's officially listed reason for his interest in Peter was a desire to offer him for scientific examination (Candland 1993, 10). Peter, it was believed, could offer scientists the unusual opportunity of studying a human in a "state of nature" and of comparing that "natural" behaviour with the behaviour of "civilized" or socialized people.

While great efforts were made to teach Peter to talk, he never learned to speak properly. The best he could accomplish was *ki sho*, meaning King George, and *qui ca*, meaning Queen Caroline. He seemed to like music and was able to hum favourite tunes. He never laughed. He did learn to do simple domestic chores, although he had to be constantly supervised when performing them.

King George and Queen Caroline eventually gave Peter to Dr. Arbuthnot, who was instructed to undertake a scientific investigation of the child. After a two-month investigation, Arbuthnot concluded that the boy could learn nothing because he lacked sufficient mental capacity. The King and Queen then settled a small pension on their charge and had him placed with a farmer in Hertfordshire. Peter died in 1785.

The story of Peter is important for a number of reasons. First, Peter's treatment at the hands of the scientists who were allowed to study him is a good indication of what the most advanced scientific thinkers of the day believed about human behaviour. They believed they had found a human being "in the state of nature," that is, free from any effects of civilization. They expected to be able to learn from Peter how a natural as opposed to a civilized person thought. But when they were unable to learn what they had expected, they categorized him in the only way that made sense to them. Peter, they decided, had to be severely mentally deficient because he could not communicate with them. As a result they quickly lost interest in studying him.

Peter's story also reveals a great deal about eighteenth-century attitudes toward persons who were in some way different from the expected or desired norm. That the King and Queen of England kept Peter as a kind of personal house pet, and then discarded him when he did not perform as expected, tells us something about the conduct of the time. Today such treatment would challenge human dignity and basic human rights.

In 1800, almost 15 years after Peter's death, another boy, first labelled "the wild boy of Aveyron" and later called Victor, was discovered in similar circumstances in rural France. Like Peter, Victor came to the attention of the authorities and passed quickly into the hands of scientists who made a study of him. But whereas the scientists who studied Peter lost interest in him once they realized he would never reveal the true nature of human existence to them, those who studied Victor persevered for much longer in their attempts to make this "wild boy" speak and reveal some of his secrets.

THE SENSATIONALISTS

This willingness on the part of French scientists to persevere in circumstances that had caused their German colleagues to throw up their hands not two decades before was due, in large part, to a new theoretical perspective that they had adopted. The scientists who studied Victor were influenced by a recent theory of human learning and behaviour called **sensationalism**. Not only did they conduct their studies of Victor for the sake of discovering something new about the human condition, they also set out quite deliberately to make Victor over into a "normal" member of society. Sensationalism (also called **radical empiricism**) maintained that all human beings acquire their ideas, beliefs, knowledge, and experiences through sensory experience—touch, smell, taste, sight, hearing. Among the best-known and most influential philosophers of this genre were the English philosopher John Locke, the French philosopher Étienne Condillac, and the Swiss philosopher Jean-Jacques Rousseau.

John Locke

John Locke (1632–1704) was an English academic, doctor, philosopher, and political theorist. While in political exile on the continent in the 1680s, Locke was asked by a relative for advice about the upbringing of her son (Cleverly and Phillips 1986, 15). He later published his recommendations as *Some Thoughts Concerning Education* (1690). It was, and continues to be, an enormously influential work. The ideas Locke expressed to his relative were further developed in *An Essay Concerning Human Understanding* (1693). There Locke argued against what he saw as "an established opinion amongst some men, that there are in the understanding certain innate *principles*, some primary notions...characters, as it were, stamped on the mind of man; which the soul receives in its very first being, and brings into the world with it" (Cleverly and Phillips 1986, 16).

But if there are no innate ideas, and if the child comes into the world with a mind like "white paper void of all characters, without any ideas," how then, Locke asked, does the mind come to be "furnished"? Locke gave a one-word answer to that question: "experience." It is on experience alone that all knowledge is founded and from which all knowledge is derived.

There were two sources of experience, according to Locke, sensation and reflection. Sensation is obtained via the sense organs and gives rise to simple ideas such as white, black, hot, cold, hard, soft, bitter, sweet. Reflection or introspection, by contrast, is the experience of perceiving the operation of one's own mind. By reflecting on our own mental processes, we come to understand thought, doubt, reason, and will. All complex ideas that humans hold, Locke argued, are derived from simple ideas, and simple ideas in turn are mental images of sense perceptions. It was the sensationalist ideas of Locke and other social philosophers that captured the attention of the fledgling scientific community in France from the mid-eighteenth century onward. Feral children became very important to those scientists who had adopted the sensationalist perspective because it was believed that those children could reveal what sense experiences alone, devoid of culture and language, contributed to human existence. When Victor was captured, he appeared almost as a godsend to members of the French scientific community who now had what they took to be a real child of nature on which to test their theories.

Étienne Bonnot de Condillac

One of the first to turn his attention specifically to the issue of feral children was Étienne Bonnot de Condillac. In his *Treatise on the Sensations* (1754), Condillac argued that social relations and language are essential to the development of what we consider to be human. For Condillac, to be human is first of all "to possess the capacity to reason and to speak." It was his opinion that if we "wish to discover what sense experience alone, without the interference of 'civilization', can produce in an individual, it is necessary to observe individuals who have been brought up in isolation." Feral children, Condillac argued, demonstrate what is naturally human as opposed to what is acquired by training and civilization.

Jean-Jacques Rousseau

Probably the most famous of the eighteenth-century philosophers to consider the meaning of living in "a state of nature" was the Swiss novelist and education theorist Jean-Jacques Rousseau. In his *Discourse on the Origin of Inequality Among Men* (1755), he argued that man in a state of nature is purely a creature of appetite and instinct, lacking morality or self-consciousness. Such a being, he maintained, lives in the eternal present, without property, without language, and without ideas, subject to his immediate needs. Rousseau greatly admired Locke's work on the influence of experience on learning in children. Following Locke he argued that at birth the mind of the child was essentially a *tabula rasa*. "We are born capable of learning but knowing nothing, perceiving nothing," he wrote in *Emile*, his novel on childhood education published in 1762. "The mind, bound up within imperfect and half-grown organs, is not even aware of its own existence. The movements and cries of the new-born child are purely reflex, without knowledge or will."

THE WILD BOY OF AVEYRON

On January 9, 1800, a young boy who fit Jean-Jacques Rousseau's description of an individual in the state of nature was captured while digging for vegetables in the garden of a tanner living in the village of Saint-Serin in the south of France. A few months after his capture, the wild boy of Aveyron, or Victor as he was later called, became one of the first feral children to come into contact with the practitioners of the newly emerging human sciences.

An eyewitness by the name of Constant-Saint-Estäve, a commissioner in charge of local government, wrote an official account three weeks after the boy's capture.

I found him sitting by a warm fire, which he seemed to enjoy, but showing signs of uneasiness from time to time, probably because of the great crowd of people around him. For a while I watched him without saying anything. When I spoke to him, it didn't take long to discover that he was mute. Soon after that, when I noticed that he made no response to various questions I put to him, in both a loud and a soft voice, I decided that he must be deaf.

When I took him affectionately by the hand to lead him to my house, he resisted strenuously. But a series of caresses, and particularly two hugs, with a friendly smile, changed his mind, and after that he seemed to trust me.

Portrait of Victor (the Wild Boy of Aveyron) from J.M.G. Itard's report of 1801. There were 26 scars about his head and body.

When we reached my house, I decided he must be hungry....To find out what he liked, I had my servant offer him on a big earthenware platter raw and cooked meat, rye and wheat bread, apples, pears, grapes, nuts, chestnuts, acorns, potatoes, parsnips and an orange. He picked up the potatoes confidently and tossed them into the fire to cook them. One at a time he seized the other items, smelled them, and rejected them. With his right hand he picked the potatoes right out of the live coals and ate them roasting hot. There was no way to persuade him to let them cool off a little. He made sharp, inarticulate, yet scarcely complaining sounds that indicated the hot food was burning him. When he got thirsty, he glanced around the room. Noticing the pitcher, he placed my hand in his without any other sign and led me to the pitcher, which he tapped with his left hand as a means of asking for a drink. Some wine was brought, but he scorned it and showed impatience at my delay in giving him water to drink....

When he had finished his frugal meal, he stood up and ran out the door. In spite of my shouts he kept on running, and I had a hard time catching him. When I brought him back, he seemed neither pleased nor displeased. This unfortunate being had already aroused my deepest interest (cited in Shattuck 1980, 6–7).

Constant-Saint-Estäve was a reasonably well-educated man. His account of his experiences with Victor reveal a deeply curious person who used scientific methods as he knew them to experiment with Victor almost from the moment of his arrival at his home. Constant-Saint-Estäve kept detailed records of Victor's reactions, as the above excerpts from his writings indicate.

The child was not toilet trained, and urinated and defecated whenever he felt the need. Constant-Saint-Estäve concluded that "from earliest childhood this boy has lived in the woods, a stranger to social needs and habits." Two days after his capture at Saint-Serin the boy was taken, still naked, to the hospice in the town of Saint-Afrique 40 kilometres away. When he was dressed, he tore off his clothing. He refused to sleep in a bed and continually tried to escape.

Soon stories about the "wild boy" spread throughout France, and he was moved once again, this time into the care of a priest by the name of Pierre-Joseph Bonnaterre, who lived in the nearby town of Rodez. Like Constant-Saint-Estäve, Bonnaterre was an educated man, and he too immediately set about experimenting with and observing the actions and reactions of his unusual charge.

From Bonnaterre we learn that the boy was about 49 inches (125 centimetres) tall and that he appeared to be 12 or 13 years old. His body was covered with scars, including one almost 4 centimetres across the upper end of the tracheal artery, right across the glottis. Bonnaterre speculated that someone probably had tried to kill the child. He further noted that the boy had no malformation of the tongue or mouth or vocal cords, which might have impeded him from speaking. While there were no serious flaws in the boy's external makeup, he did display strange behaviour. As Bonnaterre reported:

> When he is sitting down, and even when he is eating, he makes a guttural sound, a low murmur; and he rocks his body from right to left or backwards and forwards, with his head and chin up, his mouth closed, and his eyes staring at nothing. In this position he sometimes has spasms, convulsive movements that may indicate that his nervous system has been affected (cited in Shattuck 1980, 13).

Bonnaterre also observed that while there was nothing wrong with the boy's senses, he relied on those senses in a different order from others: his sense of smell came first, then taste, and finally touch. While his sense of hearing was acute, he seemed to shut out most of the sounds that people around him made and appeared to be interested only in food and sleep.

When Bonnaterre showed the boy a mirror, he apparently saw a person reflected in it, but did not recognize that reflection as his own. When Bonnaterre held a potato behind the boy's head so he could see it in the mirror, the boy first tried to reach through the mirror to grasp it. When that proved unsuccessful, he reached back over his shoulder without turning around and grasped the potato. But for all his experimenting and efforts to educate the boy, Bonnaterre really did not know what to make of him. The question soon became whether or not the child was simply an "idiot" (the eighteenth-century term used to designate a person with a low level of intelligence). Was any effort to educate the child therefore useless? After much observation, Bonnaterre concluded that the child was not without some intelligence, reflection, and reasoning power. However, in every instance that did not concern "his natural needs or satisfying his appetite," Bonnaterre observed, "one can perceive in him only animal behaviour."

> If he has sensations, they give birth to no idea. He cannot even compare them with one another. One would think that there is no connection between his soul or mind and his body, and that he cannot reflect on anything. As a result, he has no discernment, no real mind, no memory. This condition of imbecility shows itself in his eyes, which he never keeps on any one object, and in the sounds of his voice, which are inarticulate, and discordant. One can see it even in his gait—always a trot or a gallop—and in his actions, which have no purpose or explanation (cited in Shattuck 1980, 18).

It is important to note Bonnaterre's conclusion that the boy was an imbecile. Imbecile is another eighteenth-century term used to denote a person with a somewhat higher level of intelligence than an "idiot." The condition was apparent, Bonnaterre writes, in the boy's eyes, in the sounds of his voice, in his gait, and finally in his "actions, which have no purpose or explanation." Had the boy remained in Bonnaterre's care, he would have not been subject to further "scientific investigation."

The Society of the Observers of Man

Bonnaterre, however, was soon to lose custody of his charge. The boy had come to the attention of the Abbé Sicard, who had established a reputation as a teacher of deaf-mute children. Sicard held the position of director of the Institute for Deaf-Mutes in Paris, and it was here that the boy was taken. Sicard's approach to the education of deaf-mutes was closely tied to the sensationalist or empiricist ideas of the time. The impact of sensationalist theory on the study of human existence was extensive, especially in France. Through adherence to sensationalist precepts, it was believed, not only could scientific studies of humanity be undertaken, but the opportunity also existed to transform the behaviour of certain individuals who had been deprived of normal education. This goal could be achieved through the manipulation of specific kinds of sensorial input.

Based on this point of view a whole new set of institutions was created, not 10 years before the "wild boy" had been discovered. The people who ran these institutions were devoted to using sensationalist ideals to reform and control the behaviour of improperly socialized children and adults. The Institute for Deaf-Mutes in Paris was one of these new institutions.

While at the school, the "wild boy," who was still without a name, was placed under the care of a group of men who called themselves the Society of Observers of Man. Members of the society included Sicard and Dr. Pinel, who had become famous for his humane treatment of the insane. These men referred to themselves as *idéologues* and followed the teachings of Condillac. They were committed to the rigorous measurement of all aspects of human existence and to a naturalistic analysis of the origins and content of thought (Hirst and Woolley 1981, 49).

Examined by several of the more famous members of the Society of Observers of Man, including Pinel, the boy was found to be an "incurable idiot" (down a step from Bonnaterre's diagnosis of imbecile). It was Pinel's opinion that the boy would not benefit from even "lengthy and methodical instruction." It is important to note here that Pinel was committed to the "moral" treatment (or resocialization) of the insane. For Pinel, moral treatment was dependent on linguistic communication, and idiocy was held to be the result of some organic or inherited deficiency that prevented the individual from using normal language and thus from being amenable to resocialization. In Pinel's mind, and in the minds of the rest of the members of the Society of Observers of Man, the wild boy was nothing more than an idiot and not some otherwise normal child who had been abandoned and who would benefit from re-education. The boy, it was determined, could not communicate because he was "organically deficient." Because of this defect, moreover, he would never learn to communicate, no matter how much effort was expended on him. Pinel and the others concluded that the boy could safely be relegated to an insane asylum and given the minimum of care.

Philipe Pinel, 1745–1826. A doctor noted for his humane treatment of the insane, Pinel concluded that Victor was an "incurable idiot," not an otherwise normal child who had been abandoned and who would benefit from re-education.

THE SOCIALIZATION OF VICTOR

But the wild boy's story did not end there. His case was taken up by a young medical student, Jean-Marc-Gaspard Itard, who worked with deaf children at the Institute in Paris and who was not convinced by Pinel's finding that there was something organically wrong with the boy. Because he disagreed with Pinel's findings, Itard was willing to go ahead and try out Locke's and Condillac's sensationalist theories on the boy by attempting his socialization.

In Itard's mind, Victor, as he now called the boy, was not an idiot. He had simply been deprived of certain necessary formative social experiences. What he needed was a complete socialization program. As Itard himself wrote, humans are only what they have been made to be. Any human being has to learn his or her habits, needs, and ideas, and does so by imitating others under the influence of society.

Itard believed that Victor would provide him with a unique opportunity to observe how humans behave when they have been deprived of social interaction during their formative years. If Victor could be restored to the levels of learning that were expected in a normal child his age, then Locke's and Condillac's theories of learning, that the human child is born a *tabula rasa,* could be verified. Itard saw Victor as a test case against **essentialist notions** (inherent in the Great Chain of Being thesis discussed in Chapter 5) in which the nature or spirit of human beings was innate and fixed by God, or if not fixed by God, then by biological endowments.

Pinel's diagnosis of Victor as an idiot implied that he was biologically deficient and therefore beyond the help of any kind of socialization therapy. But it was Itard's belief that the boy had normal sensations that could be activated at this point in his life if the right techniques could be found. With these techniques to stimulate Victor's senses, Itard reasoned, the boy could eventually be restored to normal development for his age.

Itard was convinced that a study of the way in which Victor learned to be a "human being" could reveal much about how ideas, senses, and feelings develop in normal human beings. He hired Madame Guérin, the wife of one of the workers at the Institute, to care for Victor, and with her help, he set out to teach Victor to use all his social faculties, especially language.

Itard's *Memoire on the First Developments in the Case of Victor of Aveyron,* written in 1801, and his *Report on New Developments in the Case of Victor of Aveyron,* written for the minister of the interior in 1806, show that Victor was far from the uneducable idiot that Pinel had diagnosed. These works trace the extent to which Itard was successful in educating Victor and in shaping him into a recognizable, civilized French citizen.

Itard developed a plan, based on the work of Condillac and Locke, as well as on that of Pinel, for the moral treatment of Victor. It included:

1. Giving the boy the ability to respond to other people

2. Training the boy in the use of his senses

3. Extending the boy's physical and social needs

4. Teaching the boy to speak

5. Teaching the boy to think clearly (Malson 1964).

Itard was, in part, successful. His *Memoire* and *Report* describe his slow, difficult, and at times frustrating work with Victor. Victor learned to wear clothes and to dress himself. He became toilet trained, was able to recognize and reproduce a few words made out of metal letters. He even learned to say a very few words. Over a period of several years, Victor displayed evidence of both intellectual and emotional growth. He was able to participate in household chores such as setting the table, gardening, and sawing wood. Yet when Victor failed to meet his expectations, Itard too quickly tired of his experiments with the boy, leaving him in the car of Mme Guérin. He died in 1828, at about age 40. There is nothing in the historical record that describes the causes of his death or gives any hint of what his last years were like.

In spite of Itard's careful work and records, we have little idea of the actual nature of Victor's original condition. Was he, as Itard was convinced, a normal boy whose isolation from society had made him act as if he were developmentally delayed? Was Pinel's original diagnosis essentially correct? Was Itard's failure to completely socialize Victor the result of faulty techniques or were his attempts simply too late to be effective? (Shattuck 1980, 168)

We will never be able to directly answer these questions about Victor using the information in the historical record. But we can answer questions about how many late eighteenth- and early nineteenth-century scientists thought about human nature and the process of socialization. Victor's capture was important for the members of the Society of the Observers of Man because he afforded them a chance to test their theories of the human mind and of learning.

TWENTIETH-CENTURY CONCERNS

Some aspects of the theoretical perspective used by the scientists discussed above continue today. For example, many twentieth-century social scientists continue to accept Locke's tenets that we are all born without any innate principles, primary notions, or ideas stamped on our minds. We learn all our ideas through our social relationships with others and, as a result, we all are socialized into behaving as we do. Because we learn how to think, our ideas and behaviour are malleable and determined by our socialization. Finally, if our thoughts, ideas, and behaviours are established by socialization, then, at least in part, they can be altered through a process of resocialization.

We may be unable to answer many of the questions we would like to pose based on the historical record left to us by Victor's observers. There are, however, several more contemporary examples of children who have been abandoned that we can examine. These cases help clarify what happens to children who are deprived of social interaction and fail to acquire cultural learning. Like their earlier counterparts, these twentieth-century cases tell us a great deal about the values, beliefs, and ideals of the scientists who studied them.

ANNA AND ISABELLA

In 1947 American sociologist Kingsley Davis published an account of two cases of extreme isolation in children. One of the children, Anna, was born in 1932, the second illegitimate child of a farm girl whose father strongly disapproved of her pregnancies. Through a series of events, Anna was offered for adoption but was never placed. At $5\frac{1}{2}$ months, she was taken back to her grandfather's farm and kept there, in an attic room, with barely enough attention to keep her alive. When she was finally removed from the house at age 6, she could not walk, talk, or do anything that showed intelligence. As Davis describes her: "She was in an extremely emaciated and undernourished condition, with skeleton-like legs on a bloated abdomen. She had been fed on virtually nothing except cow's milk during the years under her mother's care (cited in Wilson and Kolb 1949, 174).

Isabella was found about nine months after the discovery of Anna. Like Anna, Isabella was the illegitimate daughter of a mother who was forced to keep her child isolated within the family home. Isabella's mother was deaf, and she and Isabella spent most of their time secluded together in a dark room. As a result, Isabella had no chance to learn to speak or to communicate except by gesture and grunts. She was afraid of strangers, especially men, made strange croaking sounds and (like Victor) seemed to be deaf. Because she had never been exposed to sunlight and had been fed an inadequate diet, she had rickets. Her legs were terribly bowed and when she stood straight the soles of her feet came almost completely together.

GENIE

Genie is the pseudonym for a California girl who was kept locked up and isolated in a room in her parents' house from about 18 months until she was discovered, in 1970, at approximately age 13 (Curtiss 1977). Genie's plight was uncovered only after her 50-year-old mother, who was going blind and who also had been kept largely confined to the house, ran away from her 70-year-old husband after a violent argument. When Genie's mother applied for social assistance, welfare authorities took one look at Genie and called the police. What they saw was a small, withered, stooped girl who could barely walk and who held her hands up as though resting them on an invisible rail. She weighed 59 pounds (27 kilograms), was 54 inches (137 centimetres) tall, incontinent, unable to chew, barely able to swallow, and unable to focus her eyes beyond 12 feet. She could not cry, salivated constantly, and spat indiscriminately. She was unable to make any movement that required fully extended arms or legs and did not seem able to perceive either heat or cold (Rymer 1992).

Although unable to speak except for "Stopit," "Nomore," and a few other negatives, she could understand about 20 words. Genie was sent to the Los Angeles Children's Hospital for tests. Her parents were charged with wilful abuse, but her father committed suicide, and charges against her mother were dropped when her lawyer pleaded that she was also a victim of Genie's psychotic father. He decided that Genie was mentally disabled when she was about 20 months old. He dreaded the idea that she would be vulnerable to exploitation by others and decided that the only way to protect her was to keep her confined (ibid., 44). As Susan Curtiss, who wrote her doctoral dissertation on Genie, tells us:

> In the house Genie was confined to a small bedroom, harnessed to an infant's potty seat. Genie's father sewed the harness himself; unclad except for the harness, Genie was left to sit on that chair. Unable to move anything except her fingers and hands, feet and toes, Genie was left to sit, tied-up, hour after hour, often into the night, day after day, month after month, year after year. At night, when Genie was not forgotten, she was removed from her harness only to be placed into another restraining garment—a sleeping bag which her father had fashioned to hold Genie's arms stationary (allegedly to prevent her from taking it off). In effect, it was a straightjacket. Therein constrained, Genie was put into an infant's crib with wire mesh sides and a wire mesh cover overhead. Caged by night, harnessed by day, Genie was left to somehow endure the hours and years of her life....

There was little for her to listen to; there was no TV or radio in the house. Genie's bedroom was in the back of the house....The father had an intolerance for noise, so what little conversation there was between family members in the rest of the house was kept at low volume. Except for moments of anger, when her father swore, Genie did not hear any language outside her door, and thus received practically no auditory stimulation of any kind....

Hungry and forgotten, Genie would sometimes attempt to attract attention by making noise. Angered, her father would often beat her for doing so. In fact, there was a large piece of wood left in the corner of Genie's room which her father used solely to beat her whenever she made any sound. Genie learned to keep silent and to suppress all vocalization....(cited in Rymer 1992, 44).

When she was first admitted to hospital, Genie was severely malnourished. She could not stand erect, straighten her arms, walk, run, or jump. Described by a psychiatrist as "unsocialized, primitive, hardly human," Genie masturbated continually and could not be dissuaded from that activity. And she was eerily silent.

In her first seven months in the hospital, she learned to walk with a jerky motion and became more or less toilet trained. She also learned several new words and began to speak single words. One month later, she was able to string two words together. A little later she produced verbs. One year after she was admitted, she could occasionally form three-word strings, such as "small two cup" or "white clear box" (Santrock 1983, 207).

Unlike normal children, however, Genie never learned to ask questions and understood very little grammar. Yet her inability to form normal sentences and to understand grammar did not seem to be the result of congenital disabilities. Instead, researchers attributed her lack of linguistic skills to the fact that she had passed a critical stage in language development without learning to speak and therefore those parts of her brain that would have been used for language had atrophied (ibid., 208).

Many twentieth-century scientists are not so quick to argue that all aspects of human social behaviour are entirely malleable. Some, for example, believe that there is an interplay between social and biological factors in the acquisition of language. Infants and young children must acquire language from caregivers in a socially interactive setting: a child who passes a "critical stage" without being exposed to spoken language looses the ability to acquire much more than a rudimentary lexicon in later years.

CONTEMPORARY CONCERNS

It is interesting to compare the observations and perspectives of the scientists who studied Peter, Victor, Anna, Isabella, and finally Genie. The scientists who studied Peter were interested in determining what was natural human behaviour in contrast to behaviour that was purely the result of civilization. A few years later, the members of the Society of the Observers of Man, using a sensational perspective, had developed interests not just in

observing and recording human behaviour, but also in modifying it. Contemporary scholars have taken much from the sensationalists. For example, most accept the view that we are capable of learning but are born knowing almost nothing of what constitutes a member of a given society.

This, for example, is the position of American sociologist Kingsley Davis. Writing in 1949 about the cases of Anna and Isabella, Davis maintained that the study cases of extreme isolation in children were of great interest to scientists. Only in such children, Davis wrote, is it possible to observe "*concretely separated*" factors of biological and social origin.

Davis believed that severely isolated children had grown up without the influence of socialization, and thus their behaviour reflected only those factors that are biologically innate or naturally occurring in all humans. He and other sociologists like him have studied feral children in order to support their point of view that, with the exception of isolated and feral children, all human behaviour available for observation is the result of social learning. For Davis and many other sociologists, social learning or socialization strongly implies that all behaviour normally seen in members of a given society is shaped by external, social forces. Society acts to suppress whatever is innate and to impose on the developing child behaviour patterns of purely social origin.

Other twentieth-century researchers have disputed this point. Child psychologist Bruno Bettelheim has maintained that socialization is a matter of *modifying* innate characteristics already present in children and not of inculcating in them external, socially constructed ones, as is claimed by sociologists. He chastises sociologists and anthropologists for wanting to see human behaviour as wholly created by society. The fact of the matter, Bettelheim insists, is that "no known society has ever done more than to modify innate characteristics" (1967, 347). All known cases of feral children, he continues, are actually cases of children with autism, and not, as sociologists and anthropologists would have it, examples of children who have missed being properly socialized.

No infant or young child, Bettelheim tells us, could live for any significant amount of time without the emotional closeness of another human being (1967, 382). Thus feral children are not examples of what happens when innate biological patterns of behaviour fail to be replaced by externally imposed ones through socialization. Rather, so-called feral children are really children who have not progressed through normal stages of personality development.

But is this really the case? Are all feral children really just autistic children who have been abandoned? Certainly it would be difficult to argue that Victor was an autistic child. Abandoned at about age 5 he lived perhaps as many as six years alone, surviving many harsh winters. Itard's records indicate that Victor welcomed human contact and did not respond either to himself or to Madame Guerin as would an autistic child.

A third point of view, one supported by new research on infant and early childhood socialization, is that there is no satisfactory way to resolve the issue of whether or not all of human behaviour is the result of the infinite malleability and educability of humans or the result of the inexorable development of a fixed human nature. Many late-twentieth-century researchers now dispute the sensationalist notion that the newborn child is purely reflex, without any social skills or will. Many suspect that the socialization process is a much more complex phenomenon than the simple imposition of external behaviour patterns on an essentially passive child—a position long favoured in traditional sociology and anthropology. For example, certain researchers insist that very young children *actively* engage in social interaction with adults and thus are active participants in their own socialization.

I give the last word on this issue to the French anthropologist Claude Lévi-Strauss who argues that "no empirical analysis...can determine the point of transition between natural and cultural facts, nor how they are connected" (1969, 8). It is impossible to make an empirical distinction between nature and culture, he contends, because we can find no presocial state in all of human evolution.

■ ■ ■

SUMMARY

So far, I have introduced the discipline of sociology and a number of different concepts, such as culture and socialization, that are the foundations of the discipline of sociology. And yet sociologists do not always agree even on what is meant by the most foundational concepts. Differing theoretical perspectives on culture and socialization have led social scientists to various kinds of understandings about culture and socialization and the relationship between human biology and socialization.

The cases of Peter, Victor, Anna, Isabella, and Genie help us to understand the significance of socialization and social interaction for the human child, if that child is to grow up and become a functioning adult member of society. These examples give some indication of the importance of early social relations in forming a child's development as a social being, and emphasize the need for sustained, supportive, and caring contact. They also indicate the extent to which the perspective of the researcher influences the kind of knowledge produced about the complex relationship between human biology, socialization, and human culture.

■ ■ ■

FOR DISCUSSION

1. Based on the case studies presented in this chapter, what are some of the consequences for a child of growing up in isolation?

2. To what extent do sensationalist ideas still shape twentieth-century understandings about child development?

3. Bruno Bettelheim has argued that feral children do not exist and that it is impossible for a child to survive without adult care. Other social scientists disagree. Which side of the debate might you support, and why?

4. Does the study of feral children really provide us with a means of establishing the extent to which human behaviour is determined by cultural as opposed to biogenetic factors? Are there other ways that might help us determine the extent to which human behaviour is biologically or socially established?

5. How are feral children and the socialization process depicted in popular stories such as *The Jungle Book* and *Tarzan*?

6. After reading this chapter, how would you go about attempting to socialize the wild boy of Aveyron?

THE SOCIALIZATION OF THE INFANT AND YOUNG CHILD

CHAPTER OPENING QUESTIONS

- How are infants and young children socialized into becoming functioning members of society?

- According to those theorists who regard infants as initially nonsocial, what forces compel humans to become socialized?

- For theorists who view even young children as active participants in their socialization, how does the process work?

- How important is the relationship between infant and adult caregiver to a child's social development?

- In what ways do contemporary theorists see social interaction and personal development as necessarily linked?

As we have discussed in the previous chapter, the importance of early social contact for the development of young children was already under investigation in the mid-eighteenth century. A century later, Victor, the "wild boy of Aveyron," had provided Jean-Marc-Gaspard Itard with a seemingly ideal subject on whom he could test sensationalist theories. Yet Itard believed he failed when he was unable to teach Victor anything more than the most rudimentary forms of speech, and along with the rest of the French intellectual community, he eventually lost interest in the project. Almost two hundred years have passed since Victor was studied. Since then a great deal of work has been done concerning the significance of early social relationships, the nature of the bonds between caregivers and young children, and the importance of socialization to human lives. In this chapter, I focus on the process of early socialization in the relationship between the infant/child and his or her immediate caregivers.

There are several different theories that attempt to explain how, why, and under what conditions the socialization of the infant and young child takes place. Probably the most significant difference among socialization theorists revolves around whether the infant begins life radically separated from society (and thus is in need of being tamed, or at least trained, before he or she can be brought into society), or whether the infant actually begins life as an already social being whose sociability is then shaped, moulded, and formed by adult caregivers. Today there is little dispute, with the exception of sociobiology (see Chapter 4), over whether the process of socialization plays the leading role in establishing the behaviour patterns of children and adults. But there is controversy over how the socialization process actually works, especially whether or not there ever is such a thing as a state of nature in which the child begins life as a passive, blank slate.

In what follows, I will present the perspectives of a number of theorists who have studied early childhood socialization, along with their specific explanations of the process. I begin with those theories that proceed from the assumption that the infant begins life radically separate from society, as an untamed, natural, self-contained, and self-referring being with little or no inclination to perceive the existence of others or to engage them in social interaction.

THE SELF AS RADICALLY SEPARATE FROM SOCIETY

Until recently discussions of how children are socialized usually depicted them as passive and even withdrawn from social interaction. According to this view, the child is like a piece of clay, acted on by adult caregivers who eventually socialize him or her into behaving in an acceptable and recognizably human way. There is a further underlying assumption that every individual is both unique and self-contained. While social bonds to others are important, these bonds are secondary to the existence of the individual who is separated from the rest of society by deeply ingrained barriers. Because of this separation, it has been suggested that society must act in ways to make the individual conform. The notion of the radical separation of individual and society was developed by theorists concerned with explaining how the "uncivilized" infant could eventually be tamed enough to become a socially acceptable human being.

Many sociologists believe that adult caregivers must act on the child to make him or her conform to acceptable social behaviour.

Sociologist Norbert Elias (1978) has pointed out that over a 300-year period beginning in the late fourteenth century, Western Europeans gradually came to view themselves as increasingly separated from other members of their society. He argues that this notion of a self separated by an invisible wall from what happens outside emerged as a result of a gradual shift in the nature of social relations among people during that period.

Political changes were occurring throughout Western Europe as the direct rule of the aristocracy declined and was replaced by ideas of equality before the law. Control began to shift from externally imposed rule to a strong sense of individualism and self-rule. This idea of the self as an independent entity, locked inside his or her own thought processes and divorced from all others, was reflected in the work of three key Enlightenment philosophers—René Descartes (1596–1650), Gottfried Wilhelm Leibniz (1646–1716), and Immanuel Kant (1724–1804).

Descartes's famous dictum "I think therefore I am" is a clear example of the belief that the real essence of the individual consists in thinking. From this perspective, the body is simply a source of automatic sensations and impulses, while all the rational conceptions of the world come from the working of the mind. Each mind, moreover, is considered to be a separate entity in its own right. Through using one's mind to the fullest, Descartes believed that each individual is able to perceive and understand the world and everything in it.

Similarly, Leibniz argued that the individual was the one indivisible entity capable of perceiving objects in the universe. Every individual had his or her unique world view. The existence of all other things, Leibniz maintained, had to depend ultimately on the existence of the individual. Thus the individual is primary, while all social relationships are secondary phenomena. Presented with the problem of explaining how social relationships could exist between independent individuals, Leibniz resorted to God. In his "doctrine of pre-established harmony," he maintained that because God created all human beings, they would naturally be inclined toward each other, in spite of their individuality.

Kant solved the problem of the relation between the essentially independent individual and society inherent in both Descartes's and Leibniz's work by arguing that certain categories of thought existed a priori, that is, prior to human existence. Human rationality is governed by what Kant referred to as "transcendental subjectivity." The human transcendental subject is made up of rules and categories that are given to all humans prior to experience and that make that experience possible. Through these a priori rules and categories, the individual is able to perceive the **phenomenal world,** yet all real objects exist independently of human consciousness in the **noumenal world.** Walled in by a priori rules and categories, the individual can never quite break through to grasp the noumenal world.

The work of all three philosophers helped to lay the foundations in Western thought of the belief in a separation between the interior life of the individual and the external social world. These ideas established what is today a taken-for-granted understanding that the individual, as a separate being, confronts the social world as something that is outside and essentially in opposition to his or her individuality and uniqueness. In this view, the individual by nature has an existence independent from any social relations but is encroached upon and eventually forced to conform to the demands of the external social world.

SIGMUND FREUD AND THE CIVILIZING OF THE INFANT

Sigmund Freud (1856–1939), a Viennese physician, is among the most influential theorists of this century to deal with the issues of the relationship between the individual and

Can we separate the environment from the child's development?

society. His work concentrates specifically on the formation of the individual's psyche and assumes a basic division between the outside or society and the inside or interior emotional and mental life of the individual. For Freud, that inside is shaped by internal, organic forces that external society demands must be regulated in culturally determined and socially acceptable ways. The individual, for Freud, is formed only in opposition to the demands of society, and the process of society's formation of the individual coincides with the child's recognition of his or her own existential separation from the mother. This realization, moreover, is also the beginning of the development of the child's sexuality and awareness of being either male or female.

Freud began his medical career as a neurologist. He soon suspected, though, that some of the patients he was treating for neurological disorders were actually suffering from psychologically induced symptoms. Freud went to Paris where he studied under Jean Martin Charcot, the most eminent psychologist of the time. Using hypnosis and purely verbal techniques, Charcot had successfully treated "hysterics," who presented what appeared to be organic illnesses.

In his own work, Freud came to understand hysteria as the result of a psychological conflict that could be expressed only in physical terms. He developed what one of his first patients called the "talking cure," or *psychoanalysis*, in which the patient (analysand) gained relief from distressing physical symptoms by remembering and verbalizing in the presence of an analyst unresolved psychological conflicts from early childhood.

On the basis of his work with patients, Freud developed a number of theories about the psychical functioning of human beings, which, he maintained, had its roots in the first few years of life. Central among Freud's contributions to the understanding of human development is his view of the relationship between the unconscious and the early frustrations of an individual's sexual life. I want to concentrate on Freud's theories of the first relationship between infant, mother, and father, and the implications of those early relationships in the creation of a social being from a self-contained infant.

PSYCHOSEXUAL PHASES, PLEASURE, AND PAIN

In part of his work, Freud laid out a series of psychosexual phases that he believed each individual passed through in the course of normal development—the oral, anal, phallic, and genital phases, and their role in the socialization of the young child. In order to understand the significance of these phases, it is important to consider first Freud's view of the human body. He regarded the body as a kind of mechanism that built up and discharged energy.

This point of view is usually referred to metaphorically as a hydraulic theory of bodily functioning. In a hydraulic system, pressure mounts as water is dammed up. The system functions only when that pressure is released. Similarly, in Freud's assessment, the body seeks to achieve homeostasis, or equilibrium, in order to keep internal energy levels from being overstimulated, causing the body to cease functioning. In the course of normal development, the *sexual drive*, which Freud believed to be an internal source of bodily energy, sets up different zones, organs, and processes that become sites of release for built-up energy. As the young child matures physically, different sites for the release of energy become available. In using these sites of tension release, the child gains pleasure. Before we discuss Freud's ideas further, it is important to settle the distinction between "drive" and "instinct" as they were used by him.

Drives and Instincts

If you are able to read Freud in the original German, you will frequently come across two words: *Trieb* meaning "drive" and *Instinkt* meaning "instinct." In his work, Freud clearly distinguishes between the two words. However, James Strachey, Freud's English translator, rendered both words as "instinct" and thus created a major confusion for anglophone readers about how Freud understood the relation between sexuality and biology (Grosz 1991, 71). Freud used the term instinct to refer to the biological need for self-preservation. He used the term drive, on the other hand, to refer only to the sphere of sexuality. In Freud's schema, biological instincts set up the bodily zones, organs, and processes that the drives then use to gain satisfaction, pleasure, and release of tension.

As the different bodily organs and functions mature in the infant, they provide the sites out of which drives emerge. As each new site matures in its sensitivity to sensations—the oral cavity during the oral phase, the bladder and bowel functions during the anal phase, and the genitalia during the genital phase—it becomes a new erotogenic zone. In order to better understand what Freud meant by his definition of sexuality and eroticism, and how they served as the foundation for all social life, we must explore further his ideas about pleasure and pain.

Pain, Pleasure, and Sexuality

It is important to keep in mind that for Freud the roots of all social interaction in human beings are to be found in *somatic* or bodily sensations. The infant gradually learns how to differentiate himself or herself from the rest of the world by experiencing bodily sensations and being able to categorize those sensations and attach their gratification or non-gratification to the presence of other human beings. Once this differentiation has taken place, the young child is then able to learn gradually how to become a full member of society.

For Freud, the most powerful of all bodily sensations were those associated with what he called the **pleasure principle** and sexuality. In the early months of life, all infants are sexual beings, although their sexuality is hardly comparable to that of an adult. Instead, their sexuality consists in sensing stimulation in some part of their body, in feeling tension build in the area being stimulated, and in finally gaining relief when that tension is released. In very small infants, the major focus of tension and release is hunger, which is satiated by feeding, and sensations in the urogenital area and around the anus, sated by urinating and by bowel movement.

In Freud's theory of sexuality, both pleasure and its opposite, pain, are defined in biological terms. Pain is defined as an increase of tension within a biological organism. While some tension is necessary for life, tension becomes pain when a certain threshold is passed. Pleasure, on the other hand, is the removal or easing of tension. For Freud, the human infant and child operate on the basis of the pleasure principle. Feeling tension as a result of built-up energy, all infants seek to release that tension and in the process experience a feeling or sensation of pleasure. One important implication of this theory of the sex drive is that there is no one fixed site of sexual excitation and no one fixed object of sexual desire that will satisfy that excitation. Any part of the body may become eroticized and any object may provide satisfaction for a drive. For example, during the oral phase, a child may get satisfaction from any object she can put into her mouth and suck on, regardless of whether or not that object provides her with nourishment (Grosz 1991, 72).

During the oral phase, the infant's social relations are exclusively with the mother and are based on the satisfaction of the oral drive. Freud maintained that there is a physiological dependency set up between the infant and its mother. The infant has several needs, for example, a need for food, and each need produces a tension until it is satisfied. When a need is finally satisfied, the infant experiences pleasure and is sated until the next bout of tension buildup and release occurs.

127

Thus, for Freud, the mother appears in the infant's world only as an *object*, as a *thing* that satisfies the infant's need to release tension, which at this point is focused on the oral cavity. The mother does not appear in the baby's world as a person in her own right. At this point in development, the child's needs are shaped only by his or her need for food and comfort, and the mother's breast represents both a source of nourishment and a source of pleasure. The infant's world does not include "any of the curiosity and responsiveness to sight and sound, face and voice, that are incipiently social" (Benjamin 1988, 16). In Freud's view, then, an infant in the oral stage is an asocial being.

The Id, the Ego, and the Superego

The infant's journey from an asocial bundle of needs and drives fixated on the mother's breast, from which she cannot differentiate herself, to an organized, repressed, and civilized adult is a complicated process in Freud's theory. As we have already discussed, the infant starts out with an undifferentiated mental life. Freud maintained that as the child grows and experiences relationships, a tripartite division of **id** (*das Es* in German or "the it"), **ego** (*das Ich* or "the I"), and **superego** emerges out of the originally undifferentiated psychic structure (Freud 1933, 57–80).

In *The Ego and the Id* (1923), Freud makes the following distinction between the three parts of the individual's psyche. The id is composed of a collection of biological urges, impulses, and processes that all strive for conscious expression and gratification. These impulses and urges (i.e., those associated with the pleasure principle) do not take reality into consideration. The ego emerges to regulate the impulse and urges (the pleasure principle) that emanate from the id. Following what Freud called the **reality principle,** the ego's role is to restrain the id. The ego forces the id into accepting compromises by presenting the id with an indirect course of action that will achieve at least partial satisfaction of its demand for release of tension but that also allows the individual to conform to social constraints.

In order to survive in society, the developing child has to learn to control her need for immediate gratification of impulses. The reality principle allows her to do this. It first intrudes into the child's growing psychic life when she experiences frustration and anxiety at not having her needs immediately satisfied. When this happens, the child begins to recognize that her mother is a separate being, with her own separate interests and activities. The reality principle is the direct result of the child's first awareness of her mother as a separate being.

As the infant experiences anxiety and frustration, she gradually differentiates herself from her mother who, up to this point, has made up her entire environment. The young child starts to erect defences against her mother and then later against the rest of the outside world. The reality principle forces the child to become more aware of the external reality of her situation and to work to control her desire for immediate gratification until the impulse can be safely discharged in a way that is socially acceptable. Induction into the reality principle means that the child must repress certain responses to external and internal stimuli and to identify with other persons in such a way as to change her own self or her experience of her self in a relationship. Freud argued that anxiety and frustration trigger the development of the ego, which emerges to deal with and help ward off those anxieties (Chodorow 1978, 69–70).

According to sociologist and psychoanalyst Nancy Chodorow, a second and equally important element of the child's induction into reality is the growing recognition of her mother's social involvement with others—especially with the child's father and siblings. Father, siblings, and anyone else of importance in the mother's life are the first to be differentiated from the child's growing sense of self. The infant's first association with them is one of envy or jealousy. She is therefore able to perceive herself in opposition to her rivals for her mother's affection and attention. The child's ego develops and the reality principle is established, Chodorow tells us, in large part as a defence against these early feelings (70–71).

Finally, in the course of development and socialization, the superego emerges as the third component part of the growing child's psyche. The superego was considered by Freud to be a modification of the ego; its function is to judge the ego. When it is first developing, an incipient superego uses the parents as its main model. In *The Ego and the Id*, Freud gives an account of the formation of the superego as the *introjection* of parental figures. The child introjects (or incorporates) into her own sense of self the values, beliefs, and ideals of her parents and makes them her own. Although parents are the first objects introjected into the child's growing superego, as the child matures she also introjects the dominant values of society at large. The superego is therefore the internalized moral commands of the child's society, which act as yet another force in addition to the ego to repress or transform the urges and needs emanating from the id.

At the centre of Freud's theory about the process of the young child's socialization lies the notion of the unavoidable tension between internal needs, urges, and desires (the pleasure principle) and external, social demands (the reality principle). The socialization of the individual entails the development of the ego and superego, which can be viewed as a process of *repression* of the individual's internal, biologically based needs, in favour of external, social demands. This repression, Freud argues in *Civilization and Its Discontents* ([1930] 1963), is necessary if civilization is to exist. In his later work, Freud also began to understand culture as a repressive structure that, of necessity, stifled some of humanity's basic tendencies such as aggression and destructiveness in order to allow it to survive. He believed that these destructive energies, which he called the death drive, were also *sublimated*, that is, were redirected to culturally and morally acceptable goals, away from their original destructive objectives.

A CRITICAL ASSESSMENT OF FREUD'S IDEAS ON EARLY CHILDHOOD EXPERIENCES

It would be difficult to exaggerate the influence of Freud's ideas, and of psychoanalytic theory in general, on twentieth-century thought. Over 100 000 books and articles on Freud and his ideas have been written during this century in over 30 different languages (Ashley and Orenstein 1990, 360). His views have had an impact on painters and writers as well as on social theorists. They have also influenced child-care specialists, including

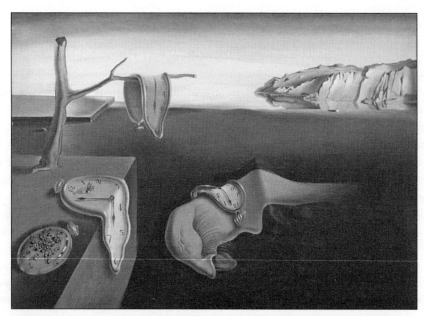

Dali drew objects as he saw them rather than interpreting what he envisioned. This work is from his Freudian stage in which he dealt with world events (the Spanish Civil War) and aspects of his subconscious.

Dr. Benjamin Spock, whose advice to parents during the 1940s and 1950s greatly affected their approach to child rearing.

While many commentators have denounced Freud and his ideas, it is impossible to deny that these ideas being denounced have helped shape the way Westerners think about themselves. By demonstrating the existence of the unconscious, Freud also showed that direct, unmediated knowledge of self and of others is impossible. Most challenging of all, as Ashley and Orenstein (1990) point out, has been Freud's observation that all human beings, no matter how "adult" they might appear to be, are in fact destined to view themselves and each other through a framework of unresolved childhood needs and conflicts. What we do as adults, the way we behave, and the wants, needs, and desires we seek to fulfil are all arrived at by a process in which the ego mediates between the infantile and untamed demands of the id and the supervisory and repressive demands of the ego and superego.

Freud's ideas continue to exercise considerable influence over many disciplines in the social sciences. Some of Freud's strongest supporters, as well as his strongest critics, are to be found among feminist scholars, who have been particularly interested in his ideas, especially as they relate to the establishment of gender differences. From the point of view of many feminist scholars, Freud's characterization of the mother as object, as having significance for the infant only as a source of milk and comfort, and as otherwise being of no social consequence in the infant's early life, is problematic. Regardless of disagreements, what most scholars find valuable in Freud's work is his attempts to understand human identity by examining the processes by which the individual is inevitably socialized into a functioning member of society.

JOHN BROADUS WATSON AND BEHAVIOURISM

A much less complex thinker than Freud, John Broadus Watson, the founder of behaviouristic psychology, opposed any notion that instincts or inborn abilities and talents exist in either animals or humans. For Watson, human beings are fundamentally passive, machinelike beings, whose socialization is accomplished wholly by external stimuli through a process he called **conditioning**.

Watson's thinking about social behaviour was strongly influenced by the famous experiment of the Russian physiologist Ivan Pavlov. In 1927 Pavlov conducted a series of tests in which he caused dogs to salivate by placing food on their tongues. In these instances, food acted as the stimulus for the salivation response. A bell was rung at the same time the food was placed on the dogs' tongues. After several repetitions of the food/bell combination, the food was withheld, but the bell still rung. Pavlov noted that, even though the dogs received no food, they still salivated when they heard the bell. He concluded that a stimulus (the bell), which originally did not elicit salivation in dogs, eventually came to do so because the dogs had been conditioned to associate the bell with food. This simple experiment by Pavlov illustrated for Watson the basic principles of all conditioning, and he made it the cornerstone of his studies of human beings (Zeitlin and Brym 1991, 34–35).

Conditioning in humans, Watson argued, constitutes the simplest form of learning and begins in early infancy. It is the basis of all other forms of learning. The infant starts life by acquiring a few simple, conditioned responses and gradually builds up a repertory of more and more complex conditioned behaviours as he or she matures and finally becomes an adult. Even emotions, Watson argued, are conditioned reactions. Only the bodily reactions of fear, rage, and love could be aroused in an infant prior to conditioned learning. Watson made an exception for these emotions because, he argued, they primarily provoke visceral reactions involving glands and involuntary muscles such as the walls of the intestines (ibid., 35–36). Watson was so convinced of the powers of conditioning that he was able to write in 1925:

> Give me a dozen healthy infants, well-formed, and my own specific world to bring them up in and I'll guarantee to take any one at random and train him to become any type of specialist I might select—a doctor, lawyer, artist, merchant, chief, yes even a beggarman and thief, regardless of his talents, penchants, tendencies, abilities, vocations, and the race of his ancestors.

With Watson's theories, we have one of the most mechanized versions of the process of socialization devised by social scientists. Not only is the infant devoid of the instincts and drives posited by Freud, but he or she is also totally passive, acted upon and shaped entirely by external social forces. This perspective was picked up on, in a modified form,

131

by some of the early American sociologists, including W.I. Thomas and Kingsley Davis (see Chapter 6).

W.I. THOMAS AND EARLY INTERACTION

The work of American sociologist W.I. Thomas displays many similarities with that of Watson concerning early childhood socialization. He, too, viewed the child as totally moulded by adult caregivers. But unlike Watson, Thomas was concerned with the social nature of the interaction between the caregiver and the child. Thomas developed a less deterministic version of Watson's ideas of early conditioning and proposed instead a process of social interaction between the child and his or her adult caregivers. According to Thomas:

> ...the child is always born into a group of people among whom all the general types of situations which may arise have already been defined and corresponding rules of conduct developed, and where he has not the slightest chance of making his definitions and following his wishes without interference (1923, 42).

Thomas's view, which is typical of traditional sociology, is that the infant or young child must quickly learn to adapt his or her activities and needs to meet the demands of adult caregivers. All the initiating of social interaction between the infant and adult occurs on the adult's part. The infant's task is to learn to respond appropriately to each new situation in a manner that eliminates "actions which either do not bring results or bring painful ones." The infant and young child also must respond by "fixing attitudes in his personality which result in the repetition of actions producing pleasurable feelings" (1923, 42).

For example, Thomas writes that "when the parent is ready to feed the child and picks him up, the child responds with sucking and other movements required for eating" (1923, 43). In this way, he argues, the child's innate drives—to eat, to eliminate—get linked to appropriate attitudes and habits, and the child begins to learn to behave like an appropriately socialized member of a given society. Thomas captures the reasoning behind this view of early socialization when he writes:

> The family is the smallest social unit and the primary defining agency. As soon as the child has free motion and begins to pull, tear, pry, meddle, and prowl, the parents begin to define the situation through speech and other signs and pressures: "Be quiet," "Sit up straight," "Blow your nose," "Wash your face," "Mind your mother," "Be kind to your sister," etc. This is the real significance of Wordsworth's phrase, "Shades of the prison house begin to close upon the growing child." His wishes and activities begin to be inhibited, and gradually, by definitions within the family, by playmates, in the school, in the Sunday school, in the community, through reading, by formal instruction, by informal signs of approval and disapproval, the growing member learns the code of his society (1923, 43).

Young children automatically accept the roles and lifestyles that their caregivers project.

Regardless of the social nature of the interaction between child and parent proposed by Thomas, the child, in this perspective, remains a passive object to be acted on and not an active participant in the process of socialization. Like that of the behaviourists, Thomas's perspective allows for the young child only to react to external social forces, never to interact or initiate social exchanges. The socialization process here is decidedly one way. In Thomas's own words, as the child's own "wishes and activities begin to be inhibited," the child "gradually learns the code of his society."

JEAN PIAGET AND COGNITIVE DEVELOPMENT

Within the perspective on socialization devised by Swiss child psychologist Jean Piaget (1896–1980), the child first appears as an interactive subject in the process of socialization, rather than as a passive object acted on by external forces. Although Piaget's work has been in print since the 1920s, it was not discovered by American child psychologists until the early 1960s. During that decade, American researchers grew curious about how human beings perceived the world, and about how they stored, retrieved, and thought about the information they gathered (Maccoby 1980, 21). At the same time, a publication of a translation of some of Piaget's work, including work on infant behaviour and moral judgment in children, made his findings accessible to a North American audience.

Like Freud, Piaget maintained that a child passed through a series of stages from infancy to adolescence. Like Freud, too, Piaget believed that passage from one stage to the next was the result of internal, bodily sensations that pressured the child to adapt to the environment. Passage from one stage to another meant that the child organized his or her relations with, and perceptions of, the world in new ways. But whereas Freud was concerned with the psychosexual stages of a child's development, Piaget focused on the cognitive or intellectual development of the child. He also saw the child as an active participant in the socialization process.

Piaget divided the cognitive development of the infant and child into four periods: sensori-motor (birth to 2 years); preoperational (2 to 7 years); concrete operational (7 to 11 years), and formal operational (11 to 15 years). In each of these stages, the child acquires new skills and advances from one stage to the next only on successful completion of the previous one. It was Piaget's belief that as the child matures, his conceptual

133

abilities develop along fairly predictable sequences. In this sense Piaget's theory shares a certain quality of inevitability with Freud's. Like Freud, Piaget viewed the child's social-ization as being carried forward by forces independent of any individual child's will.

Each child moves through the developmental sequences without skipping any of the stages and without going backward. However, Piaget also believed that the predeter-mined developmental changes each child progresses through result from structural changes that naturally take place in the child's way of perceiving and acting in the world as he or she matures. Rather than simply accumulating information, the child actively par-ticipates to organize and handle information differently at each stage. What makes Piaget's theories primarily different from those of Freud, then, is Piaget's argument that within each inevitable development stage children are not only active participants in their own socialization and learning but also set the pace of that process (Maccoby 1980, 20–21).

STAGES OF DEVELOPMENT

Sensori-motor Stage

Piaget called the first stage of human life the sensori-motor stage because during this time infants learn principally by physically relating to the world around them. At birth, Piaget argued, the infant has no sense of the difference between self and environment. Until about four months, the infant lives in a world that is timeless, objectless, and entirely aso-cial. There is no difference for the infant between self and the rest of his environment, including other human beings. In this sense, too, Piaget's theories closely parallel those of Freud who also viewed the young infant as unable to experience himself or herself as separate from the rest of the world.

This undifferentiated infant is, however, born with a number of sensori-motor sys-tems that allow him to perceive sensations either from within his body or from his imme-diate surroundings. He can make a limited number of reflexive responses such as sucking, grasping, and gross body movement. So while the baby is a completely asocial being, his or her own bodily configuration and reflexive responses actually make it impossible for him or her not to interact with the environment, including with other humans in that environment.

It is in interacting with the environment that these responses are modified and that development takes place. For example, at first the infant will suck anything that comes into contact with his lips, but he soon learns that all objects do not provide the same sat-isfaction when sucked, so his sucking behaviour is modified by the kinds of objects that he puts into his mouth. Eventually the baby begins not just to respond to his environ-ment, but actually to act on it. In Piaget's view, by the end of his first year, a child's actions are deliberately exploratory and experimental.

Preoperational Stage

During this phase of cognitive development the child comes to terms with the world of symbols and representational thought. He acquires a certain mastery over language and is able to form symbolic representations of objects and images. But the child is not yet able to use these capacities in a systematic way, and for this reason Piaget termed the stage preoperational. For example, at this stage, a child is capable of paying attention only to one characteristic or dimension of a physical object at a time. In a series of "classical experiments" Piaget studied children's judgments about the amount of water poured from a lower, wider glass into a taller, but thinner one. The preoperational child concludes that there is more water in the second, taller but thinner glass because the water level is higher than it was when the water was in the first shorter, wider glass.

Children at this stage appear to be egocentric or selfish. They are unable to consider any point of view or interpret the world in any way except in terms of their own position. They do not realize that others can see objects in the world from a different perspective than their own. A child who is looking at pictures in a book, for example, will not understand that someone who is sitting across from him can see only the back of the book and not the pictures that he sees. Thus children in the preoperational stage, while well on their way to being socialized, are as yet imperfectly so. While they are now quite capable of recognizing the distinction between themselves and others, they are still incapable of receiving others as completely independent of and different from themselves.

Children at this stage are unable to hold connected conversations with each other; rather they seem to engage in egocentric speech, and what they say to each other has little connection. They talk together, but not to one another, as do older children and adults.

Concrete Operational Stage

In this stage the child becomes capable of reasoning using logical operations. Children now understand causality and mathematical operations. Moreover, they are able to understand intellectual operations such as reversibility and ordering of things by number, size, or class. For example, a child can reverse the operation $2 \times 4 = 8$ by performing the operation $8 \div 2 = 4$. They are also able to understand the principle of transitivity, for example, if $A < B$ and $B < C$ then $A < C$.

Concrete operations are applied by the child not only to the realm of objects, numbers, time, and space, but also to social relations. By age 10, the child has developed a hierarchy of values and a well-ordered system of beliefs about rules, laws, and mutual obligations among peers. A child of this age has had time to develop the cognitive structure that makes these things possible. Finally, the child has become fully socialized in that he or she is now capable of perceiving others as different and separate, both in terms of physical existence and in terms of point of view and experience of the world.

Formal Operational Stage

During this stage, the child reaches adolescence and is able to overcome the intellectual limitations of the previous developmental stage. An adolescent is able to use hypothetical reasoning and to function at a purely symbolic, abstract level by bringing logical thought processes to bear on both concrete objects and facts and on abstract concepts. He is able to deal with both the real and the potential. An emerging preoccupation with the hypothetical is the most significant feature of this stage. The adolescent, too, is able to formulate if/then propositions as capacities to conceptualize mature. With the acquisition of this capacity, the child becomes a fully socialized member of society.

CRITICISMS OF PIAGET

Jean Piaget continues to exert influence in the field of child psychology where some believe his contributions have been far more useful than those of the behaviourists. But since the 1970s, research has proved Piaget wrong on many points in his schema of cognitive development in children. Young infants and children are very much capable of carrying out certain types of advanced thinking, which Piaget claims happens much later in the child's life. Adults, too, show a lot less logic in their reasoning than Piaget claimed. This illogicality is not the result of sloppy thinking, but is an essential response to a complex and rapidly changing world (Margaret Donaldson 1979, 152).

Piaget's view that children are highly egocentric compared with adults has also been questioned. According to Donaldson, Piaget presented children with tasks from an adult standpoint rather than from one that could be readily understood by the children. To make this point, she quotes a passage from the autobiography of the British poet Laurie Lee, describing his first day at school.

I spent that first day picking holes in paper, then went home in a smouldering temper.

> "What's the matter, Love? Didn't he like it at school then?"
>
> "They never gave me a present."
>
> "Present? What present?"
>
> "They said they'd give me a present."
>
> "Well now, I'm sure they didn't.'"
>
> "They did! They said: 'You're Laurie Lee, aren't you? Well just you sit there for the present.' I sat there all day but I never got it. I ain't going back there again" (Lee 1965).

Donaldson points out that while the parents of Laurie Lee thought he had misunderstood the instructions of the teacher, the situation looked very different from the boy's point of view. On a deeper level, then, the adults failed to understand the child by not understanding the ambiguity of the phrase "sit there for the present." The adults, and not the boy, she concludes, were guilty of egocentrism.

With Piaget we begin to see a concern with the active involvement of children in the process of their own socialization. The work of George Herbert Mead develops a view of children that recognizes them as active participants in the process of socialization.

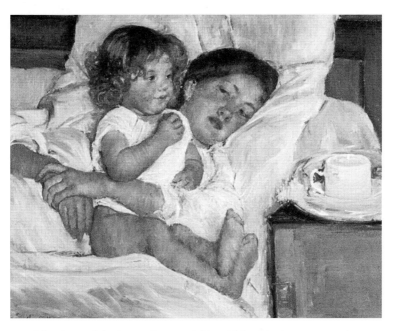

Breakfast in Bed *by Mary Cassatt, 1897. This painting suggests the supreme importance of maternal attachment. Do you agree? Or are other relationships equally important?*

GEORGE HERBERT MEAD AND THE SENSE OF SELF

George Herbert Mead (1863–1931) was a philosopher by training who spent most of his adult life teaching at the University of Chicago. Although he is recognized as one of the founders of social psychology, he rarely published anything during his life; his best-known work, *Mind, Self, and Society: From the Standpoint of a Social Behaviourist* ([1934]1967), was put together by his students from their lecture notes after his death.

Mead proposed a distinction between the self as a physical entity and the self as a social entity. Recall that for both Freud and Piaget the socialization of the infant into a functioning adult was tied, in the initial stages, to a gradual social taming and organizing of the infant's bodily sensations. For both these theorists, the physical body and its sensations were the foundation on which the socialization process could be built as those sensations were brought under the active control of the individual.

Like Freud and Piaget, Mead recognized the importance of bodily sensations in the child's process of development. But he focused his attention on the emergence of a sense of self, as opposed to managing drives (Freud) or stages of cognitive development (Piaget) in the individual child. He maintained that the development of a sense of self could take place only in a social context. For Mead, it is social relations with others and not somatic sensations that are first and foremost in the socialization process of the infant and young child.

As part of his work on what came to be called **symbolic interactionism,** Mead provided an account of the main phases of child development. He echoed the view of his contemporary, John Watson, that the environment exercises a powerful influence on the individual, and he believed human behaviour arose in response to environmental experiences. But whereas Watson and other behaviourists believed that human behaviour was the result of passive responses to external stimuli, Mead believed that humans actively determined their social environment.

It was Mead's contention that Watson and other behaviourists were wrong about the role of mental processes in socialization. Watson had ignored mental processes in favour of focusing on behaviour because he believed mental processes could not be studied scientifically. Mead, while conceding that the study of mental processes was uniquely challenging, nevertheless made them the central focus of his work. He believed that mental processes were precisely what should be studied because they distinguished humans from animals.

THE SELF AND ITS DEVELOPMENT

The basic thesis of Mead's work is that the mind and the self are formed only within the social and communicative activity of the group (Burkitt 1991). The concept of the self is central to Mead's analysis. For Mead, the self is the individual's active awareness of existing in the midst of society. Mead saw the self as a social entity distinct from, although of course dependent on, the physical organism. As a social entity, the self emerges only in and through social experience and social interaction.

Thus, for Mead, as for Freud, the self does not exist at birth but comes into existence only as the growing child comes into contact with others. A child gains consciousness, intelligence, and the ability to engage in self-determined activity only as a result of his or her interactions within the social group. If that contact is absent, the body will grow, but, as in the case of feral children, no self can emerge. The social group is the primary reality, which serves as the foundation for the development of consciousness and the self.

In Mead's view, humans are by nature social, and all of social experience is based on the exchange of "significant symbols." What differentiates humans from animals is that humans understand the intention behind any act that they or others might perform. Thus, for example, not only do we eat our vegetables because our mother tells us to, but we can also understand her intention behind the plea. We know that vegetables contain essential vitamins, minerals, and fibres, and that when our mother tells us to eat them she has our good health in mind. A dog, on the other hand, attaches no meaning to healthy eating and will often consume anything that is put before him, regardless of its nutritional content.

Language is of crucial significance in the process of social communication as well as in the emergence of the self. Mead believed that language is truly objective. It is, in his view, an impersonal system of communication through which the attitudes, beliefs, and values of the entire group, rather than just a particular individual, can be expressed. Through language each individual internalizes the attitudes of the social group to which he or she belongs. It is on the basis of these internalized attitudes that people form their own subjective or personal attitudes.

In order to understand the intentions of any other human being that we come into contact with, we must be able to assume that person's point of view. Mead called this "taking the role of the other." He explained that to engage in any social interaction means that we first must learn how to see ourselves as others see us. And to see ourselves as others see us means that we must become *self-conscious*, we must be able to adopt an objective attitude toward ourselves and experience ourselves from the standpoint of others.

The Looking-Glass Self

According to Mead the individual's first experience of self is indirect and is accomplished by taking on the attitudes of significant others—mother, father, siblings—toward oneself. One of Mead's contemporaries, Charles Horton Cooley, suggested a useful way of thinking about the process of taking the attitude of another toward oneself. Cooley used the metaphor of a **looking-glass self** to represent the idea that the individual's sense of self is gained only by seeing himself or herself reflected back through others via the process of symbolic communication.

If we think back on the examples of isolation that we discussed in the previous chapter, we can appreciate more clearly the difference between what happens to adults who are isolated later in life and what happens to children who are isolated very early in their lives. While isolated adults suffer privation, they do not lose their sense of self and will interact with others or with themselves as a socialized being (recall, for example, Selkirk dancing with his cats and goats during his period of isolation). But, from what we have seen, a social self cannot appear in the young child in isolation, outside the context of sustained social interaction. In the absence of learned ways of communicating meaning, the social self cannot come into existence.

The I and the Me

For Mead, there are two parts to the social self. He distinguishes between the self as *subject* and the self as *object*. The subjective self responds to others and initiates action, while the objective self is the presence of the self in the group to whom others react. Mead used the term *I* to refer to the spontaneous and thus subjective aspects of the individual. It is as a subject, an *I*, that the individual initiates actions. But it is as an object, a *me*, that the individual can reflect on what the *I* has done. As Mead writes, the *I*

> appears only in memory and by that time it has become a "me." The "I" of this moment is present in the "me" of the next moment. The "I" in memory is there as a spokesman of the self of a second, or minute , or day ago....If you ask, then, where directly in your own experience the "I" comes in, the answer is that it comes in as a historical figure (cited in Zeitlin and Brym 1991, 42).

While the *I* initiates action, that action is guided by the *me*, that is, by the self acting as an object to itself by taking on the role of the other. The *me* is the social self, and

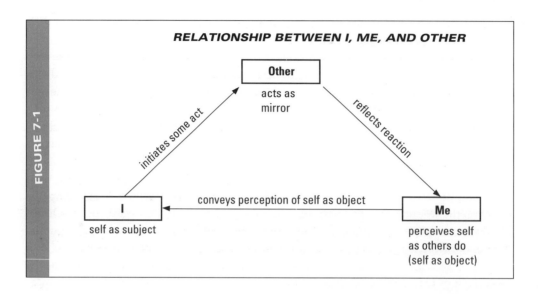

FIGURE 7-1

RELATIONSHIP BETWEEN I, ME, AND OTHER

Other
acts as
mirror

initiates some act

reflects reaction

I
self as subject

conveys perception of self as object

Me
perceives self
as others do
(self as object)

individuals develop self-consciousness by seeing themselves as others see them. All social interaction is carried out as an interplay between the *I* and the *me*. It is at the same time spontaneous yet firmly guided by the response of others (see Figure 7-1).

By age 5, Mead maintained, the child has more or less become an autonomous agent with a well-developed sense of *me,* and is therefore capable of self-understanding and of social interaction outside of the immediate family. Through taking the role of the other, the child gains more and more experience, and thus becomes increasingly sophisticated at social interaction.

The Generalized Other

While Freud and Piaget both linked the growing ability of the child as a social player to biological, developmental stages, Mead linked his theory of socialization only to the child's growing repertoire of social experiences. When young children begin to be socialized they have a very limited repertoire of social experiences with which to respond to others. They therefore respond only in terms of imitation. Lacking a fund of symbols with which to engage in social interaction, a young child is limited to mimicking the behaviour of others without understanding its underlying meaning. But as the child begins to have a facility with language and other forms of symbolic communication, he or she is able to engage in play.

When the child plays, he re-creates the complex patterns of behaviour that he observes in his environment. He does this by assuming roles modelled after the significant people in his life—mother, father, sister, brother. With further socialization and experience, the child learns to take on the roles of many others simultaneously in a single social situation. He learns to imitate different reactions of several others to the same situation. With this ability, the child then passes from play to more complex *games.* As the child's sophistication increases with his participation in games, he learns rules of play, fairness, and equality. In mastering social rules and cultural values, the child is able to grasp what Mead calls the **generalized other.** Mead used this term to refer to the general values, rules, and norms that are present in a culture and that are incorporated by the individual.

There are certain parallels between Mead's concept of the generalized other and Freud's concept of the superego. For both theorists, there is an agency in the psyche that represents social norms, values, and attitudes, and that endeavours to channel the individual's impulses toward socially acceptable outlets. There is, however, an interesting difference between the two views.

Freud saw the drives that generated the impulses as primary forces demanding satisfaction, no matter what the cost to the individual or to others. Mead, by contrast, tried to show how all aspects of the self are social and are actively acquired, including the impulses that Freud thought to be of a purely organic nature. But Mead and Freud do share the same view of the way in which the censor (the generalized other for Mead or superego for Freud) gets established, first through the attitudes of the parents toward the child and later through the generalized attitudes and behaviours of the group that are implanted in the individual's consciousness.

While Mead made it very clear that the self is always a social self, he made no study of any social group in which the individual might be active. Nor did he make any investigation into the larger social patterns of experience and activity that, as he argued, formed the basis out of which each individual self was created. Finally, Mead did little to further our understanding of how it is that the infant actually comes to be socialized. His notion that the infant first imitates the behaviour of others but understands little and only later plays or engages with others in a symbolic, social manner is challenged by new research on the social abilities of infants and young children. It is to the findings of this research that we now turn.

RECENT THEORIES OF EARLY SOCIALIZATION: THE INFANT AS A SOCIAL BEING

In recent years, a great deal of research has been done on the social abilities of infants and very young children. This research supports the point of view that infants are active rather than passive participants in the socialization process. For example, infants are able to recognize their own mothers and to recognize and remember past events. Research shows that they prefer their own mother's milk over the milk of other lactating women and that infants as young as one week prefer their mother's voice and face to that of a stranger (Benjamin 1988, 248).

In a set of experiments, Marshall Haith, a psychologist at the University of Denver, has shown that babies as young as three months are able to learn and remember what they have learned for a period of up to two weeks. In these experiments, Haith set babies inside a big black box in front of TV monitors. He then flashed a sequence of colourful objects that appeared on different sides of the monitor. Haith used an infrared camera linked to a computer to follow the eye movements of the babies. What he found is that after an

TABLE 7-1

COMPARISON OF THEORIES OF SOCIALIZATION OF YOUNG CHILDREN		
	FREUD	**WATSON**
1. **ROLE OF INSTINCTS**	• foundational to the existence of all humans • child begins life as an asocial being, radically separated from others • instincts engender drives, which ultimately must be brought under control as self emerges	• nonexistent in humans
2. **STATUS OF CHILD IN SOCIALIZATION PROCESS**	• child is radically separated from others but unable to differentiate self from the rest of the environment, including his mother • child seeks to satisfy only impulses and urges—pleasure principle	• child is passive, only acted on by others
3. **STEPS IN THE SOCIALIZATION PROCESS**	• drives and instincts are gradually brought under control of the reality principle • undifferentiated id is separated into id (source of drives, sexual energy), ego (acceptance of social constraints), and superego (moral rules and regulations acquired from society) • child learns to differentiate self from others	• socialization is accomplished via conditioning • infant gradually builds up a repertoire of conditioned responses
4. **PHASES OF DEVELOPMENT OF SOCIAL SELF**	• focus on stages of sexuality • oral, anal, genital	• focus on acquisition of conditioned responses from few and simple to many and complex

TABLE 7-1 (continued)

COMPARISON OF THEORIES OF SOCIALIZATION OF YOUNG CHILDREN

	PIAGET	MEAD
1. ROLE OF INSTINCTS	• causes child to pass from one stage of cognitive development to the next	• existence is acknowledged but not assigned a significant role
2. STATUS OF CHILD IN SOCIALIZATION PROCESS	• child is an active participant within a developmental stage but passes automatically from one stage to the next once developmental tasks have been achieved	• infant is a social being within a specific community
3. STEPS IN THE SOCIALIZATION PROCESS	• child advances through developmental stages once developmental tasks appropriate to that stage have been accomplished • each developmental stage must be completed before the child can proceed to the next one	• child gradually becomes aware of self as a separate social entity • self comes into existence through a complex interaction between the "I" (self as subject), the "me" (self as object), and the "other" (mirror for the self)
4. PHASES OF DEVELOPMENT OF SOCIAL SELF	• child automatically advances from one stage of cognitive development to the next once developmental goals specific to that stage are attained • four stages: sensori-motor, preoperational, concrete operational, and formal operational	• gradual acquisition of social self through taking the attitudes of significant others toward oneself

143

average of only five tries the babies were able to anticipate where the next object would appear. After a few more tries they could predict a four-step sequence and remember that sequence for up to two weeks.

Similar findings have been made by Carolyn Rovee-Collier, a psychologist at Rutgers University. In her experiments she first placed a baby in a crib beneath an overhead mobile. One of the infant's ankles was attached by a ribbon to the mobile. Rovee-Collier observed as the baby kicked and made the mobile move. The same scenario was then repeated one week later except that the baby's ankle was no longer attached to the mobile. If exactly the same mobile is placed over the baby, the baby will kick again, trying to make the mobile move. But if even one element of the mobile is changed, the infant remains still. However, as soon as the mobile is restored to its original form, the infant will start kicking again. Rovee-Collier concludes that for infants as young as $2 \frac{1}{2}$ months, memory is very developed, specific, and detailed (Grunwald 1993, 49).

Since the 1980s there has been sufficient research to suggest that almost from birth the interaction between infant and primary caregiver (usually the child's mother) is based on mutual recognition. As Jessica Benjamin (1988) describes it, mutual recognition includes a "number of experiences commonly described in the research on mother-infant interaction: emotional attunement, mutual influence, affective mutuality, sharing of states of mind" (26). But mutual recognition, she argues, is much more than this. It is a crucial category of early experiences. Research increasingly indicates that infants actively participate with their primary adult caregivers in creating this first social bond.

Some of the most influential work on the social relationships between infants and their adult caregivers has come from British psychologist John Bowlby. However, certain aspects of that work are problematic, especially his focus on the instinctive nature of the infant-mother bond. But his focus on the interactive nature of the child-adult relationship is of great significance, and it sets him apart from other theorists who see the mother-infant relation as little more than a one-way exchange between a passive infant and an active care-providing parent (usually the mother).

JOHN BOWLBY AND ATTACHMENT THEORY

John Bowlby served as an army psychiatrist in England during the Second World War. Afterward, he was appointed director of the Children's Department of the Tavistock Clinic. There he established a research unit to study children's responses to separation from their mothers (Eyer 1992, 57). Early on in his tenure, Bowlby became concerned with hospital practices that enforced a temporary separation of hospitalized children from their mothers. He was convinced of the real despair those children experienced and he believed that the despair lasted for a considerable time after they returned home.

As a result of his own and other research carried out during the 1950s, Bowlby began arguing that sociability, which includes social stimulation and affectionate interchange, is indispensable for human growth and development. He turned this observation into the basic thesis of **attachment theory** in a publication written for the World Health Organization entitled *Maternal Care and Mental Health* (1960). A simplified version of this report, *Child Care and the Growth of Love* (1965), was first published in 1953.

144

Attachment is the term used to describe powerful emotional ties between babies and their mothers. The original impetus for this concept came from the research done by Konrad Lorenz on geese. Lorenz observed that immediately after it is hatched, a gosling looks around for a moving object to follow. He found that the newly hatched gosling will eagerly follow any moving, honking gooselike figure that is present immediately after birth. In a similar way, lambs will follow sheep and calves will follow cows.

> Attachment in geese and in herd animals occurs very shortly after birth, while the infant is especially sensitive to such learning. If no appropriate object of attachment presents itself shortly after birth, the young gosling, lamb or calf will follow anything else that moves. Thus Mary's lamb of nursery rhyme fame followed her to school, and Lorenz was able to become "mother" to a flock of greylag geese (Scarr 1984, 84).

John Bowlby's work did much to bring this view of infant-mother relations into the study of human beings. Right from birth, Bowlby argued, the infant is capable and desirous of relating to others. The infant is an active if incipient social being who requires other social beings in order to develop, and who actively engages in social interaction with them.

Bowlby proposed that a primary social bond, which he viewed as an instinctive attachment of the infant to the mother, forms the basis of all social relations. Separation of mother and child, he concluded, has disastrous consequences because it thwarts an instinctive need. In short, nearness to the mother is essential for the infant's survival.

A child who is deprived of close, intimate social interaction with its mother, who suffers from *maternal deprivation*, Bowlby argued, will suffer from all manner of personality disturbances in later life. What is "essential for mental health," he wrote, "is that an infant and young child should experience a warm, intimate, and continuous relationship with his mother (or permanent mother-substitute—one person who steadily 'mothers' him) in which both find satisfaction and enjoyment" (Bowlby 1965, 13). A child who has been even partially maternally deprived is prone to suffer, in less severe cases, from "anxiety, excessive need for love, powerful feelings of revenge, and arising from these last, guilt and depression." Complete deprivation has even more far-reaching consequences, and "may cripple the child's capacity to make relationships with other people" (ibid., 14).

It was Bowlby's conclusion that the care of maternally deprived children was essential to the mental and social welfare of the entire community. If deprived children are not cared for, they will grow up and become poor parents as well. Bowlby saw deprived children as "the source of social infection as real and serious as are carriers of diphtheria and typhoid" (1965, 239). Mental health, he argued, is closely tied to maternal care, and maternal care should be promoted in all public sectors. Bowlby called for a public health campaign to detect and eradicate all causes of maternal deprivation.

Some Consequences of Bowlby's Theories

Bowlby's work on maternal deprivation influenced public policy regarding child welfare and early care of children both in North America and in Europe. Policy changes were made regarding hospital stays for children, institutional placement of children was discouraged, and adoptions or stable foster care was promoted. Bowlby claimed that "full-time employ-ment of [a] mother" was equivalent to the "death of a parent, imprisonment of a parent, war, famine" and other disasters, and that it was a major reason for family failure (1960, 73). His and other researchers' findings on maternal deprivation were subsequently used to discourage mothers from working or from using daycare centres (Eyer 1992).

We should note here that John Bowlby did his research and writing in the period immediately following the Second World War. At this time, women who had previously been encouraged to enter the work force as part of the war effort were actively encour-aged to stay at home and resume sole care of their children. This change in attitude allowed soldiers returning home to find employment. The phrasing of Bowlby's research report is important here. He argued that children suffer terribly from maternal depriva-tion (as opposed to deprivation of close emotional ties, regardless of the biological rela-tionship). This argument clearly reflected the beliefs current at the time that women *naturally* belonged back in the home with their children. In postwar Europe and North America, mothers, as opposed to fathers or some other adult caregiver, were deemed essential to a child's growth and adjustment. Bowlby tried to strengthen his case even fur-ther by arguing that not only was the child genetically programmed to give off signals to elicit physical closeness from the mother, but the mother was also genetically pro-grammed to respond to her infant's signals. While Bowlby did concede that an overlay of learned responses might occur to interfere with what he thought of as the natural, genet-ically programmed ones, he stuck to the idea that mothering is instinctual and that it has to be interfered with in order to be suppressed.

A Feminist Critique Of Bowlby

Probably the most salient critique of Bowlby and others who concentrate on the mother-infant bond to the exclusion of all other social relations is the extreme narrowness of their focus. Feminist scholars have criticized Bowlby's attachment theory, arguing that it has been used to establish a set of assumptions about the primacy of the mother-infant rela-tionship that incorrectly centres issues of nurturing and child rearing solely on this rela-tionship (Eyer 1992). Child rearing and child nurturing, they argue, is not "naturally" confined to the mother-child relationship, as Bowlby indicates. Rather it is a social rela-tionship that can be achieved between any adult who takes a caregiver role and the infant or child for whom he or she is providing care.

The social world the infant is born into contains many kinds of possibilities for social relationships between adults and infants, and even very young children are affected by a wide array of people who interact with them. Children do not just have mothers, they have fathers, sisters, brothers, cousins, and friends. They have parents who sometimes get along and sometimes do not. They live in communities that are sometimes peaceful, and occasionally violent. There are many different dimensions to the nurturing of children, and this process cannot simply be reduced to maternal attachment and maternal depriva-tion (ibid., 199–200). Children are also affected by the foods they eat, by the music they hear, by the television they watch, by what they see taking place in the adult world, and by the institutions—especially schools—they attend.

At the very least, then, we should be speaking of a whole array of social contacts and not just of the mother-child relationship. While the term maternal deprivation may be misconceived, as is the notion that mothering is instinctive to women, Bowlby's observations that children need to make close emotional attachments to at least one other human being have been well documented. Deprivation of close adult attachments produces deep and long-term effects.

HARLOW'S MONKEYS

During the period in which Bowlby researched and wrote about attachment and maternal deprivation, American experimental psychologist Harry Harlow conducted a series of experiments on rhesus monkeys in the animal laboratory at the University of Wisconsin. His experiments with these monkeys (which today would not pass an ethics review committee) provide shocking evidence about the effects of social deprivation in infant and young rhesus monkeys (Harlow 1958, 673–85; Eyer 1992, 58–59). (Harlow never clearly implied that his findings could be directly applied to human beings. We, too, should remain sceptical about transferring his findings about Rhesus monkeys to human behaviour. However, it is fairly safe to conclude that, like the monkeys, human are social beings and that deprivation of social contact from birth has profound consequences for human sociability and behavioural development.)

In order to explore Bowlby's ideas about the effects of maternal deprivation on young children further, Harlow separated newborn rhesus monkeys from their mothers and raised them in isolation. Because the babies were separated from other monkeys, Harlow and his fellow researchers were careful to provide for all the baby monkey's material needs. Harlow reported that the babies were kept in a "stainless steel chamber where light is diffused, temperature controlled, air flow regulated, and environmental sounds filtered" (Harlow and Harlow 1972, 276). The babies were provided with food and water, and the cages were cleaned by remote control. During the isolation period, the baby monkeys did not see another living creature, "not even a human hand."

After three, six, or twelve months of isolation, the monkeys were exposed to other monkeys. All of these monkeys showed evidence of extreme behaviour disturbance. Fear was their first and overwhelming response. While those who had been isolated for only three months recovered quickly and began to interact with the other monkeys, those who had been isolated for 12 months were "very seriously affected" (ibid., 278). They spent much of their time sitting in their cages, rocking back and forth. They were incapable of even the simplest kinds of play, and evinced only a "pitiful combination of apathy and terror as they crouch[ed] at the sides of the room, meekly accepting the attacks of the more healthy control monkeys" (278).

Harlow found that social deprivation had long-term effects on sexual behaviour. Monkeys isolated beyond 12 months of age totally failed to develop any kind of adult breeding patterns. When females who had been raised in semi-isolation were placed with breeding males, they either engaged in aggressive behaviour or they sat clutching and biting themselves. Isolated females were unable to mate, and when artificially inseminated, they showed no interest in their offspring. Harlow concluded that the sexual inadequacies of the socially deprived adult monkeys did not come from an absence of sex drive. "High arousal was often seen," he reported, "but it led to inappropriate responses—autistic behaviour, masturbation and violent aggression—all in a frenetic sequence lasting only a few seconds" (278).

In order to test if it was the absence of mothers that produced these behavioural disturbances or if it was the absence of the company of other monkeys, Harlow raised a group of infant monkeys to adulthood in each other's company. Unlike the infants raised from birth in isolation, Harlow observed no sexual disturbances in these monkeys. Baby monkeys cling to the fur of their mothers, and the peer-group-raised babies tried to replicate that behaviour by clinging to each other. But peer-group-reared monkeys clung together long after their mother-reared counterparts stopped clinging to their mothers. Harlow concluded that what mattered for normal development was that infant monkeys at least be given a chance to form attachments to other monkeys, regardless of their age, sex, or biological relation (Harlow and Harlow 1972).

As another experiment, Harlow raised some of the young monkeys with inanimate surrogate mothers made either from wire mesh or covered with towelling. His research indicated that infant monkeys sought contact more frequently with the towel-covered surrogate, who provided contact and comfort, than with the mesh surrogate, who provided milk. Harlow concluded that his observations directly contradicted the ideas of those theorists who argued that infants become attached to their mothers because they associate them with providing relief from hunger and thirst. Harlow also experimented with frightening the isolation-raised monkeys. When he startled them with a wind-up toy placed in their cage, the cloth-surrogate-raised monkeys sought refuge with their cloth surrogate mother. Those "raised" by a wire-mesh surrogate, however, clutched themselves, rocked back and forth and threw themselves on the floor (Eyer 1992, 59).

While Harlow's research supports the contention that close, intimate contact with others is a significant factor in normal infant development, it fails to support the belief that biological mothers are naturally able to provide that care. In Harlow's study, mothers raised in isolation were ill-equipped to nurture their infants. In monkeys, at least, the ability to mother is an acquired skill, dependent on previous socialization. Harlow's research, originally intended to support Bowlby's beliefs about the innate nature of mothering skills, produced some unexpected results.

THE INTERSUBJECTIVE VIEW OF THE SOCIAL INFANT

During the last 25 years, an extension and modification of attachment theory has emerged, the **intersubjective view,** which is based on the recognition of the two-way interaction between the infant and his or her caregivers. According to Jessica Benjamin, the intersubjective view of early childhood maintains that the "individual grows in and through the relationship to other subjects," and not just in relationship to a maternal figure. She compares this view with the **intrapsychic view** of Freud in which each individual is conceived of as a discrete unit with a complex internal structure (1988, 20). While the intrapsychic perspective sees being alone as the natural state of the individual, the intersubjective view holds that being alone is just one point on a whole range of relationships that the individual enters into with others. (One must have a relationship with another person in order to experience the state of being alone.) Intrapsychic theory has uncovered the unconscious; intersubjective theory focuses on the interrelations between the self and others. Benjamin suggests that intrapsychic and intersubjective theory should not be seen as opposites, but rather as complementary ways of understanding the psyche.

DANIEL STERN AND THE INTERPERSONAL WORLD OF THE INFANT

In his book *The Interpersonal World of the Infant* (1985), American infant psychiatrist Daniel Stern argues that babies are able to differentiate themselves from their mothers at birth (and not at some later stage of development, as Freud and Piaget argue). After birth infants progress through increasingly complex modes of social interaction with others. Stern argues that, far from being passive, infants exert a considerable amount of control over the "initiation, maintenance, termination, and avoidance of social contact with mother; in other words, they help to regulate engagement" (1977, 21). For example, infants as young as four months assert their independence from their mothers by averting their gaze from her. By seven months, that assertion includes gestures and vocalizations. At 14 months the child is able to escape the mother by running away, and by two years she expresses her autonomy with language. Interpersonal moments between the child and the caregiver are crucial in "forming the experiences from which the infant learns how to relate to other people" (ibid., 2).

What follows is a detailed example of the kind of infant caregiver interaction Stern is talking about. It serves to illustrate the extent to which *mutuality* plays a central role in the interaction between the child and the caregiver.

> A mother is bottle feeding her three-and-a-half-month-old boy. They are about halfway through. During the first half of the feeding the baby had been sucking away, working seriously and occasionally looking at his mother, sometimes for long stretches (10 to 15 seconds). At other times he gazed lazily around the room. Mother had been fairly still. She glanced at her baby periodically, sort of checking, and every now and then looked at him with a good long look (20–30 seconds) but without talking to him or changing the expression on her face. She rarely said anything when she looked at him....

> Until this point, a normal feeding, not a social interaction, was under way. Then a change began. While talking and looking at me [Stern] the mother turned her head and gazed at the infant's face. He was gazing at the ceiling, but out of the corner of his eye he saw her head turn toward him and turned to gaze back at her...he broke rhythm and stopped sucking. He let go of the nipple and the suction around it broke as he eased into the faintest suggestion of a smile. The mother abruptly stopped talking and, as she watched his face begin to transform, her eyes opened a little wider and her eyebrows raised a bit. His eyes

locked on to hers, and together they held motionless for an instant. The infant did not return to sucking and his mother held frozen her slight expression of anticipation. This silent and almost motionless instant continued to hang until the mother suddenly shattered it by saying 'Hey!', and simultaneously opening her eyes wider, raising her eyebrows further, and throwing her head up and toward the infant. Almost simultaneously, the baby's eyes widened. His head tilted up and, as his smile broadened, the nipple fell out of his mouth. Now she said, 'Well hello!...heello....heeelloooo, so that her pitch rose and the "hellos" became longer and more stressed on each successive repetition. The mother then paused and her face relaxed. They watched each other expectantly for a moment. The shared excitement between them ebbed, but before it faded completely, the baby suddenly took an initiative and intervened to rescue it. His head lurched forward, his hands jerked up, and a fuller smile blossomed. His mother was jolted into motion. She moved forward, mouth open and eyes alight, and said, 'Oooooh..ya wanna play do ya...yeah?...I didn't know if you were still hungry...no...nooooo...no I didn't...' And off they went (1977, 2–3).

Stern goes on to record further exchanges between this mother and her baby in which the mother walks her fingers over the baby's belly and into his neck and armpits, all the while tickling him. Throughout the baby smiled and squirmed but always stayed in eye contact with his mother. As each new cycle of play progressed, the mother escalated the level of suspense and excitement using her voice and her facial expression. The baby become more aroused and the mounting excitement of both mother and child, as Stern points out, contained elements of both glee and danger of overstimulation. During the second cycle of play the baby had slightly averted his face, but kept smiling.

By the third cycle of play, the mother and child had still not resumed full face-to-face contact, and the baby had his head slightly turned away. Stern describes what followed:

As [the mother] approached, [the baby's] face turned even further but still he kept looking at her. At the same time, his smile flattened. The eyebrows and the corners of his mouth flickered back and forth between a smile and a sober expression...he finally broke gaze with mother, appearing thereby to recompose himself for a second, to de-escalate his own level of excitement. Having done so successfully, he returned his gaze to mother and exploded into a big grin. On that cue she began, with gusto, her fourth and most suspenseful cycle, but this one proved too much for him...He broke gaze immediately, turned away, face averted, and frowned. The mother picked it up immediately. She stopped the game dead in its tracks and said softly, "Oh honey, maybe you're still hungry, huh...let's try some milk again." He returned gaze. His face eased and he took the nipple again. The "moment" of social interaction was over. Feeding has resumed (Stern 1977, 5).

Stern concludes that it is from the analysis of moments like these, sometimes called free play, that researchers have learned about the crucial significance of the social interactions that take place between caregivers and infants. These social interactions are among the most important experiences of the first phase of the infant's life. They teach him or her about how to participate in human events. By the end of the first six months, the infant not only has developed general schemas of the human face, voice, and touch, but also knows the specific face, voice, and touch of his or her primary caregiver. As Stern explains, the infant has "got" the temporal patterning of human behaviour and the meaning of different changes and variations in tempo and rhythm. He has learned the social cues and conventions that are mutually effective in initiating, maintaining, terminating, and avoiding interactions with his mother. He has also learned different discursive modes, such as turn taking. And he now has the foundation of some internal composite picture of his mother so that, a few months after this phase is over, we can speak of his having established object permanence, an enduring representation of mother that he carries around with him with or without her presence (5–6).

While an infant of six months is quite capable of social interaction, she does not do so on a conscious basis. But at seven to nine months she discovers that different individuals can share the same feelings and intentions. Like Jessica Benjamin, Stern uses the term *intersubjectivity* to designate the awareness that there are others who think and feel as I do. For example, at seven to nine months, the infant will reach for a toy and at the same time look at her mother to see if mother is sharing the excitement. The mother matches not the infant's movement, but the infant's level of excitement using a different mode of expression (for example, she says "Wow!").

In work that supports Benjamin's and Stern's view of the intersubjective infant, Colin Trevarthen (1977, 1980) has studied the nature of the distinct, unequal, but complementary nature of the contributions of infants and caregivers to social exchanges. He analyzed filmed interactions between two-month-old infants and their mothers, and observed how both mother and child played their own parts in establishing coordinated social exchanges. Trevarthen found that the mother structured the communication between herself and her child by responding meaningfully to the infant's initial cue. The infant, in turn, responded to the mother with bodily and vocal signals that matched the rhythms of the mother's communicative activity. In turn, the mother re-responded to the infant, and together the parent and child co-ordinated their activity by achieving a *mutual regulation* of expression, gesture, imitation, response, and vocalization.

Jessica Benjamin suggests that intersubjective development is best understood as a spectrum. The awareness that the other is both like and different is just one moment on that spectrum (1988, 29–30). A game of peekaboo between mother and child—based on the shared tension between expectancy and surprise—produces a sense of mutuality. Both mother and child cooperate together with one intention. The emerging intersubjectivity between mother and child emphasizes how awareness of the separate other, on the part of the infant (and the mother), enhances the feelings of connection: "This *other* mind can share *my* feeling" (ibid., 30). Yet, at the same time, the growing awareness of separate minds and the desire for mutuality can also raise the possibility of conflict. By one year, the infant can experience conflict between the desire to assert herself, maybe by pushing all the buttons on the stereo, and the desire to stay attuned to her mother's wishes.

As more research is done based on an intersubjective model of infant-caregiver relations, the model of the infant or young child as a passive being, totally manipulated by outside agents of socialization, is being replaced by a more dynamic one. In this model, infants and their caregivers interact together and cooperate to achieve what was once thought possible only through imposition. Over the last century researchers have moved away from the perception of infants and children as passive lumps of wax or clay to be moulded according to adult intentions. The late twentieth-century infant is an active participant in the socialization process—a being who is capable of initiating and sustaining social interaction, as well as of cooperation and resistance.

■ ■ ■

SUMMARY

So far I have remained focused on theories of socialization that deal specifically with the infant and his or her immediate caregivers. I have reviewed a number of theorists who have tried to answer the question "How is the infant socialized into becoming a functioning adult member of a given society?" Answers generally fall into two categories. From one point of view, the child is seen as essentially a monad—an independent and largely nonsocial being who must be acted on by society if he or she is to be socialized into being a properly functioning adult. This point of view has some of its early expression in the work of seventeenth- and eighteenth-century philosophers such as Descartes and John Locke. It was taken up (although in different ways) by early twentieth-century theorists such as Sigmund Freud and Jean Piaget, both of whom argued that the human infant starts out life as a nonsocial being and must be made by others into a socialized (civilized) adult.

But, as I have also shown in this chapter, there is reason to consider another point of view about the nature of the infant and very young child. The work of Mead, Bowlby, and of psychoanalysts Daniel Stern and Jessica Benjamin all suggest that the human infant is social right from birth. While intensive and extensive interaction with adult caregivers is required to fully socialize the infant, there is no moment of asociality, of complete isolation from reciprocal (if unequal) social interaction and engagement with adult caregivers, as there is in the theories of Freud and Piaget.

■ ■ ■

FOR DISCUSSION

1. Try to describe the sense of self that might be possessed by a person who was raised in a society where members were not considered completely discrete individuals.

2. How, in Freud's view, are the ego and the superego formed?

3. In what ways are Freud's and Piaget's theories similar? In what ways are they different?

4. Discuss some of the ways in which the "looking-glass self" might be formed.

5. Bowlby suggests that maternal care is essential to mental health in children and, as a result, should be promoted as part of public policy. Discuss some of the implications of this argument.

6. What are some of the differences between Freud's intrapsychic view of early socialization and the intersubjective view proposed by Benjamin and Stern?

7. Compare the research assumptions and research methods of the sensationalists discussed in Chapter 6 with those of researchers such as Stern and Trevarthen, discussed in this chapter.

part 3

In Part 3 we consider another important set of tools sociologists use to aid in analyzing the social relations that make up a society—theory and methods of research. Theories are perspectives or world views, templates through which we organize how we explain the world. They guide us in terms of the kinds of questions we ask and in terms of the kinds of interpretations we make. Research methods are the ways we go about studying whatever is of interest.

Like other scientists, sociologists are concerned with constructing and validating theories about the world they inhabit. But the very notion of "doing science" has become controversial in that all theories and research methods imply a set of value judgments about how research "ought" to be done. Most sociologists now recognize that by choosing a theoretical framework and a set of research methods to guide their research they are making judgments about what is an adequate or acceptable practice of inquiry into social life. In the chapters in this part we will consider the proposition that as social scientists we can never be truly objective and produce knowledge that is completely outside some paradigm or framework.

The theories and research methods sociologists use to explore human social behaviour are tools of inquiry. Like the ordinary household tools we are all familiar with, theory and methods of research reflect the intentions of the people who made them. Because the objectives of people vary so widely, the theories and methods of research they devise are also varied. In sociology, as in other scientific disciplines, there exist many

TOOLS OF SOCIOLOGICAL INQUIRY
■ ■ ■

kinds of theories and methods called research paradigms, frameworks, or approaches. These rely on different sets of assumptions and use different strategies of knowledge construction.

In Part 3, we focus on three approaches to knowledge construction: the positivist, interpretive, and critical approaches. Differences between these three are significant, and we will consider the strengths and weaknesses of each one. As well, we will examine a variety of different research methods used by sociologists.

8 SOCIAL THEORY

- How is it possible that different theoretical perspectives can exist at the same time in sociology?

- Of what significance to social theory are the kinds of questions we ask at the outset of our research and the interpretations we attach to our findings?

- What assumptions about the relation of the searcher to the objects under study are common to some natural scientists and positivist sociologists?

- In critical approaches to sociology, what is the importance of the claim that knowledge is subjective?

All of us think theoretically, although we are not often aware of it. We all seek to make sense of the myriad events, social situations, and problems, large and small, that we confront in our day-to-day lives. When we make sense of them, we use language to convey our understandings to others and to interpret the information that they send us. But most of us do not think about the social world in a rigorous and systematic manner, and this is the difference between the kind of theoretical thinking that we do on a daily basis and the kind of theoretical thinking that sociologists do.

Unlike the everyday, taken-for-granted thinking that most of us are familiar with, sociologists and other social scientists deliberately choose and apply a theoretical perspective to make sense of the social world. When we are confronted by sociological theories, we are often struck by their complexity. If that were not enough, there is an additional factor that makes learning sociological theory difficult.

No single, unified, theoretical approach has been accepted by all sociologists as the correct way of explaining social phenomena. While all theoretical perspectives used by sociologists are similar in that they attempt to systematically explain social situations, there are significant differences among them.

The existence of so many different theoretical perspectives in the discipline of sociology is often confusing for introductory students. In this chapter

I have tried to simplify matters by identifying three broad theoretical perspectives commonly used by sociologists today: **positivist, interpretive** (or hermeneutic), and **critical**. Each of these has its own strengths and weaknesses. Each simultaneously reveals and conceals different aspects of human experience.

THINKING THEORETICALLY

There are important similarities and differences between the kind of theoretical thinking we all engage in and the kind of theoretical thinking that is done by sociologists.

EVERYDAY THEORETICAL THINKING

The kind of theoretical thinking we all engage in is really an attempt to explain our everyday, immediate experience of the world in terms of something else such as other people's actions, our past experience, repressed emotions, and the like (Craib 1984, 2). Consider the following example.

Suppose for a moment that someone you know is suddenly unemployed. At first unemployment insurance, savings, or financial assistance from family and friends might help alleviate the situation. But unemployment remains a fact. It has happened regardless of whether your acquaintance wanted it or not, and it is by no means immediately apparent why it happened. In this situation people look for an explanation: "I'm unemployed because my boss was threatened by me"; or "I'm unemployed because cheap immigrant labour has taken away a job that is rightfully mine"; or "I've lost my job because the economic policies followed by the current government are ruining the economy."

Suppose, further, that this acquaintance becomes despondent after several months of unsuccessful searching for a new job. He or she might explain that despondency in simple terms such as, "I'm unhappy because I've never gotten a decent break in life." Or the explanation could become more complicated: "Relationships in my early childhood with an ungiving mother and an absent father, along with unsolved sibling rivalries, have resulted in my inability to deal with the current difficulties that I am now facing."

THEORIES AS METAPHORS

When we try to understand some thing, person, or event, we usually do so by comparing it with something familiar. In short, we try to understand the unfamiliar by using the familiar. In making this comparison, we use metaphors—figures of speech in which one kind of object or idea is used in place of another to suggest a similarity between them. When we use metaphors drawn from familiar experiences to explain unfamiliar ones, we are actually using the familiar experiences as a kind of screen through which to view the unfamiliar ones. In the example of the unemployed acquaintance, that person used everyday or common-sense thinking to explain the situation. He or she drew on previous experiences, general ideas commonly shared within the society, and emotional states to make sense of being unemployed. Black (1962) sees this interaction between the familiar (used as a metaphor) and the unfamiliar that is being interpreted as a relational event in which the familiar is used in the context of a screen:

> Suppose I look at the night sky through a piece of heavily smoked glass on which certain lines have been left clear. Then I shall see only the stars that can be made to be on the lines previously prepared upon the screen and the stars I do see will be seen as organized by the screen's structure. We can think of a metaphor as such a screen and the system of associated commonplaces of the focal word as the network of lines upon the screen (1962, 41).

All theories, whether they are common-sense or carefully worked out sociological ones, work in a similar way. Like a metaphor, any theory both reveals and conceals certain aspects of human experience (Ricoeur 1970; Sullivan 1984). When we use common-sense theoretical thinking we do so as members of a given society. We all share many common belief systems and ways of understanding the world, which we use as a template to help us give shape and meaning to our experiences. Every day each of us uses the fund of understanding that we have accumulated as the result of having been socialized. We draw on previous experiences and understandings to make sense of new experiences. To the extent that we have learned to participate effectively in a given society and have learned to communicate effectively with other members of that society, we are all common-sense theorists.

The constellation Orion. The configuration of stars constituting Orion seemingly presents a warrior figure. But in reality it is just a cluster of stars onto which someone long ago projected a human representation.

SYMBOLIC COMMUNICATION

In Chapter 4, I argued that human beings process information about their environment and communicate with each other in ways that cannot be explained by inborn, innate, or instinctual programming. Human beings communicate with each other symbolically, via language and other oral or visual clues that are learned, not inherited. A symbol is something that represents something else. Symbolic communication is rich in potential meaning but is also paradoxical; one symbol may have several different meanings, and those meanings may have contradictory or opposing significance.

For example, the phrase "she's such an interesting person" can take on a variety of meanings, including the exact opposite of its literal one, depending on the tone, inflection, and facial expression of the speaker. Virtually all interaction between humans involves the use of symbols. To become a member of a society, an individual must acquire the ability to communicate with others by using a culturally defined fund of symbols. He or she must communicate the meaning of symbols to others and must be able to understand the meaning of the symbols that are communicated in response.

Communication using symbols can take many forms: talking, writing, ritual practices (which can include activities as diverse as handshaking and religious services), dress, manners, facial or bodily expressions, and postures, to name a few. But all forms of symbolic communication (from the colour of traffic lights to the ways in which humans engage in sexual intercourse) and all meanings contained in those communications are learned.

Ferdinand Saussure and the Social Nature of Language

One of the earliest and most important contributors to our understanding of symbolic communication is French linguist Ferdinand Saussure. He distinguished between language, *langue,* and human speech, *langage.* For Saussure (1964), language is a social product made possible by the faculty of speech. It is also a collection of conventions common to members of a given society that allows each member of that society to exercise his or her ability to speak. Thus while speech is the physical, physiological, and psychological ability of the individual to make utterances, language is a social institution. It is a system of signs that expresses ideas and that is specific to a given group of people.

Saussure proposed to develop a "science that studies the life of signs within society," and called that science **semiology**. Many people, he argued, regard language as merely a naming process—a list of words in which each word corresponds to the thing it names. But this view is flawed because it assumes that ready-made ideas exist before the words and that the linking of a word to a thing is a simple process. In place of this simplistic conception of linguistic units, Saussure argued that each **linguistic sign** brings together not a thing and a name but rather a "concept and a sound-image." Moreover, the sound-image is not just a physical sound. Instead it is the impression that the sound makes on our senses. The psychological impression that these sound-images make on us is evident, Saussure assures us. Try talking to yourself, or reading a passage in a book, or reciting a favourite piece of poetry without making a sound and without moving your tongue and lips.

Saussure represented the linguistic sign by the drawing:

$$\frac{\text{signified (the concept)}}{\text{Signifier (sound-image)}} = \text{sign}$$

Defined in this way the linguistic sign has two primary characteristics. The first is that the relation between the signified and the signifier is arbitrary. The idea "tree" is not linked in any way to the succession of sounds t-r-e-e. The idea "tree" is equally well represented in French by a-r-b-r-e. Not just words, but all means of expression used in society have an arbitrary basis. For example, in North America and Europe, shaking the head from side to side indicates no. But in certain parts of Africa, it means yes.

Because we communicate symbolically, there is never a one-to-one correspondence between what is being communicated and how it might be understood (as is the case with instinctive behaviour). Human communications are always open to interpretation. When we interpret communications we are in fact performing rudimentary acts of theorizing.

I AM HUMAN, THEREFORE I THINK THEORETICALLY

Because humans rely on symbolic representations to communicate meaning, they are also able to reflect on and interpret the meaning of the information they are communicating. Each of us, for example, is quite capable of reflecting on the meaning of being male or female in contemporary Western culture. We can think about what it means to our lives to have working-class parents or upper-middle-class ones. We can consider the possible future outcome of educating our children following a certain teaching method. We can construct explanations about the effects that being born black or white might have on the kind of life we lead. In short, we all can and do think theoretically.

Common-sense theorizing is an activity that is practised by almost all of us, although most of us are unaware that we do so. Our everyday theorizing is shaped by the language we use and by our taken-for-granted understandings of how the world operates, including our religious opinions, our superstitions, and our prejudices.

The words we use in everyday conversations can hardly be thought of as neutral ones. Their meanings change depending on the context in which they are used. Take for example the words "man" and "woman." In one usage, the word man refers to someone who possesses a particular chromosomal configuration—XY—and a corresponding set of reproductive organs—testicles, penis, vas deferins, and so on. Woman refers to a possessor of an XX chromosomal combination, along with reproductive organs such as vagina, womb, and ovaries.

But used in everyday conversation the two words man and woman convey much more than a simple distinction between persons with different roles to play in the reproductive process. They also convey a whole range of religious beliefs, prejudices, and unexamined opinions—all part of the cultural inheritance that we share. In Western societies, for example, women have traditionally been viewed as possessing characteristics that are the opposite of those possessed by men. Women are viewed as passive, men as active; women are subordinate, men are dominant; women are emotional, men are reasonable.

Taken together, then, our everyday usage of the terms man and woman brings with it a series of unspoken, but nonetheless commonly understood understandings, explanations, and perspectives on men, women, and their respective behaviours and interrelations. In making sense of the social world we live in and the relationship between men and women, we draw heavily on the culturally acceptable perceptions, beliefs, attitudes, and explanations that we all learn in the process of being socialized.

While I have spent considerable time trying to persuade you that simply by being a member of any society you are also a theorist, I do want to underline the difference between taken-for-granted or common-sense theories and sociological ones. The former are based on unexamined culturally specific values, beliefs, and understandings. They are, by definition, unreflexive. Sociologists, on the other hand, strive to be reflexive, that is, to question taken-for-granted assumptions and to ask pointed questions about the evidence available to support or challenge those assumptions. While our taken-for-grant-ed theories assume that the social world is natural or inevitable, sociologists develop the-oretical perspectives that often challenge those assumptions. Theoretical perspectives in sociology, then, often offer explanations that run counter to our immediate experiences and beliefs.

For example, a young man wearing tattered blue jeans held together by safety pins, a scruffy black leather jacket covered with silver studs, and sporting purple hair, gelled into long spikes might believe that he is rebelling against parents and social authority. For functionalist theorists, however, he has simply set in motion a number of social mecha-nisms that will be used to withstand his challenge to authority, and thus to help society run even more smoothly in the future.

Similarly, a worker in a local supermarket might believe she is getting a fair wage for a day's work, but for a Marxist theorist, she is being systematically exploited. When a profes-sor fails a student on an exam, she might believe she is upholding academic standards. But a symbolic interactionist would claim that she is actually creating a failure (Craib 1984, 9).

THEORIES IN THE SOCIAL SCIENCES

All theories, whether common-sense or sociological, are perspectives or templates through which we organize how we view the world. They guide us in terms of the kinds of questions we ask and in terms of the kinds of interpretations we make of whatever we study. I emphasize that there are many different ways of producing knowledge about "how the world is." Many social scientists categorize all social theory into three broad

Andy Warhol's Elvis I and II. *The "real" Elvis was a Tennessee singer who grafted white coun-try music onto black-inspired blues. His slicked-back hair and gyrating hips enthralled young audiences. The media created a superstar.*

categories (Ashley and Orenstein 1990; Nielsen 1990; Bredo and Feinberg 1982). Those categories are positivist, interpretive, and critical approaches.

The most important difference among these three broad categories is the relationships that they assume exist between the knower or researcher and what can be known. Positivist approaches "assume a strict subject-object dichotomy in which the knower is uninvolved with the known" (Bredo and Feinberg 1982, 5). Positivists seek to discover or uncover the facts or the causes of social phenomena, and they maintain that these are independent of the subject state of either the researcher or the subjects being researched. With interpretive approaches, the knower and what can be known are closely involved with one another (ibid., 6). Interpretive sociologists are committed to understanding social phenomena from the point of view of the actors involved. For critical approaches, the relationship between knower and what can be known is taken even further. The knowledge generated in a research undertaking is viewed as part of a process of "mutual growth or evolution" for both the researcher and the subject. "The researcher is inevitably an agent of change or a reinforcer of the status quo" (ibid., 6).

I will examine in some detail the underlying assumptions of these three different approaches to knowledge. Each shares the same *ontological* basis but differs in the *epistemological* questions asked. Ontological questions ask what sorts of things exist in the world and what different forms their existence might take. For example, an ontological question might be, "Do human beings exist in the same way as inanimate objects? If not, what are the differences?" Epistemology is the study of the nature, validity, and limits of inquiry (Rosenau 1992, 109). Epistemological questions include "What methods should be used to arrive at an explanation?" and "What proofs are required?" Epistemological questions are about the validity of our knowledge. To say that each theoretical approach has a different epistemological basis, then, means that each approach is based on a different theory of knowledge.

Positivism as a theoretical approach to knowledge about society has dominated much of the social sciences in North America. This approach has its origins in the seventeenth century when attempts were made to establish a system of knowledge on the basis of unassailable, experimentally verifiable facts, which, if established in a rigorous and verifiable manner, speak for themselves. Any embellishment or interpretation is considered mere opinion, not scientific truth. The objective of most positivistic social theorists is to hold a mirror up to nature and, in so doing, to present new discoveries about society in as pristine a form as possible. Positivist-influenced theories assume that a strict separation between researcher and what is being researched is both possible and necessary.

Interpretive theorists argue that the most useful point of view from which to understand the social world is that of the social actors themselves. The objective of sociological inquiry should be to get inside those points of views rather than to impose a view from the outside. Thus a direct relationship between the observer and the observed is an essential first step in generating knowledge.

A critical approach to knowledge attempts to evaluate the contributions made by both positivist and interpretive approaches and to assess both their limitations and their possibilities. Critical approaches seek to move beyond the limitations of the other two approaches and to point to ways that progressive social change might take place (Bredo and Feinberg 1982, 272–73). Whereas both positivist and interpretive approaches are content with explaining the "what is," critical theorists are also concerned with the "what might be."

Unlike the positivists, critical theorists reject the possibility of certainty and embrace uncertainty. While the goal of positivist theorists is to distinguish fact from error by using objective, sense-based methods of observation and induction, critical theorists dispute the notion that facts speak for themselves. Some critical theorists dispute the notion that facts speak for themselves. Some go so far as to assert that there are no facts, only interpretations, and that there is no difference between "science" and "fiction" (Ashmore 1989; Game 1991).

THE POSITIVIST APPROACH

In the natural sciences, the highest level of interest is in prediction and control. Over four centuries ago, scientists such as Francis Bacon began developing a method of scientific research that would effectively establish control over nature. A good theory, from this point of view, is one that successfully predicts events and their outcomes and thus gains mastery over those events. Theories that are oriented toward prediction and control are positivist ones. In the social sciences, positivist theories are modelled after the theories and methods of research that have had great success in the natural sciences. Joyce McCarl Nielsen outlines five assumptions of positivist theories that are applicable to both the natural and social sciences.

1. The social world is knowable in the same way that the natural world is knowable. The most advantageous way to explore the social world, therefore, is by using the same principles of investigation employed in studying the physical world. The social world is studied best through observation and the recording of those observations by a neutral, independent, and above all objective researcher.

2. There is an objective, independent reality, completely detached from and external to the researcher.

3. Empirical observations based on the use of the senses is the only way to gather data about the real, external world. Data are considered objective if they can be either verified or refuted by independent observers exposed to the same phenomenon. Verification of one observer's findings by another independent observer is considered essential for the verification of conclusions.

4. The social world is ordered in a predictable way. Events don't just happen; there is a pattern to them that follows a predominantly cause and effect form. The overall goal of social science research is to construct universal laws about the social world and human behaviour that hold true across time, place, and culture.

5. There is a certain unity to all sciences, including the social sciences. All sciences share the same methods of acquiring knowledge about the world. These methods are the best if not the only way of uncovering legitimate knowledge (1990, 4–5).

Rationalism and *empiricism* are considered to be the "twin pillars" of positivist theory. Rationalism has its basis in the work of the ancient Greek philosophers and can best be characterized by the statement "What is, is; what is not, is not." The seventeenth-century French philosopher and mathematician René Descartes made the famous statement "I think, therefore I am." This statement is an example of rationalism. It is considered to be true because the first part of the statement, "I think," makes the negation of the second part, "I am," illogical. In making this statement, Descartes grounded his sense of existence in the process of thinking and not in his feelings or emotions. He did not say "I love, or I feel, therefore I am." He put his trust in rational thought (Nielsen 1990, 2).

Empiricism, the other foundation of positivist theory, is much more familiar. It is the process of directly observing, recording, or monitoring social and natural phenomena. It is a basic tenet of empiricism that a priori knowledge about the world is impossible. All claims of knowledge must be achieved and assessed only with respect to empirical evidence. According to British philosopher Karl Popper, "only observation and experiment may decide upon the acceptance or rejection of scientific statements, including laws and theories" (1969, 54). Scientific statements are useful to the extent that they are open to being refuted through reference to the realm of experience (Romm 1991, 34).

There is an important distinction between positivist-based theories and all other ways of knowing, including theology and myths. Positivist theories offer explanations that are capable of being falsified with reference to sensory experience. What is taken as evidence must be observed: all other ways of knowing are incapable of such falsification (ibid.). Popper states that "a system is to be considered as scientific only if it makes assertions which may clash with observations; and a system is, in fact, tested by attempts to produce such clashes, that is to say, by attempts to refute it" (1969, 256). Systems of knowledge such as religion or myths are not scientific because they are not testable; they cannot be refuted by reference to empirical reality.

Discovery and Positivist Theory

It is a fundamental assumption of positivist theory that there are truths about human behaviour and human society that can be discovered if we use the right methods to reveal their secrets. Positivist theorists share a high evaluation of science and the scientific method of research. The mandate of the scientist is to uncover something that was previously concealed: "To bring it into light and under scrutiny, and thereby to know that 'thing' in its unconcealed or discovered condition..." (Hazelrigg 1989, vol. 2, 12). Phrases like the "discovery of penicillin," or "the discovery of class conflict as a principle of social change," make perfect sense to positivist theorists. There are things out there waiting to be discovered and illuminated by social science researchers. Moreover, once we have discovered the truth about something, that truth is generally applicable in all similar cases.

This approach to the generation of knowledge is often referred to as *nomothetic* science, which seeks laws that will allow a scientist to predict what will happen under certain circumstances at any given time and place. Most social scientists accept that they are never going to be able to create the perfect nomothetic type of explanation, as perhaps is possible in physics or chemistry. Instead of looking for invariable cause-effect relations, social scientists who use this approach are more interested in producing **statistical correlations**. For example, those who are researching drug use among adolescents, or white-collar crime rates among bank employees, or the likelihood of university professors participating in riots, or of dentists committing suicide, are looking for trends and not for invariable cause-effect relations. They wish to predict when riots *might* occur, or who is *more likely* to commit suicide, or take drugs, or engage in criminal activity. But it is a far cry from statistical prediction to certainty about a human event. Sociologists who see their work as a search for statistical correlations can never be sure about the reliability of their conclusions.

Criticisms of Positivist Theories

A fundamental assumption of the positivistic approach is the total separation between the observed and the observer. Whatever is observed is independent of the laws or theories that might be used to explain it (Bredo and Feinberg 1982, 155). This view has been roundly criticized by those who question the sharp distinction between what we know and how we know it. A number of social scientists would agree with the statement that "What you make of any given fact depends upon how you take it."

To put it another way, facts are always relative to the way in which they are viewed, interpreted, and analyzed. What we consider to be the colour black may depend on what we are contrasting it with. This will probably vary considerably if we compare black only with white instead of with such colours as light grey and dark grey. In this case (and in all other similar cases), facts are never independent of the way in which they are viewed. We can make the same point, although at a much more abstract level, about social facts. What we observe about human behaviour and social interaction is always dependent on the world view or standpoint of the person doing the observation (Bredo and Feinberg 1982).

A positivist approach focuses only on the relationship between the scientist/observer and the external reality that scientist observes. It pays no attention to the relation between the scientist and the community to which he or she belongs. But the standards that our hypothetical scientist can adopt for judging what constitutes a fact are a product of the social interactions that he or she has experienced. Seen in this light, the rigid distinction between scientist/observer and external reality becomes problematic. The difficulty with making this distinction takes us directly to the next theoretical orientation I want to discuss: the interpretive or hermeneutic approach.

THE INTERPRETIVE OR HERMENEUTICAL APPROACH

This approach to theory can most simply be defined as a way of interpreting meaningful human action (Nielsen 1990, 7). Interpretive or hermeneutical theory is confined to the attempt to understand the meaning of other people's signs, gestures, or actions. It is based on the assumption that we can learn about the meaning of the actions of people who are separated from us by time or physical space because all humans communicate with one another using some symbolic medium. The most usual medium of symbolic communication is language. Communications that pass between people are structured and are made meaningful in terms of social rules. Interpretive theory tries to understand human action and behaviour by interpreting the symbolic meanings of human communicative interaction. Interpretive theorists share a number of assumptions:

1. Human actions are motivated by the meanings that people attach to events, people, and things.

2. These meanings are the result of social interaction between people.

3. Each individual interprets and modifies the messages that he or she receives from others in order to construct an understanding of events, people, and things.

Positivist and interpretive theoretical perspectives may be compared and contrasted on three points.

1. *The nature of reality.*
For positivist theorists, there is a tangible reality "out there" that can be divided up into variables, any of which can be studied independently. The objective of inquiry is ultimately to predict and control what is being studied. Research, therefore, must be limited to what an independent researcher is able to observe.

Interpretive theorists agree that there is a tangible reality "out there" that may be studied. The objective of inquiry, however, is to understand the meaning of that reality for the social actors themselves. Thus they argue that limiting research to only observing human actions misses out on important aspects of human behaviour. To explain human behaviour we must discover the meanings attached to behaviour by social actors themselves.

2. *The relationship of the social scientist to the object of inquiry.*
Positivists hold that the scientist and whatever he or she is studying must always be kept independent of each other. The value-free nature of inquiry is guaranteed by the use of objective methods of inquiry.

Interpretive theorists share with positivists a commitment to the distinction between subjectivity and objectivity. Max Weber, for example, argued that it is incumbent on the sociologist to always remain value-free. According to him, researchers must put aside personal concerns and take on the attitude of disinterested observers. In this way, researchers can come to understand the meanings social actors attach to their actions without being affected by their own values and beliefs.

3. *The possibility of generalization.*
According to positivists, the objective of scientific inquiry and research is to build up a body of generalizations that are truth statements, applicable anywhere and at any time.

Interpretive theorists believe that the aim of their inquiry is to develop a body of knowledge that is specific and can be used to explain an individual case.

The interpretive theorist recognizes that "social behavior is constituted by the social conventions adopted by those being studied" (Bredo and Feinberg 1982, 116). He or she wants to know how actions become meaningful for social actors and strives to see things from the other's perspective. The point of interest for the interpretive theorist, then, is not so much *what* is being done as *how* the subjects under study understand what is being done. Is the invitation "Come by and see me some time" a sincere one, a way of putting off an unwanted meeting, or a come-on? The objective of the interpretive theorist is to clarify exactly what the interaction means to the participants. To do this, the interpretive theorist seeks to "get to know" the people under study.

From this perspective, sociological research is essentially a translation from one language to another. Rules that are meaningful to members of a culture and define how they behave serve as raw data to the sociologist, who must translate these data into something understandable to a wider audience. To the extent that we cannot translate from one meaning system into another, the behaviours and actions of the people being studied remain alien or even bizarre and disgusting. (These form the basis of prejudice, discussed in Chapter 1, and racism, to be discussed in Chapter 18.)

Although it shares much with the positivist perspective, the interpretive one does provide certain alternatives to researchers who wish to stay within the scientific tradition, but who also wish to incorporate elements of subjectivity into their research. Like the positivist approach, the interpretive approach is frequently criticized. The most frequent criticisms are that it says virtually nothing about social structures, class conflict, and social change. A second point that is often made is that interpretive theorists see humans as purely cognitive beings. If we understand how people think about the world, what they mean and their self-conceptions, then we understand all that is important to know about human behaviour. Critics claim that the interpretive approach grossly underestimates the complexity of human existence.

THE CRITICAL APPROACH

Critical theories try to bridge the gap between positivist and interpretive approaches by synthesizing the contributions made by each and by "viewing knowledge in the context of human social evolution" (Bredo and Feinberg 1982, 272). The promotion of a higher stage of social evolution, or what Habermas (1970) calls an "emancipatory interest" is the ultimate goal of a critical inquiry.

The roots of the critical approach to knowledge are found in German philosophy, especially in the writings of Karl Marx and Frederick Engels. Recently German philosopher and sociologist Jurgen Habermas has tried to advance the critical approach to knowledge within sociology. In his work, Habermas seeks to incorporate the concerns and insights of both positivist and interpretive approaches, but also to go beyond what he views as the limitations of both. For example, both positivist and interpretive theories are constrained to treat knowledge gained by scientific inquiry as objective knowledge. For both, scientific knowledge is unconnected with any value orientation. Critical theorists take the opposite stance. They argue that it is impossible to produce objective knowledge because no knowledge can be severed from human interests and practices.

Critical theorists maintain that all social inquiry is value-bound in a variety of ways. It is always influenced by the values of the inquirer and by his or her choice of theoretical perspective. This point of contention is a difficult one to deal with because it requires us to question the epistemological basis of scientific inquiry, a daunting task. When Descartes, Bacon, and Newton began developing the theories and methods that we now understand as modern science, they did so with an express purpose in mind. As we have already seen, that purpose is to provide humanity with the ability to exercise effective mastery over nature. In the intervening centuries, modern science has indeed matured to the point where the domination of nature, as envisaged by its original proponents, seems like child's play in comparison with what we are now capable of achieving.

The implications of an objective approach to research, one which views research as value-free, may be best summarized by an anonymous young scientist who said to his interviewer in the late 1970s: "What I'm designing may one day be used to kill millions of people. I don't care. That's not my responsibility. I'm given an interesting technological problem and I get enjoyment out of solving it" (Hazelrigg 1989, 11).

From the point of view of a critical theorist, if the young physicist is not responsible for the weapons of mass destruction he is creating, who is? Who is responsible for the consequences of this man's research? The canons of scientific research clearly do not call for public debate over the desirableness of his research nor even over the use to which his findings might be put. In fact, this physicist and anyone like him could easily achieve awards for the rigour and importance of their discoveries while at the same time remain absolutely assured that they are doing the right thing by disclaiming responsibility for the destructive uses of their discoveries.

While it is hard to argue that positivist-inspired science has not done a great deal to improve the lot of many people, it is also clear that much of science today is conducted not with the interests of a community in mind, but with the interests of a bottom line of profit. As Michael Crichton, medical doctor and author of the science fiction thriller *Jurassic Park* (1990), writes in his introduction:

> The late twentieth century has witnessed a scientific gold rush of astonishing proportions: the headlong and furious haste to commercialize genetic engineering. This enterprise has proceeded so rapidly—with so little outside commentary—that its dimensions and implications are hardly understood at all.

The premise of Crichton's book is that a technique for recovering and cloning dinosaur DNA has been parlayed into a fantasy park complete with living dinosaurs. Chaos soon rules as human greed and mismanagement bring the project to the verge of disaster. While the book is a fanciful extension of a what-if hypothesis, Crichton's critique of modern science rings true for critical theorists. Pursuing profit and "value-free" science simultaneously, without regard for the community, is a sure recipe for disaster. In *The Social Construction of Reality* (1966), sociologists Peter Berger and Thomas Luckmann comment that humans are capable of producing a world that they then experience as something other than a human product. Critical theorists argue that we must strive to overcome this perception of the world as a "not human creation."

169

The manufacturing of nuclear weaponry has created the potential for global destruction. Do you think the scientists who harnessed this capability considered its future implications?

A sociological theory is a critical theory when it departs from, or questions, the prevailing world view. It does this by rejecting the point of view that there can be such a thing as "objective" knowledge (a position shared by both interpretive and positivist theories). Critical theorists share the position that there is no such thing as an objectively neutral or disinterested perspective. Everyone, including the critical theorist, is located both socially and historically. This location inevitably influences the knowledge that they can produce.

The major criticism to be raised of the critical perspective is that, if all knowledge is historically and socially relative, whose point of view about some social event, relationship, or problem should prevail? What criteria should we use to judge the validity of our knowledge? The dilemma of critical theorists is that once they have rejected objectivism, the alternative seems to be a kind of relativism (anything goes). This is not a very satisfying proposition. The question that is always in the forefront for critical theorists is whose standards will prevail, and what criteria do we use to decide between competing or differing explanations?

Some critical theorists have tried to respond to this telling criticism. Gadamer, for example, has argued that as critical theorists we make decisions and develop knowledge through an interplay between our existing values (that he calls prejudgments) and new elements that we draw on from other cultures or from new theories. We are doing our jobs as critical theorists if we are willing to test our existing values (prejudgments) against those of others. Prejudices, Gadamer contends, are "biases of our openness to the world. They are simply conditions whereby we experience something—whereby what we encounter says something to us" (1986, 9).

As critical theorists we can never transcend our prejudices. Rather we must become aware of what they are and use them as essential building blocks from which we can construct knowledge. The objective of critical theorists should always be to move back and forth between old theories and new ones; between familiar world views and those obtained from new cultural contexts. It is in this way that critical theorists are able to create new understandings of human behaviour.

Gwen Jacobs led a protest against barring women from baring their breasts in public in an effort to illustrate inequality between men and women. In our culture, why are women's breasts considered sexual objects? Who defined them as such?

UNDERSTANDING FOOTBALL:
POSITIVIST, INTERPRETIVE,
AND CRITICAL APPROACHES COMPARED

As critical sociologists, must we carefully avoid positivist and interpretive approaches to knowledge? The answer is clearly no! Positivist and interpretive understandings of social events, relations, and processes are often foundational to a critical approach to understanding. The popular North American game of football offers another illustration.

If we want to analyze football and its place in American and Canadian culture, we might begin by gathering and analyzing all sorts of statistics on the game itself, the players, the owners of football clubs, the amount of money generated in an average professional football game, the fans, media coverage—the potential list is extensive. As football fans, we might choose to sit in the stands for a game and keep statistics: how many touchdowns, passes, interceptions, yards gained in first downs, and so on. Or we might decide to collect statistics on the owners of professional football clubs; who the owners are, what their other business connections might be, how much income is generated from any given operation.

But sitting in the stands or researching the financial records of a club would present a different body of knowledge from what an interpretive theorist would seek. The interpretive theorist will want to know what a football player's experience of playing the game is like. What are the sights, feelings, smells, and emotions of playing football? What is it like to see "the visual patterns of lines going by as he runs down the field, bodies looming up in front and tackling, and so on" (Darroch and Silvers 1982, 34)?

While gathering statistics and trying to understand the experience of playing the game from the player's perspective give different views of football, they are not antagonistic explanations. But neither of these two approaches allows us to question the culturally accepted understanding of the role of football in North American society. For that we will need to take a critical stance and ask such questions as, Why is football so popular? Who profits? What is done to keep fans loyal and spending their money? We would probably gather statistics and seek out information about players' experiences. But as critical theorists, we would be interested in determining relations of power between players and owners of the football clubs, and between those who pay to watch (fans) and those who profit from the game (owners, advertisers).

■ ■ ■

SUMMARY

We started this chapter by comparing common-sense theories and sociological ones. All theories, whether they are common-sense or scientific ones, reveal and conceal certain aspects of human experience. But common-sense understandings are by definition based on unexamined values, beliefs, and understandings. Sociological theories, by comparison, are carefully constructed and often challenge common-sense assumptions.

There has never been a single theoretical perspective or template through which all sociologists have organized how they view and explain human social interaction. There exists a wide variety of theoretical perspectives available to sociologists, including those based on positivist, interpretive, and critical approaches.

Positivist approaches have dominated much of sociology theory, especially in North America. Those who use positivist theories believe that an objective reality exists, external to any influence the observer might exert, and that the role of the social scientist is to discover what already exists. Interpretive theorists, by contrast, argue that the objective of sociological inquiry should be to understand the social world from the point of view of the social actors themselves. Interpretive theorists share certain assumptions with positivist ones, including the point of view that it is possible and desirable to make an objective study of society.

Critical theorists seek to move beyond the limitations of both interpretive and positivist perspectives and to point out ways of achieving progressive social change. For them, all knowledge must be viewed in the context of its potential contribution to human emancipation.

■ ■ ■

1. In what ways are common-sense theories and sociological theories similar? In what ways do they differ?

2. To what extent do positivist, interpretive, and critical perspectives share the same epistemological basis? In what ways do they differ?

3. Identify three or four common, everyday experiences. Construct an explanation for each, first from an everyday, taken-for-granted perspective, and then from each of a positivist, interpretive, and critical perspective.

RESEARCH METHODS

- Why do sociologists use different methods to study society?

- What common assumptions underlie positivist and interpretive research methods?

- What are the distinguishing characteristics of relativistic research methods?

At least since Plato's time, questions have been posed about how we acquire knowledge about things and how we know if the knowledge we have acquired is true. These questions make up the traditional task assigned to methodology in both the natural and social sciences.

In the social and natural sciences, theories that explain human conduct are the outcome of inquiries that use specific kinds of methods for information gathering and assessment. From its Greek origins, the term **method** means "way" or "path." In the social sciences today, the concept of method refers to the way research is conducted.

Like other concepts, method is a metaphor. In this case, method is seen as a path leading us toward a destination of knowledge. This metaphor suggests that there may be many routes and many different kinds of knowledge or understandings. But in the Western intellectual tradition, at least since the eighteenth century, there has generally been only one path taken toward arriving at *true* knowledge and understanding. That path has been via objective, value-free scientific research.

Assertions such as "Human language is learned, rather than genetically inherited," or "Human emotions and feelings are expressed in culturally mediated ways," or "Without consistent interaction with adults human babies will not be socialized" are all arrived at by following particular procedures or methods for gathering, interpreting, and presenting information. These methods are subject to certain rules of progression and presentation. They are also informed by a specific ontological and epistemological stance.

Until recently, conventional wisdom had it that if properly pursued the scientific method of inquiry afforded a value-free, objective way of obtaining information about both the social and natural worlds. Because of this, the scientific method has been considered the best way humans have yet devised to answer the question "How do we know what we know?" (Neilson 1990, 1). But many social scientists now question this belief. There is a growing sense

Arnold Gesell, a psychologist, attempted to gather data on child development. Is it possible to study human behaviour in a controlled environment for "scientific purposes"?

that the scientific method of inquiry is never value-free; that it is incapable of excluding the influence of social and cultural values in establishing knowledge.

As feminist research methodologist Joyce McCarl Nielsen has pointed out, there are a growing number of researchers who argue that all knowledge is understandable and valid only within a specific cultural or historical time and place, or only within a specific theoretical perspective. It is impossible, therefore, to arrive at some final, or ultimate, value-free measure of the truth that everyone can agree on and accept. Some theorists even argue that there is no basis on which to choose between competing theories and their explanations. Because everything is relative, every explanation, idea, or claim to truth is equally valid.

There is a growing sense among many social theorists that it is possible and necessary to move beyond the traditional claim that following the scientific method guarantees that knowledge will be value-free and objective, toward a practice that incorporates the personal and political context from which knowledge springs as an important part of the data-gathering process. The construction of knowledge is a political act, and research should be done by, for, and with people, not on them (Kirby and McKenna 1989, 22). As anthropologist Maria Mies wrote:

> Research, which so far has been largely the instrument of dominance and legitimation of power elites, must be brought to serve the interests of dominated, exploited and oppressed groups (1983, 123).

In what follows, I will examine a variety of research methods that currently exist in sociology. These methods may be divided into two broad categories—methods based on the premise of value-free, objective research, and **relativist** methods that acknowledge the influence of social and cultural values in structuring knowledge. Within the first category are both positivist and interpretive research methods. In spite of significant differences, both of these research methods accept the proposition that objective, scientific research is both possible and desirable.

Within the second category are those methods that acknowledge the relativist basis of knowledge, including feminist research methods, participatory research methods, and methods of discourse analysis.

Different research methods have different objectives or purposes in producing "knowledge." In sociology, positivist research methods are generally used by sociologists who are concerned with the prediction and control of social behaviour; interpretive methods are employed by those who wish to establish how social actors understand their own and others' actions; and relativist methods are used by those who accept the premise that all knowledge is socially constructed. Relativist methods are particularly relevant to those who work from a critical perspective.

I have situated each method in the context of the kinds of research questions it is able to address. "Method," as Auguste Comte once wrote, "does not admit of being studied apart from the research in which it is used" (1970, 23).

SCIENCE AND SOCIOLOGICAL INQUIRY

The identification of sociology as a science is so commonplace that it appears in most introductory sociology texts. Open almost any introductory sociology textbook written in the last decade and you will find a definition of sociology like:

Sociology is the science that constructs theories about the social relations making up a society....For sociologists, the word *science* means much the same as for physicists or

If sociology is considered a science, how do we quantify human grief and emotion in the face of tragedy such as that in Bosnia?

biologists: namely, the construction and validation of theories about the real world. A science of social relations is more complex than one concerned with atoms or amoebae. But, in principle, the goals of all sciences are the same (Tepperman and Richardson 1986, 1).

Some sociologists have noted that sociology is similar to the natural sciences to the extent that "it involves systematic methods of investigation, the analysis of data, and the assessment of theories in the light of evidence and logical argument" (Giddens 1991, 21). But they also note that sociology differs from natural sciences to the extent that the object of sociological study—human beings—are self-aware and act in a purposeful fashion.

Thus, unlike the physicist or biologist, a sociologist first has to be aware that his or her subjects of study apply a sense of meaning to what they do. Moreover, human beings are quite capable of changing their actions to please, annoy, or confound the sociologist who observes them. While this kind of behaviour would be totally unexpected from atoms or neutrons, it is an everyday occurrence among humans.

ASSUMPTIONS UNDERLYING THE USE OF POSITIVIST AND INTERPRETIVE RESEARCH METHODS

There are at least six basic assumptions about what constitutes knowledge and how best to acquire it made by sociologists who use positivist or interpretive research methods.

1. The social and the natural worlds can be known in the same way by using the same scientific method of inquiry. This method includes both rationality and direct observation.

2. Use of scientific method will eventually lead to the discovery of true knowledge about both natural and social worlds.

3. An objective reality exists in both the natural and social worlds independent of any observer.

4. Once the truth has been discovered about something, that truth is generally applicable to all similar instances.

5. The salient characteristics of scientific researchers are objectivity, neutrality, and detachment.

6. Facts, whether about the social or natural world, should be reported in neutral, plain language. Facts should be allowed, as much as possible, to speak for themselves.

7. Any truth claim is only provisionally accepted. It is open to refutation and can be replaced by a better claim.

These assumptions are associated with an approach to the generation of knowledge that emphasizes rationality (allows no contradictions to exist); objectivity (no personal interests allowed); and prediction and control of the observed events or phenomena. Let's examine each of these assumptions.

The social and natural worlds are knowable in the same way, via direct observation and rationality. In both social and natural sciences, evidence is gathered through observation. This observation may be made directly, in an experimental setting, or by comparison with other known phenomena. In direct observation, the scientist simply observes what is happening without intervening. In an experimental setting, events are under the control of the scientist, and circumstances or conditions can be modified at will to see how they will affect the phenomena under study (Popper 1961, 139). In comparative observation, a scientific observer "compares different phenomena manifesting different levels of complexity, in order to discover the way in which a phenomenon alters as it assumes a more complex structure" (Romm 1991, 53).

Knowledge and truth about any phenomena are discovered by the scientist. A scientist, according to this view, is a person involved in the process of **discovering** the secrets of nature or of human behaviour. The mandate of the scientist is to uncover something that was previously concealed, "to bring it into light and under scrutiny, and thereby to know that 'thing' in its unconcealed or discovered condition..." (Hazelrigg 1989, vol. 2, 12).

This notion of discovery is, in turn, dependent on the notion that there is an objective, independent reality completely detached from, and external to, the researcher (Nielsen 1990, 4). The prevailing view of science is that there is an independent reality, detached from all of us, and filled with objects that have an independent existence. Independent reality *can* and indeed *must* be studied as if it were an object. This idea of the separation of the world into two different kinds of things—objects and subjects—with no properties in common can be traced to René Descartes. Descartes divided the world into two kinds of things—humans who are pure subjects, or mind, and the rest of the physical world, which is pure object and in no way related to human minds. As mind, humans share with God the subjective properties of life, creativity, and order. Everything else that exists is separate from humans and, even if it is living, can be treated as nonliving, as being profoundly disconnected from human subjectivity.

Once we have discovered the truth about something, that truth is generally applicable in all similar cases and may be considered to be a "scientific law." Both social and natural worlds are ordered in regularized, and thus predictable, ways. Events don't just happen. There is a pattern to all events, whether they are social or natural, that follows a predominantly cause and effect form. The overall goal of all scientists is to construct universal laws about the nature of events. The specific goal of sociologists, as scientists, is to construct universal laws about the social world and human experience that will hold true across time, place, and culture (Nielsen 1990, 5).

As generalizations, scientific laws are rules that govern scientists' expectations about what is reasonable. For example, the statement "Language is part of all human cultures" is a generalization of what social scientists reasonably expect is the case. It is a generalization, however, that is also open to verification or refutation.

In order to produce scientific knowledge, scientific researchers are required to be objective, neutral, and detached in both the way they think about what they are doing and the way that they conduct their research. In its common-sense everyday meaning, to be objective is to be "fair," to not let personal prejudice interfere with the kinds of judgments or decisions one makes. Scientists are required to put aside prejudices and values. By doing this, it is argued, they will be able to do research in an open-minded and neutral way. Many sociologists recognize that no one can be expected to be completely open-minded or neutral on all topics. However, they continue to be committed to the idea of objectivity, arguing that objectivity does not depend solely on the individual researcher, but has to do with the public character of scientific research and reporting.

Scientific researchers publish their findings in scholarly journals and other peer-assessed publications. These findings are available for scrutiny so others can check the conclusions. Objectivity in any science, sociology included, is thus guaranteed by the mutual criticism generated among members of the scientific community as a whole. Because information, ideas, and arguments are circulated among a group of professionals, those professionals, as scientists in whatever discipline, will keep the researcher honest.

The facts, produced by independent and objective scientists, must be allowed to speak for themselves through the neutral language of scientific reporting. The dispassionate transmission of facts, motivated by a commitment to representing scientific discoveries as accurately as possible, in a plain style, with as little distortion as possible, is what distinguishes the work of a true scientist from that of a politician, a lawyer, or even a preacher. It is a commonly held opinion that politicians, lawyers, and preachers use rhetoric—the language of conviction—to present their case and to sway their audience into believing their version of reality. A scientist, on the other hand, is objective, uses neutral language, and reports only the facts. Scientific knowledge is held to be untainted by tricks, passions, or manipulative intentions.

All truth claims are provisional. Positivists place emphasis on refutation as well as on verification. They claim to be open-minded in that they accept truth claims only provisionally. If a better claim based on the process of doing scientific research is put forward, that new claim will eventually replace the older, less accurate one. Karl Popper, one of the best-known proponents of positivism, insists that because the aim of positivist research is to refute truth claims, we can avoid any system of thought that claims to possess absolute, inviolable knowledge of the truth.

All data in the social sciences consist of social meanings, a point that we have already discussed in Chapter 2. This has led some social scientists to make a distinction between positivist methods (also called quantitative methods) through which the researcher collects and processes data using statistical procedures, and interpretive research methods (also called qualitative methods) which allow the researcher to collect and analyze data that are rich in description and therefore not easily handled using statistical procedures.

SOCIOLOGY AND POSITIVIST RESEARCH

The nineteenth-century founders of sociology admired the perceived successes of researchers in the field of physics. They adapted physics and its positivist methods of research as the ideal model for sociology to follow. But the true precursors of

179

empirical, statistically oriented studies of society were done by sixteenth-century constructors of mortality and actuarial tables for the insurance industry and by seventeenth-century census-takers. It is not well known that the first comprehensive census of a population took place in Quebec in the 1630s. Other fields of study, such as astronomy, the study of odds in gambling, and the distribution of the sexes at birth, also contributed ideas on how to quantify human qualities. Given the wide range of human behaviours and the unpredictability of individual persons acting the same way in any given situation, early sociologists seized on the mathematics of probability as a statistical tool that would allow them to assign numbers to the people that they studied. In order to do this, they had to construct the idea of a norm for any given human characteristics.

STATISTICAL NORMS

The **statistical norm** is a nineteenth-century concept that developed out of a combination of probability theory and the political ideologies of Belgian astronomer Adolphe Quételet. In the eighteenth century, probability became a "moral science" used to judge the credibility of court testimony and criminal evidence. The eighteenth-century French philosopher Voltaire wrote an essay on the subject. According to him, almost any aspect of human life could be reduced to a problem of probability. Condorcet, another Enlightenment thinker, expressed a similar belief that truths in moral and political science could be arrived at in exactly the same way, and with the same degree of certainty as those of physical science (Walker 1929, 30).

But for our purposes, the key event in the history of positivist research was the development by Quételet of the concept of *l'homme moyen*—"the average man." Quételet proposed that instead of making a series of observations on one individual over time, as he or she progressed through the various stages of life, changes from one stage to another could be ascertained by observing large numbers of people of different ages. Quételet was convinced that all that was missing were good procedures for collecting data in order to discover that the distribution of all human traits conformed to the law of normality (ibid., 41).

Francis Galton, a cousin of Charles Darwin, was the first to advocate use of the **normal curve** (also known as a bell curve because of its shape) in assigning marks in school. Galton believed that all children should be subjected to complete psychological and physical examinations on a regular basis and that a cumulative record card of the measurements taken should follow each child through school (ibid., 45). In his book *Hereditary Genius*, Galton claimed to be the first to suggest a "law of deviation from the average," and his student, Karl Pearson, coined the term **standard deviation,** which is a measure of the scatter of observations around their mean. As well, Galton developed the idea of grades as a device for ranking by classification. This and other ideas were soon widely adopted. Theodore Porter (1986) in *The Rise of Statistical Thinking* notes how group characteristics measured as an average came to take precedence over individual behaviours. In the nineteenth century, Porter says:

Statistical writers persuaded their contemporaries that systems consisting of numerous autonomous individuals can be studied at a higher level than that of the diverse atomic constituents. They taught them that such systems could be presumed to generate large-scale order and regularity which would be virtually unaffected by the caprice that seemed to prevail in the actions of individuals. Since significant changes in the state of the system would appear only as a consequence of proportionately large causes, a science could be formulated using relative frequencies as its elemental data (5).

It was only a short step from average to normal and abnormal, and that step was made in the mid-nineteenth century by Émile Durkheim. In his book *The Rules of Sociological Method* (1895), he associated the average with "normal," and any deviation from the average with the "abnormal" or "pathological." The average, for Durkheim, represented the "group mind," and statistics, he believed, could serve as a way to measure "currents of opinion" that would "impel certain groups either to more marriages, or to more suicides, or to a higher or lower birthrate, etc." (Durkheim [1895] 1964, 8, 56). It is interesting to note how Durkheim turned a statistical concept of norm—or most frequently occurring—into a moral concept of normal or abnormal.

SCIENCE AND THE RESEARCH CYCLE

How does a sociologist who follows scientific methods of inquiry go about producing knowledge about the social world? Briefly, the scientific method is usually thought of as a sequential research process with the following steps:

1. Define a problem;

2. State the hypothesis to be tested;

3. Operationalize key concepts;

4. Collect and analyze data;

5. Interpret the results and draw conclusions about the problem (Schumacher and McMillan 1993, 8).

These four steps are often referred to as the **research cycle** or the "wheel of science." The assumption has been that if the appropriate steps are followed in a rigorous fashion and in the correct sequence, then the result will always be the production of knowledge that is trustworthy, valid, and value-free.

The following is an example of how the research cycle might be followed by a sociologist conducting, from a positivist perspective, a comparative analysis of suicide in Denmark and Spain.

1. *Define a problem*
Statistics published between 1960 and 1964 indicate that the rate of suicide in Denmark is higher than that in Spain. Why might this have been the case?

2. *State hypothesis*

In stating a hypothesis sociologists often refer to the results of similar kinds of research that have already been reported by other sociologists. Émile Durkheim's pioneering study of suicide is one such important reference work. Durkheim made the observation that the suicide rate among Protestants is generally higher than that among Catholics because Protestants are generally less socially embedded than Catholics and therefore more likely to take their own lives. Given that Denmark is a predominately Protestant country, while Spain is a primarily Catholic one, we can deduce that Durkheim's explanations for the differences in suicide rates between Protestants and Catholics might be applicable to the specific case of Denmark and Spain during the early 1960s. Deduction is inference that follows necessarily from premise to conclusion.

The hypothesis "Protestants are generally less socially embedded than Catholics and therefore more likely to take their own lives" links two variables or characteristics. The variable that is taken to be the cause of some relationship is labelled the independent variable. The variable that is taken to be the effect or result of some relationship is labelled the dependent variable. In our hypothesis, rate of suicide is the dependent variable (what the researcher wants to explain) and religious affiliation is the independent variable (what the researcher uses to explain the dependent variable).

3. *Operationalize key concepts*

To operationalize a concept means to translate it into language that will allow empirical measurement. The researcher must devise a way of observing and measuring the dependent variable—in this case suicide. In operationalizing suicide, we want to make sure that our definition is valid, and that it truly can measure what it claims to measure. We also want to make sure that our measure is valid. If we make the same measurement over again would it be equivalent to the previous measurements we have made?

4. *Collect and analyze data*

Using published statistics for both countries, we learn that between 1960 and 1964 the suicide rate in Denmark averaged 18.8 per 100 000 inhabitants, compared to 5.1 per 100 000 Spaniards.

5. *Interpret results and draw conclusions*

At first glance it would appear that with a suicide rate in Denmark of 18.8 per 100 000 inhabitants compared with 5.1 per 100 000 in Spain, Protestants are more likely to commit suicide than Catholics.

But can we safely conclude that this is sufficient evidence to maintain that Protestants are more likely to commit suicide than Catholics? Most likely not. According to Russell Keat, suicide statistics cannot be regarded merely as "observational data." A suicide is not simply a dead body (1979, 82). That is to say, a suicide cannot be defined without reference to the intentions of the person involved to end his or her life. So to describe a death as suicide is not simply a matter of observation. It is also a matter of attributing motive or intention to the person who makes up the bit of data under study. And to explain why this or any other person killed himself is to say something about how he perceived his situation. Making reference only to the religious affiliation, marital status, or degree of social integration of a person who commits suicide has little meaning except in relation to how that person perceived herself.

INTERPRETIVE METHODS AND RESEARCH

Interpretive methods is an umbrella term used to refer to different research methods and strategies that share certain characteristics. Data collected using interpretive methods of research are usually referred to as "soft"; they are rich in descriptions of people and their social interactions, and are not suited to statistical procedures. In the broadest sense of the term, interpretive methods refer to research methods (such as field research, case studies, and ethnomethodology) that produce descriptive data, including people's own written or spoken words as well as descriptions of their observable behaviour.

All interpretive research shares the following characteristics:

1. Interpretive research is inductive. Unlike positivist researchers who use deductive reasoning where all research questions are clearly formulated at the outset, interpretive

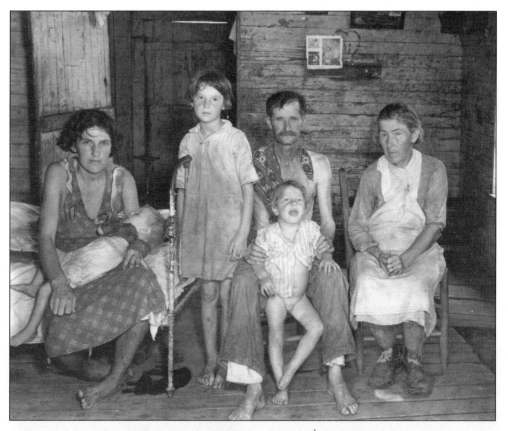

Who knows or understands poverty better than those who have experienced it directly?

researchers often develop their research questions in the process of carrying out their research. Interpretive researchers use inductive reasoning, moving from the particular—usually some observation made in the course of carrying out this research—to more general statements.

2. Interpretive researchers treat settings and people holistically. People and their settings are not reduced to categories of dependent and independent variables, as is the case in positivist research. Instead, interpretive researchers analyze people in the context of the settings in which they interact.

3. Interpretive researchers strive to be sensitive to their subjects. They seek to minimize their effects on the people they study. (The exception is ethnomethodology, where the objective is to act in such a way that a reaction is provoked, which then may be studied for what it reveals about everyday assumptions.)

4. Interpretive researchers try to understand people from their own frame of reference. As Herbert Blumer, a well-known proponent of interpretive research, wrote:

Trying to catch the interpretive process by remaining aloof as a so-called "objective" observer and refusing to take the role of the acting unit is to risk the worst kind of subjectivism—the objective observer is likely to fill in the process of interpretation with his own surmises in place of catching the process as it occurs in the experience of the action unit which uses it (1969, 86).

5. A interpretive researcher must be willing to suspend his or her own beliefs, perspectives, and predispositions. In interpretive research, events must be viewed as if they were happening for the first time. Nothing can be taken for granted or judged.

6. All perspectives are valuable to an interpretive researcher. The objective of interpretive research is to detail other people's perspectives. That being the case, all people and their points of view must be considered equally valuable and important. Interpretive researchers seek to "give a voice" to people who are rarely heard (Lewis 1966, xii).

7. Interpretive methods are humanistic. Those who follow an interpretive perspective are committed to the idea that, if we reduce people's words and acts to statistical equations, we lose sight of the humanness of social life. By studying people using interpretive research methods, we get to know people as they are—their inner lives, moral struggles, hopes, and ideals.

8. Interpretive research is a craft. Interpretive research methods are neither refined nor standardized. As a result, researchers are flexible and are afforded a great deal of latitude in how they conduct a study. While there are guidelines for interpretive researchers to follow, there are no set rules; research methods are there to serve the researcher (Taylor and Bogdan 1984, 5–8).

Those who use interpretive methods, then, are committed to a research approach that emphasizes the importance of meaning in human social interaction. Specifically, they argue that if we want to understand human behaviour, we need to know the meaning attached to that behaviour by the participants themselves. To limit research to "observable" behaviour and actions misses out on the most important part of human social existence. The following two examples will give you some idea of how interpretive research might be carried out.

"DOING" WALKING

While very few of us give much thought to the procedures involved in walking, that is precisely what A. Lincoln Ryave and James N. Schenkein chose to study (1972). All of us possess routine practices that we use when we walk, and we use those practices in conjunction with other people who walk with, by, past, in front of, behind, around, and even on top of us. "Doing" walking, then, is the result of the concerted efforts of members of a community. It is a profoundly social act. In conducting their study, Ryave and Schenkein used a series of videotapes of people walking . They were interested in finding out how it was that people navigated and avoided collisions with each other. In their opinion, in order for successful walking to take place in a social context, all parties involved must not only recognize that they are walking, but also create an appropriate walking strategy.

To walk together, Ryave and Schenkein assert, means that people as a collective must produce some pattern of walking. They must maintain a certain proximity to one other. If one person falls behind, or gets ahead, that person usually initiates "corrective measures" or "repair work" to restore the walking pattern. They either hurry up, slow down, or offer an explanation as to why they were out of step. To refuse to engage in repair work means that walking together is not possible.

All sorts of other social activities are made possible by the act of walking together. As Ryave and Schenkein note: "...such activities as conversing, being available for conversation, touching, laughing, offering of offerables such as cigarettes or sweets, parting and so on, are made relevant, and expectable, by the sheer fact of walking together" (272).

Walking alone is also a social accomplishment. Ryave and Schenkein present the dilemma of how a lone walker avoids the appearance of walking together with another walker that he or she is merely passing on the street. Videotapes of such events suggest that the individuals involved manipulate their direction, pace, speed, and bodily attitude so that the appearance of walking together is minimized to a moment.

Avoiding the violation of social norms when walking is another accomplishment. Individuals try not to give the impression that they are "following" someone on the street. They also try not to give the impression that their approach to someone else might be threatening.

PERSONS WITH MULTIPLE SCLEROSIS (MS)

Canadian sociologist Susan Russell conducted a study of 35 persons with multiple sclerosis (MS), a chronic, progressively debilitating disease whose onset usually occurs in early adulthood. In this study, Russell (who herself has MS) wished to understand how persons with MS adjust to such an illness "in terms of a dynamic process involving physical and social constraints...as well as the social response to both of these" (1989). Russell was concerned with establishing individual responses of persons with MS to the experience of being confronted with physical constraints, as well as with establishing the response of nondisabled persons and institutions to persons with MS.

While a questionnaire format would have allowed her to gather a larger sample and to perform statistical analyses on responses, she chose an "interpretive" approach using a small sample. Her reasons for using an open-ended discussion for data gathering instead of a structured questionnaire centred on the appropriateness of each of these two approaches to understanding the experiences of the respondents themselves. The open-ended discussion format advocated by an interpretive approach allowed categories of analyses to "emerge from the respondents themselves rather than being imposed upon them by an impossibly omniscient researcher" (279). The results of her research, says Russell, "confirm the value of the interview method."

> [It] would appear that the adjustment to chronic illness involves a dynamic process. Those with MS respond to both physical and social constraints. The constraints themselves change, the response changes and both must be perceived in a dialectical relationship with each other (280).

The complexity of the relationship between social and physical constraints made an interpretive approach to this study the only real choice for Russell. A strictly positivist research approach would not have been flexible or sensitive enough to capture the kinds of nuances that she was able to uncover using a less structured, more personal approach.

Russell's study was based on data taken from a series of "wide-ranging, semistructured interviews" with individuals ranging in age from 24 to 67 and living in Montreal (278). Although her sample was a nonrandom quota sample, she paid particular attention to ensuring that the sex-ratio of her sample matched the reported sex-ratio of people with MS in the Canadian population. She also tried to ensure that her sample contained persons with a range of manifestations of MS. As well, the employment status of respondents was taken into consideration.

By using an interpretive approach, Russell found that, while some of the people she interviewed had given up trying to respond to the physical constraints of MS, others persevered. What became clear to her was that the difference in responses to physical constraints on activities was very often related to social factors that accompanied the physical condition (281). MS is a slow, debilitating disease, with an unpredictable trajectory. This offers hope to some of those diagnosed with MS, Russell says, because they are able to maintain some "disbelief that one's body will continue to decline in physical abilities"

(282). Russell's research methods allowed her to capture some of the sense of how hope and disbelief work together for persons with MS.

> One young woman expressed the feelings of many by saying, "I never thought I was going to get bad, you know." While another said, "It's strange, I know, but I keep thinking, 'They have *that* wrong with them, but I'll never be like that.'" This disbelief persists. As one young man using a wheelchair almost permanently said, "I keep telling myself the disease will not get worse...maybe it will" (282).

A second way of dealing with the physical constraints of the disease, Russell found, is "anticipatory socialization"—often involving social withdrawal on the part of the individual with MS. This withdrawal, Russell says, is both voluntary and involuntary. In part, withdrawal is a result of the person with MS being aware of the impact that he or she has on others. Many people with MS are aware of their "presentation of self," and are guided in their behaviour by the responses of others around them. Many express shock at no longer being able to control their bodies, at no longer being able to walk or speak properly.

Russell also wanted to establish the social constraints affecting the responses of persons with MS. In her study, she found that of the 23 marriages that had been established prior to the onset of the disease, eight ended in divorce shortly after the diagnosis. At 35 percent, this is lower than the rate of divorce in Canada. But while a high proportion of divorced people remarry, none in Russell's sample did. Moreover, she found that husbands were more likely to leave wives diagnosed with MS than wives were to leave husbands. For diagnosed women, 6 out of 15 marriages ended in divorce, while only 2 out of 8 marriages of diagnosed men ended in divorce.

One older woman who said that she had had a wonderful marriage until being diagnosed with MS spoke about her husband's withdrawal:

> I think he knew what was going to happen and he thought, "I'd better get out while the going is good." He didn't even know I'd ever be in a wheel chair. I was walking then. That was pretty hard to take—finding out you had MS....Your marriage going on the rocks (284).

One young man in Russell's sample quoted his wife who said she wanted a divorce "because I don't want to spend the rest of my life with a cripple" (285). In this case, she forced him to give up his role as husband because she felt his physical disability meant he was no longer of use to her in his social role as her spouse.

A marriage that persists, however, indicates two things. First, persons with a disability do not themselves decide that the physical disability means they should give up their social roles as spouses. Second, it means that the persons' spouses are willing not to force them to give up their social roles (Russell, 285). This, in turn, has an effect on the way people with MS are able to deal with their physical disability.

Russell found that while men diagnosed with MS were advised by their physicians to continue working and living as normally as possible, married women were advised to stop working and to avoid the stress of a paid job. Unmarried women, however, were never advised by their doctors to stop working. Russell concludes that "medical advice operates differently with women and men, and in a way that emphasizes man as active agent and woman (particularly if married) as passive subject" (287).

Through her interview techniques and discussion groups, Russell determined that employers, faced with employees who were partially or fully restricted in their job activities, generally encouraged them to retire or dismissed them out of hand, rather than employing them in a more appropriate situation. The experience of working-class men, however, was different from that of white-collar workers: the latter maintained their jobs for much longer. In Russell's sample, out of a total of 11 women and 14 men who were working at the time of diagnosis, three (two women and one man) passed as "normal." The others who continued to be employed (two women and four men) worked for agencies with specific policies about maintaining workers with disabilities or for companies where management took a personal interest in them. One of the things learned from the interviews was that persons with MS who continued to work reported that their co-workers tended to resent the preferential treatment accorded them by management.

Russell concludes that while chronic illness may "ruin life...it gets a lot of help from mundane social practices." Because the social environment remains hostile to persons with chronic debilitating diseases like MS, the easiest response is to withdraw socially and to give up maintaining social roles altogether. Indeed, as Russell finds, many persons with disabilities are encouraged to do just that. She ends with the observation that interpretive research can help bring to light the extent to which physical disability and the inability to fulfil social roles are socially constructed.

A CRITIQUE OF INTERPRETIVE METHODS

It is important to note that many of those who use interpretive methods assert that objective research is possible. Max Weber, whose work initially inspired this perspective, forcefully argued that to study social behaviour is to study the meanings that conscious human agents attach to their behaviour. To this extent, he argued, the social sciences and natural sciences differ. In the social sciences, a full understanding of social action involves what he identified as *verstehen* or empathetic understanding. While Weber was aware that complete objectivity for social scientists was never achievable, he firmly believed that they must, nonetheless, strive to remain unbiased in conducting research.

In the mid-twentieth century, Schutz (1967) has done the most to develop the interpretive or hermeneutic perspective for sociologists. Schutz is committed to the belief that human action is endowed with meaning by human intention (that is, by human consciousness). While it is true that we continually use interpretive schemes provided by our culture, we nonetheless can achieve some measure of objectivity by consciously suspending our own subjectivity. Interpretive research methods have been valuable to sociologists because they provided an alternative to the positivist approach during a period in sociology's history when the latter perspective was widely accepted as the only way of producing scientific knowledge. For positivists, research done from an interpretative perspective is less rigorous and discriminating than their own. Yet those following an interpretive perspective share significant common ground with positivists: both maintain an underlying assumption that there is an objective reality "out there" that is both separate from and independent of the (subjective) researcher.

Thus, the benefit of the interpretive or hermeneutic perspective has been the development of a strong critique of positivist methods, without replacing their common focus on objectivity. Interpretive research methods have provided a legitimate alternative to those who wish to stay within the scientific tradition and at the same time hear directly from the people they study (Nielsen 1990, 9).

THE RELATIVIST APPROACH

As Yvonna Lincoln and Egon Guba have pointed out:

> We are so imbued with the tenets of science that we take its assumptions utterly for granted, so much so that we almost cannot comprehend the possibility that there might be other ways of thinking. And when other ways are suggested, we are inclined to shut our ears, feeling that merely to listen to them is, quite literally, a heresy (1985, 8).

Yet there is a growing uneasiness and suspicion that objective, value-free research is neither possible nor desirable. This realization is having profound consequences for the discipline of sociology. Writing done in the history and sociology of scientific knowledge has challenged the traditional view of how scientific studies are conducted, as well as how the results of science are "replicated" and passed on to successive generations of scientists. New writing suggests that a relativist approach to research might be more accurate.

In the traditional view of research shared by positivist and interpretive researchers, scientists investigate a concrete reality by using theories to develop hypotheses, by testing their hypotheses through observation and experimentation, and by revising their theories based on their results. Some researchers, committed to the traditional view, go so far as to contend that they use pure observation only to develop a set of "facts" concerning the phenomena under study. New knowledge is the result of "discovery" rather than "invention," and "progress" is the slow accumulation of knowledge in a particular field.

Yet even in the disciplines of physics, chemistry and biology, astronomy, geology, and mathematics, there are acute differences in methods employed. While physics is an experimental science, mathematics and astronomy are not. As feminist scholar Sandra Harding (1986) has pointed out, the discipline of physics, which is considered to be the "most real of sciences" (Haraway 1981) is in fact quite different from the other disciplines we call scientific. Physics relies on experimentation and formal logic; its subject matter is comparatively simple in that it is neither self-reflective nor intentional (as is human behaviour); and it makes minimal use of interpretation. Thus the discipline of physics is a poor candidate to use as a model for the social sciences. The sociologists who took physics as their model made the assumption that the social world could be explored in the same ways as the physical world; they also chose a model that was not very representative of the other sciences.

The relativist view, by contrast, says that "science itself is an eminently social accomplishment. Rather than science standing independent of the social world by virtue of the methods it employs, those very methods, on a practical day-to-day level, are whole-heartedly social" (Doran 1989, 515). From a relativist point of view, the production and reproduction of scientific knowledge is *framed* by historical and cultural locations, and by social interests (Habermas 1971). It is an accumulated "story" that feeds and informs the methods and interpretation of empirical data gathering. From the relativist point of view, the world is "made" rather than "found." In its most radical form, this view of research is self-reflexive. All research can be turned back on itself to question its own social interests and cultural/historical position.

These two conceptions of science—value-free and relativistic—are ultimately about two types of epistemology or ways of knowing reality: the value-free view contends that there is a concealed but regularized reality that can be revealed through careful study; the relativist view contends that there is only a chaotic reality that can never be known except through human interpretation, and that such interpretation is always a human product, not an ultimate truth or absolute reality.

On the level of the production of scientific knowledge itself, knowledge has been shown to be highly influenced by preconceived philosophical and theological ideas, as well as by human desire for power and recognition. Arriving at knowledge through research is not necessarily (or perhaps even usually) a rational process based on the careful collection and examination of evidence. Rather it is the application of preconceived positions and theories, using whatever means are available to find support for a particular position.

Just what might research look like that is not driven by the notion that objectivity is both possible and highly desirable? In the following sections I discuss some of the research methods now available that focus on the meaning of social actions, have an emancipatory interest, or deliberately promote research done from a specific point of view. Relativist methods encompass a wide variety of approaches. In general, they are used by researchers to detect and expose beliefs and practices that limit human freedom. The relativist perspective differs from value-free scientific ones by permitting researchers to question and challenge the dominant belief system of their society. From a relativist perspective, everyone, including the researcher, has a social, historical, and cultural location. And it is in the context of this location that all knowledge is socially produced. This perspective has provided a true alternative to the assumptions of the value-free scientific one.

EMANCIPATORY INTEREST AND RELATIVIST RESEARCH

Social inquiry, which acknowledges the influence of social and cultural values, often has an emancipatory interest in empowerment and social ethics based on such principles as justice, beneficence, nonmaleficence, and autonomy (Beauchamp and Childress 1989). Such emancipatory interests are behind most feminist criticisms of traditional sociology, for example. Canadian feminist and sociologist Dorothy Smith (1990) criticizes conventional social science research as practices "that convert what people experience directly in their everyday/everynight world into forms of knowledge in which people as subjects disappear and in which their perspectives on their own experience are transposed and subdued by the magisterial forms of objectifying discourse" (4).

Others interested in using their research to aid emancipation note that calls have come from governments of Third World countries to change the way in which information is gathered, processed, and released; such calls have also come from literacy workers and popular educators like Paulo Freire who use the context of popular education as a means of transforming consciousness and social relations (Kirby and McKenna 1989). In place of traditional research, those influenced by a relativist perspective argue in favour of research that is done by people who are "on the margins of the production of knowledge." By designing and carrying out their own research, these people will be able to "create knowledge that will describe, explain or help change the world in which they live" (Kirby and McKenna 1989, 17). According to them, even graffiti like "If voting could change the system it would be illegal" or "We're poor and we know why" come from individuals who are analyzing their experience. Making sense in this way, they argue, can lead people to take action and claim space to express their analysis (ibid.).

This point of view has much in common with that expressed by social scientists who argue that all research and knowledge production is directly related to the vantage point

The propaganda we see about war is markedly different from the battlefield.

or social location of the researcher. Several different approaches to research that draw on a relativist approach to knowledge construction are discussed below.

FEMINIST RESEARCH INTERESTS AND STANDPOINT EPISTEMOLOGY

According to Joyce McCarl Nielsen, **standpoint epistemology**

> begins with the idea that less powerful members of society have the potential for a more complete view of social reality than others, precisely because of their disadvantaged position. That is, in order to survive (socially and sometimes even physically) subordinate persons are attuned to or attentive to the perspective of the dominant class (for example, white, male, wealthy) as well as their own. This awareness gives them the potential for…."double vision," or double consciousness—a knowledge, awareness of, and sensitivity to both the dominant world view of society and their own minority (for example, female, black, poor) perspective (1990, 10).

Feminist researcher Nancy Hartsock (1983) argues that a standpoint is based on the following premises:

1. The material life of the researcher—what they do for a living and related facts such as standard of living and quality of material surroundings—structures and limits that researcher's understandings. Being a secretary in a company leads to a different standpoint than being that company's Chief Executive Officer;

2. Powerful members of society and less powerful members of the same society often have opposing understandings of, or standpoints on, the social world;

3. Accepting the premise that one's everyday life has epistemological consequences, standpoint theorists argue that the standpoint of the less powerful group has more potential for competing than that of the more powerful group. It is in the interests of the members of the more powerful group to maintain and legitimate their position. Thus their understanding of the social world is limited to what is needed to accomplish that legitimation.

Research conducted from a particular standpoint is based on the premise that the point of view of both the researchers and the researched is shaped by their social positioning and material activities.

PARTICIPATORY RESEARCH

Participatory research grew out of a liberating method of teaching the poor in Third World countries, known as popular education. Participatory research is a combination of research methods drawn from Paulo Freire's efforts in adult literacy education in Brazil, Catholic liberation theology, and the views of the neo-Marxist Antonio Gramsci (Lapatpí 1988).

Budd Hall defines participatory research as "a three-pronged activity which integrates a research process (social investigation) with educational work through an action designed to deal with specific problems (1984, 291–92). According to Hall, participatory research is based on the following six principles:

1. Research should involve people in the entire process beginning with identification of issues, through discussion of how to get the information, to analysis and use of results within the context of action.

2. Research should result in some direct and positive benefits for those communities and people involved.

3. Research is a process of systematic creation of knowledge which may or *may not* involve people who have been professionally trained as researchers.

4. Knowledge is deepened, enriched, and made more socially usable when it is produced collectively.

5. Research involves a combination of methods designed to facilitate social, cooperative, or collective production of knowledge.

6. Research, learning, and knowledge production are often aspects of the same intellectual processes in the context of action.

According to L. David Brown and Rajesh Tandon (1983), participatory research involves exploited or oppressed groups who define the central problem of the research as uncovering and opposing oppression. This research perspective, they note, has at least three implications: participatory research clients will define problems differently from dominant groups; authority and resources will be controlled largely by other interest groups; dominant interest groups can be expected to resist or attack problem definitions that threaten their positions" (284).

Participatory research methods can include a diversity of research approaches and can be used to serve many purposes, depending on the problems and issues identified by participants. Most participatory research is a group effort, and community building among the participants is one of the objectives of participatory research. Group discussions, public meetings, community seminars, open-ended surveys, the forming of research teams, fact-finding tours, collective production of audio-visual materials, and popular theatre can all be part of the process.

GENEALOGY AND DISCOURSE ANALYSIS

An important contribution to research methods in the social sciences has been made by Michel Foucault, whose work has focused on the analysis of discourse. Discourse analysis is an analysis of the language used in any social interaction setting. It is one method of revealing, and calling into question, some of the most strongly held and cherished assumptions about daily life. It can be used effectively to reveal biases, ideologies, and relationships that usually remain hidden. By holding the language used in any social interaction up to scrutiny, understanding can be advanced through fresh perspectives on the underpinnings of dominant theories and practices.

Foucault called his method of discourse analysis genealogical—meaning that he was interested in searching for differences that occur as social practices are transformed. We have already considered some of Foucault's work in Chapter 2, where we looked at the differences in the discourses concerning the treatment of prisoners from the eighteenth to the nineteenth centuries. In presenting these two discourses on the treatment of prisoners, Foucault uses his genealogical method of juxtaposition to search out and highlight the different ways in which power is manifest in all social relations. For Foucault, the genealogist "must be able to recognize the events of history, its jolts, its surprises, its unsteady victories, and unpalatable defeats—the basis of all beginnings, atavisms, and heredities" (1977, 144–45).

Dreyfus and Rabinow (1982) observe that Foucault's research method is powerful because "as a method of isolating discourse objects, it seems to distance and defamiliarize the serious discourse of the human sciences. This, in turn, enables Foucault to raise the genealogical questions: How are these discourses used? What role do they play in society?" (xxi). This approach differs from the traditional mandate of historians who are mostly concerned to write narratives, compile facts, and generally show how things really were.

Foucault's genealogical method of discourse analysis is particularly relevant to the study of human services because of his treatment of social institutions such as asylums and prisons, which isolate and exclude individuals. Social institutions do not exist in a vacuum; neither do they appear suddenly without warning. They "emerge," to use Foucault's term, out of a particular historical situation, as a response to a particular set of social pressures.

■ ■ ■

SUMMARY

Research methods currently used by sociologists may be divided into two broad categories—methods based on the premise of value-free, objective research, and those that acknowledge the relativist basis of all knowledge. Until recently the belief that the scientific method of inquiry would guarantee value-free research dominated all of the sciences, including sociology. In following the scientific method, a problem is defined, a hypothesis is formulated and tested, data are collected and analyzed, and the results are interpreted and conclusions drawn.

This approach has been exemplified in sociology by research done from both positivist and interpretive perspectives. Using quantifiable observations made by what they believe to be objective, detached, and disinterested observers, sociologists have unveiled what they consider to be the truth about the social world. Sociologists with a positivist perspective use statistical techniques to gather and process data. Those with an interpretive perspective emphasize the importance of meaning in human social interaction and seek to discover the meanings that social actors themselves attach to their behaviour.

Recently, however, the dominant model of value-free research shared by positivist and interpretive theorists has been strongly challenged. Many sociologists are now using a relativist approach. These sociologists accept the premise that all knowledge is socially constructed.

Research methods that acknowledge the relativist basis of knowledge include feminist and participatory methods, and methods of discourse analysis including genealogical analysis. Relativist methods permit researchers to question the dominant beliefs of their society, creating the possibility for the researcher to act to implement change. It is for this reason that researchers who work from a critical perspective have been so interested in relativist research methods.

■ ■ ■

FOR DISCUSSION

1. Has most research been "largely the instrument of dominance and legitimation of power elites," as Maria Mies claims?

2. Should sociologists continue to strive to emulate physics as a model for scientific research? What are some of the strengths and shortcomings of that model?

3. One of the cardinal assumptions of positivist researchers is that an objective reality exists, independent of any observer. Discuss this assumption.

4. To what extent do qualitative research methods differ from quantitative ones? What are some of the similarities?

5. What is the relativist view of research methods and the production of knowledge? Compare this view with the positivist and interpretive views.

6. Design one or two research projects based on qualitative research methods. Then approach the same topic using only quantitative research methods. Compare the kinds of questions and understandings that each approach might yield.

7. What are the aims and objectives of critical research? What kinds of research projects might be conducted using critical research methods?

8. Can research carried out by researchers with specific interests ever be valid research?

10

SHAPING SOCIAL RESEARCH

CHAPTER OPENING QUESTIONS

- In what way does our theoretical perspective structure the way we define and study social phenomena?

- How are positivist research methods used in the studies of primary socialization outlined in this chapter?

- In what ways do interpretive research objectives influence the results of the studies of secondary socialization discussed in this chapter?

- How might a critical approach to the subject of socialization bring together elements from both positivist and interpretive methodologies?

In Chapter 7, I pointed out that the concept of socialization is used by sociologists to refer to the learning process whereby a human infant gradually acquires cultural fluency and becomes skilled in the ways of the culture in which he or she is being reared. I also indicated that, while the concept of socialization is widely accepted among sociologists as foundational to the discipline, the actual processes by which socialization occurs, especially in infants and young children, are widely contested. In this chapter I wish to explore how researchers using different theoretical perspectives approach the study of socialization. By comparing how we might study the process of socialization using interpretive and critical perspectives, I hope to help you understand how, as sociologists, we are able to produce such widely differing understandings of a single social process.

PRIMARY AND SECONDARY SOCIALIZATION

During the 1960s, sociologists Peter Berger and Thomas Luckmann proposed the distinction between **primary socialization** and **secondary socialization**. According to them, primary socialization is the most important form of socialization for the individual. Primary socialization is "the first socialization an individual undergoes in childhood, through which he becomes a member of society." Secondary socialization, on the other hand, is defined as "any subsequent process that inducts an already socialized individual into new sectors of the objective world of his society" (1967, 130).

Each individual is born into an **objective social structure,** where he or she encounters others who are in charge of their socialization. Both primary and secondary socialization impose definitions on the individual. These definitions exist ready-made and emanate from an already defined social world. **Socializers** mediate between this exterior, already existing social world and the individual who is being inducted into it. The socializers present different aspects of the exterior social world to the infant or child, and these are chosen on the basis of the others' own "individual, biographically rooted idiosyncrasies" (Berger and Luckmann 1966, 130).

In primary socialization, there is no question of choice of others. As Berger and Luckmann put it, "Society presents the candidate for socialization with a predefined set of significant others, whom he must accept as such with no possibility of opting for another arrangement." Secondary socialization, on the other hand, occurs afterward, and is built directly on the experience of primary socialization. Thus secondary socialization always proceeds with an already formed individual, and whatever else there is new to learn

School is an important agent of secondary socialization for children.

"must somehow be superimposed upon this already present reality" (ibid., 134, 140). The recipient of secondary socialization may recognize the extent to which this process represents only one out of a number of different possible perspectives on the world.

The process of secondary socialization is something that continues throughout each individual's life. Going to university, moving away from home, starting a job, learning a profession, getting married, becoming a parent and eventually a grandparent—these and myriad other life situations require that we learn new roles and accept new responsibilities. In short, what sociologists call secondary socialization affects all of us, in all stages of our lives.

Clearly both primary and secondary socialization include different kinds of learning. Moreover, that learning happens in a wide variety of contexts and over an extended period of time. Socialization takes place at the dinner table, in the streets, in the movie theatres, the classroom, and the schoolyard, to name just a few. Socialization can take place as a result of a deliberate attempt to teach a child behaviours and beliefs that are considered of great importance to his or her life. This kind of primary socialization or teaching occurs, for example, when parents, teachers, or religious leaders deliberately impart knowledge or types of values to children.

But socialization can take place informally also. Cultural knowledge, norms, beliefs, values, and expectations can be well transmitted by less obvious teachers. Media super-stars from Madonna to Barney can convey strong cultural messages, but school friends and neighbourhood children, classmates, and sports team members can all be very effective **agents of socialization.** Agents of socialization are individuals and groups who carry out some process of socialization and pass on norms, beliefs, and social practices from one generation to another. While socialization of one generation is generally consistent with its predecessor, change is quite possible. Any aspect of social life can be modified and transformed from one generation to the next.

Different agents of socialization play different roles in the lives of children and adults. Sometimes they reinforce each other. It is often the case that the values parents teach their children are reinforced by teachers, religious leaders, or even politicians and media stars. But different agents of socialization can also be contradictory. Parents might teach their children concern for the environment, and this value may be reinforced by teachers and by television programs. At the same time, big logging companies might use television or magazine ads to promote the position that too much conservation puts company employees' jobs at risk and interferes with the company's ability to make a profit.

Finally, we can distinguish between **intended** and **unintended socialization.** Parents may intend to raise their children to be nonracist and to promote the worth of each individual. But these same parents may invite only members of their own racial or religious group into their homes, join only racially or religiously exclusive groups, and generally make comments about the superior value of their own race, religion, or lifestyle, thus unintentionally socializing their children to be raised.

A POSITIVIST APPROACH TO PRIMARY SOCIALIZATION EXPERIENCES

Of all the agents of socialization, sociologists consider the family to be the most influential in shaping a child's sense of self, values, and beliefs. The family is the first social world encountered by the infant: it usually serves as his or her first introduction to personal relations. The significance of the family to primary socialization can be seen in the intensity, scope, and sheer amount of interactions that take place between parents and children. The kind of socialization that occurs in the family, as well as the way that it is conducted, has an enormous impact on the child's sense of self and self-worth, his or her personality characteristics, as well as beliefs, values, norms, and morals. The family is the first reference group for most children. Through the family the child is first introduced to social life and to the rest of society.

Birth into any given family is already a position on the social map. Children, of course, have no influence over the income and social status of their parents. Nevertheless, the status of the family into which a child is born will have a lifelong influence on how others—neighbours, teachers, co-workers—will treat that child. Moreover, the family's race, ethnicity, religion, and even regional location all affect the kinds of life experiences a child is likely to have. Through the family the child acquires not all that is available in that culture but one version of what is available, strongly mediated, selected, and interpreted by the family.

Socialization has been studied by many sociologists, using a wide variety of theoretical perspectives and methods of analysis. I begin with a look at the impact of primary socialization within the family on the individual's sense of self, values, and beliefs. The first example is drawn from a wide body of literature on socialization that uses a positivist approach. In this example, child socialization practices and their outcomes are established by gathering data from a crosscultural sample. The second example uses a data base of American blacks to report on the effects of primary socialization on the racial identity of this group. Again, a positivist approach has been used in gathering and analyzing data.

A CROSSCULTURAL COMPARISON OF PARENTAL SOCIALIZATION TECHNIQUES

There is a large body of research on socialization and parent-child interaction. Much of it focuses on parental values and the ways in which parents transmit those values to their children (see Maccoby 1980; Ellis and Petersen, 1992, 39). One approach to the question of parental values and child socialization practices has been established with the survey work done by Melvin Kohn (1951, 1969, 1977). He found that there was an observable difference between the ways in which members of the working class and members of the middle class socialized their children. In his study, working-class parents tended to stress obedience and conformity from their children, while middle-class parents emphasized self-direction and autonomy. Working-class parents placed more value on manners, neatness, honesty, and obedience. Middle-class parents, by contrast, taught their children to be interested in finding out why things happened, as well as to be considerate, responsible, and self-controlled (Kohn and Schooler 1982).

Working-class parents were less concerned with children's motives than with the consequences of their actions. Valuing conformity much more than middle-class parents, working-class parents punished their children for breaking rules, even if the child did not mean to do wrong. Middle-class parents, on the other hand, often tried to determine if an act was deliberate or not and to reason with the offending child to make him or her understand why the action shouldn't be repeated.

Kohn reasoned that the class-based differences in parenting and socialization styles had to do with the structural differences between working-class and middle-class jobs. Working-class jobs, he pointed out, are usually closely supervised. The work is highly routine, and success is largely defined by conformity. Middle-class jobs, by contrast, stress self-reliance and are more complex and variable. It was Kohn's opinion (1969) that parents determine what characteristics bring them success in their occupations and in turn want to pass those characteristics on to their children.

In a study done on a sample of 122 societies drawn from the Standard Cross-Cultural Sample (SCS), Godfrey Ellis and Larry Petersen (1992) built on Kohn's findings to conceptualize and carry out their own crosscultural comparison of parental values and child socialization techniques. The SCS is a nonrandom sample of 186 world societies at all levels of economic development from all geographic and cultural regions of the world. None of the societies in the sample is geographically proximate, thus the possibility that cultural traits observed in one society are the result of intersocietal contact is greatly reduced (ibid., 44).

Ellis and Petersen examined the relationship between child socialization techniques of corporal punishment and lecturing and parental values of conformity and self-reliance. Their research confirmed their expected finding based on Kohn's earlier work that the more a society values the inculcation of conformity or obedience in children, the more it is typified by the use of coercive socialization including lecturing and corporal punishment (52). In cultures where conformity is stressed, high levels of parental control are expected, and parents rely on the most effective techniques available to exercise that control. By contrast, in cultures where self-reliance and autonomy are valued, parents tend to avoid severe and frequent discipline. Instead, the emphasis is on "indulgent permissiveness with minimal punishment" (52). The use of most control techniques appears to be inconsistent with the concern that children act on the basis of their own decisions (52–53).

Thus, Ellis and Petersen conclude, differences in the ways in which conformity and self-reliance are valued not only affect class-based child-rearing practices (as Kohn found) but also reflect cultural values for adult roles. In cultures where adults are expected to conform to the demands of their superiors, children likewise are expected to be obedient to their parents. But in cultures where adults have more autonomy, self-reliance becomes a dominant cultural value, and children are less controlled by their parents.

The Positivist Approach to Studying Socialization

The Ellis and Petersen study of socialization is based on a positivist approach to the generation of knowledge. We can use this study as an opportunity to discuss the relative strengths and weaknesses of positivism by focusing on the kind of analysis that this approach to the socialization process allows us to generate. The positivist method of inquiry is always made up of two parts—a proposition and some type of research to test that proposition. In their study on socialization techniques, Ellis and Petersen began with the proposition that parents' values strongly affect the socialization techniques they use with their children. They sought to pinpoint a cause and effect (or casual) relationship between observable facts. Ellis and Petersen took Melvin Kohn's conclusions and used them to generate their own proposition that child socialization practices vary not only from class to class but also from culture to culture. They then set out to test this proposition.

Their proposition linked two variables or characteristics: cultural values and socialization techniques. To review, a variable is something that varies from individual to individual, or social group to social group, such as income, political affiliation, social class, gender, religion, or, in this case, socialization technique. They began their research by proposing a relationship between the two variables, socialization techniques and cultural values, suggesting that in some way they are tied together and that when one changes the other does so as well. The variable a researcher wants to explain is called the dependent variable, while the variable or variables used as explanations are called independent variables. The cultural values of conformity, obedience, self-reliance, and autonomy are all treated as independent variables in Ellis and Petersen's study. It is these variables that can be used to predict different types of socialization techniques, or the dependent variables. Ellis and Petersen conclude that the variations found in socialization techniques crossculturally (the dependent variables) may be explained by the independent variables of self-reliance and dependency.

An interpretive approach to secondary socialization experiences

The positivist approach certainly allows us to make statements about expected behaviours among the members of specifically defined populations. But research conducted in this manner lets us say very little about the actual experiences of any given individual or individuals. Although the family clearly exerts enormous influence on the young child and strongly influences his or her values, beliefs, and behaviour, agents of socialization outside the family can play a very significant role in secondary socialization. In 1949, American sociologist Kingsley Davis wrote about the significance of **peer groups** to the child's induction into society. Children are almost always subordinate to adults, Davis argued, but they are able to see the world through the same eyes as their peers (Davis 1949, 217). While adults already know the societal rules and are able to enforce them in themselves and in others, children often make up the rules as they go along. In peer groups children are able to create their own rules and norms and to enforce those rules and norms on one other. Moreover, members of peer groups often teach each other about things that parents consider inappropriate or are unwilling or unable to discuss: drugs, dress, speech (what is "awesome"), as well as romantic love and sex.

THE PARTICIPANT OBSERVER: LEARNING ABOUT ROMANTIC LOVE

Many sociologists have noted that in North America, romantic love is considered an important emotion (Cancian 1987; Swidler 1980; Simon, Eder, and Evans 1992). In a study entitled "The Development of Feeling Norms Underlying Romantic Love Among Adolescent Females" Simon, Eder, and Evans (1992) demonstrate just how important peer groups are in regulating the romantic behaviour of high-school girls (30). To carry out their study, Simon, Eder, and Evans selected a middle school (a school that enrols grades 6, 7, and 8 students) in a medium-sized, Midwestern community in the United States. Students at the school came from a wide range of socio-economic backgrounds and were mostly white. There were approximately 250 students in each grade. Rather than administer a questionnaire to these students, Simon, Eder, and Evans opted to do field work over a period of three years. They used many different methods to collect their data, including participant observation, audio and audiovisual recording, and in-depth group interviews. They observed a total of 10 female peer groups during lunch periods twice a week. The groups were representative of different status levels in the school.

They observed that romantic love was a frequent topic of conversation among members of the peer groups. By Grade 7, most of the girls in the school had become concerned with romance and had begun to form relations with boys (32). At this stage, girls shared normative information with each other about romantic love, but the feelings and behaviour that peer group members considered appropriate were still being negotiated.

Simon, Eder, and Evans argue that adolescent girls obtain from members of their peer groups information about romantic feelings and how to express them. These peer groups therefore serve as a major source of emotional socialization for the girls. In negotiating their social world, adolescents must draw on the norms and beliefs that are available to them in the wider adult culture. But they make those norms and beliefs personal by interpreting them within the context of their everyday concerns and activities (Simon, Eder, and Evans 1992, 31).

In their study, Simon, Eder, and Evans used an interpretive perspective and research methods to observe that, at the same time as adolescent girls are acquiring cultural knowledge about romantic love, they are creating, perpetuating, and modifying their own local set of norms to govern their behaviour: norms that focus on the concerns of their specific peer culture.

Peer group discussion is crucial to the socialization of adolescent girls.

Through their research, Simon, Eder, and Evans were able to demonstrate that peer group members used a number of strategies to communicate feelings and to clarify and negotiate their group norms. One norm that Simon, Eder, and Evans saw emerge was that, while romantic relations were important, they should not be all-consuming in a girl's life (33). By grades 7 and 8 the girls had become critical of friends who made boys their primary interest. How this was achieved is illustrated by an excerpt from a lunch-room conversation that took place between members of a Grade 8 peer group.

The girls were discussing romance novels when the researcher asked them how important romantic love was to them. One of them, Ellen, began by expressing her view that boys were the most important thing in her life. This view ran counter to the emerging group norm. What follows is a fragment of the conversation that was recorded after Ellen made her statement. All names are pseudonyms.

Ellen: Boys [are] the most important thing in my life. That's what I marked
on my value chart today.

Hanna: Yes. I know.

Researcher: Why? Why are boys the most important // thing?

Hanna: Boys, um (pleasure)

Ellen: You can't live without 'em!

Natalie: You can't live // with 'em and you can't live without 'em.

Peg: You can't live with 'em.

Ellen: You can too.

Tricia: That's // a matter of opinion.

Ellen: There is no way—there is no way a girl could live her whole life without a boy.

Tricia: I can.

Ellen: You can live your whole life without a boy?

Tricia: Yeah. // I'm not going to, though.

Peg: Uh uh!

Ellen: (... be isolated) you never kissed one or nothin'.

Natalie: Lesbies can.

Researcher: That's true.

Tricia: You wouldn't know, Natalie. ((laughing))

( ) refers to an uncertain or unclear utterance or speaker

(( )) refers to nonverbal behaviour

// refers to the point at which the next speaker begins talking during someone else's turn

/1/ first interruption; /2/ second interruption

refers to a brief pause

In this segment of the conversation, although the girls disagree about the relative importance of romance with boys, they express their conflict in a playful and nonserious way (Simon, Eder, and Evans 1992, 33). However, sometimes the conflicts were quite serious and the exchanges became heated, especially when lighter disputes were not successfully resolved by some emerging normative consensus. A bit later in the same interview, Ellen repeatedly stated that boys were her central interest, thus violating emerging group norms. She reinforced this statement by flirting with some boys at a nearby table.

> Researcher: What about you, Tricia? How do you feel // about it?
>
> Peg: Ellen, // I'm only teasin', gosh! ((singsong voice))
>
> Tricia: I feel the same way that Peg does. Especially now when we're just about to go into high school, our grades are more important than // boys.
>
> Natalie: See, we may be friends // with them but we're not sluts.
>
> Hanna: Will you repeat that, please? ((angry voice))
>
> Tricia: No, /1/ you /2/ don't qualify.
>
> Natalie: /1/ I know, but we're not sluts.
>
> Ellen: /2/ ( ) Fuck you (you guys)! ((Ellen stomps off, angry and upset)) (1992, 33–34).

In this conversation, some of the girls become increasingly annoyed when what they considered a group norm—that boys should not be their central interest—was repeatedly challenged by Ellen's attitude and behaviour. Simon, Eder, and Evans point out that responses to norm violators are important ways in which peer group members develop and communicate norms and expectations with each other. They conclude that while the conflict was not resolved in this case, the girls did learn through these debates what their friends viewed as appropriate feelings and behaviours with respect to romantic love.

The other prevalent norms concerning romantic love that these researchers discovered included:

- One should have romantic feelings only for someone of the opposite sex.

- One should not have romantic feelings for a boy who is already attached.

- One should have romantic feelings for only one boy at a time.

- One should always be in love.

Simon, Eder, and Evans suggest that while girls obtain normative information about romantic love from their friends, they don't always abide by those norms. Romance is very important because having a boyfriend enhances a girl's popularity with her peers. At this age, popularity is crucial to a girl's self-image. Interestingly, teenage girls seem to feel that they should always be in a romantic relationship with a male as a means of validating their attractiveness and worth to themselves and to their female friends. Finally, Simon, Eder, and Evans note that focusing on emotional socialization among adolescent peers is important for understanding emotions in general. While **affective socialization**—socialization that influences how feelings are expressed—is a fluid, negotiated process, it often leads to conformity to social norms. Not only do adolescents acquire cultural knowledge about romantic love from many sources, including family, peer groups, and the media, they also challenge, refine, and alter this knowledge in the course of their daily lives.

Discussion of the Interpretive Approach

With the work of Simon et al. we have moved a long way from the idea of the complete separation of the individual and society, and of society acting on a resistant or conversely open individual. Instead, what emerges from their work on secondary socialization is a clearer picture of the intricate give-and-take nature of the relationship between all social actors. What is important here is not so much the notion of the individual struggling against society, or being coerced by society, as a picture of the ways that social norms and individual beliefs, values, and practices are all part of a single negotiated process.

We can also see that to uncover and study the intricate negotiations that are constantly going on between individual members of any given social group requires research objectives and methods that have little to do with collecting data on a large scale. In the case of these adolescent girls, Simon et al. were able to uncover information about how the socialization process works by engaging in participant-observation field work. Such research methods are central to an interpretive project. As the recorded excerpts from the girls' noon-hour conversations attest, being a participant-observer requires not only that the researcher gain acceptance from those being studied, but also that he or she pay close attention to what is being said and done by them. The goal of this method of gathering information, on which an interpretive understanding of the social world depends, is to produce as thorough a description as possible of settings, language, tone of voice, posture, gestures, clothing, and arrangement of movable objects, and to learn how all this changes from one interaction to another (Traweek 1988, 9). In conducting their research, Simon et al. sought to develop such an "extensive" description of how their informants developed local, everyday understandings of what constitutes romantic love, and how the ways that they determined those feelings should ideally be expressed.

One underlying assumption that should be examined here is that as long as the observer remains marginal to whatever is being studied, he or she will be potentially able to produce an objective, accurate, and reliable study. As long as the researcher is able to keep his or her distance from the sociocultural assumptions shared by the members of the study group, those assumptions will ultimately catch her attention and form part of what is studied. At the same time, the researcher must develop close and complex relationships with her subjects. She must learn what they find interesting, boring, useful, troubling, exciting, or catastrophic: what they believe to be the right responses for each social situation that arises. And she must learn what the consequences are for giving a response that does not meet with established expectations.

The strengths of using an interpretive approach to generating knowledge about any social group are apparent from the study done by Simon et al. As a result of their work, we have a clearer appreciation of the complexities of how young high-school girls are socialized into knowing about and acting out feelings of romantic love. We can also see how mechanisms of social control work in the process of socialization and how violations of group norms mean risk of public humiliation or even expulsion from the group. But while interpretive studies can tell us a great deal about the process of socialization, they are unable to offer any kind of critical insight into why a particular group is structured the way it is, why it occupies a specific place within the larger social structure, or even what changing the group's rules and expectations would entail.

Interpretive analyses of social processes such as socialization can offer us a fine-tuned picture of how certain aspects of social life work. What they cannot do in and of themselves is question why a particular process, institution, or set of social relations exists in the first place, or what has to be done in order to change them. In the next example, we look at socialization from a critical perspective.

A CRITICAL APPROACH TO STUDYING SOCIALIZATION—*LEARNING TO LABOR*

We have already seen that critical approaches to understanding the social world are not tied to any one method of inquiry. An analysis of any social situation begins to be critical when it attempts to illuminate those aspects of human social interaction that take place outside the conscious control of the actors themselves. Unlike an interpretive approach, a critical approach to social analysis recognizes that while the intention and meaning of social actors are in themselves important and worthy of study, human action is also strongly influenced by structural conditions over which no single social actor has conscious or intentional control.

Critical, positivist, and interpretive approaches all require that a researcher pay strict attention to structural dynamics such as social class, gender, employment, age, and race, along with the life experiences of the social actors who are participants in these historically and culturally specific structures. But unlike either a positivist or interpretive approach, the objective in making a critical analysis, ultimately, is an interest in human emancipation. Paul Willis's (1977) study of the peer-group socialization process of working-class English boys is an excellent example of the ways in which critical inquiry, combining both positivist and interpretive research methods, can explain both individual actions and the larger social context in which these actions occur.

Willis and his co-workers undertook to study the transition from school to work experienced by white, nonacademic working-class boys in an industrial town (Hammerstown) in England. The issue framing the study was the difficulty in explaining why working-class boys settled for the jobs they did, without striving for the jobs of their middle-class counterparts.

Working-class life from home to school to factory floor is often a self-fulfilling prophecy.

In order to conduct the study, Willis used a number of different data-gathering methods including interviews, group discussions, and participant observations made over a period of two years. The use of these methods was dictated by the nature of his interest in cultural issues. For him, the informal culture shared by the working-class teenagers in his study was not merely transferred from adults to passive children. Rather the boys actively participated in creating their own informal culture and in socializing newcomers into its belief systems, values, and rules of conduct (Willis 1977, 4).

Willis carried out one main and five comparative studies. The main one concentrated on a group of 12 teenagers attending a working-class, all-male high school twinned with an all-girls school in the same area. The boys are shown in constant rebellion against the school system and very disdainful of "ear-oles"—the name they gave to their conformist working-class peers. As well, they actively express their disregard for girls, teachers, and middle-class values.

The 12 boys are observed in all school settings—halls, classrooms, lunch—as well as outside of school. In addition, Willis conducted regular group sessions with them and interviews with individual boys, their parents, teachers, and school officials. All interviews were recorded.

In the course of his research, Willis became convinced that together the boys developed and enforced on each other a cultural project of apparent opposition or resistance to the middle-class norms and values that dominated the lives of teachers, school officials, and members of the society at large. In developing their oppositional culture, Willis contends, the boys were trying to go beyond the rules of the school and of society and to defeat the school's main purpose of making students "work." As one of the boys, called "July," told Willis:

> I don't think the school does fucking anything to you....It never has had much effect on anybody. I don't think (after) you've learnt the basics. I mean school, it's fucking four hours a day. But it ain't the teachers who mould you, it's the fucking kids you met. You're only with teachers thirty percent of the time in school, the other fucking two-thirds are just talking, fucking pickin' an argument, messing about (26).

Asked midway through the school term about when he last did some writing, another boy, "Fuzz," responded: "Oh, er, last time was in careers 'cos I writ yes on a piece of paper, that broke me heat." When Willis pressed Fuzz about why it broke his heart, Fuzz responded: "...'cos I was going to try and go through the term without writing anything. 'Cos since we've cum back, I ain't dun nothing" (27).

In interpreting their behaviour, Willis contends that the boys developed a class culture that is distinct from the dominant one, one intended to defeat the formality of that dominant culture through informal modes of interaction. The boys identify themselves by their opposition to learning, to girls, and to ethnic minority groups. In all three cases, they held themselves to be superior.

The local culture that they created for themselves and socialized each other into took them from school to the shop floor. Far from being defeated and passively accepting their lot, these working-class boys tried at every step of the way to assert their own kind of control. They disdained girls and expressed chauvinistic attitudes that were later reflected at work as masculine toughness. They attempted to control the classroom situation by substituting their own timetables for those of the teachers, and in general by controlling their daily routines. This later was mirrored on the shop floor in their attempts to gain control of workspace and of definitions of work processes from authority figures, such as shop-floor managers. Finally, while at school, the boys developed an in-group language and humour that they continued to use at work.

Willis maintains that while they were in school the boys were preparing themselves, systematically, for the kind of work they would do once they got jobs. They disdained vocational counselling and the kind of knowledge teachers tried to give them; instead they developed a socialization process among themselves that prepared them for the jobs they would very shortly hold. In that sense, there is a direct link between their resistance to doing mental work in school and their later resistance to middle-management authority at work. As one of the boys, "Spike," expressed his disdain for "ear-oles":

...it gets me mad to see these kids working in a fucking office. I just dunno how they do it, honestly. I've got freedom, I've got...I can get money, it's hard to explain (104).

Willis concludes that it is the boys themselves and not any formal schooling that carries them from school into specific kinds of jobs within the capitalist economy. Although they take on the lowest-paying, most menial jobs in society, they do it in such a way that it appears to them to be a free choice, a clear expression of their resistance to dominant culture.

In order to understand how this might happen, Willis combines a form of Marxist class analysis with his observations of the boys and how they become socialized to take on working-class jobs. In so doing, he interprets the findings of his research into the social life and culture of working-class boys through the use of a theoretical perspective that focuses on the larger structural dynamics of capitalism. Unlike researchers who work solely within an interpretive perspective, Willis not only wants to understand group dynamics; he also wants to understand why such an unfree condition as working as a labourer could be entered into so freely. He wants to determine why the boys' apparent resistance to dominant middle-class values does not produce any kind of social change but leads instead to their taking on working-class jobs.

On the one hand, Willis observes that the personal world the boys create together and socialize each other into holds out the possibility for social change, in the sense that the counterculture they create challenges the school system and clearly points out their real lack of options in British society. The boys resist the dominant values of the system in which they are forced to take part. They refuse to acknowledge an emphasis on qualifications and resist the school system's demand that they make sacrifices to obtain recognition. They are well aware of their lack of real possibility for upward mobility or for ever having a really satisfying job.

On the other hand, however, he also observes that the boys are never able to do anything more than move into uncreative, highly controlled manual-labour jobs once they leave school, and that they are divided among themselves, as well as from women and from ethnic minorities who share their class position. In securing their own positions, the boys overvalue manual labour, their gender, and their racial origins, and make these badges of distinction from others they consider even lower in the social hierarchy. They align despised effeminate traits with mental work, which they discredit as being passive and "lacking robust masculinity" (150). Willis sought to understand the structural reasons behind why this happens. He turned to Marx's theories of social class to help construct that explanation.

Discussion of the Critical Approach

It is in explaining how and why the working-class boys in his study take on menial jobs that Willis's account exemplifies a critical approach to analyzing socialization. He uses an interpretive approach to capture the intimate world of the boys. But he takes this knowledge much further than do Simon et al., for example, who simply described their subjects' world, their goals, and how the girls socialized each other into certain kinds of behaviour. Willis, by contrast, provides a critical view of the socialization process by linking the personal world of the boys to the larger social and economic order of which they are a part.

His account of peer socialization of working-class schoolboys also raises the issue of **agency** (the ability of the individual to reason and act). Some sociologists write as if the cultural setting in which we are born and socialized so greatly influences our behaviour that we are without any free will or individuality. Willis's work indicates that such a view is fundamentally misguided. He is able to show that the personalities, values, and behaviours of the schoolboys are directly linked to the socialization process, and that the socialization process is also the source of their individuality, their sense of agency, and personal freedom. Willis provides an indication of the extent to which the boys themselves are partly responsible for the creation of the social world they live in.

SUMMARY

In this chapter, I have compared how socialization might be studied from three different theoretical perspectives: positivist, interpretive, and critical. While research conducted using only positivist methods allows us to make statements about expected social behaviours among members of specifically defined populations, it allows us to say very little about individual experiences.

This problem is corrected in the interpretive approach. I have used the example of the role of peer groups among high-school girls in creating local sets of norms to govern behaviour. In a study published in 1992, Simon, Eder, and Evans undertook to find out how a group of high-school girls generated and shared a common understanding of how romantic love should be experienced and expressed. To get this information, they conducted field work in a setting arranged and structured not by the researchers themselves, as would have been the case had they employed positivist methods, but by the community they were studying. As a result of their study, Simon et al. were able to point out that peer-group members use a number of different strategies to clarify and negotiate group norms. Violation of those norms often has painful consequences.

A third perspective examined in this chapter is a critical one, and the work of Paul Willis (1977) on peer group socialization among working-class English boys was used as an example. Willis undertook to study the transition from school to work of 12 working-class boys from Hammersmith. In addition to studying them using interpretive methods, Willis provides a critical analysis of the daily lives of his subjects by using a Marxist perspective on the larger social and economic order of which they are a part.

■ ■ ■
FOR DISCUSSION

1. List five or six settings in which primary socialization might take place and another five or six in which secondary socialization might occur.

2. To what extent does the Simon, Eder, and Evans study conform to your own experiences about high-school peer-group pressure?

3. Develop a critical perspective for Ellis and Petersen's crosscultural comparison of parental values and child socialization techniques.

4. Develop a critical perspective for the Simon, Eder, and Evans study of romance and high-school peer groups.

5. To what extent is the world of working-class teenagers that Willis studies their own making? How is that world structured by larger economic, social, and political forces?

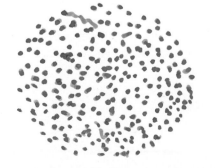

part 4

Sociology is a relatively new discipline. The term "sociology" was first used by Auguste Comte in 1822. Comte sought to create a new science with which to study human social interaction and intended to fashion it after the methods of inquiry current in the natural sciences. In this part, we examine the development of sociology from its roots in the beginnings of the scientific study of nature to its current iterations, including postmodernism and feminism. While many sociologists today continue to emulate the methods and theories of the natural sciences, others seek to go beyond the limitations they see inherent in them.

As with other academic disciplines, the methods and theoretical perspectives that dominate sociology today have been shaped by the social, economic, and political circumstances in which they emerged. But early sociologists were not just affected by the political, economic, and social revolutions that took place during the eighteenth and nineteenth centuries. They also took those major revolutions as their basic subject matter for study.

Early sociologists like Karl Marx, Émile Durkheim, and Max Weber tried to understand the speed and direction of the social changes taking place in Europe. In spite of differences in theoretical perspectives and methods of analysis, each spent his professional life studying and confronting the problems inherent in capitalism and the Industrial Revolution. All three were concerned with the effects of the rapid social transformations that accompanied industrialization.

Karl Marx actively supported the overthrow of capitalism as the only real solution for eliminating the misery of the majority of nineteenth-century Europeans. Marx was both a social theorist and a political activist. He wrote extensively on the subject of capitalism; at the same time, he personally engaged in many political activities that he hoped would help bring about a socialist revolution.

Marx's theoretical position and his activism were strongly opposed by Durkheim and Weber. While they both recognized that there were serious problems with capitalism and capitalist society, Durkheim and Weber both sought to reform society from within rather than by fomenting revolution. They actually feared socialism, and their ideas about what constitutes society and how it should be analyzed have dominated mainstream sociology much more than those of Marx.

Taken together, Marx, Weber, and Durkheim have been responsible for generating many of the often conflicting ideas, concepts, and theoretical frameworks that have inspired the work of several generations of their successors. Today, new approaches to the study of society call into question many of the basic assumptions of the discipline. But in so doing, they create new problems and issues for sociologists and other social scientists. Some of the more recent challenges to "modern" sociology have come from postmodern and feminist theorists. The last two decades have been exhilarating and frustrating times for sociologists, as the foundations of knowledge have been questioned, reworked, and often rejected in favour of more open, tentative, and questioning approaches.

11

THE BEGINNINGS OF THE SCIENTIFIC STUDY OF SOCIETY

CHAPTER OPENING QUESTIONS

- Why did Copernicus and Galileo's discovery that the earth revolves around the sun cause disruption in their societies?

- How did Bacon and Newton, by insisting on the importance of observation and experiment, lay the foundations for Western scientific thinking?

- What did the prevailing world view of Enlightenment thinkers contribute to the origins of the science of society?

- Of what significance were the ideas of progress and evolution in the Enlightenment?

- How does contemporary sociology deal with the legacy of the Enlightenment?

In this chapter, I begin an inquiry into the changes that have taken place in the discipline over the last century, with a specific look at the history of scientific inquiry, which helped the discipline of sociology begin. But in order to understand the influence of science on early sociological inquiry, it is important to understand first the early history and nature of scientific inquiry itself. But why begin a study of sociology, which is a nineteenth- and twentieth-century phenomenon, by turning to feudalism, theology, and the Middle Ages? As Billig (1987, 91) has noted, in order to understand the meaning of something, it is useful to do comparative analysis, especially to compare with an opposing position. Comparative analysis is a good way of examining the current context of the concepts and theoretical perspectives or approaches we all use. If we want to understand the scientific approach to knowledge, for example, we can begin by examining the context in which the approach arose, especially the arguments against which it was posed. Most of the themes of the scientific approach to knowledge production had their origins in opposition to a theological approach.

FEUDALISM AND THE MEDIEVAL CHRISTIAN WORLD VIEW

Most of us have grown up in a modern nation state with its own standing army, national tax system, and unified market economy. As citizens of Western nation states, we take certain rights for granted: the right to vote in elections, to express our ideas, to be free to move from one geographic location to another. Many of us have always lived in a society dominated by an economy where almost everything we need for our daily existence can be bought and sold in the marketplace. Finally, most of us have been raised with the belief that we are free to make almost anything we choose out of our lives and that our choices are limited only by our abilities.

This illumination in the fifteenth-century manuscript Très Riches Heures of Jean, Duke of Berry *is a reflection of the ordered world view of medieval life.*

But this social organization, these ideas about what constitutes a "good life," and the rights and freedoms that we have come to expect are, in fact, very recent. Four hundred years ago, the people of Western Europe lived in a society still dominated by feudalism.

The beginnings of science and the methods of producing knowledge about the social world originated in feudalism and, more important, in the transformation of feudal economies into capitalist ones. Understanding the intellectual and historical roots of science can provide an important vantage point from which to understand critically the theories and methods of inquiry that underpin today's sociological research efforts.

People who lived in the Middle Ages were divided into estates—social classes that were regulated by tradition, custom, and law. Members of the dominating class—the aristocrats—were accorded various forms of power, honour, immunity, and privileges. The majority of people in feudal society were serfs or vassals who were tied to the land and to a life of servitude. As such, most owed rents, tithes, labour-services, and allegiance to the lord of the manor, seigneur, or suzerain. They in turn owed allegiance and military service to a hierarchy of nobles who had the right, or the military force, to claim the land. (In some rare cases, land was held by a female noble.) Ultimate ownership of the land rested with the king. Only a few people resided in towns and made their living as merchants or artisans.

Feudal society was relatively stable. There were few changes in individuals' lives or in the way in which society was organized over a period of several hundred years. Members of one generation lived much the same way as their parents and could expect that their children would live very similar lives to their own. Hardly anyone ever moved more than a few kilometres from their birthplace. Most lived, worked, and died in one small area. They performed the same economic tasks, using the same tools and methods of production as their ancestors. Succeeding generations lived and worked within an established pattern of rights and obligations that was fixed by tradition and by established social hierarchies.

Under feudalism, all intellectual life was controlled by a priestly class. But by the fifteenth century, there were profound changes happening in the way in which medieval theologians viewed the relationship between nature and God. Unlike the ancient Greeks who made a clear distinction between sacred and profane spaces, medieval Christian theologians argued that the "Divine Essence" of God was part of everything and existed everywhere simultaneously. While the Greeks viewed the world as an imperfect imitation of the perfection that they believed existed in the heavens or celestial sphere, nothing in the world of the medieval theologians was viewed as strictly profane, imperfect, or opposed to God. Instead all things that humans perceived through their senses were believed to have a sacred aspect. With the development of a theology that did not make a distinction between sacred and profane space came the notion of a universe that is limitless, unbounded, and infinite.

THE COPERNICAN REVOLUTION

What we now know as modern science began with disputes between medieval thinkers trying to make sense of an infinite and entirely sacred universe. We refer to these beginnings today as the **Copernican Revolution**, named after Nicolas Copernicus (1473–1543), a clerical administrator in the bishopric of his uncle and guardian, Lukas Watzenrode. Watzenrode's bishopric was in an area that at the time was part of Prussia but is today part of northern Poland. Under his uncle's patronage, Copernicus studied medicine and canon law in Italy before taking up his clerical post (Westman 1975).

Of course, it was not just Copernicus who was the driving force behind the founding of what we now call modern cosmology. But it was the rethinking of the relationship between the earth and the heavens and how to go about studying them, begun by Copernicus and those who followed him, that set the foundations of modern science, including the basis for sociology as the science of society.

Ancient cosmology, against which medieval theologians were beginning to develop their own ideas, held that the earth and the heavens constituted two separate worlds and that the earth was immobile and at the centre of the universe. Copernicus challenged this view in *On the Revolutions of the Heavenly Spheres,* published in 1543. He argued that the earth had a rotational motion on its axis and that its orbit was heliocentric, that is, that the earth was in orbit around the sun and not vice versa.

In making this argument, he contested the prevailing view of the separation between terrestrial and celestial space. He also argued that the universe was infinite and without a preferred position or centre. In an infinite space, all points are equidistant from all other points. While the heavens might appear finite to the senses, it is only with the mind that we can begin to grasp their infinity (Galgan 1982).

At the same time that Copernicus was challenging long-held beliefs, other equally profound changes were taking place in feudal Europe. Beginning in the fourteenth and fifteenth centuries, growing economic instability, increased military activities, climatic changes, the invention of the printing press, and new means of transportation (especially by water) laid the groundwork for major changes to feudal social organization.

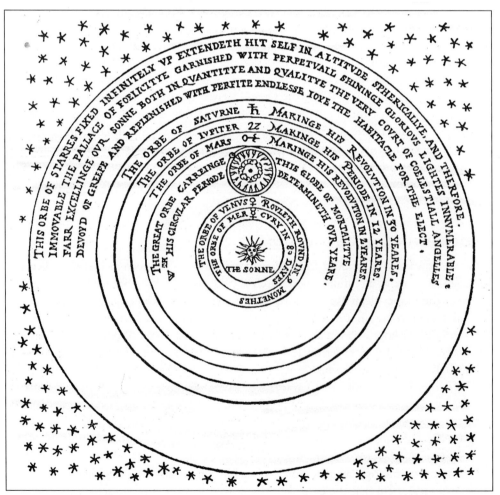

The Copernican universe: the sun at the centre, the moon revolving about the earth, surrounded by an infinite number of stars. Woodcut by Thomas Digges, London, 1576.

The appearance in fifteenth-century Europe of the absolutist state headed by a single monarch who ruled by Divine Right was another important development. With the rise of the absolutist state, the power of one king was increased at the expense of local nobles. Tax collecting and armies began to be centralized under his control. Simultaneously, traders and adventurers were setting out to reach distant lands in order to establish new sources of wealth through trade, conquest, and even enslavement of people living in "newly discovered" territories such as Africa, India, and the New World. The growth of trade, industry, and material wealth in Western Europe resulted in a growing concern with material things. At the same time, education became more secularized, and learning was no longer the sole preserve of the Church. An educated, secular class of doctors, lawyers, and administrators began to emerge. Thus, by the sixteenth and seventeenth centuries, the ideas of the old feudal order were losing credibility, religion had lost its place of supreme authority, and science was being invented. Many thinkers who lived during the late sixteenth and early seventeenth centuries contributed to the invention and elaboration of science and the scientific method of research. In the section that follows, we will consider some of their contributions.

SCIENCE AND MODERNITY

Modern science, for which the Copernican Revolution helped lay the foundations, was well established in Western Europe by the eighteenth century. The appeal of science over other ways of establishing knowledge was its promise to dispel the darkness of myth, superstition, and theology that had previously dominated people's lives. In the seventeenth and eighteenth centuries, thinkers promised that science would be able to liberate people from the barriers that controlled their existence. They claimed that by following the scientific method of discovery they would be able to discover "true knowledge" about the ways that all things work in the universe.

GALILEO AND THE BEGINNINGS OF THE NEW SCIENTIFIC METHOD

The first attempts to make sense of the new Copernican cosmology and to develop a scientific method with which to study it were undertaken by the university professor and astronomer Galileo Galilei (1564–1642). A committed Catholic, he nonetheless confronted the Church's opposition to his ideas. He was a mathematician with an equally strong interest and commitment to observation, measurement, and design. In 1609 he constructed the first astronomical telescope, which he used to discover the large satellites of Jupiter and the stellar configuration of the Milky Way.

In Italy where Galileo lived, the Catholic Church felt threatened by the Protestant Reformation and was trying to resecure its dominant position by looking backward to its basic doctrines. All change was regarded with suspicion and the Church committed itself to supporting what it believed was the clear connection between Aristotelian and Ptolemaic systems of cosmology and Catholic doctrine (Galgan 1982; Westman 1975).

Galileo's attempt to define the new scientific method in a way that might be consistent with the Christian faith created one of the most famous controversies in Western history. He wanted the Church's approval of the new scientific method, which he considered to be a matter of public interest for all of society. In order to obtain the hoped-for approval, he made the distinction between ordinary language and modern scientific discourse.

God, Galileo argued, used ordinary language to make His word understandable to humanity. While this language might produce certainty about humanity's relationship to Him, it could not produce certainty about the physical universe. Just as the Scriptures were invincible in terms of the ethical and religious dimensions of reality, scientific discourse was invincible with regard to physical reality (Galgan 1982). Galileo reasoned that, while God always knows a great deal more than humans do, the knowledge that scientists have of mathematics is the same as a part of God's knowledge of mathematics. Because of this, scientists are able to help raise the rest of humanity out of their ignorance toward further perfection of their knowledge.

This assumption of a public, educative role for scientists led Galileo into much difficulty with Church authorities. He claimed that the distinction between celestial and terrestrial bodies could not be maintained, based on the certainty of mathematics corroborated by empirical observation. By using a telescope, Galileo gathered what he believed to be evidence supporting his mathematical theories. Through his telescope, he observed that the moon had craters and that there were blemishes on the sun. He thus had empirical evidence that the celestial bodies were not perfect, as had been claimed by Aristotle.

But now Galileo faced an even greater challenge: he had to persuade his contemporaries that what could be seen through the telescope was really what was there. To late twentieth-century university and college students, this is hardly an issue that requires reflection: an instrument like a telescope will help rather than hinder us when it comes to observing what is in the sky. But stop and think about what this view really means. It implies that we believe that what the telescope allows us to see actually exists. It requires a leap of faith that we accept what we see through the telescope as real. This leap of faith was Galileo's methodological revolution.

In 1633 Galileo was called to Rome and summoned to the Holy Office. On June 22, he was made to kneel in order to hear his sentence, which condemned him to imprisonment. While still kneeling he was forced to recant his theory that the earth moved around the sun, swearing that he would "neither say nor assert in speaking or writing such things as may bring upon me similar suspicion." Instead of imprisonment, Galileo was confined to his estate and his *Dialogue* was consigned to the Church's list of prohibited publications.

Galileo had limited his vision of the application of scientific methodology to the physical world, the only area where he saw fit to challenge the privileged authority of the Catholic Church. But once the question was posed, once authority, privilege, and common-sense knowledge of the physical universe were challenged, other areas of privilege and authority could not remain untouched. If the hierarchical nature of the universe was successfully challenged, it was only a matter of time before the new scientific method would be used to challenge the inevitability of the social hierarchy on which feudal society depended.

Galileo discusses the scientific method with his students and peers.

RENÉ DESCARTES AND THE NEW UNIVERSE

Like Galileo, the French philosopher René Descartes (1596–1650) was committed to Christianity. However, Descartes made an explicit show of always deferring to the Church in questions of faith (Westfall 1993). After Galileo's condemnation, Descartes altered his work on natural philosophy, which he published under the title *Principles*, to conform to the notion that the earth did not turn on its axis. Descartes sought absolute certainty for his beliefs, and in order to find it he became the first of the new scientific thinkers to describe the philosophical foundations of the scientific method. He saw that the basis of the ancient, classical theories of knowledge was secured in Aristotelian metaphysics. He perceived that, as yet, there was no such metaphysical ground—no ultimate rational foundation—for science. He set out in search of that foundation by questioning the foundations of knowledge (Galgan 1982).

Descartes became convinced that the metaphysical foundation of science he was searching for could be found "within ourselves." In his book *Meditations of First Philosophy*, 1641, he parallels his technique for finding the metaphysical basis of science with the techniques of religious meditation developed by Ignatius Loyola, founder of the Society of Jesus (Jesuits). As Descartes describes it, the technique is one of self-doubt:

training the mind not to take ordinary, everyday understandings of phenomena as definitive. What Descartes searched for were those principles that could unconditionally withstand doubt. He found those principles in the **scientific method**, which he designated as "nothing more or less than pure thought confronting the conditions of its own truth" (Galgan 1982, 66). In identifying those principles, Descartes established the modern metaphysical subject—the *res cogitans* (thinking subject)—on a belief in the existence of a truthful God.

Having convinced himself through the application of the scientific method of the veracity of the statements "I am" and "God exists," Descartes felt free to assert that the "possibility of attaining knowledge of innumerable other propositions whose truth is certain" was also secured (Galgan 1982, 64). Mathematics, he argued, is the most obvious example of this.

But how do we get from pure thought to the actual, physical world? For Descartes, the scientific method could establish directly only the existence of a thinking being. It could, however, offer indirect support to the claim that science deals with objects that have an existence independent of the scientist's thought. Because a truthful God exists, Descartes reasoned, He would not allow the scientist to be deceived. Thus the correlation between pure thought and existing physical nature is indirectly guaranteed by the existence of a truthful God (Ashworth 1989).

Descartes viewed "man" as a finite being characterized by "an infinite aspiration that is embodied in scientific method." While "man" can never know everything in the universe, he can know the whole of what he examines via the scientific method. By using the scientific method, which Descartes saw as a set of "certain and easy rules," he was convinced that anyone can arrive at perfect knowledge of everything that is not beyond his understanding. The only limit to the scientific method's revelation about the universe is each individual's imagination, emotions, and attention. Thus while scientific reason is infallible and incapable of error, human beings are not.

This desire to improve the lot of humanity and to allow for its full enjoyment of a bountiful nature would serve as a focal point for thinkers and social activists for centuries to come. It was the promise of control over nature and daily life that gave the scientific method of inquiry such a powerful attraction. By using the scientific method, people would be able to become "the masters and possessors of nature."

FRANCIS BACON AND SCIENTIFIC INDUCTION

Some of the earliest formative statements of the benefits to humanity of rational, scientific inquiry were made by the English monk Francis Bacon (1561–1627). While both Bacon and Descartes were committed to the practice of science and to the development of the scientific method, there is an important distinction between the two. Descartes believed that truth could be established in the mind, but Bacon wished to establish the certainty of what was known on the basis of experimental verification.

True knowledge, as Descartes envisaged it, could be achieved by beginning with clear, distinct, doubt-free ideas and by then linking these together using the method of proof and inference (Shotter 1993, 7). Bacon retained Descartes's concept of reason but rejected his start-

English philosopher and statesman Francis Bacon was among the first proponents of the scientific method: "True knowledge" could be obtained only through observation and experiment, untainted by historical and cultural factors.

ing point. He believed that the place to begin inquiry was not with abstract ideas but with concrete, sense-based observations and experience. Bacon began his scientific inquiries by rejecting the authority of tradition as the means of determining truth. It was his opinion that "men have been kept back, as by a kind of enchantment, from progress in the sciences by reverence for antiquity, by the authority of men accounted great in philosophy, and then by general consent." He complained that those devoted to traditional ideas and practices "tend to nothing less than a wicked effort to curtail human power over nature and to produce a deliberate and artificial despair. This despair in its turn confounds the promptings of hope, cuts the springs and sinews of industry, and makes men unwilling to put anything to the hazard of trial" (cited in Hampson 1982, 36).

Human thought, in Bacon's view, must be purged of all uncertainty based on historical and cultural factors such as myths, religion, and superstition. In this way, eternal truths can be separated from historical and cultural prejudices. Pure knowledge can be obtained only through results based on observation and experiment, as opposed to impure knowledge, which is shaped and warped by historical and cultural factors (Hekman 1986). Bacon was among the first to use the method of experiment and induction, which he argued could provide humanity with an infallible means of distinguishing between what was true and what was false. It is ironic that Bacon himself died as a result of his convictions about scientific experiments. In an effort to demonstrate that cold preserves meat, he became ill after spending time outdoors collecting snow to stuff the cavity of a chicken. He took to his bed, which he decided should be in a dark, damp place in order to cure his illness. In this case Bacon had incorrectly induced what would cure him. Exposed to the cold and damp, he contracted pneumonia and died.

SIR ISAAC NEWTON AND THE SCIENTIFIC METHOD OF INQUIRY

Bacon's ideas concerning experiment and empirical observations were elaborated on by the English Protestant physicist Sir Isaac Newton (1642–1727). Newton wrote in his *Principia* that "in experimental philosophy we are to look upon propositions inferred by general induction from phenomena as accurate or very nearly true, notwithstanding any contrary hypotheses that may be imagined, till such time as other phenomena occur by which they may either be made more accurate, or liable to exceptions."

Newton's law of gravity, which is a simple, elegant explanation of every kind of movement on the earth and in the heavens, appeared as a triumphant example of the possibilities of this new learning. His work in physics seemed to prove that observation and experiment could actually reveal the inner workings of nature. Like Descartes and Bacon, he consciously formulated his theories of knowledge not in opposition to but in support of the existence of a Christian God who in his mind was solely responsible for the creation of the universe.

Nature, for Newton, was the revelation of God, in much the same way as the Bible was also God's revelation (Westfall 1993). As such, nature could be studied. Thus nature ceased to be unintelligible, God became a "mathematician whose calculations were accessible to man's intelligence," and every aspect of the universe was susceptible to being understood and mastered.

Like Descartes, Newton deduced the basic principles on which his scientific method was to be founded. He divided the world into active and passive principles. In this world, nature was an inactive, passive principle, devoid of vitality in and of itself. Nature, however, was permeated by the life of God, who, as the active principle, provided vitality to the otherwise senseless, inert matter that constituted nature. Thus for Newton, matter possessed active qualities only through God's energy. Unlike Descartes, however, Newton rejected the ability of mathematical deduction alone to supply proof that some scientific conclusion was indeed factual. Instead, he argued that whatever might be deduced also had to be demonstrated by experiments (Galgan 1982, 77). The result of the experiment guaranteed that what had been deduced mathematically was factual. As Newton wrote:

> The theory which I propounded was evinced to me, not by inferring "Tis thus because not otherwise," that is, not by deducing it only from a confutation of contrary suppositions, but by deriving it from experiments, concluding positively and directly.

With Descartes the metaphysical foundations of modern science had been put in place; with Bacon and Newton, the experimental basis of scientific research and knowledge had been established. After this the questioning shifted from how the universe could be known by humanity to what the limits of human knowledge might be (Galgan 1982, 95). It was a shift from metaphysics to epistemology; from an attempt to lay the foundations for modern science to the question of how we know what we know. That shift took place during the period we call the Enlightenment.

THE ENLIGHTENMENT: FROM FEUDALISM TO CAPITALISM

During the period from the seventeenth century until well into the late eighteenth century, a number of significant changes took place in the ways that European and North American societies were organized. Those changes included:

1. The replacement in Western Europe and North America of the ultimate authority of the Church with science, reason, and social laws devised "by the people, and for the people."

2. The replacement of social systems based on hierarchical gradations of rank and privilege with ones based on the equality of each citizen before the law.

3. The replacement of political systems based on the personal allegiances of serfs to lords with ones based on the impersonal allegiance of each "equal" citizen to an abstract nation state.

In feudal society, an individual was born, lived, and died within a prescribed set of social relationships. He or she lived and worked within an established pattern of rights and duties, fixed by existing hierarchies, that gave honour and power to one group—the aristocracy—and confined the others—serfs, peasants, servants—to a life of bound service. But with the rise of capitalism and its attendant class system based on ownership or nonownership of property, where the majority of the population worked for wages, the traditional arrangements of feudal society were progressively undermined. Instead of a society dominated by rural landowners and their serfs and peasants, urban life, nation states, and ever-expanding systems of communication, exchange, and technological developments were being established.

The transition from feudal to capitalist society in Western Europe and the establishment of market-based, capitalist economies gave many thinkers reason to hope for the future liberation of all humanity from traditional religious systems of thought and attendant social constraints. Thus the dominant theme in the work of many eighteenth-century theorists was the release of the individual from the traditional ties that had bound him or her—ties that were at once economic, social, emotional, intellectual, and religious. A new form of authority was to be sought in a historical experience, with an emphasis on people's ability to find within themselves the means to be autonomous, self-willed, and independent citizens of a nation state.

While science first emerged as a way of generating knowledge about the natural world, by the early eighteenth century, it was apparent to some thinkers that the methods of science and its goals could equally well be applied to the study of humanity. The Catholic Church's influence was on the decline: in its place appeared a growing interest in secular reform and a willingness to take risks to bring it about. Thus, in the late seventeenth and early eighteenth centuries, many social thinkers turned their attention to the scientific study of humanity. It is to this period, the Enlightenment, with its recognition that humanity could be taken as a proper object of study, that we can trace the next important step in the establishment of the discipline of sociology.

THE DISCOVERY OF THE SOCIAL NATURE OF HUMAN EXISTENCE

Today most philosophers occupy official posts in universities and have to submit to lengthy training to obtain doctoral degrees. By contrast, the philosophers of the Enlightenment had few such formal qualifications. There were a diverse collection of independently educated lay people who were bound together in their determination to gain control of intellectual life from the priestly class that had dominated during the Middle Ages (Shotter 1993, 9).

Most Enlightenment thinkers held in common two basic tenets, which they applied to all social life:

1. Social laws exist in the same way that laws of nature exist, and they can be discovered using the same scientific methods used to disclose natural laws.

2. Human history is one of progress toward the scientific enlightenment of humanity and away from social oppression and the tyranny of religion and superstition. Human history, moreover, is the result of the progressive unfolding of human nature.

In addition to these tenets, Enlightenment thinkers also shared two other views:

1. Societies should be studied in relation to one another as well as on their own merits. (This position is called **cultural relativism**.)

2. Social reform is the ultimate objective of the scientific study of society.

During the Enlightenment, many thinkers sought to develop a concept of "society" and to interpret the history of Western society in relation to the history of other forms of social organization (Aron 1965). Enlightenment thinkers were acutely aware of the social nature of human existence. They believed that people were naturally social, and that societies were the "natural state" in which all of humanity existed. They reasoned that if science could bring about new ways of understanding and controlling the forces of nature, it could be equally helpful in illuminating the basic mechanisms of human social life and in liberating humanity from irrationality. This highly desirable transformation in human social life could be brought about by scientific research, which would establish the scientific principles upon which society should be founded. Once the natural laws that governed the world had been discovered using the scientific method of inquiry, society could be properly aligned with those laws.

History as Progress

One of the objectives of Enlightenment thinkers was to provide a comprehensive intellectual system of human existence and development with which to contest traditional, medieval Catholic and even Reformation Protestant world views. To do so, they had to devise a plausible story of humanity's past, present, and future to replace the religious belief in original sin, fall from grace, an afterlife in heaven, and hell or purgatory commensurate with the deeds of one's lifetime on earth.

Enlightenment thinkers were able to transform their anti-Christian polemic into a positive platform from which to redefine nature and thus human nature. What they settled on was the idea that a common human nature existed, found in all people and based on shared basic human feelings. The search for what might be defined as a common human essence began with this idea.

Enlightenment thinkers in both Europe and in North America were committed to humanity as a whole and considered themselves emancipated citizens of the world. They viewed the world in the fresh light of Enlightenment thought, which, they believed, could make everything visible and intelligible to an inquiring human mind. They also believed that human nature was limitless in its perfectibility. With this idea they introduced the notion of progressive change—human societies evolving over time toward ever-greater perfection.

As part of developing a new "story" for humanity, many early sociological thinkers focused their efforts on discovering the laws of evolution. As a result, a variety of different **stage theories** were proposed, all with the intent of describing the evolution of human societies on their route toward increasing complexity and development. Evolutionism is really the oldest part of sociology, and it dominated sociological thinking throughout the nineteenth century and well into the twentieth. While there have been many different theorists of social evolution, they all focused on two common elements:

1. *Progress.* Theorists of social evolution all believed that every human society undergoes progressive or positive change over long periods of time.

2. *Stages.* As each society changes, it passes through a series of stages that follow in orderly, logical progression. Disagreements exist, however, over whether a society can skip one or more stages and over whether alternative stages are possible.

Social evolutionary theories fell out of favour in the early twentieth century but made something of a comeback in the 1960s and 1970s, especially within sociobiology. While they have largely been discredited, the practice of considering human history and behaviour in terms of social relations and social life, as well as concerns about emancipating humanity from all oppression, continues to underlie much of contemporary sociological inquiry.

In what follows, I present some of the specific ideas, theories, and proposals of a number of key Enlightenment thinkers whose work contributed to the founding of the science of society. While we might be tempted to view the background history of ideas leading up to the establishment of contemporary sociology as steps toward the "correct version" of understanding what we do today, I urge you to reconsider. As with the medieval theologians, eighteenth-century Enlightenment philosophers developed their ideas within specific social, economic, and historical contexts. Their beliefs, world views, and ways of interpreting events and phenomena were strongly influenced by those contexts.

The same considerations apply today, of course. Contemporary views of knowledge and truth are equally influenced by the objectives, values, beliefs, and world views that prevail in our society. While this does not mean that change is impossible, or that every thought we have is always culturally predetermined, it does mean that we need to be mindful of the context in which ideas emerge and are used. Keep this caution in mind as you examine some of the history of the discipline's development.

GIAMBATTISTA VICO

The earliest version of stage theory in human progress was developed by Italian theorist Giambattista Vico (1668–1744) in his *Scienza Nuova* published in 1725 and revised in 1730. It was Vico's conviction that there was an "ideal eternal history" that all nations

227

followed through "rise, progress, maturity, decline and fall." This eternal history was divided into several stages—the divine or religious, the heroic or mythical, and the civil, scientific, reasonable, or adult. While this scheme is cyclical, it is also progressive: the beginnings of humanity were thought by Vico to have been "small, crude and quite obscure," while the present was considered "enlightened, cultivated and magnificent." Vico believed that because European nations were Christian, they were more civilized than earlier barbarian ones at a similar stage of their cycle. Vico's insights have been especially important for contemporary sociologists who use interpretive or hermeneutic approaches to understanding social life.

Table-talk by Voltaire (upraised arm) and his friends, the Abbé Maury, Father Adam, Condorcet, Diderot, La Harpe, and d'Alembert. From an eighteenth-century engraving. In such a privileged setting, discussion of reason seemed sensible and realistic.

CONDORCET

In *Sketch for a Historical Picture of the Progress of the Human Mind* (1795), Marie Jean Antoine Nicolas de Caritat, Marquis de Condorcet (1743–1794) maintained that human progress included the domination of the passions by reason and the reorganization of society on a rational basis for continuous growth. Along with Vico, Condorcet was firmly convinced that natural laws, including the law of human progress, governed the world. The ultimate result of establishing the law of human progress, he argued, would be equality among all people in achievement, wealth, education, and social status. Freedom for all would naturally follow from this equality, and he believed that the French Revolution would further these ends.

In developing his model of human progress, Condorcet argued that humanity had passed through 10 different stages:

1. a primitive, tribal stage characterized by the "hunting and fishing horde";

2. a pastoral stage;

3. a settled agriculture stage, which included a class system and a population vulnerable to domination by conquerors;

4. the Greece stage, which culminated in the division of the sciences;

5. the rise of Christianity and concomitant decline of science;

6. the early Middle Ages and Crusades, the further decay of science, but end of slavery in Europe;

7. the late Middle Ages and the slow revival of science, including the invention of the printing press;

8. the fall of Constantinople and the discovery of the New World;

9. Descartes to the French Revolution, the founding of the French Republic;

10. the future.

Condorcet was concerned with writing a new kind of history, not a history of "a few individuals" but a history based on observation about "that which really constitutes the human race" (Condorcet 1955, 170). He believed that all of human history led up to the emergence of the French people "as the supreme product to date of the progressive principle."

Condorcet was convinced that there were certain factors, specific to each stage of development, that had held civilization back. In the primitive stage, for example, progress was slow because everyone's time was devoted to finding food. In later stages, it was a priesthood or a corrupt government that held civilizations back. But he felt that changes, including the development of agriculture, private property, exchange, industry, and the division of labour, all made possible the appearance of scientists and philosophers, the growth of population, and the invention of writing. He was also convinced that all this would soon lead to the creation of a new scientific language. This new language, in turn, would lead to more and more systematic rather than accidental advances, and the benefits of these advances would eventually spread to the "moral" and "social" sciences.

Condorcet felt that new scientific techniques, such as the calculus of probability, would be applied to politics and decision making and that advances in science would also lead to the development of an entirely new set of moral and mental attitudes on the part of the French population. He envisaged a near future where improvements in medicine, food, and housing would lead to the establishment of a healthier way of life in which human physical powers would be developed "by exercise" instead of being ruined "by excess." He identified misery and excessive wealth as "the two most virulent causes of deterioration," and he envisaged a future in which these would be eliminated, thereby extending human lives and ensuring better health (Condorcot 1955, 199).

Condorcet's interests in eliminating misery and improving the lives of everyone continues to form an important part of the rationale behind the work of many critical sociologists. While his ideas about progress and stages of human development have proved to be problematic, his commitment to bettering the lot of the majority endures.

The Enlightenment and Cultural Relativism

During this period, optimism about the destiny of humanity reached a high point. While it began with the concept that progress was possible in science and technology, many were convinced that progress in other areas, particularly economics, social organization, civilization, culture, and even human nature and biological makeup was inevitable. Although the term "sociology" was not yet used, many of the Enlightenment thinkers were nonetheless keen students of the study of society. A large part of the interest in applying scientific principles to the study of human societies was stimulated by European explorers who brought back stories, drawings, and descriptions of exotic peoples whom they had encountered as a result of trade, colonization, and attempts at conversion.

Confronted with the astonishing variety of human social life, Enlightenment theorists tried to explain the similarities and differences between their own society and the newly "discovered" ones. Most important, many among them understood the differences between their own and other societies to be the result not of individual or racial differences but of socially induced, cultural differences.

Those who wrote about non-Western societies used the growing body of travel literature, reports, diaries, and letters of missionaries, colonizers, and administrators as their major source of information to support a cultural relativist position, which maintained that each human society, while affected by universal laws, also had to be considered on its own merits. Drawing from a wide variety of human societies and cultures, they were able to support cultural relativism by demonstrating the astonishing and complex range of possible beliefs, practices, customs, institutions, and behaviours existing in human societies.

One example of cultural relativism can be found in the work of John Locke. In his *Essay Concerning Human Understanding*, 1690, Locke used evidence from

230

An idealized representation of Swedish colonists trading with the Delaware Indians.

non-European societies to argue that differences among humans resulted not from "blood," but from cultural and environmental differences.

JOHN LOCKE

Locke begins his *Essay* (1690) by arguing against Descartes's notion of innate, pre-existing ideas in the human mind. Instead, he suggested that all our complex ideas are the results of many simple impressions being written on the empty mind by the outside world. Knowledge, Locke maintained, is gained by individuals, via their efforts, abilities, and opportunities. He used the analogy of the mind being "white paper, void of all characters," a *tabula rasa*. Marks or knowledge are made on this paper only through experience.

It was Locke's opinion that however we choose to classify things, the resulting classification system is always the outcome of social conventions that are imposed by human actors. The aim of classification is convenience of communication. Abstract ideas that allow classification are constructs of the human mind, the results of cultural and environmental differences, and therefore are neither fixed nor rigid. In place of Descartes's certainty, Locke introduced the notion of "probability," meaning the likelihood that something is true. Probability, he argued, is content with arguments or proofs that "persuade us to receive it as true, without certain knowledge that it is so." Experience serves as the ultimate measure of truth. Anchored in experience, the behaviour of the individual can be studied because the human mind develops from infancy to adulthood in the context of testable and culturally specific experiences (Galgan 1982, 107).

With John Locke, the study of the relationship between the individual and society received another important boost. His insistence on the social nature of human behaviour and his attempts to understand the relationship between the individual and a particular society continue to be a primary objective for many sociologists.

MONTESQUIEU

Probably the best example of the use of cultural relativism in Enlightenment social thought can be found in the works of Charles de Secondat, Baron de la Brède et de Montesquieu (1689–1755). Montesquieu was a significant figure of the French Enlightenment, and his social theories are laid out in *The Spirit of Laws*, 1748.

In this book, he reasons that there are certain fundamental laws of nature that are common to all humans and that explain social and historical behaviour. What differs, from society to society, is the way these laws are expressed. They are shaped, Montesquieu contends, according to circumstances, including geography, climate, customs, and religion. The task of the social scientist is to discover both what these laws are and their appropriate application in different situations. For example, Montesquieu held that political and civil laws of a given society bore a marked relation to "the degree of liberty which the constitution will bear; to the religion of the inhabitants, to their inclinations, riches, numbers, commerce, manner, and customs" ([1748] 1989, 108, 169).

231

REFORM AND THE (PASSIONATE) STUDY OF SOCIETY

The study of society was invented in the eighteenth century as a science designed "to substitute reliable information and rational theory for guessing and metaphysics, and to use the newly won knowledge in behalf of man," according to historian Peter Gay (1966). The phrase "and to use the newly won knowledge in behalf of man" is central to the kind of "protosociology" that the Enlightenment thinkers developed. While it seems like a contradiction to many of us who are convinced that there is a direct connection between science and objectivity, Enlightenment thinkers accepted the necessity of a link between science, on the one hand, and reformist or revolutionary intentions on the other.

These thinkers, who were among other things cultural critics, religious sceptics, and political reformers, were in agreement, in spite of their many differences, in their pursuit of freedom of all sorts: freedom from arbitrary power, freedom of speech, of trade, of aesthetic response, freedom of all individuals to realize their capacities. In short, they were united in their desire for the freedom to pursue their own way in the world (ibid.). Moreover, they were concerned with what might be called "moral philosophy," the reformation of society for the benefit of humankind. These concerns raised a number of new questions about human nature, society, and the relationship between the two, as well as questions about religion, the state, authority, the origins of law, and the nature of social change. The questions they asked struck at the heart of feudal society—especially at the religious, political, and economic bases on which it rested.

John Locke is a good example of the commitment many Enlightenment thinkers had to change. A friend of Sir Isaac Newton, he was involved in the movement to end the Divine Right of Kings in England, which culminated in the overthrow of James II. His book *Treatise on Civil Government,* 1690, provided a theoretical justification for the view that the relations between the monarch and the people were contractual and as such were limited and revocable.

It is important to note that the intellectual roots of all social sciences, including sociology, are not to be found exclusively in what we think of today as objective and detached scientific research. The philosophers of the Enlightenment were not at all indifferent to their project of spreading "enlightenment" to others, and thus of improving the lot of all humanity. Many of them shared the belief that it would take much effort to secure the freedom of humanity.

French philosopher and reformer Condorcet perhaps best expressed this new vision of the infinite perfectibility of humanity and the companion belief in the upward development of human nature when he wrote: "Our hopes for the future condition of the human race can be subsumed under three important heads: the abolition of inequality between nations, the progress of equality within each nation, and the true perfection of mankind" (cited in Galgan 1982, 177).

A belief in the indefinite perfectibility of humanity was possible, Condorcet maintained, because by the end of the eighteenth century, a few thinkers had discovered "how to learn nature's secrets, and therefore how to be happy." Because there were no limits in nature to the progress that humanity could make, it naturally followed that humanity would one day obtain perfect happiness. What had once been only a promise of a perfected life after death in the heavenly City of God was now seen as obtainable on earth as part of the regeneration of society (Becker, 49). In praise of these possibilities Voltaire wrote:

> I shall not be a witness to this fine revolution but I shall die with the three theological verities which are my consolation: the faith which I have in human reason which is beginning to develop in the world; the hope that ministers in their boldness and wisdom will at length destroy customs which are as ridiculous as they are dangerous; the charity which makes me grieve for my neighbour, complain of his bonds, and long for his deliverance (cited in Galgan 1982, 179).

These are some of the dispossessed whom Voltaire had no intention of enlightening.

ENLIGHTENMENT IDEALS AND SOCIAL REALITY

Many Enlightenment thinkers called for the total transformation of the consciousness of all members of society, but it was really only the consciousness of the members of the nobility, the bourgeoisie, and the intellectuals that was considered important enough to be changed. While these people read and adopted the ideals of Enlightenment writers, peasants, workers, and colonized peoples inhabited a very different world. Many thinkers, drawn from the aristocracy and the upper bourgeoisie, seemed to like the ideal of equality. But when it came to actually putting it into practice, either at home or in their colonies, it was an entirely different matter.

Voltaire (1694–1778), one of the best-known and most influential Enlightenment thinkers, expressed his whole-hearted commitment to the idea of equality. Yet he also wrote disparagingly about the capacity of certain kinds of people to be enlightened. "It is not the worker we must instruct," he wrote, "it is the *bon bourgeois* of the townsmen. We have never pretended to enlighten shoemakers and servant girls, that is the portion of the apostles" (Galgan 1982, 182).

Although Enlightenment thinkers wrote about "universal laws" and about humanity as a whole, it is clear that they had a select group in mind. In the end, their audience was bourgeois or aristocratic European males. In today's terms, Enlightenment thinkers

233

were, for the most part, racist, sexist, and classist. They argued for radical social reform from a position of privilege that viewed reform in terms of the benefits that might come to those most like themselves.

When it was a question of abolishing slavery, for example, as was the case in the French colony of San Domingo (today's Haiti) in the late 1700s, few bourgeois or aristocratics could be found among the ranks of the supporters. There was simply too much at stake in terms of income to allow humanist ideals to interfere with the possibility of profits from slave labour.

	NAME	KEY WORK	IDEAS	LINK TO SOCIOLOGY
TABLE 11-1	Nicolas Copernicus	*On the Revolutions of the Heavenly Spheres,* 1543	Contested prevailing view of separation of terrestrial and celestial space Argued that universe was infinite, without a centre	Rethinking of the relationship between the earth and heavens set foundations of modern science
	Galileo Galilei	*Dialogue Concerning the Two Chief World Systems,* 1632	First attempt to develop a scientific method with which to study the new Copernican cosmology Assumed a public, educative role for scientists	Challenged the Church's view of the hierarchical nature of the universe Inadvertently set the groundwork for the scientific method that would challenge the inevitability of the social hierarchy on which feudal society and the Church's authority rested
	René Descartes	*Meditations of First Philosophy,* 1641	Defined the scientific method as "pure thought confronting the conditions of its own truth" Use of the scientific method would result in humankind becoming masters of nature	Method of establishing the truth solely in the mind via pure thought was replaced by the notion of experimental verification

TABLE 11-1 (continued)

NAME	KEY WORK	IDEAS	LINK TO SOCIOLOGY
Francis Bacon	*Novum Organum,* 1620	Replaced Descartes's notion of beginning scientific inquiry with abstract ideas with concrete, sense-based observations and experience Among the first to use the method of experiment and induction	Bacon's scientific method of experiment and induction continues to influence much of sociological research today
Sir Isaac Newton	*Principia,* 1687	Elaborated on Bacon's ideas concerning experiment and empirical observation	Along with Bacon, helped to establish the experimental basis of scientific research and knowledge
John Locke	*Essay Concerning Human Understanding,* 1690	Used evidence from non-European societies to argue that differences among humans were the result of cultural and environmental differences	Notion that cultural and environmental differences rather than biological ones cause differences among humans is still accepted by contemporary sociologists
Giambattista Vico	*Scienza Nuova,* 1725	All of human history is divided into progressive stages Each nation follows a single, ideal path of development through each stage, which includes rise, progress, maturity, decline, and fall	Stage theories are no longer popular among contemporary sociologists although they played a significant role in the development of the discipline Vico's notion that human behaviour is not the result of chance or human nature continues to inform sociology

NAME	KEY WORK	IDEAS	LINK TO SOCIOLOGY
Montesquieu	*Spirit of Laws,* 1748	There are fundamental laws of nature common to all humans that explain social behaviour These laws are expressed differently from society to society	Along with Vico, one of the first social scientists to try to explain human behaviour on the basis of social life
Condorcet	*Sketch for a Historical Picture of the Progress of the Human Mind,* 1795	Argued that all humanity passes through 10 stages, including primitive, pastoral, settled agriculture, Greece, Christianity, early Middle Ages, discovery of the new world, the founding of the French Republic, the future Believed that all of human history led up to the emergence of the French people as the highest expression of human development to date	Although his theories of stages are no longer given credence, Condorcet's interest in eliminating misery and improving human lives continues to inform the work of many sociologists today

TABLE 11-1 (continued)

CONTEMPORARY SOCIOLOGY AND THE LEGACY OF THE ENLIGHTENMENT

A large part of the task of contemporary sociology has been dealing with the Enlightenment legacy. That legacy includes an apparently contradictory call for the emancipation of *all* humanity with the implicit understanding that only a part of humanity is really worthy of enlightenment. Left out of the utopian vision of these thinkers were women, workers, the poor, the uneducated, the non-European. Sociologists today continue to struggle to come to terms with the implications of the exclusion of so many.

A second inheritance from the Enlightenment, one that forms a major theme today not only in sociology but in the social sciences in general, concerns the role of science, and in particular empiricism, in providing knowledge about human behaviour and social organization. On the one hand, Enlightenment thinkers seized upon empiricism and the scientific method as a route to salvation. Having abandoned religion, they turned to science as the sure means by which humanity (at least that part of humanity that counted) could be set on the road to rational organization and escape misery and domination. On the other hand, what eighteenth-century Enlightenment thinkers meant by science and the use to which it should be put was different from the ideas dominating the social sciences in the nineteenth and twentieth centuries. The question of what role science should play in sociology, especially whether we can ever be expected to generate objective knowledge, continues to be a central concern in the discipline. After many years of pursuing objective, scientific knowledge and "social laws" applicable to all societies at all times, sociologists have come once again to consider the historically and culturally specific nature of social life. Moreover, many now regard the study of society not in terms of the search for absolute, universal truths achieved by objective scientific methods, but in terms of critical understandings constructed on the basis of moral, ethical, and culturally contingent considerations.

A third factor, the belief that social change is not only possible but desirable and even inevitable, is also one of the legacies of the Enlightenment. Some sociologists have embraced this notion of change, while others have acted strongly against it. It is with this notion of unparalleled development and progress that an interesting split exists between the "progressive" and the "conservative" thinkers of the eighteenth and nineteenth centuries. The progressive thinkers favoured infinite advance, while the conservatives, sensing a plateau was about to be reached, argued that beyond a certain point no improvements would be possible.

Sociology, as a separate discipline, was founded as part of the reaction to the ideas promoted by Enlightenment thinkers. Many of the earliest sociologists, appalled by what they saw as the decline in social organization and tradition after the French Revolution, began to harken back to the "good old days" when life was more regulated and everyone knew his or her place. Although many of the influences that continue to work within sociology today rest on the Enlightenment call for change and progress, the earliest sociologists reacted to the change they saw taking place around them with a nostalgic look backward to happier and less alienated times.

■ ■ ■

SUMMARY

Enlightenment thought is central to the study of the discipline of sociology for several reasons. First, it was during this time that social thinkers turned to the scientific study of human society in order to discover ways of making society more rational and egalitarian. Science, as we have seen, had quickly eclipsed all other means of generating knowledge about the world and humanity's place in it. With scientific inquiry, rational intelligence could at last conquer the "treadmill of human existence."

But this emancipatory project was never a straightforward one, nor did it include all of humanity. Enlightenment thinkers were selective about whom to enlighten. Thus, while they celebrated what were to become the basic tenets of modern individualism, including personal liberty, freedom of individuals to pursue their own interests, and absence of authoritarian constraints, these rights and freedoms were reserved for Western, white aristocratic or bourgeois males.

Finally, we discussed how Enlightenment thinkers believed that science would help to facilitate the social changes they believed would advance the cause of human liberation. At the core of their thought was the view that all (white male) humans were rational beings, capable of creating a free and just society (Hearn 1985, 32). They therefore supported the French and Industrial revolutions for contributing to the abolition of irrational society and the introduction of a new one based on reason, freedom, and progress. They were ready to accept science and scientific inquiry as the means of generating knowledge about the social world but were clear about their political and moral objectives in using science.

■ ■ ■

DISCUSSION QUESTIONS

1. Discuss how comparative argumentation might be a useful way of examining the current concepts, theories, and methods of inquiry used in sociology.

2. In what ways was the rise of science and scientific methods of inquiry tied to social changes occurring in Western Europe from the fifteenth century onward?

3. Must the scientific study of society be tied to objectivity?

SOCIOLOGY AND THE NINETEENTH-CENTURY REACTION TO THE ENLIGHTENMENT

CHAPTER OPENING QUESTIONS

- What social conditions precipitated the development of the discipline of sociology?

- What contributions did Émile Durkheim, Karl Marx, and Max Weber each make to establishing sociology as a "human science"?

- In what ways has the work of Durkheim, Marx, and Weber influenced their successors?

In this chapter I will explore the work of the first sociologists of the nineteenth and early twentieth centuries whose ideas, theories, and work are often thought of as constituting classical sociology. The most important among these thinkers are Karl Marx, Émile Durkheim, and Max Weber whose work I will present in some detail. But the work of two late eighteenth-century French writers—Claude Saint-Simon and Auguste Comte—also helped establish the discipline of sociology.

HISTORICAL CIRCUMSTANCES

All academic disciplines taught in universities and colleges today have been profoundly shaped by the social, economic, and political circumstances in which they emerged. Sociology in particular has been affected by the political, economic, and social revolutions that occurred in the late eighteenth and nineteenth centuries, and has taken those major revolutions as its basis for study (Ritzer 1992, 5).

According to Philip Abrams:

> The generation that gave birth to sociology was probably the first generation of human beings ever to have experienced within the span of their own

lifetime socially induced change of a totally transformative nature—change which could not be identified, explained and accommodated as a limited historical variation within the encompassing order of the past (1972).

The discipline of sociology developed as a result of the concerns of several social thinkers to understand and control the direction of the social changes taking place in eighteenth- and early nineteenth-century Europe. As one of the "social" or "human sciences" that included economics, political science, and psychology, sociology emerged during this time in response to "the problems of order" in the economy, in political organization, and in the newly emerging forms and structures of social life (Foucault 1970; Donzelot 1979; Hazelrigg 1989).

SOCIAL, ECONOMIC, AND POLITICAL CONTEXTS

American sociologist and specialist in sociological theory George Ritzer has identified six social conditions of the nineteenth and early twentieth centuries that were of the utmost significance in the development of the discipline of sociology.

University students, 1890: white, privileged, male. From this environment sociology as an academic discipline evolved.

Political Revolutions

Beginning with the French Revolution in 1789 and carrying over into the nineteenth century, a long series of political revolutions made an enormous impact on Western

European and North American societies. Nineteenth-century commentators were affected by the chaos and disorder that occurred in their midst, especially in France. They were intent on doing everything possible to restore order to society, and some of the most conservative among them even advocated a return to a medieval form of social organization.

Those less conservative, however, realized that a return to feudalism was not only impossible but highly undesirable. They sought a new basis on which to organize society, and this search directly influenced their interest in its study. For many, including Comte and Durkheim, the issue of social order was foremost.

Women in the forefront of the French Revolution. On June 20, 1791, they invaded the Assembly, demanding the death penalty for members of the aristocracy.

The Industrial Revolution and the Rise of Capitalism

By the late nineteenth and early twentieth centuries, the Industrial Revolution had transformed the economies of most Western countries from an agricultural basis to ones based overwhelmingly on industrial production. People, thrown off the land or unable to survive as agriculturalists, left farms to work in the ever-increasing number of factories. These fac-

tories were constantly changing because of the continual invention of new and more "efficient" technologies.

At the heart of this new economy and production system was capitalism, powered by the ideal that goods and services could be exchanged on a free market. But while the new economy meant huge profits for a very few, the majority worked long hours for low wages in appalling conditions. As a reaction, labour movements emerged in several countries, along with a variety of more radical movements all aimed

The Industrial Revolution brought workers from farms to the factories. Pictured here are women manually sewing silk top hats.

at overthrowing the capitalist system and establishing a new economy controlled by workers. Karl Marx, Max Weber, and Émile Durkheim spent much of their lives studying and confronting the problems inherent in capitalism and the Industrial Revolution.

The Rise of Socialism

Socialism, as an economic, political, and social ideal, emerged during the nineteenth century as a specific means of coping with the excesses of industrialization and capitalism. Karl Marx actively supported the overthrow of capitalism as the only real means of alleviating the misery of the majority of nineteenth-century Europeans. He developed and wrote theories about capitalism as a mode of production and personally engaged in several political activities that he hoped would help bring about a socialist revolution.

Marx's position on socialism, however, was strongly opposed by Émile Durkheim and Max Weber. Although Durkheim and Weber recognized there were serious problems with capitalism, they sought to reform society from within rather than to support the kind of revolution advocated by Marx. Weber and Durkheim actually feared socialism, and their ideas have dominated sociology much more than those of Marx. Especially in the United States, the discipline of sociology developed in reaction to Marx's ideas, particularly the advocacy of socialism and communism as possible alternatives to capitalism.

Urbanization

Vast numbers of people were uprooted from their rural homes by industrialization and forced to migrate to urban areas. The rapid expansion of cities produced an almost endless list of urban problems—overcrowding, noise, pollution, poverty, crime, unemployment, alcoholism. The nature of urban life under an industrialized and capitalist system attracted the interest of many sociologists, including Marx's collaborator and friend, Friedrich Engels. In the early twentieth century, American sociologists at the University of Chicago focused on the city of Chicago as a kind of laboratory for studying urbanization and its problems.

Religion

As political and economic revolutions destroyed the fabric of medieval society, the religious basis on which it stood was also challenged. Some of the early sociologists were concerned with the diminution or disappearance of religion in people's lives. Durkheim wrote one of his most important works on religion. Comte went so far as to propose that sociology be transformed into a new kind of religion. Weber made a point of studying religion from a crosscultural perspective. Even Marx was concerned with religion, although his famous phrase "religion is the opiate of the masses" gives some idea of the critical perspective he took on the subject.

The Growth of Science

Early sociologists were preoccupied with science. By the end of the nineteenth century, it had acquired authority as the sole means of producing true knowledge about any subject. Scientists associated with physics, chemistry, and biology were accorded enormous prestige. Comte and Durkheim, in particular, sought to model sociology after the highly successful natural sciences. Marx, too, was impressed with scientific research, especially with the work of Charles Darwin. Others, such as Weber, thought that human social life was distinctive enough that a wholesale adoption of the models used in the natural sciences was difficult and unwise (Ritzer 1992).

Taken together, then, these six factors set the parameters for the emergence of sociology as a separate discipline. As already indicated, from the beginning of its development, there have been strong disagreements about how to make sense of the social world. As a result, there are many different theoretical and political orientations toward social life that vie for sociologists' support. Sociology's "founding three" sustain different perspectives: the work of Durkheim exemplifies a positivist perspective connected to a conservative political orientation; that of Weber an interactive perspective connected to a liberal orientation; and that of Marx a critical perspective tied to a radical orientation.

LIBERAL, CONSERVATIVE, AND RADICAL ORIENTATIONS

At least three different political orientations to human social relations informed sociology at its inception, and they continue to influence the discipline. These can be characterized as liberalism, radicalism, and conservatism (Nisbet 1966).

The liberal orientation of sociology drew heavily on individual autonomy. It was devoted to defending and expanding the individual's civil, political, and social rights. Liberals shared the belief that progress lay in the emancipation of the human mind and spirit from religious and traditional bonds. This orientation was well developed by Enlightenment thinkers who promoted a belief in the self-sustaining nature of individuality once it was released from corrupting and fettering institutions. Nineteenth-century liberal thinkers included Alexis de Tocqueville and John Stuart Mill.

Radical thinkers also drew on the works of Enlightenment theorists and argued that redemptive possibilities for humanity lay in the capture and use of political power to promote the social, economic, and political emancipation of the downtrodden. Like the liberals, radical thinkers placed their faith in the power of reason to fashion a new social order. They saw the need for revolt against existing power in secular rather than religious terms. Power, once obtained, could be used to realize the goal of liberty for everyone from the tyranny of inequality.

The final tradition that played a role in establishing sociology was a strongly rooted conservatism that looked to reinstitute an ethos believed by its proponents to have been present in traditional, medieval society, but that was in danger of complete elimination under industrial capitalism. Conservative thinkers were quick to defend those social traditions that emphasized community, kinship, hierarchy, authority, and religion. In particular, they wished to stop the chaos they believed liberalism and radicalism were causing by wrenching individuals from the social, political, and economic contexts in which these social traditions had existed. Saint-Simon, Auguste Comte, and Émile Durkheim can be placed in this category.

Most conservative thinkers wished to re-establish forms of social organization and control that would permit an educated elite to manage decision making for the entire

TABLE 12-1

PHILOSOPHICAL, ECONOMIC, POLITICAL, AND SCIENTIFIC WRITERS FROM THE SIXTEENTH TO NINETEENTH CENTURIES

1561–1626	Sir Francis Bacon, English philosopher
1588–1679	Thomas Hobbes, English political philosopher
1596–1650	René Descartes, French philosopher
1597	*Essay* by Bacon
1597	Galileo writes his agreement with the Copernican system
1605	*Advancement of Learning* by Bacon
1609	Kepler defines laws of planetary motion
1610	Galileo discovers Jupiter's moons and the phases of Venus
1620	*Novum Organum* by Bacon
1632	Galileo presents evidence for a heliocentric solar system in which the earth revolves around the sun
1632–1704	John Locke, English philosopher
1637	*Discourse de la méthode* by Descartes
1638	*Two New Sciences* by Galileo
1640	*Elements of Law* by Thomas Hobbes
1642	*Meditations de Prima Philosophia* (2nd ed.) by Descartes
1646–1716	Gottfried von Leibniz, German philosopher
1657	Academica del Cimento, first scientific research institute founded in Florence
1660	Royal Society founded in London
1664–66	Newton defines the laws of gravity
1666	French Académie Royale des Sciences founded by Colbert
1666	Newton discovers the spectrum
1667	Paris National Observatory founded
1668	Newton constructs first reflecting telescope
1687	*Principia* by Newton
1689	*On Civil Government* by Locke
1689–1755	Charles de Montesquieu, French philosopher
1690	*Essay Concerning Human Understanding* by Locke
1693	*Ideas on Education* by Locke

244

con't

TABLE 12-1 (continued)		
	1694–1788	François-Marie Voltaire, French philosopher
	1695	*Système nouveau de la nature* by Leibniz
	1712–1778	Jean-Jacques Rousseau, Swiss philosopher
	1715–1780	Étienne de Condillac, French philosopher
	1724–1804	Immanuel Kant, German critical philosopher
	1734	*Lettres philosophiques* by Voltaire
	1734–48	*The Spirit of Laws* by Montesquieu
	1735	*Systema Naturae* by Carolus Linnaeus
	1750	*Défense de l'esprit des lois* by Montesquieu
	1754	*Traité des sensations* by Condillac
	1756	*Essay on Morals* by Voltaire
	1759	*Candide* by Voltaire
	1762	*The Social Contract* by Rousseau
	1770–1831	Georg Hegel, German philosopher
	1781	*Critique of Pure Reason* by Kant
	1788	*Critique of Practical Reason* by Kant
	1798–1857	Auguste Comte, French sociologist, founder of positivism
	1807	*Phenomenology of Spirit* by Hegel
	1818–1883	*Karl Marx*, German political philosopher
	1821	*Philosophy of Right* by Hegel
	1830–1842	*Cours de philosophie positive* by Comte
	1848	*Communist Manifesto* by Marx
	1897	*Suicide* by Émile Durkheim

society. Based on observations of the social, economic, and political conditions of their society, conservatives asked questions that basically challenged Enlightenment ideals and optimism. In view of the current state of society, they demanded, where were the reason, freedom, and progress that the Enlightenment had promised?

In reacting to the unfounded optimism of the Enlightenment, the conservatives pointed to the disorganization, misery, disease, and violence of their time. The Enlightenment's emphasis on individual rights, freedoms, and reason had done nothing but weaken the social bonds that had traditionally held people together. Far from liberating humanity, it had merely produced social chaos and individual misery. Their solution was to replace the Enlightenment ideas of individual freedom and reason with a reaffirmation of traditional values and practices, including traditional authority, hierarchy, inequality, religious revelation, and the sanctity of the group over the individual (Zeitlin 1984, 34–35; Hearn 1985, 33).

Unrelated as these three orientations appear, commonality can be found in two regards: the stability-seeking motives of the authors of each position and their commitment to using scientific language and reasoning. Comte, Saint-Simon, and Durkheim were troubled by the French Revolution and its aftermath. With Karl Marx and Max Weber, they shared a strong concern with the implications of industrialization for European societies. All of these early contributors to the discipline of sociology saw how dehumanizing industrialized society could be; all but Weber thought that a better world for future generations was possible.

THE CONSERVATIVE REACTION TO THE ENLIGHTENMENT

Two French thinkers, Saint-Simon and Comte, formulated a version of sociology from a synthesis of conservative fears and aspirations and the Enlightenment concern for the scientific study of society.

CLAUDE-HENRI DE ROUVROY, COMTE DE SAINT-SIMON

Born into an aristocratic family, Saint-Simon (1760–1825) was by all accounts a wild and uncontrollable youth who spent part of his earlier years imprisoned by his family as a way to control his behaviour. He ran away from home at 19 and later became an officer in the French army. His king, Louis XIV, supported the Americans in their struggle for independence from the British. Saint-Simon was sent to America to fight in the American Revolution.

Upon his return to Europe, he tried unsuccessfully to promote canal-building schemes in Central America and Europe. When the French Revolution broke out in 1789, Saint-Simon gave it his full support, renounced his title, made revolutionary speeches, proposed reforms, and befriended the peasants. He continued, however, to promote his private affairs, buying up the confiscated lands of aristocrats and the Church at a fraction of their value. He acquired then lost a fortune and was confined to a mental asylum for a time.

Released from the asylum Saint-Simon became a publicist, advancing the cause of industrialists and the reconstruction of French society. In writing papers and pamphlets, Saint-Simon introduced the term **industrial society** into European social theory. It was his contention that industrialism heralded the beginnings of a new society and would bring about a new era of human history. The outgrowth of a declining feudalism, this incipient industrial society would provide the basis for solving all the problems inherent in feudalism.

As one of the first to discern the emergence of a new social order, Saint-Simon was concerned with explaining how it would work. He proposed the term **social physiology** as the guiding principle by which the new society should be organized. The basic premise of social physiology is that a new order can be established only on the basis of careful concern about and consideration for the old order. The objective of social physiology, therefore, is to identify the laws of progress that are inherent in society (Hearn 1985, 36). These laws, Saint-Simon believed, are inevitable and uncontrollable, and they guide the process of social development. All that anyone can hope to achieve is to know what the laws are, adapt to their demands, and do whatever is possible to support their course of development.

In his book *Industrial Systems*, 1821, Saint-Simon argued that the new industrial society should be organized on scientific, positive principles with the economic and political systems working in harmony. Politics, in his view, had to become the "science of production" (Hearn 1985, 37–38). Because it used the principles of prediction and verification, science would form the basis of all social practice in the new industrial society, as envisaged by Saint-Simon. Decision making would be given over to those institutions that were associated with science and technology. The state would be replaced by those men most able to manage the affairs of the nation, that is, by a council of scientists, artists, financiers, and industrialists who would plan and coordinate for the good of all.

One of the more interesting aspects of Saint-Simon's work is his significance to the development of both conservative sociological theorists such as Comte and radical theorists like Marx. On the one hand, Saint-Simon wanted to preserve society, and strongly supported using the same methods for studying social and natural phenomena. On the other hand, he saw a pressing need for socialist reforms, especially ones leading to the central planning of the economy. Unlike Marx, though, he did not believe that the working class would one day supersede the capitalists (Ritzer 1992, 14).

ISIDORE AUGUSTE FRANÇOIS-XAVIER COMTE

Born to middle-class, conservative, Catholic, monarchist parents in Montpellier, France, Auguste Comte (1798–1875) enjoyed a comfortable childhood. In Paris as a young man, he eked out an existence as a private instructor. He was so poor he could afford only two meals a day, but he did manage to attend public scientific discussions and debates. There he met Henri de Saint-Simon, 40 years his senior. Comte served for several years as Saint-Simon's secretary, finally leaving his employer in 1824 after a bitter dispute over ownership of ideas. Comte went on to develop a number of Saint-Simon's ideas about science, technology, and society, although he often did not credit his former mentor. He never held a secure academic position, and although he taught courses from time to time, he remained on the fringe of French academic circles (Swingewood 1984, 40).

Like his former employer, Comte suffered from bouts of insanity, was confined for a time to a sanatorium for depression, and twice attempted suicide. In 1825 he married Caroline Massif, a registered Paris prostitute. It was not a happy marriage and they separated several times before parting for good in 1841. After his marriage ended, Comte lived for a while on subsidies from English social theorist John Stuart Mill and others who admired his work.

In 1844, at 46, Comte fell in love with Clotilde de Vaux, a 36-year-old unpublished novelist and descendant of an aristocratic family, whose husband had abandoned her several years before (Ashley and Orenstein 1990, 69). When they met, Clotilde de Vaux

247

was already terminally ill. On her death in 1846, Comte erected an alter to the memory of "my Saint Clotilde" and visited her grave every Wednesday. He then dedicated himself to formulating a new religion, which he called the "religion of humanity." He assigned himself the title "Great Priest of Humanity" and lived an austere existence, giving up wine, tobacco, and coffee.

Like many of his contemporaries, Comte believed that European society was in a state of crisis brought about because one form of society was disappearing and another was struggling to replace it. But unlike Enlightenment thinkers who preceded him, Comte did not think that something new, exciting, and hopeful was happening to society. Instead, he had an anguished sense that the old system was breaking down, being gradually engulfed by anarchy. Far from being the herald of a new era, as it had been for Enlightenment thinkers, Comte saw the French Revolution as little more than "social disorganization presided over by political tyranny" (Nisbet 1966, 51).

Disturbed by the chaos that followed the French Revolution and critical of the Enlightenment thinkers whom he blamed for the disintegration of society, Comte proposed a new scientific approach. This he called "positivism" or "positive philosophy." Its purpose was to combat the negative and destructive aspects of Enlightenment thought. He developed what he first called "social physics" and later, in 1822, "sociology."

The use of the term social physics is a good indication of Comte's intention to model his new science of society after the hard sciences. He believed his new science would dominate all others. Sociology, as he conceived it, would be the study of both "social statics" (existing social structures) and "social dynamics" (the processes of change). Comte was particularly concerned with social reform, especially with correcting the social ills that the French Revolution had introduced. But he did not urge another revolution; instead, he believed that only reforms were needed to encourage the natural evolution of society toward something better.

The basis of Comte's sociology was a commitment to evolutionary theory, what he called the "law of three stages." All human societies must pass through a series of developmental stages—a theological stage, a metaphysical stage, and a positivistic stage. Not only do societies all progress through these three stages, Comte argued, so do groups, individuals, and even minds.

The theological stage, he claimed, characterized the world prior to 1300 and emphasized belief in supernatural powers and religious figures. The metaphysical stage lasted from 1300 to 1800 and produced the conviction that abstract forces, such as nature, rather than supernatural forces, like God, were responsible for almost everything and could be used to explain all changes. Finally the positivist stage, entered around 1800, was characterized by a belief in science. In this last stage, people would give up the search for absolute causes and focus on observing the world and seeking to discover the laws that governed it (Ritzer 1992, 15).

Comte was convinced that when positivism gained complete domination, all social revolutions and upheavals would cease. He also believed that there was no need to foment social revolution. Because positivism was part of a natural, evolutionary process, it would inevitably come to dominate the thinking of the entire world. Moreover, Comte believed, what changes were needed were intellectual ones, so there was little reason to support social or political revolutions. For him, society was strongly characterized by consensus rather than conflict. Finally, Comte was an elitist in that he believed that sociology would eventually dominate all of science because of its ability to discover and interpret social laws and to develop programs of reform to help ameliorate the problems within the system.

The sociology of both Saint-Simon and Comte was intended to foster respect for the existing status quo and to promote stability, cohesion, and solidarity as the basis for social progress. In Comte's opinion, it was the "false dogmas" of the French Revolution—egalitarianism, popular sovereignty, and individualism—that were responsible for the spread of moral disorganization in Western Europe. Those false dogmas had to be countered with positive sociology and the discovery of the true laws of society.

Comte's view of the world and his vision of what society should be were quite agreeable to the newly emerging middle class. Concerned with preventing popular unrest, the new bourgeoisie was content with Comte's arguments that change was necessary and inevitable but that it had to be tempered with respect for stability and order if it was to be beneficial (Hearn 1985, 46). In spite of his popularity with members of the bourgeoisie, Comte was never able to build a school of Comtian sociology. His contributions to the scientific study of society, moreover, were quickly eclipsed by others, among them Émile Durkheim, Karl Marx, and Max Weber.

MARX, WEBER, AND DURKHEIM: THE "SECULAR TRINITY OF SOCIOLOGY"

The names of Karl Marx (1818–1883), Max Weber (1864–1920), and Émile Durkheim (1858–1917) are often cited together as a "secular trinity" of sociologists—the founding fathers of the discipline, so to speak (Alexander 1987, 1). Each of these social theorists made major contributions to the establishment of the discipline of sociology, both in terms of defining what sociologists study and in terms of setting many of the parameters by which future generations of sociologists have conducted their analyses. All three theorists wrote about industrial capitalist society, and the work of each was strongly informed by concerns about its future. But their objectives for undertaking the study of society, the methods they employed to make their analyses, and their theoretical approaches were markedly different.

Both Weber and Durkheim share the distinction of having occupied academic posts as sociologists. Although Marx earned a Ph.D., he was never given an academic appointment. In fact, his political activities excluded him from that possibility. Nor was he ever a sociologist in the sense of either profession or intellectual allegiance. In spite of this, his work on society and social interaction had an enormous impact on the discipline of sociology and continues to influence present-day critical thinkers in the field.

Marx devoted his life to social revolution and to the task of realizing the full potential of all humanity for a more equitable and just existence. Durkheim's work, by contrast, exemplifies the positivist approach to social analysis. He was opposed to revolution and devoted much time to establishing sociology as an academic discipline, complete with teaching institutions, learned societies, and journals. Max Weber, like Durkheim, was opposed to sudden revolutionary change. Despite mental health problems (Weber was often incapacitated by emotional difficulties), he published extensively and contributed to the founding of a sociological journal. His work did much to help establish the interpretive approach to sociology.

Taken together, Marx, Weber, and Durkheim have been responsible for generating many of the often conflicting ideas, concepts, and theoretical frameworks that have inspired the work of those who followed them.

ÉMILE DURKHEIM

Born in Lorraine, France, the son of Moise Durkheim, chief rabbi of the Vosges and Haute-Marne regions of France, and Melanie Durkheim, Émile was encouraged to follow the rabbinical calling of his father and grandfather. He was given a thorough secular and religious education by his parents. However, as a young student, Durkheim was strongly influenced by a form of Catholic mysticism and turned away from the rabbinate toward more secular interests.

Émile Durkheim, first French academic sociologist.

Durkheim studied philosophy and history at the prestigious École Normale Supérieure in Paris and read Comte's texts on sociology. It was here that he broke with Judaism and dedicated himself to academic studies, especially philosophy (see Lukes 1985). Another significant influence on Durkheim's ideas about society was the political circumstances of mid- and late nineteenth-century France. Throughout his life, he witnessed repeated political changes and upheavals. His concerns as a sociologist with stability and his abhorrence of sudden change may be directly linked to his personal concerns with the fragility of the French Republic and his desire to see the French state preserved. Durkheim hated social disorder, a subject to which he devoted most of his work. In his view, social disorder was not a necessary part of the modern world. Like Comte, he believed that all social disorders could be greatly reduced through the introduction of social reform.

Durkheim was the first French academic sociologist. During his lifetime he published over 500 articles, books, and reviews, including *The Division of Labour* (1893), *The Rules of Sociological Method* (1895), *Suicide*, (1897), and *The Elementary Forms of the Religious Life* (1912). He also founded a respected, although controversial, sociology journal, *L'Année sociologique*. In his books and his journal, Durkheim developed his ideas about sociology, which he called "the science of institutions, their genesis and their functioning" (Durkheim [1895] 1982, 45).

CONCEPTS AND IDEAS

Durkheim used the concept of society in a variety of ways, but certain central themes run through all his work. Essential to his use of the concept of society is the idea, borrowed from Comte, that society is a reality in itself. Durkheim often used the Latin phrase *sui generis* to refer to society. By this he meant that society cannot be reduced to or explained in terms used to describe other realities. The properties of society cannot be borrowed from expressions of other realities, such as biology or psychology.

Durkheim believed there were many levels of reality manifest in the universe, including social, physical, chemical, biological, and psychological ones, and that each level emerged out of a previous, simpler one. He also believed that the social level was the most complex. While it emerged from the interrelations of individuals who possessed symbolic communication and reflection, it had unique properties that extended beyond those available to any one individual. According to Durkheim:

> Society is not the mere sum of individuals, but the system formed by their association represents a specific reality which has its own characteristics. Undoubtedly no collective entity can be produced if there are no individual consciousnesses: this is a necessary but not a sufficient condition. In addition, these consciousnesses must be associated and combined, but combined in a certain way. It is from this combination that social life arises and consequently it is this combination which explains it. By aggregating together, by interpenetrating, by fusing together, individuals give birth to a being, psychical if you will, but one which constitutes a psychical individuality of a new kind. Thus it is in the nature of that individuality and not in that of its component elements that we must search for the proximate and determining causes of the facts produced in it. The group thinks, feels and acts entirely differently from the way its members would if they were isolated. If therefore we begin by studying these members separately, we will understand nothing about what is taking place in the group ([1895] 1982, 129).

The defining task of sociology, Durkheim argued, is to discover and interpret what is external to the individual. Moreover, the laws governing this external world are no different from the laws governing nature: the way that a sociologist discovers those laws is the same as the way used in other sciences (Swingewood 1984, 107; Lukes 1985, 68). But Durkheim claimed that sociology is an autonomous science because the ability to discern social reality and to grasp social facts intelligently, vital to the sociologist, can be achieved only through distinctly sociological training and the application of the sociological method of inquiry.

251

The first point Durkheim makes is that the sociological method must be strictly empirical, represent positive science, and have nothing to do with what he calls "philosophy." Second, the sociological method must be objective. Social facts, Durkheim cautions, are "things and must be treated as such." In short, the subject matter of sociology must be treated in exactly the same way that the subject matter of physics or chemistry is treated. Third, social facts must be explained only in relation to other social facts. The properties of social facts cannot be understood in terms of attributes of individual members of a society.

Following these methods of sociological inquiry, Durkheim became a pioneer in the use of **statistics**. In *The Rules of Sociological Method* ([1895], 1982), Durkheim developed his conception of the proper subject matter of sociology—social facts. In *Suicide* ([1897] 1951), he tested his notions in an empirical study. Durkheim reasoned that if he could demonstrate that a seemingly individual behaviour like suicide was actually linked to social causes (social facts), he could make a persuasive case for sociology as the science of society.

In writing *Suicide*, Durkheim used a series of government records containing statistics on suicide rates, across time periods, for different ethnic and religious groups, arranged according to gender and marital status. He used these statistics to demonstrate by a series of comparisons—Protestants vs. Catholics; males vs. females; married vs. the unmarried—that suicide rates were a good indication of the degree of social integration of the members of any particular social group. The greater the degree of integration of the members of a particular group, the lower the suicide rate. Using statistical indicators of rates of suicide as his evidence, Durkheim concluded that modern society was not sufficiently integrated to give the support that individuals needed for a sense of well-being. A high rate of suicide, he contended, was proof of a low level of social integration within a society. It was also proof that the members of that society had a weak sense of social unity and purpose.

In his last major work, *The Elementary Forms of Religious Life* ([1912] 1965), Durkheim focused on religion as a social fact. Believing that "primitive" societies, as he labelled them, were simpler than complex modern ones, and thus easier to study, he examined these societies with the expectation of finding the roots of all religion. By the end of his research into religion, Durkheim was convinced he had found the source of all religion—society itself. In the end, he argued, society and religion are one and the same thing. In identifying society with religion and God, Durkheim took a very conservative stance toward social change. Not inclined to support social revolution, he championed social reforms instead as a way of improving the functioning of society. Despite identifying society with God, Durkheim did not take the same route as Saint-Simon and Comte in proposing a new religion of humanity based on a scientifically determined social morality. He did, however, seem to share their notion that sociologists have access to the truth about society. He proposed, moreover, that it was the duty of politicians to listen to sociologists.

Given his deification of society, Durkheim's suspicion of freedom, which had been a major focus of the Enlightenment philosophers, is understandable. For him, as for Comte, the issue of individual freedom was a red herring: freedom, he believed, only came from submission to the laws of society or to social facts. It was never to be found in emancipation from the dictates of society. If such a thing were to happen, human desires and wants would be unbridled, something that could lead only to dissatisfaction and unhappiness. Following Comte, Durkheim argued that the major problem facing modern society was the absence of a morality appropriate to the new social conditions. Old traditions and practices had gone, but there was nothing to replace them. The result was a state of **normlessness** or **anomie**.

All individual members of society, Durkheim contends, have their personal goals. Society provides them with norms or rules about how they should go about achieving those goals. As long as members of society recognize those rules and respect their authority, they are unwilling to pursue their personal desires beyond certain limits. But in the rapidly industrializing society of the nineteenth century, Durkheim felt that societal norms governing the moral consciousness of society's members were greatly weakened. The rapid economic development that European society had undergone produced what Durkheim determined to be a state of crisis, in which economic relations had become separated from traditional forms of religious, occupational, and social regulation. When this happened, the aspirations of individual members of the society were no longer held in check, individual greed was allowed to run rampant, and a state of anomie or normlessness pervaded the entire society. Normlessness, Durkheim felt, is a pathological state that

Marx, Engels, and Lenin emblazoned on a banner at a traditional May Day parade in Red Square before the collapse of communism.

had to be eradicated. The first obligation of sociology, therefore, was to establish the scientific basis for a new, and more appropriate, morality.

Durkheim's work on method, suicide, religion, and division of labour helped to establish sociology as a separate academic discipline and earned him a central position in the new field. By 1910 he had done much toward establishing the legitimacy of sociology in France. But while the discipline had a fairly coherent line of development in that country from the Enlightenment, through the French Revolution, and on to the ideas of Comte, Saint-Simon, and Durkheim, what happened in Germany was somewhat different. There a split emerged between Karl Marx and his supporters, who remained on the fringes of mainstream sociology, and one of the early giants of the discipline, Max Weber (Ritzer 1992, 19).

KARL MARX

Of all the thinkers and writers of the last two centuries, Karl Marx has probably affected more people in this century than any other social theorist. His writings have inspired thousands of books and articles on subjects ranging from social and economic relations in hunting and gathering societies, to detailed treatises on the operations of capitalist economies, to fomenting revolutions. Major political and economic revolutions have been made in Marx's name—the Russian and Chinese revolutions of this century are two. In many countries, Marxism became institutionalized; political parties and state administrations promoted and developed their own versions of Marxist theory and Marxist politics.

Karl Marx, journalist, social analyst, political revolutionary.

In countries where Marxism took hold as the basis for state organization, it was supported by many who were attracted to Marx's ideas concerning an ethical denunciation of inequality and exploitation and his celebration of universal brotherhood (Worsley 1982, 14). In other countries, specifically the United States, entire federal government administrations have devoted themselves to combatting Marxism and communism both at home and throughout the world.

Karl Marx was born and grew up in Trier, a small town in Prussia. His father, a lawyer, converted from Judaism to Protestantism shortly before his son's birth. As a young man, Marx attended university in Bonn and distinguished himself by running up debts, drinking too much, fighting (he was wounded in a duel), and being arrested for carrying a deadly weapon. His father, who had hoped his son would become a lawyer, worried that Karl was becoming a spendthrift and a "slovenly barbarian" and had him transferred to the University of Berlin. Before he set off, Marx became secretly engaged to his next-door neighbour and childhood sweetheart, Jenny von Westphalen, the daughter of Baron von Westphalen, himself a follower of Saint-Simon.

At the University of Berlin, Marx quickly became interested in philosophy. When he submitted his doctoral thesis on Greek philosophies of nature, he hoped to win a post as a university lecturer. But he soon learned that he had been blacklisted by the Ministry of Education because of his radical tendencies. He turned to journalism as a way to support himself. As a journalist, he met his lifelong friend and collaborator, Friedrich Engels. Engels was the son of a wealthy German manufacturer who owned textile factories in Germany and in England. Throughout the rest of his life, Marx would depend heavily on monetary support from Engels, who managed his father's textile company in Manchester and was thus able to finance Marx's writing.

In 1844 Marx was charged with high treason by the Prussian government. He was expelled from Paris where he had been living and writing and moved first to Brussels and later to London. By 1847 he and Engels were actively involved in the Communist League, and together they wrote the *Communist Manifesto* in 1848. In 1849 Marx was involved in promoting a workers' revolution in Cologne, Germany. Put on trial for insulting the authorities and inciting rebellion, he was acquitted by a jury but he was now bankrupt, having spent his inheritance on buying arms for the failed workers' revolution.

In 1849, Karl and Jenny Marx moved to London, where they lived in a series of rented rooms in Soho, a poor district in the centre of the city. They lost three of their six children in early infancy. Marx's only surviving son was born in 1851 to Helen Demuth, a servant who helped run the Marx household for over 30 years. Jenny Marx never knew about this child, who was adopted by a working-class family in London.

Marx became the London correspondent for the New York *Daily Tribune*, although much of what he signed his name to was actually written by Engels. He spent a great deal of his time at the British Museum reading government statistics and reports of factory inspectors, which described in detail the horrible conditions under which most of the working class laboured. In London he remained active as a political revolutionary. Marx was responsible for putting together the rules and statutes of the International Working Men's Association, which supported workers' rights. The first volume of *Capital* was published in 1867 and was translated into Russian. It sold briskly in Russia, although it did not fare so well in England. Marx died at home in 1883 after a lengthy illness.

IDEAS AND INFLUENCES

At the University of Berlin, Marx was originally influenced by a group of students and university lecturers called the "Young Hegelians." These men tried to apply the work of the recently deceased German philosopher Georg Wilhelm Friedrich Hegel (1770–1831) to an understanding of human existence. Two concepts, the dialectic and idealism, form the basis of Hegel's philosophy. Both are complex and are only briefly outlined here.

Basically the dialectic is a way of thinking about the world. It focuses on relations, dynamics, conflict, and contradiction. Idealism emphasizes the importance of the mind and ideas over material conditions of existence. As a philosopher, Hegel espoused a form of philosophical idealism in which ideas played the central role in human history and in which social and historical events were represented in highly abstract terms. Following Hegel's lead, the young Hegelians carried on their intellectual discussions and writing as if humans acted and existed only in the realm of pure thought.

Marx soon abandoned this group, convinced that it was necessary to go beyond metaphysical speculation. Although he remained influenced by Hegel's interest in human emancipation, he became convinced that human history was the result of practical human activity, especially the ways in which humans exercised technical and cognitive control over their natural environments. He argued that because the problems of modern life can be traced to real material sources, the solutions to those problems are also based in real, material activities involving revolutionary acts on the part of large collectivities of people. In Marx's words, while Hegel had "stood the world on its head" by focusing on ideas and consciousness, he himself intended to put things right by embedding his dialectical approach in a concrete material base.

Thus Marx developed a **dialectical materialist** method of studying society. The major problem with Hegel and the young Hegelians, Marx was convinced, was that they failed to inquire into the connection between their philosophy and the real material conditions in which they lived. By material conditions, Marx had in mind economic, political, social, and cultural factors.

But Marx did not abandon all of Hegel's philosophy. He kept what he considered to be its "rational kernel"—that is, the emphasis on the *active*, or dialectical nature of human existence. Hegel, Marx noted, had given human beings a creative and active role in his philosophy. The problem was that this role allowed people to be only producers of ideas, and thus abstracted from their material surroundings. What Marx found most useful in Hegel, however, was that in developing the dialectical aspects of his philosophy, he had focused both on the positive, existing state of things and on their *negation* or opposite states. As well, Hegel focused on the inevitable transformation and breakup of all social forms. For him, history was the process whereby social forms came into existence, developed, were destroyed by internal contradictions, and gave way to new social forms. These aspects of Hegel's dialectical philosophy were retained by Marx. But Marx replaced Hegel's focus on ideas as the motor force in history with a focus instead on the material conditions of existence.

Marx quickly came to the conclusion that human history was the result of a constant struggle that took place between differently advantaged groups or social classes. In order to understand human history, it was essential to "set out from real, active men" who were engaged in "real-life processes" ([1859] 1971). But to understand how Marx conceived of the social relationships between different classes and the inevitable struggle that had to take place between conflicting class interests, we must first consider another set of concepts developed by him—**mode of production, social relations of production,** and **productive forces.**

Mode of Production, Social Relations of Production, and Productive Forces

"The subject of our discussion," Marx wrote in the *Grundrisse*, "is first of all material production. Individuals producing in society, and thus the socially determined production of individuals, naturally constitutes a starting point." In the processes of producing and reproducing the material conditions necessary to live, human beings interact with the natural world via their labour. Marx used the various ways in which the relationship between the individual labourer and the natural world of objects was organized and mediated through social relations of production and the technical means of production to characterize different epochs of human history.

It was Marx's opinion that the organization of human labour had undergone a series of changes over the course of human history. He described a series of economic stages, or modes of production, which followed one another sequentially: primitive communism, ancient societies, feudalism, capitalism, and finally advanced communism. A sixth stage, Asiatic societies, could also exist in the same time frame as primitive communist and ancient societies. As Marx wrote in his Preface to *A Contribution to the Critique of Political Economy* [1859] 1971):

> In the social production of their existence, men inevitably enter into definite relations, which are independent of their will, namely relations of production appropriate to a given state in the development of their material forces of production. The totality of these relations of production constitutes the economic structure of society, the real foundation, on which arises a legal and political superstructure and to which correspond definite forms of social consciousness. The mode of production of material life conditions the general process of social, political and intellectual life (20–21).

Marx argued that all societies in human history can be classified in one of the six categories or modes of production. Any given mode of production is made up of a combination of the productive forces and the social relations of production. Productive forces are made up of two parts: **labour power** and the **means of production.** Labour power consists of the "mental and physical capabilities" of any given human being to work. The means of production are made up of all the tools, machinery, scientific and technical expertise, and raw materials—coal, water, iron ore—in short, everything that is needed for production to take place.

The social relations of production are the relations that exist among individuals with respect to ownership of and access to the productive forces. In their legal form, social relations of production are *property* relations. A change, or transition, from one mode of production to another happens as a result of the development of the productive forces, which in turn bring about changes in the social relations of production. This can be illustrated by the transition from the feudal to capitalist modes of production.

Social Class and Exploitation

Understanding how Marx conceptualized the interplay of social relations of production and access to the productive forces in any given mode of production is central to an understanding of his conceptualization of **class,** and the exploitation of one class by another. For Marx, the organization of the productive process in a class society—capitalist or not—is based on social relations of production in which individual members of that society have different abilities with which to gain access to the means of production.

Any given individual's class position is determined by his or her relationship to the means of production. A social class is made up of all individuals who have the same relation to the means of production. In slave societies, for example, the slave owner has exclusive ownership of the slave's labour power (ability to work) and thus exclusive rights to everything that is produced by the slave. In feudal societies, the feudal lord has the right to a certain portion of the labour power of the serfs under his jurisdiction, and thus the right to a specified portion of whatever those serfs produce.

In feudalism, Marx points out, there are two main social classes—feudal lords and their serfs. A serf is not free to produce just as he or she wills, nor is a serf free to consume all that he or she produces. Instead, serfs are obliged to meet certain economic demands made by their overlords. Those economic demands take several different forms. A serf might be obliged to pay an overlord dues in the form of money, produce, or military service, for example. At the same time, a serf is not a slave. The serf, as Marx tells us, is "in possession of his means of production, of the material labour conditions required for the realization of his labour and the production of his means of subsistence. He carries on his agriculture and the rural house-industries connected with it, as an independent producer" (*Capital*, vol. 3).

The instruments of production used by feudal serfs were simple, readily available, and inexpensive. Moreover, while a portion of what each serf produced went to the overlord, the rest was used to meet the daily consumption needs of the household or the immediate community. Under feudalism very little was produced for exchange in a market, and so the feudal economy was not an exchange economy.

This began to change by about the thirteenth century when, slowly, production for self-consumption was increasingly replaced by production for market exchanges. These changes were accompanied by new social relations of production in which serfs were gradually transformed into a peasantry who worked with their own instruments of production and who had the right to use common lands to pasture animals and gather wood.

Economic changes were accompanied by other, more far-reaching social, cultural, and political changes, including new ways of thinking. With increased production for markets, social relations between producers and consumers gradually changed from personal relations, to impersonal ones, based on contractual agreements. By the late fifteenth century, however, things changed once again, as powerful monarchs confiscated the lands of local overlords and forced masses of peasants and serfs from the soil, confiscating common lands.

The earliest exchanges, based on commodities and money, were not yet *capitalist* exchanges. For the capitalist mode of production to appear, Marx argues that

> two very different kinds of commodity-possessors must come into contact; on the one hand, the owners of money, means of production, and means of subsistence who are eager to increase the sum of values they possess, by buying other people's labour power; on the other hand, free labourers, the sellers of their own labour-power and therefore the sellers of labour (*Capital,* vol. 1, 714).

The conditions for the emergence of capitalism, however, were quickly established once the more powerful feudal lords and the monarch began evicting peasants and serfs from the land. What had formerly been the peasants' means of production became capital in the hands of the new lords, and former peasants now had nothing to sell but their ability to work for wages.

For Marx, labourers under the capitalist mode of production are free in two senses of the word. First, they are free in that they are neither slaves nor bondsmen. Second, they are free because they are "free of the means of production." That is, they are not owners of any means of production. They have been "freed" or separated from their traditional means of production—the land and the tools needed to work the land—and are now entirely dependent on selling their ability to work to someone else who owns the means of production. Without free labour in this sense, the capitalist mode of production could never have developed. The origins of the capitalist mode of production, Marx insists, lie in the historical process of separating the worker from the means of production and means of subsistence, and placing those means in the hands of a small group of people—the capitalist class.

Alienation of Labour

Marx defined the capacity to labour as "man's self-confirming essence" (*Economic and Philosophic Manuscripts* (1843–44). All that human beings produce, including their beliefs, religion, arts, and music, is the result of human labour. **Alienation** occurs when human beings are separated from direct enjoyment of, and direct ownership over, their labour and the products of that labour. This is precisely the case under the capitalist mode of production, which alienates all humans from the products of their own labour. Instead of owning themselves and what they produce, workers labour to produce commodities that they neither own nor (often) can use. In Marx's words, under capitalism, the worker "puts his life into the object, and his life then belongs no longer to himself but to the object. The greater his activity....the less he possesses. What is embodied in the product of his labour is no longer his own. The greater this product is...the more he is diminished" (cited in Swingewood 1984, 65).

259

The possibility of freedom for all humanity is enhanced, Marx contends, through the development of technology. In societies where technological developments are at a low level, humans live in miserable conditions. But with the maturation of capitalism, productive forces are developed enough to allow individuals to satisfy more easily their material needs and to escape some of the drudgery of their previous existence.

And yet, according to Marx, societies based on a capitalist mode of production are also dehumanizing because the relations of production prevent workers from achieving the freedom and self-determination that the advance in the productive process has made potentially possible. Private ownership of the means of production, as is the case under capitalism, meant for Marx that workers continue to be alienated from the ownership of whatever they produce. This alienation, in turn, means that workers do not have control over the very thing that Marx believed made them fully human—their own labour power. He believed that work should be an end in of itself. Work done for any other purpose—especially work done in order to make profit for an employer—is always alienated work.

Ideology

The term **ideology** was first used at the end of the eighteenth century by the French philosopher Destutt de Tracy. Marx used this concept to mean distorted thought or *false consciousness*, which mystifies real social relations in order to defend and perpetuate the interests of the dominant social class (Swingewood 1984, 72). Marx's ideas about ideology, therefore, are closely connected with his ideas about social class and the necessarily conflictive nature of relations between classes.

Recall the discussion above of Marx's view that all societies are divided along class lines, which are formed on the basis of the relations individuals have to the ownership of the means of production. It was his contention that domination of one class (the owners) over another (the nonowners) is not a natural occurrence. Domination has to be supported by an ideology, held by the majority of a given society's members, that the economic relations that exist are both right and for the common good. Marx termed the holding of a position not in the "class interest" of the majority to be an ideological position resulting from false consciousness. It is false consciousness, Marx pointed out, for people living in a capitalist economy to believe that the division of society into bosses and workers, or into owners and nonowners of the means of production, is right, inevitable, and natural.

Marx stated that while these beliefs are "false" in the sense that they do not reflect the real interests of the majority of people, they are also accurate in that they mirror the day-to-day conditions of living and working under a capitalist mode of production. Appearance and reality, he noted, rarely coincide. If that were the case then all science would be superfluous. For Marx, the task of anyone engaged in making a scientific analysis of society was to uncover and analyze the underlying forms or structures of society on which both false consciousness and true scientific understanding could be based.

The Relevance Of Marx's Theories

During the twentieth century, a great number of revolutions have been fought in many societies in the name of Marx and Marxism. As a political philosophy and as a theory of revolutionary change, Marx's ideas have had, without doubt, an extensive and far-reaching impact on the entire world. His theories about the organization and functioning of capitalist societies have been widely studied and written about. Since 1960, over 400 scholarly books on Marx and his work have been published in the United States.

Marx never held an academic post and never considered himself to be a sociologist. While his work is much broader than the field of sociology commonly encompasses, there is, nonetheless, much of what might be properly considered sociological theory in his work. Many European (and some North American) sociologists have been strongly influenced by his writing. But until fairly recently in the United States, and to a lesser extent in Canada, Marx's work was either ignored or treated with hostility.

In part, rejection of his ideas in North America has been governed by the fear many conservative thinkers share about his revolutionary ideas and his predictions of, and support for, continuing and extensive social transformation. As a result, many mainstream sociologists classify his work as ideological. Yet at the same time they have accepted the conservative ideology proposed by Comte, Durkheim, and others. In particular, these sociologists have been hostile to Marx's ideas promoting social revolution, but cling strongly to conservative ideals about orderly, controlled change.

In the 1970s it was entirely possible to graduate with a degree in sociology without ever considering anything that Marx wrote. However, this is not usually the case today in major Canadian universities. At the same time, Marx is held by some to be personally responsible for the problems, excesses, and economic difficulties experienced by large numbers of people in Eastern Europe, the former Soviet Union, and in China. His work and ideas are often confused with the outcomes of the revolutions that have been made in his name. Marx believed communism was the necessary solution to the inequalities and abuses inherent in capitalism and that only under advanced communism could each individual actually develop his or her full abilities. Yet he would have hardly recognized the many communist revolutions that were made in the twentieth century.

Marx has made significant contributions to sociological theory that continue to influence many contemporary sociologists. One of the most important has been his philosophical understanding of the production of knowledge, which is different from that held by more conservative thinkers. Most conservative thinkers who established the discipline of sociology were strongly influenced by the philosophy of Immanuel Kant. Among other things, their philosophical underpinnings led them to emphasize a linear cause-and-effect relationship between events and phenomena. For example, a change in the ideas brought about by Enlightenment philosophers led immediately to major political changes brought about by the French Revolution. Instead of seeing a cause-and-effect relation between the ideas of the Enlightenment and the political changes of the French Revolution, for example, a dialectical thinker such as Marx focuses on the ongoing interplay of ideas and politics (Ritzer 1992, 23).

By emphasizing the relationship between theory and social practice (praxis) Marx provided future generations of sociologists with a way to conceptualize the interaction of individuals with one another and with existing social structures. In so doing, he also gave them a powerful tool for understanding the ways in which social structures are reproduced or transformed.

Finally, Marx offered a view of capitalist society based on his particular way of understanding human nature. He believed that the defining characteristic of all humans is their capacity to labour productively—to produce food, clothing, tools, shelter, and other necessities. Moreover, all human labour is done in relationship to others, so to this extent people are inherently social. But throughout human history, this natural sociability has been subverted. In capitalist societies, its breakdown is most obvious. Marx expended much effort in trying to bring about the end of capitalism. He contended that in the next mode of production—socialism—human beings would once again interact harmoniously with one another and with nature to create a society without alienation.

Max Weber

Max Weber came from a well-to-do, upper-middle-class German family. His paternal grandfather was co-founder of a profitable linen firm; his maternal grandfather was a wealthy, high-ranking Prussian civil servant. Weber's mother, Helen, was a devout Calvinist who followed a rigid moral code. His father, also named Max, was an authoritarian figure whom Max Weber Jr. was never able to oppose openly.

In 1882 Weber left home to attend university in Heidelberg, where he studied jurisprudence. He was (like many of the other founders of sociology whom we have studied) wild and impetuous, spending much time drinking and brawling. He joined a duelling fraternity and like Marx acquired a scar across one cheek.

Weber was very successful at university and at 30 received an appointment as professor of economics at Freiberg University. Two years later he was appointed chair in political science at the University of Heidelberg. He married Marianne Schnitger, the daughter of a cousin, in 1893. In 1897 he had a nervous breakdown after an argument with his father, in which he accused him of being a tyrant and mistreating his mother. The elder Weber was ordered out of his son's house and died suddenly a few weeks later. Consumed by guilt and remorse Max Weber Jr. suffered an emotional collapse from which he never fully recovered.

In 1903, partially recovered, he took over as editor of the journal *Archiv für Sozialwissenschaften und Sozialpolitik* (*Archives for Social Science and Social Policy*), along with two other academics, Edgar Jaffe and Werner Sombart. In the first issue, Weber noted that the journal would focus on "the historical and theoretical recognition of the general cultural significance of capitalist development." Among other disciplines to be represented in the journal, Weber listed sociology.

On a rest-cure trip to the United States in 1904, Weber was intrigued by the pace of life in America and by its strange democratic customs. He was convinced that the "spirit of capitalism" was alive and flourishing in "ideal-type purity" here. He later wrote that "with almost lightning speed everything that stands in the way of capitalistic culture in the United States is being crushed." Much of his inspiration for his book *The Protestant Ethic and the Spirit of Capitalism* came from this visit.

In 1910, along with Georg Simmel, Werner Sombart, Ferdinand Tönnies, and Robert Michels, Weber helped organize the first meetings of the German Sociological Society. Weber had originally been sceptical about sociology, but in the years following

Max Weber emphasized people's understanding of their actions.

his breakdown he became more interested in sociological theory. After 1911 his central focus of concern was the sociology of religion, especially the relationship between religious beliefs and economic development.

In 1910 Weber fell in love with Else Jaffe, the wife of Edgar Jaffe and the best friend of his wife, Marianne. Most likely Weber's marriage had never been consummated, but with this new relationship, he had finally discovered passion and physical love (Ashley and Orenstein 1990; Mazlish 1993). Probably the new relationship affected Weber's sociological writing, making him aware of the role of emotions in social life. How else might we explain why, in the otherwise dry prose of *Economy and Society*, we find Weber saying such things as:

263

For sexual love, along with the "true" or economic interests, and the social drives toward power and prestige, is among the most fundamental and universal components of the actual course of interpersonal behaviour (Weber cited in Mazlish 1993, 223).

After the First World War, Weber joined the German Democratic Party. He firmly opposed the "crazy" left-wing revolutionary element of the Marxist Social Democratic Party and wished to prevent them from making a *putsch*. Weber was concerned about the future of his country, wanting to "restore Germany to her old glory." He died suddenly at 56, a victim of an influenza epidemic that killed millions following the war.

Weber had once remarked that he became a sociologist because he wanted to see just how much he could stand—just how much he could bear to look directly at the contradictions of human existence. He was convinced that the only option open to modern individuals was to learn to live with the inconsistent and incompatible demands of making a reasoned analysis and an ethical commitment. The complexities of Weber's life help us to understand the complexities of his thought. He synthesized national and global commitments. He championed rationality, yet he was able to analyze the role of the irrational in history. Given his psychological problems and his short life, the amount and scope of his sociological writings is truly impressive.

INTELLECTUAL BACKGROUND

Unlike Marx who had been strongly influenced by the dialectical thinking of Hegel, Weber was influenced by the philosophy of Immanuel Kant (1724–1804). Kant made a distinction between the kinds of knowledge one could have in the natural sciences and those in the human sciences. In the natural sciences, he argued, scientific methods of study will give us true knowledge about the external world as we experience it through our senses. But the knowledge that human beings have about themselves is something different. Because human beings have free will, their actions are not determined in the same ways as the actions of things in nature. Hence it is necessary to analyze moral philosophy to understand human behaviour.

Unlike the natural sciences, the moral laws that underlie the human sciences are not based on the meaning or significance of empirical data. Rather, the moral laws are innate and are understandable without reference to human experience. Weber agreed with Kant on this issue. He believed that human intellect could not distinguish between good and bad. It was not the task of intellectual activity to make moral judgments. Sociology, therefore, cannot derive ethical imperatives from the study of cultural values. While sociology can tell us about the consequences of our actions, it is unable to say whether those consequences are good or evil.

CONCEPTS

In spite of illness, Max Weber wrote a great deal in his lifetime on a wide variety of topics. One authority on Weber, Raymond Aron (1967, 219–20), has divided his work into four categories.

1. Studies in methodology, criticism, and philosophy. In these works, Weber considered the relationship between science and human action.

2. Historical works, including a study of the relations of production in agriculture in the ancient world, a general economic history, specific studies on economic problems in Germany and the rest of Europe.

3. Studies in the sociology of religion, including his most important study on the relationship between Protestantism and capitalism, as well as a comparative analysis of the great religions of the world and the reciprocal influence of economies and religions.

4. A treatise on general sociology entitled *Economy and Society*. Unlike Marx, Weber was not interested in developing a theory of human society. He was more concerned with showing why Western capitalist societies developed in ways that were different from all other types of societies. Unlike Comte, Hegel, and Marx, Weber did not believe that all societies followed general laws of development. He therefore did not develop any general categorizing schema (as Marx did concerning the development and transitions of different modes of production).

The Concept of Social Action

Weber believed that only individuals are capable of meaningful social action. For the purposes of sociology, he argued, "There is no such thing as a collective personality which 'acts.' When reference is made in a sociological context," he continued, "to a state, a nation, a corporation, a family or an army corps, or to similar collectivities, what is meant is...only a certain kind of development of actual or possible social actions of individual persons" (*Economy and Society*, 14). Weber's point was that only individuals could think, feel, and act. Collectivities were incapable of such things. The objective of sociology should be to comprehend the subjective understandings of the individual. Weber was mainly concerned with the actions of real-life people, particularly with how social actors conceptualized their social actions.

Although he strongly emphasized individual action, Weber was in no way a simple-minded idealist; that is, he did not believe that ideas and beliefs, individually generated and held, solely determined social action. Especially in his later work, Weber was very clear that the social action of any given individual was affected by both the psychological state of that individual and the external, cultural constraints that surrounded him or her. The action of the individual, he insisted, is always performed in relationship to some external order. He wrote:

> The satisfaction of our most ideal needs are everywhere confronted with the quantitative limits and the qualitative inadequacy of the necessary external means, so that their satisfaction requires planful provision and work, struggle with nature and the association of human beings (1949, 64).

Despite this stance, Weber strongly rejected the "materialist conception of history," which Marx favoured, and which placed the final emphasis on economic factors as the determining factors in human interaction. It was Weber's contention that "political, religious, climatic, and countless other non-economic determinants" were not accidental, but, rather, that they "actually follow their own laws."

His emphasis on the individual, and the individual's understandings of his or her actions, contrasts with the kinds of sociology that Durkheim and Marx developed. For Durkheim, the only unit of study that counted was the collectivity. To make individual motives and subjective understandings of behaviour the central focus of sociology was in direct conflict with Durkheim's ideas about "society" and "social facts" having an existence independent of any given individual. For Weber it is individuals alone who create meaning out of the "meaningless infinity of the world process."

The Concept of "Ideal Types"

According to Weber, different kinds of meaningful social actions make up human social life. It is the task of the sociologist to describe these highly complex actions and develop "ideal types" as heuristic devices or means of helping the researcher to make sense of social phenomena. Sociologists might wish to talk about capitalism, or feudalism, or Protestantism. But patterns of behaviour like those characteristic of capitalist or feudalist societies are made up of many interconnected elements. In order to understand such complex social phenomena, sociologists must decide first on the most essential aspects of what they are studying. Weber called these abstract categories ideal types.

An ideal type is not intended to be a complete or accurate description of some social reality. Rather, the investigator must abstract from that reality aspects that most interest him or her. All sociological writing is selective in that it emphasizes certain aspects of human social action while disregarding others. By using ideal types, Weber argued, sociologists can acknowledge that all reality is seen from a point of view. The central point Weber is making here is that it is an illusion to believe we can capture the true essence of social reality. Social reality is capable of being constructed and represented in countless different ways. What constitutes reality, Weber says, largely depends on the conceptual categories we use to view it in the first place.

Here Weber's position can be directly contrasted with Marx's. Marx believed there was a distinction to be made between surface reality and a deeper, essential reality. Indeed, as Marx contended, all science would be superfluous "if the outward appearance and the essence of things directly coincided." Although there may be many different ways of depicting capitalism or feudalism, or any other mode of production, Marx was convinced that some of these depictions were false while others were true and therefore scientific. Weber, on the other hand, believed that the most sociology could hope to achieve by seeking general and abstract knowledge about such things as capitalism, feudalism, or Protestantism was to isolate some of the possible and probable causes of some historical developments. He believed that complex events and circumstances were responsible for the occurrence of any single event in society. For example, the emergence of capitalism in Western Europe was the result of a combination of class formation, technological developments, religious transformations, and other cultural factors. Thus, while it is possible to use positivist methods to study human social interaction, the resulting knowledge, he argued, was not the kind of knowledge that sociologists should *want* to have. Instead, sociology is best suited to interpreting human social action.

The Concept Verstehen

For Weber, sociology "is a science which attempts the interpretive understanding of social action in order thereby to arrive at a causal explanation of its course and effects" (*The Theory of Social and Economic Organization*, 88). Thus, in developing the notion of ideal types, Weber pointed to understandings of large-scale social phenomena: but he did so with the ultimate objective of better constructing an interpretive understanding of human social action. Because subjective meaning is a part of social action, sociology necessarily must be an interpretive science.

Weber explained taking the subjective meanings of individuals as the starting point for sociological inquiry by using the concept of **Verstehen,** a German term that means "understanding." Weber used the term to imply an understanding of social action arrived at through a kind of empathetic connection with the actor on the part of the observer. The investigator tries to put him or herself into the shoes of the person under study and to imagine how that person might act in a similar circumstance. As an interpretive science, then, sociology is concerned with reconstructing the meaning of action from the actor's point of view.

Like Marx, Weber had doubts about the individual's capability to understand fully the meaning and significance of his or her own actions. To this end he wrote:

> In the great majority of cases actual action goes on in a state of inarticulate half-consciousness or actual unconsciousness of its subjective meaning. The actor is more

likely to "be aware" of it in a vague sense than he is to "know" what he is doing or be explicitly self-conscious about it....Only occasionally...is the subjective meaning of the action, whether rational or irrational, brought clearly into consciousness. The ideal type of meaningful action where the meaning is fully conscious and explicit is a marginal case (*Economy and Society,* 16).

The Concept of Bureaucracy

One ideal type of social organization that Weber discerned in many societies was the bureaucracy. Weber selected several distinctive features of a bureaucracy, including "a formal hierarchy of rank and officialdom, the application of rules according to the book, promotion by merit or seniority, strict control of the files and information and so on...." (Parkin 1992, 34). It was Weber's opinion that these characteristics gave bureaucracies a certain kind of *technical* superiority over other forms of organization (*Economy and Society,* 937).

A bureaucracy, according to Weber, is an official jurisdictional area regulated by definite rules and administered by bureaucrats who are trained to be impartial so that all clients are treated in the same manner. The bureaucrat carries out all work-related obligations in a dutiful manner and owes allegiance to the office held rather than to any particular individual. The bureaucrat obeys rules not as the personal servant of a superior but as a member of an organization from which he or she draws a salary commensurate with his or her rank and status in the organization. Within bureaucracies, individuals aspire to move up from lower positions to higher ones and by so doing to increase their salaries.

The rules for the operation of the bureaucracy administration are general ones. Neither the people within the bureaucracy nor the people outside of the organization that the bureaucracy administers are treated as individuals with unique situations. Rather they are treated as members of certain categories. Because of this bureaucracies can operate speedily, fairly, precisely, and at reduced costs. In modern societies, bureaucracies have become well established in all aspects of government: the creation of large standing armies, the administration of state budgets, the delivery of health-care services and social programs including education, welfare, and even religion.

Weber was convinced that all bureaucracies tend to develop highly inflexible and formalized rules where personal intentions had no place. As he wrote:

> Bureaucracy develops the more perfectly the more it is "dehumanized," the more completely it succeeds in eliminating from official business love, hatred, and all purely personal, irrational, and emotional elements which escape calculation (*Economy and Society*, 975).

Whereas Marx saw the most serious problems of capitalism inherent in the contradictions between the bourgeoisie and the proletariat, Weber thought that the most pressing problem was the emergence of bureaucratic administration. Certainly bureaucracies had existed before modern capitalism, but in capitalist society, he argued, each bureaucracy took on an a "seemingly cancerous life of its own" (Mazlish 1993, 234). Modern

267

bureaucracy, he announced, was "escapeproof" (*Economy and Society*, 1401). While Marx saw capitalism as depersonalizing all social relations, reducing them to cash exchanges, Weber saw bureaucracy as the depersonalizing agent. "[A bureaucracy] does not establish a relationship to a person...but rather is devoted to *impersonal* and *functional* purposes." Weber believed that the capitalist entrepreneur was a representative of the only ideal type in capitalist society "who has been able to maintain at least relative immunity from subjugation to the control of rational bureaucratic knowledge" (*Economy and Society*, 959).

WEBER'S SIGNIFICANCE TODAY

There is little doubt that the work of Max Weber continues to have a significant impact on many sociologists, particularly in North America. Certainly American sociologist Talcott Parsons (1902–1979) was strongly influenced by Weber's ideas, and in his turn Parsons did much to interpret and present Weber's work to an American audience. He translated some of Weber's major works from German into English. He also developed his own theory of society, which he called structural-functionalism, and which he based on Weber's work. Parsons went so far as to claim that if Weber had lived only a bit longer, he too would have probably become a functionalist (Parsons 1964).

In 1964, at the Fifteenth German Sociological Congress held in Heidelberg to commemorate the centenary of Weber's birth, Parsons praised Weber for rising above the "ideological disputes" of the late nineteenth and early twentieth centuries and for showing how the science of sociology might play a "major role" in shaping the future of the world. Indeed, Parsons went so far as to claim that Weber's sociology foreshadowed the end of "ideology."

That same conference was attended by another American sociologist, Herbert Marcuse. Marcuse, having fled Hitler's Germany during the 1930s to escape the horrors of anti-Semitism, had a very different perspective than did Parsons on the effects of Weber's sociology. Marcuse argued passionately that Weber's ideas about value-free sociology, far from marking the "end of ideology," in fact merely supported the domination of one class of people over another (Ashley and Orenstein 1990, 290).

Throughout the twentieth century, Weber's sociology has influenced many important social theorists of both left and right political leanings. Moreover, his work has been adapted by Americans such as Alfred Schutz (1899–1959) as the basis for interpretive theory. Schutz took Weber's emphasis on subjective understanding (*Verstehen*) as central to any sociological understanding. Others, including Herbert Marcuse, have used Weber's analysis of bureaucracy and legal-rational modes of thought as the basis for their own understanding of social class and class oppression in advanced capitalist societies. Generally in North America, theories of class and explanations of social stratification have, for the most part, drawn on Weberian rather than Marxian modes.

One of the reasons that Weber's work has been so widely adopted stems in part from the fact that he was "a brilliant and profound apologist for liberal capitalism" (Ashley and

Orenstein 1990, 292). His popularity stems, too, from the fact that he seems to have been much more aware than were the many "Marxists" who succeeded Marx of the various tensions and contradictions inherent in Western capitalist societies.

■ ■ ■

SUMMARY

In this chapter, I have examined the work of the first sociologists of the nineteenth and early twentieth centuries. Their ideas, theories, and work are often thought to constitute classical sociology.

The most important among these thinkers are Karl Marx, Émile Durkheim, and Marx Weber. The work of two late-eighteenth-century French writers, Claude Saint-Simon and Auguste Comte, has also been discussed.

The originators of sociology found much of their inspiration in the liberal and radical extensions of the Enlightenment tradition, where hope was sought for the emancipation of all humanity. However, many social thinkers also realized that with the emergence of industrial capitalism came grave possibilities for exploitation—especially through a bureaucratic system that constantly undermined the conditions necessary for people to enjoy their lives fully.

Those who helped found the discipline of sociology were concerned with what they perceived to be the unsettling consequences of the collapse of traditional society. For Durkheim, the most significant problem facing modern society was the absence of a morality appropriate to the new social conditions. With old traditions gone, and nothing new to replace them, Durkheim contended that normlessness or anomie prevailed. It was his opinion that the new discipline (sociology) he helped found had an obligation to establish the scientific basis for a new and more appropriate morality.

Karl Marx focused on the material conditions of human existence to develop his dialectical materialist method of studying society. Marx viewed capitalist society as based on social relationships between two very different social classes—workers and owners of the means of production. The interests of these two classes conflict, and the ensuing struggle between them, Marx predicted, would result in capitalism being replaced by a new kind of society based on socialism.

Like Marx, Max Weber was concerned with showing why Western capitalist societies have developed differently from all other known societies. Unlike Marx, however, Weber rejected a materialist conception of history. Instead he believed that politics, religion, climate, and other determinants followed their own laws, independent of economic considerations that Marx considered central.

According to Weber, the objective of any sociologist should be to comprehend the ways in which social actors understand and conceptualize their own actions, because it is individuals alone who make sense of world processes. By investigating the consequences of different types of social actions that individuals engage in, along with the conflicts that arise between and among individual members of a society, sociologists can come to understand how individuals reason and act.

■ ■ ■

FOR DISCUSSION

1. Discuss the social conditions that were significant for the development of the discipline of sociology. What are some of the conditions today that might lead to a further revolution in thinking about society?

2. Compare the political orientations of sociologists who promoted positivist, interpretive, and radical perspectives on society.

3. Discuss Marx's dialectical materialist method of studying society. How is it different from the dialectic of Hegel?

4. Apply Marx's concept of the capitalist mode of production to analyze Canadian society today.

5. Compare Marx's explanation for the emergence of capitalism with that of Max Weber.

6. Discuss Durkheim's concept of a "social fact." How did this concept help shape the way in which he viewed "society"?

13

SOCIOLOGY IN THE TWENTIETH CENTURY – MODERNITY AND ITS CRITICS

> **CHAPTER OPENING QUESTIONS**
>
> - What is the modern vision of sociological inquiry?
>
> - What does a postmodern perspective have to offer sociologists?
>
> - What contributions do feminist scholars bring to the discipline of sociology?

"There is a mode of vital experience," says American cultural theorist Marshall Berman, "—experience of space and time, of the self and others, of life's possibilities and perils—that is shared by men and women all over the world today" (1982, 15). Berman calls this experience **modernity**. To be modern, he continues, is to live a paradox: one is aware of living in an environment that promises to transform each and every individual and, indeed, the entire world. At the same time, one is also aware that everything could easily be destroyed.

The experience of modernity, Berman continues, cuts across all ethnic, political, geographical, national, and class boundaries. In this sense, the experience of modernity can be said to unite all of humanity. However, this unity

> pours us all into a maelstrom of perpetual disintegration and renewal, of struggle and contradiction, of ambiguity and anguish. To be modern is to be part of a universe in which, as Marx said, "all that is solid melts into air...."
> (16)

Berman goes on to note that the maelstrom of modern life is fed from a number of sources—new scientific discoveries, changes in the way we conceive of the universe and our place in it, industrialization, new technologies that create new human environments and destroy old ones, the speeding up of the tempo of life, new forms of class struggle, new means of mass communication, new political structures, struggles, and mass social movements. He concludes that, in the twentieth century, "the social processes that bring this maelstrom into being, and keep it in a state of perpetual becoming, have come to be called "modernism" (ibid.).

Needless to say, opinion about these momentous transformations that make up "the maelstrom of modern life" is polarized. Certainly the founders of the discipline of sociology viewed these transformations with a mixture of fear and pessimism, but also, as did Marx, with a sense of inevitability in the world-historical movement toward a more equitable society. Today we are still trying to understand and control those immense forces of change that began in the seventeenth century and that have been developing ever since.

In this chapter I extend the history of the discipline of sociology forward. I begin with a look at the early twentieth-century American version of scientific sociology and then consider the work of the mid-century structural-functionalists. Although structural-functionalism was enormously popular from the 1940s to the 1960s, it fell out of favour by the 1970s, unable to respond satisfactorily to challenges from other perspectives, including conflict theory.

As complex and paradoxical as modernity has been over the last several centuries, until recently the basic premises that modern scientists have held about knowledge production, truth, morality, and what constitutes a good and desirable society have remained quite constant. The second part of this chapter discusses some of the challenges to modern society and to the science of sociology via "postmodern" theories and feminist inquiry. The last two decades have been exhilarating and frustrating times not only in sociology but also in other social and natural sciences, as the foundations of knowledge have been questioned, reworked, and often rejected in favour of a more open, tentative, and questioning approach.

THE SCIENTIFIC STUDY OF AMERICAN SOCIETY

When Americans began to establish sociology departments in their universities, they were caught up in the hopes and fears of "modernity." Early American practitioners of sociology were convinced, as were their European counterparts who had influenced them, that the conscious management of society was something no complex society could do without. They believed that, as the science of society, sociology quickly would become a useful tool for resolving societal problems even as they emerged. Society for them was a collection of problems in need of scientific resolution; sociology was the only science through which this task could be accomplished.

American sociologist W.I. Thomas declared that the aim of sociology was "the abolition of war, of crime, of drink, of abnormality, of slums, of this or that kind of unhappiness." While it is difficult to say exactly when sociology began to be taught in the United States, by the 1880s courses bearing the title "sociology" were appearing. The first university sociology department was established at the University of Kansas in 1889.

These initial courses were oriented toward issues of social problems, with lectures and seminars that focused mainly on poverty, child labour, women wage earners, dependent children, insanity, juvenile delinquency, immigration, race relations, temperance, and labour movements. For Americans, it was soon clear that the new science of society was intended to be both reformatory and managerial and that it was to accomplish this goal through the rigorous use of scientific methods of inquiry. But even as the discipline was being established, the managerial and social-order objectives of sociologists, along with the scientific methods they were using, were being challenged.

That challenge has intensified during the last two decades with the rise of postmodern theories and with feminist critiques of science and society. But in the first decades of this century, American sociologists believed in a future shaped by scientific inquiry. As Luther Bernard wrote in 1919:

> We, as scientific workers in sociology, are so definitely launched upon the trend toward objectivism and definiteness of method...that it is needless to argue in its defense (298).

Bernard wrote at a time in the history of American sociology when interest in science and the scientific method of inquiry was experiencing a real growth. Lester Ward (1841–1913), the acknowledged founder of American sociology, had set out two separate tasks for the fledgling discipline. First, he argued that sociological inquiry begins with "feelings" because feelings alone produce social change, and social change is what sociology was all about. At the same time, Ward maintained that the dynamic laws of any society could be gathered only from empirical data. Sociology, from this perspective, was to be the collection and classification of what he called "statistical facts." In Ward's work, the same kinds of concerns appear that the earlier European founders of the discipline had faced: questions about how to deal with feelings, emotions, and other nonquantifiables, and at the same time how to gain the status of science for the new discipline. By the 1920s these questions were resolved in the United States in favour of science, and the notion that the natural and social sciences should be governed by similar concepts and methods prevailed. While debates were carried out over the usefulness of case studies, participant observation, and comparative methods of study, statistics had become the favoured method of sociological inquiry by 1939 (Bannister 1987, 3).

Moreover, it was a generally accepted proposition that sociologists should maintain strict neutrality in all matters concerning public policy and ethics. As students they were instructed not to pass moral judgments or to set any standards for human conduct. As a result of these widely accepted standards, early American sociologists

- focused on individual behaviour rather than on the ways in which larger social structures (the family, the education system) were formed and changed over time;

- emphasized an inductive model of science;

- promoted a bureaucratic vision of research done by teams of social scientists tied to established institutes of social science research.

Many took an **objectivist** approach to sociology. Objectivist meant a sociology conducted by trained, unbiased observers using statistical methods. In this sense, early American sociologists drew heavily on the work of Max Weber.

273

But Weber had specified that a different methodology was needed for the study of humanity (*Verstehen* or sympathetic understanding) than was needed for the study of nature. Moreover, by positing a stance of value-free neutrality, Weber had not meant that only social statistics and their manipulation should be the methods of research used by sociologists. Yet this was the stance taken by the American objectivists. Not surprisingly, then, even as they got started, there was growing opposition from others who employed different kinds of perspectives, such as those being developed under the rubric of the "Chicago School of Sociology."

THE CHICAGO SCHOOL

The department of sociology at the University of Chicago was established by Albian Small in 1892. In 1895, he founded the *American Journal of Sociology,* which continues today as one of the disciplines leading journals. He also founded, in 1905, the American Sociological Society (A.S.S.), which became the major professional association for American sociologists. In 1959 the A.S.S. changed its name to the American Sociological Association, A.S.A., for obvious reasons.

Early members of the sociology department at the University of Chicago included W.I. Thomas and Florian Znaniecki. Znaniecki and Thomas co-authored a famous study, *The Polish Peasant in Europe and America*, one of the first empirical studies published by American sociologists. The book took eight years to research and chronicled social disorganization among Polish migrants to America.

Another early member of the department, Robert Park, helped establish an area of research that the Chicago School became well known for—urban problems. But the School became famous for the work done by its members on the theory of **symbolic interactionism.**

SYMBOLIC INTERACTIONISM

Beginning with the work of W.I. Thomas, Charles Horton Cooley, and George Herbert Mead, symbolic interactionism has been one branch of American sociological theory that continues to attract a large following. Thomas and Mead have been discussed in Chapter 8. In this section I will deal only with the work of Erving Goffman (1922–1982), who became symbolic interactionism's best-known proponent. Although he spent his professional career teaching at the University of California, Berkeley, and later at the University of Pennsylvania, Goffman was born in Alberta and obtained his undergraduate degree from the University of Toronto. He did graduate work at the University of Chicago and was influenced greatly by social anthropologists and the symbolic interactionists.

Goffman's work was especially influenced by Mead's discussion of the tensions between the "I," the spontaneous self, and the "me," the socially constrained self. In *The Presentation of Self in Everyday Life,* he focused on this "crucial discrepancy between our all-too-human selves and our socialized selves" (1959, 56).

The assumptions of symbolic interactionism are outlined as follows:

1. Human beings act toward things on the basis of the meanings that the things have for them;

2. These meanings are the product of social interaction in human society;

3. These meanings are modified and handled through an interpretive process that is used by each individual in dealing with the signs each encounters (Craib 1984, 73).

The metaphor that guided Goffman's work on human action and interaction was that of dramaturgy. Goffman compared social life to a series of performances given by actors on a stage. The social self was not something that each social actor possessed but was the result of the dramatic interaction between actor and audience. The self, Goffman wrote, "is a dramatic effect arising from a scene that is presented" (1959, 253). It only appears to emanate from the actor.

Developing this metaphor further, Goffman argued that because the self is the product of an interaction between a social actor and his or her audience, the self is always vulnerable and susceptible to disturbances, which must be either prevented or dealt with. Actors need to control their audiences, especially disruptive ones. They need to make their audience do what they want them to do. Goffman talked about the **front stage,** the part of a social performance that is used to define the situation in a general way for an audience. He also discussed the **back stage,** where whatever is pertinent to the performance but not allowed on the front stage might appear, and an **outside,** which is neither front nor back stage. For example, a doctor's office is front stage when he or she examines patients, back stage when no patients are present, and outside when the doctor is vacationing in Hawaii.

In developing the dramaturgical metaphor, Goffman also referred to **settings,** the physical props and scenery that had to be present if a social actor were to give a credible performance. For example, firefighters usually require trucks, hoses, and other equipment to be taken seriously in their work. Doctors usually conduct examinations in an office filled with equipment, medications, and other signs of their profession. In both these cases the social actors go about their business in well-defined settings that are associated with them in everyone's mind.

Finally the **personal front** of any actor consists of those props that he or she needs to make the audience believe that the role being played is genuine. Firefighters wear hats, boots, and coats, which identify them as legitimate practitioners; doctors wear lab coats and often a stethoscope around their necks. University professors stand behind lecterns, carry lecture notes, hold chalk in their hands, use blackboards, overheads, and videos, all as a means of presenting a personal front that identifies them.

Goffman focused on what he called **teams** rather than individuals in any interaction setting. A team, for Goffman, is a set of individuals who cooperate together to stage a single performance. Thus an actor and audience form a team, and each member is reliant on the others to make the performance at hand run smoothly (Ritzer 1992, 359). A doctor, patient, nurse, and additional patients in a waiting room might form one team. A university professor and her class might form another.

In other works, such as *Stigma: Notes on the Management of Spoiled Identity* (1963), Goffman analyzed the gap between a person's *virtual social identity*, what he or she sets out to be, and *actual social identify*, what he or she actually is. Anyone who has a noticeable gap between these two kinds of identities, he claimed, is *stigmatized*.

ETHNOMETHODOLOGY AND PHENOMENOLOGICAL SOCIOLOGY

Ethnomethodologists have focused on the everyday, taken-for-granted social world we live in. Simply put, the term **ethnomethodology** refers to the "study of common-sense practical reasoning" (Collins 1988, 274). A more complex definition of ethnomethodology is offered by John Heritage, who contends that it is the study of

> the body of common-sense knowledge and the range of procedures and considerations by means of which the ordinary members of society make sense of, find their way about in, and act on the circumstances in which they find themselves (1984, 4).

Ethnomethodology was "invented" by American sociologist Harold Garfinkel in the late 1940s, but not systematized until he published *Studies in Ethnomethodology* in 1967. The perspective, along with its founder, continues to have a controversial reputation among other sociologists. According to social theorist Randall Collins:

> Ethnomethodology is widely regarded as a cult, cantering on outrageous theatrical claims and bizarre nonscientific "experiments." It is often claimed to be boring and commonsensical, poring over the details of everyday life in their endless banality (1988, 273).

Garfinkel makes two main replies to his critics. First, it is his conviction that the social world does not exist except in so far as it is constructed by people. Second, people account for their world and act in it using the same practical reasoning. These he refers to as *ethnomethods*, methods of accountability that everyone uses in their daily lives.

For example, when one person says "Hi," and the other responds "How ya doin'?" both greeters are involved in what Garfinkle terms **reflexive work**—they are engaging with each other through thoughts and actions to create a specific social reality. In this example, two people are trying to create a friendly or at least a neutral social reality by exchanging civil greetings. Garfinkle's point is that we all do this kind of reflexive work, but, for the most part, we remain unaware of what we are doing.

We become aware that we are trying to create a specific social atmosphere only when things don't turn out as expected. If, in response to a neutral or friendly "Hi," the other person turns away or yells an obscenity, there is a real opportunity to become aware of the reflexive work that was already going on but that failed. When reflexive work fails, Garfinkle says, we look for alternative explanations: "He didn't hear me"; or "He must have got up on the wrong side of bed."

The early methods he advocated are rarely used today, but they do tell us much about the approach. One of the methods used by Garfinkel is **breaching experiments.**

Three generations of a refugee Muslim family in Bosnia peer out as truckloads of new refugees file past. What ethnomethods do these people use as they view the carnage and mayhem that surround them?

In breaching experiments, ethnomethodologists deliberately violate social order in the hope of learning about the ethnomethods that ordinary people use to construct their social reality. In one infamous experiment, Garfinkel asked his students to spend from 15 minutes to an hour pretending to be a boarder in their parent's home. He instructed them "to conduct themselves in a circumspect and polite fashion," to "avoid getting personal," to use "formal address," and "to only speak when spoken to" (1967, 46).

Family members reacted strongly to this behaviour. "Reports were filled with accounts of astonishment, bewilderment, shock, anxiety, embarrassment, and anger, and with charges by various family members that the student was mean, inconsiderate, selfish, nasty or impolite." Garfinkel concluded that the reaction of family members served only to indicate the importance of acting within the bounds of taken-for-granted assumptions about behaviour.

He was most interested in finding that family members often sought common-sense ways of coping with the odd behaviour of the student. Questions like "Did you get fired?" "Are you sick?" or "Are you out of your mind or are you just stupid?" (Garfinkel 1967, 47) were common. If students did not acknowledge the validity of family members' explanations for their behaviour, family members themselves began to react more strongly. Withdrawal, denouncement, or retaliation were all means by which family members tried to deal with the inexplicable behaviour of the student. When the student finally explained the situation, harmony was restored in most cases, although in some families hard feelings lingered (Collins 1988, 398–99).

STRUCTURAL-FUNCTIONALISM

Although symbolic interactionism and ethnomethodology have some followers, the paradigm that came to dominate American sociology from the 1930s to the 1960s was known as **structural-functionalism** or, more briefly, as functionalism.

Structural-functionalists think in terms of systems. A system is a very general concept referring to anything that has parts that are connected to each other. A machine is a system. So is any biological organism or any organized collection of information. Within structural-functionalist theory, the connections between the parts of any social system can be material or ideal, living or inorganic, imaginary or actual; it can also be a combination of different sorts of elements such as an ecological system that involves both living species and geological features. Connections between parts can be physical ties or flows (pipes, electrical currents, chemicals); communications, signs, or acts of meaning; or even purely abstract mathematical or conceptual connections" (Collins 1988, 46).

Put as simply as possible, the basic metaphor underlying all structural-functional theory is that society is a large, living organism made up of a number of different, interrelated structures. Just as the internal organs (structures) of any human being's body function together to contribute to the survival of that body, so do presumably all parts of any given society function together to contribute to the maintenance of that society.

Like a living organism, a society has certain needs that must be met if that organism is to continue to exist. The structures of society—its institutions, culture, belief systems—contribute to the functioning of that society. All its institutions must work harmoniously if the society is to continue to exist.

Zeitlin and Brym (1991, 82–83) have defined the key concepts of structural-functionalism as follows:

1. Structure—any regular social pattern of conduct. This social pattern of conduct might be something as complex as a belief system or the institutional structures supporting specific religious practices. It might also be something as simple as the patterns of daily interaction between people in public spaces, i.e., a shopkeeper and her customers. Any given social structure,

Order, control, structure, civility: the cornerstone of early structural-functionalism. The family as a social institution was conceived as a harmonious system.

however, must contribute toward the maintenance of the social system in which it operates, if that social system is to continue to survive.

2. *Function*—what any given structure contributes to the smooth operation of the society. While Talcott Parsons recognized only the positive contributions of a structure to the functioning of society, Robert K. Merton (1968) allowed for negative consequences. He called these negative functions *dysfunctions*.

3. *System*—the relatively stable interaction between two or more persons or two or more structures. Thus a married couple might be considered a system, but so might something as large and complex as an entire society.

4. *System need*—whatever must take place to permit the system to maintain itself. Functionalists argue that every system has **integration** and **adaptation** as basic needs. All parts of a social system must work together smoothly (integrate) as well as adapt to the external environment.

The example of romantic love will give you an idea of how these different elements all might work together to form a functioning system. From a structural-functionalist perspective, romantic love would be considered a structure of Western society, that is, a relatively stable pattern of social conduct that persists. The function of romantic love in Western societies, then, might be seen as preparation for young people to leave the security of their families of birth in order to set up their own independent family units. One negative function might be that romantic love can lead not to happiness and a strong family unit but to disappointment and the subsequent refusal or inability to enter into a marriage relationship.

Proceeding with our example, the system would be the courting relationship between two young lovers, followed, supposedly, by a marriage relationship. Finally the larger societal system needs of integration and adaptation would be achieved as the young couple moved from dependence on parental units to establishment of their own family unit and thus toward perpetuating the heterosexual family as a basic social structure. From a structural-functionalist perspective, the heterosexual family promotes the emotional and economic well-being of the couple, as well as the biological continuation of the society.

A structural-functionalist answer to the general question of what causes any particular social pattern to exist is that each social pattern can be explained by the functions it serves in society. Paying doctors well, for example, is explained by the need to attract the best people to that position. The traditional restriction of women to the home and men to the workplace can be explained by the need to socialize children and the need to feed them.

TALCOTT PARSONS

Probably the best known of all the American structural-functionalists is Talcott Parsons (1902–1979), who pioneered structural-functionalist theory and was its leading architect and proponent. In developing his grand theory of society, Parsons drew heavily on the work of Durkheim and Weber, especially on their insight that social integration is the most significant aspect of any society. Parsons first formulated his theory during the

Nighthawks *by E. Hopper (1942) is an artist's depiction of fragmentation, malaise, and meaninglessness.*

Depression of the 1930s. It appeared to him that cherished American values were under strain, and social disorganization was rife. The answer to this situation, he believed, lay in promoting moral values, which in turn would act as a kind of glue that would hold society together. Parsons later modified his theory, and by the 1950s the basic tenets of American structural-functionalism could be summarized as follows.

1. Societies are whole systems made up of interrelated parts. Each part has meaning only in relation to the whole. Each part, too, performs a specific function within the system and contributes toward the integration and adaptation of the system as a whole.

2. Each element or part that makes up the whole system is indispensable to that system. Each part performs a specific function that is related to the overall "need" of the system.

3. Despite the first two points, the integration of all elements of a system into the whole is usually less than perfect. In reality, the system is fragile and unstable. Elements of disharmony and malintegration are present. These elements necessitate the presence of social control mechanisms.

4. Deviance and other forms of malintegration are dysfunctional in that they strain the existing social system. These dysfunctional elements tend to be resolved eventually through integration, thus restoring equilibrium to the system.

5. Social change is always adaptive and gradual.

6. Social integration is achieved through individual members of a society sharing common values, including a set of principles that legitimize the existing social, economic, and political order.

The system devised by Parsons is extremely abstract, and what I present here is only a small part of his elaborate theory. It does, however, give you some idea of what Parsonian theory entails. Parsons was interested in determining the basic functions that had to be fulfilled by any social system. Knowing these functions in advance makes it possible to classify every social institution according to its societal function. Parsons devised a four-part diagram, called the L-I-G-A scheme or the A-G-I-L scheme, depending on which way you read it.

Randall Collins explains what each letter stands for. **L** stands for latent pattern maintenance; it refers to the necessity for any system of action to have some basic pattern. Metaphorically speaking, it is a guiding script. **I** stands for integration and refers to a system's need to actively keep its parts together. **G** stands for goal attainment and refers to the fact that every system has some output or goal that it achieves in relation to its environment. **A** stands for adaptation and refers to the way the system supports itself as a physical entity in relation to the material environment.

The scheme is generated very abstractly by the two dichotomous dimensions, Internal/External and Means/Ends. Everything in a system may be regarded as operating in either internal or external directions, and can be either a means or an end. By crosscutting these two dimensions, we create four boxes, which Parsons labels L-I-G-A (Collins 1988, 57–58).

In the L box, Parsons placed those institutions—family, education, religion—that he believed produce basic cultural patterns and serve to socialize children. In the I box went all those institutions that actively promote social integration (e.g., legal institutions). In the A box, Parsons placed economy, which he decided was a system means. The social system deals with the external world by taking material inputs and transforming them into economic means that serve the physical needs of the system. Finally, the ends of the system, as it acts externally, is G or goal attainment, accomplished through the polity. To

FIGURE 13-1

L-I-G-A SCHEME

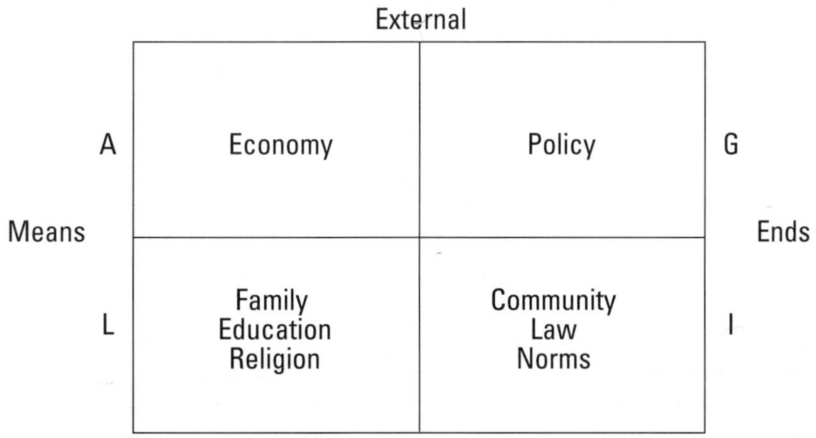

	External	
A	Economy	Policy	G
Means			Ends
L	Family Education Religion	Community Law Norms	I

make matters more complex, each of the four boxes could be divided again into another four boxes and treated as a separate system with its own L-I-G-A functions.

THE REVOLT AGAINST PARSONS AND FUNCTIONALIST THEORY

By the 1950s, structural-functionalism was regarded by many as the only desirable socio-logical theory, and sociologists such as Kingsley Davis proclaimed that the methods of functionalism were simply the methods characteristic of any sound scientific undertaking. However, contemporaries of Davis were voicing their dissent, claiming that functionalism was anything but a neutral, value-free, objective method for sociological inquiry. One of the most telling criticisms came from those who argued that, due to an overemphasis on social order and stability, structural-functionalists had failed miserably to provide any rea-sonable analysis of social conflict and social change.

Jeffrey C. Alexander suggests that while Parsons's theory of society was by no means simply an ideological diatribe, it is fairly clear that it was linked closely to his own hopes for a revitalized postwar society (1987, 112). Parsons believed that his theory of society would better explain social instability and that it would contribute to a process whereby political consensus and social equilibrium could be achieved.

Parsons began in the 1930s by emphasizing negative data and by criticizing American society, but by the 1950s a not-too-subtle shift had taken place. During this decade, the positive elements of his program for ideological renewal began to predomi-nate as he used his theory to highlight what he considered to be the "stabilizing features of Western society." These features, he argued, formed the basis of what the "good" soci-ety was all about. Moreover, he was convinced that the United States was the leading world model of what constituted that society. By the 1950s, Parsons had linked his own reputation and stature to that of the United States. As Alexander comments:

> You can easily understand, in light of these strong ideological links, that any significant change in the social environment of the postwar period would greatly affect the recep-tion of Parsons's work. To put the connection crudely and simply, if the prestige of the United States were fundamentally challenged, if it looked less like the model for a good society, then the prestige of Parsons's own theorizing would falter (1987, 113).

When Parsons first began to formulate his functionalist theory immediately follow-ing the Second World War, he did so within a social atmosphere of hope and a belief that a new era had dawned on human social relations. The threat of Nazism had been broken by an alliance of capitalist and communist nations, holding out for many the hope of a future world without strife. In capitalist countries, glaring disparities between the social classes were softened somewhat by social welfare legislation. But by the end of the 1950s, Americans were once again embroiled in class and race-based conflicts.

Third World nations also began experiencing conflicts. By the 1960s, it was appar-ent that the American commitment to spreading capitalist development in so-called "underdeveloped" nations was not going to be easily accomplished. Instead, these nations had become a source of instability and revolution and not, as had been anticipated, the testing place for American ideals of democracy and economic progress.

Finally, intellectual and philosophical critiques of Western ideologies and culture were appearing during the 1950s and 1960s. The beatniks and then the hippies criticized postwar society for holding up the ideals of individualism, democracy, and personal freedom while at the same time demanding conformity from its youth. Postwar youth, now relatively affluent and independent, became the ideal carriers of "the sensual, rebellious culture of rock-and-roll music" (Alexander 1987, 16).

Because Parsons had tied his theories to a particular vision of a positive, fulfilling society, his theories were also open to question once that vision was in doubt. By the 1960s many were criticizing, not praising, Parsons.

American sociologist Alvin Gouldner's critique of functionalism in general and of Parsons in particular is telling in this respect. Functionalism, Gouldner wrote, favours the preservation of privilege. Because this theory takes as its central problem the preservation of social order, it is attractive to those who have the most to lose should society change (1971, 252–54).

In the 1950s, C. Wright Mills raised an important criticism of Parsons's theories when he wrote that functionalism was an example of a "grand theory" that reflected the dominant values of American capitalism while failing to address the realities of the division of power in that society. His theories, Mills argued, neglect to consider that the social consent necessary for the functioning of society might be achieved through manipulation (Mills 1959, 232).

THE RISE OF CONFLICT THEORY

C. Wright Mills was one among many postwar American sociologists whose writings challenged Parsons's focus on the problem of social order. Although Mills is not properly classified as a conflict theorist, his work has much in common with that of those who first challenged the Parsonian vision of society. Conflict theorists, such as John Rex, David Lockwood, Ralf Dahrendorf, and Lewis Coser, took their inspiration from the work of Marx and Weber. All insisted, contra Parsons, that sociology be a public and political undertaking, rather than a private,

Two young boys tinkering with their identity are also a part of today's social reality. They have positioned themselves outside any "mainstream" structural system. Conflict theorists view this behaviour as understandable because society is composed of many groups with competing and conflicting interests.

academic one. The emphasis that conflict theorists place on power and domination is what strongly differentiates their work from that of structural-functionalists. In contrast to the functionalists, conflict theorists view society as being composed of a number of groups and organizations with competing and even conflicting interests. The system of power and domination at the root of every social system is characterized by a division of society into the rulers and the ruled. The division is backed up by each group's recognition of its own and other groups' relative power.

In the 30 years or so since conflict theory was first proposed, it has made a substantial impact on the field of sociology. In light of the propositions of conflict theorists, the concept of deviance has been reinterpreted so that it is no longer considered something dysfunctional, but rather a result of the control exercised by some group over the definitions of acceptable behaviour. Professionals are thought of as people who hold a monopoly over certain kinds of knowledge, not as ones who hold key functional positions. Racism, too, is seen as the outcome of struggles between colonizers and those they are attempting to dominate. Status differences between groups are considered to be the result of one group's ability to control material goods or information and not as a

	MODERNIST THINKERS		
THEORETICAL PERSPECTIVE	**KEY THEORIST**		**MAIN ASSUMPTIONS**
Symbolic Interactionism	Erving Goffman		Humans act on the basis of meaning.
			All meanings are product of social interaction.
			All meanings are subject to being modified through a process of interpretation.
Ethnomethodology	Harold Garfinkel		The social world exists only in so far as it is constructed by people.
			Members of a given society account for and act in their world on the basis of a shared system of practical reasoning.
Structural-Functionalism	Talcott Parsons		Societies are whole systems made up of interrelated parts.

TABLE 13-1

TABLE 13-1 (Continued)		
MODERNIST THINKERS		
THEORETICAL PERSPECTIVE	**KEY THEORIST**	**MAIN ASSUMPTIONS**
		Each part contributes toward the integration and adaptation of the system as a whole.
		Each part performs a specific function that is related to the overall need of the system.
		Integration within a given system is often imperfect, rendering the system unstable.
		Due to malintegration, mechanisms of social control are necessary.
		Social integration is based on shared values.
		Social change is adaptive and gradual.
Postmodern Theories		
Deconstruction	Jacques Derrida	Meaning originates both in the production of a text and in its reception by a reader.
		All understanding is interpretive; there is no objective position possible.
		The objective of any analysis is to disrupt and question authority.
Genealogy	Michel Foucault	All social practices are contingent, historically specific, and socially instituted.
		Power in modern societies is ubiquitous. It is constructive rather than repressive.
		The human sciences, including sociology, contribute to the proliferation of new techniques of power.

285

functional prerequisite to social cohesion. Yet even as conflict theory was being devised, new critics were showing dissatisfaction, arguing that it is as crude and unsatisfactory a framework as structural-functionalism.

CHALLENGES TO MODERNIST APPROACHES TO KNOWLEDGE

In the last two decades, new approaches to knowledge construction have emerged to challenge the basic premises that underlie *all* the approaches to the social world that we have dealt with. Up to this point, the theories under consideration fall within what might be called a "modernist" perspective. Despite their great differences, sociologists from Auguste Comte to the structural-functionalists, conflict theorists, and symbolic interactionists held certain fundamental premises in common. These premises are characteristic of what has been called modernity.

MODERNITY

Modernity refers to the long epoch that emerged after the decline of feudalism and the Middle Ages. For some the term "modern" designates all societies that stand in opposition to "traditional" ones. To be modern therefore has connotations of being dynamic, progressive, and innovative. But that dynamism and innovativeness are not without their drawbacks. To be modern

> is to find ourselves in an environment that promises us adventure, power, joy, growth, transformation of ourselves and the world—and, at the same time, that threatens to destroy everything we have, everything we know, everything we are" (Berman 1982, 15).

With the demise of the religious view of the world, the modern world emerged along with a growing realization that human social order was vulnerable, contingent, and devoid of reliable foundations (Bauman 1992, xi). This discovery was shocking to many, and modern science emerged as an attempt to make the world solid and reliable again. Reason, as opposed to superstition and religion, was to be the vehicle for establishing security and reliability. All modernist discussions of the social world, from Descartes to twentieth-century sociologists, have accepted the premise that reason is "the source of progress in knowledge and society, as well as the privileged locus of truth and the foundation of systematic knowledge" (Best and Kellner 1991, 2).

The modern world view that emerged during the seventeenth century was that nature, and indeed all of life, was spontaneous, chaotic, and in need of taming. Chaos, it was feared, would overwhelm all if vigilance was let up for one moment. As Bauman states, "The war against mystery and magic was for modernity a war of liberation leading to the declaration of reason's independence" (1992, x). Because the natural world was viewed as an enemy to be controlled and vanquished, nature had to be deprived of autonomous will and the power of resistance. To win against chaos and disorder, the modernists set about de-spiritualizing the world, and in the process refused to consider nature as an independent subject. Objectified, the world could be acted on wilfully by humans. The world became a source of raw material; natural resources would be given form only by human designs. Against such a disenchanted world the postmodernist criticism of modernism has taken aim.

Critics of modernism have pointed out that modernity has produced, along with many advances, oppression and misery: the subjugation of peasants, proletarians, and artisans by capitalist industrialization; the exclusion of women from the public sphere; genocide as a result of imperialist colonization (Best and Kellner 1991, 3). German-American critical theorists Max Horkheimer and Theodor Adorno (1972) use the term "dialectic of Enlightenment" to describe the process whereby "reason" has been turned into its opposite, and modernity's promise of liberation has been used to mask acts of domination and oppression. Some of the strongest criticism of traditional sociology and modernist approaches to analyzing social relations have come from late twentieth-century feminist theorists.

FEMINISM

Early sociologists paid little attention to gender; however, it now merits serious consideration. Alison Jaggar (1983) points out that, while feminism has always existed because women have always resisted subordination, only in the last two or three centuries has a visible feminist movement emerged to struggle against women's oppression in an organized way.

According to British sociologists and feminists Pamela Abbot and Claire Wallace (1990), between the 1960s and the 1970s many women began expressing the opinion that sociology for the most part ignored the experiences of women. Although sociology was to be about "understanding the relationship between our own experiences and the social structures we inhabit," the experiences discussed by sociologists were almost always men's. If women appeared at all it was as men saw them and not as they saw themselves. In this way, sociology actually contributed to the subordination and exploitation of women. While claiming to put forward a detached and objective view of women, male sociologists promoted their own biased positions (1990, 4).

The reason for this, Canadian sociologist Dorothy Smith has argued, is that women's concerns and experiences had traditionally been viewed as subjective, while the experiences of men had been thought of as objective, and thus as the basis on which true knowledge could be produced (1979).

FEMINIST CRITICISM OF TRADITIONAL SOCIOLOGY

Criticisms of traditional sociology by feminist scholars since the 1960s are summarized by Abbott and Wallace as follows:

1. Sociology has been mainly concerned with research on men and by implication with theories for men;

2. Research findings based on all-male samples are generalized to the whole of the population;

3. Areas and issues of concern to women are frequently overlooked and seen as unimportant;

4. When women are included in research they are presented in a distorted and sexist way;

5. Sex and gender are seldom seen as important explanatory variables (1990, 4–5).

Sociology, they conclude, has at best been sex-blind, at worst sexist. There has been little recognition that women's structural position and therefore experiences in society are different from those of men and that, as a result, gender is an important explanatory variable in social research. The result has been a particular view about men, women, and their differences and interrelations.

Feminist scholars have proposed at least three different solutions to rectify the situation. The first is simply to remove the sexist bias that has always been inherent in the discipline. Women need to be brought into sociology through research that incorporates them and by reforming existing theories to remove their sexist biases. Other feminists have argued that a separate sociology is needed by women for women. Feminists who support this approach argue that, since the world is always interpreted from a specific point of view, the best solution is to develop a sociology that sees the world from a woman's perspective. Moreover, because women share more with each other, regardless of other differences, than they share with men, feminist research should be devoted to improving the conditions under which all women live. Finally, some feminist theorists argue that it will never be enough to integrate feminist sociology into existing perspectives. Instead, a complete revolution in sociological theories is needed. Existing theories are sexist and as such beyond reform. A total reformulation of sociology is necessary (Abbott and Wallace 1990, 10).

The word "feminism" is of French origin. It was introduced into the United States at the beginning of this century to refer to a group of women's rights activists who proclaimed the uniqueness of women and the mystical experiences of motherhood. These activists were opposed to women's subordination because of what they believed to be women's "superior purity."

But they were not the only group of women struggling for emancipation. Another group of women, the "sexual rationalists," were also opposed to women's subjugation to men, not on the grounds of their differences, but rather because of the similarities between the two sexes (Ehrenreich and English 1989). Today the term feminism is used to refer to "all those who seek, no matter on what grounds, to end women's subordination." And the term "women's liberation movement" is the major political form that feminism has taken in contemporary Western society (Jaggar 1983, 5).

Sometimes feminist theorists make a distinction between "liberal feminism," "radical feminism," and "socialist feminism." Liberal feminism is concerned with the day-to-day discrimination that every woman faces living in a Western society, not with an analysis of women's subordination in terms of overarching structures such as biology or capitalism. Liberal feminists are concerned with women's unequal access to education and to employment opportunities. They combine this concern with a further one in the "sexist attitudes towards women that often act to sustain discrimination against them in Western societies" (Walby 1990, 4–5).

Politically, liberal feminists focus on the reform of legislation and on the promotion of women's equality. One criticism of liberal feminism is that it is unable to deal with either the origins or the persistence of discrimination against women. A second criticism is that this approach has benefited only those women who are already privileged because of their class and race.

Radical feminists argue that differences between the sexes constitute a universal basis for the oppression and domination of women, known as patriarchy. It is a system in which men as a group benefit from the subordination of women as a group. Male violence against women is considered an integral part of patriarchy. One main criticism raised against radical feminism is that it reduces everything to essential biological differences. A second criticism follows from the first. Because radical feminists see differences between men and women almost exclusively as biological differences, they place all women in one category and all men in another. However, this fails to take into account the divisions that exist within the category *women* or the category *men* because of differences in race, class, ethnicity, economic status, or sexual orientation.

Socialist or Marxist feminists contend that inequality between men and women derives not from essential biological differences but as a result of the way in which capitalism organizes labour. Within the family, women as housewives do unpaid work—cleaning, providing meals, raising children. This unpaid work provides capitalists with a cheap work force. Housewives are essential to capitalism, but they receive only enough for their subsistence from their husbands. The main criticism against socialist or Marxist feminists is that they focus too narrowly on capitalism, incorrectly reducing inequality between men and women to economic relations. Not only does this ignore issues of beliefs and cultural practices, but it also ignores gender inequalities in noncapitalist societies.

Recently some feminist writers have come under attack from other feminist writers for their failure to address issues of either racial differences or differences in sexual orientations. Feminist theorists such as Elizabeth Spelman, for example, argue that there has been a tendency in Western feminist thought to posit the existence of a generic "woman." Spelman contends that there are racial, class, religious, ethnic, and cultural differences between women. Western feminist thought, she argues, "has taken the experiences of white, middle-class women to be representative of, indeed normative for, the experiences of all women." This has reinforced the privileges that white, middle-class, heterosexual women enjoy (1990, x).

POSTMODERN APPROACHES

In opposition to what they consider the gross failings of the modernist perspective, postmodern theorists claim that new high-tech mass media and the accompanying social, economic, and cultural transformations have produced a new society. Postmodernity, they claim, constitutes a fresh stage in human history, one that requires new concepts and

symbolic interactionism, where the meanings we attach to social relations are human constructs, not objective realities (Goffman 1959; Berger and Luckmann 1966). They have drawn from **anarchism,** especially in its questioning of authority and the arbitrary imposition of any one given systematic point of view. Finally **romanticism** has contributed to postmodernism a focus on fantasy, feelings, emotions, the unusual, the sacred. Romanticism has also contributed the troubling stance that there are no universal criteria for beauty, goodness, or truth. Like the romantics, postmodernists feel they are living "between" times, in a society where conventional social practices no longer hold meaning, but where new ones are yet to be developed.

Because the term postmodern is used in so many different fields and disciplines, the definitions and conceptualizations are often at odds with one other. To cut down on some of the confusion and to help simplify discussion, Pauline Rosenau (1992) has divided postmodernist approaches into two broad categories: the **sceptical postmodernists** and the **affirmative postmodernists.** Sceptical postmodernists focus on the negative, tend to offer no hope for anything, and are inclined to anticipate the worst. They argue that the postmodern age is one of fragmentation, disintegration, malaise, meaninglessness, and absence of moral parameters. In short, the postmodern age is one of social chaos (Baudrillard 1983; Scherpe 1986–87, 101) where nothing new is possible (Gitlin 1989, 103); it is an era waiting for a catastrophe.

While the affirmative postmodernists agree with the sceptics' general critique of modernity, they also offer hope and have a more optimistic view of the postmodern age. They are open to positive political action, to struggle and resistance. They do not shy away from being positive about the social world they inhabit, or from making choices based on established social norms. Nor do they avoid arguing that some value choices are superior to others. Because the term postmodern generates so much controversy in the field of social sciences, many people avoid its use altogether.

The Role of the Expert

One of the criticisms that postmodernists make of modern approaches to knowledge concerns the relation between the *expert* and the *student*. In the modern view, the expert always holds a privileged position with respect to the generation of knowledge. The expert takes the role of the final arbiter of meaning; the true meaning of any text is deemed to be whatever the expert or author intended. If the student wishes to understand a text, it is up to him or her to discover that intent.

From this point of view, the role of the modern expert is to educate by communicating meaning to an as yet uneducated *reader* and to instil moral values or to offer enlightenment. The expert, by virtue of his or her position as intellectual, educator, professional, or specialist, is assumed to have privileged access to truth, reason, and scientific knowledge. He or she decides what is true by looking at conflicting points of view, weighing their positive and negative aspects, and then presenting his or her understanding as the only correct one.

From the modernist perspective, an expert's selection is always considered to be correct and binding, at least until some other expert comes along with more compelling arguments (Bauman 1987). Postmodernists question this role of the modern expert by challenging the authority and the power of the expert to deliver a definitive statement on some event or idea. In place of claims of truth, postmodernists call for the activities of "listening, questioning and speaking" (Ashley and Walker 1990, 259–68).

The Relationship between Theory and Reality

The relationship between theory and data is significant for postmodernists. They maintain that every fact is always already "theory laden" because facts are invented by the community and have little or no meaning outside that community (Smith 1988, 105). Take, for example, the case of the present-day myths of the Maori of New Zealand. Early in this century, Western anthropologists who visited and studied the Maori created their own versions of these people's history. In inventing their account of Maori history, these anthropologists used documents of doubtful origins. But today these histories created by Western anthropologists have become interwoven into the myths of the Maori people themselves so that for them it is meaningless to talk about a "true" as opposed to an "invented" myth (Hanson 1989, 890; Rosenau 1992, 87–88). Postmodernists argue that the "truth" of any text depends on the creative activity of the reader and not on the intentions of the original author (Clifford 1988, 520).

This example illustrates how "facts" are invented by communities rather than "discovered" by impartial observers trained in the scientific method of inquiry. As such, facts always have original meaning only inside the community in which they were invented. Using examples such as the Maori history, postmodernists are able to insist that rigid truth claims can no longer be considered viable.

Postmodernists, Rosenau claims, reject all modern views about science, epistemology, and methodology. They have little or no faith in reason. Modern social science, like modern natural science, operates by assuming that there is an independent reality out there, and that we can use theory to test our assumptions about that reality. Modern social scientists strive to discover and explain what they call that external reality. Postmodernists (Latour and Woolgar 1979, 153; Edelman 1988, 6) argue that if reality does exist, it does so as a result of the activities of scientists. In this view, *signs* (what can be observed via the senses) are not representations of reality; rather they produce reality (Ryan 1988, 565–66).

Modern science assumes that causality and predictability are essential to any explanation. The world, in this view, is predictable and can be understood as a system of causal relations where independent variables predict dependent ones with certain statistical regularity. Those who follow the scientific model admit that complete knowledge of all causal variables is impossible. As a result, they endeavour to make a general assessment of how specific phenomena are interrelated. Usually this interrelation is based on temporal proximity of the independent and dependent variables. (Simply put, this means that some event "A" happens, the independent variable, and as a result event "B" follows, the dependent variable.) Postmodernists, on the other hand, contend there are no methods or rules of procedure to which they must conform. In place of the scientific method, they look to personal experience, empathy, emotion, intuition, subjective judgment, imagination, creativity, and play (Rosenau 1992, 117).

By way of comparison, recall that modern social science understands the act of interpretation to be a careful reading of any data source, with the objective of discovering already existing patterns. Meaning is never arbitrary, never dependent on the observer or on circumstances. Rather it is acceptable to say that some interpretations are better than others because they are based on a correct reading of the existing data. Postmodernists recognize that many different interpretations might be possible for any given body of information.

DECONSTRUCTION

One of the postmodernists' methods of choice for dealing with the production of knowledge is called **deconstruction**. The term was introduced by French philosopher and literary theorist Jacques Derrida in the mid-1960s. Deconstruction is intended to be an act of demystifying a text. The text is figuratively torn apart in order to reveal its internal arbitrariness, hierarchies, and presuppositions. Deconstruction lays out the flaws of a text, examines margins, and looks for what is repressed, masked, excluded, or concealed. The objective is to transform, redefine, undo, and reconstruct. Derrida (1967) has argued that when we read a text, what we read has very little to do with what the author intended. Meaning originates not only in the production of a text by its author, but also in its reception by a reader. According to Derrida and his followers, the reader interprets any given text in the act of reading, so there is no single true meaning. In the words of political scientist and feminist theorist Jane Flax,

> Deconstructive readers are disrespectful of authority, attentive to suppressed tensions or conflicts within the text, and suspicious of all "natural" categories, essentialist oppositions, and representational claims. They are willing to play with the text, to disrupt its apparent unity, to rescue its heterogeneous and disorderly aspects and its plurality of meanings and voices. They are not to think of themselves as authorities or as un- or discovers of Truth, but rather as potentially interesting members of an ongoing conversation (1990, 38).

Flax suggests that there is a certain affinity between postmodernist use of deconstruction and the method of hermeneutic (or interpretive) inquiry (see Chapter 8). Both accept that all understanding is interpretative and that there is no objective, value-free position from which to observe or to speak or write about something. To this extent, no speaker can claim special or privileged authority. Each speaker and each reader offers an interpretation of what is under study.

Whereas interpretive or hermeneutic thinkers argue that there is a "deep" meaning that can be uncovered and reconstructed, those who use deconstruction argue that there is no single meaning to be uncovered. For Derrida, no ultimate authoritative or correct interpretation exists that must be deferred to. Rather than recovering deep meaning—the objective of interpretive theory—Derrida's deconstructive approach calls for a constant, open-ended disruption of and disputation with the text's authority by constantly creating new meanings and interpretations of that text (Flax 1990, 39).

MICHEL FOUCAULT'S "GENEALOGICAL" CRITIQUE OF MODERNITY

Michel Foucault's writings on society, knowledge, power, and the body have all made major contributions to postmodern thought. Until his untimely death from AIDS in 1984, he reflected on and wrote about the appearance and nature of "modern societies." He called his method of reflecting **genealogy.** Foucault conceived of culture as a specific set of social practices. Contrary to hermeneutics, which looks for hidden meanings in how social practices are discussed, the genealogical method assumes that everything is interpretation from beginning to end. Foucault believed that all cultural practices are contingent, historically specific, and socially instituted. The genealogical method of inquiry allowed Foucault to construct unusually rich accounts of the emergence and operation of power relations (1977).

One of his most important insights concerns the ubiquitous operation of power in modern societies, power even in the most simple social practices. Power in modern societies is not essentially repressive, Foucault says. Rather it is constructive, and it touches people through their social practices—those that constitute everyday life in modern society. Like other postmodernists, Foucault rejects the equation of reason with human progress and emancipation, arguing instead that modern forms of power relations and ways of producing knowledge have created new forms of domination.

This theme is sustained throughout his writings on a wide variety of topics, including medicine, psychiatry, crime and punishment, sex and sexuality, and the rise of the so-called human sciences. Foucault's major objective, which is fairly consistent in all his work, has been to criticize our own historical era by questioning modern forms of knowledge, rationality, and social institutions that seem to be "natural" but that are in fact sociohistorical constructs of power and domination.

Foucault's work concentrates on the domination of the individual through social institutions and practices. He analyzes knowledge and truth as integral components of domination and not as neutral, objective, and universal means to progress. In his book *Discipline and Punish*, for example, Foucault describes historical changes in the way that

Correction officer at a maximum security prison.

the individual, the body, and the soul have been conceptualized, and their changing relations to the social institutions that control them.

He argues that as the conceptualization of the individual, body, and soul changed in history, so too did the "disciplinary techniques" for keeping them in order. In modern society, the life of the prisoner, the student, and the soldier are

295

racial groups, genders, and age groups. When we study inequality, we seek to explain why these valuable attributes are distributed in a particular way as well as the consequences of that distribution.

One kind of inequality that has been widely studied by sociologists is what Eric Olin Wright calls "inequalities of material welfare." Sociologists have used two different perspectives to understand these inequalities—the achievement and exploitation approaches. Depending on the approach chosen, sociologists have produced different kinds of explanations about the distribution and consequences of social class inequalities.

From the perspective of the achievement model of social inequality, individuals acquire material wealth differentially on the bases of their own efforts. Two individuals pursuing the same occupation may easily end up with very different amounts of income. As Wright (1994) explains:

> The paradigm case would be two farmers on adjacent plots of land: one works hard and conscientiously, the other is lazy and irresponsible. At the end of a production cycle one has twice the income of the other....The conscientious farmer saves and reinvests part of the income earned during the first cycle and thus expands production; the lazy farmer does not have anything left over to invest and thus continues production at the same level. The result is that over time the inequality between the two farmers increases....(26).

Eventually the conscientious farmer's holdings increase to the point where he must employ others to help him work his farm, while the lazy farmer, having wasted his resources, is unable to support even himself adequately and therefore has to go to work for the conscientious farmer as a wage labourer.

In sociology this kind of model of individual achievement is referred to as a **status attainment model of stratification,** and deviations from the expected societal norms are usually attributed to some obstacle that is placed in the way of the individual—such as race, gender, sexual orientation, ethnicity—and that acts as an obstacle to "equal opportunity."

By contrast, **exploitation models of inequality** regard disparities in material wealth distribution as the result of social relations, not of individual effort. Again, Wright explains:

> In order to obtain income, people enter into a variety of different kinds of social relations. These will vary historically and can be broadly classified as based in different "modes of production." Through a variety of different mechanisms, these relations enable one group of people to appropriate the fruits of labor of another group. This appropriation is called exploitation. Exploitation implies that the income of the exploiting group at least in part depends on the efforts of the exploited group rather than simply their own effort (27).

In this model individual effort can have some effect on wealth distribution since some individuals prefer to spend more time at leisure activities than others, but these issues are secondary to the more fundamental mechanisms of exploitation. From this perspective, the material wealth that any individual acquires is a result of social relations between a wide variety of people, and only to a much smaller degree the result of individual effort. As we will see below, the approach that is taken to the issue of inequalities between individuals greatly affects the kind of analysis of social class that different sociologists have made.

	MODELS OF SOCIAL INEQUALITY	CHARACTERISTICS
TABLE 14-1	**1. STATUS ATTAINMENT**	• Disparities in material wealth between individuals are the result of efforts of individuals. • Obstacles to equal opportunity include factors such as race, gender, and sexual orientation.
	2. EXPLOITATION MODEL	• Disparities in social wealth between individuals are the result of the kinds of social relations between society members. • Exploitation occurs when members of one group are able to appropriate the benefits of the labour of members of another group.

SOCIAL CLASS DEFINED

When it comes to analyzing issues of social inequality, social classes and the differences between them are probably the most discussed topics in all of sociology. Whether sociologists use an achievement or an exploitation approach to understanding social class, they all share a common assumption that the concept of class can be used in constructing theories about observable regularities in social organization and behaviour. American sociologists H. Gerth and C.W. Mills ([1954] 1964) summed this up best when they wrote:

> No matter what people believe, class structure as an economic arrangement influences their life chances according to their positions in it. If they do not grasp the causes of their conduct this does not mean that the social analyst must ignore or deny them (340).

Because of the significance of class to sociological theory, it should not be surprising that the concept is used in many different ways and has a wide variety of meanings.

Marx and Engels claimed that while every society had its characteristic class antagonisms, the resolution of which led to a higher level of human development, it was only with capitalism that the conflict between social classes could lead ultimately to the end of all class conflict.

Socialism and later advanced communism, in the view of Marx and Engels, were the necessary resolutions to internal conflicts generated by what they designated as the **capitalist mode of production**. Once advanced communism had been achieved, however, all class conflict would cease because there would no longer be any class inequalities. With the accompanying rise of the advanced communist mode of production, they were convinced that human history, as the history of class struggles, would end.

Winnipeg General Strike, June 4, 1919. Confrontation between labour and management led to a massive city shutdown in which public-sector employees and workers in private industry protested together for collective bargaining, better wages, and improvement of working conditions. Government forces ended the strike, leaving a legacy of bitterness.

THE CAPITALIST MODE OF PRODUCTION

Much of Marx's writing was devoted to an analysis of what he termed the capitalist mode of production: he contended that it is characterized by private ownership of the means of production. Societies dominated by the capitalist mode of production are made up of two great, opposing classes, the proletariat or working class, and the capitalist class or

bourgeoisie. Members of the proletariat own nothing except their ability to work (their labour power), which they are obliged to sell to the bourgeoisie, who own and control the material means of production.

Marx also recognized other classes in capitalist societies, which he variously identified as the **petite bourgeoisie**, the **lumpenproletariat**, the financiers, the peasantry, the landed aristocracy, and the middle class. The petite bourgeoisie, for example, was said to be made up of small business owners and the term lumpenproletariat was used to refer to marginal and often criminal people who lived on the "crumbs of society."

While Marx recognized that there were more than two antagonistic classes in capitalist societies, he nonetheless contended that, as capitalism developed, the two main classes—the proletariat and the bourgeoisie—would increase in size and gradually absorb the other subsidiary classes. Ultimately there would come a time when the conflict between the two antagonistic classes would lead to revolution. As Marx and Engels wrote in *The Manifesto of the Communist Party:*

> When, in the course of development, class distinctions have disappeared and all production has been concentrated in the hands of a vast association of the whole nation, the public power will lose its political character. Political power, properly so called, is merely the organized power of one class for oppressing another. If the proletariat during its contact with the bourgeoisie is compelled by the force of circumstances to organize itself into a class; if by means of a revolution it makes itself into the ruling class and, as such, sweeps away by force the old conditions and production, then it will along with these conditions have swept away the conditions for the existence of class antagonisms and of classes generally, and will thereby have abolished its own supremacy as a class.

> In place of the old bourgeois society, with its classes and class antagonisms, we shall have an association in which the free development of each is the condition for the free development of all (1848 [1962], 35).

Membership in the capitalist class, for Marx, has nothing to do with prestige, or income, or ever power. It is based solely on the social relations that exist between those who own the means of production and those who own only their *labour power,* or ability to work.

Under capitalism, the employer pays a wage, by which he purchases exclusive rights over a worker's labour power (and thus rights over everything the employee produces) during those hours that the employee has contracted to work for the employer. Profits are extracted because the capitalist is able to buy the labour power of others at a price that is cheaper than the price realized when the product is sold on the market. Even when the worker receives a wage that is entirely "fair," that is, he or she receives market value for labour power, and thus has not been cheated, in Marx's view the worker has still been exploited. This is so because labour power purchased by the capitalist is used only for part of the day to create value that is equivalent to its price. (i.e., to the wage). The rest of the day is spent in creating what Marx called *surplus value*, value over and above the price of labour, which is retained by the employer.

Marx pointed out that in all societies economic production and the exchange and consumption of the goods produced are always social activities. Individuals are never merely isolated producers or consumers. Production, exchange, and consumption take place under established, well-regulated social relations.

Social Classes as Forces for Change

Marx was not just interested in providing a description of the exploitation of one class by another under the capitalist mode of production. He was also a revolutionary concerned with understanding and bringing about social change. He believed that social classes played the central role in the transformation of societies. For Marx, then, social classes were actually social forces. It was his opinion that as members of a particular social class, men (and, it should be added, women) make their own history, although not gratuitously. The Preface to *A Contribution to the Critique of Political Economy* is a very well-known summary of his position, which has been called a theory of *historical materialism*. Marx writes:

> In the social production of their life, men enter into definite relations that are indispensable and independent of their will, relations of production which correspond to a definite stage of development of their material productive forces. The sum total of these relations of production constitutes the economic structure of society, the real foundation, on which rises a legal and political superstructure and to which correspond definite forms of social consciousness. The mode of production of material life conditions the social, political, and intellectual life process in general. It is not the consciousness of men that determines their being, but, on the contrary, their social being that determines their consciousness (*Selected Works*, 1962, 362–63).

Scholars have drawn two related and contentious points from this passage. First, it is the economic base—the material means and conditions under which commodities are produced—that sets the stage for the political, social, and cultural life of the society, including that society's belief systems or ideology. Second, the material conditions of life, especially the means of production that people have at their disposal and the social relations of production into which they enter, determine how, and about what, they think.

To illustrate this, let's turn to the account of the transition from feudalism to capitalism provided by Marx and Engels in *The Communist Manifesto*, as summarized by Rosemary Crompton (1993). Recall for a moment the description of feudal society in Chapter 11. The feudal mode of production consisted of a system of manorial holdings, held by a lord through the right of inheritance, and the unfree peasants and or serfs who were attached to that land and obliged to render labour and services. This system of hierarchically arranged classes and property holding through birthright was justified by an ideology sanctioned by the Catholic Church: divine will decreed things should be so.

We have also seen that feudal society was encumbered by a system of customary rights and duties. But, as Marx and Engels point out, ultimately the feudal aristocracy, which benefited greatly from the system, was unable to resist the power of the rising bourgeoisie, who in the context of feudalism constituted the "revolutionary class."

While the bourgeoisie succeeded in breaking with feudal restrictions and in bringing about the transition to capitalism, it also created a large class of people—peasants "freed" from the land—with no property except their capacity to labour, which they were continually forced to sell in order to gain a livelihood. In Marx's view, in ushering in capitalism, the bourgeoisie created the proletariat, and in so doing it also created the seeds of its own destruction. As Marx and Engels wrote: "Society as a whole is more and more splitting up into two great hostile camps, into two great classes directly facing each other: Bourgeoisie and Proletariat"(1962b, 35). And the proletariat, in their view, was the next revolutionary class, destined to bring about the transition from capitalism to socialism and eventually to advanced communism: the class destined, moreover, to stop the cycle of human history as the history of class struggle by putting an end to class differences forever. Since the time Marx and Engels wrote, many have sought both to apply their theories and to interpret their theories.

A Marxist Analysis of the Toronto Garment Industry

Production, exchange, and consumption under a capitalist mode of production take place primarily on the basis of commodities. Commodities are goods and services that are produced not to meet the immediate needs of those who produce the goods and services but for later sale on an open market. This means that at the point of production and when commodities are consumed, they are evaluated in relation to how well they do on the market.

Take the example of buying an article of clothing in a store. To you, the consumer, that article of clothing may be one way you feel you can express your individuality. Canadian sociologist Charlene Gannagé has looked at clothing not as the expression of individual identity, but in its prior existence as a commodity, one among many that a particular clothing manufacturer has brought to market to sell. Looked at this way, it is possible to trace many of the social relations that exist among the people who produce clothing for sale in the marketplace: (1) those who produce the clothing; (2) those who own the factories where clothing is produced; (3) those who sell the clothing; and (4) the end buyers.

Just how does a piece of clothing get from the producers into the hands of the final consumer? In Toronto, for example, many of the workers in the garment industry are immigrant women and men. In *Double Day, Double Bind* (1986), Gannagé describes what she saw on a visit to a garment manufacturer. In 1984 (the time of the visit), Gannagé was conducting research for her doctoral thesis, and was accompanied in her rounds by "Matt," a union representative. She describes what she saw:

> The next stop was a shop where sections of the garment were made by individual operators. The coats were of poor quality. Matt called them "garbage." Because this shop was working at full production, my ears were assaulted by incredible noise. The pace of

Women garment workers in New York. In 1981, 12 employers in the garment district were charged with running sweatshops and depriving workers of basic rights and benefits.

the work appeared to be very fast. There were no windows, the shop was dimly lit and material was strewn everywhere. The owner complained about a presser who had walked off the job. According to the owner, the presser was a "$26,000 a year man." The owner's son laughed as his father described the "crazy" presser. I looked around and noticed a presser with sweat pouring from his face and cheeks puffed as he pushed down the lever of his machine. "For some reason, all the pressers go crazy," the owner informed us.

In the business for thirty years, the owner had switched from a *conventional* way of production (in which skilled tailors made the whole garment) to a *sectional* method (in which the garment is made in sections by different operators) because it was difficult to find skilled tailors. He showed us the button hole machine. (In conventional shops, button holes are made by hand.) The operator looked up at me and pointed out, "You just have to make sure you don't lose a finger." The owner announced proudly, "We pay the pressers good money." "Why is that?" I asked. "Because they are more skilled?" "No, anyone can be a presser," he retorted. "It's the job, especially in the summer, it's hard work." "He has lots of trouble with his pressers," interjected Matt. "I don't cause any trouble," the owner defended himself, "I don't care if they go to the union." As we were leaving a woman shouted at Matt to get out of the way because she had to make some money (29–30).

Each worker in this particular garment shop has a social relation with other workers, with the boss, with the union representative, and with the people to whom the garments are sold. But none of these relations, with the possible exception of that with the union representative, are based on a concern with the immediate satisfaction of a human need.

It might be the case that the "crazy presser" or the woman who shouted at Matt to get out of her way help to make a product that ultimately ends up satisfying somebody's need for a warm winter coat or that conveys just the right fashion statement. However, the capitalist mode of production under which that coat is produced is insensitive to the need of any individual for a winter coat, except in so far as that need can be translated into a *commodity*.

The relations between the workers and their boss, between the boss and his suppliers, between the boss and the retail stores that buy the finished coats, and between the retail stores and their customers are all based on impersonal exchanges. The relations between people in these exchanges are indifferent to personal qualities, except in so far as those qualities might determine whether or not a particular commodity is going to have success on the market.

Even when the market brings sellers and buyers together in a face-to-face relationship, when you enter a retail store and are confronted with a sales clerk who wishes to help you choose a coat, this relationship is hardly a personal one. The sales clerk is interested in you only as a customer—as someone who will spend money. It is almost invariably a desire to make some profit and not a concern that the customer get the best coat possible, for the best price possible, that motivates the salesperson's interest in the customer. This is especially the case if the salesperson receives a commission for each sale.

It was Marx's point that, with the rise of the capitalist mode of production and the decline of feudalism, personal relations were destroyed and replaced by relations that were to a large extent mutually indifferent. In the capitalist mode of production, he noted, "personal relations flow purely out of relations of production and exchange." Marx and Engels wrote decisively about the instrumental and impersonal nature of social relations under the class system of capitalism:

> The bourgeoisie, wherever it has got the upper hand, has put an end to all feudal, patri-archal, idyllic relations. It has pitilessly torn asunder the mostly feudal ties that bound man to his "natural superiors," and has left remaining no other nexus between man and man than naked self-interest, than callous "cash payment"...In one word, for exploitation, veiled by religious and political illusions, it has substituted naked, shameless, direct, bru-tal exploitation ([1848] 1962, 52).

Under the class system of capitalism, people came to see each other only as a means of satisfying market needs rather than as individual human beings. This state of affairs in turn encouraged people to think of themselves as autonomous and independent. Such an ideology of bourgeois individualism, Marx contended, is in fact *false consciousness*. In reality, our life chances are strongly influenced and structured by the pattern of social relations that is predetermined by the market economy.

The logic of production and consumption that operates in the capitalist mode of production is based on the existence of individuals who are separated from one another and from ownership of the means of production, and who strive to accumulate private property, believing that goal to be in their best interests. The illusion of personal independence that many of us living under capitalism hold dear is based on our ability to own things, including owning our own ability to work—our labour power. The real chance for having any control over our identity and existence under capitalism hinges on our ability to own property, especially to own the means of production.

It was Marx's firmly held conviction that the capitalist mode of production would eventually be transformed as a result of internal contradictions between social relations of production and the forces of production. He believed that economic crises were opportunities for the proletariat to seize control of the means of production. As capitalism matures, he noted, it becomes more and more unstable, and opportunities for social

313

revolution are more apparent. He predicted that eventually the capitalist mode of production would be entirely replaced by socialism, which in turn would pave the way for advanced communism.

Marx thought that an advancement in technology would make a final transition to communism possible. The forces of production had to advance sufficiently so that an organized division of labour was no longer necessary. Once such a thing happened, the organization of labour would be such that no one member of society would have "one exclusive sphere of activity." There would be no socially regulated task that would require any specialized knowledge or labour. Thus no occupational task would be the sole responsibility of any one single person. In the communist society that he envisaged, people would be freed to enter into very individualized forms of self-expression, not on the basis of their economic status and ability to pay to buy consumer goods, but on their real abilities, needs, and desires.

MARXIST THEORIES OF CLASS SINCE MARX

I Learn from the People *illustrates the spirit of cooperation between soldiers and civilians, both called out to sweep snow off the streets, 1973. This is an example of government-approved propoganda.*

Many writers and theorists have taken up and elaborated on Marx's work. Antonio Gramsci stressed the humanist aspects of Marx. He used Marx's analysis to help develop a critique of the dehumanizing aspects of modern capitalism. Gramsci's work—a large part was written while he was a prisoner of war in the 1920s—places the social actor at the centre and seeks to provide an understanding of capitalism that he or she can use to transcend the alienation induced by capitalism.

During the 1970s and early 1980s, the work of French structuralist Marxists (scientific Marxists, as they called themselves) such as Louis Althusser (*For Marx*, 1969) and Nicos Poulantzas (*Classes in Contemporary Capitalism*, 1975) enjoyed considerable popularity. These writers and theorists argued that we can never know anything about social classes merely by observing them. Rather, knowledge has to be constructed through theoretical practice or "science," and the best science with which to achieve this is Marxism.

The objective is to identify the class structure that underlies every society. Once that structure is identified, the theorist is in a position to determine the real interests of each individual in society, based on his or her location within the structure. Different classes can then be identified on the basis of the functional relationship to the capitalist mode of production as a whole. Although very popular for a time, this approach to Marxist analysis of social class, which has much in common with structural-functionalist thinking, quickly fell from favour.

Throughout the 1980s and early 1990s, as the left lost electoral favour and the right gained it in Western Europe and in the United States, and as communist regimes in Eastern Europe toppled, Marxist theorists reconsidered the ways in which they thought of social class, including arguing that there is no necessary connection between class position and political action.

Marx had predicted socialism as an intermediary stage between capitalism and advanced communism brought about through the political struggles of the proletariat against the bourgeoisie. Somehow Marxist theorists now propose that socialism can come about without the agency of the working class. Socialism, they claim, is about universal human goals that exceed the boundaries of material class interests and address issues of broad public concern. In their opinion, the struggle for socialism can be seen today as an amalgamation of several different democratic struggles—gender, race, sexual orientation— all of which are concerned with resistance to various forms of inequality and oppression.

In addition to concerns with class struggle and the emergence of socialism, a number of sociologists, including R. Dahrendorf (1964) and F. Parkin (1979), have taken exception to Marx's division of capitalist society into two polarized and conflicting classes. While the model might have been accurate for nineteenth-century Europe, they contend it is not applicable today. First, the revolutionary potential of the proletariat is in question: the major transformations that Marx predicted under the leadership of the proletariat have simply not taken place. Second, the middle classes seem to be expanding at the expense of the working class.

In addition, sociologists have found two other reasons to be critical of Marxist analyses. There is still much debate within sociology over whether the economy and the class antagonisms it generates are the most significant sources of social differentiation in shaping society today. Also, many are unconvinced that consciousness is an integral part of the identification of a social class. Some sociologists who are critical of Marx find Max Weber's analysis of class more to their liking (Edgell 1993, 10–11).

MAX WEBER

Social class and relations between classes were important issues for Weber as for Marx. They agreed that all class divisions are property divisions. "Property or lack of property," Weber wrote, "are...the basic categories of all class situations"(1968, 927). But Weber's position on the significance of economic relations, as compared with other sources of differentiation in shaping social class, was significantly different from that of Marx.

I have already discussed how Weber and Marx differed markedly in terms of their approach to social science (Chapter 13). Weber was critical of Marx's revolutionary commitment and promoted instead value-free social sciences. Moreover, he found Marx's views about classes as social forces distasteful. Weber disapproved of socialism and preferred the rationality of modern capitalism. He thought that bureaucracy was the most efficient form of administration and that modern capitalism favoured its development. While Weber feared the impersonalization of the world that capitalism fostered, he feared socialism's potential to weaken the incentive to work even more (Edgell 1993, 12). Extolling the merits of bureaucracy under capitalism, he wrote:

> It [bureaucracy] is superior to any other form in precision, in stability, in the stringency of its discipline, and in its reliability....Capitalism is the most rational economic basis for bureaucratic administration and enables it to develop in the most rational form (1968, 223).

Weber was committed to understanding the individual and argued that all collectives were reducible to their individual constituents.

> We may speak of a "class" when (1) a number of people have in common a specific causal component of their life chances, in so far as (2) this component is represented exclusively by economic interests in the possession of goods and opportunities for income, and (3) is represented under the conditions of the commodity or labour markets (1968, 927).

Elsewhere he wrote that class refers to any group of people who share a common class situation defined as:

> [t]he typical chance for a supply of goods, external living conditions, and personal life experiences, in so far as this chance is determined by the amount and kind of power, or lack of such, to dispose of goods or skills for the sake of income in a given economic order (1968, 181).

With this statement, we can see how Weber considered "class" to be composed of people who have life chances in common that include material possessions and income, all market-determined. He distinguished between what he saw to be two positively privileged class positions, ownership or propertied classes—those who owned land, buildings, and people—and acquisition or commercial classes—those who possessed goods, skills, or services that they could offer on the market. He also identified three types of negatively privileged property classes—the unfree, the declassed, and the paupers; three types of negatively privileged commercial classes—the skilled, semi-skilled and unskilled workers; in between were various middle classes—peasants, professionals, craftspeople, and public officials (1968, 303–4).

The hallmark of a Weberian perspective on social class is its multidimensionality. Class, for Weber, is a combination of positions including property, occupation, education, authority, income, and prestige. Moreover, class is both objective and subjective, and it can be understood as an aspect of consumption and as an aspect of production. Finally, where Marx focused on ownership of the means of production as a way of identifying class position, Weber was concerned with the ability to acquire and consume as class and status group markers.

As McNall, Levine, and Fantasia (1991) have pointed out, a Weberian perspective can "draw a map of society that locates people in terms of differences in property, skills or authority." Weberian analyses, too, can "compare with relative ease the class composition of different countries." And they can determine "whether some category of people sharing the same life-chances is expanding or contracting"(3).

But unlike Marx, who put exploitation and the resulting class struggle at the centre, Weber and his followers have shown little interest in placing either exploitation or class struggles as the social means whereby capitalism was brought into existence. This limits their ability to conceptualize social change as a large-scale, class-based social process. Moreover, by focusing on individual attributes, those who follow a Weberian perspective ignore what Marx and his followers believe to be the abilities of a social class to become a social actor. For the former, it is simply not a possibility for the working class to act as one and to liberate itself from subordination to the capitalist class (ibid., 2).

Despite differences, the analyses of Marx and Weber share certain commonalities. Neither offered a static perspective of social class. Both identified roughly the same social classes as constituting modern, industrial society. Classes identified by Weber included the working class, the petty bourgeoisie, technicians, specialists, lower management, and classes privileged through property and education (1968, 305). Like Marx, Weber believed that class differences were closely connected to power differences among society's members. Weber defined **power** as the "probability that one actor within a social relationship will be in a position to carry out his own will despite resistance" (1964, 152).

Weber also agreed with Marx that the relationship between workers and owners was one of great inequality in which the capitalist definitely exercised most of the power. Entering into a contract to work for an employer, he argued, in no way gives the worker "even the slightest freedom in the determination of his own conditions of work." Rather the employer, as "the more powerful party in the market," is in a position to set the terms of employment (1968, 729–30).

But unlike Marx, Weber felt that **status** as well as class affected an individual's ability to exercise power over others (Gerth and Mills 1946, 181). Weber defined status as the evaluations made of one individual by others in terms of the honour and prestige (negative and positive) that might be accorded to a specific individual. He even argued that under certain circumstances status could be the predominant basis on which access to material rewards is awarded (Crompton 1993, 31).

While class and status usually overlap, Weber contended that they were separate dimensions of the process of **stratification**—the division of society into separate groups. Thus, while a low-caste person in India may have a higher income or more property than a high-caste person, he or she is less highly esteemed. In this case status and class do not overlap.

Weber added a third dimension of stratification, **political party**, to class and status, in order to further explain power differentials. Because of the way that the state is run, he

317

argued, high-ranking members of a dominant political party exercise power that is derived from neither their own status nor class but from their position within that dominant political party.

While Weber expected to find a very high degree of correlation between class, status, and party positions (i.e., an economically well-off person was more likely to have a high status and to occupy a position as a high-ranking member of a political party than was an unemployed factory worker), he insisted that each dimension should be studied separately. Only by making the separation could the sociologist be assured of discovering and understanding the interrelations among them.

Weber and Marx differed profoundly over the question of class action. Whereas Marx saw classes as social actors, Weber regarded status groups as much more likely to be the basis for collective action. For Weber class position in relationship to property need not result in class struggles and revolutions. This point is made even more clearly when he wrote that "every class may be the carrier of any one of the innumerable possible forms of class action, but this is not necessarily so" (Gerth and Mills 1946, 184).

We can sum up the crucial differences between their accounts of social class as follows: whereas Marx grounded class relations in "exploitation and domination within production relations," Weber viewed class situations as reflecting "differing life chances in the market." Marx gave class a primary position in his view of historical evolution and saw class action as inevitable. Weber, by contrast, saw class as only one among many bases for communal action (Crompton 1993, 32–33).

Since the Second World War sociologists have developed both Weberian and Marxist class analyses. In general, they have expressed concern with what they call class structure or the diverse economic positions—white-collar, blue-collar, managerial—that make up society. Authors such as Lockwood, Dahrendorf, and Braverman have generated accounts of how specific jobs and occupations are located within a structure of class positions.

MEASURING SOCIAL CLASS

Once we move from the theoretical formulations of Marx or Weber, we are faced with questions concerning how social researchers can translate the abstract concept of social class, however formulated, into a measurable concept. By far the greatest number of empirical studies of social class that have been carried out by sociologists define the concept of class in terms of occupation. These studies also assume that the family is the basic unit of class analysis and that the occupation of the (usually male) head of the family determines the class status of the rest of the members of that family.

But employment titles do not pinpoint many of the dimensions of inequality that are experienced in modern society. Furthermore, only a fraction of all members of a society will be employed at any one time. The question then arises concerning how to categorize those who are economically inactive. Finally, employment categories do nothing to help uncover the significant role that differences such as race, gender, sexual orientation, ethnicity, or physical ability play in structuring labour force and occupation experiences.

The problems with subjective assumptions about class positions and occupations are evident in critiques that have been raised about the treatment of social class by structural-functionalists. In Chapter 13, I pointed out that the dominant paradigm established in the United States after the Second World War was structural-functionalism. Associated with structural-functionalism is the view that occupations are hierarchically arranged on the basis of a system of rewards and prestige. Members of society, it is argued, are sorted into positions in the hierarchy on the basis of their capabilities. Individuals achieve occupations that are higher or lower on the scale of rewards and prestige on the basis of their abilities. The greater the abilities of individuals, the higher occupational category they are capable of achieving, and the greater the rewards they can obtain.

Structural-functionalists such as K. Davis and W.E. Moore ([1945] 1964) believed social inequality to be the mechanism through which the best and most qualified persons got allocated to the most important positions in society. This position has been criticized by many, even by those who continue to support structural-functionalist analyses. For example, Tumin (1964) argued that it was impossible to think of some occupations as being more important than others in a society where all occupations are necessary for the society to function. Consider, for example, what happens when garbage collectors (who are poorly paid and thus, according to functionalists, of little value to society) go on strike. At the same time, there are movie stars and professional sports players who are grossly overcompensated considering the kind of contribution they make to society.

TASTE, CONSUMPTION, AND LIFESTYLE

Obviously there is a link between social class, patterns of consumption, and lifestyle. Throughout human history, consumption and the display of scarce material goods have been markers of difference, especially of power and domination. In modern capitalist societies, a growth in the capacity for wealth creation since the Second World War has focused attention not on production and acquisition of basic needs but rather on consumption. "Consumer culture" rather than economic class is now seen as shaping attitudes and behaviour.

In keeping with this, there has been a growing interest on the part of social scientists to study patterns of consumption, taste, and consumer culture. Sociologists who study taste are interested in establishing the ways in which it is used as a resource by a specific social class to enhance its social standing. The work of the French sociologist Pierre Bourdieu focuses on the significance of what he calls **cultural capital** or the deployment of taste in establishing or enhancing a social group's location within the social order.

PIERRE BOURDIEU AND TASTE

The work of Pierre Bourdieu (1984, 1987) has received a growing amount of attention from American sociologists in the last decade. While he is influenced by both Marx and Weber, his work is distinctive.

Bourdieu identifies what he calls four different "forms of capital"—economic, cultural, social, and symbolic as opposed to the economic capital identified by Marx. These

319

four forms of capital empower or impede individuals in their attempts to gain a position in society. Bourdieu uses the term "habitus" to indicate what he calls a "system of dispositions," which are "shared by all individuals who are the products of the same conditioning" (Bourdieu 1984, 1–18).

In his book *Distinction: A Social Critique of the Judgement of Taste* (1984), Bourdieu demonstrates how social differentiation actually takes place, focusing on the way in which differences in taste, or the choice of cultural practices and objects that people make as part of their daily lives, help to establish their class position. Contrary to taken-for-granted understandings, Bourdieu argues, "taste" is not an individual attribute or something that is achieved, but rather is largely the result of social learning and is highly correlated with social class. For example, Bourdieu identifies a single dominant middle class, but within that class makes a distinction between the bourgeoisie—who, he says, are high in economic capital but low in cultural capital—and the intellectuals—low in economic capital, high in cultural capital. Tastes within these two groups differ enormously. While intellectuals display a preference for aesthetic modernism, the bourgeoisie prefers the flamboyant and baroque. But Bourdieu also notes that there is an amalgamation taking place between the two groups. Members of the bourgeoisie in France now send their children to American business schools or to elite schools in France. Thus the children of the bourgeoisie tend to be high in both economic and cultural capital.

Bourdieu identifies these young bourgeoisie members as a new middle class that responds to a new economy in Europe, one that depends "as much on the production of needs and consumers as on the production of goods." There is a real difference between the economy of their parents' generation and that of their own, and, as a result, the cultural capital of this generation is unique. As Bourdieu writes:

> The new logic of the economy reduces the aesthetic ethic of production and accumulation, based on abstinence, sobriety, saving and calculation, in favour of a hedonistic morality of consumption, based on credit, spending and enjoyment (1984, 310).

Moreover, Bourdieu argues, this new bourgeoisie has made natural allies out of the petty bourgeoisie—those people who work in sales, marketing, advertising, public relations, fashion, interior design, journalism, media, crafts, and those concerned with body and emotional regulation—dietitians, psychotherapists, marriage counsellors, physiotherapists, sports and exercise experts, vocational counsellors. These "indeterminate" positions, Bourdieu argues, are of interest to

> those individuals endowed with a strong cultural capital (that is, superior family background) imperfectly converted into educational capital, or rising individuals who have not obtained completely the educational capital needed for the top positions, and lack the cultural and social capital required to make this final leap (Crompton 1993, 179–80).

Thus the new petty bourgeoisie is made up of those who are downwardly mobile, and those who are upwardly mobile.

In carrying out his research on class and taste Bourdieu and his associates questioned over 1200 subjects from Paris and Lille and from a small provincial town in two separate surveys undertaken in 1963 and 1967–68. These large surveys were then supplemented with a series of smaller ones. Survey respondents were asked questions about their knowledge of and preferences for a wide variety of topics, including painting, music, books, film, food, sports, home furnishing, and clothing.

Bourdieu was concerned with illustrating the relationship between the socio-economic class of individuals (their access to economic capital) and their status (their access to and use of cultural, symbolic, and social capital). He wished to be able to establish the relationship between a person's economic power and the power of the cultural and social symbols with which he or she most identified.

Like Marx, Bourdieu maintains that members of different social classes struggle with one another over resources in order to maximize their interests. In each generation, the members of these social classes are presented with or acquire different kinds of economic, social, cultural, and symbolic capital. Each person engages in social life on the basis of these endowments.

It is Bourdieu's contention that taste is an important part of the cultural capital that each individual acquires as a result of being a member of a particular social class. Moreover, he points out that all people learn their taste (unintentionally), and that taste serves as a powerful means of distinguishing the members of one social class from those of another. Occupying a higher social class is not merely the capacity to consume more. Nor is it simply the social relations that one has to property and to others in the productive process. An individual's social class, from Bourdieu's point of view, shapes every aspect of that individual's life, including the most seemingly personal and intimate aspects, such as food.

While individuals modify what they receive as part of the cultural *habitus* as they age, the scope that they have available to them to make those changes is also circumscribed by what they have inherited and by the social expectations of the groups that they associate with. Every action is culturally imbued with meaning, and the practice of day-to-day living reinforces group membership.

Each one of us is a member of formally organized groups such as clubs, political or religious organizations, or informally organized groups, such as friendship groups. We adopt the identifying marks of those groups—manner of dress, style of eating, speaking, walking, the kind of music we listen to, the movies we see, and what we have to say about them. By so doing, we confirm our social identity and our membership. We also confirm our distinction from other groups.

In acquiring cultural and social capital, members of different social classes learn class-specific dispositions toward seemingly personal choices such as music, food, literature, and clothing. These dispositions then serve as the means by which individuals establish their orientation to the rest of society and by which their class membership is recognized.

321

Bourdieu's Study of Social Class and Food

Common sense tells us that there is a very simple relationship between the types of food consumed and social class. As one goes higher up the socio-economic scale, a smaller portion of total income is spent on food. Moreover, the portion of money spent on more expensive foods such as fresh meats, fruits, and vegetables rises, and the portion spent on cheaper foods, such as pasta, beans, and processed meats, declines.

But Bourdieu counters this simplified relationship between food consumption and taste with the observation that there are several different consumption patterns possible for the same level of income. In his study, he found that those who worked as "foremen" generally remained attached to popular tastes in food, even though they earned more than clerical and commercial employees. And the food tastes of clerical and commercial employees were closer to those of teachers (well-educated members of French society) and far from manual workers, even though their incomes were closer to those of manual workers than of teachers.

In order to explain this, he argues, we have to consider what he calls the "tastes of luxury (or freedom)" and the "tastes of necessity." The clerical workers spent less money on their food than did the skilled manual labourers both in absolute and relative terms. They spent their money instead on "health and beauty care and clothing, and a slight increase in spending on cultural and leisure activities" (1984, 180). Bourdieu argues that the manual workers spend more money on food and embrace an ethic of being in the present, a readiness to take advantage of good times and to affirm solidarity with others because they recognize no reason to subordinate present desire to future fulfilment. They do not expect that a sacrifice in the present will result in a superior future.

The clerical worker of Bourdieu's study, however, is a different matter. By abstaining from having a good time now with others, the clerical worker, Bourdieu says, "betrays his ambition of escaping from the common present" to a future of greater individual self-sufficiency (1984, 180–81).

While popular taste is defined by the heavy, the fat, and the coarse, by contrast the taste of the professional or senior executive tends toward the light, refined, and delicate. As economic constraints disappear, social constraints take their place, forfeiting "coarseness and fatness, in favour of slimness and distinction," a cuisine rich in expensive foods, such as fresh vegetables and meat.

Finally, Bourdieu points out, teachers, who are richer in cultural capital than in economic capital, opt for exoticism—eating Italian or Chinese cooking—or for populism, eating peasant dishes. "They are almost consciously opposed to the (new) rich with their rich food...gross in body and mind, who have the economic means to flaunt, with an arrogance perceived as vulgar, a life-style which remains very close to that of the working classes as regards economic and cultural consumption."

Moreover, eating habits and the taste for particular kinds of foods are associated with a particular domestic economy and the division of labour between men and women. In France, traditional, elaborate cooking involves casserole dishes such as *pot-au-feu* (made with inexpensive meat boiled for a long time), *blanquette* (veal stew), or *daube* (beef stew), which all take much preparation time and are linked to a traditional role for the

322

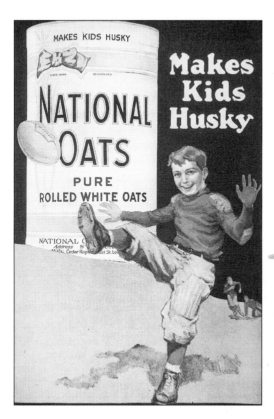

This 1919 American advertisement forges the connection between diet and social status. At the time, huskiness was an ideal for children; today we prefer that our children be slim and fit.

wife and mother, especially among the working classes. Higher-class women, Bourdieu tells us, devote their spare time to "child care and the transmission of cultural capital," not to cooking. The aim of these women seems to be to save time and labour in food preparation; they combine this aim with a search for "light, low-calorie products," such as grilled meat and fish, raw vegetables, frozen foods, and dairy products (1984, 185–87).

Tastes in food, too, depend on the idea that each social class has of the body, and what it believes are the effects of particular foods—especially on the body's health, strength, and beauty. Working-class people in Bourdieu's survey tended to pay attention to the strength of the male body and were not so concerned with its shape. Professionals in his study, however, were concerned with the shape of their body and were interested in eating nonfattening foods. The body, Bourdieu concludes, "is the most indisputable materialization of class taste."

The distinctions between the ways different classes regard the body is apparent in many ways, including the ways it is fed, cared for, exercised (or not), and the desired size, shape, and appearance that is sought. Distributions of bodily properties are greatly influenced, Bourdieu found, by class-specific preferences for food, exercise, and maintenance as well as the use of the body in work and leisure.

But it is more than just a partially conscious notion of what is or is not a desirable form and condition for the body to take. Distinctions between social classes are more profound, Bourdieu tells us, based on a deeper level of cultural understanding regarding the whole body schema. In particular, Bourdieu cites the actual physical act of eating as a culturally constructed mark of distinction between social classes. This construction affects not just the act of eating but also the selection of foods.

In the France of the late 1960s and early 1970s that Bourdieu studied, a working-class meal was characterized by the impression of abundance on special occasions, at least for the men, whose plates were always filled twice. Restrictions, however, usually applied to the women, who often shared a plate between them or ate leftovers. While a boy's accession to manhood was marked by the privilege of having his plate filled twice, a girl's accession to womanhood was marked by doing without.

Bourdieu noticed a kind of freedom both in the sequencing of the meal and in labour-saving steps. In a working-class household, for example, dessert might be served on pieces of the cardboard box that it came in; one spoon could be used to stir everyone's coffee; plates need not be changed between courses. In a bourgeois household, by contrast, the concern is to eat with "all due form." Form is first a matter of rhythm, which implies expectations, pauses, restraints; waiting until the last person served has started to eat; taking modest helpings; not appearing overeager.

A strict sequencing of courses is always observed, and all traces of the previous course are removed from the table before the next course is brought. Prior to the dessert, for example, all dishes, even the salt, pepper, and butter, are removed from the table. Rigorous rules of this sort are extended into everyday life, and the distinctions between the home and the exterior world get blurred much more than in the working-class household.

This, Bourdieu tells us, is an expression of a bourgeois *habitus* of order, restraint, and propriety, which cannot be overstepped. Although habits of eating serve as the primary model, all of the bourgeois *habitus* is permeated with forms and formalisms that are imposed on immediate appetites. There is a "gentle, indirect, invisible censorship imposed which structures the art of bourgeois living. Correct eating practices, exercised when one is invited out to dinner, are seen as a way of paying homage to one's hosts, as a sort of tribute to the care and effort expended by them" (1984, 196–97).

Even with something so seemingly natural as food consumption, we can see that culture plays a significant role in establishing and maintaining class differences. Bourdieu's study found many similar distinctions between social classes in their approaches to clothing, grooming, beauty, sports, art, and other cultural objects and practices such as home care and decoration. His work is important because it shows clearly how taken-for-granted knowledge about people's "natural" characteristics, such as tastes in food and even manners, are really the cumulative result of the kind of *habitus* in which they have been raised. Individuals receive cultural identity from previous generations, and that identity greatly affects almost every aspect of their lives. Bourdieu has been able to show that there are very different aspects of what is desirable in terms of human excellence: what would be viewed by the bourgeoisie as slovenly and shameless is viewed by the working class as straightforward and unpretentious.

THE CULTURAL FRAGMENTATION OF THE MIDDLE CLASS

Many sociologists have been influenced by Bourdieu's work on social class. In a study published in 1990, Wynne, for example, makes a distinction between the "economic petty bourgeoisie" and the "cultural petty bourgeoisie" (21–34). The former he describes as the "drinkers." Their lifestyle includes regular convivial drinking, packaged family holidays,

324

dining out at steak houses, comfortable household furnishings, and a preference for musical comedies and spectacles. The latter, described as "sporters," are concerned more with style than comfort, and prefer personally planned holidays, avant garde theatre, and classical music. What both have in common though is that they construct and affirm their social position through their different lifestyles.

Savage (1992) comes to similar conclusions in his work about the taste differences between members of the petty bourgeoisie who are high in cultural capital vis-à-vis those who are high in economic capital. Savage points out that cultural assets have become commodities practices once reserved for people of "quality" by a previous generation (skiing holidays, opera, exotic food) are now available to those who have the money. In nonsociological language, what we are seeing here is the rise of yuppie culture (Crompton 1993, 181).

CONTEMPORARY CLASS MAPS

Despite all the questions concerning the legitimacy of the concept of social class, the continued existence of material differences among people living in contemporary industrial societies strongly suggests that the theories of classical theorists such as Marx and Weber are still relevant. For example, one can still say that social classes in Western society are characterized by differing means of access to and participation in commodity production. This differential access, in turn, produces varying kinds of advantages and disadvantages for members of a particular class.

Class factors are not alone in contributing to the generation of advantaged or disadvantaged positions (race, gender, sexual orientation, and physical abilities are also contributors, as we will see in later chapters). However, class factors do contribute to life experiences and chances.

Today, sociologists studying class all agree that the basic map of class distribution is hierarchical, with fewer numbers at the top in the small dominant upper class. Beneath the upper class is the middle class, made up of a variety of different groups with assorted marketable skills. The working class (beneath the middle class) includes manual labourers, as well as white-collar workers who are employed in sales or clerical positions. The poorest and most disadvantaged at the bottom of the hierarchy are usually labelled an "underclass"—a concept linked with failure and dependency.

Several well-known studies of contemporary class structure in Canada have been written. In 1965, for example, John Porter published *The Vertical Mosaic: An Analysis of Social Class and Power in Canada*. Porter made the simple distinction between those with power, who constitute elites, and those without power who make up the nonelites (27). Using these two concepts as his theoretical perspective, he identified and investigated five major groups of elites controlling Canadian society, which he called the economic, political, bureaucratic, ideological, and labour elites.

Porter's data on these elites showed that, with the exception of the labour elites, membership in any one of the other groups was drawn from a very narrow segment of the population. When he conducted his study, the majority of members of the Canadian elite were white, Anglo-Saxon men with middle- and upper-class backgrounds who were in no way representative of most Canadians. Canadian society, Porter concluded, was run by a select few powerful people who shared common backgrounds, education, and values.

Ten years after Porter, Wallace Clement published another study that updated Porter's original one, entitled *The Canadian Corporate Elite: An Analysis of Economic Power*. He found that economic power in Canada had become even more concentrated, and the economic elite more important in controlling significant decisions about Canadian society. Clement discovered an important distinction between two parts of the economic elite in Canada: those who controlled Canadian corporations and those who managed the Canadian branches of multinational corporations. According to Clement, the indigenous elite head corporations mainly engage in commercial- and transportation-related activities. The comprador elite, by contrast, manage the Canadian branch plants of multinational corporations. But, as Clement notes, the two segments of the elite play complementary roles in the Canadian economy, and the boards of directors of the companies controlled by each type of elite are highly interlocked.

Dennis Forcese (1975) argued that inequality is a fundamental aspect of Canadian life where class differences exist in areas as diverse as level of health care, quality of life, operation of the justice system, and working conditions. He also saw these inequalities mirrored in people's political attitudes and levels of education.

One increasingly common experience for a growing portion of Canadians has been living in poverty at some point. If, as Porter and Clement have shown, economic power and control in Canada are concentrated in the hands of a few, lack of power and little control seem to be the lot of more and more people.

According to the Economic Council of Canada, about one in three Canadians will be poor at some point in their working lives (1992, vii). One in five Canadian taxpayers received unemployment insurance benefits at some point during 1989, and there are now more food banks (1110) in Canada than McDonald's outlets (Duffy and Mandell 1994, 49). Added to this is evidence that the gap between the rich and the poor is increasing both in Canada and the United States.

Pat Armstrong and Hugh Armstrong (1993) argue that while the per capita income of Canadians has risen substantially since 1951, this rise actually camouflages an increased inequality. The disparity between those with high incomes and those with low incomes has increased significantly. In addition, there is a strong pattern of decline in incomes, which penetrates deeper as we move toward the present.

Using deciles — ranking families by income and then dividing them into 10 groups of equal numbers — Armstrong and Armstrong have graphically illustrated the growing disparity in income distribution among Canadian families for the period 1973–1991. Over this period, six of the ten deciles experienced decreasing shares of the total market income, while the top four deciles increased their shares. Even when government transfer payments such as unemployment insurance, social assistance, pensions, and the like are considered, six of the ten groups still experienced a decline in their share of income.

SUMMARY

Whatever way we consider it, the persistence and growth of material differences between large numbers of people indicate that class processes identified by social theorists such as Marx and Weber are still major factors in shaping the contours of social inequality in Canada as well as in other capitalist societies. Despite many differences in approach, contemporary theorists of social class all agree that class structure in Western industrialized countries can be mapped into hierarchical structures, with proportionally more people in the lower categories than in the higher ones.

Almost all class theorists, regardless of their chosen perspective, identify a relatively small upper class, which includes the very wealthy and the owners and controllers of industry. They also identify a much larger middle class or classes—those with marketable skills and professions. Finally, all identify a working class or classes, which include both nonmanual workers such as office and sales personnel, and manual workers. Some theorists even identify an underclass. Despite Margaret Thatcher's pronouncements about the conceptual bankruptcy of the concept of social class, the analysis of social class has as much if not more significance today than it did in the past when Marx and Weber formulated their different analyses of the problems inherent in capitalist society.

DISCUSSION QUESTIONS

1. What differentiates an achievement model of social inequality from an exploitation model of inequality?

2. Develop your own model of social class using whatever criteria you find appropriate. Explain why you chose those criteria.

3. What special role in history did Marx and Engels assign to the working class? Is there a chance that the working class will fulfil the role that Marx and Engels expected?

4. What is a commodity? What role does surplus value play in Marx's analysis of commodity production and exchange in the capitalist mode of production?

5. In what ways does Weber's conceptualization of social class differ from that of Marx?

6. Following Bourdieu's example, analyze how "taste" can be used to define your own class position.

SEX, SEXUAL DIFFERENCE, AND SEXUALITY

CHAPTER OPENING QUESTIONS

• What is the relationship between biological sex and gender identity?

• Are male and female the only sexes, or is it possible to consider other categories?

• What is the relationship between sexual orientation and gender roles?

• To what extent is sexual orientation a cultural status?

Male and female. Feminine and masculine. Western culture has provided us with two different templates or sets of acceptable and distinct attributes, one considered specific to and appropriate for women, and another for men. We all know what these templates are: distinctions between the two are stereotypical, familiar, and widely shared. Women should be passive, nurturing, dependent, weak, and emotional while men should be aggressive, independent, strong, and stoic.

These distinctions have had a long history in Western culture. They are based on three prevalent beliefs: (1) that men and women have fundamentally different psychological and sexual natures; (2) that males are the dominant or superior sex and females the subordinate, inferior sex; and (3) that male domination and female subordination are based on biological differences and are therefore both natural and inevitable (Bem 1993, 1).

In most societies, being male or female greatly influences the life chances of an individual, including the economic and social roles he or she might expect, or be allowed, to take on. Gender affects the ways that each person is encouraged to express emotions, and it shapes the quality of relations that individuals might be expected to have with others. Being male or female is so fundamental to the identity of an individual that the first determination we make when meeting some new person is gender. Our language tells us there are only two sexes; our laws tell us that every birth must be registered as either male or female.

For most of us, the determination of our maleness or femaleness takes place decisively at the moment of birth when the attending medical practitioner observes the appearance of our genitals. The fact that almost all infants born with male genitals turn out to be socially recognizable as men in later life and that almost all infants born with female genitals turn out to be recognizable as women is a powerful common-sense support for the argument that there are two dichotomous sexes and that the relationship between an individual's biological sex and her social gender is both natural and inevitable.

But even in the history of Western thought there have been some doubts about the existence of only two sexes. Although the ancient Greeks believed that human nature was characterized either by masculine or by feminine attributes, their system of classification was open to other possibilities. In his *Symposium*, Plato proposed that three sexes were originally part of human nature. Images of hermaphrodites (persons with both male and female sex characteristics) are common in Greek and Egyptian art. In addition, Greek Hippocratic theory maintained that there were three kinds of men and three kinds of women. According to this theory, each kind of man or woman was produced as the result of different combinations of male and female seed. For example, when female seed from a male got overpowered by male seed from a female, the result was an androgynous or "manly" woman (Lloyd 1984, 91).

Greek polytheism accepted the possibilities of fluid sex categories as well as a variety of sexual practices, including homosexuality. The later Romans, however, were much more restrictive. Exposed to more diverse cultural standards as a result of their empire building, the Romans became rigid, maintaining that human nature dictated only two sexes (Hoffman 1984). This strict adherence to two dichotomously opposed sexes came to prevail in later Western societies.

Portrait of a hermaphrodite.

In this chapter, I explore some of the most widely held and strongly defended taken-for-granted beliefs of Western culture: that there are only two sexes; that each of us has one, true biological sex; that there is a natural and inevitable relationship between biological sex and social gender; and finally, that a heterosexual orientation is the natural outcome of the existence of two sexes, an outcome, moreover, that is fundamentally necessary for the reproduction of the species.

In this chapter I deal with five interrelated questions:

1. Is there a direct and natural relationship between biological sex, on the one hand, and **social gender,** including **gender identity** and **gender role,** on the other?

2. Are there only two sexes, or is it reasonable to consider categories other than the dichotomous pair, male/female?

3. Is there a connection between sex, gender identity, and **sexual orientation** such that heterosexuality might be deemed to be "natural" to the human condition, while other types of sexual orientation might reasonably be considered aberrant?

4. What causes gender differences and gender inequalities?

5. What sustains those differences and inequalities today?

The issues of "biological sex" and "social gender" have been closely intertwined in academic discussions and in the press. Much has recently been published in the popular media asserting the biologically determined nature of most aspects of male and female behaviour. Everything from divorce to parenting styles to sexual orientation and sexual fidelity have been attributed to genetic, heritable factors, while social influences are frequently downplayed. For some people, relying on a biological determinist argument to explain the most complex aspects of human behaviour is both simple and satisfying, but in this chapter and the next I caution against such a solution. Instead, I look at biological and cultural/social factors that might affect human behaviour and social interaction concerning sex, sexuality, and sexual orientation. While I am convinced that, as a species, the behaviour of *Homo sapiens* is *not* ruled by genetic factors alone, I am cognizant of the fact that we are embodied beings and that bodies do matter. But socialization and culture are powerful influences on human behaviour, and even things as seemingly biological as sex, sexuality, and sexual orientation are best explained in a social context.

Sex, sexuality, and sexual orientation are complex issues that continue to be widely debated in the social sciences, natural sciences, and humanities. In this chapter, the tensions between accounts of male and female differences, whether of a biological or social nature, will not be fully resolved. Nor will the question be resolved of whether sexual attraction between persons of the same biological sex can be traced to biological or social factors. But it is my intention to help you understand that your gender identity, the gender roles you play as a matter of course, and the sexual attractions you feel are not feelings and behaviours that you were destined to have at birth. Rather, they are all part of a complex process that is strongly shaped by social and cultural factors.

The best solution for a critical approach to understanding biological sex, gender identity, and sexual orientation is to develop a perspective that includes both biological and social factors, and to consider sex, sexual orientation, and sexuality in crosscultural and historical perspectives. A man, from this point of view, is never simply and naturally a man, nor is a woman simply and naturally a woman.

SEXUAL DIMORPHISM IN BIOLOGY, SOCIOLOGY, AND ANTHROPOLOGY

At least since Darwin, who wrote over a century ago, most Westerners believe that *Homo sapiens* is divided into only two sexes—and that this sexual dimorphism is necessary for the reproduction of the species. Sexual dimorphism, and heterosexual behaviour, it is believed, exist solely to serve the purpose of the reproduction of the species. Anthropologist Gilbert Herdt points out that sexual dimorphism is "a phytogenetically inherited structure of two types of human and sexual nature, male and female, present in all human groups" (1994a, 25). In Western societies, Herdt states, the principle of sexual dimorphism serves as a "uniform law of nature, like gravity" that most people accept without question. Since the late nineteenth century, thinking of both the popular and scientific variety has held that the differences between the two sexes are innate. Moreover, this innate nature can be demonstrated by measuring the differences between males and females in such things as brain size, tool use, and even in the evolution of speech (27). (As we will see in Chapter 18, the obsession with measuring differences in order to establish superiority and inferiority extended to differences between races as well as to differences between the sexes.)

Herdt also points out that it was a short step from the notion of the centrality of sexual dimorphism in human evolution and the survival of the species to the invention of the science of sex or sexology. The coinage of the terms homosexuality around 1870 and heterosexuality around 1890 underscore how important the notion of sexual dimorphism had become in understanding human evolution. Sexology emerged as the scientific study of what were considered to be the innate sexual structures underlying all of human life. Heterosexuality was considered necessary to human existence and was touted as the highest stage of sexual evolution that the species could achieve (ibid., 28). Sexologists, such as Sigmund Freud, argued that the distinctions between the two sexes were natural and necessary and that they emerged out of the biology of human beings and out of the different kinds of mental and emotional abilities that those biologies entailed for men compared with women (Gay 1989, 516).

Sexual dimorphism is a cornerstone of many societies. Traditional marriage is the formal recognition of the different yet complementing natures of the two sexes because it fosters reproduction. Challenges to traditional ideas of marriage have come from common-law arrangements and the union of same-sex couples.

It was not only nineteenth-century sexologists who were strongly influenced by ideas of sexual dimorphism. Traditionally, sociologists as well as anthropologists and historians have focused on sexual dimorphism in such areas as kinship, family, gender roles, and sexual practices. As well, they have been concerned to establish the rules and regulations that guide heterosexual reproductive practices in a variety of different societies at different points in time, seeing them as foundational aspects on which all societies rest. In *Elementary Forms of Religious Life*, Émile Durkheim argued that the dichotomy of male and female is so fundamental to the structure of all human societies that it should be treated in the same way as the dichotomy between sacred and profane ([1912] 1965, 161–62). American anthropologist Margaret Mead was of the same opinion, noting that "in all known societies sexual dimorphism is treated as a major differentiating factor of any human being, of the same order as difference in age, the other universal of the same kind" (1961, 1451). Mead also suggested that "mating and reproduction by physically mature, child-rearing human beings" is the ultimate purpose of sex (1457). She did, however, contend that personality traits denoted as either masculine or feminine are only "lightly linked" to sex differences ([1935] 1963, 1280).

QUESTIONING SEXUAL DIMORPHISM

In the late twentieth century, most medical practitioners continue to assume that sexual dimorphism is the natural state of the human species and that anything else is a deviation or mistake of nature. In our daily lives, most of us will never have occasion to question this two-sex model. For most Westerners today, everything in our culture tells us there are only two sexes. Everyone should fit, at birth, into either of the two categories, and everyone should be able to naturally acquire both the identity and the behaviour appropriate to their biological sex. Anything else is seen as something that should be "corrected."

But historical and contemporary medical, literary, and sociological records indicate that the matter of what is and what is not "natural" to the human species is anything but simple. There are some individuals who are born with ambiguous genitals; there are others whose external genitalia change as they go through puberty. Still others are born with external genitalia of one sex, but internal genitalia that might be considered appropriate to another. And, finally, there are those who are born with the visible genitalia of both sexes.

Persons born with ambiguous sex characteristics (they do not easily fit into either one of the two sex categories recognized in Western thought) are important for our understanding of the relationship between biological sex and social gender. As we will see, the connection between biology, on the one hand, and behaviour and identity as a male or female, on the other, is anything but a foregone conclusion. In understanding what happens to those people who do not easily fit into either of the two recognized biological sexes, we can gain a new perspective on the relationship between biological sex, gender identity, and behaviour.

In the June 1992 issue of *Discover* magazine, Jared Diamond tells the following story:

> Barbara grew up as an apparently normal girl enjoying a happy childhood. As her teenage years approached, she looked forward to experiencing the same sexual development she saw in older girls. Gradually, however, she began to have a vague sense that the expected changes weren't happening in her. By the age of 14 she was really worried: she had not yet menstruated and her breasts showed no signs of growth. What she did have was pain in her left groin that eventually subsided, only to be replaced by the appearance of a mass in the left side of her labia. With growing shock, she felt her voice dropping, her facial hair growing, and her clitoris enlarging to become more and more like a penis (71).

After Barbara's sixteenth birthday, her penis developed erections, she produced ejaculations, and she found herself feeling a sexual interest in girls. By now she had become con-

332

vinced that she was really a boy and that the mysteriously shifting mass within her was in actuality a testis. But Barbara still struggled with the problem of how to present herself to her parents and friends, before whom she avoided being caught naked. She knew they had to suspect something. When they found out, would they ridicule her—or him—as a freak?

In 1993, American geneticist and professor of medical science at Brown University Anne Fausto-Sterling published an account of Levi Suydam, a mid-nineteenth-century resident of Salisbury, Connecticut. The events that brought Suydam to the attention of the town authorities and ultimately to Fausto-Sterling's attention began with Suydam's request to the town council that his right to vote as a Whig in a hotly contested local election be recognized. As Fausto-Sterling tells us:

> The request raised a flurry of objections from the opposition, for reasons that must be rare in the annals of American democracy: it was said that Suydam was more female than male and thus (some eighty years before suffrage was extended to women) could not be allowed to cast a ballot. To settle the dispute a physician, one William James Barry, was brought in to examine Suydam. And, presumably, upon encountering a phallus, the good doctor declared the prospective voter male. With Suydam safely in their column the Whigs won the election by a majority of one (1993, 20).

Barry's diagnosis was soon thrown into question. A few days later he discovered that, phallus notwithstanding, Suydam also had a vaginal opening and menstruated regularly. Barry remarked on Suydam's "feminine propensities, such as a fondness for gay colours, for pieces of calico, comparing and placing them together, and an aversion to bodily labour, and an inability to perform the same...." (20). Yet Barry also noted that Suydam had male characteristics, including occasional feelings of sexual desire for women.

While the vast majority of people are born with unmistakable male or female parts, there are people like Barbara or Levi Suydam who do not fit into either of the two categories on the basis of physical characteristics. Medical researchers have for some time recognized the existence of **intersexed individuals**, that is, individuals with some mixture of male and female characteristics. In the true intersexed condition, also known as true hermaphroditism, both ovarian and testicular tissue are present in either the same or in opposite gonads.

The word *hermaphrodite* comes from the name Hermaphroditus. In Greek myth, Hermaphroditus was the son of Hermes, known as the messenger of the gods, and Aphrodite, goddess of sexual love and beauty. According to myth, at 15 Hermaphroditus fell in love with a nymph and became half male, half female when his body fused with hers. Continuing with mythology, hermaphrodites have also been featured in stories of human origins. Early biblical scholars, for example, believed that Adam began his life as a hermaphrodite and divided into separate male and female parts only after he fell from grace. Even Plato mentions that there were originally three sexes, but that the third—hermaphrodites—were lost with the passage of time. Both the Talmud and the Tosefta, books of Jewish religious and civil law, give extensive regulations to control the social roles and behaviours of intersexed persons.

333

Only about 5 percent of all intersexed individuals are true hermaphrodites (Castro-Magana et al. 1984). In most other cases, the infant is born with either ovaries or testes inside the body, but with external genitalia that do not appear to correspond with internal sex organs. If the infant has ovaries, but also has some aspects of the male genitalia (although not testes), the condition is called **female pseudohermaphroditism**. If the infant has two testes, but also some aspects of female genitalia (although not ovaries), the condition is called **male pseudohermaphroditism** (Kessler 1990, 5).

Given these criteria, Barbara would be considered a male pseudohermaphrodite, born with what appeared to be female genitalia, but with testes hidden inside, which descended at puberty. Levi Suydam, on the other hand, was most likely a true hermaphrodite.

It is very difficult to estimate the frequency of intersexual births. One authority has estimated that as many as 4 percent of all births may be intersexuals (Fausto-Sterling 1993, 21). Today, in keeping with the view that there are only two sexes, and that anything else is aberrant and must be corrected, most persons who are born with ambiguous genitals are screened at birth and receive hormonal and surgical treatments designed to allow them to become "normal" males or females.

The study of intersexuals is challenging to the social sciences, particularly because it is with hermaphrodites that the ordering of nature seems to clash with what Western culture, and most of Western science as a result, has dictated must be in nature. Michel Foucault has noted that for a long time in Western history hermaphrodites were considered criminals since their anatomical configuration clashed with the established law of nature "that distinguished the sexes and prescribed their union" (1980, 38). Indeed, sexual dimorphism is so prominent in Western thinking that Western culture and Western science have "scarcely considered the absolutism that this piece of common sense exercises over sexual research" (Herdt 1994b, 421).

Far from telling us only about medical curiosities, then, the study of intersexuals allows us to make a critical inquiry into the assumptions of Western cultural and scientific models of sex, sexuality, and gender. To begin with, persons who cannot be readily fit into either male or female categories are of interest to us because they help shed a great deal of light on a number of basic questions about how we come to be born with certain external and internal sex organs. Together with persons who have been surgically altered so that their external genitalia does not correspond to their chromosomal makeup, but that allows them to be sexually active as adults—for example, boys who are born with micropenises are often surgically altered and given vaginas and clitorises—these individuals also help us to understand the complex relation between biological gender, gender of identity, behaviour, and sexual orientation.

None of these—gender identity, behaviour, or sexual orientation—it turns out, is naturally or inevitably determined merely by the presence or absence of biological characteristics. Nor is there such a tidy and obvious distinction between males and females after all. To understand why this might be, we must examine the complex issues of how biological sex is established in our bodies. In discussing the complexities of how biological sex is established, I want to point out how close male and female really are, and how relatively easy it is to switch from male to female and female to male during fetal development. In doing this, I hope to help you understand the very contingent nature of biological sex. It will then be easier to understand the even more contingent nature of the relationship between biological sex and social gender.

BIOLOGICAL SEX OR GENDER

The first thing to understand about biological sex determination is the role of genes. In each cell of the body, genes are collected together along 23 pairs of microscopic packages called chromosomes. In each of us the paired members of chromosomes one through 22 appear identical to each other, although different from all other pairs. It is only with the sex chromosomes that there is any visible difference between the two members of the pair, and that difference occurs only in males. The twenty-third pair of chromosomes in males are of unequal sizes and shapes: a large X chromosome is paired with a much smaller Y chromosome (the X and Y refer to the shape of the sex chromosomes). In females two X chromosomes are present.

Many of the genes found along the sex chromosomes affect traits that are not specifically related to biological sex, such as the ability to distinguish green from red. However, a Y chromosome carries genes that serve to specify the development of testes. Between the fifth and seventeenth week after fertilization, the human embryo begins to develop two all-purpose gonads that will later become either testes or ovaries. If an X and a Y chromosome are present, the all-purpose gonads will begin to develop into testes by the eighth week. If two X chromosomes are present, the all-purpose gonads will begin to develop into ovaries by the thirteenth week.

The original direction of development of the all-purpose gonads is as ovaries. It is necessary for the Y chromosome to intervene in that development and to turn them into testes. To put it more directly, the "natural" form of the human body is female. It requires a biochemical intervention, instigated by the presence of the Y chromosome, to change that course of development away from the female form and toward the male form. As developmental biologist Alfred Jost put it, "Becoming a male is a prolonged, uneasy, and risky venture; it is a kind of struggle against inherent trends toward femaleness" (cited in Diamond 1992, 73).

Of course, being a female is more than having ovaries, just as being male is more than possessing testes. To form a penis, or a vagina and clitoris, the human embryo also possesses other all-purpose sex structures. But unlike the testes, these sex structures do not develop as the direct result of the possession of a Y chromosome. Instead, other primordial sex structures are directed toward the male model of development (and thus away from the female model) because of the secretion of hormones by the testes. In the absence of testicular secretions, or if there is an insensitivity to those secretions, other sex structures continue to develop along the female path.

Let's return to the eighth week of gestation of an embryo with X and Y chromosomes. At that time, testes form and they in turn begin to produce a hormone called

335

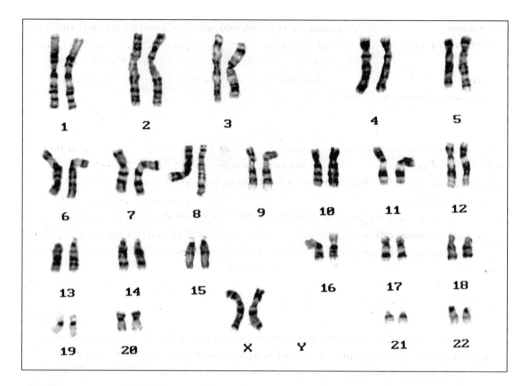

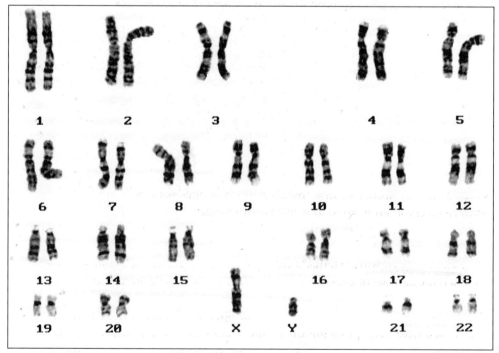

336

Male and female human karyotypes.

testosterone. Some of this hormone gets converted into an androgen called dihydro-testosterone or DHT. It is DHT that acts on the other all-purpose sex structures to convert them into the glans penis, penis shaft, and scrotum. Without the DHT, or in the face of insensitivity to DHT, those all-purpose sex structures would go on to develop into the clitoris, labia minora, and labia majora.

A similar process happens to those structures that will become either Fallopian tubes in females or seminal vesicles, vas deferens, and epididymis in males. Up to week eight of gestation, the developing embryo has two different sets of ducts, Müllerian ducts and Wolffian ducts. If a Y chromosome is present and testes develop, the androgens produced cause the Wolffian ducts to develop into male seminal vesicles, vas deferens, and epididymis. At the same time, the testes also produce a protein, called the Müllerian prohibiting factor, which prevents the Müllerian ducts from developing. If two X chromosomes are present, however, it is the Wolffian ducts that atrophy, while the Müllerian ducts develop into a uterus, Fallopian tubes, and the inner part of the vagina.

Whether an embryo develops as a male or female might seem like an relatively simple matter. If a Y chromosome is present, testes develop; if testes develop, other male structures develop and the embryo takes the path of male development. The problem is that there are a long series of biochemical steps, programmed by chromosomes other than the Y chromosome, that require the production of a variety of substances called enzymes. If one of the genes involved in the process is in some way damaged, or altered by mutation, the enzyme that it is to produce may be either defective or absent. In male pseudo-hermaphrodites, for example, some of the male structures develop along the expected line because they are dependent on enzymes and hormones that remain typical. Other male structures, those dependent on altered enzymes, may be completely missing or replaced by female equivalents.

BIOLOGICAL SEX AND SOCIAL IDENTITY

Now that we have had a closer look at how biological sex is established and at some divergent paths to that development, we can return to the question of the relation between biological sex and gender identity and behaviour. There are a number of cases in recorded medical history of male pseudohermaphrodites who, as a result of an altered androgen receptor, grow up to look like normal women. Cases of such "women" turn up repeatedly as fashion models because they conform so well to ideals of feminine beauty—long legs, well-developed breasts, flawless complexion (Diamond 1992, 73). Because such a child is born with external female genitalia, the condition is usually recognized only when the adolescent consults a doctor when she fails to begin menstruating. At that point, the doctor discovers that the patient has no Fallopian tubes or uterus, and that the vagina is short and ends abruptly. The patient does have active testes, buried inside the groin, which have been programmed by the Y chromosome and which actively secrete testosterone. The adolescent develops externally as a female, however, because of a biochemical inability to respond to that testosterone.

Barbara's case exemplifies a second type—a 5-alpha reductase deficiency (5AR) that produces male pseudohermaphroditism. 5AR pseudohermaphroditism is quite rare and results in delayed anatomical maleness. Children are born genetically males, with typical Y chromosomes, testes, and production of Müllerian inhibiting factor. They do not produce Fallopian tubes, a uterus, or the internal part of a vagina. But at birth their external male genitalia are very tiny or are entirely absent, and the child is mistaken for a female. At puberty, however, many of these children begin to develop external male genitalia.

A child is born with this syndrome only if he inherits the genetic code from both parents. Thus most of the known cases of 5AR pseudohermaphrodite children come from parts of the world where marriages between close relatives are common. One example of such an area is a previously remote village in the Dominican Republic. Until 1960 this village had no paved road to the outside world. A total of 38 5AR pseudohermaphrodites, all descendants of a common female ancestress, have been identified by physicians. A second area, in the New Guinea highlands, was also isolated until a few decades ago. A comparison of what happens to children born female but who later turn into males in each of these two societies is very revealing in what it has to tell us about the relationship between biological sex, social gender, gender identity, and behaviour.

The Treatment of Pseudohermaphrodites in Two Different Cultures

In the village in the Dominican Republic prior to the early 1950s, all pseudohermaphrodites born were raised unquestioningly as girls. But by 1950 enough cases had appeared that the villagers began paying very close attention to the baby's genitals at birth. Since that time, most have been recognized at birth or in early childhood and have been raised as boys. Among the older pseudohermaphrodites, however, 19 were raised as girls, and 18 of those 19 were studied. According to medical doctor Juliane Imperato-McGinley and her associates who studied these children, "of the 18 subjects, 17 had successfully changed to a male-gender identity, and 16 to a male gender role" (Imperato-McGinley et al. 1979, 1234). This change occurred at around age 16, and was indicated by sexual interest in women.

Only one of the subjects studied was reported to have maintained her original "gender identity" as a female. This person had an unsuccessful marriage as a teenager and then went to work as a housemaid, wearing false breasts. The others quickly became convinced they were male, and adopted male gender identity and gender roles. At first they and their families were astonished and confused. They were ridiculed in the village, but eventually 15 of them married and took on traditional gender roles, typically working as labourers, while their wives took on the traditional roles of keeping house, tending the garden, and looking after any children there might have been from a previous marriage.

Imperato-McGinley and her associates claimed that individuals not only switched their gender identities and their sexual desires from one conforming with the expected female norm to one conforming with the expected male norm, but also did so spontaneously, without either psychological or social pressure from others (1974). She and her collaborators claimed that this spontaneous change in gender identity and sexual desire was directly caused by the existence of prenatal hormones that had "masculinized" the brains of the fetuses. Because the children under study had masculinized brains, Imperato-McGinley reasoned, they were compelled quite naturally toward adopting their true sex once it was made known. Her study concluded that "the extent of androgen (i.e., testosterone) exposure of the brain in utero, during the early postnatal period, and at puberty has more effect in determining male gender identity than does sex of rearing. This experiment of nature emphasizes the importance of androgens, which act as activators, in the evolution of male gender identity" (1979, 1236).

If Imperato-McGinley and her colleagues are to be believed, the pseudohermaphrodite children of the Dominican Republic adjusted with astonishing rapidity to their new gender identities and roles. The female gender in which they had been reared seemed to have little effect on their development as adolescent males and their ability to adopt male gender roles and identity in later life.

But these conclusions fly in the face of what has become the accepted theory of gender acquisition shared by the North American medical community, especially those who deal with cases of intersexed infants and children, and many social scientists. That theory was first proposed in the 1950s by John Money, now professor of medical psychology and professor emeritus of paediatrics at Johns Hopkins University Hospital, and his associates J.G. Hampson and J.L. Hampson (1955, 284–300). The theory was later developed by Money and Anke Ehrhardt in a 1972 publication entitled *Man and Woman, Boy and Girl.* According to this theory, gender identity and the ability to assume gender roles is changeable until approximately 18 months of age. After this time, the authors argue, the child is faced with a great deal of trauma and may never make an adequate adjustment. While support for this theory is based on only a few repeatedly cited cases, it has been accepted across North America because of the prestige of the researchers and because the theory fits with currently held ideas about biological gender, gender identity, and gender roles (Kessler 1990, 7–8). But before we use Imperato-McGinley's evidence to conclude that Money and his associates are mistaken and that there really is a direct relationship between sex and gender, let's consider another example of pseudohermaphroditism that offers clearly contradictory evidence to that presented by Imperato-McGinley.

In Papua New Guinea, highland tribal people began sustained contact with outsiders only about 30 years ago. Among the most feared were the Sambia, a warrior tribe of about 2400 who live in the isolated rain forest in the southeastern part of the Highlands (Herdt 1987). It is among this group that one of the world's largest concentrations of 5AR-deficient pseudohermaphrodites are to be found.

Anthropologists Gilbert Herdt (1987, 1993, 1994a, 1994b) and Maurice Godelier (1986) have remarked that gender role differences between the men and women of the New Guinea highlands are among the sharpest and most rigid of any in the world. The male sex is clearly preferred and valued. Men are fighters and hunters, while women's economic and social roles are gardeners and mothers. These people divide the world into men's space and women's space. Men and women have different footpaths within villages, and husbands and wives occupy separate living spaces within their small huts. Children are segregated by sex after about age 7, and boys are eventually forbidden to talk with or even to look at women who, because they possess vaginas, are considered to be "dirty polluters."

But only women can grow sweet potatoes (men are considered incapable of such an accomplishment because they have penises). Only women can secrete milk. All sons, therefore must be entrusted to their mother's care. But at 7, a boy's care is taken over by the men of the village, and he is forcibly initiated into the life of the communal men's house where no women are permitted.

Pseudohermaphrodites, not unexpectedly, don't easily fit into tribal life, although the Sambia do recognize three sexual categories, male, female, and *kwolu-aatmwol*, roughly translated as "transforming into a male thing" (Herdt 1994b, 436). They are usually rejected by both parents and by their peers. In one study of ten such pseudohermaphrodites, only half were married, and one had committed suicide. Of those who had tried to retain their female gender identity, two who had married were rejected by their husbands after attempts at intercourse. In a separate project, Gilbert Herdt (1994b) has identified and studied 14 pseudohermaphrodites (*kwolu-aatmwol*) over three generations since 1910. In several of the cases known to Herdt, the switch from one sex category to another took place only after marriage, and humiliation. But in these cases the switch was not from female to male, but from female to *kwolu-aatmwol*.

The reported relative ease with which gender identity behaviours are changed among the pseudohermaphrodites of the Caribbean from gender of rearing (female) to the new gender corresponding to changes to the external genitalia (and also to the already-present chromosomal and hormonal profile of a male) might suggest that the adoption of male identity and behaviour patterns was easily accomplished because of a true, although previously masked, biological sex. The difficulties experienced by the pseudohermaphrodite children of New Guinea, however, suggest a more complex relationship between biological gender, gender identity, and behaviour than common-sense understandings lead us to believe. As Gilbert Herdt comments:

> Surely, some elements of sex/gender development are internally motivated or hormonally time loaded in ways that can influence the outcome of a life. However, we are reminded of the importance of social classification of sexual dimorphism and of the resistance to the creation of a third sex that is so enduring in Western culture....We do not have to alienate human culture and history from biology to accept that, in some places and times, a third sex has emerged as part of human nature; and in this way, it is not merely an illusion of culture, although cultures may go to extreme lengths to make this seem so (1994b, 445).

Gender identity and behaviour, it seems, are very strongly influenced by the social relations of which we are a part. But if identity and behaviour are not directly linked to biological sex, and if, as we have already seen, there are numerous persons who do not fit into either of the two standard categories in Western cultures, just how many sexes might there be?

How many sexes are there?

On the basis of what is known about intersexed individuals, Anne Fausto-Sterling has suggested that there are not two but five sexes—males and females, true hermaphrodites, and two categories of "pseudohermaphrodites," the "merms" and the "ferms." But, as Fausto-Sterling comments, "Sex is a vast, infinitely malleable continuum that defies the constraints of even five categories" (1993, 20–21).

Until recently, feminist scholars were content to distinguish biological sex from gender roles and identity. In distinguishing between what they believed to be socially and culturally generated differences and differences brought about by biology, they signalled their concern with analyzing social rather than biological differences. The most prevalent reason for the distinction was the chance that such a separation (allowing an analysis of male privilege and women's subjugation) could be the result of historically and socially constituted systems of gender inequality, and not the inevitable and natural outcome of biological differences between males and females (Yanagisako and Collier 1990, 131).

More recently, however, researchers and theorists have presented convincing arguments that it is not just gender identity and gender roles that are culturally and historically specific and subject to change. The body and therefore sex and sexuality also have a history and are subject to different interpretations and representations. The body, as American social historian Thomas Laqueur tells us, "has also been lived differently, brought into being within widely dissimilar material cultures, subjected to various technologies and means of control, and incorporated into different rhythms of production and consumption, pleasure and pain" (Laqueur and Gallagher 1987, 1).

The dominant view in Western culture since the eighteenth century has been that there are only "two stable, incommensurable, opposite sexes" and that the political, economic, and social lives of men and women, including both their gender identity and their gender roles, are somehow based on these "facts" (Laqueur 1990). It may, therefore, surprise you to learn that the notion that males and females are two fundamentally different sexes is of fairly recent vintage. Until the eighteenth century, the most commonly held view was that women and men had the same genitals with the exception that women's were inside the body and men's were outside. During that century, a lengthy transition took place in which the "one-sex model," where only one archetypal body—male —was considered to exist, was replaced by the "two-sex model" in which males and females were considered to have distinctly different bodies (Gould 1991, 11–13).

The "one-sex model" has had a long history in Western thought. According to Galen, the second-century A.D. Roman court physician to Marcus Aurelius, women were essentially imperfect men who lacked the vital heat necessary to bring about the expulsion of the sexual structures from the body. "The female is less perfect than the male for one principal reason—because she is colder," Galen wrote, "for if among animals the warm one is the more active, a colder animal would be less perfect than the warmer" (Galen 1968, 296). He also asserted that "the female is less perfect than the male by as much as she is colder than he (ibid., 288).

While the female of any species was considered a degenerate or imperfect male, it must be emphasized that she was not thought to possess sex organs that were significantly different from those of the perfect male. Galen invites his readers to try to conceptualize how, turned inwards, the man's external genitalia becomes a woman's, and how, pushed outside, a female's becomes a male's.

> Think first, please, of the man's [external genitalia] turned in and extending inward between the rectum and the bladder. If this should happen, the scrotum would necessarily take the place of the uterus with the testes lying outside, next to it on either side....

> Think too, please, of the converse, the uterus turned outward and projecting. Would not the testes [*note:* today we call these the ovaries] then necessarily be inside it? Would it not contain them like a scrotum? Would not the neck [today called the cervix] hitherto concealed inside the perineum but now pendant, be made into the male member? (1968 628–29).

342

Galen compared the "degenerate" female organs to the eyes of the mole. Like other animal's eyes, the mole's eyes have "vitreous and crystalline humours and the tunics that surround them." Yet moles do not see. The eyes remain but are left imperfect. In the same way, the uterus is an imperfect version of what would exist if there was enough bodily heat to expel it outward.

This view of the lack of significant differences between male and female sexual parts was reflected in language. What we, today, distinguish clearly as ovaries and testes, or semen and ova, were referred to by the same terms in Greek and Latin and in early European vernaculars. All this changed, however, in the late eighteenth century, and by the beginning of the nineteenth, a wide variety of writers were making fundamental distinctions between males and females on discoverable biological differences. Doctors now identified the distinguishing features of females. All parts of a female's body were held to express this essential difference, from her facial features to her organs, tissues, and fibres.

Londa Schiebinger (1989) tells us that by the middle of the eighteenth century, doctors in Germany and France began defining and describing sex differences "in every bone, muscle, nerve, and vein of the human body." Although anatomists had drawn the human skeleton from observation and dissection since the sixteenth century, it was not until the mid- to late eighteenth century that those drawings portrayed a marked difference between male and female skeletons. Specifically, the differences emphasized were a smaller skull and a larger pelvis size for females compared to males. The focus on these, and not other parts of the body, says Schiebinger, was not arbitrary. Anatomists focused on the parts of the body that were to become politically significant. Thus the depiction of female skeletons with smaller skulls and larger pelvises than those of male skeletons was not the result of a growth in realism in anatomy. Rather, as Schiebinger tells us:

The depiction of a smaller female skull was used to prove that women's intellectual capabilities were inferior to men's. This scientific measure of women's lesser "natural reason" was used to buttress arguments against women's participation in the public spheres of government and commerce, science and scholarship. The larger female pelvis was used in parallel fashion to prove that women were naturally destined for motherhood, the confined sphere of hearth and home (1989, 43).

Given that the two-sex model we all take for granted was only recently invented, Fausto-Sterling's call for a five-sex model (or more) does not seem so utterly preposterous.

THE TWO-SEX MODEL

Why, we might very well ask, did the two-sex model come to predominate when the one-sex model lasted for so many centuries? To answer that question requires that we consider the rather contradictory nature of the social reforms that were promulgated during the Enlightenment. In an earlier chapter, I discussed some of those ideals—the most prominent of which were appeals to individual freedom and to equality. But even as those appeals were being announced, counter appeals were being made that, in fact, not all humans were equal. According to this view, some (Caucasian males) are more suited to produce equality among themselves, while others, including women and persons from other races, are of a lesser order, and should therefore be placed under the authority of the superior males.

Ideas of "nature" played a pivotal role in the development of liberal political thought during the eighteenth century. Philosophers such as Locke and Kant based their ideas about social order on appeals to "natural reason" and "natural dignity." If social inequalities were to be justified, scientific evidence would have to show that human nature varied and was not uniform. The areas of focus were race, sex, and age. Finding sex-based differences between males and females became a priority during the late eighteenth century as a means of prescribing different gender roles for women and men within the social hierarchy. As Londa Schiebinger writes:

> In the course of the eighteenth century, some anatomists were even moved to believe that women held a lowly rank in the natural hierarchy; it became fashionable to find in women the qualities of children and "primitives." By locating woman's social worth in her physical nature, anatomists hoped to provide a sure and easy solution to the "woman" problem (1989, 46).

By the nineteenth century, those differences were being perceived, not just in visible bodies, but at the microscopic level. Patrick Geddes, a prominent biologist, argued that the cells that made up males were fundamentally different from those that made up females. Male cells, he argued, are "catabolic," that is, they put out energy. Female cells, by contrast, are "anabolic," meaning that they store energy. These differences demonstrated that

women were passive, conservative, and sluggish compared to men who were more ener-
getic, passionate, and variable (Laqueur 1990, 6).

From the eighteenth century onward, "scientific" discoveries, shaped by a definition
of "human nature," were used to justify different social roles for different sexes. With the
two-sex model, it could be "scientifically" shown that men should naturally dominate in
public spheres and in matters concerning reason and intelligence. Women, on the other
hand, could be shown to be "creatures of feeling" who, by their very nature, were destined to be mothers and the conservers of tradition and home life.

What might the historical change from a one-sex model to a two-sex model mean
for a critical understanding of the relationship between biological sex, gender identity,
and behaviour? Most important, it underscores the need to be cognizant of the fact that
any talk about sex and the differences between males and females is "inevitably about the
social order that it both represents and legitimates" (Laqueur 1990, 11). As French
anthropologist Maurice Godelier has observed, "Society haunts the body's sexuality" (1981, 17). The ancient, one-sex accounts of the differences between males and
females were based on the metaphysical belief in the co-existence of perfection and its
opposite, the absence or deformation of perfection. The entire social order was thought
to rest on this principle, and differences between males and females simply reflected this
understanding.

The new biology of the eighteenth century emerged at the same time that the foundations of society were being profoundly shaken by social, economic, and political revolutions. All of the radical changes that have taken place since the beginning of the
eighteenth century, including the factory system, the rise of a class system based on ownership of the means of production, and the restructuring of the sexual division of labour,
affected the remaking of biological gender or sex into two sexes. As Thomas Laqueur has
pointed out, on the basis of historical and crosscultural evidence, it is fairly clear that
almost all of what we can say about biological sex, regardless of how we understand it, is
already based on a prior claim about gender identity and behaviour. "Two sexes are not
the necessary, natural consequence of corporeal difference. Nor, for that matter, is one
sex" (1990, 243). The treatment of intersexed persons in Western society today has been
strongly affected by the two-sex model that currently prevails in both scientific and popular thinking.

EXPLORING THE TWO-SEX MODEL

In this century, the medical community has moved toward completely erasing any form
of embodiment that does not strictly conform to the standard two-sex, male/female heterosexual pattern. Fausto-Sterling points out correctly that the more sophisticated our
understanding of the complexity of sexual systems has become, the more that understanding has suppressed those complexities and promoted a rigid two-sex model (1993,
23). In 1969, two English physicians, Christopher J. Dewhurst and Ronald R. Gordon,
wrote in *The Intersexual Disorders*:

One can only attempt to imagine the anguish of the parents. That a newborn should have a deformity...[affecting] so fundamental an issue as the very sex of the child ... is a tragic event which immediately conjures up visions of a hopeless psychological misfit doomed to live always as a sexual freak in loneliness and frustration (cited in Fausto-Sterling 1993, 23).

Yet not 30 years earlier, American urologist Hugh H. Young had described the case of Emma, a hermaphrodite who had grown up as a female. Emma, endowed with both a penis-size clitoris and a vagina, was able to enjoy heterosexual sex with both males and females. At 19 she married a man who, she complained, did not give her any sexual pleasure. As a result, Emma kept a number of girlfriends on the side with whom she had pleasurable sex. When she expressed to Young a desire to be male, he informed her that this could be accomplished relatively easily. Emma's reply is interesting:

Would you have to remove that vagina? I don't know about that because that's my meal ticket. If you did that, I would have to quit my husband and go to work, so I think I'll keep it and stay as I am. My husband supports me well, and even though I don't have any sexual pleasure with him, I do have lots with my girlfriends (Fausto-Sterling 1993, 23).

In North America today, most children born with ambiguous genitals are treated by medical practitioners in such a way that they conform as soon as possible to the two-sex model of sexual dimorphism. In a study of practitioners who deal with intersexed infants, Suzanne Kessler (1990) found that the guidelines for making decisions about infants' external genitalia reflect the general cultural model for the construction of gender-role differences.

Despite much evidence to the contrary (all the infants these physicians see have some combination of male and female reproductive and sexual features), the physicians continue to believe that there are only two natural options, male or female. This belief seems, in Kessler's opinion, to be fuelled by the cultural assumption that it is biological differences between males and females that underlie cultural differences. Physicians also determine how they are going to handle each case by considering factors in addition to biological ones. As Kessler found out, "Biological factors are often pre-empted in their deliberations by such cultural factors as 'correct' length of the penis and capacity of the vagina" (1990, 3). At the same time, physicians make every effort to convince parents that what they are doing is revealing the infants' "true sex," rather than relying on a cultural interpretation of what male or female should mean.

The Aesthetic of the Penis
John Money argues that while it may be difficult for a male to have a smaller than average-sized penis, it is absolutely devastating to the male psyche to have a micropenis (Money 1974). Although the psychological consequences of having a micropenis have

never been documented, Money and his colleagues have suggested that boys with micropenises should be reassigned and given external female genitalia. Here, it would seem, penis size, much more than chromosomes, is what the medical profession considers significant in determining a male/female distinction. The implication is that male "is defined not by the genetic condition of having one Y and one X chromosome or by the production of sperm but by the aesthetic condition of having an appropriately sized penis" (Kessler 1990, 12).

Kessler points out an important and interesting contradiction in the medical profession's treatment of biological gender or sex, on the one hand, and gender identity and gender roles, on the other. In their treatment of intersexed children and especially in their explanations to their parents, physicians almost always impress upon them that the most important factors in gender development are social and not biological. One psychoendocrinologist who participated in Kessler's study paraphrased his explanation to parents of intersexed children this way: "It will depend, ultimately, on how everybody treats your child and how your child is looking as a person....I can with confidence tell them that generally gender identity clearly agrees with the assignment." Another pediatric endocrinologist explained, "I try to impress upon them that there's an enormous amount of clinical data to support the fact that if you sex-reverse an infant...the majority of the time the alternative gender identity is commensurate with the socialization, the way that they're raised, and how people view them, and that seems to be the most critical" (Kessler 1990, 17).

While the implication of these medical practitioners' words is that gender identity and behaviour are determined almost exclusively by social rather than biological elements, the message that parents of "normal" children receive is different. In these cases doctors and parents alike treat gender as naturally determined by the child's biological makeup. It is important to note, as Kessler does, that the equation of gender with genitals could happen only in an age where biological science is capable of creating "credible-appearing and functioning genitals." It is astonishing that the equations "good-sized penis equals male" and "absence of good-sized penis equals female" can be treated in the literature as objective criteria for determining gender. The only attention paid to the size and shape of the vagina, in intersexed cases, is that it be able to accommodate a penis.

The treatment of intersexed children by the medical profession during this century is a clear example of what Michel Foucault has called the exercise of biopower. Physicians and surgeons, using the knowledge developed by many branches of medicine, can control the external appearance of the body, specifically the genitalia. This attempt to manage intersexuality has grown out of two different impulses: to relieve the psychological trauma and suffering believed to go along with having ambiguous genitals, and to make all bodies conform to the binary classification of male/female.

But why should we care, asks Anne Fausto-Sterling, if a "woman" who has breasts and a vagina also has an organ large enough to penetrate another woman's vagina? Why should it matter to us if the external genitalia of some people allow them to have heterosexual sex with *both* men and women? Why does it matter that a penis "look right" before an infant is raised as a male? The answers, says Fausto-Sterling, lie in our cultural need to maintain a clear distinction between two sexes. We need to control the intersexed body because those bodies blur the sharp division that our culture demands between two and only two sexes. By embodying both sexes, hermaphrodites challenge that division. And by being able to live sometimes as a male, sometimes as a female, they also challenge the notion that heterosexuality is the natural condition of all humanity.

The Cultural Recognition of a Third Sex

The efforts of some anthropologists, sociologists, historians, and biologists to reconfigure the sexual dichotomy of male/female have been largely unsuccessful. The reproductive dimorphic perspective on males, females, and their interrelations is very powerful in the biomedical sciences and in popular Western culture as a whole. But observers like Kessler that have noted that in some non-Western societies, categories of male/female are not based on anatomical or morphological criteria, but on gender role. One such example are the berdaches, found among many Native North American societies.

Berdaches may be defined either as men who adopt woman's dress and do woman's work or as women who adopt man's dress and do man's work. They have been documented in almost 150 Native North American societies (Roscoe 1987). (There are male berdaches in all these societies and female berdaches in about one-half of these).

According to Will Roscoe (1994), the key features of male and female berdaches in order of importance are

> *productive specialization* (crafts and domestic work for male berdaches and warfare, hunting and leadership roles in the case of female berdaches), *supernatural sanction* (in the form of an authorization and/or bestowal of powers from extrasocietal sources) and *gender variation* (in relation to normative cultural expectations for male and female genders) (332).

Berdaches have been documented in almost 150 Native North American societies.

Often cross-dressing (that is, wearing male clothes if female, and female clothes if male) was a common and visible marker of berdache status, but this was not always the case. Some berdache cross-dressed at all times, others on specific occasions (women especially cross-dressed only when they were hunting or warring), others not at all. Sexual behaviour was also varied. Many berdache were homosexual in the sense that the term is used today. Others were bisexual or heterosexual. In sum, Roscoe says, berdache status was economic and religious foremost and not based on gender or sexual differences alone. Common characteristics, however, were that the berdaches were associated with exceptional productivity, achievements, and were well integrated into their communities. Finally, Roscoe argues that far from being conceptualized by their societies as **transvestites** or **transsexuals**, as would be the case in contemporary Western societies, male and female berdaches were seen as constituting third, and sometimes fourth, genders (335–38).

The religious functions fulfilled by berdaches and the life-cycle rituals they underwent were specific to their status. Berdaches did not simply exchange one gender status for another, but actually entered into an entirely different one. As late as the 1930s among the Navajo, children with berdache tendencies were welcomed and encouraged. As adults they were often given control of family property, and they acted as the head of the household, supervising agricultural and domestic work (355). According to one Navajo elder, recorded in the early 1930s:

> If there were no *nadle* (the Navajo word referring to a berdache) the country would change. They are responsible for all the wealth in the country. If there were no more left, the horses, sheep, and Navajo would all go. They are leaders just like President Roosevelt. A *nadle* around the hogan will bring good luck and riches. You must respect a *nadle*. They are, somehow, sacred and holy (Hill 1935, 274).

Berdache status, concludes Roscoe, was neither a "niche for occasional (and presumably 'natural') variation in sexuality and gender, nor was it an accidental by-product of unresolved social contradictions" (Roscoe 1994, 370). It was, rather, a "distinct and autonomous social status on par with the status of men and women." A berdache gender designation, like that of a man or a woman, entailed a specific pattern of behaviour, emotional profile, and social duties and responsibilities. Among Native North Americans, social learning and personal experiences, including religious and supernatural ones, were just as important as anatomy in defining an individual's social identity. It would therefore be wrong, Roscoe concludes, to categorize berdaches by using Western concepts of cross-dressers, or transvestites, or even as men or women who assume the role of the opposite sex.

Writing about the approach taken to intersexuals by Navajo and Pokot peoples, American anthropologist Clifford Geertz notes that these Native Americans take the view that "intersexuals are a product, if a somewhat unusual product, of the normal course of things." It is a view, Geertz says, which contrasts starkly with that held by Americans, "who apparently regard femaleness and maleness as exhausting the natural categories in which persons can conceivably come: what falls between is a darkness, an offense against reason" (Geertz 1984, 85).

BIOLOGICAL SEX AND SOCIAL NORMS

The final issue to be broached in this chapter is the relation between biological sex and sexual orientation. In 1896, English socialist and homosexual radical Edward Carpenter wrote: "The subject of sex is difficult to deal with" (*Love's Coming of Age*). Since Carpenter penned those words, the subject of sexuality and sexual orientation, though difficult, has become a major focus of academic and public attention. In 1948, American sexologist Alfred Kinsey wrote that "there is no aspect of human behaviour about which there has been more thought, more talk, and more books written." Thirty years later, Michel Foucault commented that, while Westerners like to maintain that we live in a sexually repressed society, we in fact expend a great deal of time and energy discussing all manner of matters sexual.

In *History of Sexuality*, Volume 1, Foucault points out that, contrary to common belief, it is because sex is treated as a forbidden topic, and as something to be repressed, that talk about sex has so much power in structuring social behaviour. In Western cultures, what Foucault refers to as the "repressive hypothesis"—that sex is a forbidden topic, and our true sexual desires are largely barred from our conscious knowledge—actually serves to mystify, or hide from direct view, the fact that sex is socially constructed and historically specific.

Freud argued that repression is a major psychic mechanism of defence, one that is put in place in order to ensure that our sexual drives are controlled and that sexual energy or libido is harnessed for other means, especially the founding and maintaining of "civilization." For him, one of the most significant acts of repression occurs with the resolution of the **Oedipus complex,** when the boy's original sexual desire for his mother is repressed and replaced by an identification with the father and, more generally, with the laws of society. The unconscious is founded on this and other acts of repression, particularly sexual repression.

While many people in Western societies do not accept Freud's concept of the Oedipus complex as the reason behind sexual repression, they do firmly believe that most people in Western societies are sexually repressed. But as Foucault maintains, whether in its Freudian or popular guise, this "repressive hypothesis" focuses on the unconscious and ignores the social context in which repression occurs. And yet, Foucault argues, ideas about repression do not spring naturally from the unconscious but are socially constructed.

Modern society, in spite of all the denials, is consumed with talk and writing about sexuality. Yet the subject of sexuality and sexual orientation does not seem to have grown either less difficult or less complex. Today many researchers are occupied trying to understand what Jeffery Weeks (1985) has called "that bundle of sensual possibilities we know as our sex, and through which we claim to know ourselves."

HOMOSEXUALITY

In Western industrialized societies the positively sanctioned norm for sexual orientation is heterosexuality. The term heterosexuality comes from the Greek *hetero*, meaning "the other of the two." The term reflects the dominant thinking about sex and

349

sexual orientation in Western culture. "Normal" sexuality can be expressed only in terms of sexual practices and orientations that serve to bring members of the two mutually exclusive categories, male and female, together, ultimately for the purposes of reproduction.

Other sexual practices that are not directly intended for reproduction, but that are practised between two consenting adults of the opposite sex have also received varying degrees of tolerance or approbation, depending on the historical time period and the level of acceptance that is currently in vogue. There are, as British social historian Jeffery Weeks writes:

> ...a host of sexual practices, falling short of reproductively successful coition, that while incurring ecclesiastical or legal injunctions, are still regarded as "normal" in heterosexual relations: fellatio, cunnilingus, buggery, biting and so on. They only become "abnormal," when they substitute themselves for reproductive sexuality, when they become ends in themselves rather than "fore pleasures" (Weeks 1985, 85).

Certain kinds of sexual practices, specifically sexual relations between two members of the same sex, have long been considered unacceptable in Western culture. However, the treatment of those practices has varied considerably over time. For example, *sodomy*, anal intercourse between two males or a male and a female, or *beastiality*, intercourse with animals, have been considered crimes punishable by both ecclesiastical and secular authorities since the twelfth century. In a study of sodomy trials beginning in 1300, Theo van der Meer (in Herdt 1994, 137–212) notes that it was only in the last quarter of the seventeenth century that sodomy trials began to appear on a regular basis in Dutch court records (139–40). By the 1730s, the court of Holland was vigorously pursuing, convicting, and putting to death men convicted of sodomy. By the beginning of the nineteenth century, women were also being prosecuted on the grounds that they had had sex with one another.

While the occurrence of sexual relations between members of the same sex has had a long history in Western cultures, the use of the term **homosexual** is relatively recent. The term was coined in 1869 by K.M. Benkert who wrote under the pseudonym of Kertbeny. According to Benkert:

> In addition to the normal sexual urge in men and women, Nature in her sovereign mood has endowed at birth certain male and female individuals with the homosexual urge, thus placing them in a sexual bondage which renders them physically and psychically incapable—even with the best intention—of normal erection. This urge creates in advance a direct horror of the opposite sex, and the victim of this passion finds it impossible to suppress the feeling which individuals of his own sex exercise upon him (cited in Money 1988, 9).

By the twentieth century, sexologists such as Havelock Ellis and Sigmund Freud, and later Alfred Kinsey, developed the concept of a continuum of sexuality. Kinsey went so far

In San Francisco, gay and lesbian couples celebrate new laws recognizing domestic partnerships. As yet these laws have no legal benefits. In Ontario since 1993, spousal benefits have been available to all provincial government employees. However, no law exists yet in any province that allows gays the same financial benefits as heterosexual couples.

as to argue that there was nothing intrinsically perverse or harmful to the human species in any act that was biologically possible. At the same time, however, a growing and concerted attempt continued to tie social differences between two sexes to biological differences. Thus there remained a determination on the part of most researchers to divide all humanity into either the category of male or female and to justify that division on the basis of biologically based, intrinsic, and obvious differences. Those differences formed the basis for justifying social differences between the two sexes, and for justifying the position that sexual orientation must be toward a member of the opposite sex (what Freud called sexual object) and for the purpose of reproduction (what Freud called sexual aim).

Within this view, there was no place for talk about homosexuality as a cultural status that could be considered normal and healthy. Rather, in Western culture, same-sex sexual relationships have been defined historically as a sin and a crime against nature and humanity or at best as a kind of sickness or perversion or pathological deviance. Only within the last 50 years have major changes taken place in the way that we understand homosexuality. During the 1940s, medical models dominated talk and theories about homosexuality. Homosexuals were seen as suffering from a social pathology, and homosexuality was construed as aberrant behaviour, something that had to be "cured."

In 1948 and again in 1953 Alfred Kinsey published reports that revealed to the American public that the incidence of homosexuality was much higher than had been previously thought. His reports were written in neutral, nonjudgmental language and suggested that homosexual behaviour was part of normal human experience. At the same time, another researcher, Evelyn Hooker, conducted tests that showed there were no cognitive differences between homosexuals and heterosexuals. During the 1950s, the Gay Rights movement was started, and in 1969 gay activists rioted in New York (The Stonewall Riots). Since then, much has been published by gays and lesbians about their own lives and experiences to ascertain how same-sex behaviour is culturally expressed and the reactions it brings.

351

Gay and Lesbian Gender Roles Today

Even among persons who have homosexual and lesbian encounters, how those encounters are defined and experienced in terms of gender roles has changed enormously in the last 70 years. Research done on the Amsterdam homosexual and lesbian bar culture since the 1930s gives some indication of the ways in which gay relations have been experienced over time.

Until the 1950s, sexual relations between men in the bar scene was often between one man who presented himself as effeminate ("queen"), and another who presented himself as heterosexual ("trade"). The system here was based on a prostitution model with the effeminate man submitting to the masculine one. But in the 1950s homosexual men started to give up trying to imitate feminine styles and began to develop a style of their own. By the next decade, a new model of gay life and sex emerged, based on the model of marriage and friendship. This change in lifestyle brought with it discussion of legal reform, the depathologizing of homosexuality, and eventually gay and lesbian marriages and parenthood.

By the 1960s, many gay men had discarded the older-style practice based on opposites (queens and trade) and had adopted new possibilities that allowed masculine men to have sex with one other. Queens did not disappear from the gay world, but they became a minority. Gert Hekma notes:

> Much of the social support for feminine styles foundered. Nowadays, such styles are part of the diversity of the gay world. The revolution in forms of desires and identities that has occurred since the 1950s has meant not a transition from one style to another but the addition of new models to the older ones that were already evolving themselves. The young queen of the 1950s may still be living in the 1990s, but he is quite a different figure from the young queen of the 1990s who may have adopted a punk or Madonna style (Hekma 1994, 238).

While Western cultures have made such sharp distinctions between males and females and have promoted normal, healthy heterosexual relations as those directed toward reproduction, other cultures, both historical and contemporary, do not make such sharp distinctions. We have already considered the Sambia people of the eastern highlands of New Guinea, and I want to return to this example.

A Crosscultural Example: The Sambia

The Sambia have traditionally promoted a policy of homosexual relations among prepubescent and pubescent boys. Until marriage *all* Sambia boys are expected to engage in homosexual relations in order to ensure that they grow to full manhood. At age 7, when they are removed to the men's house, Sambian boys are initiated into sexual relations with older boys. In place of milk from their mothers, the young boys are now told that daily consumption of older boys' semen is essential for their maturation to adulthood. Gilbert Herdt describes the Sambian understanding of differences between maleness and femaleness and the ritual practices that are the consequence of those differences:

Sambia are preoccupied with the differences between maleness and femaleness. Men perceive these differences to be the product of biological forces active both in natural species and in humans. On the one hand, Sambia believe femaleness to be an innate, natural essence, which in humans inevitably results in adult femininity and parturition. Maleness, on the other hand, is a weak and tenuous essence and does not naturally produce adult masculinity. Unless men intervene with ritual procedures that protect boys from female contamination, boys stay small and weak and ultimately die. Only through oral homosexual inseminations that artificially create maleness are boys believed able to attain manhood....For some 10 to 15 years, Sambia boys engage in homosexual activities on a daily basis, first as the fellator (insertee) and then as the older fellated (insertor). At marriage (usually between the ages of 18 and 25 years), youths become true bisexuals for a time. With fatherhood, however, homosexuality should cease; men should become exclusively heterosexual in their sexual behaviour (1987, 6).

Like the Sambia, the Baruya, another mountain tribe, have institutionalized the same sexual practices. Maurice Godelier, who has lived among the Baruya for many years, tells us that the knowledge that swallowing sperm gives men their strength and power and allows them to dominate and manage women is "the holiest of secrets" (1986, 52).

Any boy who reveals the secret to women or any woman who trespasses in the men's house is punished with the threat of death. The young boys are taught that, at this point in their lives, any heterosexual involvement is unacceptable. Other unacceptable forms of sexual behaviour include masturbation (semen is to be ingested, not expelled) and same- sex anal intercourse. Marriages, however, have been arranged at birth and are expected to be consummated when the girl reaches menarche. Just before they are to be married, the young bachelors are told about heterosexual procedures. After marriage the young men are expected to have sexual relations with their wives but also to continue ingesting male semen. But once the first child is born, homosexual activity is considered as harmful as heterosexual activity was before the birth of the child.

Among the Sambia, the attainment of manhood necessarily entails a period of sexual relations that, in Western culture, would be considered and dealt with as either pedophilia (sexual relations with young boys) or as "enforced" homosexuality. But in Sambian culture, the omission of a homosexual phase of development would stigmatize a young man as deviant and would be considered clearly detrimental to his heath and his ability to become a man. This kind of institutionalized sequence of sexual orientations not only appears aberrant within Western culture but it remains unexplainable using conventional theories about sexuality. Conventional theories view anything other than heterosexuality as a sign of *individual* pathology or deviance. What sense can we make of Sambia culture in relation to everyday taken-for-granted understandings of human sexuality that are prevalent in Western cultures? According to John Money:

353

Culturally institutionalized bisexuality signifies either that bisexuality is a universal *potential* to which any member of the human species could be acculturated; or that bisexuality is a unique potential of those cultures whose members have become selectively inbred for it. There are no data that give conclusive and absolute support to either alternative. However, genetically pure inbred strains are an ideal of animal husbandry, not of human social and sexual interaction. Therefore, it is likely that acculturation to bisexuality is less a concomitant of inbreeding than it is of the bisexual plasticity of all members of the human species (1988, 11).

■ ■ ■

SUMMARY

In the last few decades, the issue of sexual orientation has become a political one concerning human rights and equity. Public debates on the rights of gays and lesbians with respect to marriage, adoption, family benefits, inheritance, insurance, and even military service have become prominent. The question of what determines sexual orientation is no longer simply a question of interest to "scientists"; it has also become a question that has implications for who we include or exclude as full members of our society.

Today, certain scientists argue that sexual orientation is largely a matter of biology. Some neurobiologists such as Richard Gorski and Simon LeVay support the contention that sexual orientation in humans has a biological basis. Human brains, they and others argue, are sex differentiated, not only on male/female lines but also in terms of sexual orientation. The brains of heterosexuals and homosexuals, LeVay argues, are morphologically different in the same way that the brains of males and females are morphologically different.

Others, such as Anne Fausto-Sterling and neurobiologist William Byne, dispute these findings. Data from studies, they contend, are inconsistent, the studies themselves are methodologically questionable, and the results are open to alternative interpretations. Yet many researchers would agree that biology sometimes does play some role in sexual orientation. That role, however, is strongly affected by social and cultural factors. The practice of institutionalized homosexuality among the Sambia contrasted with institutionalized heterosexuality among Westerners is a good case in point.

A very important point for discussion emerges from all of this: how can we continue to justify discrimination against people on the basis of their sexual orientation? Many people answer we cannot. But we should not rely on science to provide us with answers about fundamental questions involving human rights, freedoms, and tolerance. As Chandler Burr has pointed out, the issue of the role of homosexual and lesbian people in society did not first appear in the scientist's laboratory. The principles needed to resolve this issue will not come from the scientist's laboratory either (1993).

■ ■ ■

FOR DISCUSSION

1. What are some of the ways that being male or female might influence an individual's life chances in Canada today?

2. What role might biology play concerning human sex, sexuality, and sexual orientation?

3. To what extent might gender identity, gender roles, and sexual orientation be affected by social and cultural factors?

4. Discuss the role of sexual dimorphism in human reproduction. Does sexual dimorphism necessarily mean that sexual relations are meant only for the purpose of reproduction?

5. How many sexes are there?

6. What might the differences in life experiences of pseudohermaphrodites from the Dominican Republic and from the New Guinea highlands tell us about the role of biology compared with the role of culture in shaping gender roles and gender identity?

7. Is discrimination against people based on their sexual orientation ever justifiable?

16

GENDER INEQUALITIES

CHAPTER OPENING QUESTIONS

- Why do gender inequalities exist, and what sustains those inequalities today?

- What contributions have feminist scholars made to the study of gender?

- To what extent are gender-based behaviours biologically determined or social constructed?

In spite of gains made in the last several decades, gender stratification remains a fact for Canadian women and men. Men tend to have more powerful, prestigious, and high-paying occupations than women, who are often relegated to relatively low-paying, powerless positions. This stratification carries over into the home where, over the last three decades, men have not increased their share of housework, although 75 percent of married Canadian women between 24 and 44 are part of the labour force. As a result, women work longer hours than men and have less free time. Finally, women are much more likely than men to be poor at some point in their lives, either as single parents with sole support of their children or as widows in old age without a pension.

While the causes of gender inequalities have not been resolved, it is clear that researchers hold different opinions on this issue. Some favour social constructionist arguments, while others strongly believe that inequalities are the result of biological differences being played out at the societal level. Certainly this belief that gender inequalities result from biological differences has a long history in Western culture.

At least since Aristotle (384–322 B.C.), Western philosophers have argued that the differences between men and women are philosophically significant and that men are naturally superior. It was Aristotle's view that male and female were opposites, that female was the privation of male, and that this justified the devaluation of women, especially in the area of the kinds of contribution each made to the reproductive process. Women, he argued, do not contribute any active "seed" to the generative process. Instead they contribute passive matter that is acted on by the active seed contributed by men. On the basis of this "evidence," Aristotle concluded that women were passive while men were active, women were irrational and men were rational, and that while the virtue of men was to rule, the virtue of women lay in their obedience to men (Allen 1985, 84).

In large part Aristotle's views, elaborated and altered by later Christian theologians, continue to permeate Western culture's taken-for-granted understandings of men, women, and their interrelations. While we have abandoned the notion of the male's "active seed" and the female's "passive matter," we nonetheless continue to accept the notion that there is some connection between biology and behavioural differences demarcating the boundaries between the two sexes.

The position of feminist scholars, by contrast, is strongly in favour of social rather than biologically based arguments to explain gender differences and inequalities, and it is this position that I find appealing for a variety of reasons. Feminist scholars point to an impressive collection of historical and crosscultural research as an indication of just how strongly connected perceived differences between men and women are to cultural ideals, which vary considerably from one society to another, and even within one society, over extended periods of time. And they argue that, until recently, the experiences and social realities of women have been either downplayed or ignored by sociologists as well as other social scientists.

Sociology and gender

According to British sociologists and feminists Pamela Abbott and Claire Wallace (1990), between the 1960s and the 1970s several women expressed the opinion that sociology for the most part ignored the experiences of women. If sociology was to be about "understanding the relationship between our own experiences and the social structures we inhabit," the experiences sociologists discussed were almost always those of men. When women appeared at all in the writings of sociologists, it was as men saw them and not as they saw themselves (4). In this way, feminist scholars argued, sociology actually contributed to the subordination and exploitation of women. While claiming to put forward a detached and objective view of women, male sociologists were promoting their own biased positions (ibid.).

DURKHEIM AND PARSONS: ANOTHER LOOK

The writing of Émile Durkheim on women is a case in point. In his work *Suicide*, Durkheim discovered what he considered to be an anomaly between the suicide rates of men and women in most Western European countries. He found that when a marriage ended either in divorce or in the death of a spouse, men had a much higher tendency to kill themselves than did women. But during a marriage, women had a higher suicide rate than did their husbands. Durkheim concluded from these empirical observations that marriage affects women differently than men, and that men have more complex and aggressive natures than do women and therefore need more societal bonding. In short, he followed Aristotle's understanding that women are less developed. While men commit suicide for societal reasons, because they are bereft of their social bonds, women commit suicide because those social bonds have become too complex and constraining for them. In Durkheim's own words:

357

This is also why woman can endure life in isolation more easily than man. When a widow is seen to endure her condition much better than a widower and desires marriage less passionately, one is led to consider the ease in dispensing with the family...a mark of superiority....It is said that woman's affective faculties, being very intense, are easily employed outside the domestic circle, while her devotion is indispensable to man to help him endure life. Actually, if this is her privilege it is because her sensibility is rudimentary rather than highly developed. As she lives outside of community existence more than man, she is less penetrated by it, society is less necessary to her because she is less impregnated with sociability. She has few needs in this direction and satisfies them easily. With a few devotional practices and some animals to care for, the old unmarried woman's life is full. If she remains faithfully attached to religious traditions and thus finds ready protection against suicide, it is because these very simple social forms satisfy all her needs. Man, on the contrary, is hard beset in this respect. As his thought and activity develop, they increasingly overflow these antiquated forms. But then he needs others. Because he is a more complex social being, he can maintain his equilibrium only by finding more points of support outside himself, and it is because his moral balance depends on a larger number of conditions that it is more easily disturbed (Durkheim [1897] 1965, 215–16).

358

Talcott Parsons, whose general theories I presented in Chapter 13, also turns to biology to explain the different roles that men and women take within the family. It was his opinion that the nuclear family—a biological mother, father, and their children living together in their own household—was the family unit most suited to industrial society. In this way men could be liberated to work outside the home, while women could exercise their maternal destiny and look after home, children, and husband. In Parson's view, a father is destined to bridge the boundary between the home and the outside world, acting in his capacity as *instrumental* leader of the family unit. A mother, on the other hand, is destined by her biological makeup to take on the *expressive* role.

In our opinion the fundamental explanation of the allocation of roles between the biological sexes lies in the fact that the bearing and early nursing of children establishes a strong presumptive primacy of the relation of mother to the small child and this in turn establishes a presumption that the man, who is exempted from these biological functions, should specialize in the alternative instrumental direction (1955, 23).

The reason for women being ignored or treated as inferior by traditional sociology, according to Canadian sociologist Dorothy Smith, is that their concerns and experiences have been viewed as subjective, while the experiences of men have been thought to be objective and thus the basis on which true knowledge could be produced (Smith 1979). Feminist scholars' criticisms of traditional sociology are summarized by Abbott and Wallace (1990, 4–5) as follows:

1. Sociology has been mainly concerned with research on men and by implication with theories for men;

2. Research findings based on all-male samples are generalized to the whole of the population;

3. Areas and issues of concern to women are frequently overlooked and seen as unimportant;

4. When women are included in research, they are presented in a distorted and sexist way;

5. Sex and gender are seldom seen as important explanatory variables.

Sociology, they conclude, has at best been sex-blind, at worst sexist. There has been little recognition that women's structural position and therefore experiences in society are different from those of men and that, as a result, sex is an important explanatory variable in social research.

Anne Oakely (1982), a British feminist, has maintained that from the beginning sociology was biased against women, that it has been dominated by men, and that this has resulted in a particular view about men, women, and their differences and interrelations. Feminist scholars have proposed at least three different solutions to rectify the situation. One solution is to remove the sexist bias that has been inherent in the discipline by bringing women into sociology through research that incorporates them and by reforming existing theories to remove their sexist biases.

Other feminists have argued that what is needed is a separate sociology for women, by women. Supporters of this approach argue that, since the world is always interpreted from a specific point of view, the best solution is to develop a sociology that sees the world from a women's perspective. Moreover, because women share more with one another, regardless of other differences, than they share with men, feminist research should be devoted to improving the conditions under which all women live. Finally some feminist theorists argue that it will never be sufficient to integrate feminist sociology into existing perspectives. Because existing theories are sexist and as such beyond reform, what is needed instead is a complete revolution in sociological theory (Abbott and Wallace 1990, 10).

One way that feminist scholars have approached these contentious problems is to consider questions of gender differences in both crosscultural and historical perspectives. In this way, they have explored the varying degrees to which patriarchy, the subordination of women to men, prevails throughout the world. Crosscultural explorations are also helpful in determining the extent to which culture determines the allocation of specific but different roles and responsibilities between men and women.

MARGARET MEAD'S WORK: A MIX OF SCIENCE AND POLITICS

One of the first to address the significance of culture in establishing gender differences was American anthropologist Margaret Mead (1901–1978). She carried out field work in Samoa and New Guinea. At both locations her objective was to challenge the existing models of biological determinism and **eugenics** (biological engineering aimed at improving the quality of the species) that were prevalent in academic circles during the 1920s. Mead intended to demonstrate that American women had a much wider range of possibilities available than just the seemingly inevitable roles of mother and housewife. She was

Margaret Mead exposed the fact that social research is often difficult to isolate from personal beliefs and values.

also determined to challenge the prevailing Social Darwinist view that certain people (white males) were naturally superior to others (women and nonwhites). This view was behind American and Canadian legislation of the day restricting immigration. Mead and her mentor, Franz Boas, believed that Social Darwinism was being used to support an otherwise untenable belief in the biological superiority and inferiority of different races and to justify unfair social policies.

Mead arrived in Samoa in 1925 to study how children grow up on that South Pacific island. Her research resulted in the publication of her first book, *Coming of Age in Samoa* (1928). In this book she reported that, unlike American teenagers, Samoan adolescents experienced little upheaval and emotional turbulence. Mead concluded that it was the environment, in the form of culture, and not biology, that determined the different kinds of experiences of Samoan and American adolescents. She made similar claims regarding the role of sex in determining what we call masculine or feminine behaviour. In 1935, she published *Sex and Temperament in Three Primitive Societies*, the results of her research among three neighbouring New Guinea societies.

One of the societies Mead studied was the Arapesh, who lived in the highlands. Among the Arapesh, she reported, there were very few gender differences. Both men and women displayed remarkably similar attitudes and behaviour patterns, which included passivity, cooperation, and sensitivity toward others. Men and women were equally likely to initiate sex and to care for children. Among these people, the term "to bear children" was applied to men and women—a parental role was equally important to both.

The Mundugumor, who lived just south of the Arapesh, were a striking contrast to their neighbours. Mundugumor men and women displayed the same attitudes and behaviour patterns, but there the similarities with the Arapesh ended. Whereas the Arapesh were gentle and warm, the Mundugumor, according to Mead, were head-hunters and cannibals. Both men and women were selfish, aggressive (especially in their sexual encounters), and equally jealous and vengeful. By North American standards, Mundugumor women lacked any of the nurturing characteristics considered typical of women: they disliked pregnancy and breast feeding and were less than tender toward their children, especially daughters.

Whereas the Arapesh and the Mundugumor made little distinction between male and female roles, the third New Guinea society Mead studied, the Tchambuli, defined male and females roles as distinctly different from each other. Moreover, the roles, behaviours, and attitudes that the Tchambuli ascribed to men and women were the reverse of those in North America. Tchambuli men shopped, looked after the children, spent time choosing clothing and jewellery, and liked to gossip. Women, by contrast, were expected to be domineering, rational, practical, and the main economic providers for their families.

Shortly after Mead's death, Derek Freeman, an anthropologist who had also conducted research in Samoa, published a book challenging her conclusions (1983). Freeman claimed that Mead presented only that information about Samoian society that fit with her personal politics. He accused Mead of **cultural determinism**—giving culture priority over biology. Because of her cultural orientation, Freeman argued, Mead's presentation of Samoan society is biased. His own research, by contrast, revealed that growing up in Samoa was not the stress-free experience that Mead claimed it to be. Freeman concluded that his observations on Samoan society provided support for the position that Mead had hoped to defeat with her research: that biological forces do play an important part in determining human behaviour.

Freeman's book has generated much lively debate among scholars. Some have taken his work as supporting a sociobiological approach to understanding human behaviour. Others argue that Mead's work continues to be basically sound and that it is Freeman who is rigidly committed to promoting a particular view of the world—one where human behaviour is largely biologically determined. Eleanor Leacock (1993), for example, criticizes Freeman, arguing, among other things, that his critique of Mead has two major shortcomings: it ignores history, and it ignores the structure of gender relations. For example, Leacock points out that Freeman bases his refutation of Mead's findings concerning a carefree adolescence among the Samoans on police records on violence and delinquency. The problem, Leacock points out, is that the records Freeman refers to are from the 1960s, while Mead's own work was carried out during the 1930s.

Arguments based on sociobiology such as the one put forward by Freeman have increased in popularity in the last several years. Often these arguments appear as an easily understandable way of explaining the sometimes perplexing differences between men and women. Because of the acceptance of these arguments and their considerable use in everyday, taken-for-granted understandings of male/female relations, it is to sociobiology's explanations of gender differences that I next turn.

EGGS, SPERM, AND PARENTING

One of the most familiar distinctions made between men and women in Western culture is that men are naturally aggressive, while women are naturally nurturing and maternal. Both of these behaviours, sociobiologists argue, can be explained by biological differences, and they affect the degree to which males and females are capable of parenting. Based on observations of insect societies, sociobiologists have argued that the reason women care for children can best be explained by the concept of **parental investment.** In brief, parental investment refers to actions on the part of a parent toward his or her offspring that increase the offspring's chances of survival but that are costly to the parent.

Female parents, sociobiologists argue, are naturally more nurturing than are male parents because they have from the moment of conception a greater investment in the survival of the child. According to sociobiologists, while male sperm are "cheap" (a single male ejaculation contains about 300 million sperm, which can be replicated within 24 to 48 hours), female eggs are "precious." The female usually produces only one egg every menstrual cycle. Moreover, the female invests nine months of her bodily resources in carrying the fetus to term. Thus, as one sociobiologist claims, it would be "evolutionary insanity" for any female to give up responsibility of a new-born child to anyone else. Hence females nurture while males are allowed the luxury of philandering (Shibley-Hyde 1985). Furthermore, because male sperm is cheap and female eggs are expensive, male promiscuity is an evolutionary adaptation that allows each male to try to impregnate as many females as possible and thus to ensure that his genes will be passed on to the next generation. By the same token women must be careful in selecting a mate with whom she will intermix her genes. Aside from dif-

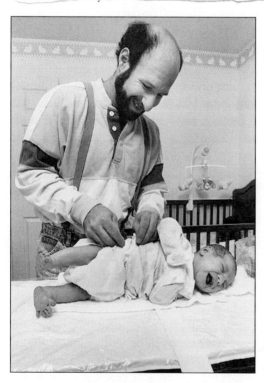

Because of changing gender roles, more and more fathers are taking part in the nurturing and daily care of their children.

ferent parenting investments as a biological cause of differences in male and female behaviour, sociobiologists point to another biological difference—hormones.

HORMONES AND GENDER-SPECIFIC BEHAVIOUR

There have been numerous studies that link aggressiveness to the presence of the male hormone testosterone (see Wilson, 1975; Fedigan 1982; and, for a critique, Brettell and Sargent, 1993). Two psychologists, Eleanor Maccoby and Carol Jacklin, for example, found in favour of testosterone as an explanatory factor in male/female behaviour differences. They concluded that:

> (1) Males are more aggressive than females in all human societies for which evidence is available. (2) The sex differences are found early in life, at a time when there is no evidence that differential socialization pressures have been brought to bear by adults to "shape" aggression differently in the two sexes....(3) Similar sex differences are found in man and subhuman primates. (4) Aggression is related to levels of sex hormones, and can be changed by experimental administrations of these hormones (1974, 242–43).

Feminist Critiques of Sociobiology

We have already considered some of the general problems that sociologists might have with sociobiology. Feminist social scientists have noted in particular that sociobiology can serve as a convenient rationalization for perpetuating existing relations of subordination and domination between men and women. Shibley-Hyde notes: "The sociobiologists' belief is that the greater aggression and dominance of males is a result of sexual selection and is controlled by genes. Therefore, men are genetically dominant, and women are genetically subordinate, and the subordinate status of women will have to continue because it is genetic" (1985, 60–62).

Eleven years after Maccoby and Jacklin published their findings supporting a biological basis for differences in male and female behaviours, feminist biologist Anne Fausto-Sterling published *Myths of Gender: Biological Theories About Women and Men* (1985), in which she roundly criticized them. Citing numerous studies, Fausto-Sterling points out that the earliest perceived sex differences in physical aggressiveness and willingness to engage in "rough and tumble" play could well be the result of differential treatment of boys and girls on the part of early caregivers. She notes that Maccoby and Jacklin themselves cite studies showing parents treat their sons more roughly than their daughters as early as three weeks of age.

In addition, much more information is now available, which indicates that, among our close primate relatives, sex differences in physical aggressiveness is *not* universally present among all species. When sex differences are present, it is only under specific environmental conditions. Finally, while there is good evidence to support the claim that the presence of testosterone is related to physical aggression among rats and mice, there is no good evidence to support such a claim for humans or other primates (see Bem 1993, Chapter 2).

If male aggression is socially learned, is the same thing true about female nurturing? Are females everywhere predisposed to care for infants and children because of their genes or the presence of female hormones? Or is it possible that like male aggression, female nurturing and motivation to care for children is strongly fostered by cultural expectations and experience?

Behavioural psychologists frequently use experiments done on rats as an indication of what might be considered natural behaviour—that is, behaviour uninfluenced by culture. They then often apply their findings to human beings by extension. A series of studies of rat behaviour by Rosenblatt (1967) and Rosenblatt and Siegel (1981) are relevant to our search for conclusions about the "naturalness" of the relationship between females and nurturing. While this study demonstrates nothing about parenting behaviour in humans, it is instructive because it challenges taken-for-granted assumptions about the naturalness of mothering in female animals and thus challenges the sociobiological concept that mothering is a naturally occurring phenomenon in all female animals.

In the Rosenblatt studies, researchers were concerned to establish how contact with newborns might foster parental behaviour in adult rats. They placed newborn rats inside cages with single adult rats. The adults were either intact males or females, or males and females who had their testes, ovaries, or pituitary glands removed. None of the females had given birth before the experiment. Researchers observed how much each adult rat engaged in four different kinds of parenting behaviours: retrieving, crouching over, licking, or building a nest. The results are startling. While none of the adult rats began parenting behaviours toward the newborns as quickly as did a control group of mothers after giving birth, all rats, regardless of sex or of the presence or absence of male- and female-circulating hormones, eventually engaged in all four parenting behaviours. What is more important is that researchers found no discernible differences among any of the adult rats. It would appear that while the birth process does something to speed up the onset of parenting behaviour in rats, the facts of being in proximity or of having responsibility for parenting infants is sufficient to motivate males and females alike to engage in behaviours usually seen only in mother rats (Bem 1993, 36).

A study done on human mothers is more directly informative. In this study, mothers of premature babies were divided into two groups; one group was allowed to interact with its infants, while the other group was not allowed contact until the babies had reached normal birth weight (Leifer, Leiderman, Barnett, and Williams 1972; Leiderman 1981; Myers 1984). At the time of the study (early 1970s) the standard procedure in American hospitals was to separate premature babies from their mothers until normal birth weight had been obtained. The results of the study clearly indicate that the mothers of premature babies who were allowed contact from the time of birth were more attached to their offspring than were the mothers who were prevented from having contact right after birth. "Contact" mothers were better able to stimulate the babies to feed; these mothers smiled at, talked to, maintained eye contact with, and caressed and held their babies more than did "non-contact" mothers.

On the basis of these and other studies Bem (1993) concludes that "women and girls are everywhere more motivated to take care of infants and children than men and boys, not because of any 'maternal instinct,' but because the sexual division of labour always places women and girls in the contact condition and men and boys in the no-contact condition." While it very well might be the case that males and females differ biologically with respect to specific abilities or predispositions, those differences are poorly matched to the job requirements of men and women in contemporary Western society. For example, it might indeed turn out that women are more nurturing than men. But that alone should make them psychiatrists, not secretaries. Whatever subtle differences we might find could never justify the sexual inequality that has been a part of social life for many centuries.

YET ANOTHER TAKE ON THE NATURE/NURTURE DEBATE

American feminist and biologist Ruth Hubbard (1990) has suggested that we need to get away from "futile arguments about whether nature or nurture is more significant in shaping behaviour." The effects of genetics and environment are both important and cannot be easily separated. Just as we cannot predict the physics and chemistry of water from the properties of its components, hydrogen and oxygen, we cannot predict the relationship between individuals and their genes, or between societies and the individuals that make them up. Instead Hubbard proposes a dialectical model of **transformationism**. The basis of this model is that "biological and environmental factors can utterly change an organism so that it responds differently to other concurrent or subsequent biological or environmental changes than it might have done" (1990, 67).

Consider this example of the interplay between biological and cultural factors as they affect the ways in which boys and girls have grown up in Western societies.

> If a society puts half its children into short skirts and warns them not to move in ways that reveal their panties, while putting the other half into jeans and overalls and encouraging them to climb trees, play ball, and participate in other vigorous outdoor games; if later, during adolescence, the children who have been wearing trousers are urged to "eat like growing boys," while the children in skirts are warned to watch their weight and not get fat; if the half in jeans runs around in sneakers or boots, while the half in skirts totters about on spike heels, then these two groups of people will be biologically as well as socially different. Their muscles will be different, as will their reflexes, posture, arms, legs and feet, hand-eye coordination, and so on (Hubbard 1990, 69).

As long as people have differential access to resources and live in different environments, it is impossible, Hubbard tells us, to separate nature from nurture when we confront differences between two groups. We are all aware that the grandchildren of immigrants to Canada are taller, on average, than their grandparents. We know that men who do physical labour are stronger, generally, than male college professors.

We tend to think of menstruation as something that is commonly experienced by almost all women of child-bearing age. Yet menstrual patterns are affected greatly by the way in which women live, the exercise the get, the food they eat. Female athletes in the Western world experience menstrual changes because of changes introduced by food and

practices of the child's social community have made it perceptually and emotionally compelling" (1993, 114). She points to two empirical findings, replicated in numerous studies, to support her claim. First, many studies have indicated that 80 percent of American children are fully able to distinguish male from female on the basis of purely cultural cues, such as hairstyle and clothing, by age 2. But, even by 3 or 4, up to 50 percent of American children will fail to distinguish male from female if all they have to go on are "natural," biological cues such as genitalia or body physique. In short, Bem insists, it is not biological cues that children first use to distinguish male from female, but cultural ones (see Bem 1989; Carey 1985; Goldman and Goldman 1982; Katcher 1955; Levin, Balistrieri, and Schukit 1972; Thompson and Bentler 1971).

The second body of evidence comes from studies that indicate that by age 2, preschool children have already generated much more restrictive gender rules for their male peers than for their female peers. While there is no obvious reason for this in either cognitive or biological development, there is an obvious cultural reason. As Bem points out, Western culture "prescribes much harsher treatment for male gender deviance ("sissies") than for female gender deviance ("tomboys") (Bem 1993). Kohlberg's theory of gender acquisition, then, is problematic in that he naturalizes gender polarization and situates the motivation for making such a polarization within the mind of the child. Bem and others, by contrast, have shown that far from being a natural, preoperational stage, the acquisition of gender identity and the recognition of gender differences are part of a learning process that is highly structured by the cultural context in which it occurs.

PATRIARCHY AND ANDROCENTRISM

Gender differences in Western societies have historically been shaped by some degree of patriarchy. Feminists of the 1960s and 1970s identified **patriarchy** as one of the most serious impediments to the achievement of egalitarian relations among all human beings. In writing *Sexual Politics*, American feminist and social activist Kate Millett announced:

> Our society, like all other historical civilizations, is a patriarchy. The fact is evident at once if one recalls that the military, industry, technology, universities, science, political office, and finance—in short, every avenue of power within the society, including the coercive force of the police, is entirely in male hands (1970, 34–35).

A few years later, Adrienne Rich, another American feminist and social activist wrote:

> Patriarchy is the power of the fathers: a familial social, ideological, political system in which men, by force, direct pressure, or through ritual, tradition, law and language, customs, etiquette, education, and the division of labor, determine what part a woman shall or shall not play, and in which the female is everywhere subsumed under the male. It does not necessarily imply that no woman has power, or that all women in a given culture may

Pope John Paul II, *the supreme head of the Roman Catholic Church, touches the head of a newly ordained priest. Within the Church hierarchy only men hold positions of recognized power.*

not have certain powers....Under patriarchy, I may live in *purdah* or drive a truck;...I may become a hereditary or elected head of state or wash the underwear of a millionaire's wife; I may serve my husband his early-morning coffee within the clay walls of a Berber village or march in an academic procession; whatever my status or situation, my derived economic class, or my sexual preference, I live under the power of the fathers, and I have access only to so much of privilege or influence as the patriarchy is willing to accede to me, and only for so long as I will pay the price for male approval (1986).

The concept of patriarchy makes it abundantly clear which sex holds power in Western societies. The concept of *androcentrism* or male centredness goes beyond noting who is in power to describing how that power is culturally and emotionally reproduced. Feminist writers, beginning with Simone de Beauvoir who first published *The Second Sex* in 1949, have described how, under androcentrism, men see the world only from their own point of view, defining everything in terms of similarity or dissimilarity from themselves. Under the sway of androcentrism, men take their own experiences to be the standard for the species as a whole. Anyone whose experiences differ from the standard is inferior.

Men also define everything in terms of its meaning for them alone. Thus women are defined only in terms of their meaning for men—their domestic, sexual, and reproductive functions within the male-headed household. Under androcentrism, men are in a position to create both cultural understandings and social institutions that automatically privilege male experiences and denigrate female ones.

Many feminists have argued that maintaining patriarchy and androcentrism is costly, not only for women, but for society as a whole. First, limiting opportunities for more than half a society's population prevents the full talents of women to be developed—talents that could well serve the interests of all. Second, while males derive a certain benefit from androcentrism, especially a disproportionate amount of power, they also suffer as a result. At least since the 1950s, medical opinion has shown that there is something wrong with the way men live. Death rates from coronary disease have been linked to "Type A" personalities—impatient, driven, hostile, and competitive—the very epitomy of masculinity in our culture (Ehrenreich 1983). Men not only suffer from a higher death rate from accidents, heart attacks, and other diseases; masculine gender identity and roles also seem to prevent men from establishing relations based on intimacy and trust (French 1985).

Is patriarchy inevitable? While there have never been any known societies in human history based on *matriarchy*, or rule of women, there have been societies in which women and men have held different but egalitarian positions. In North America, records from the seventeenth and eighteenth centuries indicate that several Native peoples including the Iroquois, Hurons and to a lesser extent the Montagnais-Naskapi, all had egalitarian forms of social organization prior to and shortly following the arrival of European colonizers (Anderson 1993).

Anthropologists Mona Etienne and Eleanor Leacock (1980) have convincingly argued that an implicit or explicit belief in the "universal subordination of women, if not in its inevitability, continues to obstruct efforts to understand both other societies and our own" (2). Etienne and Leacock point out that women's social and economic responsibilities and prerogatives have varied greatly from society to society and that a rough correlation exists between women's subjugation to men and the degree of economic inequality in the society as a whole. Egalitarian relations between men and women are most likely to thrive in those societies where economic equity is achieved.

To help understand how gender differences and inequalities are achieved and maintained in Western society today, I want to consider why gender differences are so deeply embedded and so widely established. How do children begin to think of themselves as either male or female? How do the differences between being male or female affect men and women in society today?

LEARNING TO BE GENDER SPECIFIC

Certainly the most familiar and prevalent theory about the acquisition of gender identity and roles within sociology is **social learning theory,** which views gender identity as a result of various forms of learning. The basic premises of social learning theory are simple. Boys become aggressive, outgoing, active, and dominant, and girls become nurturing, passive, and submissive because each child is rewarded for behaviours seen as appropriate to his or her sex, and conversely is punished for behaviours seen as inappropriate to his or her sex. Moreover, children learn their same-sex behaviours from a number of different sources, the most important of which is their parents and immediate family, although school, television, and other media and peers also play a significant part.

Social learning theory begins with the observation that boys and girls are accorded differential treatment—from the way they are handled by their caretakers, to the toys, clothes, and games they are given, down to the language they hear—right from birth. All adults, whether male or female, are the products of the child's encounter with caregivers whose own behaviour is structured in turn by the cultural norms and expectations about gender differences that they learned when they were children. The point should be clear. The kinds of human beings that children and adults become is closely tied to the kinds of experiences they have on a daily basis. These social experiences in turn are structured by already existing cultural practices and social institutions.

Nancy Chodorow

In the late 1970s, American psychoanalyst and sociologist Nancy Chodorow combined psychoanalytic and sociological and feminist theories to answer the question of "why women mother." Not satisfied with social learning theory as a means of explaining how women become emotionally capable of taking on the role of mothers, Chodorow turned to psychoanalytical theory in an attempt to create a more nuanced answer. According to her, there is something in the act of being "mothered" by a female that produces different experiences for boys and girls, leading to the creation of girls who take on the gender identity and roles of being mothers and boys who take on the identity and role of being male, including dominating and devaluing women.

Following classical Freudian psychoanalytic theory, Chodorow begins her analysis by maintaining that infants and very young children are completely self-centred, unable to distinguish between themselves and their primary caregivers—most often their mothers. In this world, the infant believes that the mother is there only to meet his or her needs as they arise. Only later, when they grow a little, and are confronted with others who vie for maternal attention—siblings, father, other relatives—do children come to recognize that their mothers have independent lives.

The important thing, Chodorow notes, is that both little girls and boys begin life with a similar attitude and set of expectations: women are to be nurturing and self-sacrificing. As children grow and are socialized, they develop their own sense of self and turn to the same-sex parent for their models. A girl's sense of self continues to be shaped by her expectations about what a woman is supposed to offer; she moulds her sense of gender identity around being self-sacrificing and nurturing. It is a different story for the boy. To achieve an appropriate gender identity little boys must renounce their intense attachment to their mothers and adopt masculine roles. In establishing their separateness from their mothers (a task, by the way, that Chodorow says little girls do not have to accomplish), little boys devalue women and idealize men, especially their fathers, as superior beings. In all of this, girls retain their potential for nurturing and mothering, while little boys deny those aspects of themselves in order to establish their separate identities as males. While many feminists today dispute Chodorow's claims, her insistence that one cannot simply learn a social role or identity, but must accept it as

371

part of oneself and feel it at some deeply emotional level, continues to merit consideration.

Gender socialization begins with the initial labelling of a newborn child as a boy or a girl and continues throughout childhood into adulthood. Even in middle and old age, adult men and women learn new roles—grandparent, widow or widower, resident of a home for "senior citizens." But let's begin with the child's earliest experiences of gender socialization.

Has this image of a little girl at play been created by her caregivers or did she choose these gender-specific toys and apparel?

PARENTS AS SOCIALIZING AGENTS

The earliest gender-role socialization—the process whereby the child acquires a gender identity along with culturally defined appropriate ways of acting, feeling, and self-expression—usually occurs in the family. In North America, as in many other societies, parents have power over the material and psychological conditions available in the early years of their child's life. This places them in a uniquely powerful position to shape their children's behaviour in keeping with the expectations that they already hold, including expectations about gender-appropriate behaviour. Research indicates that even before the child is born, would-be parents anticipate the sex of their child and express strongly held, stereotypical beliefs about the differences between the sexes. In most societies, including North America, parents usually prefer male children and express this preference in terms of stereotypical and culturally specific notions about sex differences (Steinbacher and Holmes 1987). Parents who express a preference for male children are more likely either to use sex selection technology to assure that their next-born child is a male or to continue to have children if they have not yet had a male child (Steinbacher and Gilroy 1990; Richardson 1981).

In their classic review of empirical research, Maccoby and Jacklin (1974, 338–39) reported that they found "surprisingly little differentiation in parent behaviour according to the sex of the child," although they did note that in some areas parents did some differential "shaping." This finding has been criticized by J.H. Block (1978, 29–87). Block suggested that Maccoby and Jacklin found little evidence for differential general socialization in the first few years of a child's life because the measuring devices used were not sensitive enough to pick up on the subtle but nonetheless pervasive methods that parents actually do use.

For example, in 1974 J.Z. Rubin, F.J. Provenzano, and Z. Luria reported on their research in which they interviewed 30 first-time parents within 24 hours of their children's birth. They found that a significant amount of sex stereotyping had already begun: girls were seen as softer, finer, smaller and boys as stronger, firmer, and more alert. More recent research on middle-class parents has come to similar conclusions: parents expect sons to be more aggressive, noisy, rough, and daughters to be more emotional. They expect sons to do better in maths and sciences, and cross-sex activities were viewed more negatively for boys than for girls. It is worse to be an effeminate boy—a sissy—than it is to be a little girl who acts like a boy—a tomboy (Eccles 1989).

While the evidence might be inconclusive for parents' differential treatment of infants, by the first year those differences are quite clear. Fagot and colleagues (Hagan, Leinbach, and Kronsberg 1985) found that caregivers of one-year-old children respond to them differently, depending on their gender. Caregivers react more readily to boys' assertive behaviours and to girls' attempts to communicate verbally. What is interesting is that Fagot and colleagues found that in the beginning the children in the study did not differ in either their assertive or verbalizing behaviours. But after 10 months, clear differences had emerged; boys were more assertive, and girls had increased their amount of verbalizing to adults.

Parents provide their children with very different living environments; young girls' bedrooms typically contain dolls, fictional character toys, children's furniture, and the colour pink, while boys' rooms have more sports equipment, tools, toy vehicles of all kinds, and the colours red, white, and blue. Toys designed specifically for boys and those specifically for girls elicit different types of parent-child interaction. Boy toys do not require close physical proximity and demand low levels of verbal interaction, while girl toys require closer proximity and more verbal interaction. Thus boys and girls learn from a very early age to develop different patterns of interpersonal interaction, simply as a function of playing with sex-specific toys provided by parents and other caregivers.

Numerous studies indicate that as early as age 5 boys and girls are assigned different tasks by their caregivers. As they mature, boys typically are given maintenance kinds of chores—fixing things, cutting the grass—while girls, predictably, are assigned domestic tasks—cooking, cleaning, shopping. These differences are more pronounced among working-class families than they are among middle-class ones. They are also less pronounced among black children where gender stereotypes seem to be less prevalent, and where both sons and daughters are socialized toward independence, work, and domestic responsibilities.

Based on her extensive survey of gender-role socialization research, Susan Basow (1992) concludes that a general picture emerges in which boys and girls are treated differently by their parents in terms of the specific kinds of toys and chores available to them and in terms of parental reactions and modelling. Boys are more intensely socialized than girls, receiving more praise, punishment, and pressure to conform to gender stereotypical behaviour than do girls. Boys also receive more attention than do girls, more encouragement to undertake independent exploration, and more pressure to excel in athletics and in school achievements in general.

TEACHERS AND SCHOOLING

While parents clearly influence gender-role socialization among young children, by the time they are 5, most children in North America have entered the school system. It is there that gender-role differences first learned at home receive some of their strongest support and reinforcement. Teachers are particularly important here. They provide strong messages about sex-role typing as well as sex-role modelling. But even before children get to school, other aspects of the social environment may convey strong messages about gender. In those societies where school attendance is voluntary, boys are much more likely to attend than are girls (Basow 1992). According to United Nations figures (1991), 63 percent of all illiterates are female. Boys, much more than girls, receive attention from teachers. Boys are more likely to dominate the class, to speak out in class, and to insist on getting help and attention. They are also more likely to be praised by a teacher for their accomplishments (Sadker and Sadker, 1988). Girls, quite predictably, get praise for being quiet and compliant. These findings are consistent across kindergarten, elementary, and middle school. Sadker and Sadker found that boys dominated classroom interaction in all grades. Teachers called on boys more often than girls and encouraged them more. When a boy calls out in class, the teacher is more likely to accept his intervention than if a girl does the same thing; girls who call out are more likely to be reprimanded. In short, teachers send the message that girls should be quiet, passive learners, while boys should be assertive and active (Basow 1992, 136). Even at the college level, teachers tend to pay more attention to male than to female students (Sadker and Sadker 1988).

Other aspects of the education system where gender-specific socialization occurs include instructional materials, counselling, curricula, and general atmosphere. For example, students receive strong messages about gender from the way that teaching is organized and assigned to men or women. Based on American figures, the percentage of male teachers generally rises with grade level, while the percentage of female administrators falls. Women make up 86.2 percent of all elementary school teachers, but only 18 percent of the principals. They make up 47.0 percent of all senior high-school teachers but only 2 percent of all high school principals (Basow 1992, 153).

In high schools women predominantly teach subjects in the humanities and languages while men teach maths, sciences, and vocational education. The same underrepresentation of women in the maths and sciences is extended to colleges and universities.

GENDER INEQUALITY AT WORK AND AT HOME

There have been many important changes in women's position in Canadian society over the last several decades as women have been drawn into the paid labour force in increasing numbers. While only about 16 percent of Canadian women over 15 were in the paid work force in 1913, that figure had grown to 60 percent in 1991 (Employment and Immigration Canada 1985; Armstrong and Armstrong 1993). In 1991 women made up 45 percent of all those counted as members of the labour force. In 1951 fewer than 10 percent of all married women were counted as working outside the home. By 1991, a full 75 percent of married women between 25 and 44 were counted as gainfully employed

(Armstrong and Armstrong 1993, 77). Today women with children are more likely to be working than childless women, especially if they are divorced women who head single-parent households.

But while women have moved into the paid work force in great numbers, the jobs that they have continue to be characterized as "women's work" with corresponding low pay, poor benefits, and poor working conditions. Two-thirds of women in the labour force are employed in job categories in which over 70 percent of the workers are women. Women are highly concentrated in just 35 of 200 occupations listed by Statistics Canada (Armstrong and Armstrong 1993, 9). Women work as stenographers and typists, babysitters, maids, service workers, nurses, nursing assistants, and telephone operators—all occupations with low income levels and few opportunities for promotion. In 1991, 85 percent of all dental hygienists, assistants and technicians were women, while only 15.4 percent of all dentists were women (Armstrong and Armstrong 1993, 32, 38).

A great many women work part time. But with the current restructuring of the Canadian economy, men who cannot get jobs in their traditional fields are taking the best jobs that used to go to women. Men were offered half of all new teaching jobs between 1990 and 1992 even though they made up only one-third of all teachers during those years. They also took over 50 percent of the new jobs created in the health occupations, where women have traditionally held more than 80 percent of the jobs.

From figures published by Statistics Canada, Pat and Hugh Armstrong (1993, 46) have compared the average earnings in the 10 highest and 10 lowest-paying full-time occupations. The results reveal great discrepancies between the percentages of males and females in these occupations: men dominate in high-paying ones, while women dominate in low-paying ones. But the statistics also reveal discrepancies between men and women within each occupational category. Regardless of occupation, men earn significantly higher wages than do women employed in the same job. These figures strongly indicate that gender stratification continues to be a fact for Canadian men and women.

Gender stratification also carries over into the home, especially into housework. American sociologist Jessie Bernard (1982) has pointed out that in North America housework has always been viewed in a contradictory fashion. On the one hand, it has been held up as an essential component of family life; on the other, it carries little rewards or social prestige. Sociologists who do research on division of labour in the family largely concur on one thing: over the last 25 to 30 years men have not increased their portion of housework. While women have entered the work force in growing numbers, they are now confronted with a double working day. In most Canadian households, while men do such tasks as home repairs or mowing the lawn, women return from paid jobs and cook, clean, take care of children, shop, and do "emotional" counselling.

Canadian research in the 1970s found that across Canada women consistently were responsible for the majority of regular household and child-care tasks (Meissner, Humphreys, Meis, and Scheu 1975; Clark and Harvey 1976). Two decades later research still indicates that little has changed for women in terms of the hours devoted to domestic labour. A study done in 1992 in Sudbury, Ontario, found that women spent 4 hours and 45 minutes per week on domestic chores, compared with 1 hour and 15 minutes spent by men (Wilkinson 1993, 79).

TABLE 16-1

1990 AVERAGE EARNINGS FOR MEN AND WOMEN[1]
FROM THE TEN HIGHEST-PAYING AND TEN LOWEST-PAYING OCCUPATIONS

Occupation[2]	Female earnings as % of male earnings	Female % of all workers	% of all male workers	% of all female workers
Ten highest-paying occupations[3]	61.2	19.3	4.6	1.8
Judges and magistrates	72.5	22.2	—	—
Physicians and surgeons	65.7	23.3	0.5	0.2
Dentists	68.5	11.2	0.1	—
Lawyers and notaries	58.1	25.3	0.7	0.3
General managers and other senior officials	54.6	19.0	2.2	0.8
Other managers and administrators, mines, quarries, and oil wells	53.4	24.5	0.1	—
Air pilots, navigators, and flight engineers	46.9	5.0	0.2	—
Osteopaths and chiropractors	66.3	17.8	—	—
Management occupations, natural sciences, and engineering	62.7	12.8	0.3	0.1
University teachers	74.6	21.6	0.5	0.2
Ten lowest-paying occupations[3]	72.8	72.3	1.4	5.6
Livestock farm workers	61.1	35.7	0.2	0.2
Sewing machine operators	69.3	91.4	0.1	1.0
Other farming, horticultural, and animal husbandry workers	62.3	45.0	0.3	0.4
Crop farm workers	62.7	49.0	0.1	0.2
Bartenders	75.2	54.1	0.1	0.2
Lodging cleaners, except private household	78.9	86.8	—	0.2
Service station attendants	82.8	19.8	0.2	0.1
Housekeepers, servants, and related	73.2	91.7	—	0.4
Food and beverage serving workers	73.2	77.8	0.3	1.6
Child-care workers	63.1	96.6	—	1.3
All other occupations	71.3	38.7	94.0	92.6
Totals	67.4	39.1	100.0	100.0

[1] *The data in this table are only for those men and women who worked 49–52 weeks in 1990, mostly full-time.*

[2] *Although athletes were in the top ten occupations, and trapping and hatmaking were in the bottom ten occupations, their very small numbers rendered their income statistics unreliable. Hence the individuals in these three occupations were excluded from the high or low groups and included in "all other occupations."*

[3] *Ranked in order of average earnings for both sexes taken together.*

Source: Pat Armstrong and Hugh Armstrong. 1993. The Double Ghetto: Canadian Women and Their Segregated Work. *McCelland & Stewart.*

Analyzing a 1986 Canada-wide survey, Michel Ornstein and Tony Haddad found that women spent on average 204 minutes per day on domestic work, compared with 99 minutes for men (1991). In Toronto, Ontario, Michelson found that women who were employed in full-time jobs spent nearly three times as much time on housework and child care than their husbands (Michelson 1989, 81–101). Research from Newfoundland concurs with other Canadian findings. Even in the 1990s, women perform "almost all the routine housework and most of the child-care" (Sinclair and Felt 1992).

Research from Britain, France, and the United States indicates that women work much longer hours than do men and that men have much more free time than women. But more than the demand of their time in actual hours, women are faced with doing work that is necessary and inflexible. Long hours of unchanging domestic work can be harmful to women's health, causing fatigue, depression, and other illnesses (Lowe 1989). Men, on the other hand, work at more flexible tasks and have greater discretion over when these are to be performed.

Nor has there been much of a reduction in the actual number of hours that are spent on domestic work. Labour-saving devices such as washing machines, vacuum cleaners, and dishwashers notwithstanding, research indicates that these mechanical aids have not reduced the number of hours devoted to housework. Instead they have allowed housekeeping standards to rise (Vanek 1994).

FEMINIST CONTRIBUTIONS TO THE STUDY OF GENDER RELATIONS

Feminism and feminist studies have only recently gained acceptance within some university systems. However, women's questioning of and struggle against patriarchy and domination by men has had a much longer history. Until the mid-nineteenth century, the differences between men and women, including women's subjugation to men, was seen as part of God's plan for humanity. With the triumph of science, the reasons for those differences have been transferred from the result of God's creation plan to the consequences of biology or evolution. The appearance of the first wave of the women's rights movement in North America and in Europe during the mid-nineteenth century forced men to see a conflict between a commitment to human equality on the one hand and the denial of women's right to vote on the other.

Eighteenth-century writers such as Mary Astell, who published *Some Reflections upon Marriage* in 1730, and Mary Wollstonecraft, who published *A Vindication of the Rights of Women* in 1792, were among the first to call attention to this conflict. In the nineteenth century, suffragists campaigned in the United States, Canada, and Europe for the extension of the vote for women. In Canada, women were finally given the vote in national elections with the passage of the federal Women's Franchise Act in 1918. But even then, women were still not equal under the law. Under the terms of the British North America Act, 1867, women could not be appointed to the Senate because they were not judged to be "qualified persons" in the legal sense. Judge Emily Murphy appealed to the Supreme Court of Canada and lost her case. She then appealed to the

377

Judicial Committee of the Privy Council of England, and in 1929 that committee overturned the judgment of the Supreme Court of Canada, ruling that the word "persons" in Section 24 of the BNA Act did include women as well as men.

Feminism, as an approach to scholarship, appeared in Canada in the 1970s, a response to the women's liberation movement already under way since the 1960s in the United States. Women were identified as an oppressed group, and feminists across North America demanded equality for women in all social, economic, cultural, judicial, and sexual matters. At the same time, they critically assessed scientific theories, pointing out that while those theories claimed to be neutral and value-free, they actually promoted the oppression of women (Eichler 1987).

Today feminist approaches and courses on women's studies and gender issues have been established in many North American universities. Feminist research focuses on areas of work socialization, sex and sexuality, politics, violence against women, media, family, social policy, education, the sociology of knowledge, and race, to name just a few. Canadian feminist and sociologist Margrit Eichler (1987) notes that feminists share four central propositions:

1. Most knowledge has been constructed by men for the benefit of men;

2. The dominant approaches to sociology bolster and maintain patriarchy;

3. Social science in general has so far largely been the handmaiden of sexism;

4. Women and men generally have different positions within society. Women and men, therefore, have different perspectives on the same issue. Women's perspective is of equal, if not more value, to that of men. This is so because, having been in an inferior position in society women tend to have keener insight into society's workings.

This situation has occurred because issues of importance to women have until recently been trivialized. Male concerns were considered the norm, while those of females, when studied at all, were seen as deviations from the norm. Feminist scholars produce knowledge intended to confront the belief that there are basic and unchangeable differences between men and women that determine their relative value to society as well as their behaviours. Feminist scholarship produces knowledge that is not only about women, but that is also intended for women. Its objective is to produce knowledge that can be used to empower women to confront and change a sexist world.

Feminist challenges to "old" knowledge about men and women and their interrelationships have met with much success. But they are also increasingly meeting with opposition. There is a renewed emphasis, for example, on the continuing segregation of the sexes in Christianity, both among Catholics and Protestants. New cultural themes are emerging of the ever-popular hypermacho male—Rambo, Robocop, the Terminator—all-American males out to protect the world and keep it safe. Today there is a backlash against feminism, as women's abilities in business, the professions, and blue-collar jobs become increasingly evident.

Even ten years ago, North Americans felt ambivalent toward the gains made by feminists. In a *New York Times*/PBS survey conducted in 1983, one-quarter of those sampled felt their lives had been improved by the women's movement. But two-thirds were unconvinced that things had changed for the better, and many felt that the women's movement had "led women astray" (Epstein 1988, 239–40). Whether under the banner of feminism, women's suffrage, women's liberation, or no banner at all, many women have refused to accept their unequal position in society as inevitable. In Canada, the United States, and Western Europe, there is a long history of women struggling together to make significant changes in women's lives. Yet, as we approach the twenty-first century in Canada, significant differences in women's work and men's work still clearly exist. Women continue to work in specific "female" job categories, and men continue to hold more prestigious jobs, earning higher average wages than women do. This segregation cannot be explained in terms of differences in biology or ideas. As Pat and Hugh Armstrong have pointed out:

> Women's domestic responsibilities, their economic needs, and their integration into a larger consumption unit mean many women form a cheap and relatively flexible pool of labour. Desegregation of the labour force would require fundamental changes in those sectors that rely on a cheap and/or flexible labour force supply. It is therefore in the interest of many employers to maintain the division of labour by sex. Strategies for change, then, must not only take both kinds of women's work into account but must also recognize that employers will resist such change (1993, 225–26).

Armstrong and Armstrong call for "radical alterations in both the structures and ideas that perpetuate the division of labour by sex." If women's position in Canadian society is to change, they note, strategies for change must be worked out collectively, as people actively "engage in altering their daily lives," and especially as they engage in altering the economic structure of society (228).

■ ■ ■

SUMMARY

In this chapter, we have seen that gender inequalities have had a very long history in Western societies. At least since the time of Aristotle, it has been common-sense knowledge that women and men differ significantly in their abilities, emotions, and life roles. Aristotle argued that women were men's opposites—passive while men were active, irrational and submissive while men were naturally rational and dominant. And he justified this argument on the basis of what he perceived to be their differing roles in the reproductive process.

While we have long ago abandoned Aristotle's rationale for explaining how women and men differ in their reproductive roles, it continues to be taken-for-granted knowledge that some natural connection exists between biology and behavioural differences to demarcate the two sexes. This common-sense understanding, however, can be challenged in a number of different ways. Feminist scholars have persuasively argued that sex differences in physical aggressiveness is a direct outcome of the different ways that parents treat their children: boys are taught to be aggressive, girls to be nurturing.

Gender inequalities persist both at work and at home. While there have been many important changes in women's position in Canadian society over the last several decades, on average women continue to hold low-paying jobs with few opportunities for promotion. Moreover, Canadian women are still responsible for the majority of regular household and child-care tasks. Feminist challenges to taken-for-granted knowledge about men and women and their interrelationships have met with much success. But there is also growing opposition, and many North Americans express ambivalence toward the gains made by the women's movement.

■ ■ ■

FOR DISCUSSION

1. Is a separate sociology for and by women necessary to correct biases in the discipline?

2. In what ways do parents, teachers, and other agents of socialization encourage different behaviour in boys and in girls?

3. Discuss the extent to which aggressiveness and nurturing might be learned rather than instinctual in humans.

4. Is Canadian society patriarchal? Justify your response.

5. Nancy Chodorow has claimed that one cannot simply learn a social role or identity, but must accept it and feel it at some deeply emotional level. To what extent might this affect sex-role socialization and gender identity?

6. Make a list of the extent to which gender inequality might exist within your family and among your friends and acquaintances.

7. Is feminism outmoded, or does it continue to have an important role to play in Canadian society?

17

*DISABILITY AS DIFFERENCE**

CHAPTER OPENING QUESTIONS

- What informs our cultural understanding of disability?

- From where do our attitudes and images of persons with disabilities come?

- How do the patterns of social relations of persons with disabilities differ from those associated with mainstream society?

- What are the most common models of disability used by researchers today?

Among the cultures of difference in our society is the emerging recognition of persons with disabilities as a distinct minority group, with their own unique history, traditions, understandings, and responses to others. In this chapter, we will see how our understanding of disability has changed over the years from mostly negative mythologies in the premodern era, to a scientific study after the Enlightenment, and recently to a minority-group model of persons with disabilities in which human rights are paramount. We shall also see how a new sociology of disability is being constructed, often by sociologists who are themselves persons with disabilities.

DISABILITY: HISTORICAL BACKGROUND

Persons with disabilities have always existed in human societies, but their treatment by the nondisabled majority has varied greatly across different historical periods and different cultures. Indeed, what has been defined as a disability is culturally and historically specific. Persons with disabilities, at various times, have been viewed as a sign that the gods were unhappy, as a source of entertainment and amusement, or as less than human. Many of our fairy tales, for

---

* This chapter was written by Gary Woodill and Karen Anderson. Portions of the chapter appeared in modified form in Gary Woodill, *Independent Living and Participation in Research: A Critical Analysis*. Toronto: Centre for Independent Living, 1992.

example, portray people with physical or mental differences as "monsters" or as fearsome. Even today, some medical journals still refer to fetuses that differ significantly from the norm as "monsters."

In Western societies before the Enlightenment, persons with disabilities were commonly found in communities, often as beggars. Over the course of the scientific revolution, disability came under study by a number of emerging professional groups who saw in disabled people a "problem" that could be corrected by the application of scientific principles (Victor, the "wild boy" of Aveyron, whose story was presented in Chapter 6, is a case in point). In this regard, we can say that much of the approach to the study of disability by the professional community has been decidedly positivistic. However, as we shall see, both interpretive and critical views of disability have been introduced in the past few years.

Over the past two hundred years, disability and persons with disabilities have been objects of study by social scientists. Such scientific study has several roots, including developments in anatomy, neurology, and germ theory; the rise of statistics in sociology and

Originally portrayed as a monster, Quasimodo, the hunchback in The Hunchback of Notre Dame, *emerges as a compassionate man when he is helped by a caring, beautiful woman. Victor Hugo's famous 1831 epic reveals the importance of looking beyond an individual's disabilities.*

psychology; and the demands of social insurance to discriminate between those who should receive benefits and those who should not. Medicine is the oldest profession to study scientifically persons with disabilities. In fact, when the first state welfare offices were opened in the 1530s in France, it was the "barber-surgeons" who were hired to examine those who were applying for benefits, in order to determine who was really disabled and who might be faking.

GERM THEORY

The development of medical knowledge has a long history, but in the seventeenth and eighteenth centuries important changes that affected persons with disabilities included the discovery of the electrical nature of the brain, the invention of new technologies for examination, such as the stethoscope, and the switch from humoral theory of disease to germ theory. In particular, germ theory gave medical practitioners immense power because, unlike humoral theory, which required the patient's cooperation to "balance the humors," germ theory had as its metaphor a war against invaders. The doctor was the heroic soldier and the patient was the battleground. Here whatever small amount of power and control a patient had was lost to the "medical gaze" (Foucault 1973), as this life and death struggle between germs and the doctor was waged. Patients who had their own opinions about what was happening inside their bodies were often seen as dangerous impediments in this all-out war. For persons with disabilities, this increased power of the medical professions resulted in the **rehabilitation model** of treatment, in which the medical practitioners had most of the control over the disabled person's body, in order to "treat" the symptoms of the *impairment* that had caused the disability. In this situation, individual persons with disabilities had very little control over what was done to them.

The model of control over the bodies and minds of persons with disabilities was reinforced by an appeal to the overriding validity of science, particularly with respect to testing, measurement, and "treatment." Much of the definition of disability has been based on comparisons with norms and the so-called normal functioning of human beings. This idea, too, is a social construction and has its own history. During the eighteenth and nineteenth centuries social statistics were developed and used to formulate theories of human functioning. In the 1840s, Belgian astronomer A. Quételet first suggested the concept of "the average man," for him, the place of human perfection. From the average, the idea of tables of norms arose, which could be used to make comparisons on many aspects of human performance. Of course, those who fell outside the average range on either side of the middle became the abnormal or pathological (being precocious was as problematic for Quételet as being mentally deficient). This statistical idea of abnormality (also called error) came to be applied in medicine, sociology, and psychology. Statistics were used in the nineteenth and twentieth centuries for drawing up mortality tables and making predictions about sickness and accidents for life insurance companies, workers' compensation schemes, and social welfare benefits. In this context, disability came to be defined as "an inability to work," and compensation was paid on the basis of elaborate formulae that calculated the degree of impairment for various body organs (Stone 1984).

383

EUGENICS

The beginning of the twentieth century marked the rise of **eugenics**, a scientific approach to human reproduction that sought to have the "less fit" removed from the "human stock" (see Chapter 18). Many studies of mentally handicapped persons and their families were carried out to prove pro-eugenic arguments, all supposedly based on scientific methods. The results included the incarceration of hundreds of thousands and involuntary sterilizations in many countries including the United States, Italy, and Canada.

The eugenics movement had many supporters, particularly among the medical professions and among those in charge of asylums for persons with intellectual disabilities. Dr. Martin Barr, one of the early presidents of the American Association on Mental Deficiency, was a strong advocate of sterilization, wanting "the surgeon's knife in place of sentimentality, and a nurse instead of a keeper" (Scheerenberger 1983, 117). The American Breeders' Association, which normally concerned itself with the optimal mating of cattle, suggested in 1913 that the following classes must generally be considered as socially unfit: (1) the feeble-minded, (2) paupers, (3) criminaloids, (4) epileptics, (5) the insane, (6) the constitutionally weak, (7) those predisposed to specific diseases, (8) the congenitally deformed, and (9) those having defective sense organs (ibid., 139). The association argued that the supply of these classes should, if possible, be eliminated from the human stock in order to maintain or raise the level of quality essential to the progress of the nation and the human race.

Sterilization laws were passed in most states in the United States and in British Columbia and Alberta in Canada. While official records are likely to underestimate the numbers of persons who were sterilized, it is believed that over 50 000 Americans and 4000 Canadians were subjected to involuntary sterilization as a eugenic measure.

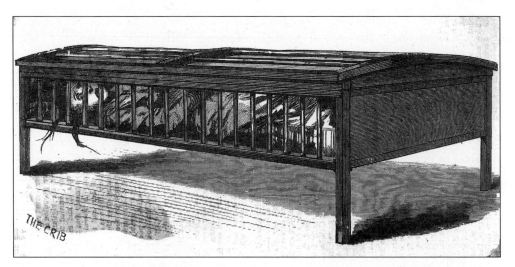

This crib, used for treating mental illness in a New York institution in the 1880s, is a cruel device for restraining difficult cases.

A much larger number of people in Canada and the United States were confined to segregated, locked institutions as a way of preventing them from reproducing. One strong proponent of this approach was Dr. Helen MacMurchy, the province of Ontario's first inspector of the feeble-minded. In 1908 she defended segregation by stating in her official report:

> Thus we shall cut off the supply of probably 80 per cent of the mentally defective for the next generation, and we shall save all the time and money we now waste by classifying them as paupers, prostitutes, criminals, tramps, when they are not anything but irresponsibles (1908, 15).

The culmination of the eugenics movement was the murder of many sick or disabled persons by the Nazi regime. As Robert J. Lifton has documented in his book *The Nazi Doctors*, the German eugenicists of the 1930s looked to the United States for their models. He also notes that the killing of persons who were disabled or sick was carried out *before* the mass killing of Jews. In a real sense, the murder of persons in hospitals in prewar Germany and the lack of any outcry was a practice run for the Holocaust.

DISABILITY: THE POSITIVIST VIEW

While much of the study of persons with mental or physical disabilities has resulted in less drastic treatment than death, even in the recent past many persons with disabilities have been confined, subjected to treatments without consent, and abused with the tacit or explicit approval of professionals trained in scientific research. Of course, many professionals have not acted like this, but many *have* objectified the person with a disability in the course of research or treatment. One of the reasons for this objectification is that both medicine and the social sciences borrowed much of their research methodology from nineteenth-century physics and chemistry. As we have already discussed in Chapter 7, the success of these sciences impressed researchers in the new fields of psychology and sociology. In particular, science was seen as studying objects in a value-free, unbiased manner. Applied to the social sciences, this became a set of ethics that included treating humans as discrete objects, using numbers to describe behaviours, and maintaining as objective as possible a stance in relation to the subjects of study.

Today, several journals on disability in both social sciences and medicine are distinctly positivist. Articles on persons with disabilities appear with charts and tables and report statistical tests that decide whether or not the results of the tests are "significant." The results are often presented in cryptic jargon, making it difficult for the nonexpert to read. A recent article on skills training for mothers of children with disabilities in the *American Journal on Mental Retardation* reported these results:

In the follow-up sample, the distribution of male children to female children was 51% to 48%, respectively. In the original sample, however, the distribution of males to females was 62% to 38%, X2 (2, N=215) = 7.85, p<.02. Further examination of this age difference at the two test times within the two treatment groups revealed that the significant difference was within the comparison treatment group, X2 (2, N=72) = 11.76, p<.05, but not in the skills-building group. A chi-square analysis of child's age by sex was not significant....(97(2) (Kirkham 1993, 513).

The problem with this type of research, besides being difficult for the uninitiated to understand, is that it usually leaves out the perspective of the individual person who is being studied, and the meaning of his or her life in any discussion of the design, methods, or results of the research. It can be argued that this method of research in medicine, psychology, and sociology has been oppressive for persons with disabilities, and does not fit with a philosophy of Independent Living or considerations of a person's quality of life. Medical practitioners often focus on the presenting problem and its treatment without taking into account all aspects of the patient's life or considering if the treatment proposed, and its hoped-for results, will improve the person's life. As one writer put it, "Questions about the quality of life have sometimes been portrayed as something of an intrusion upon the purely medical equation" (Brisenden 1987, 176).

DISABILITY: THE INTERPRETIVE VIEW

In the past 30 years or so, there has been a shift to understanding disability from the point of view of the person *with* a disability, rather than from the detached clinical view that has dominated most writing on this subject. This interpretive point of view has tried to show that disability is a *lived experience* and that persons with disabilities construct their own meaning of the world and even their own culture.

There are, of course, a number of well-known persons with disabilities who have written autobiographies or who have had books written about them. Perhaps the most famous is Helen Keller, a gifted woman who became deaf and blind as a young child. Through the intervention of her teacher, Anne Sullivan, Helen Keller became an accomplished speaker and public figure. Yet, Helen Keller's experiences as a disabled person are quite likely very different from those of other disabled people, since most do not become famous world travellers. Most live quite ordinary lives in the sense that their everyday experiences, needs, and desires do not differ greatly from those of the nondisabled population. Yet most nondisabled people view persons with disabilities as objects of pity, sympathy, fear, and curiosity; much of this probably stems from the two groups' separation, and is not based on real information about disabilities.

What follows are excerpts from writings by four people with different disabilities. These excerpts are interpretive: they are intended to provide a sense of what it is like to be a person with a disability.

Ed Murphy (not his real name) was born with cerebral palsy but was labelled mentally retarded as a child. At 15 he was placed in a large state institution. Here he speaks of the overprotection that is often a prevalent feature of a disabled person's life.

> The doctors told my mother that I would be a burden to her. When I was growing up she never let me out of her sight. She was always there with attention. If I yelled she ran right to me. So many children who are handicapped must be in that position—they become so dependent on their mother. Looking back I don't think she ever stopped protecting me even when I was capable of being self-sufficient. I remember how hard it was to break away from that. She never really believed that after I had lived the first six months that I could be like everybody else (Taylor and Bogdan 1984, 158–59).

By contrast, Sondra Diamond, a psychologist who also was born with cerebral palsy, had a very different experience growing up. While her father was very protective of her, her mother was determined that she should be independent.

> I recall the first time I used a Kotex. My mother handed me the sanitary belt and Kotex, and said, "It's time you learned to put this on yourself." I sat on the toilet for three hours, struggling, sweating, and swearing. Every few minutes, I heard my father yelling at my mother, "Rose, go in there and give her a hand." Since it was the weekend, the usual flow of neighbours and friends were coming in and out of the house. Noticing my absence, they asked what I was doing in the bathroom so long. I remember hearing her explain, and hearing each of them say, in different ways, "Rose, how can you be so cruel?" My father was in a rage. The neighbours were outraged by my mother's treatment of me. My mother never wavered. Amid this commotion, I learned how to use a Kotex, secretly admiring my mother's fortitude, and getting a kick out of the fuss that was being made over me (Diamond 1981, 28).

As noted above, many persons with disabilities have been institutionalized for much of their lives. Although not all stories are unhappy ones, many residents remember the physical and mental abuse and neglect they suffered. Peter Park, one of the leaders of Canada's "People First" movement, writes:

> In 1960, I entered the institution to have my epileptic seizures controlled. After eighteen years, they still hadn't succeeded in controlling them. "Oh," you say, "Why so long?" Well, I originally went into the institution to have my seizures brought under control with medication. There were two doctors who admitted me. After three days, one doctor died. I said to myself: "Old age, likely." About six days later, the second doctor passed on, and I became a name and a number on a piece of paper that was conveniently lost for eighteen years. I was given Dilantin and phenobarb, plus other drugs. We were used as guinea pigs to try out new drugs that aren't normally

387

available through the CPA [Canadian Pharmaceutical Association] or in Merck manuals. Okay, I said that I was institutionalized for eighteen years. I am estimating that I was in a lock-up for nine of eighteen years. A lock-up is a form of aversive therapy. I was held by a staff member while another staff squirted lemon juice in my face (Park 1988, 13).

Carol Padden and Tom Humphries are both Deaf professors who write about deafness not as a disability but as a different culture. From this perspective, people who identify with Deaf culture (the capital on Deaf is important in designating Deaf culture rather than being unable to hear) see themselves as culturally different from the hearing culture. Deaf culture has its own language (signs), history, and traditions. Padden and Humphries tell of how Sam, born into a Deaf family, with several Deaf older brothers, came to realize that some people were not like him.

As his interests turned to the world outside his family, he [Sam] noticed a girl next door who seemed to be about his age. After a few tentative encounters, they became friends. She was a satisfactory playmate, but there was the problem of her "strangeness." He could not talk with her as he could with his older brothers and his parents. She seemed to have extreme difficulty understanding even the simplest or crudest gestures....One day, Sam remembers vividly, he finally understood that his friend was indeed odd. They were playing in her home, when suddenly her mother walked up to them and animatedly began to move her mouth. As if by magic, the girl picked up a dollhouse and moved it to another place. Sam was mystified and went home to ask his mother about exactly what kind of affliction the girl next door had. His mother explained that she was HEARING and because of this did not know how to SIGN; instead she and her mother TALK, they move their mouths to communicate with each other. Sam then asked if this girl and her family were the only ones "like that." His mother explained that no, in fact, nearly everyone else was like the neighbours. It was his own family that was unusual. It was a memorable moment for Sam. He remembers thinking how curious the girl next door was, and if she was HEARING, how curious HEARING people were (Padden and Humphries 1988, 15–16.)

There is also an interpretive literature on disability written by nondisabled social scientists. One of the earliest works of this type is *The Cloak of Competence: Stigma in the Lives of the Mentally Retarded*, written in 1967 by anthropologist Robert Edgerton. Edgerton shows how people who have been stigmatized try to make themselves appear "normal" to others and deny their status as persons with mental handicaps. This concept of *passing* can be applied to any stigmatized group that tries to cover up certain aspects in order not to suffer at the hands of the majority. Edgerton describes how ex-patients of a mental hospital try to construct a normal past:

For one thing, the ex-patient lacks the ordinary souvenirs of a normal past. When he leaves the hospital he ordinarily has few if any souvenirs that could be displayed in the outside world. The ex-patients recognize this lack and make efforts to remedy it. It is quite common for souvenirs, photos, and oddments of all kinds to be picked up in junk shops or trash cans. Others are borrowed from friends. And more or less legitimate memorabilia of trips or experiences are collected with a passion, as though to make up for lost time. For example, one married woman had a photograph album filled with photos of assorted relatives, friends and family—and not a single photograph was legitimate. She had accumulated the photos from several old albums at a church rummage sale and was now happily representing the album to be a record of her allegedly normal, almost illustrious, past (Edgerton 1967, 157).

Another woman had over 40 china cups, saucers, and dishes, each one with a history of travel, good friends, fine memories, and the happy exchange of gifts. All these tales were false also—she had picked up the lot for a few dollars in a junk shop. A man had over a dozen trophies of supposed skills in golf, bowling, tennis, and even archery, presumably dating back to a happy, athletic boyhood; these too were acquired in junk shops.

These and other interpretive analyses of the lives of persons with disabilities give some indication of the extent to which many lack legitimation and place in society. In order to acquire a place and to be treated like everyone else, they are forced to go to extraordinary lengths to cover their real histories and present ones that are more accommodating.

DISABILITY: A CRITICAL VIEW

In his book *The Politics of Disablement*, Michael Oliver (1990), a British sociologist who is disabled, lists three main problems with previous social science research that uses disabled people as subjects.

1. Most research questions given to disabled persons in questionnaires "ultimately reduce the problems that disabled people face to their own inadequacies or functional limitations";

2. Most research with disabled persons as subjects "has failed to improve the quality of life for them, while doing no harm to the career prospects of the researchers";

3. "The theoretical underpinnings of much research on disability have usually been so divorced from the everyday experience of disabled people that they have felt victimized by professionals" (7–9).

Oliver concludes that "for these reasons more and more disabled people are refusing to participate in research over which they have no control and which they regard as likely to further their oppression" (9).

THE "REALITIES" OF DISABILITY

Oliver's work is a good example of a critical approach to disability, and his theoretical base is *neo-Marxism*. In a 1988 article, he identified four principal accounts of treatment of

Terry Fox, marathon runner, 1958–1981.

persons with disabilities operating in social science and social policy research in Western societies.

The first is the humanitarian account where disability is seen as personal tragedy (or its converse, personal heroism). Because having a disability is seen as tragic, humanitarian perspectives on disability tend to focus on helping the person with a disability to *overcome* his or her individual situations. Those disabled people who are recognized as high achievers take on the cultural status of heroes; Canadian examples include Terry Fox and Rick Hansen, two disabled athletes whose exploits raised money for research and heightened Canadians' awareness of persons with disabilities. While the achievements of these athletes needs to be recognized, their stories tend to reinforce the view that disability is something to be overcome or "conquered."

Another account of disability used in social policy research is the metaphor of social investment. In this functional approach, persons with disabilities are seen as human capital, and investment in the welfare of disabled persons is based both on cost-benefit analysis and the need for social and political stability. Such an approach would argue that it is more economical to place persons with "special needs" in the community rather than in institutions, particularly when such people can be now controlled with drugs, therefore posing little *threat* to the general population.

A third account of disability used in social policy research is based on several **conflict theories**. The pluralistic view of conflict theory sees persons with disabilities as one more social group clamouring for scarce resources who must compete for funds with other groups in society. Marxist conflict theory reduces this struggle to conflict between classes—labour and capital, workers and bosses.

Finally, a **social control** view of disability argues that groups that can be demanding need to be pacified and controlled through minimal benefits, legislation, forced exclusion, and professional power. For example, legislation on benefits for those who are unable to work is structured so that only the bare necessities are given, in order to ensure that those who can work will continue to rather than apply for welfare benefits. Thus, both those unable to work and those able to work are kept in their "proper" places in society (for an economic analysis of disability, see Deborah Stone, 1984).

These four accounts of treatment are accompanied by three different definitions of disability. In the individualistic definition, the person with the disability is seen as having a problem, and efforts are made to help the individual cope with life. In the social construction definition, disability is said to exist because it is defined as disability by other people. If categories of disability are not thought about or defined, then the problems of disabled people are seen to disappear. In the social creation definition, it is argued that society "disables people with impairments by the way it responds to those impairments" (Oliver 1990, 17). Thus inaccessibility is a result of how buildings are designed and not the inability of some people to walk.

Oliver, along with leaders of many organizations of disabled people, favours the third definition of disability—that society creates disability by neglecting to account for the needs of those who are mentally or physically different from the majority. An even more radical position is to see disability in its negative meanings as a *fiction*, and to view being mentally or physically different as a positive state of being, or as simply a matter of being *culturally distinct*. This view has been most recently articulated by members of the Deaf community, who sometimes argue that prevention programs are a form of cultural genocide, and that more deaf children need to be produced in order to keep a healthy Deaf culture. Similarly, Jean Vanier (1971) has argued that the world needs mentally handicapped persons in it in order to teach those who are not mentally handicapped about caring and generosity of spirit.

Today, sociologists and disability rights activists such as Harlan Hahn and Michael Oliver have taken the position that disability is not a misfortune but a positive and often creative experience. The problem, according to them, is not that disability should be prevented, but that the world simply has to be better designed to accommodate persons with disabilities. However, Paul Abberley, another sociologist and disability rights activist, has argued that, while Western society should drop its oppressive stance toward persons with disabilities, disabilities themselves should be prevented. The late Irving Zola, also a sociologist and disability activist, agreed with Abberley, pointing out that for most of their history organizations of persons with disabilities have not been very successful in producing viable subcultures. The reasons for this, Zola maintained, have already been outlined by Talcott Parsons. Parsons, according to Zola, accurately laid out the dilemma facing groups who are dependent on others for their survival. And while Parsons referred in the following excerpt to the "sick" and the "sick role," Zola felt the same observations apply to persons with disabilities.

> The sick role is...a mechanism which...channels deviance so that the two most dangerous potentialities, namely group formation and successful establishment of the claim of legitimacy, are avoided. The sick are tied up, not with other deviants to form a "subculture" of the sick but each with a group of nonsick, his personal circle, and, above all, physicians. The sick thus become a statistical status and are deprived of the possibility of forming a solidary collectivity. Furthermore, to be sick is by definition to be in an undesirable state, so that it simply does not "make sense" to assert a claim that the way to deal with the frustrating aspects of the social system is for everyone to get sick (Parsons 1951, 477).

To understand what this might mean in terms of persons with disabilities organizing to fight for disability rights, Zola suggested we consider some of the rallying cries of the different liberation movements of the last several decades. "Black is beautiful" and "Sisterhood is powerful," he said make perfect sense. But, he asked, what about those with chronic disabilities? Could they yell, "Long live cancer," "Up with multiple sclerosis," "I'm glad I had polio," "Don't you wish you were blind?" In the case of persons with disabilities, the reversal of stigma, Zola pointed out, "will not so easily provide a basis for a common positive identity" (1993, 16). But we should not be too hasty in dismissing the ideas of Oliver and Hahn. Their critical stance reminds us that meaning *is* constructed and that it is possible to view disability as a "beautiful and creative experience" (Hahn 1993).

A COMPLEX VIEW OF DISABILITY

How does one decide among all the above competing accounts of disability and social policy toward disabled persons? One might argue that each position is a partial view that contains some merit but is incomplete because it excludes other valid points of view. A fuller account of disability is complex in that there are many different aspects to consider in order to gain a complete picture of the disabled person's life situation.

There are no essential qualities that warrant a person being labelled disabled. "Disabled" says nothing about a person that clearly distinguishes that person from someone who is not described as such. What we mean by this term is culturally and historically specific, and therefore relative. The value placed on the person who is labelled disabled, the roles expected of that person, and the behaviours of others toward him or her are also culturally and historically relative. One Swedish philosopher, Lennart Nordenfelt (1992), has suggested that we cannot properly speak of disability with any real meaning unless it is in the form of a statement such as: person A is disabled given that he or she has vital goals X and is prevented from realizing these goals by circumstances Y.

Having a disability, as defined now in Western societies, applies mainly to individuals rather than groups defined by some other criteria. Groups of disabled persons are seen as groups of individuals with disabilities. One reason for this view is the recognition that having a disability is possible regardless of class, race, or gender. There is a certain truth to the perception that disability is a personal issue, and given that most disabilities involve a loss of some area of human capacity, it is not unreasonable to expect that most people would not want to have a disability if it could be prevented. But neither does it necessitate describing a disabled person as having a *tragic* life. Paul Abberley (1987) notes that we must hold two separate attitudes to disability simultaneously. On the one hand, we should do everything possible to prevent a person from becoming disabled, and on the other hand, we must affirm and not devalue persons who already have a disability.

From another more sociological perspective, no one is an isolated individual; rather, we all live in relation to others, and to an entity we term society. As well, we occupy **multiple subject positions** in society; we do not just have one identity. We act as individuals with **agency**, but almost always with regards to others' views of us and with regard to our perception of our social status in society. Thus the attitudes of others do make a difference in how we are seen, labelled, and treated. From this point of view, all problems of disability are social problems that can be removed through technological or social solutions.

But this too is an incomplete account for a number of reasons. First, it does not recognize that many (but not all) disabilities are either caused by technology (weapons, airplanes, cars) or are aided by medical advances that allow some severely disabled persons to live who would have died in previous times; nor does it recognize that the problems of persons with disabilities cannot simply be reduced by the removal of barriers to accessibility in a society. Second, this view is limited to the extent that it doesn't recognize its cultural relativity. Not all human capacities are restorable through technology or through removal of barriers. As well, in societies without advanced technology, where the natural environment is more prominent in daily life, it would not be reasonable to see all problems of disability as created by the society. While it is reasonable to suggest that steps *create* a disability for persons in a wheelchair, it is not reasonable to suggest that the lack of ability to move through the jungle in a wheelchair is equally a society-created problem. The attraction of the social-creation position is that it counters the common tendency in Western culture to blame the victim with a reversal. Attractive as that may be, the limitations of this account need to be acknowledged.

A better, critical understanding of disability must explain how the category of disability occurs socially, how it is maintained, and how it may be modified, while recognizing that persons exist as individuals in relation to society. We begin with an analysis of how some human differences are recognized in Western societies today and are then turned into the category we term disability.

"I AM NOT WHAT YOU SEE"

American ethnomethodologist David Goode tells of his encounter as a graduate student with a severely handicapped person while on a tour of a local state hospital for persons with mental handicaps.

> I went into one of the rooms near the end of the hall and saw a huge bedboard at the head of the bed whose occupant was hidden from view. The room was empty, without objects on the walls or toys. It was brightly lit. I walked toward the bed and peeked over the edge and was as intensely horrified as I have ever been in my life at what I saw. A *huge* head, later I was told over forty pounds, attached to this stunted body. Horrible bedsores covered what appeared for a moment as an almost unreal monstrosity—like a Hollywood inspired nightmare, though *too* real, too much an actual sensory experience to ignore as fantasy. He, it turned out to be a he, was the most profane looking human being I had ever seen (1984, 229–30).

David Goode's immediate reaction was nausea and feeling faint. A nurse appeared suddenly and took Goode's arm to steady him and reassure him. She said, "Oh, I see you've found Johnny, my favourite. I've been here three and a half years and he's my special favourite. He's eighteen and I'm his mommy during the day....He loves rock and roll, I usually open the window up so it's bright and put on the music loud. He loves when I take his hands and clap them to the beat. He has his likes and dislikes, you know. He loves his red flashlight...."

A few moments later, back out on the ward, David met a young physician who informed him that this young man "was hydrocephalic," born before the invention of the shunt operation, and that the intracranial pressure had made him deaf, blind, and completely paralyzed. "The clinical profile was hopeless—no possibility existed for remediation, therefore the case was essentially custodial, the person as low functioning as one could find" (230).

From this story we can see that there are many different understandings of disability and many different reactions to meeting a person with a disability. First, there is the cultural understanding exemplified by David Goode who looks and reacts with horror at what he sees. (Other culturally established understandings and reactions to disability include the evocation of pity or a patronizing attitude.) The nurse exemplifies a second understanding of disability—the intimate or caring understanding: she identifies herself as Johnny's "mommy during the day." But this understanding, though caring, can have its patronizing and pitying elements. A third understanding is the professional or clinical understanding of the doctor, which allows no room for emotion. A fourth understanding—one that in Goode's story is nearly absent—is the understanding of the person with the disability. In Western societies today, this understanding is often marginalized and has only recently been given any credence. Finally, there is the analytical understanding, again provided by David Goode, but also provided by the authors of this chapter and by others who write on disability issues, about what happens when a nondisabled person encounters a person with a disability.

In keeping with the critical perspective in this book, it should be no surprise to learn that our understanding of disability is both a social and a historical construction. The idea of the social construction of disabilities can be linked to the ground-breaking work of Erving Goffman in *Asylums* (1961), which introduced the concept of the "moral career of the mental patient," and in *Stigma* (1963), with its concept of "spoiled identity." A stigma, writes Goffman, is any attribute that is "deeply discrediting."

> While the stranger is present before us, evidence can arise of his possessing an attribute that makes him different from others in the category of persons available for him to be, and of a less desirable kind—in the extreme a person is quite thoroughly bad, or dangerous, or weak. He is thus reduced in our minds from a whole and usual person to a tainted, discounted one. Such an attribute is a stigma, especially when its discrediting effect is very extensive; sometimes it is also called a failing, a shortcoming, a handicap. (1978, 103).

Among the different types of stigma Goffman notes are "physical deformities." Whatever the stigma, however, Goffman maintains that the same kinds of sociological features are found. A person who is stigmatized has some trait that becomes the focus of attention of others. Because of this trait, an individual who would otherwise be treated in a normal fashion is instead perceived as "not quite human." This perception in turn allows others to feel justified in their discriminatory actions, which reduce the life chances of the person so stigmatized (ibid., 105).

Many times in our society persons with disabilities are treated as children or as less than fully human. Consider the fact that McDonald's, the well-known restaurant chain, has trade-marked the term McJobs to refer only to the employment of persons with disabilities. In reaction to this, Vic Willi, a leader in the disability community in Canada, commented:

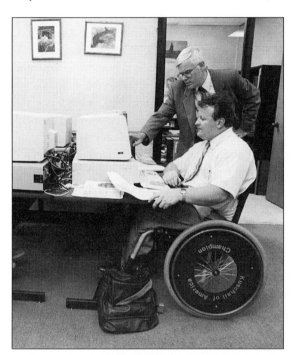

Job retraining focuses on skill development.

> They are in a state of denial if they think that "McJobs" is not patroniz-ing and humiliating to people with a disability. We want to integrate in an equal fashion, and not through some fancy public relations label. Do they have McXecutives, too? (personal communication, August 1994).

Images of disability are all around us. Historically, persons with disabilities have been portrayed as monsters and freaks, and this image has stayed with us until the present day in cartoons, fairy tales, horror films, and the circus sideshow. Recently an American company published an interactive CD-ROM called *Freak Show* as an "entertaining" way to experience the circus sideshow on your home computer. Persons with disabilities have been portrayed as "objects of pity" on telethons, charity advertising, and in popular films.

But, as Vic Willi has indicated, persons with disabilities don't want to be seen as less than full citizens in our society and don't wish to be stereotyped into a particular set of roles. The anger of disability rights activist Joseph Shapiro is palpable when he writes, "Nondisabled Americans do not understand disabled ones" (1993, 3). Shapiro goes on to recount what happened at a memorial service for Timothy Cook, "a disabled attorney who, at thirty-eight years old, had won landmark disability rights cases." At the service longtime friends got up and paid Cook heartfelt tribute:

> "He never seemed disabled to me," said one. "He was the least disabled person I ever met," pronounced another....But more than a few heads in the crowded chapel bowed with an uneasy embarrassment at the supposed compliment. It was as if someone had

tried to compliment a black man by saying "You're the least black person I ever met," as false as telling a Jew "I never think of you as Jewish," as clumsy as seeking to flatter a woman with "You don't act like a woman" (3).

To be fair to the well-meaning friends, says Shapiro, their sincere words were "among the highest accolades that Americans routinely give those with disabilities" (4). And they are words that until 15 years before, most persons with a disability would have gladly accepted as a compliment. Indeed, as stigmatized individuals many persons with disabilities have attempted to ameliorate their position in society "by devoting much private effort to the mastery of areas of activity ordinarily felt to be closed on incidental and physical grounds to persons with their shortcomings (Goffman 1963, 10). But increasingly, persons with disabilities have begun to think differently. As a result of an ongoing revolution in self-perception, persons with disabilities no longer see their physical or mental limitations as a "source of shame or as something to overcome in order to inspire others. Today they proclaim that it is okay, even good, to be disabled" (Shapiro 1993, 4).

Persons with disabilities represent a highly variable cross section of different personalities, desires, and abilities. This sentiment is well expressed in the following poem by Cheryl Marie Wade:

> **I Am Not One of The**
>
> **I am not one of the physically challenged...**
>
> **I'm a sock in the eye with a gnarled fist**
>
> **I'm a French kiss with cleft tongue**
>
> **I'm orthopedic shoes sewn on the last of your fears**
>
> **I'm not one of the differently abled.**
>
> **I'm an epitaph for a million imperfect babies left untreated**
>
> **I'm an icon carved from bones in a mass grave at Tiergarten, Germany**
>
> **I'm withered legs hidden in a blanket**
>
> **I'm not one of the able disabled.**
>
> **I'm a black panther with green eyes and scars like a picket fence**
>
> **I'm pink lace panties teasing a stub of milk white thigh**
>
> **I'm the Evil Eye**
>
> **I'm the first cell divided**
>
> **I'm mud that talks**
>
> **I'm Eve I'm Kali**
>
> **I'm The Mountain that Never Moves**
>
> **I've been forever I'll be here forever**
>
> **I'm the Gimp**
>
> **I'm the Cripple**
>
> **I'm the Crazy Lady**
>
> **I'm the Woman with Juice**

THE CREATION OF THE CATEGORY OF DISABILITY

Human differences are produced in many ways. Sexual reproduction ensures that off-spring are different from their parents: genetic codes produce offsprings not identical to either parent; the random matching of recessive genes develops characteristics that have been dormant in the family line for generations; genetic mutations sometimes occur. Yet it is the parental similarities that are noticed first in newborn infants. The human infant is recognized as fully human to the extent that it is in the likeness of other human infants (i.e., its characteristics fall within the norms for the species). The concept of species and species boundaries is important to the definition of humanness, and if a child departs too much from the norms of the species, then he or she may not be recognized as human. Indeed, the first requirement of life is the recognition by some adult humans, usually the parents, that the child belongs to the human race and will receive care.

Differences are produced a second way through physical means such as accidents, abuse, war, or cosmetic surgery. The injury of a child in the prenatal/perinatal/postnatal environment is not part of biological reproduction but is due to the intervention of a destructive force. Drugs, alcohol, tobacco, malnutrition, and physical injuries, as well as genetic factors, may all contribute to produce differences that are interpreted as impairments. Such destructive influences are a major focus of prevention programs. Accidents that leave permanent injury, a feature of industrial societies, are another source of disabilities.

War injuries also contribute to the production of impairments, although generally the war-injured have been honoured and treated better than those who were born with a disability. Many of the social benefits for disabled people, for example, occurred first as provisions for the war-wounded: pensions were allocated in ancient Greece, and social insurance benefits for war veterans are provided in our time.

Our society makes a clear distinction between those who have been injured in war as soldiers and those who have suffered civilian injuries. Sustaining a war injury has often resulted in medals and pensions for soldiers. But becoming disabled as a result of land mines, gunshot wounds, and other war-related injuries has never in any way been a positive experience for civilians. War-injured civilians receive no pensions or other honours, yet their lives are often radically changed.

Finally, differences are produced through chronic diseases, which are those with long duration and uncertain outcomes. Most chronic diseases are manifest in early adulthood (Mathews 1985) and come to affect even the most minor aspects of daily life. (See the discussion of multiple sclerosis in Chapter 9.)

THE SOCIAL CONSTRUCTION OF DIFFERENCES

While biological and physical factors can produce differences in humans, the recognition and perpetuation of meanings of specific differences allow us to speak of the social production and reproduction of differences. Even if a person has a specific impairment, it is a social act to recognize oneself or others as a "disabled person." Many people who are eligible for certain disability benefits simply refuse to register as disabled. This shows how

397

disability and need are relative terms: the effects of a particular physical, mental, or social condition cannot be defined in the abstract, but rather in relation to individual expectations, attributes, reactions of others, and one's self-concept. Thus, a lawyer who is blind may have more in common with a lawyer who can see than with a newsagent who is blind, but in the perceptions of the general public the attribute of blindness may be the classifying factor. The possibility of stigma attached to the use of an aid is also culturally relative—glasses are acceptable, and may even project a desired maturity, while hearing aids and wheelchairs may mark a person as defective.

Categorization and Perception

The beginning of a disability category is the recognition of an important difference by those who have the power to define the situation, followed by a labelling of the recognized difference. For example, while it might seem obvious that a person who is blind is disabled, this fact rests on several social constructions. There is the recognition of difference in terms of a sensory ability, but contrary to common belief, most legally blind people retain some sight. Those termed blind have passed an arbitrarily set threshold of the measurement of visual functioning. This threshold has little to do with a person's ability to function in the world, which is dependent on the person's adaptation to his or her loss of sight and to the demands of the specific situation on that person. The perception that blindness results in a different experience of the world, that blind people are abnormal or have special needs, is a majority point of view based on the rarity of finding blind people in one's daily life and on living in a world that has not been specifically designed for blind people.

The philosopher Wittgenstein once asked, "What would a society all of deaf people look like?" One answer to his question is found in Groce's (1985) book, *Everyone Here Spoke Sign Language*, which documents a 250-year period when hereditary deafness was very common in Martha's Vineyard. Almost every family had at least one deaf member, and everyone interacted on a daily basis with deaf people. Rather than marginalization and stigma, the presence of many deaf people resulted in widespread bilingualism. A vernacular sign language developed and was used throughout the island. In the nineteenth and early twentieth centuries, almost everyone in the community used sign language in all social and personal contexts. Because signing was learned early in life, it was commonly adopted by hearing people, and sometimes even preferred in situations where secretiveness was advantageous or where distances made speech difficult. Sign language was so common that the elderly men and women who were Groce's principal sources had difficulty in remembering who was deaf and who could hear in their community.

Social Construction

Several writers have argued that the way a disabled person is perceived is a social construction; so much so that after a period of "adjustment" or training, he or she is forced to act as a disabled person.

> When those who have been screened into blindness agencies enter them, they may not be able to see at all or they may have serious difficulties with their vision. When they have

been rehabilitated, they are all blind men. They have learned the attitudes and behaviour patterns that professional blindness workers believe people should have. For the intensive face-to-face relationships between blindness workers and clients that make up the rehabilitation process, the blind person is rewarded for adopting a view of himself that is consistent with his rehabilitators' view of him and is punished for clinging to other self-conceptions. He is told that he is "insightful" when he comes to describe his problems and his personality as his rehabilitators view them, and he is said to be "blocking" or resisting when he does not. Indeed, passage through the blindness system is determined in part by his willingness to adopt the "experts'" views about self (Scott 1969).

Special education and rehabilitation derive their legitimacy as institutional forms from both the need for exclusion of those who are perceived to be different and from the religious ethic of helping those in need. Exclusion is always masked with love because open admission of administered inequality would contradict the public ethics of the administrator. "For their own good" has been a key phrase when people are being institutionalized as well as deinstitutionalized. In both cases, the existence of a professional group and a client group is maintained. In the case of deinstitutionalization, modern drugs are sometimes able to create an institution without walls.

From a general confinement of all the "unwanted" elements of society, there has developed an increasing differentiation of categories with corresponding service systems. There has also been a concomitant growth of professional influence on the definition of experience that is not strictly normative. Thus the mildest deviations now have diagnostic labels and specialized programs. The result has been a proliferation of professional discourses, training programs, and legislation.

Large custodial institutions often confined people from age one or two years until death; deinstitutionalization has resulted in the service system for disabled children moving in two directions: from school-age programs to adult programs and to preschool, infant, and perinatal or prenatal programs. A general philosophy of "the earlier the better" has prevailed with regard to the timing of the initial intervention. The implication of the trend to earlier intervention, however, may be that a younger child is more likely to be vulnerable to professional definition and control and less able to resist the induction into the "moral career" (Goffman 1961) of disability, which refers to the development of identity that takes place when one becomes disabled.

These trends reflect the changing powers of various professional groups to define and control the situation of the "deviant" person in society. The role of doctors was extremely important in policy making in the nineteenth and early twentieth centuries because of doctors' reputations for "high moral character and discerning judgment...a person whose experience with human failings and weaknesses bestowed on him the kind of wisdom inaccessible to other professionals" (Simmons 1982, 177).

With the rising prestige of science, other groups such as psychologists, social workers, teachers, and occupational therapists could also register a claim to legitimacy in the treatment of persons with a disability. Further, as medicine shifted more toward a scientific base and away from moral prestige, doctors tended to confine themselves to those they could cure, leaving others to work with nonmedical problems. These shifts in power were reflected in changing concepts and vocabulary about the disabled. As educators became more prominent, words like "educable" and "trainable" replaced "idiot," "imbecile," and "moron." As psychologists gained influence, terminology of assessment, behaviour modification, and therapy entered the field. Like the doctors, the new professionals invoked the power of science to justify their interventions into the lives of disabled people. The "clinical method" (also known as the "medical model") became *the* way of operating to ensure the maximum scientific respectability and the least resistance. One of the results of professional social control of disabled persons has been their relative silence in explaining their own lives to others. As well, professional control leads to dependence, a state that has often been reinforced by the use of scientific research. Finally, as objects of study, disabled persons have sometimes been subjected to dehumanizing treatment in the name of science. The story of Peter Park, cited above, is just one of the many instances in which persons with disabilities are treated as if they were simply objects, without rights or feelings.

But scientific methods have come under increasing scrutiny over the past 20 years, and there are now approaches to research that promote subject input and control and that are used for emancipatory goals. Given that Independent Living is a form of emancipation, these forms of research hold out the promise of compatiblity with the goals of the Independent Living Movement.

THE SELF-ADVOCACY MOVEMENT

The Independent Living Movement seems to have started in 1962, when four severely disabled students at the University of Illinois were transferred from a campus-isolated nursing home to a modified home closer to campus. In 1972 the Berkeley Center for Independent Living (Berkeley CIL) was incorporated as a self-help group, with its management under the control of persons who were themselves disabled. Other centres followed in the United States, each with its own blend of services and features. Unlike the Berkeley CIL, many offered residential programs. The Independent Living Movement spread to Canada in 1980 when Gerben DeJong spoke about the American movement at the Coalition of Provincial Organizations of the Handicapped (COPOH) Conference in Vancouver, B.C.

Disabled athletes, like their able-bodied counterparts, push the limits of physical endurance.

As DeJong noted in his 1979 article, "Vocational rehabilitation professionals...have a different conception of independent living than do their consumer counterparts in the IL movement" (438). The leaders of the IL movement had adopted the model of *consumerism* as a metaphor for how they saw disabled persons' relationships with professionals. As a consumer, the disabled person would, in theory, have the right to choose his or her services and service providers, and reject those providers who did not give good service. This model "asserts that because disabled persons are the best judges of their own interests, they should have the larger voice in determining what services are provided in the disability services market" (ibid., 439). As a consequence of this choice of image, the term "disabled consumers" has entered the mainstream of professional vocabulary within the past five years.

TABLE 17-1	PERSPECTIVES ON THE TREATMENT OF PERSONS WITH DISABILITIES	
	PERSPECTIVE	**DEFINING CHARACTERISTICS**
	1. Humanitarian	• Disability viewed as a personal tragedy • Focus on helping person with disability overcome his or her individual situation
	2. Social investment	• Persons with disabilities viewed as human capital • Focus on cost-benefit analyses and the need to promote social and political stability within society
	3. Conflict	• Persons with disabilities are among many social groups demanding scarce resources • Focus on competition with others for scarce funds
	4. Social control	• Persons with disabilities viewed as demanding resources and services • Focus on providing minimal benefits in order to pacify and control

■ ■ ■

SUMMARY

All persons, disabled or not, have many things in common. We all use professional services to some degree, we all learn to do many things for ourselves. We all choose certain aspects of our existence, we all face many things that are beyond our control. We all are capable of being in relationships with others, however similar to us or different. For example, David Goode has shown that it is possible to develop a meaningful two-way communicative relationship with a deaf-blind adolescent who uses no formal language system.

As the name of the association of persons with intellectual disabilities states, disabled persons are "People First." They have the same needs, desires, and reactions to the world as most people, but because of nondisabled prejudices, they tend to have patterns of social relations that are different. This is slowly changing as more persons with disabilities become included and integrated into the mainstream of society.

■ ■ ■

FOR DISCUSSION

1. To what extent does the rehabilitation model continue to dominate the treatment of persons with disabilities in Western societies?

2. What are some of the problems inherent in using a positivist approach to study disability?

3. Oliver (1988) identified four principal theories of treatment of persons with disabilities—humanitarian, social investment, conflict, and social control. Discuss the kinds of research that each theory might support.

4. What are some of the ways that disability might be defined? How would each of those definitions affect the way in which research on disability is carried out?

5. List some of the most common images of disability that exist today. Discuss the meanings each of those images conveys about persons with disabilities.

6. What are the goals of the Independent Living Movement? Are those goals achievable in Canada today?

18

THE MANY FACES OF RACE AND RACISM*

CHAPTER OPENING QUESTIONS

- How might we understand the changes that have taken place in the way "race"[1] has been understood within the social sciences?

- What do these changes mean in terms of the relationship between scientific discoveries and the social conditions in which those discoveries are made?

- What are the broader implications for Western societies of the new approaches, as well as the return by some scholars to the older approaches, to issues of race and racism?

Race and **racism** are pervasive aspects of Western thought and experience. The two permeate Western cultural meanings, practices, and expressions. Because of this, both the meaning and the reality of these two concepts are rarely challenged in day-to-day living. But what is meant by race, who is considered to be a member of a given race, and what being a member of a given race entails have changed over time in Western societies and differ from culture to culture.

Audrey Smedely has pointed out that in countries such as Canada and the United States the perceived biological race of someone is an important factor in establishing social identity and strongly influences social interactions. We

---

* This chapter has been strongly influenced by many of the articles collected in *The Anatomy of Racism*, edited by David Theo Goldberg and published by the University of Minnesota Press, Minneapolis, 1990. The authors of the articles examine the conceptual and historical background of different kinds of racism in historical and crosscultural perspectives.

[1] In this chapter "race" (in quotation marks) will be used to refer to the concept of biologically or physically significant differences between populations of people. Race (without quotation marks) will be used to refer to the social construction of a category of difference between populations of people. While in Western society race (as a socially constructed category) is believed to reflect "race" (as a biological or physical category), I argue strongly against such a conflation.

How do these children's faces reflect both race and "race"?

perceive different racial identities on the basis of what we assume are obvious, easily recognizable biological and physical differences. And we believe these physical differences to be concrete evidence of the existence of different races. "We have been conditioned," Smedely asserts, "to respond automatically to the presence of certain varying physical features as indicators of race and the differences race connotes" (1993, 1).

The common-sense, taken-for-granted view shared by many North Americans today is that scientists have confirmed that biological "race" is part of the natural order. Certainly the first textbook published in the discipline of anthropology by E.B. Tylor in 1881 defined anthropology as the study of "man and the races of man." "Race" began and stayed a central concern of anthropology well into the 1960s. Yet since 1970 the term "race"—referring to physiological differences between human populations—has been progressively eliminated from introductory North American textbooks on physical anthropology (Littlefield, Lieberman, and Reynolds 1982, 642). Indeed, American authors of these texts now claim that "races" do not exist in the sense that they are social and not biological constructs (Smedely 1993, 2).

It would seem that today the "progressive" opinions of social scientists are at odds with public opinion, experience, and realities. It should be noted, however, that while progressive social scientists have jettisoned the concept of "race" as a useful analytic concept for understanding human social existence, others, such as Philippe Rushton of the University of Western Ontario and Richard Herrnstein and Charles Murray for their controversial book *The Bell Curve: Intelligence and Class Structure in American Life,* have received a great deal of publicity for claiming the opposite. Rushton has reasserted not only that races *do* exist, distinguished from one another by clearly defined biological characteristics, but also that biologically based racial differences are a significant factor in establishing behaviour patterns in individual members of a given race.

In this chapter, race and racism are treated as a sociocultural phenomenon, quite separate from any biophysical variations that might exist among human beings. Following Smedely, I am convinced that "to comprehend the nature and meaning of race in our society, it is necessary and essential to distinguish physical diversity in the human species from culturally based perceptions and interpretations of this diversity" (1993, 14). "Race" is one of the many concepts that we take from our culture to use as a means of perceiving, interpreting, and handling social interaction. The view of race that many North Americans share is perpetuated by the continual use of the concept in daily life, by the kinds of stereotypes that we share and that are present both explicitly and implicitly everywhere in our culture.

In stressing the cultural and social nature of race and racism, however, I do not intend to avoid the empirical reality of physical variations that exist between human beings. Nor do I mean to suggest that those physical variations have nothing to do with the origin and the persistence of race categorization or with the treatment of the people identified as belonging to one or another race category. But I do want to emphasize that the concepts of race and racism, as they now exist in the taken-for-granted world of most Westerners, are the result of the "imposition of an arbitrary value system on the facts of biological (phenotypic) variations in the human species" (ibid., 22). In this chapter, I will consider three issues. The first is the history of what might be called "race formation" and a corresponding history of the kinds of racisms that have accompanied each change. Here I will look at the successive transformation of the ways that race has been conceptualized in Western cultures and the different kinds of domination and exclusion that have accompanied those transformations. The second issue will be "racialization." Here I will address the issue of how individuals become defined by others, as well as how they come to define themselves as belonging to specific racial categories. I will consider the implications that this kind of identity has for the social practices of racism as well as for the resistance to racism. Finally, I will consider some of the forms that racism has taken in Western society.

THE CONCEPT OF "RACE"

Many scientists today reject the concept of biological "race" as not being useful to either biological or social analyses. At the end of the Second World War in 1945, UNESCO (United Nations Educational, Scientific, and Cultural Organization), stunned by the use of the concept of "race" in Nazi Germany, commissioned biologists and sociologists to give an exact meaning to the word "race." After much research and debate, the biologists concluded that as a species *Homo sapiens* had one single origin and that all the so-called "races" were statistically distinguishable as groups only. While it is possible, they found, to classify human beings in terms of the predominance of certain kinds of physical

405

characteristics—nasal index, skin colour, hair type—even this kind of classification had to be made with the recognition that boundaries between categories could never be clearly defined.

But, they continued, under no circumstances were such physical differences correlated with behavioural or psychological ones. The idea that "race" could be used to justify unequal treatment of different peoples was rejected outright as irrelevant to any explanation of social, economic, emotional, behavioural, or political differences among human beings. Explanations for why such differences were regarded as the result of race, they concluded, should be left to sociologists to determine.

UNESCO notwithstanding, one of the more pervasive taken-for-granted assumptions of North Americans is that humanity can be divided into different "races." Supporting this belief is the fact that North Americans are frequently faced with the need to resolve perceived threats to the stability of their societies that appear to have "race" as the point of contention. The seriousness and pervasiveness of what are seen to be "racial" differences help to reinforce the belief shared by many North Americans that "race" is both self-evident and significant.

From this point of view, it matters little if race has any real meaning as a biological category. It is a fact of life in Western societies that physical diversity is a means of categorizing and separating people into groups that are then subjected to different kinds of social and economic treatment.

Without doubt, then, race continues to be an obvious and real concept employed in the day-to-day lives of most North Americans. But how the "racial" differences that appear to be so significant have been thought about and the treatment that has been accorded persons of different "racial" backgrounds have not remained constant. "Race," writes American social scientist David Theo Goldberg, "is one of the central conceptual inventions of modernity" and the meaning and significance of the concept has been transformed "theoretically and materially as modernity is renewed, refined, and redefined" (Goldberg 1993, 3).

BIOLOGY, RACE, AND CULTURE

Consider this simple exercise. Try to decide, by looking at a crowd of people, which individuals in that crowd belong to which "race" (use the standard categories developed by social scientists of the nineteenth century: Negroid, Caucasian, and Mongolian, or black, white, and yellow. Use only physical characteristics—skin colour, hair type, nose and skull shape—as marks of identification.

It should become apparent that the taken-for-granted and culturally acceptable categories of white, black, and yellow can never be made up of people with exactly the same combinations of physical characteristics. The colour variation in people's skin tones alone is enormous, let alone nose shape, hair type, and colour. Deciding who belongs in which category on the basis of physical attributes is a purely arbitrary procedure. (Are green-eyed, straight-haired redheads, with very fair skin and long noses, a different race than green-eyed, curly-haired redheads with very fair skin and short noses? What about olive-skinned, hazel-eyed, curly-haired brunettes with upturned noses?) Something else happens when we categorize people on the basis of physiological characteristics. What we are really doing is using physical attributes—pigmentation, hair colour, nose shape, and the like—as reference points for a whole range of other encultured characteristics, including mode of dress, hairstyle, speech, music preferences, food preferences, religious practices, and family type. In short, we are relying on obvious biological variations to define cultural distinctions.

Consider two other examples, one drawn from the experiences of American historian David Roediger comparing his experiences when he lived in Ghana with those when he lived in the London borough of Brent. The excerpt is a superb example of the extent to which race is socially constructed rather than biologically determined. Writing first about his experiences living in the Ashanti region of Ghana, Roediger (1994) recounts how, whenever he and his companion went out walking, they were

> greeted on the streets by children who chanted, *Oburoni koko maakye.* English-speaking Ashantis often translate this as "Red white man, good morning"….However, *oburoni* derives from *Aburokyere,* the Akan word for "from across the waters," and is thus not equivalent to Euro-American usages of *white.* The many Chinese, Koreans and Japanese now in Ghana are called *oburoni.* But in discussing translation, Ashantis will point out that this is not just because they are "from across the sea" but because they are "white"— that is, they are perceived as looking and acting like Europeans and Americans….

> Other transatlantic experiences demonstrate the ways the social construction of race enters politics. In 1984, when we lived in the London borough of Brent, immigrants and descendants of immigrants of many nationalities often called themselves "Blacks" because that "racial" category came close to becoming what A. Sivanandan's work has characterized as a "political colour" of the oppressed. Asian Indians, Pakistanis, Malaysians, Turks, Chinese, Bangladeshis, Arabs and even Cypriots and some Irish so identified themselves (4).

A SHORT HISTORY OF THE USES OF THE TERM "RACE"

The actual origins of the word "race" are disputed, with some claiming Arabic, others Latin, and still others German as the source of the word. The first recorded use of the term in the English language, however, has been traced to a poem, *The Dance of the Sevin Deidly Synnis,* written by William Dunbar, a Scot, in 1508 (Banton 1987, 1). Aside from its use in Dunbar's poem, the term race was rarely applied to humans during the rest of the sixteenth century. "Race" appeared in the English language as a technical term, referring to human groups, only in the seventeenth century. Shakespeare, for example, uses the term to mean the inherited disposition or temperament of an individual (Smedely

1993, 37). From the sixteenth to the eighteenth centuries, "race" developed as a classifying term meaning "people," "nation," "stock." It was not until the eighteenth century that it came to be used to identify groups perceived as strange to the European eye, different from what they were used to, in short, as the "other." The term came increasingly to be identified with behavioural propensities and physical characteristics that were considered inherited, permanent, and unalterable except through calculated breeding.

THE EIGHTEENTH CENTURY

Most eighteenth-century authors who wrote on the subject of human differences drew on the Great Chain of Being thesis. We have already considered some of the broad parameters of this hierarchy; with God at the apex of the Great Chain and human beings ranked just below angels (see Chapter 5). Despite the fact that eighteenth-century men of science claimed to use empirical evidence in their deliberations, the Great Chain of Being thesis had no basis in empirical evidence, yet it was accepted without question (Lovejoy, 1936, 227).

I have pointed out that biologist Carolus Linnaeus believed that in the Great Chain of Being an intermediary classification would be found between apes and humans. He classified *Homo sapiens* into four varieties: *Americanus, Asiatius, Europaeus,* and *Aser.* Europeans were described as "light, lively and inventive"; American Indians as "choleric and perservering"; Asiatics as "yellow, melancholic, inflexible"; and Africans as "phlegmatic, indulgent, crafty, lazy, and negligent (Count 1950, 357).

RACE AND BIOLOGY IN THE NINETEENTH CENTURY

Not until the nineteenth century did the term "race" come to signify groups that could be distinguished biologically from one another (Banton and Harwood 1975, 13). In 1800 French zoologist Baron Georges von Cuvier wrote a memorandum advising a French expedition to the Pacific that research should be carried out "relative to the anatomical difference between the diverse races of man" (Stocking 1968, 13). Cuvier believed that the species *Homo sapiens* could be divided into three subspecies: Caucasian, Mongolian, and Ethiopian. Each subspecies could be further divided on geographical, linguistic, and physical bases. While all humans constitute one species in that they are inter-fertile, nonetheless, Cuvier wrote in *Le règne animal* (1817), we can note certain hereditary similarities "which constitute what are termed races."

Michael Banton has pointed out two features of Cuvier's conception of human "race" that have become part of Westerners' taken-for-granted world view. First, Cuvier represented "races" as being arranged in a hierarchy, with whites at the top and blacks at the bottom. He further contended that cultural differences and differences in mental capacities were the result of physical differences between the races. Caucasians, he asserted, had "gained domination over the world and made the most rapid progress in the sciences." The Chinese were less advanced, with skulls shaped more like those of animals. Finally the Negroes were "sunken in slavery and the pleasures of the senses." Yet at the same time, Cuvier maintained that Negroes were "rational and sensitive creatures" and that "slavery was degrading for both slave and master and must be abolished" (Coleman 1964, 166).

During the nineteenth century, more and more scholars drew on Cuvier to discuss differences between "races," while skirting the question of whether or not the "races" they proposed were actually different species (Banton 1987, 32). But Charles Hamilton Smith took that step and extended Cuvier's arguments with the publication of *The Natural History of the Human Species* in 1848. In his book, Smith argues that humans are one genus, with three different species: the "woolly-haired" or "Negro," the "beardless" or "Mongolian," and the "bearded" or "Caucasian." He was eloquent on the extraordinary virtues of the Caucasian, who was able, he wrote,

> to endure the greatest vicissitudes of temperature in all climates; to emigrate, colonize, and multiply in them, with the sole exception of the positive extremes...he alone of the races of mankind has produced examples of free and popular institutions...he has ascended to the skies, descended into the deep, and mastered the powers of lightning....He has instituted all the great religious systems in the world, and to his stock he has been vouchsafed the glory and the conditions of revelation (Smith 1848, 371–72).

"Negroes," on the other hand, held a much lower place in Smith's version of the human hierarchy because of their (supposedly) smaller brain volume. Indeed, the human brain, Smith argued, "successively assumes the form of the Negroes, the Malays, the Americans, and the Mongolians, before it attains the Caucasians" (125–27). The notion of brain volume differing by "race" persisted in the popular press even as late as 1964. No less an authority than the *Encyclopedia Britannica* listed "a small brain in relation to their size" as well as "woolly hair" as characteristics of black people (Gould 1981, 111). It wasn't until 1970 that South African anthropologist P.V. Tobias wrote an article exposing as myth the idea that group differences in brain size had any relation to intelligence. Tobias also showed that group differences in brain size had never been demonstrated, despite concerted efforts on the part of many researchers (Tobias 1970).

Another nineteenth-century writer, the French Count Joseph Arthur de Gobineau, published a four-volume work, *Essay on the Inequality of Human Races* (1853–55), in which he divided humanity into three "races"—white, yellow, and black. Gobineau was especially concerned with the decline of the "high civilizations" of Europe and argued that "race" mixing was "leading to the inevitable deterioration of humanity." Adolph Hitler later used Gobineau's claims to support the notion of the superiority of the "Ayran race" (Gould 1981, 29–30).

Swiss naturalist Louis Agassiz, an ichthyologist specializing in fish fossils, was struck by what he considered the ugliness of Negro waiters, whom he met on a trip to the United States, and began a lecture tour arguing that Negro and white "races" were morphologically and physiologically so distinct that they constituted separate species. Agassiz eventually gained a post at Harvard University, where he and his students promoted the idea of the inequality of human "races." (Agassiz also became one of the most prominent leaders of the opposition to evolutionism) (Smedely 1993, 241).

Even Charles Darwin, a passionate supporter of the abolition of slavery, accepted the notion that some "races" were closer in evolutionary terms to apes than were Caucasians.

Darwin looked forward to a future time when the distance between humans and their nearest ape ancestors might be widened by the extinction of such intermediaries as chimpanzees and Hottentots. In his own words,

> The break will then be rendered wider, for it will intervene between man in a more civilized state, as we may hope, than the Caucasian, and some ape as low as the baboon, instead of at present between the Negro or Australian and the gorilla (1871, 201).

As a result of many efforts by nineteenth-century scientists to classify humanity into different types, the concept of "race" became legitimized in academia. Moreover, the belief that different racial groups were related to each other through a logic of the natural hierarchy of groups was strongly promoted, as was the belief that the behaviour of individual human beings was determined by their particular place in that hierarchy (Outlaw 1990, 63). The most popular of the positions taken by the "scientific racists" of the nineteenth century was that human races were "separate biological species, the descendants of different Adams." One significant conclusion followed: As other forms of life, those races different from Caucasians need not be considered participants in the "equality of man." Proponents of this position were called "polygenists," supporters of the idea that different races of humans came from different stock, as opposed to monogenists, who opined that all human races descended from the same stock, but that some had degenerated, while others had progressed (Gould 1981, 39).

During the nineteenth century, then, *Homo sapiens* became a species divided into biologically different racial groups characterized by different capacities and temperaments. From the perspective of race scientists, "Human affairs could be understood only if individuals were seen as representatives of races first for it was there that the driving forces of human history resided" (Banton and Harwood 1975, 30). Following empiricist principles, these race scientists sought to measure human differences in a wide variety of ways. And they used those measurements to "prove" the supremacy of one "race" over all others and to support the principles of racial separation.

Anders Retzius, for example, invented the cephalic index, which differentiated people with roundheads from those with longheads. Longheaded populations were interpreted as being more advanced than roundheaded ones. Retzius's measure was widely used until it was discovered that the cephalic indices of many so-called "savages," including some black Africans, were similar to the indices of Scandinavians (Smedely 1993, 259). (The cephalic index was used by French anthropologist Paul Broca, who advocated racial determinism. But Broca's own cephalic index, it turned out, made him a roundhead.) (Gould 1981, 99).

Others, such as Samuel Morton, measured the differences between "races" on the basis of cranial capacity. He measured these differences by filling skulls with mustard seeds or lead shot. On the basis of his "research," he concluded that there were five different "races"—Caucasian, Mongolian, Malay, American, and Ethiopian. Each of these, he contended, could be further subdivided into families (Gould 1981, 54–55). J.C. Nott and G.R. Gliddon (1854) proposed that there was a correlation between increasing cranial capacity and level of innate intelligence.

By the beginning of the twentieth century, the rediscovery of Mendel's experiments on heredity and a growing understanding of the role of genes and chromosomes led scientists to new ways of conceptualizing "race." But this new interest in and understanding of heredity inspired the growth of the eugenics movement, which was influential during the first three decades of the century. The word **eugenics** was first coined by Francis Galton, a cousin of Charles Darwin, in 1883. He defined it as the "science of improving the stock" (1883).

The basic objective of eugenicists was to encourage the "breeding" of supposedly genetically superior persons while discouraging or even prohibiting inferior ones from having children. In short, the objective of the eugenics movement was to improve the race by selective breeding. Eugenicists were especially interested in seeing individuals with "defective genes" sterilized. They imagined that all sorts of traits were inheritable, including criminality, feeblemindedness, poverty, and various mental diseases.

Race and IQ

Along with a growing interest in genetics and selective breeding for intelligence, another measurement that fascinated scientists of the nineteenth century was the **Intelligence Quotient** or **IQ**. The foundations of psychometrics were laid by Galton. In the 1880s, he established a laboratory to study differences among individuals. For a small fee, visitors to his lab could be tested on a number of dimensions—visual and auditory capabilities, reaction times, colour discrimination, and other sensory abilities. Individual performance on these tests was then compared to the performance of the "average" person. Differences between an individual's performance and that of the average person were thought to relate to intelligence level.

In *Hereditary Genius* (1869), Galton noted that "it is in the most unqualified manner that I object to pretensions of natural equality." He wished to establish a meritocracy, where the most able would rise to the top and the less able would remain at the bottom. It was his concern to improve the human species by selectively breeding members of the superior "race" and sterilizing inferior ones. The use of intelligence tests, especially tests that showed whites to be of superior intelligence to blacks, was a "scientific" measure that could be easily used to justify the racial discrimination Galton proposed as a necessary safeguard for the health of the superior "race."

Intelligence testing was brought to the United States in 1908 by Henry Goddard. As director of research at the Training School for the Feebleminded in Vineland, New Jersey, Goddard was an enthusiastic supporter of eugenics. By the 1920s, intelligence testing was being used in the United States as a means of separating the "feeble-minded" from the "robust." In the process, entire "races" were ranked on a hierarchical scale of IQs. But by the late 1960s, most progressive social scientists agreed with American psychologist I.I. Gottesman's sceptical assessment of IQ tests. It is obvious, Gottesman wrote, that IQ tests "do not directly measure innate gene-determined intellectual capacity but do measure

411

current intellectual performance as defined by a particular culture or at least by its psychologists" (1968, 25).

One prominent social scientist who did not agree with Gottesman was Arthur A. Jensen, professor of psychology at Harvard University. It was Jensen's opinion that blacks are genetically inferior to whites in IQ. He based his argument on two observations. Studies with identical twins (produced by the splitting of a single fertilized egg cell), he claimed, show that the correlations between their IQs are higher than the correlations between the IQs of fraternal twins (produced when two eggs are fertilized by two different sperm in the same time frame). As well, the IQs of siblings are more highly correlated than are the IQs of randomly selected children. He further claimed that if all other factors are held constant, racial differences in IQ still remain (1969, 1–123).

Jensen attempted to prove that black intelligence was different from, and inferior to, white intelligence by arguing that there are two different kinds of learning abilities: Level I, or associative abilities, which blacks are good at, and Level II, or conceptual abilities, where whites excel. Level II abilities are, in Jensen's opinion, higher-order abilities because an individual must be proficient in Level I abilities to perform well at Level II. What Jensen was arguing then was not that blacks are intrinsically of inferior intelligence, but that they are at a genetically less advanced stage of intellectual development than are whites.

There are two kinds of criticisms that have been levelled at Jensen's hereditarian theory of IQ. The first is quite simply put. IQ tests measure the ability of individuals to manipulate abstract symbols and concepts. The notion that this ability is the measure of intelligence is a culturally biased one. Stephen Jay Gould takes exception to hederitarian arguments for other reasons. While he has "no doubt" that intelligence is "to some degree heritable....the degree has clearly been exaggerated by the most avid hereditarians..." (Gould 1981, 155). In the first place, hereditarians equate "heritable" with "inevitable." To a biologist, however, "heritability refers to the passage of traits or tendencies along family lines as a result of genetic transmission" (156). This says little about the kinds of environmental modification that these traits might be subject to. What gets measured as low IQ on one test may be the result of the cultural biases of the test, and "low IQ might be subject to extensive improvement through proper education" (156).

Moreover, there is confusion, Gould claims, over within- and between-group heredity. The common fallacy has been that if IQ tests can explain a certain percentage of variation among individuals within a group (white Americans for example), they can also be used to explain a similar percentage of difference between groups (whites and blacks). But the two are separate phenomena.

A hypothetical and noncontroversial example will suffice. Human height has a higher heritability than any value ever proposed for IQ. Take two separate groups of males. The first, with an average height of 5 feet 10 inches, live in a prosperous American town. The second, with an average height of 5 feet 6 inches, are starving in a Third World village. Heritability is approximately 95 percent in each place—meaning only that relatively tall fathers tend to have tall sons and relatively short fathers short sons. This high within-group heritability argues neither for nor against the possibility that better nutrition in the next generation might raise the average height of Third World villagers above that of prosperous Americans. Likewise, IQ could be highly heritable within groups, and the average difference between whites and blacks in America still records only the environmental disadvantages of blacks (156–65).

Race and twentieth-century scholarship

In the mid- to late twentieth century, much has happened in North America to help introduce attitudes toward race that are significantly different from those expressed by nineteenth-century scientific racists. It is not simply the case that newer attitudes have replaced older ones, for many North Americans still believe in the natural superiority of one race over another and support treating different "races" unequally.

At the same time, however, many social events have occurred in North America this century that call older attitudes and practices into question. The presence of new immigrants, the fact that many blacks and Native peoples served in both American and Canadian armies during the First and, more important, Second World War, the increasing involvement of Natives, blacks, and new immigrants in national economies all have been significant. But the racial component of Nazism and the atrocities committed during the Second World War in the name of racial purity shocked many North Americans into rethinking their beliefs, values, and attitudes. After the war, many began to support antiracist sentiments (Smedely 1993, 273).

When the Nazis—the National Socialist Party—led by Adolph Hitler came to power in Germany in 1932, they were able to adopt a perspective on race that had been developing over several decades in Europe and North America. That perspective distinguished between "superior" and "inferior" races, and the Nazis took that distinction to extremes with the belief that Germans constituted a "master race" destined to rule the world. At the same time "inferior" races, especially Jews, were cast as destroyers of civilization who had to be exterminated. But once one group of Europeans started characterizing another as racially inferior and treating them the same way as they had previously treated non-Europeans, reactions against such ideas about "race" and the genocidal practices they entailed soon followed (Smedely 1993, 279).

Belongings left behind by inmates at the concentration camp Auschwitz-Birkenau.

413

BOAS'S CHALLENGE TO ANTHROPOMETRY

In the early decades of the twentieth century, American anthropologist Franz Boas began questioning nineteenth-century ideas about "race." One of the many studies that Boas undertook was one of American schoolchildren in order to establish mental and physical growth patterns and to determine the influences of heredity and environment on growth. **Anthropometry** is the study of the measurements of the human body.

Boas measured the bodies of children from all sorts of backgrounds, including Italian and Jewish immigrants, Native Americans, and mulattoes. He found that the body measurements of immigrant children varied significantly from those of their parents; for example, the cephalic index could change from roundheads to longheads in one generation. His findings shocked the scientific community because they challenged the notion of the permanence of physical racial characteristics and demonstrated the plasticity of the human skeleton. Boas's findings pointed to nutrition and climate as major determinants of many physical traits (1940).

Boas and later his students, including Ruth Benedict, Margaret Mead, and Melville Herskovits, began research and writing that was overtly hostile to all forms of racism. He and his followers tried to limit the concept of race to purely biophysical characteristics. In *The Mind of Primitive Man* (1911) Boas developed several themes that today have been incorporated into much of anthropological thinking. First, he argued that hereditary racial purity does not exist; races are never stable, but rather are susceptible to change because of environmental factors, mutation, and selection. The average physiological differences between races are small, he asserted, compared to the differences among those classified as members of the same race. Second, all races can participate in, or even create, any culture. Thus there is no relationship between physical heredity and any given language or culture. Finally, Boas argued that some groups "are not primitive by reason of hereditary inferiority but because the circumstances of their life were more static than those of civilized men, the differences being products of their variant history and traditional equipment" (Spier 1959, 147).

BUT RACE STILL MATTERS

By the mid-twentieth century, the basis for classifying human races had changed from the morphological and topological variables (skin and hair colour, cephalic index), to genetics (differences expressed in terms of the proportions of genetic expressions of given traits) (Smedely 1993, 285). With a new interest in genetics came an interest in breeding populations. For example, in *Physical Anthropology*, a textbook published in 1973, G.W. Lasker defines race as "a breeding population whose members share a higher degree of common inheritance than they share with other members of the species" (384).

The question that has been raised by many biologists and physical anthropologists is what constitutes a "breeding population." Do people of a small and relatively endogamous town in Saskatchewan and another in British Columbia constitute separate breeding populations and therefore separate races? If races are breeding populations, are all breeding populations races? What do we do with information from researchers such as

Nel and Roychoudhury (1974) who have found that only minor variations in known genetic traits actually exist between the major traditional racial groupings? As such questions become increasingly difficult to answer, it becomes clearer that "race" has little or no value in a sociological analysis. While "race" as a biological concept has been discredited, the social consequences of being classified as belonging to one or another "race" are very real.

American historian David Roediger recounts a joke that has made its way among several African-American scholars: "I have noticed that my research demonstrating that race is merely a social and ideological construction helps little in getting taxis to pick me up late at night" (1994, 1). Roediger points out that while the joke is not intended as a rejection of the idea that "race" is socially constructed, it does focus on the point that "race may be more easily demystified on paper than disarmed in everyday life" (ibid.). "Race" (as a biological category) may be insubstantial, it may be discredited as a viable concept among most scholars in North America, but race as a social category is nonetheless still very potent indeed.

Racism

Racism, writes Tzvetan Todorov, "is a matter of *behaviour*, usually a manifestation of hatred or contempt for individuals who have well-defined physical characteristics different from our own" (1993, 90). Racism is a disposition involving beliefs and attitudes. It puts as much emphasis on the positive attributes of one's own race as on the perceived negative attributes of the race of the other. According to UNESCO,

> Racism falsely claims that there is a scientific basis for arranging groups hierarchically in terms of psychological and cultural characteristics that are immutable and innate. In this way it seeks to make existing differences appear inviolable as a means of permanently maintaining current relations between groups (1975).

In spite of much opposition, there are a few academics who find racist theories attractive. In fact, since the 1980s, a revival of interest in hierarchical theories of race has occurred, supported by the research of a few scholars in Canada and the United States. Philippe Rushton, professor of psychology at the University of Western Ontario, for example, has argued that whites and Asians are in general more family oriented and more intelligent than blacks (1988). Robert Gordon, professor of sociology at Johns Hopkins University, has written that the high crime rate among American blacks is strongly correlated with their low intelligence level compared to that of other races (1980, 1987). And anthropologist Roger Pearson published *Race, Intelligence and Bias in Academe* (1991) as a defence of scientific racism (Kühl 1994). These authors have been harshly criticized for their poor research and unsupportable conclusions. Nonetheless, they continue to find support among those whose own prejudices make them susceptible to the appeal of racist arguments.

RACISM AS A SOCIAL CONSTRUCT

The term "racism" is of even more recent origin than the term "race." The *Oxford English Dictionary* of 1910 shows no entry for the word, although it does define race and racial. The *OED* supplement of 1982 records the first appearance of the term "racism" in the English language to have been in the 1930s. Although Friedrich Hertz referred to "race hatred" in a book published in 1928 (1–19), the term racism was first used in a book by Magnus Hirschfeld published in German in 1933–34 and in English in 1938.

But while the term racism is a very recent one, the practice of emphasizing one's own positive attributes compared to the negative attributes of others has had a long history in Western societies. What follows are a series of quotations, beginning with some writing commissioned by Henry II of England, king from 1154 to 1189. The descriptions are of a people that he was considering invading.

> This people, then, is truly barbarous, being not only barbarous in their dress, but suffering their hair and beards to grow enormously in an uncouth manner, just like the modern fashion recently introduced; indeed all their habits are barbarisms (cited in Curtus 1968, 124).

Nineteenth-century descriptions by English observers of the same peoples are even less flattering:

> They are more like tribes of squalid apes than human beings...as unstable as water...an impatience of control, a deliberate preference for disorder, a determination in each individual man to go his own way, whether it was a good way or a bad, and a reckless hatred of industry (ibid., 84).

Segregated drinking fountains were a feature of public life in the American South until the 1960s.

Other nineteenth-century descriptions by English writers of the same people insist that evidence of their "lowly descent" can be traced "in their blighted, stunted forms—in their brassy, cunning, brutalized features." The same writer insists that these people "are the missing link between the gorilla and the Negro" (Lebow 1976, 40).

The people so reviled by the British, over so many centuries, were the Irish. When the twelfth-century Welsh monk Giraldus Cambrensis was sent to Ireland by Henry II, he reported back to his king that the Irish were "eaters of human flesh, murderers and thieves who revelled in sodomy and incest" (ibid., 75). By the seventeenth century, the idea of a degenerate Irish race provided the justification the British felt they needed to dominate Ireland. Unlike the Anglo-Saxon English, the Irish were held to be members of a degenerate but highly prolific Celtic race. This belief was even supported by Charles Darwin who wrote in *The Descent of Man* (1871):

> Given a land originally peopled by a thousand Saxons and a thousand Celts—and in a dozen generations five-sixths of the population would be Celts, but five-sixths of the property, of the power, of the intellect, would belong to the one-sixth of Saxons that remain. In the eternal "struggle for existence," it would be the inferior and *less* favoured race that had prevailed and prevailed by virtue not of its good qualities but of its faults (141).

These concepts of degeneration followed the Irish when they emigrated to America. In 1910 a full-scale movement was begun in the United States to block further immigration, fuelled by the belief that any more Irish in the country would dilute the superior Anglo-Saxon stock. Today few people would think of claiming that the Irish are a separate race from the British. But the example clearly indicates how beliefs about what constitute race have changed, even within this century. It also indicates that while the original objective of the English in promoting the notion of a separate race of Celts or Irish was political, the consequences have been very real. Finally, the example underlines the disparities between official political ideas about rights, freedom, and equality and the reality of the experiences of many peoples identified as racially inferior who emigrated to America and to Canada (Shanklin 1994, 7).

Because racism is frequently related to prejudice and exploitation, the two are often conflated. "Racism," says Thomas Powell, "serves to *justify* aggressive behaviour such as discrimination and other forms of abuse. Discrimination, exploitation, segregation and other forms of discriminatory and abusive behaviours are *expressions* of racism. Racism itself is an underlying assumption that others are inherently inferior or disagreeably different in their fundamental behavioral, mental or moral characteristics or capacities" (1992, 1).

Racism is not, of course, just a European or a North American phenomenon. "We/they" or "them/us" thinking has been practised by people of the most diverse cultural backgrounds, and the distinctions made are usually on the basis of assumed deficiencies in others. Many Native North American groups, for example, make distinctions between themselves—usually identified as human beings—and others, defined as less than human. But racism in North America is particularly conspicuous because cultural values and beliefs that would seem to militate against racism have been used, instead, to support it.

Many American cultural heroes, participants in the founding of a country devoted to "life, liberty, and the pursuit of happiness" for everyone, were racists. In his *Observations Concerning the Increase of Mankind*, published in 1751, Benjamin Franklin expressed the hope that America would become a place exclusively for whites and reds, undarkened by "all blacks and tawneys." "Why increase the Sons of Africa," he wrote, "by planting them in America, where we have so fair an opportunity, by excluding all blacks and tawneys, of increasing the lovely white and red?" (cited in Gould 1981, 32).

Other American heroes like Thomas Jefferson wrote in favour of the biological inferiority of blacks. "I advance it, therefore, as a suspicion only, that the blacks, whether originally a distinct race, or made distinct by time and circumstance, are inferior to the whites in the endowment both of body and mind" (cited in Gossett 1965, 44). Nor is there much question about the beliefs of Abraham Lincoln:

> I am not, nor ever have been, in favour of bringing about in any way the social and political equality of the white and black races; I am not, nor ever have been, in favour of making voters or jurors of Negroes, nor qualifying them to hold office....I will say in addition to this that there is a physical difference between the white and black races which I believe will ever forbid the two races living together on terms of social and political equality. And in as much as they cannot so live, while they do remain together, there must be the position of superior and inferior, and I as much as any other man am in favour of having the superior position assigned to the white race (1894, 369–70, 457–58).

418

Racism and canadian society

Although popular myth holds otherwise, Canadian society and politics have been replete with racism. In Chapter 1, I referred to the attitudes and practices of Canadians, including Prime Minister Sir John A. MacDonald, toward Chinese immigration at the time of Confederation. Although Canada is a young country, there have been many instances where racism has played a central role in official governmental policy. And while federal and provincial governments today no longer promote official racist policies, racism continues as part of the general cultural heritage and experiences of many people.

From Confederation in 1867 to the end of the Second World War in 1945, the policies of both federal and provincial governments emphasized the perceived need to reject "unassimilable" immigrants. The 1910 Immigration Act specified race as grounds for admission or rejection of immigrants. Black children in Ontario and Nova Scotia were segregated well into the twentieth century. Chinese immigrants faced a head tax of $500 in 1904 and were almost completely excluded from between 1923 and 1947 with the passage of the Chinese Immigration Act. Because of restrictive labour laws and pervasive racism, often the only work available for Chinese was their own small, family-run businesses—restaurants, laundries, hothouses. Women worked alongside men and were also responsible for housework, child rearing, and holding small communities together (Lee 1993, 3–37). One woman, born in British Columbia in 1908, speaks about her mother: "It was always a steady routine of work, work, work for my mother. She'd have a child in her arms or on her back, because there were eight of us. She had to help with the laundry, farmwork, to cook and maintain us" (Guo 1992).

The Chinese were disenfranchised in British Columbia in 1872, the Japanese in 1895, and East Indians in 1907. During the First World War, racial minorities were deemed inferior and barred from military service. During the Second World War, the Japanese were deprived of their property and physically interned in detention camps (Elliott and Fleras 1992, 45). A small token redress agreement was reached as late as 1994.

ANTI-SEMITISM IN CANADA

Racist or anti-Semitic views toward Jews have a long history in Canada. Anti-Semitism includes "acts of physical violence against Jews, desecration of Jewish cemeteries, and mass anti-Jewish rallies." But it also includes "negative attitudes and everyday discriminatory acts that are directed against Jews and harm them" (Brym and Lenton 1992, 179). Anti-Semitism has taken a number of different forms, including violence and outright prejudice, as well as less overt forms of discrimination. Intolerance of Jews was openly accepted in Canadian society prior to the First World War. One of this country's very few race riots occurred at a baseball game at Toronto's Christie Pits in 1933, and involved Jews and non-Jews.

In response to the question "How should anti-Semitism be defined?" Canadian sociologists Robert Brym and Rhonda Lenton give this answer:

> There is an old Jewish joke about an anti-Semite who was asked to define anti-Semitism. "Anti-Semitism," he replied, "is hating the Jews more than you absolutely have to" (1992, 179).

Historically, Jews were routinely prevented from working in banks, insurance companies, and department stores, and universities imposed quotas on the number of Jewish students allowed to enrol (Abella 1989). In 1939 the Canadian government refused to grant political asylum to a boatload of 900 German-Jewish refugees who had already been rejected by the United States and several Latin American countries. The refugees were forced to return to Germany where many were put to death in concentration camps (Abella and Troper 1982).

Today, blatant anti-Semitism is not tolerated in Canada, but for some, racist attitudes remain deeply entrenched. Under the Canadian Charter of Rights and Freedoms, as well as under various human rights codes, discrimination that denies access to housing, employment, education, and club membership is illegal (Elliott and Fleras 1992, 51). But Holocaust denial theories, attempts to reject the existence of Nazi concentration camps where millions of Jewish people were incarcerated and gassed, continue to circulate. These and other "polite" forms of racism are as devastating as the older, direct varieties. "Polite racism," as defined by Elliott and Fleras, is

> a deliberate attempt to disguise racist attitudes through behaviour that outwardly is non-prejudicial or discriminatory in appearance. This politeness is especially evident when ethnic minorities are ignored or turned down for jobs, promotions, or accommodation on

a regular basis....Canadian racism is often depicted as polite and subdued. Racism in Canada is rarely practised by raving lunatics who engage in beatings, lynching, or graffiti. Rather, racism among Canadians is unobtrusive, often implicit and embedded in everyday language, thought and behaviour. Derogatory references to ethnic minorities continue to be expressed, but these are likely to be circulated only among friends, often as jokes, or outside public discourse. This subtlety makes it difficult to confront, let along eradicate, expressions of racism (59–60).

In a study published in 1991, Robert Brym and Rhonda Lenton present a synopsis of the distribution of anti-Semitic attitudes by Canadian province based on the results of the 1984 Canadian National Election Study, which was administered to a random sample of 3377 Canadians. Among other questions, respondents were asked to indicate on a scale of 0 to 100 their feelings toward Jews, with 0 representing the most negative feelings, and 100 the most positive feelings. Results of the survey showed that overall "86% of Canadians held positive or neutral attitudes towards Jews; only 14% held negative attitudes" (412). In some provinces, however, the percentage of people who disliked Jews was well above the national average, while in others it was below. The three provinces with the highest levels of expressed anti-Semitism were Newfoundland, with 29 percent expressing negative attitudes, New Brunswick with 23 percent, and Quebec with 21 percent. The province with the lowest percentage of people with negative attitudes toward Jews was Alberta with only 7 percent.

Brym and Lenton found that religion played an important role in influencing anti-Semitic feelings. In Canada as a whole, 9 percent of those identifying themselves as Protestant, but 19 percent of those identifying themselves as Catholic, expressed negative attitudes toward Jews. A full 44 percent of all Newfoundlanders in the survey who identified themselves as Catholic expressed negative attitudes toward Jews, while 24 percent of Catholics in Prince Edward Island and 22 percent in Quebec expressed negative attitudes. Language spoken at home was another factor. In Quebec, 24 percent of those who identified themselves as speaking only French at home held anti-Semitic attitudes, while 0 percent of those who reported speaking only English at home held those attitudes (417). Brym and Lenton conclude that low levels of anti-Semitism in Canada are associated with populations that are "relatively affluent, highly educated, non-Catholic, and non-French" (412). That is the case in Alberta, and to a lesser extent in Ontario (10 percent expressed anti-Semitic attitudes) and British Columbia (11 percent expressed anti-Semitic attitudes).

FIRST NATIONS (NATIVE PEOPLES)

The terms First Nations and Native peoples refer to the more than 55 different peoples who established themselves in North America thousands of years prior to the arrival of Europeans. In Canada, Native peoples have been systematically discriminated against at least since the seventeenth century. European countries that colonized New France, New England, New Sweden, and New Holland operated under the doctrine of the right of "first discovery." By this doctrine, Christian nations were mandated to subjugate non-Christian "primitives" and given the right to appropriate any "unoccupied" lands. By the

Royal Proclamation of 1763, the British Crown "unilaterally asserted its sovereignty over self-governing indigenous nations in North America, and claimed proprietary title to lands on which Indians had lived and survived from time immemorial" (Boldt 1993, 3).

Since then, although Native peoples have interacted with Canadian society on economic, political, and social levels, they have remained marginalized and have not been assimilated into mainstream society. According to James Frideres, the "behaviour or characteristics of most Indians are stereotyped and systematically condemned by the dominant or majority group members of Canadian society" (1991).

Aboriginal Canadians are defined under the Constitution Act of 1982 as status Indians, Inuit, and Métis—a total population of over one-half million people (about 2 percent of Canada's population). If nonstatus Indians are added, there are nearly 2 million Aboriginal people living in Canada. About 70 percent of all status Indians live on 2272 reserves—lands set aside for Natives' use, but held in trust for them by the federal government. The size of the nonstatus First Nations population is diminishing because of a reinstatement clause added to the Indian Act in 1985.

Status or registered Indians are enrolled in the register of the Department of Indian Affairs and are subject to the Indian Act. About 33 000 Inuit who live in the newly created province of Nunavut in the Eastern Arctic and in Northern Quebec are also dealt with under provision of the federal Indian Act. Métis are the offspring of Native-white marriages and, as of the 1986 census, about 129 000 people identified themselves as such. Métis are not considered Native and are ignored by the Indian Act, but they are officially regarded as Aboriginal people, with subsequent rights to make claims on the Canadian state. For example, the Alberta government has recently recognized the Métis right to self-government, along with the right to some limited institutional autonomy (Elliott and Fleras 1992, 160).

Native-white contact became sustained in the early 1800s, and at that time a concerted attempt was made on the part of whites to "civilize" them. In a bid to allow white settlement and agricultural development, several treaties were signed, creating reservations for Natives and extinguishing Aboriginal land rights for those who signed. The policy of the Canadian government toward Native peoples from this point on was to integrate them into the rest of society. The expectation was that Natives, as a people, would soon become "extinct," and the Canadian government put itself in a temporary "caretaker role" to expedite that end.

Even as late as 1969, the federal government, under the leadership of Pierre Trudeau, developed a policy in a White Paper that declared its aim to be the total assimilation of Natives. The proposal met widespread resistance from Native peoples who strongly protested against what they believed to be the government's attempt at cultural genocide.

Many measures, including health, education, and economic opportunities, indicate that Native peoples have continually experienced systematic institutional racism. For example, figures from 1986 show that the mortality rate for Natives stood at 5.2 per 1000, twice the national rate. In the age group 4 to 19 years the mortality rate is four times the national average (Frideres 1991, 116). About 70 percent of Natives are without a high-school degree, compared to the national average of 45 percent. They are chronically underemployed, and their income levels are substantially lower than those of other Canadians.

421

Until recently, overt discrimination toward Native peoples was common in Canada, and many employers refused to hire them (ibid., 127). While open discrimination has decreased, the social position of Native Canadians has not increased substantially, and institutional discrimination continues to exist in jobs, housing, and education. No matter how

RACISM IN CANADA, RESULTS OF A GALLUP POLL

In the early 1980s, the Multicultural Directorate of the Government of Canada commissioned the Gallup organization to undertake a national poll on racial attitudes in Canada. The preliminary results of the poll were released at the Race Relations and the Law conference held in Vancouver in April 1982. The poll demonstrated that there was some reason for optimism to the extent that the majority or respondents did not display racially prejudicial attitudes. However, the poll did show that a significant minority of Canadians hold racist attitudes. More recent polls have tended to support these earlier findings.

	General Agreement %	General Disagreement %	Neither Agree nor Disagree %
1. Riots and violence increase when nonwhites are let into a country.	19	64	13
2. Nonwhite immigration has made Canada a culturally richer country.	67	21	8
3. Racial mixing violates the teaching of the Bible.	14	70	11
4. I would maintain a fairly open immigration policy with few limitations.	65	16	13
5. I would support organizations that worked towards preserving Canada for whites only.	31	50	13
6. I would limit nonwhite immigration and those who were let in would have to prove themselves before they were entitled to government-supported services.	58	23	14

TABLE 18-1

7. A culturally diverse country is a strong country.	56	19	19
8. I would limit immigration in general, but not base it on racial origin.	43	37	15
9. The people of this country are looking less and less Canadian.	12	74	9
10. I would support local organizations that worked toward multiculturalism and harmony among races.	34	43	19
11. I would cut off all nonwhite immigration to Canada.	12	71	10
12. We are all immigrants in one way or another.	49	28	18
13. I don't mind nonwhites but I'd rather see them back in their own country.	28	52	16

TABLE 18-1 (continued)

Source: Peter S. Li and B. Singh Bolaria. Contemporary Sociology: Critical Perspectives. Mississauga: Copp Clark Pitman, 1993.

the situation is assessed, Native peoples remain at the bottom of any socio-economic measure of Canadian society. Housing on most reserves is inadequate—fewer than 50 percent of Native homes have sewer or water connections, and houses are overcrowded. The unemployment rate is three times the national average. Up to 95 percent of those living on reserves subsist on welfare or unemployment benefits. Only about 20 percent of all Native students finish high school, and fewer make it to university. "As a group...most [Native people] live in conditions that evoke images of grinding Third World poverty" (ibid., 165).

Infant mortality rates are about 60 percent greater than the national average; rates of violent deaths and suicides are much higher than in the rest of the population—six times the national average for certain age-specific groups. Almost 70 percent of all status Indians have been incarcerated in a correctional institute by age 25, and Native peoples constitute 40 percent of all inmates in prairie prisons, although they make up only 12 percent of the prairie population. Together, these constraints and experiences have "robbed many Native Indians of any positive self-concept, and have led to self-fulfilling cycles of despair and decay" (ibid.). Indeed, Native Canadians are one of the most self-destructive populations in the world today.

Living conditions on a reserve in northern Manitoba. Poverty has become the norm among many Native communities.

Not unexpectedly, for many Canadians, Native peoples constitute a social problem, or at least are seen as having problems in desperate need of solution. The question that is frequently raised is "Who is responsible?" According to Elliott and Fleras (1992) there are three ways of answering this question. The first is that the problems Native people confront are Native problems for which they alone are largely responsible. The second is that the so-called "Native problem" is really a white problem. Whites sought to dominate, control, and exploit Natives and in the process created the terrible devastation that now exists. The third answer is that the problem is a combined Native-white one, originating in the clash between culturally different peoples.

Until recently the first approach has been the one taken by a succession of Canadian governments. Over the past 125 years, Canadian governments have remained strongly committed to a policy of assimilation and civilization. The prevalence of poverty has been considered central to Native problems, and only the elimination of poverty will alleviate the situation. To facilitate this, governments have encouraged Native people to move off the reserves, which they see as breeding grounds for violence, poverty, and apathy, and to get exposure to "modern" values, institutions, and culture.

But Native leaders vociferously reject their people being labelled as social problems and the easy solution of calling in "experts" to analyze the situation. Moreover, they reject the idea that Native cultures and values are an impediment to security and to a satisfying life. Native cultural values, they insist, must be retained because they provide valuable sources of identity as well as a basis for community renewal.

The second approach, that the plight of Native peoples in Canada is the fault of white people, assumes that Natives have been victimized by a system of colonization imposed on them by European conquest and settlement. From this point of view, Natives have been exploited by whites for land, resources, and labour power. As well, the Canadian government stands accused of consciously promoting the destruction of Native culture. The assimilationist pressures exerted on Native children within the education system are a case in point. Native cultures have been seen as "primitive" and irrelevant to modern societies. Natives have been treated as children, prohibited from deciding for themselves how they should handle their affairs. From this perspective, a massive restructuring of white society in general is needed in order to stop it from subverting Native attempts at self-regulation.

The third perspective identified (and favoured) by Elliott and Fleras is one that incorporates "a more dynamic approach to the Native Indian problem without ignoring the broader context, which involves aboriginal/government interaction" (1992, 173). From this viewpoint, neither whites nor Natives are entirely responsible for the plight of the Native people. Rather it is a problem of Native-white interaction, a problem of contested power between competing groups, exacerbated by the imposition of a capitalist system on a noncapitalist population.

While historically government policy toward Native peoples has been one of segregation, guardianship, and control, that policy was changed after the Second World War to one of "normalization": the government offering Native peoples equal rights and opportunities. Today Native peoples have fought to be considered "First Nations," an approach that recognizes their right to self-determination and control over their lives and future. Attempts to devolve power and define self-government have been convoluted, complex, and often elusive, but currently there is a process underway to redefine, once again, relations between Native peoples and the rest of Canadian society (Elliott and Fleras 1992, 174). Today Native peoples have taken the initiative in demanding a fundamental redistribution of power and resources in the form of the establishment of self-government within the framework of Canadian federalism. While this is perceived as a threat by many non-Natives, an important point to consider is that, in light of past history and contemporary realities, what other alternatives are there?

SOLUTIONS TO RACISM

The term racism is widely used in everyday, common-sense discussions as well as in academic ones. Descriptions of the effects of racism are common, as are calls to rid society of its influence. One approach often taken is that the persistence of racism results from

425

TABLE 18-2

REGISTERED INDIAN POPULATION BY REGION, 1989		
Region	**No.**	**%**
Atlantic	18,433	4.0
Quebec	45,742	9.8
Ontario	107,862	23.1
Manitoba	67,092	14.4
Saskatchewan	72,111	15.5
Alberta	57,590	12.3
BC	80,742	17.3
Yukon	5,973	1.3
NWT	10,792	2.3
Canada	466,337	100

Source: Department of Indian Affairs and Northern Development, Basic Departmental Data, 1990 *(Ottawa: Minister of Indian Affairs and Northern Development 1990), 8.*

lack of information or misunderstanding. A practical solution to ending the problem might be mounting a campaign to inform and educate otherwise misinformed and uneducated people. But as Thomas Powell (1992, 1) points out, like most common-sense, popular solutions, this one overlooks a great deal. To begin with, the education solution to racism treats racists as being deficient in some way—in character, morality, intellect, or in all three. This approach assumes that the misguided beliefs and attitudes held by racists are susceptible to reversal or revision on the basis of new and more reasonable information and evidence.

If this were in fact the case, the persistence of racism would be easy to understand. We could simply attribute it to lack of education, poor information, and self-interested rationalizations on the part of racists. But the persistence of racism is "difficult to grasp, and its explanation is hard to accept, because our most cherished conceptions of reality have made it seem justified, attractive and even necessary" (ibid., 5). Racism, Powell goes on to say,

has always been supported by American religious, social, economic and political thought, and even by our formal philosophy.... In short, racism rests firmly on American individualism, with its cherished values of will-power and individual responsibility for shaping one's own life (6).

Soldiers guard black students at Little Rock Central High School in the late 1950s. Was this a solution to racism?

We hold to our beliefs and associated attitudes with great tenacity, since to change them is deeply disturbing and means questioning the nature of who we are and how we define ourselves. We accept and perpetuate explanations of social phenomena that feel "right" and that appear to be "natural" because they allow us not to question our fundamental conditions of existence. For some, racist characterizations have become comfortable, they are part of their daily lives. Racism is supported, therefore, because it still works as "truth" for those people, even in the face of opposing religious ideals and cultural values such as democracy, equality, and fairness.

Resisting racism, then, is a complex undertaking. "Resistance to racism," writes Goldberg (1993, 224), "consists in vigorously contending and disputing exclusionary values, norms, institutions, and practices, as well as assertively articulating open-ended specifications and means for an incorporative politics." To resist racism, we must give up our dislike of change and our feelings of security in having things the way they have always been. We must also learn to make a distinction between cruelty and coercion. We cannot presume that, if institutional cruelty of a racist kind has been prohibited by law, all repugnant forms of racism have been eradicated. Very often (for example, in Canada with so-called visible minorities), while violence is no longer practised, impoverishment, exclusion, and the dismissal of "others" as irrelevant in a "white" world are all part of the lived experiences of nonwhite people. To eliminate racism means actively opposing coercive, as well as cruel, practices.

Writing about her experience as a woman from India in Canadian society, sociologist Himani Bannerji points to the paradox of being labelled a "visible minority" in an academic system that until recently made her invisible:

> The invisibility of "visible minority women" in Canada is such that, until recently, readers and scholars residing elsewhere could perhaps justifiably conclude from published evidence that: (a) Canada does not or did not have a significant non-white population; or (b) if they at all existed, women (or men) among them were/are incapable of writing or not significant enough to be written about; and (c) understanding Canadian society is possible without any consideration of colonialism and (sexist) racism (1993, ix-xxiv, xii-xiii).

Bannerji asks how this can be, given the past history of Canadian society as a white settler colony, the dispossession of indigenous peoples, labour history including indentured labour, head taxes, and selective immigration policies. Canadian history and political economy have been filled with incidents of racism and violence toward nonwhite people. "What creates such an invisibility," Bannerji asks, "while ironically, or paradoxically, handing us the appellation of 'visible minorities'?"

Putting an end to racism requires changing the socio-economic conditions under which people live, including eliminating any political or legal structures that promote or sustain racist exclusions and racist expressions. It also requires that the mechanisms by which people identify themselves racially, and by which they discriminate against those seen as racially different, be dismantled and replaced.

■ ■ ■

SUMMARY

Taken-for-granted understandings of the concept of "race" assume that biological differences among human populations are part of the natural order and have a significant bearing on individual behaviour. Progressive social scientists, however, maintain that the concept of "race"—physiological differences between human populations—has little analytic significance for the understanding of human social existence. But "race" does have meaning in the context of everyday life in Western societies. Physical diversities continue to be used as a means of categorizing and separating people into groups that have different life experiences in terms of social, political, and economic opportunities, as well as life chances.

In this chapter, I have argued that, far from being an obvious biological phenomenon, "race" is an arbitrary social construction that has meaning and value for those who use the concept, but has no intrinsic value in itself. But while "race" may be insubstantial as a biological category, it continues to be a very powerful social category. One consequence of the use of the concept of "race" is racism: the manifestation of hatred or contempt for those who are perceived as being "other."

There are many examples of racism in Canadian society, including the discriminatory treatment of Native peoples and most non-European immigrants. Ending racism requires changing not only the conditions under which people live, but also the ways that we identify ourselves as members of specific racial groups.

■ ■ ■

FOR DISCUSSION

1. To what extent is Canadian society racist? What are some examples of racism in our society?

2. Discuss the concept of "race." Assess the claims made by Philippe Rushton and others that biologically based differences are a significant factor in establishing behaviour patterns in individual members of a given "race."

3. What is the taken-for-granted view of race that is most commonly held by Canadians today?

4. What are some of the factors that contribute to our everyday taken-for-granted views of race and our attitudes toward "others?"

5. To what extent is race a social construct?

6. Many Canadians see Native peoples as constituting one of the most pressing social problems facing Canada today. But Native leaders reject the idea that Native cultures and values have no place in society. Discuss some of the potential solutions to this impasse.

429

part 6

Since the inception of sociology, most sociologists have been concerned both with the present moral, social, and political climate of human society and with humanity's future. More particularly, they have been concerned with defining what constitutes the "good life" and determining what can be done to help people achieve it. The final two chapters that make up Part 6 focus on mass culture, popular culture, and communications (Chapter 19), and on computer technology and the kinds of social interactions emerging from it (Chapter 20).

The mass culture we consume for pleasure—via television, print media, recordings, the purchase of cultural artifacts or attendance at concerts and theatres—delivers strong statements about underlying cultural values, morals, and accepted social practices, Conversely, it also can deliver messages about how to resist those values, morals, and practices. At the same time, we are not simply cultural sponges consuming mass culture in a vacuum and doing as we see or hear.

One aspect of popular culture that has recently become a reality for many people is the use of computers as a tool for facilitating communication among people who do not have to be physically present in the same location. Analysts talk about "the age of intelligent machines" and about the fact that we are now truly living in a "global village," connected to one another through the Internet.

Although there are physical devices such as computer screens, keyboards, and fibre optic networks involved in making this connection, the reality that a sociologist might study in approaching the use of information technology is much more nebulous because that reality has no physical presence. It has been created through use of a computer and it can be seen as imaginary or artificial because it is located in the user's mind as a result of interaction with an electronic device rather than in the material world as we know it. This artificial reality, whether it is created by a single comput-er running a pro-gram that interacts with the user or whether it is created by the experience of instantaneous connection with hundreds of people simultaneously in a global conversation, has been referred to as *cyberspace*, a term coined in 1984 by novelist William Gibson to denote a future where we are all connected by digital com-munication.

POPULAR CULTURE AND FUTURE DIRECTIONS

■ ■ ■

The implications of communications in cyberspace among "cyborgs" is fast becoming a new area of study for sociologists inter-ested in popular culture and in the future of Western society.

CHAPTER 19

MASS MEDIA AND THE CULTURE INDUSTRY

CHAPTER OPENING QUESTIONS

- How do mass media affect our social lives and behaviours?

- What role does mass culture play in the construction of popular culture?

- How do popular cultural meanings get relayed to, interpreted, and used by the individual?

- What is the relationship between popular culture, mass culture, and mass media?

Mass culture, culture that is produced for mass consumption, **popular culture,** culture produced by the masses, and **mass media** are closely connected and play increasingly important roles in contemporary Western societies. Not surprisingly, all three are subjects of intense and often controversial sociological inquiry. They impact on everybody's life on a daily basis. Videos, CDs, television and radio broadcasts, the cinema, magazines, and newspapers are all well-known examples of mass media that transmit mass culture. But more recently mass communication technology has been rapidly transformed to include technologies such as electronic mail, computer conferencing, and "virtual reality." These new forms, in turn, influence the ways in which mass culture is consumed and in which popular culture is created and spread.

Mass culture and mass media are most often linked in people's minds with entertainment. Very few North Americans have not watched television or a video, attended a movie theatre, listened to recorded music on a stereo system, CD player, or broadcast on the radio, or even read a newspaper or magazine. Considered in this way, it is easy to see how mass culture might appear to be little more than entertainment, mass media merely the means of delivering that entertainment to consumers, and popular culture just an act of mindless consumption of mass culture. But to take such a limited view of the relationship between mass culture, mass communication, and popular culture would be a mistake. To begin with, popular culture involves much more than just playing CDs or computer games, watching videos, television or films, or listening to the radio. Popular culture includes all those ways we are organized daily to interact: it surrounds our lives and is something with which we actively engage continually. As Nachbar and Lause (1992) point out, popular culture includes

> the clothes you are wearing (mass produced, advertised, sold for profit), the mall or store you purchased them in (and the ritual of shopping which shaped the process and got you there and back), the food you eat (from restaurants or grocery store chains), the television programs which inform and entertain you (beamed to over 98% of American homes to be watched for an average of seven and a half hours each day), and the very textbook you are holding in your hands right now (2).

Certainly mass culture, popular culture, and mass media are closely linked. The fact that North American children recognize Ronald McDonald more often than any other figure with the exception of Santa Claus results from the interaction of mass culture, popular culture, and the way in which mass culture is delivered, via mass media, into the homes of almost everyone on the continent.

POPULAR CULTURE, MASS CULTURE, AND MASS MEDIA: SOME DEFINITIONS

Popular culture reflects the accepted values, beliefs, and morality of large numbers of people. They are attracted to elements of mass culture—Madonna, Santa Claus, printed T-shirts, the nuclear family—because they perceive that those elements fulfil a need or want. Thus mass culture is not forced on an unwilling population; in order for any element of mass culture to exist, it must be attractive, and to be attractive it must satisfy a perceived desire. But individual members of society take the elements of mass culture and construct meanings with them, often ones that bear little relation to what the original, commercial producers intended.

The German word *Zeitgeist* means "the spirit of the times or era." It describes major beliefs and values that help define the viewpoint, outlook, or even the atmosphere of a particular culture during a specific period of time. Today, popular culture is a kind of mirror of the *Zeitgeist* of our time. While it forms the vast majority of all the artifacts and events that make up our daily lives, it does not make up our entire culture. Nachbar and Lause (1992) explain that there are at least two other kinds of culture that we can identify—**folk culture** and **elite culture**.

Folk culture develops within a limited community and is usually communicated orally. For example, we participate in folk culture when we learn a family recipe for baking bread from Grandma, or when we hear stories about the adventures and exploits of Great-Uncle Charlie as a young man. Elite culture, on the other hand, is produced for a limited number of people with exclusive, specialized interests. It is produced for "the ages"—for example, the work of painters such as Van Gogh or Rubens—rather than for the immediate use and enjoyment of a local group. Elite culture is limited to those willing and able to learn enough about it to be able to appreciate it.

Examples of mass media expand their reach at the world's largest permanent video wall installation in Mississauga, Ontario.

THE EMERGENCE OF MASS CULTURE AND MASS MEDIA

Mass culture, as we know it today, emerged during the late eighteenth century when three conditions were met that were necessary for its rise: masses, money, and technological advancements. At that time, the population of Europe and North America increased rapidly, and large numbers of people congregated in growing urban areas. The rapid growth of population, the movement away from rural areas, and the increasing mechanization of production and general industrialization disrupted old patterns of culture and called forth new ones. As the Industrial Revolution progressed, a new class emerged that was neither peasant nor aristocrat, but workers and professionals who were paid wages, and who, through long struggles, had won increased levels of pay, better education, and more leisure time. These people were ready for new cultural forms on which to spend time and money.

Mass media means of communicating cultural forms to this new class were also developed. Mark Poster (1990) defines mass media as "systems of communication that structure an unknown group of receivers." Mass media function as "centres of information, distributing discourses and images to a broad public." They are "systems of cultural transmission without ties to any community...emitters of signals received by a tele-anomic society." In the late eighteenth century this was accomplished by the invention of high-speed printing presses. Much later the means of mass communication expanded to include all of the methods we now associate with mass media, including radio, television, movies, CDs, and CD-ROMs (Nachbar and Lause 1992, 12). Today new forms of mass communication, such as electronic mail and the Internet, are beginning to have an impact that some feel will change the way we communicate as radically as did the introduction of printing presses.

According to British sociologist John Fiske, popular culture in Western societies is constantly undergoing change (1989, 1). It is always "in the making," that is, it is something that everyone engages in and that acts as a kind of glue to hold society together, even as it undergoes constant change. The same can be said for mass media. Mass media are used to communicate entertainment but enter into our social interactions in many other ways. For instance, today most people do their banking in front of a video monitor, which provides the same prompts for each customer: withdrawal or deposit; savings or chequing account; amount of transaction.

When you deposit money into your bank account at a designated terminal, the information is transferred electronically from the terminal to a central computer. That computer connects not just different branches of the same bank but many different banking systems around the world. Thus a customer who normally does her banking at a local branch in Toronto can make a transaction anywhere in the world where a specially dedicated computer terminal can be found. Some credit cards also link into an equally complex system of electronically stored and transmitted information that allows you to carry out financial transactions around the world.

Obviously, mass media such as television, radio, newspapers, and magazines are not confined to carrying information that has an entertainment value. Vast quantities of information—everything from community news and weather, to the proposed policies of political candidates, to the latest scientific discoveries in astrophysics, to advertising—transmitted locally, nationally, and internationally.

In this chapter we will discuss several aspects of mass media, mass culture, and popular culture. We begin with the controversial topic of the effects that mass media exert over viewers, readers, and listeners. Some social science researchers are concerned with the role of mass media in shaping public opinion, especially about political issues, or in determining the fate of public figures, politicians, and governments. Some have argued that the mass media are totalitarian and nondemocratic; that they destroy both individualism and the community. The more mass culture comes to dominate popular culture, they argue, the more likely society will fall into patterns of decline, similar to what happened in ancient Rome. Others, such as the late Marshall McLuhan, have taken the opposite approach and argued that the mass media are in the process of making the world into a "global village"—a sort of electronic utopia (Brantlinger 1983, 9–10).

In addition, many sociologists have become increasingly absorbed by attempts to uncover the relationship between representations of violence, crime, and sex in the mass media and the violent or sexual behaviour among audience participants, especially youthful ones. Does watching television or even reading about violence or sex influence the actions of the individual? Is the behaviour of the individual directly dictated by what he or she watches, reads, or listens to? Or is the relationship between the consumption of popular culture and individual behaviour less straightforward?

TELEVISION AND VIOLENCE

From its first commercial appearance in the late 1940s, television, more than any other medium, has been accused of contributing to cultural and political decadence. The television has been viewed as a sort of "fake magic mirror on the wall forever distracting, infantilizing, and consequently barbarizing its viewers" (Brantlinger, 252). In its short history, there have consistently been proposals before governing bodies for television reform and for a reduction in the amount of violence shown, especially to children.

In August 1994, for example, the Federation of Women Teachers' Associations of Ontario passed a resolution calling for federal and provincial governments to bar the access of minors to all forms of violence in the media. The federation especially singled out television, video games, and music videos as sources promoting violence among young people. This resolution echoes a policy unveiled by the Ontario Ministry of Education two months earlier to develop antiviolence measures in schools. Educators in Ontario, it appears, are firmly convinced that the blame for violence among young people can, in large part, be attributed to the violence they watch on television.

The Federation of Women Teachers' Associations of Ontario and a number of other concerned citizens might agree with the sentiments expressed by Martin Kettle in *Guardian Weekly* (March 14, 1993):

> For years, we have had to listen to the pretentious, ambitious, amoral and above all, cynical cultural hustlers trying to bully us into thinking that the violence and hatred in the heart of modern mass popular culture is something we should admire, even if or even because we don't sympathize with it ourselves. Those of us who...actually detest Freddy Kruger, are revolted by Hannibal Lecter, are ashamed of the Terminator, are humiliated by the degenerate, inhuman rubbish of the martial arts movies, who don't find the endless blowing up and mutilation of human beings amusing, trendy, or streetwise and who want to turn away from all the baseness that they represent and protect our children's innocent minds from it have been mocked mercilessly and opportunistically with any weapon of abuse that came to hand—as hippies, oldies, lefties, righties, racists, or elitists. Well, who cares what we are, except that we are people? All I know is that at least we're fighting back...
>
> *Hasta la vista,* you bastards.

Some sociologists who have studied the effects of TV violence on aggression argue that watching violence on television promotes aggressive behaviour in viewers

(Huesmann et al). The argument usually put forward is that the amount of television violence viewed globally affects the aggressive behaviour of viewers. For example, in a review of the literature on children, TV viewing, and aggressive behaviour, Comstock and Strasburger (1990) found that the majority of studies correlate TV viewing with aggressive behaviour. They reviewed a number of studies that used many different research methods, including laboratory experiments, field studies, and longitudinal studies, and concluded that, regardless of the method used, all studies seemed to suggest that television makes a small but significant contribution to violent behaviour in children. But Comstock and Strasburger also found that the effects of TV viewing on aggressive behaviour in children could be reversed if parents and teachers stressed their disapproval of the violence depicted. School-based programs about how to view television critically also helped mitigate the effects of its violence.

In another series of studies, Freedman (1984, 1986) has shown that the effects of viewing television violence are short-lived and rarely transferred into the television viewer's everyday social behaviour. Moreover, a study by Hennigan et al. (1982) indicates that there were no changes in crime rates before and after the introduction of television into various regions of the United States.

While a study done by Gerald Hopkins (1989) of 310 residents of Billings, Montana, suggests that there might be some relationship between viewing TV violence and an increase in antisocial behaviour, many other studies have failed to demonstrate anything but the weakest relationship between exposure to TV violence and violent behaviour. A survey by Steven Messner (1986) of the relationship between exposure to TV violence and rates of violent crime reported in the United States FBI Uniform Crime Reports (1982) failed to confirm the author's hypothesis that populations with higher exposure to television violence would be more likely to display criminal violence. What Messner found, instead, was that high exposure to television violence was consistently related to lower levels of reported criminal violence in the populations under study.

Public perception to the contrary notwithstanding, the rate of violence in Canada has been declining or in the case of homicide has remained stable over several years. Moreover, there is less violence on television now than in the past, and fewer children are watching television. In 1992, A.C. Nielsen rating service reported a 13 percent decline in Saturday morning television viewing among children ages 2 to 11. This parallels the decline in television viewing by all age groups, but especially among adolescents for whom music sources and interactive computer games have become the recreation of choice (McCormick 1993).

If we want to understand the relationship between television viewing and violence, we should be paying attention to children's popular culture. Children do not live in isolation, according to Canadian sociologist Thelma McCormick. First of all, "They belong to groups, and second, they share a symbolic culture of language, games, sports, secret passwords, songs, music, rhymes, books, jokes, stories, comic books, slang, codes and private signals, board games, Disney films, puns and a whole underground of fart-jokes, scatological stories and verses..." (26). Television, McCormick insists, is only a small part of the larger cultural matrix in which children live. If we only talk about violence on television that children watch and somehow absorb, we miss what she points out are "the series of filters between the child and the screen."

We know that television watching is a regular part of the activities of most children. But generally they do not watch television alone; they watch with siblings, friends, and adults. By the time children are 5, they also understand that television is make-believe. By the time they are 7, they prefer adult programs to those constructed specifically for children. Preschool children do like cartoon programs, which usually are very violent. Older children, however, like "adult violence" but still prefer watching comedy. What is clear, McCormick insists, is that children do not passively absorb what adults believe to be the "message" of what they are watching. Moreover, the level of cognitive development attained by a child seems to determine what that child sees and how he or she understands what has been seen (McCormick 1993, 22).

In a study of educational television that McCormick conducted, children in a Grade 2 class watched a CBC telecast on the making of an igloo. She found that what the children remembered about the program depended on when and where they watched it.

> The programme was seen first in the early afternoon during school hours and again in the late afternoon as part of a children's programme. Children who saw it at school thought it was about how the igloo was constructed; those who saw it at home thought it was about the Eskimo community and how fortunate the children were to play outdoors all the time and have their own dogs. When we asked them about how long it took to build an igloo, the children who saw it in school speeded it up, reflecting a highly structured, task-oriented environment, while those who saw it at home, where they are less pressured, slowed it down (1994, 32).

439

McCormick concludes that studies of the effects of television aggression on children are "superficial, misleading and adult-centred." And she insists that such studies "should not ever, by themselves, be the basis of social policy" (32).

We can conclude that empirical evidence of a link between viewing television violence and aggression in either children or adults is, at best, questionable. The direct effects of viewing television violence on violent behaviour would appear to be either very low or nonexistent. But if there is not a direct causal relationship between what viewers see or hear or read and their behaviour, what is the relationship between popular culture, mass media, and individual behaviour?

MASS MEDIA, POPULAR CULTURE, AND BEHAVIOUR

The most simplistic argument about the influence of mass media is that it conveys dominant cultural meanings from which audiences construct their understanding of the social world and their place in it. But a number of cultural theorists have argued against this interpretation, maintaining instead that there is an interactive social process that occurs between an audience and the content that is conveyed to it through mass media. If we want to understand critically any aspect of popular culture, we must also consider it in relation to the audience. We cannot just ask what it means; we also must ask what it means for whom (Brown and Schulze 1990, 89). In spite of claims to the contrary, watching violence on television does not directly appear to make little Johnny violent. Nor does simply watching violent pornography on the satellite sex channel directly turn the middle-aged guy next door into a crazed serial sex slayer. In short, we are not "cultural dopes" (to use John Fiske's term), incapable of doing anything except mindlessly absorbing and parroting the content of mass media. Instead, the meaning of what we see or hear or read is the result of a negotiation between producers and consumers of what is carried through the media.

This complex relationship between producers and consumers of mass culture and the popular cultural meanings and practices that are circulated through mass media are illustrated by a discussion of three examples of popular American mass culture—*Miami Vice*, Batman, and Madonna. Each example will illustrate specific aspects of the ways in which popular cultural meanings are negotiated in response to mass cultural offerings.

MIAMI VICE OR MIAMI VIRTUE?

440

The stars of Miami Vice *(left to right): Don Johnson (Detective Sonny Crockett) and Philip Michael Thomas (Detective Ricardo Tubbs). The show epitomized the triumph of morality played out in a glamorous setting.*

The 1980s television series *Miami Vice* was a popular serial about two Miami undercover cops who drove fast, expensive cars, lived in upscale accommodations, were fashion trendsetters, regularly killed, blew up, or beat up bad guys, and were beaten up in turn. But it can be argued that *Miami Vice*'s explicit message of violence, glamour, drugs, and sex was not what ultimately attracted and held the weekly attention of the viewing public. Rather, the audience was drawn into the show by the underlying moral code that the series promoted, and by the tension created when that code was at first violated and then reaffirmed during the dénouement of each episode.

Certainly, as a mass cultural product, *Miami Vice* pulled out all the stops in an attempt to capture the attention of as wide a range of viewers as possible. It was the first television series to make use of neurophysiological research on the viewing process, carried out in the communication technology laboratory of the University of Michigan. This research showed that American viewers easily became impatient with elaborate stories and complex characterizations. To capture their viewers' attention, *Miami Vice* resorted to constant visual and sound excitement through a series of aesthetic devices that included rapidly changing images, pastel and florescent colour schemes, and mood music. Plot and dialogue were reduced to a minimum (Buxton 1990, 140).

The series' two main characters, Sonny Crockett and Ricardo Tubbs, were equally sketched out in broad, stereotypical strokes. David Buxton (1990) describes them as follows:

> Sonny Crockett is white, divorced, an ex-alcoholic beach bum of dubious antecedents, who lives in elegant negligence on a houseboat with his pet alligator and drives a Ferrari Daytona. His partner and buddy is Ricardo Tubbs, a "dude" of mixed, black-Hispanic descent, a charmer with a diamond in his ear, who has moved to Miami after the killing of his policeman brother in a gangland murder. Crockett is tough and down-to-earth; a Vietnam vet and ex-football star, he represents "regular-guy" small-town values. Tubbs is romantic, sensitive, and intellectual: epicurean and impeccably dressed, he represents New York sophistication (143–44).

What holds these two characters together, in spite of racial and personality differences, is their common loyalty to each other, to their captain, and to their fellow police officers. This is the ultimate value expressed by the series and held up against the powerful counterinfluence of "vice." Each episode of *Miami Vice* is a story of crime and its punishment, murder and retribution for murder, the breaking of laws and the punishment meted out for such transgressions. Each is a story of "vice's" threat to police integrity being met and overcome. Illegal, "dirty" money and the dissipated life and sorry end it inevitably leads to (i.e., "vice") presents an always unsuccessful challenge to the virtuous life of legitimate affluence, defended by men and women of the Miami Vice Squad whose stellar personal qualities emphasize their loyalty to their own image and to one other.

In one episode, "Honor Among Thieves" (1988), members of a Miami crime syndicate set out to track down the psychopathic murderer of teenage girls. This murderer is giving the syndicate's cocaine business a bad name by raping the girls and then killing them with lethal injections of cocaine. The leader of the syndicate, Palmo, appears in the episode with all the trappings of refined respectability: he has his own personal French chef, listens to classical music, and plays golf. But Palmo also keeps an uncouth, uneducated bodyguard by the name of Cyril. Palmo's respectability is therefore easily seen as hypocritical, and he is just as responsible for the murders of the teenage girls as is the psychopath that both he and Crockett and Tubbs are hunting. In the dénouement of the episode, the psychopathic killer leaps to his death and in the act also kills Palmo. Responding to a police officer who arrives on the scene and asks which one is the murderer, Crockett wearily replies, "Take your pick" (Buxton 1990, 145).

In short, *Miami Vice* stressed the two most prevalent themes of 1980s American popular culture—law and order and conspicuous consumption. It could have just as easily been called *Miami Virtue,* a celebration of all that is estimable in American culture. In each episode, crime and economic crisis are found to be the result of moral weakness. At

441

the same time, the message is clear that there is nothing wrong with, and indeed everything to be gained from, the conspicuous consumption of private, legitimate wealth. Crime and poverty are moral issues (not social ones). Political issues are "old-fashioned" and "unstylish" and the only solution left is the cultivation of personal style and identity.

VIOLENCE AND VIRTUE IN SUPERHERO COMIC BOOKS

Another prevalent example of the intertwining of themes of violence and virtue and the legitimation of dominant social values in mass media products can be found in many superhero comic books. The superhero comic book industry, originally aimed at children, got started in 1938 with the publication of the first superhero comic book, *Action Comics*, featuring Superman. Shortly afterward, a comic book devoted solely to Superman was issued by the same publishers. By 1941, 1.4 million copies of *Action Comics* and *Superman* were being sold every two weeks. Two years later, 95 percent of boys and 91 percent of girls between the ages of 6 and 11 in the United States regularly bought comic books (McAllister 1990, 57). Designed and marketed for children, the comic books of the 1940s idealized dominant cultural ideals—especially that good and evil were clearly demarcated and could be easily recognized. The American war effort of the 1940s only served to increase the importance of reinforcing dominant social values and of separating good (the Americans) from evil (the Germans and Japanese). Comic books were not only sold to children; over 44 percent of enlisted men in American training camps also reported reading them regularly (Fader 1955, 59).

During the 1950s, the comic book industry expanded its themes to include science fiction, crime, and horror, and all became popular. But with the growing popularity of horror and crime comics came pressure from parent groups, church groups, and educators for industry regulation of comic book content. In the postwar era, moreover, comic books were subjected to anticommunist hysteria, as well as to deliberate attempts to promote family values and domesticity. In 1949 Fredric Wertham, a child psychiatrist, published *The Show of Violence* in which he claimed that comic books were part of a growing conspiracy to corrupt the morals and values of American youth and thus to destroy the American family (12). His second book, *Seduction of the Innocent* (1954), claimed that the comic book industry was undermining American civilization. In that book, he accused comic books of promoting juvenile delinquency, romanticizing criminal and sexual deviancy, and demeaning authority.

Wertham believed that superhero stories "undermine the authority and dignity of the ordinary man and woman in the minds of children." He also claimed that the Batman and Robin series "helps to fixate homoerotic tendencies by suggesting the form of adolescent-with-adult or Ganymede-Zeus type of love relationship." The relation between Batman and Robin, the Boy Wonder, Wertham argued, conveys the feeling that "we men must stick together because there are so many villainous creatures who have to be exterminated." He likened this feeling to "the wish dream of two homosexuals living together" (1954, 12).

Wertham's books echoed suspicions held by the general public that comic books had a negative impact on children. These suspicions are understandable if we take into

Batman, the evolution of a popular hero. Pictured above is Batman in his high-tech Batcave from the 1989 movie.

consideration the political climate of the 1950s. Americans had just come out of a 15-year period of deprivation and fear, a result of the combined effects of the Depression and the Second World War. What was most sought was cultural stability and security. Anything that might be perceived as a threat to those desires elicited a very strong response.

A 1954 U.S. Senate investigation into the relationship between comic books and juvenile delinquency recommended that the comic book industry begin self-regulation. In order to meet the criticisms and to forestall external censorship, the publishers of comic books created the Comic Book Code Authority, intended to mainstream the values and messages presented in comics. The Comic Book Code Authority seal of approval appeared only on those comics reviewed by it. The preamble to the "Code for Editorial Matter" speaks of the need to "see that gains made in this medium are not lost and that violations of standards of good taste, which might tend toward corruption of the comic book as an instructive and wholesome form of entertainment, will not be permitted" (Weiss et al. 1976, 819).

During the 1960s, comic superhero characters, such as Batman, appeared in television series, which emphasized the satirical or campy side of comics. As well, designers, writers, and artists collaborated to deal with themes that had formerly been banned by the Comic Book Code Authority, such as drug addiction or the questioning of public officials. In one issue of *Captain America*, the discovery of corruption in the presidency of the United States was explored. At this time, an underground comic book industry emerged that clearly questioned mainstream values and institutions. Foremost among these was Robert Crumb's *Zap Comix*, which first appeared in 1967. Crumb's central character, Mr. Natural, lived in a world of free love and readily available drugs—both of which were portrayed as highly desirable (McAllister 1990, 64). At the same time, the average age of the comic book reader increased to about 20 (Eichenwald 1987, 1), with the majority of readers falling between 15 and 28 (McAllister 1990, 65). With the adult reader increasingly targeted, comic book themes have become more sophisticated than they were when children were the main consumers. In the example of Batman, we can see the changing roles that this American superhero has played in relation to the *Zeitgeist* of American culture over a period of a half-century.

BATMAN: A SHORT HISTORY[1]

Comics are certainly an important part of North American popular culture, and *Batman* is among the most popular. Although the comic character of Batman has been around for over 50 years, it continues to hold great relevance today—a major movie starring Jack Nicholson, one of the highest-paid American movie actors, another starring Danny DeVito, and a third featuring Jim Carrey. In the spring of 1989 Americans became obsessed with all manner of things to do with Batman. That obsession, "Bat-mania," included the consumption of a wide variety of commodities: T-shirts, key chains, jewellery, buttons, toys, trace and colouring books, magic plates, magazines, watches, posters, records, cups, and the ubiquitous Batman series of toys and games. *Batman*, the film, drew record-breaking crowds to movie theatres across the country; Prince's *Batdance* video played heavily on MTV. In short, there seemed to be something for everyone regardless of race, age, or gender (Meehan 1991, 47).

And while the late 1980s and early 1990s Batman craze was carefully coordinated and promoted by a profit-motivated media giant, this in itself is an insufficient explanation for the intense interest on the part of North Americans for consuming anything related to this comic book character. Understanding the appeal of Batman, one of the longest-lived cultural heroes in North America, is a complex undertaking. Batman was introduced to comic book readers in May 1939, the next superhero after Superman. Superman was a calculated response to the Nazi ideal of the *Übermench*, a superman who would lead the masses to victory. The American version, however, was endowed with a social conscience and used his talents to "benefit mankind." The success of Superman led to Batman, created by artist Bob Kane and writer Bill Finger.

Like the criminals who fascinated the American public, the character that Kane and Finger created operated outside the law and on his own terms. But instead of operating at the expense of the status quo, Batman worked on its behalf. Nor did he work by himself; rather he was aided by a number of supporting characters. His opponents, too, often mirrored aspects of Batman's own character and personal history. Kane and Finger gave their superhero his origins in a criminal act. As young Bruce Wayne is walking home from

---

1 This section draws extensively from Aileen Meehan's 1991 work on Batman.

a movie with his wealthy, upstanding parents, Thomas and Martha Wayne, they are brutally slain by a faceless thug who attempts to rob them. Young Bruce is traumatized and this trauma leads him to adopt the alter ego of Batman. Young Bruce swears to avenge the death of his parents by combatting crime, and his great inherited wealth helps him to achieve this purpose (ibid., 7). Like Batman, his opponents often had their origins in some traumatic event that forever altered their lives. These characters also share his respected position in society. But unlike him, their traumas have driven them into madness and crime, or even into a quest for world domination. The Penguin, for example (played by Danny DeVito in *Batman Returns*) was constantly harassed by his schoolmates because he reminded them of that bird. The Joker (Nicholson in *Batman*) personifies the irrational and chaos, everything that Batman opposes (8–9).

In the origins of the Batman character, we can see the impact that Nazism had on American culture during the late 1930s and 1940s. That impact is also clear in the series of movies produced during the 1940s in which Batman and Robin are said in the voiceover to represent "American youth who love their country and are glad to fight for it...against...Axis criminals" (10). Comic book superheroes created during the Second World War reflected the nationalism and war fervour of the times. With the end of the war, however, interest in superheroes declined, but comic books as a popular cultural phenomenon expanded with the addition of new characters and themes, including mysteries, romances, Westerns, and especially Disney figures.

With the adoption of the Comic Code, Batman underwent a decided personality change, becoming both happier and unmistakably heterosexual. In the 1950s, he became "a sort of ebullient scout master...a bright, sunny fellow who would walk down the street in the middle of the day and people would say, 'Hey, Batman, hi, how's it going?'" (Pearson and Uricchio 1991, 19–20). During the 1950s and 1960s, the Batman stories became increasingly focused on sci-fi scenarios, consistent with the Cold War period in American history. The "caped-crusader" was often called on to fight off the menace of alien invaders. Here the villains become less ominous and more like pranksters, and Batman himself was transformed into a campy sort of prankster.

In the mid-1960s, artists like Andy Warhol and Roy Lichtenstein raised popular culture to a high-art form with representations of formerly ignored aspects of American culture. Warhol's renderings of Campbell soup cans and Lichtenstein's giant comic book panel paintings turned commonplace, everyday items into art. Comic books were at the centre of this new aesthetic, and the inevitable happened: a television series was inaugurated based on a comic book character—Batman. The show had a stunning success and ran 120 episodes. Moreover, an animated cartoon version of Batman was aired Saturday mornings between 1968 and 1969. As a result, comic book sales revived, but then immediately began a decline and hit an all-time low in 1985.

In an attempt to revive interest in the comic books, the character of Batman was reinvented yet again during the late 1960s and 1970s. Batman was transformed from the campy comedian of the television series back to the "Dark Knight Detective," an "obsessed loner" who goes after criminals but cannot take a life (Pearson and Uricchio 1990, 18). The resurgence in popularity of the Batman character was greatly aided by the 1986 publication of Frank Miller's graphic novel *The Dark Knight Returns.* In this book,

445

a troubled, suicidal, mid-fiftyish Bruce Wayne struggles with his impulse to once again take on the Batman persona after 10 years of retirement. Everything around him has deteriorated—Gotham City is corrupt, the world is on the brink of nuclear war, and the Joker, Batman's archenemy, has been released from a mental asylum. The novel is a gloomy story about the fall of the superhero in a world that has made him obsolete. Miller's vision for a sequel to *The Dark Knight Returns* is in his words "as preposterous as the original." In the sequel, the Batman hero is transformed to meet the changing cultural requirements. This reinvented Batman is "much more direct in his actions, much more willing to mess with the order of things. He wouldn't be going after the poor bastards who are the muggers. He'd be going after the people who make them muggers."

To sum up, changes to the Batman story and to his character over the last 50 years reflect the past and current state of cultural anxieties, fears, and concerns of North Americans. They also tell us much about what is of value and morally beyond question in that society.

THE ECONOMICS OF NORTH AMERICAN MASS CULTURE

Most of the production of cultural artifacts in Canada and the United States is done by privately owned corporations that are run for profit. These corporations make up the entertainment and information sectors of the North American economy. They include publishing, television, film, music, cable television, and radio industries (Meehan 1991, 48). Profit is a major constraint in shaping and organizing the creation and consumption of mass-produced cultural artifacts. In order for a popular cultural craze such as Batmania to sweep the continent as it did in 1989, the material objects that mark the craze had to be mass-produced. Much of what constitutes the mass culture industry in North America is governed by corporate motives: stocks, market shares, and market control.

When casting decisions were made for the film *Batman,* negative reactions to the choice of Michael Keaton to play the Bruce Wayne/Batman character hit the front page of the *Wall Street Journal* (Meehan 1991, 54; Pearson and Uricchio 1991, 183–84). Tensions over the various ways in which the Batman persona had been portrayed for 50 years exploded in the summer of 1989. As the scriptwriter Sam Hamm claimed: "What you wind up doing when you're putting an existing character in a major Hollywood film is essentially *defining* that character for a whole generation of people (Pearson and Uricchio 1991, 182).

Prince's *Batdance* video, which played out the usual Prince themes—androgyny, punishment, sexuality—was featured frequently on MTV, targeting middle-class white youths and adults. The rap-style choice also meant that the song was played on radio stations aimed at black audiences. More specifically, the choice of Prince to do the movie's theme also targeted Prince's fans—white women in their 20s and 30s, an audience that was not typically comic book fans—and further deepened the pool of potential *Batman* moviegoers. The question of the extent to which consumers of popular culture are "cultural dopes," manipulated out of their money by clever multinational moguls, is one that warrants more careful consideration.

MADONNA

Madonna has been an American and world-popular cultural phenomenon throughout the late 1980s and into the 1990s. As such, she provides some rich terrain to explore, especially because it has become clear that what her fans are most concerned about is Madonna herself—her appearance, clothes, what she does and says, and what she represents. Her music is of much less importance. John Fiske (1989) focuses on these aspects of Madonna, arguing that her appearance, personality, and the words and images of her songs are the "main carriers of her most accessible meanings." While the music provides an underlying emotional intensity without which the other aspects would not matter to her fans, it is the words and the images themselves that are essential to the production of the mass cultural phenomenon known as Madonna (95).

Madonna arrives at a party celebrating her book Sex.

In 1984, before her image was widely circulated, Madonna was not a success. Her first LP, *Madonna*, was selling slowly and her second, *Like a Virgin*, had been recorded but not released. Only with the release of the rock video "Lucky Star" did *Madonna* become a popular icon. *Like a Virgin* was released shortly afterward and stayed in the number one position for weeks. The release of the film *Desperately Seeking Susan* in March 1985 supported the video in launching the "Madonna look." Madonna established her own Boy Toy label, selling such items as crucifix earrings and fingerless lace gloves—visual symbols she had made her own. There was a concert tour, the release of an old film for the home video market, publication in *Playboy* of old art school nude pictures, and her marriage to Sean Penn (Fiske 1989).

One interpretation is that Madonna had become "a fine example of the capitalist pop industry at work creating a (possibly short-lived) fashion, exploiting it to the full, and making a lot of money from one of the most powerless and exploitable sections of the community, young girls" (ibid., 96). This account supports the view that Madonna fans are indeed manipulated by leaders of the mass cultural industry both economically and ideologically. Her videos exploit her sexuality, and there are those who argue that she is in fact just teaching her young female fans to see themselves as they are seen by men—as sexually exploitable objects.

447

But there is another way to look at Madonna and her fans. If her fans *actively* choose to listen to and imitate her, then they are not just being manipulated. Rather they see in Madonna meanings that connect to their own social experiences—in this case powerlessness and subordination. Madonna offers her fans a model not for submitting to powerlessness, but for struggling against it and for subverting it. We can come to this understanding about the relationship of mass culture and popular culture by studying the significance that fans actually attribute to her. We can also come to this understanding by paying attention to the symbols that Madonna presents to her viewers and what those symbols mean in the everyday interpretations provided by Western culture.

Analysis of the role played by Madonna in popular culture requires that we pay attention to the symbols that are present in her work and to the ways in which her audience reacts to, uses, and finds meaning in them. The main question is, "How does mass cultural meaning get relayed to, interpreted by, and used by the individual?"

An interpretive approach to understanding Madonna can yield interesting insights about the meanings attached to her, as they are constructed in popular culture by her audience. While Madonna's mass cultural offerings contain references to domination that simply repeat existing cultural values such as the subjection of women to men, those images are read in a variety of ways by her audience. Madonna's audience is not only diverse in terms of class, race, ethnicity, gender and sexual orientation, it is also often socially powerless and subordinate. The messages that Madonna conveys have popular appeal because her fans see and hear meanings that are at once related to dominant values, beliefs, and morals, and that offer opportunities for evading or avoiding domination (Brown and Schulze 1990, 88).

The example of Lucy, a 14-year-old fan of Madonna, is instructive. Commenting on a Madonna poster Lucy says:

> She's tarty and seductive...but it looks alright when she does it, you know, what I mean, if anyone else did it would look right tarty, a right tart you know, but with her it's OK, it's acceptable...with anyone else it would be absolutely outrageous, it sounds silly, but it's OK with her, you know what I mean (Fiske 1989, 98).

As Fiske points out, while Lucy uses the words of the dominant patriarchal culture to describe Madonna's sexuality, "tarty" and "seductive" and "outrageous," she is also struggling against that dominant view, arguing that Madonna, in being a "sexy tart," is presenting a positive view of feminine sexuality. Her sexuality is acceptable if not to the dominant culture then at least to Lucy and girls like her who are struggling to establish a satisfactory sexual identity (ibid., 98–99). Madonna's sexuality can and does offer a challenge to long-held, dominant views of masculinity and femininity, and it does this in a mocking, ironic, confrontational way. The sexualization of her navel is a case in point.

> The most erogenous part of my body is my belly button. I have the most perfect belly button—an inny, and there's no fluff in it. When I stick a finger in my belly button I feel a

nerve in the centre of my body shoot up my spine. If 100 belly buttons were lined up against a wall I would definitely pick out which one was mine (cited in Fiske 1989, 99).

In choosing to sexualize parts of her body that patriarchal culture has ignored, in taking pleasure in her naval for herself and not for some masculine voyeur, Madonna is declaring that her sexuality is for her pleasure and under her control. In so doing, she invites fans to discover their own feminine sexuality in a way that suits them and that is independent of patriarchal culture. Young teenage girls, in adopting Madonna's style, are attempting to align themselves with a source of power. By choosing to adopt the mass-marketed "Madonna look," fans are not just superficially playing with appearances; rather they are attempting to construct and control social relations and social identity (Fiske 1989, 100–102).

Madonna offers her fans access to social power. At some basic level, this access works through fantasy, which, in turn, may empower a fan's sense of self-worth and change, if only subtly, her behaviour in social situations. When fantasy connects to real, everyday life, then that fantasy becomes achievable. It is not simply escapism, as many critics of Madonna's fans have noted. Thus Madonna's popularity is a "complexity of power and resistance, of meanings and countermeanings, of pleasures and the struggle for control" (Fiske 1989, 113). Nowhere is this last statement as evident (along with the concerted attempt by a media giant to separate the public from its money) as it is in the 1992 Time-Warner release of the coffee-table book *Sex*, featuring Madonna and a cast of others in fantasy scenes of ambiguous sexual orientation. As it did for the release of the Batman movies, Time-Warner conducted a "spectacular six-figure multimedia marketing campaign" in the months leading up to the release of *Sex* (*Publishers Weekly*, June 15, 1992). A series of news items were released that kept the forthcoming publication in the public's eye. In one prepublication story, Madonna elicited the help of the FBI in recovering photos for the book that were stolen from a photo studio. In others, Madonna appeared in risqué photo spreads in magazines such as *Vanity Fair* and *Vogue* (Frank and Smith 1993; Ross 1993). The well-publicized fact that the forthcoming book was threatened with censorship in the United States and impounded by nervous customs officials in Europe only served to further heighten anticipation.

The marketing ploys worked. When *Sex* was finally published, it was reviewed everywhere: in magazines catering to every sexual orientation, in mainstream and industry newspapers, on television and radio, and, of course, at academic conferences. By the time *Sex* was actually released, few people were indifferent to it; everyone either wanted to see it or refused to see it. Designed by Fabien Baron, art director at the upscale magazine *Harper's Bazaar*, the book was presented to the public in a mylar wrapping. As Baron said about this particular marketing "hook," "We wanted there to be an act of entering."

Sex sold half a million copies within weeks of its release in North America, and another half a million were put up for sale in Europe and Japan. Profits were "astronomical" (Frank and Smith 1993), but as one reviewer protested: "*Sex* is less a book than a slickly contrived, shrewdly marketed happening." After all the prepublication hype, the book itself elicited an immense yawn once the public actually took off its wrapping. In

449

short, *Sex* was created as a public spectacle, an extraordinary event to command public attention. Once that attention was commanded, the result was just sufficient interest to sustain a purchasing frenzy as consumers sought to discover the forbidden secrets behind the mylar covering. A lot of books were bought, and a lot of people said so what?

Madonna herself clearly generates much mass media attention. She functions, in Andrew Ross's words, like a "charismatic megafauna: a highly visible and lovable species, like the whale or the spotted owl, in whose sympathetic name entire ecosystems can then be protected and safeguarded through public patronage" (1993, 52). Madonna, it seems, has taken on an avowed task of bringing "subversive sexuality into the mainstream." For example, when asked about homophobia in the music industry in a 1991 *Advocate* interview she replied: "They're not going to be when I'm finished with them." With the publication of *Sex*, Madonna, it seems, might have been trying to make politics out of sexual diversity. Certainly *Sex* is filled with homoerotic imagery.

The question is, How can Madonna get away with this? More than that, how can she bring decidedly homoerotic/homosexual images before the consuming public in a climate that continues to be homophobic and that does not brook challenges to heterosexuality? The answer, according to bell hooks (1993), is that the willingness of today's mass markets to consume homoerotic or homosexual images does not correspond to "a cultural willingness to stand against homophobia or challenge heterosexism."

We live in a culture that has a longstanding fascination with cross-dressing. There has been a tradition in American cinema of male superstars appearing in drag as female characters. Dustin Hoffman in *Tootsie* and Robin Williams in *Mrs. Doubtfire* are two recent examples. But does all this fascination with consuming images of cross-dressing mean that Western popular culture is any less committed to maintaining heterosexism and perpetuating homophobia? According to bell hooks, what a book like *Sex* offers is simply a means of appeasing the voyeuristic desire to "look at, or experience through fantasy, sexual practices that in one's everyday life might be perceived as taboo" (1993, 71). Madonna, then, in presenting homoerotic images to the masses, is doing nothing subversive at all. Indeed, all that she is doing is framing gay subculture and gay experiences in a stereotypically heterosexist and homophobic manner, so that they can be safely consumed by mass audiences who will spend their money in order to catch a glimpse of something forbidden and slightly naughty.

■ ■ ■

SUMMARY

In this chapter, I have brought together three separate analyses of aspects of mass culture, popular culture, and mass media. In keeping with John Fiske's observations (1989), each one of the examples is intended to illustrate how culture-making and the circulation of cultural meanings and understandings is a social process. In our society, there are many diverse aspects of popular culture that, taken together, help knit the diverse aspects of our social life into some coherent, although often conflicted, whole.

As we have seen, part of the contradictory and conflict-riddled nature of popular culture is apparent in the different kinds of interests it serves. On the one hand, large multinational conglomerates play a significant role in developing the content and drumming up the mass appeal of various aspects of popular culture by making them salable commodities. But popular culture is not just something that is, in John Fiske's words, "imposed from without or above....There is always an element of popular culture that lies outside social control....Popular culture...always involves the struggle to make social meanings that are in the interests of the subordinate." Thus popular culture is also a resistance to, or evasion of, domination. Madonna fans may be naive when they hand over a portion of their disposable income to purchase mass cultural items made for them by a multinational conglomerate. At the same time, these fans use Madonna to resist domination and to construct their own meanings of female sexuality (1989, 2).

In his book *The Mode of Information: Poststructuralism and Social Context* (1990), Mark Poster suggests that mass media alter the time-space parameters of social interactions, making it possible for anyone to communicate with anyone else across time and space. In this sense, Marshall McLuhan's prediction of a global village emerging as a result of new methods of communication has in fact already been realized as a technical possibility.

But such forms of communication are very different from the older, face-to-face communications. The structure and conditions of symbolic exchanges have been profoundly altered. While anyone can talk to anyone else at any time, what is being exchanged via mass media is clearly different from what happens in a direct interaction. In the first place, electronically mediated exchanges profoundly alter context. What is conveyed when one watches a news event on television is clearly different from what might be conveyed, contextually, from hearing about that event personally, or from being there oneself. We are all aware that camera angles, choice of colours, music, background lighting, and the like can profoundly alter the meaning of the content. Second, electronically mediated exchanges are primarily *monological* and almost never *dialogical*. For example, as we sit mutely in front of the television, our active involvement is limited to choosing which of the messages being transmitted we will receive. And yet, as we have seen, the viewer is not just a passive "dope" who will mimic everything he or she sees on the screen. In order to attract a large audience, a television emission must bring together a mass audience composed of different races, classes, and genders, concerning some *positive* project, one that can be neither reducible to nor explicitly opposed to dominant cultural values and ideals (Buxton 1990, 17).

But today television, a monological medium, is being transformed into something that is potentially dialogic. The information highway is already here for many. Well beyond the capabilities of television to bring together a mass audience, it may provide the means whereby interacting participants can find a place to come together in creative and liberating ways. The new information technology necessary for such an undertaking is discussed in the final chapter.

■ ■ ■
FOR DISCUSSION

1. How pervasive a role do the mass media play in shaping popular culture?

2. Analyze a favourite television series for the values, beliefs, and morality it reflects. To what extent do you share that morality? Do the same for a number of rock videos by different recording artists.

3. What would you identify as the *Zeitgeist* of today? Give examples drawn from popular culture.

4. Do mass media exert an unwarranted influence over the lives of Canadians? Explain.

5. Are we all just "cultural dopes," easily separated from our money by clever manipulators of popular culture? Or do we get good value for our money when we buy items associated with our favourite popular culture heroes?

20

SOCIAL RELATIONS IN CYBERSPACE

CHAPTER OPENING QUESTIONS

- Are we now involved in a social and technological upheaval that will be as profound as the Industrial Revolution?

- Has the global village that Marshall McLuhan envisioned several decades ago finally become a reality for many people?

- Is true love possible in cyberspace?

- What new areas might sociologists of the near future want to study?

" Where is cyberspace?...Cyberspace is like Oz—it is, we get there, but it has no location" (Stenger, 48–49, 53).

"I come into LambdaMOO through the closet. The closet is the port of entry....to this virtual world....I can see the metal doorknob in front of me....I type "open door." Text marches across my screen, telling me I'm in the living room" (Quittner 1994, 92).

One of the earliest social thinkers to speculate about the impact of global communications on industrial economies was Karl Marx. He declared that technological innovations, such as railroads, steamships, and telegraphs, served to accelerate the circulation of capital, thus promoting the growth of industrial economies. With the growth of capitalism would also come an underlying contradiction in social relations. These contradiction could only be resolved, he predicted, in a revolution that would lead us toward socialism, the next stage of human social evolution.

University of Toronto sociologist Marshall McLuhan took much from Marx (avoiding, however, any predictions of socialist revolution) and dressed up the ideas with phrases such as "the global village" and "the medium is the message." Television, radio, telephones, and jet airplanes, McLuhan told us, were weaving the post–Second World War period into a single community—a "global village." Today, this global village seems even closer to becoming a reality, at least for those who possess the means to connect with the global computer network. This network, also known as the Internet, had 20–30 million users in over one hundred nations as of the end of 1993, and is rapidly growing. Its users speak of a "network culture" and of "virtual communities."

Because a growing number of people around the world now possess the means (a computer, a modem, and an e-mail address) to access vast data banks of electronically stored information and to send out queries and receive answers, a new "social space" is available for sociologists to study. Although only a few anthropologists, sociologists, and computer buffs have studied the changing nature of social relations that has resulted from the use of computers and computer networks, virtual communities (as well as our relations with, and the personal and social impact of, computer-based technologies) are soon likely to become areas of study for many more sociologists.

In this chapter, I will first take a brief look at the computer itself and then at one of computing's fast-growing and more trendy offshoots—*cyberspace*. Cyberspace is a place that has "no location," a computer-generated, interactive, "virtual" environment. In the words of Canadian artist and anthropologist David Thomas, cyberspace is a place that has "recently engaged the creative imaginations of a narrow spectrum of government, corporate, and academic researchers from various disciplines, as well as an assortment of other individuals including artists and science fictions writers" (1992, 31).

COMPUTERS: MACHINES THAT "THINK"?

To get into cyberspace, one needs to use a computer, a modem, and some communications software. Like writing, computers facilitate communication between people. Both rely on symbolic languages to fix meaning. They are tools whose symbols represent ideas or knowledge constructs. Once presented, those ideas and constructs are open to discussion, review, alteration, and development.

As Edward Barrett (1988, xvii) points out, "There is a family of relationships that unites thinking, writing, and computers." But Barrett also cautions against "anthropomorphizing the machine and mechanizing the uniquely human." His concern is that we not conflate humans and machines, but that we use computers to facilitate our communications with ourselves and with others (xviii).

Seymor Papert (1980) and Sherry Turkle (1984) are two of the earlier writers concerned with the role of computer-mediated communications. Papert analyzed the cognitive basis for computer-mediated instruction and argued that, unlike other instruments of communication, the computer is unique in its ability to stimulate. He is convinced that it is dangerous to anthropomorphize the computer and maintains that it is not a thinking object itself. Instead a computer provides us with "an object to think with." It is a means for displaying the cognitive or thinking processes of its users (Barrett 1988, xix). According to Turkle (1984), the computer is not simply a neutral means to access electronically stored information. While she sees it as a machine, it is unique. The computer challenges "our notions not only of time and distance, but of mind." In this way, computers are "evocative objects." They change what we do as well as how we think, includ-

A laptop computer provides efficient use of commuting time. How does this constant access to work affect us?

ing our awareness of ourselves, of one another, and of our relationships with the world.

One of the initial questions to ask ourselves is, How does the computer affect the way we think? First, computers often have a holding power over children and adults, perhaps because they simulate human encounters. The computer is a projective device: we speak to it, get angry with it, even call it names. Allucquere Rosanne Stone, director of the Group for the Study of Virtual Systems at the Center for Cultural Studies at the University of California, Santa Cruze, writes about some of the conceptual problems she faces in studying cyberspace, its users, and the computer technology necessary to get there:

I, for one, spend more time interacting with Saint-John Perse, my affectionate name for my Macintosh computer, than I do with my friends. I appreciate its foibles, and it gripes to me about mine. That someone comes into the room and reminds me that Perse is merely a "passage point" for the work practices of a circle of my friends over in Silicon Valley changes my sense of facing a vague but palpable sentience squatting on my desk not one whit. The people I study are deeply imbricated in a complex social network mediated by little technologies to which they have delegated significant amounts of their time and agency, not to mention their humor. I say to myself: Who am I studying? A group of people? Their machines? A group of people and/or their machines? Or something else? (1992, 81).

455

Second, there are important differences between television and computers. Television is something you watch. Accessing games or virtual realities through a computer, by contrast, is something you do. Cyberspace is a world that you enter actively, a world where you interact with others.

Third, the computer changes our patterns of thinking because it is a device that enhances creativity. Computer programming is like experimenting or problem solving. As a tool for manipulating information, the computer opens up new ways of writing and of exploring information. Those who have switched from using a pen to using a word processor know that it isn't just a matter of increased efficiency or having a spell check. The ease with which we can make changes provides a new freedom to move ideas around, to be hasty about wording (we can make improvements later), and to get ideas down as quickly as possible.

Fourth, computers can become a part of one's personality, identity, and even sexuality. Computer talk can be incorporated into everyday language. We speak of "reprogramming" ourselves (or someone else) or of "pulling the plug." The computer has become a metaphor for brain functioning in a field of study known as *information processing theory* in psychology. So even before we enter cyberspace through our computers, the very fact that we use them has already affected the way we think, how we use ideas, and how we might relate to "others" that we find in this new space.

The changes in patterns of thinking and relating that using computers implies are not, of course, without their critics. Cultural critic and sociologist Neil Postman in his 1992 book *Technopoly* contends that the most dangerous metaphoric use of computers is to see ourselves as machines:

> The computer redefines humans as "information processors" and nature itself as information to be processed. The fundamental metaphorical message of the computer, in short, is that we are machines—thinking machines, to be sure, but machines nonetheless (111).

Postman claims that once we are defined as machines, our human attributes—biology, emotions, spirituality—become subjugated to things that machines do better, such as processing information. Not only do we become machines, he maintains, we become inferior ones to computers.

But other social researchers are not as concerned as Postman about computers taking over from humans. Indeed, researchers such as feminist biologist and cultural theorist Donna Haraway advocate the creation of "cyborgs" out of the union of nature, society, and technology. In her work, Haraway goes so far as to tell us that given the choice, she would "rather sleep with a cyborg than with a sensitive man." On a less personal note, Allucquere Rosanne Stone points out that the usual analytical categories for making distinctions between "the biological and technological, the natural and artificial, the human and mechanical are all unreliable" (1992, 101). The dichotomy between nature and technology, or nature and culture, she argues, is a false one.

It is this latter understanding of human/computer relationships that underlies the attitudes of many computer users who use them as a means of accessing virtual communities where they relate to other virtual presences. These communities have no physical existence, but are, nonetheless, very real for their participants.

THE NEW COMMUNITIES

Sociology, as we have seen, emerged out of the concerns of late eighteenth- and nineteenth-century scholars over the changes that were happening to social relations and to community as Europe underwent a complete economic, social, and political transformation. When Marx, Weber, and Durkheim wrote, community was largely limited to those people who had face-to-face interactions with each other, who lived in the same physical space, and whose interactions were based on a common culture and on mutual concerns. Even if they did not share the same class position, and thus the same class interests (as

Marx so clearly pointed out), those interests and positions were at least related on the basis of material interactions that produced daily existence.

While all of this is still true today, our sense of community is being changed. Consider the following excerpt from computer journalist Howard Rheingold as he tries to convey what constitutes community for him and his seven-year-old daughter:

"Daddy is saying 'Holy moly!' to his computer again!"

Those words have become a family code for the way my virtual community has infiltrated our real world. My seven-year-old daughter knows that her father congregates with a family of invisible friends who seem to gather in his computer. Sometimes he talks to them, even if nobody else can see them. And she knows that these invisible friends sometimes show up in the flesh, materializing from the next block or the other side of the planet (1993a, 1).

What constitutes community for Rheingold and his daughter is not something that the early founders of sociology had in mind. The people making up Rheingold's community do not necessarily have to occupy the same physical space, or even any space at all. Certainly there are commonalities among those who occupy "real" communities and those who get together only in cyberspace: in both cases people do communicate with each other, share information and experiences, help each other out, and develop a sense of belonging. But in cyberspace all of these shared experiences are based on the use of new communications technologies and not on all the old cultural markers—race, class, gender, religion, nationality, physical proximity.

CYBERSPACE: ARTIFICIAL REALITY?

Although there are physical devices like computer screens, keyboards, modems, and fibre-optic networks involved, the reality that a sociologist might study in approaching the use of information technology is much more nebulous. It is the reality created by using a computer, a reality that can be seen as virtual or artificial in the sense that it is located in the user's mind as a result of an interaction with an electronic device, rather than one in the material world.

This artificial reality, whether it is created by a single computer running a program that interacts with the user, or whether it is created by the experience of being instantly connected with hundreds of people simultaneously in a global conversation, has been referred to as *cyberspace*, a term coined in 1984 by novelist William Gibson to refer to a future where we are all connected by digital communication.

Cyberspace. A consensual hallucination experienced daily by billions of legitimate operators, in every nation....A graphic representation of data abstracted from the banks of every computer in the human system. Unthinkable complexity. Lines of light ranged in the

Chess was once a game played face-to-face by two opponents. What are the implications of a cyberspace competitor?

nonspace of the mind, clusters and constellations of data. Like city lights, receding... (Gibson cited in Harasim 1993).

Gibson continues his definition of cyberspace: "[a] desperate, dystopic vision of the near future," a vision of "corporate hegemony and urban decay, of neural implants, of a life in paranoia and pain...." Others, unhappy with his negative connotations, prefer more positive definitions. Michael Benedikt, for example, sees cyberspace as

a new universe, a parallel universe created and sustained by the world's computers and communication lines. A world in which the global traffic of knowledge, secrets, measurements, indicators, entertainments, and alter-human agency takes on form...(1992, 1).

This new space, virtual reality, virtual community, or cyberspace—whatever we call it— is likely to disturb our present theories of how the world works and our social relations with others. In *The Mode of Information* (1990), sociologist Mark Poster notes that with the spread of electronic communication, the body has ceased to be the "effective limit of the subject's position" (15). Instead we can now enter into virtual spaces and interact with other virtual social beings, any or all of whom may be fictional characters, created for the purpose of these kinds of "interactions."

CYBERSPACE AND THE INTERNET

Once connected through the telephone system, space is abolished as you talk to people all over the world, browse through libraries in distant countries, or access a data base stored halfway around the globe. The first thing you notice about cyberspace is that time constraints are almost absent. Once in you can access what you want, when you want it, whether it is information, entertainment, or a chat. Many university professors and researchers already live in this space created by the Internet. The Internet is an unplanned weaving together of several hundred thousand computers used by over 25 million people. It grew out of an earlier communications system called ARPAnet (Advanced Research Projects Agency), which was originally set up by the American Department of Defense. The Internet has grown so fast that no one really knows exactly how many people use it. But according to *Scientific American,* one bulletin board where high-energy physicists post their results gets up to 10 000 hits every day ("The Computer in the 21st Century," Special Issue, 1995, 4–9). More recently, ordinary people have begun using the Internet. On-line services like America Online offer over five million customers such choices as access to information bases, the contents of magazines and periodicals, and on-line shopping services.

Most of the major countries in the world are now connected to the Internet. Use of the Internet varies from country to country. In North America, most people with a modem (a device that allows information to be sent between computers across phone lines) and a personal computer can connect to the Internet, either through a commercial service or through computers owned by nonprofit organizations such as universities, colleges, governments, and research agencies. Above all, the Internet has become a social network (Harasim 1993) consisting of electronic-mail networks, computer conferencing, and commercial videotext systems. Networks are places to conduct work or to socialize. People "meet" each other there to do business, collaborate on a project, share information, or just chat (Harasim, 1993).

Interestingly, the social community aspects of the Internet seem to appear when the network is organized using metaphors based on familiar ideas such as neighbourhoods and collective activities. Thus we see such forms of organization as "townhall meetings," "cafés," "treasure hunts," "classrooms," and "malls." As well, many people use the Internet as commercial networks to telecommute to their workplace without leaving home. Education administrators have invested heavily in computer networking, with the result that there are now virtual classrooms, learning circles, and on-line access to many university and college libraries around the world. Increasingly, university faculties are using the Internet for research and for collaborative writing projects. Children in school classrooms, from kindergarten to the end of high school, use the Internet in a variety of ways. Already there are worldwide discussion groups for children, such as KIDSNET and KIDSCAFE. As well, many classrooms now connect to subject experts through e-mail.

EDUCATION

Through the Internet, education has the potential for being global and multicultural. By easily crossing national boundaries, networking promotes an understanding of the interconnectedness of the world and the common humanity of those who live on this planet. One vehicle for networked global education is the use of **learning circles,** which involve participants from many countries discussing a common topic of interest. As Margaret Riel (1993) notes, this new approach to education requires a change in the role of both the teacher and the learner. Perhaps its most important change is in the promotion of collaborative problem solving.

Learning circles are small electronic communities that form to accomplish a common goal. Students and teachers from classrooms located around the world work together for a specified period of time. The AT&T Learning Network is organized into learning circles because this task-oriented grouping provides an effective way to integrate communication technology, classroom curriculum, and the aims of global education. Six to nine classes form a learning circle. Students in these classes design and organize curriculum-based activities using computer telecommunications. Learning circles on the Learning Network help students share written information with distant peers in much the same way as circle time or sharing days are used in primary grades to help young students share verbal information. Students conduct research on society's problems and global issues; compare historical, geographic, and environmental concerns; and share local news, events, and opinions. Learning circles in the educational community, like "quality circles" in the business community, involve participatory management by teachers. No one teacher controls a learning circle. It is a collective construction by the participants (Riel 1993, 223–24).

SOCIAL CONFLICT ON THE INTERNET

But all is not completely smooth on the Internet, and as its use grows exponentially, serious conflicts are emerging among users with very different agendas. Probably the most publicized conflict to date has been between Lawrence Canter and Martha Siege, a husband-and-wife law firm, and thousands of other Internet users. Canter and Seige made themselves the "most hated couple in cyberspace" when, in April 1994, they wrote a program that sent out an ad to some 6000 user news groups offering their legal services to aliens living in the United States who were interested in getting a green card. In Internet jargon, what Canter and Seige did was to "Spam" the Net: what they did had the effect of dropping a can of processed meat into a fan.

The response was quick and angry. Enraged Internet users sent thousands of angry e-mail messages called "flames" to the offenders. By the third day, the company that provided Canter and Siege with their Internet access had pulled their account. This incident brought forth many issues associated with the Internet's rapid growth. It is not designed for commercial use. New arrivals, who are not properly socialized into the existing customs, language, and protocols, or who openly defy them, are dealt with mercilessly.

Until recently, access to the Net was restricted to those with some connection to a university or a government research lab. But since 1993 dozens of small businesses have emerged selling access to the Net for as little as $10 a month. With the new arrivals have come new issues and conflicts. Started by the United States military as a means for scientists to keep in touch with each other, even in the face of a nuclear attack, the Net has no central command authority. Nobody owns it, nobody runs it, and nobody has the power to remove anyone. In *Hackers*, Steven Levy describes the mind-set of the users who set the original rules to govern the Net: access should be total and unlimited; information should be free; authority is to be distrusted and decentralization promoted. Is a virtual community possible on the Internet? Howard Rheingold insists that it is more than possible, it is a reality:

> A virtual community is a group of people who may or may not meet one another face-to-face, and who exchange words and ideas through the mediation of computer bulletin boards and networks. In cyberspace, we chant and argue, engage in intellectual discourse, perform acts of commerce, exchange knowledge, share emotional support, make plans, brainstorm, gossip, feud, fall in love, find friends and lose them, play games and metagames, flirt, create a little high art and a lot of idle talk. We do everything people do when people get together, but we do it with words on computer screens, leaving our bodies behind. Millions of us have already built communities where our identities commingle and interact electronically, independent of local time or location. The way a few of us live now might be the way a larger population will live, decades hence (1993a, 58).

There are, of course, those who strongly disagree with Rheingold and who remain cautious or even downright negative about the benefits of this new technology and the possibilities for community that it brings. Arthur Kroker, a professor at Concordia University, Montreal (and member of the rock band Sex Without Secretions) is pessimistic about the vision of the future presented by what he calls the "technical specialists" or "technocrats." In an interview in *Mondo 2000* he says:

> I call [these times] "the Age under the Sign of the Will to Virtuality"—that's what VR is all about. It's about closing down the world in subordination to technical will...the real power and privilege resides in a class of specialists, technical specialists, who are the theorists of digital reality. There's no place where they congeal with greater ferocity and density than in a city like San Francisco, or in Silicon Valley, or Chiba City outside Tokyo, or around Toronto, or MIT....They very happily view themselves as servomechanisms of digital reality. If you talk to these missionaries in their research labs, they'll say to your face, "This new kind of monitoring device—in, like, the new office of the future—will make possible godlike surveillance techniques and will make it possible to get rid of ourselves, and who needs a self anyway, because your body will ultimately betray you and die" (1993, 62).

Who's right? Rheingold with his joyful experience of community without geographical limits or Kroker with his bleak take on technocrats and technological fetishists addicted to technological euphoria? Do electronic virtual communities represent "flexible, lively and practical adaptations to the real circumstances that confront persons seeking community" in what Haraway (1989) refers to as "the mythic time called the late twentieth century"? Are they innovative solutions to a total human drive for sociality—one that has often been thwarted by geographical and cultural distances and by

461

economies structured by powerful interests? Or are they about "closing down the world in response to technical will," as Kroker insists?

One consequence of computer-assisted communications has been the decline in employment of middle managers and highly paid workers. At the same time, the new technology is putting an end to the traditional way in which people have climbed into management jobs and middle-class identities. In many industries, there are fewer jobs, and those that remain often lead nowhere.

A second consequence is the concern over the interplay of intellectual freedom and the right to property. Does the government have the right to access private citizens' computer files while investigating illegal activities? How can the work of authors or publishers or artists be protected from being copied at will or deftly altered beyond recognition? Will students want a printed copy of a textbook when one is available on-line, complete with moving images and illustrations, one that can be quickly updated to reflect the latest information?

Certainly there are many things today that make us seriously consider Kroker's warnings and his bleak view of the new technology. Some of the issues that confront the residents of cyberspace include issues of privacy and surveillance. Already we are hearing stories of bosses in companies who are secretly able to read their employees' e-mail. As well, credit companies maintain large files on cardholder purchases; each time a purchase is made with a credit card, the details are noted and electronically stored. From this information, police and less scrupulous people can track your movements and build a picture of your personality based on your purchasing patterns.

Stone, on the other hand, argues strongly that virtual communities are "complex and ingenious strategies for survival." But, she cautions, it remains to be seen "whether the seemingly inherent seductiveness of the medium distorts the aims of those strategies, as television has done for literacy and personal interaction..." (1992, 111).

Virtual Relationships?

Some social analysts have noted that because of the real possibility of never actually meeting the people with whom one is interacting, many networkers lack any constraints about themselves. Mark Poster describes how this works on the messagerie service (a place to leave and receive personal messages) of the French Minitel network.

> Connected to the messagerie, one's subjectivity flowers. "Computer cafes," "electronic singles bars," the messageries provide a new form of sociability, a "community" in the era of the mode of information. So attached have people become to their electronic village that, for his August vacation in Britanny, one Parisian would bring only his Minitel. A single woman in Besançon chalked up a record Minitel bill for one month of $11 666, requiring a connect time of 500 of the total 720 hours for that month. As the success of the messageries mounts...conflicts emerge between the old and the new social forms. Spouses become jealous over their partners' electronic flirtations; one husband furiously cut the wire to prevent his wife's "affair" over the Minitel (though she was able to splice the wires, upon which he threw the contraption out of the window) (1990).

463

However, the same lack of constraint may allow people on the Internet to reinvent themselves with a new identity. Stone (1992) tells the story of Julie:

> Let us begin with a person I will call Julie, on a computer conference in New York in 1985. Julie was a totally disabled older woman, but she could push the keys of a computer with her headstick. The personality she projected on the "net"—the vast electronic web that links computers all over the world—was huge. On the net, Julie's disability was invisible and irrelevant. Trapped inside her ruined body, Julie was herself sharp and perceptive, thoughtful and caring (82).

After several years, something happened that shook the conference to its core. "Julie" did not exist. "She" was, it turned out, a middle-aged male psychiatrist. Logging onto the conference for the first time, this man had accidentally begun a discussion with a woman who mistook him for another woman. "I was stunned," he said later, "at the conversational mode. I hadn't known that women talked among themselves that way. There was so much more vulnerability, so much more depth and complexity. Men's conversations on the nets were much more guarded and superficial, even among intimates. It was fascinating, and I wanted more." He spent several weeks developing the right persona. A totally disabled, single older woman was perfect. He felt that such a person wouldn't be expected to have a social life. Consequently, her existence only as a net persona would seem natural. It worked for years, until one of Julie's devoted admirers, bent on finally meeting her in person, tracked her down.

The news reverberated throughout the Net. Reactions ranged from humorous resignation to blind rage. Most deeply affected were the women who had shared their innermost feelings with Julie. "I felt raped," one said. "I felt that my deepest secrets had been violated." Several went so far as to repudiate the genuine gains they had made in their personal and emotional lives. They felt those gains were predicated on deceit and trickery (Stone 1992, 82–83).

The story of Julie illustrates the phenomenon of "computer cross-dressing." A few years ago on the Qualitative Research List (QUALRS-L), there was a posting by a person named Jean. Someone wanted to know if Jean was male or female. A lengthy debate ensued on whether or not this information was important to network discussion. Jean never did reveal his or her gender identity. With virtual reality, sex can be simulated with a digitized object of one's fantasy or with an erotic object created and controlled by another person. With body suits or other yet-to-be-invented sensory interfaces (perhaps direct brain stimulation devices), virtual sex (also known as "teledildonics") will be available in the twenty-first century. One version of how this might work is given by Howard Rheingold:

> The first fully functional teledildonics system will be a communication device, not a sex machine. You probably will not use erotic telepresence technology in order to have sexual experiences with machines. Thirty years from now, when portable telediddlers

Café patrons surf the Internet. This new medium has greatly altered social interactions.

become ubiquitous, most people will use them to have sexual experiences with other *people,* at a distance, in combinations and configurations undreamed of by pre-cybernetic voluptuaries. Through a marriage of virtual reality technology and telecommunication networks, you will be able to reach out and touch someone—or an entire population—in ways humans have never before experienced. Or so the scenario goes (1991, 345).

However, John Perry Barlow, co-founder of the Electronic Frontier Foundation, says that one thing that is essential to community is some sense of physical proximity. A problem with network communities is that "all they've got is a shared interest, not a shared necessity." Barlow makes the point that while it's easy to drop out of network discussion groups, it is not so easy "to leave my little town in Wyoming. There, we have to learn to stick it out and make it work." He says that "if you look at the overall trend, not just in cyberspace but everywhere, it's toward globalization and localization. What seems to be coming apart is everything in the middle" (1993).

Mark Poster agrees that "electronically mediated conversation cancels contexts, creating new speech situations" (1990, 45). He continues: "With computer message services, language use is radically separated from biographical identity....For the first time, individuals engage in telecommunications with other individuals, often on an enduring basis, without considerations that derive from the presence to the partner of their body, their voice, their sex, many of the markings of their personal history" (117).

MUDS, MUSES, MOOS, MUCKS, AND MUSHES

MUDs (Multi-user dimensions or multi-user dungeons), along with variants MUSEs (social MUDs that include a class system and combat), MOOs (object-oriented MUDs with education or research orientations), MUCKs (a social MUD), and MUSHes (Multi-user shared hallucinations) are computer programs accessed through the Internet. MUDs use text descriptions to created the illusion of rooms, worlds, and time periods. A player enters these virtual spaces and interacts with other virtual characters, solves quests and/or fights monsters.

LambdaMOO is one such program, set up in 1991 by Pavel Curtis at Xerox's Palo Alto Research Centre. Curtis designed LambdaMOO as an experiment, but it has become one of the biggest and most versatile "virtual community" on the Net.

Once into the program, a would-be participant must first create and name a character. Wired magazine writer Josh Quittner describes his character, "Johnny Manhattan," as "out of work, underfed, full of jazz." To this he added "tall and thin, pale as string cheese, wearing a neighbourhood hat." He chose male as his character's gender (the choices were male, female, and neuter). Once described and gendered, "Johnny Manhattan" was ready to interact with other characters he might meet in LambdaMOO.

Quittner's first interaction was with "Jongleur," described by his creator as "a wiry fellow in orange and black motley who carries a sack with juggling balls and a diabolo slung over his back." Quittner describes his reaction to his first interactions in LambdaMOO as a feeling of the "shock of communication....the organic sensation that you're connected to people" (1994, 93).

Not only are virtual characters created, but players can also describe the environments in which their characters interact. One character encountered by "Johnny Manhattan" was "Legba" (the name of a Haitian shape- and gender-shifting voodoo god). Legba him/herself has multiple personalities, but at this particular meeting with Johnny Manhattan she was described as "massive and magnificent as an antique schooner, wearing a muumuu bright with flowers of a variety and color not often found together in nature. Her hair floats in a frowsy black halo around her face. She has a deep, rich laugh and very small feet which are usually wedged into pink mules" (94).

Many players find MUDs like LambdaMOO addictive, and they play in cyberspace for many hours a day. One limitation is that all MUDs are entirely text-based. There are no visual cues. Yet some users feel that it is easier to make things happen with text than to try to present some visual representation. In the three years that it has been in operation, LambdaMOO has developed a means for all members of the "community" to become involved in a petitioning and balloting system, giving the "public" of LambdaMOO a voice. Pavel Curtis is referred to as "god." Programmers who help administer the virtual space are called wizards. New MOOs are being launched all the time, and with each new MOO a new community is launched, and new kinds of social interactions are made possible. In the information age, says Quittner, people are using their computers to communicate (138).

THE BODY AND CYBERSPACE

Ways in which computer-mediated communication are different from face-to-face interchanges include the possibility of playing with identity, the lack of gender, race, disability, and age cues, the reordering of social hierarchies according to new criteria, and the difficulties of displaying emotion in purely textual communication. For some people, the lack of bodily cues is appealing, because people can get to know one other based on ideas rather than personal appearance.

The last word on the question of community in cyberspace comes from Allucquere Rosanne Stone. "No matter how virtual the subject may become, there is always a body attached. It may be off somewhere else—and that 'somewhere else' may be a privileged point of view—but consciousness remains firmly rooted in the physical. Historically, body, technology, and community constitute each other" (1992, 111). Participants in electronic virtual communities exist in both virtual and physical spaces, participate in both virtual and physical cultures. Their social interactions include other people in real space and virtual people in virtual space. But their interactions with other people, whether in real space or in virtual reality or cyberspace, are in real time. While cyberspace developers, buoyed by sci-fi imagery, assume that the human body is "meat," something to be discarded as soon as consciousness can be uploaded into the Net, the virtual community does originate in and has to be cognizant of the physical body.

We cannot forget that we are embodied, no matter how much we try. As Stone forcefully says, "No refigured virtual body, no matter how beautiful, will slow the death of a cyberpunk with AIDS. Even in the age of the technosocial subject, life is lived through bodies" (113).

This is just a glimpse of how the world is changing around us. It is impossible to foresee all the new developments that might result from the introduction of information technology into our lives. But for sociologists, the immediate future will continue to be "interesting times."

■ ■ ■

SUMMARY

In this chapter we have considered some aspects of the impact of new information technology on life in the late twentieth century. Some analysts argue that we have now entered an "age of information" or, perhaps more to the point, an "age of intelligent machines." Certainly there has been an explosion in the amount of information produced in various media, and much of this information is now stored in data banks and distributed on a worldwide basis through almost instantaneous electronic networks. The idea of the "global village," first proposed by Marshall McLuhan in the 1960s, has become a reality, at least for those who

467

have access to the Internet. This global network has 20–30 million users in over one hundred nations as of the end of 1993, and is rapidly growing. Users of the Internet speak of a "network culture" and of "virtual communities."

A few anthropologists and sociologists have studied the changing nature of social relations that has resulted from the use of computers and computer networks. Clearly, this development is likely to be an object of study for many more sociologists in the near future. Already some social scientists perceive that, along with benefits, the pervasive use of computer-mediated communications carries certain risks. Sociologist and cultural critic Neil Postman, for example, cautions that the most dangerous metaphoric use of computers is to see ourselves as machines. Others, however, have noted that, at least on the Internet, social communities are best formed when the network is organized using metaphors that are based on familiar ideas such as neighbourhoods and collective activities.

■ ■ ■

FOR DISCUSSION

1. What kinds of challenges might the use of computers present to traditional ways of thinking?

2. Is a virtual community possible over the Internet? Or do humans need face-to-face contact for real communities to develop?

3. Discuss some of the differences between William Gibson's view of cyberspace as a "consensual hallucination" and Michael Benedikt's version of it as a "new universe."

4. What are some of the ways in which the use of the Internet might affect education?

GLOSSARY

■ ■ ■

The number in brackets after each term refers to a chapter in which the term is discussed or used.

Words that appear in **boldface** in the definitions accompanying each term are defined elsewhere in the glossary.

Adaptation (13)   In **structural–functionalist** theory, adaptation is something that permits the social system to maintain itself. All parts of a social system (and the system itself) need to adapt to the external environment in which they exist in order to survive.

Affective Socialization (10)   Socialization processes that influence the expression of emotion or teach acceptable ways of expressing emotion. See also **socialization.**

Affirmative Postmodernists (13)   A **category** based on a distinction made by Pauline Rosenau between affirmative and skeptical postmodernists. Affirmative postmodernists are critical both of **modernity** and its consequences and of the postmodern age, but argue that positive political choices and value commitments are still possible. See also **skeptical postmodernists**.

Agency (10, 17)   The ability of an individual to reason and act. Agency is something we express in our actions, but it is also a social **category**; some people may be affected by perceptions of age, gender, race, or level of ability.

Agents of Socialization (10)   Individuals, groups, or organizations that carry out some process of **socialization** and thereby perpetuate beliefs, **norms,** and social practices.

Alienation (12)   In Marxist theory, a loss of control over, or connection with, some aspect of one's being or activity; particularly as a result of the organization of wage labour. Under capital-ism, wage labourers are alienated from their work, from the product of their work, and from their fellow workers because they give up control over their work in return for a wage.

Anarchism (13)   A tradition of political and social thought that is critical of institutional forms of authority (like the state) and that advocates forms of decentralized self–government.

Anomie (12)   In Durkheimian sociology, the weakening or absence of **norms** governing social life, which allows free rein to destructive (or self-destructive) exercises of will in pursuit of expanding or unrealistic personal goals. See also **normlessness**.

Anthropometry (18)   The study of physical measurements of the human body.

Attachment Theory (7)   A theory of early **socialization** developed by John Bowlby based on the idea that sociability (social stimulation and affection) is necessary for human growth and development, especially in the early stages of life. Bowlby emphasized the importance of the mother-infant bond.

Back Stage (13)   Term developed by Erving Goffman to describe actions or interactions not intended for public view but that support a public role performance (for example, a consultation between doctors for dealing with a particular patient, carried on "out of earshot" of the patient). See also **Front Stage**, **Outside**.

Bio–Power (13)   A term developed by Michel Foucault to describe a form of disciplinary control that emerged in the **modern** period as a strategy for controlling human populations through precise knowledge of the human body and its functions, especially sexual ones.

469

Bipedalism (5)   The ability to walk upright on two feet. The origins of bipedalism are the focus of much controversy among anthropologists as are its consequences for the subsequent social development of the human species.

Bourgeoisie (14)   In Marxist sociology, the ruling class in capitalist society. The bourgeoisie is defined as the class that owns and controls productive property (the **means of production**). Members profit from the labour of workers, whom they employ at a wage rate that allows them to accumulate a surplus. See also **labour power, proletariat, class, mode of production**.

Breaching Experiment (13)   A form of sociological experiment used by Harold Garfinkel to make visible the ways in which we construct or create a social atmosphere or a sense of social order. It involved deliberately behaving in ways at odds with expectations. This form of experiment has serious ethical ramifications: breaching can be disturbing to those subjected to it.

Capitalist Mode of Production (14)   According to Marxist theory, in the capitalist mode of production, productive property is held privately and used for private gain. Those who own the means of production profit by employing wage labour. Typically, capitalist production is industrial in nature. See also **mode of production, forces of production, social relations of production, class, bourgeoisie, proletariat**.

Categories (3)   Classes of similar things or characteristics. Categories are basic to the process of giving meaning to social life, recognizing patterns, and making comparisons. Categories are culturally specific: different cultures categorize social and cultural reality in different ways. Sociological **concepts** are special categories that have been carefully designed and constructed to help make sense of social life.

Class (12)   Class is a term used by sociologists to designate differences between groups of people in a given society based on income, wealth, or property. It is important to note that class is defined differently by different social theorists. Karl Marx (and Marxist sociologists generally) define class in terms of ownership of the **means of production**. Max Weber argued that in addition to a division between bourgeoisie and pro-

letariat, there are internal divisions within each group. Both Marx and Weber argued that people belong to classes whether or not they believe they are members of a particular class.

Concept (3)   A term designating a **category** of things or characteristics. A basic element of classification and comparison. See also **metaphor**.

Conditioning (7)   In behaviouristic psychology (e.g. Watson), conditioning is said to be the process by which **socialization** occurs through repeated application of external stimuli. This model of socialization treats the child essentially as a passive, machinelike being who acts only in response to external inputs.

Conflict Theories (17)   Conflict theories note that social order is imposed by some groups against others groups. Pluralist conflict theory sees society as composed of a number of groups competing for scarce resources. Marxist conflict theory sees social conflict as an expression of a fundamental contradiction in social life, usually expressed in terms of conflict between two **classes**, one of which seeks to **exploit** the other.

Copernican Revolution (11)   Nicolaus Copernicus (1473–1543) was one of the first astronomers to propose that the earth revolved around the sun, and that the universe was infinite. This change in perspective was a revolution in human thinking because for the first time the earth came to be seen, not as the centre of the universe, but as one small part of it.

Critical (8)   A critical approach to knowledge involves an attempt to assess the contributions and limitations of other approaches to knowledge and to move beyond them. Critical approaches attempt not only to make sense of "what is" but also to suggest "what might be." See also **critical thinking, relativist**.

Critical Thinking (1)   A way of thinking about the social world that involves questioning **taken-for-granted** assumptions and beliefs, and recognizing and exploring the constructed nature of social reality. Critical thinking tends to be tentative in its conclusions, fluid, and marked by an ethic of responsibility for its own motivations and commitments. See also **critical, relativist**.

Cultural Capital (14) A term used by Pierre Bourdieu to stand for types of knowledge, typically taught in family settings, but also in schools and other institutional settings, that give certain persons an advantage in social life or mark them as members of a distinctive **social status** or **class** group. Distinctions made on the basis of "taste"—in food, clothing, choice of holidays, housing, and furnishing, etc., are expressions of cultural capital.

Cultural Determinists/Cultural Determinism (4, 16) Cultural determinism holds that cultural factors influence all aspects of social life, including the economic sphere. Generally speaking, cultural determinists argue that almost all human behaviour must be explained in terms of its cultural meaning rather than in terms of genetic factors or instinctual factors.

Cultural Relativism (11) A point of view arguing that judgments of value, or of right and wrong, are culturally specific. The study of culture thus necessarily entails suspending one's own cultural assumptions, at least provisionally, and studying cultures in relation to each other rather than on their own merits. Cultural relativism is often contrasted with **ethnocentrism**.

Deconstruction (13) A postmodern method of analyzing statements or texts, focusing on features that are excluded, masked, or repressed in the explicit message, but that are at the same time necessary to that message. Deconstructionists tend not to believe in a single, unified standard truth, but in the existence of heterogeneity and plurality.

Dialectical Materialism (12) The philosophical orientation underlying the work of Karl Marx. Marx argued that ideas, values, and beliefs respond to the circumstances of material life (the organization of work, class position, etc.). At the same time, Marx treated ideas as having the power to alter material circumstances. He argued that social life had to be understood as a web of relations or connections in terms of which **social actors** were defined. These relationships are dynamic and changing, driven by changes in the organization of production in social life.

Discovering (9) In **positivist** sociology and positivist science more generally, the world of objects to be studied is **taken for granted**. The notion that reality exists independently of the observer who is able simply to "see" and then make sense of what is there is emphasized strongly. See also **objective knowledge**.

Ego (7) In Freudian psychology, a part of the psychic structure that develops to restrain the **id** and to integrate the id and the **superego** into one personality.

Elite Culture (19) Elite culture is produced for and appreciated by a limited number of people with specialized interests. It tends to be evaluated in terms of "universal" criteria of artistic merit and to be seen as a sign of prestige. Appreciation of elite culture usually entails a process of learning and the acquisition of specific tastes. See also **cultural capital**.

Essentialist Notions (6) Any theory of human nature, gender, or race that argues for the innate nature of certain characteristics rather than their being the product of social interaction or socialization.

Ethnocentrism (4) A belief in the superiority of one's own culture; an inability to see or accept the existence or validity of cultural differences. See **cultural relativism**.

Eugenics (16, 17, 18) A set of theories and also a series of social movements in Western countries in the nineteenth and twentieth centuries. Eugenics theories argue that certain human characteristics or tendencies are genetically inherited, and that those who exhibit negative traits should be kept from having children in order to increase the general "health" and "strength" of the population. See also **biopower**, **racism**.

Experimental Verification (11) Experimental verification is a belief that truth is not established in the mind on the basis of clear ideas but on the basis of observation; in particular, observed patterns of action and reaction that can be replicated under controlled conditions. See also **scientific method**, **objective knowledge**.

Exploitation Models of Inequality (14) The theory that the prime causal factor for inequalities in wealth is unequal social relations; for example, the exploitation of one class by another.

471

Female Pseudohermaphroditism (15) A person born with ovaries as well as some aspects of male genitalia (except for testes). See also **male pseudohermaphroditism**.

Folk Culture (19) The knowledge, customs, and art, associated with everyday life and ordinary people within a specific, limited culture, transmitted person-to-person by example or word of mouth. See also **popular culture**.

Folkways (3) Everyday **norms** or conventions of little moral significance (for example, informal dress codes for particular occasions).

Front Stage (13) In the work of Goffman, social performances meant to be seen and that define the situation in a general way for an audience. See also **back stage**, **personal front**, **settings**, **outside**.

Gender Constancy (16) An awareness that gender is a permanent part of one's identity. Kohlberg maintains that it develops between the ages of 4 and 6 in most children.

Gender Identity (15) A gendered sense of self. This may be experienced subjectively or imposed as a social category, or both. Gender identity is challenged by the existence of individuals who exhibit physical signs that place them in one sex category but who nonetheless identify with another sex category. See also **gender role**.

Gender Role (15) A set of expectations governing social behaviour that is specific to one sex. See also **gender identity**.

Genealogy (13) A method of inquiry used by Michel Foucault. The genealogical method rests on a belief that culture is a specific set of social practices whose origins are not to be found in any hidden meanings. Foucault argued that values or beliefs assumed to be universal in modern culture (e.g., truth, reason, sexuality) have their origins in a series of specific practices through which some ideas were developed and celebrated and others were discouraged or disappeared. See also **social constructionist perspective**.

Generalized Other (7) A term used by G. H. Mead in his theory of **socialization**. Children learn to take part in social life by developing an identity as members of social groups. They inter-nalize the general rules, values, and expectations of the larger culture, and come to define themselves in relation to them. These general rules, values, and understandings constitute the generalized other. See also **symbolic interactionism**.

Homosexual (15) A term coined in 1869 by Benkert to refer to people sexually repelled by the opposite sex and attracted to members of the same sex. The term homosexuality has undergone a number of shifts in definition since then, particularly in the characteristics attached to people labelled homosexual.

Id (7) In Freudian psychology, the id is composed of the urges, impulses, and processes that drive human behaviour.

Ideology (12) A term first developed in the eighteenth century by Destutt de Tracy. Marx redefined it to mean distorted thought or false consciousness, in which consequences are treated as causes and real social relations are mystified in order to perpetuate the status quo or the interests of a dominant **class**.

Industrial Society (12) A term first used by St. Simon in the early nineteenth century to stress the uniqueness of new forms of social organization that were developing along with industrial production in France.

Instincts (4) Complex patterns of behaviour that are genetically preprogrammed and that regulate the activities of members of a species. Instinctual behaviours tend to be found in all members of a species and are innate. Instincts differ from reflexes in that instinctual behaviour is complex whereas reflex actions are simple. See also **sociobiology**.

Integration (13) In **structural–functionalist** theory, the idea that all parts of a social system must work together in order for the system as a whole to survive.

Intelligence Quotient/I. Q. (18) A standard measure of intelligence based on standardized tests. **Statistics** based on intelligence testing were (and sometimes still are) used to link genetic differences in intelligence to racial differences or class differences. Critics point out that intelligence testing reflects cultural biases and that it measures not genetically inherited intelligence, but cultural knowledge and learning.

Intended Socialization (10) Explicit **socialization** messages and practices consciously intended to generate a particular result. The opposite of **unintended socialization**.

Interpretive (8) Interpretive theorists argue that the most useful point of view from which to understand the social world is that of the social actors themselves. Interpretive theorists believe that an understanding of social reality must include an account of how that reality is subjectively meaningful to those who participate in it. See also **verstehen**, **positivist**, **relativist**.

Intersexed Individuals (15) Individuals whose bodies possess some sexual characteristics from both male and female sexes.

Intersubjective View (7) An extension of **attachment theory**, which focuses on the two–way interaction between infants and caregivers in the **socialization** process. The intersubjective view emphasizes the role played by subjects other than the maternal figure in early socialization. The intersubjective perspective defines individuals in relation to others, not as discrete or isolated units.

Intrapsychic View (7) The intrapsychic view focuses on the individual as a distinct unit with a complex internal structure. Relations to others are seen as affecting the individual's development rather than as part of the basic structure of individuality.

Labour Power (12, 14) In Marxist sociology, labour power is the physical or mental capacity for work that an employee sells to an employer in return for a wage or salary. This sale of labour power was, for Marx, the basis of the **exploitation** of the worker, and of **alienation** in the **capitalist mode of production**.

Learning Circles (20) Informal groups of students who meet electronically via the Internet and form virtual communities. While these may constitute electronic versions of the traditional study group, they have the potential to be more wide ranging and diverse.

Linguistic Sign (8) In **semiology** linguistic signs are defined as the combination of a concept with a sound-image. A linguistic sign is composed of the impression made on a listener when he hears the sound of a word as well as the mental image or concept that the word brings to mind.

Looking-Glass Self (7) A term used by Charles Horton Cooley to stress the point that we become social beings by developing the ability, through **socialization**, to see ourselves as others might see us in any given social situation. We only gain a sense of self by seeing ourselves reflected back through the responses of others in symbolic communication. See also **generalized other**, **symbolic interactionism**.

Lumpenproletariat (14) A term used by Marx to designate those who, in the **capitalist** society, fell outside of **class** boundaries. In particular, the term was used to refer to people who existed at the margins of society on the basis of crime, handouts, and occasional employment.

Macrolevel (1) A sociological approach that focuses on the study of large-scale social phenomena such as social institutions, populations, demographic trends, **modes of production**. See also **microlevel**.

Male Pseudohermaphroditism (15) A person born with testes as well as female sexual features. See also **female pseudohermaphroditism**.

Mass Culture (19) Mass culture stands for cultural phenomena (music, dance, symbols, values, consumer goods, etc.) propagated by the mass media. For mass culture to exist, there needs to be a large and concentrated population (the masses) with money to spend on consumer items and technologies of mass communication and transportation to disseminate ideas and products to this population. See also **mass media**.

Mass Media (19) A term used to refer to modern means of communication, such as newspapers, radio, television, and computerized communications, which can transmit identical messages to large numbers of people in a very short time. Mass media are carriers of **mass culture**. Today, older definitions of mass media that "broadcast" uniform messages to mass populations are being shaken by the development of interactive media.

Means of Production (12) In Marxist sociology, those things needed for production to take

473

place: in the **capitalist mode of production** these include energy, raw materials, tools, facilities, and expertise. Along with **labour power**, these constitute what Marx called the **forces of production**.

Metaphors (2)   Words or images used figuratively to associate different **concepts**, ideals, or values. For example, the use of the metaphor of *society as an organism* in **structural-functionalism** takes "organism" out of its biological context and modifies the meaning of the term "society."

Method (9)   The way in which research is conducted. In the Western intellectual tradition, it has often been assumed that **objective**, value-free scientific research is the only basis on which to build research methods (as in **positivist** social science). Today, research methods reflecting **interpretive** and **relativist** approaches to sociological knowledge are increasingly employed.

Microlevel (1)   In sociology, a focus on personal experience of social life or on small-scale social interactions between individuals. See also **macrolevel**.

Mode of Production (12)   In Marxist sociology, the characteristic way in which human labour is organized and carried out in a given era. The mode of production encompasses both the material and the technological organization of production as well as its social organization (i.e., ownership and control). See also **capitalist mode of production**, **social relations of production**, **forces of production**.

Modernity (13)   A mode of cultural experience shared by members of Western societies in the twentieth century (but with roots going back at least three or four centuries). The experience of modernity has been fed by changes in the ways we conceive of our place in the universe. See also **sceptical postmodernism**, **affirmative postmodernism**.

Mores (3)   Plural of **mos**. Mores are normative expectations governing conventional behaviour. They have great significance (e.g., prohibitions against killing, rape, incest). Breaking a mos leads to severe consequences.

Multiple Subject Positions (17)   The fact of having more than one identity. We live in a web of

social relationships in which we respond to different perceptions and expectations on the part of others and cultivate different aspects of our "selves" in those responses. See also **social roles**, **social status**.

Myths (2)   As used by anthropologists and sociologists, myths refer to a complex of values, beliefs, and expectations to tell a story about some aspect of social life. They are often represented **metaphorically**. Myths refer to ways in which meaning is constructed and reproduced. See also **social constructionist perspective**, **social reproduction**, **ideology**.

Nomos/Nomi (1)   A Greek term, related to the modern term **norm**, referring to shared, taken-for-granted beliefs, customs, and traditions of primal beliefs and understandings. They serve as the basis for judgments of right and wrong in a particular culture. See also **taken-for-granted**, **social norms**.

Normal Curve (9)   Also known as a bell curve. Popularized in the nineteenth century by Francis Galton. The normal curve is based on the idea that the distribution of human capacities across a population clusters around an average score. See also **statistics**, **standard deviation**.

Normative Perspective (13)   A set of criteria for distinguishing between acceptable and unacceptable actions or forms of power. One criticism of the work of Foucault and other postmodernists is that it does not allow adequately for making judgments about the goodness or badness of investigated social features. See also **sceptical postmodernism**, **affirmative postmodernism**.

Normlessness (12) See **Anomie**.

Norms (1) See **social norms**.

Noumenal World (7)   In the philosophy of Kant, a term standing for the world of real objects as they exist in themselves, independently of human consciousness. Kant contrasts this realm to the **phenomenal** world: the world of things as they appear in consciousness. Implicit in this distinction is the idea that consciousness and perception are governed and structured by transcendental rules and categories that are given prior to all experience.

Objective Knowledge (2)   Knowledge that is said to be based on unbiased scientific observation. The problem with any conception of objective knowledge, especially in the social sciences, is that researchers are in a relationship with their subjects, and they bring to their research assumptions that affect their research by shaping the questions they ask. See also **positivist**, **research cycle**, **objectivist**.

Objective Social Structure (10)   The social context or exterior social world into which we are born. It is imposed on us in our **primary socialization** and beyond.

Objectivist (13)   An approach to sociology relying on trained, and supposedly unbiased observers using statistical methods.

Oedipus Complex (15)   In Freudian psychology, an early sexual desire by a male child for his mother that is eventually repressed and replaced by an identification with the father and more generally with the laws of society. The concept of the Oedipus complex is subject to some controversy: some argue that, while individuals in Western culture are repressed, the Oedipus complex is not the primary mechanism. See also **ego**, **id**, **superego**.

Outside (13)   In Goffman's sociology, areas irrelevant to the performance of a particular **social role** or to a particular social situation. See also **front stage**, **back stage**.

Palaeoanthropologists (5)   Anthropologists whose primary concern is the study of the origins of humankind. Most of this work takes place from fossil records. It is also linked to comparative studies of humans and primates in order to hypothesize about evolutionary paths from early primates to modern apes and humans.

Pangenesis (5)   A nineteenth-century attempt to explain how physical traits could be inherited or how evolutionary variations could take place. According to this view, all organs produce tiny replicas of themselves, called pangens, which find their way into the bloodstream and eventually into the sex cells. The idea of pangenesis has been replaced by genetic theories in the twentieth century.

Parental Investment (16)   A concept used by some **sociobiologists** to refer to actions on the part of parents toward their offspring that increase the offspring's chances of survival but are costly to the parents. Sociobiologists argue that females have a greater investment in the survival of a child than do males, because while males can produce a great many sperm, females usually produce only one egg per menstrual cycle and, if fertilized, carry the fetus to term.

Patriarchy (16)   A term denoting social and cultural systems predicated on the subordination of women to men. In a patriarchal society, positions of political, social, and cultural power are held by men. The division of labour favours men over women in the attainment of prestige occupations and high income.

Peer Groups (10)   A term developed in 1949 by Kingsley Davis to refer to groups of children of roughly the same age. Davis argued that, while children tend to be subordinate to their parents, they see the world through the same eyes as their peers. Thus peer groups can have a strong effect on a child's **socialization**.

Personal Front (13)   In Goffman's sociology, the props needed by an actor in a social situation to make others (the "audience") believe that the role being played is genuine. See also **settings**.

Petite Bourgeoisie (14)   In Marxist sociology, a third class existing in capitalist societies between the working class (**proletariat**) and the capitalist class (**bourgeoisie**). The term refers to people who own and work in their own small businesses (farmers, self-employed professionals) and employ few, if any, other workers. Marx hypothesized that the petite bourgeoisie would eventually be squeezed out of existence by competition and by the development of large-scale businesses.

Phenomenal World (7)   In Kantian philosophy, the world of objects as it appears to our senses. Contrast with **noumenal** world: the world as it is in itself, apart from our conscious apprehension of it.

Pleasure Principle (7)   In Freudian psychology, the urge to fulfil a desire for pleasure, a given of human life. Freud argued that pleasure was primarily biological in nature and that the most

475

powerful pleasurable sensations were sexual. In very young children, sexual pleasure is generalized over the whole body, not concentrated in the genital area. Pleasure takes the form of stimulation leading to tension and then release. See also **ego, id, superego, reality principle**.

Political Party (14)   A third dimension of **stratification**, proposed by Max Weber. Weber argued that in modern societies, parties develop as means to advance **class** or **status** interests in an increasingly competitive and impersonal social arena. Those who lead such parties have their own basis of **power** as a result, regardless of their class or status position. Weber's conception of party could also be applied to organized interest groups, such as unions.

Popular Culture (19)   Culture created by masses of people in modern urban-industrial societies. Popular culture is closely related to **mass culture**, and many creations of mass culture become part of popular culture through the mass media. However, popular culture may develop in ways unforeseen by those who market mass culture items.

Positivist (8)   An approach to scientific inquiry that argues that the world exists independently of the observer and that it is discoverable through the use of rigorous scientific methods and unbiased observation: the result is **objective knowledge**. The word "positivism" refers to the contrast drawn between positive knowledge of real things or events and speculation based on preconceptions. See also **research cycle, objectivist**.

Power (14)   Defined by Max Weber as "the probability that one actor within a social relationship will be in a position to carry out his own will despite resistance." Weber and Marx both agreed that power differences and **class** differences were closely related.

Primary Socialization (10)   The earliest stage of **socialization**, lasting from infancy through early childhood (and perhaps later, depending on who defines the term and in what context). Primary socialization is the most important stage in socialization. It is the stage in which the formation of a self and of personal identity first takes place.

Productive Forces (12)   In Marxist sociology, the elements needed for production to take place in any **mode of production**. The forces of production are composed of the **means of production** (raw materials, tools, facilities, energy, technological expertise) and **labour power** (the physical and mental capacity to work), which is sold to employers in return for a wage or salary.

Proletariat (14)   In Marxist sociology, one of the two main **classes** in capitalist society, the other being the **bourgeoisie** (the owners of the **means of production**). The proletariat, or working class, is composed of those who do not own or control the means of production and who must therefore sell their **labour power** in return for a wage. According to Marx, because the wage relationship is exploitative and alienating, the proletariat and the bourgeoisie are set up in an antagonistic relationship.

Race (18)   A term generally used to refer to supposedly inherited biological characteristics that distinguish different human populations. In racist **ideologies**, such biological differences are often linked to psychological and behavioural characteristics and are used to judge different populations either positively or negatively. See also **eugenics, ideology, systemic racism**.

Racism (18)   A set of beliefs concerning supposedly biologically inherent characteristics pertaining to human populations. Usually, racist theories entail judgments about the superiority and inferiority of particular people. Racism often serves to justify **exploitation** and serves as an underlying belief system expressed in forms of prejudice. See also **race**.

Radical Empiricism (6) See **Sensationalism**.

Reality Principle (7)   The principle according to which, in Freudian psychology, the role of the **ego** is to restrain the **id** and to channel human desire into acceptable behavioural forms. The development of the ego is necessary for effective control of immediate gratification. See also **superego, pleasure principle**.

Reflexive (13)   In the work of Garfinkel (ethnomethodology), a term that designates the way in which individuals involved in social interaction engage with each other's thoughts and actions to create a specific social reality. The point Garfinkel makes is that we don't just perform interactions according to role expectations; we are also constantly engaged in creating and reproducing for ourselves and others the reality and meaningfulness of those normative expectations. In discussions of scientific methodology, reflexivity has a somewhat different and more general meaning: it refers to the need to account for one's own standpoint in the conduct of research. See also **relativist.**

Rehabilitation Model (17)   A way of looking at disability, prominent among medical practitioners, which focused on disability as an impairment that needed to be treated or fixed. This viewpoint commonly gave disabled person little power to control what was done to them.

Relativist (9)   Research methods that stress ways in which the relationship between the observer and the observed affects the results of research. Relativist research does not assume that a reality exists to be discovered; instead knowledge is accumulated. In the process of its development, it affects research methods and forms of interpretation. Relativist research thus is distinct from both **positivist** and **interpretive** research in that it is **reflexive**: it focuses on identifying assumptions, biases, and interests and attempts to account for them (rather than to hide or erase them) in the course of research.

Research Cycle (9)   A sequential research process followed by those who believe in the possibility of scientific research in a **positivist** sense. The assumption is that, if the sequence is followed rigorously, and in the correct sequence, the result will always be trustworthy, valid, and value-free knowledge; in other words, **objective knowledge**.

Role Set (3)   A set of roles attached to a particular **social status**. Sometimes the roles in a particular role set can conflict with each other.

Romanticism (13)   An intellectual and artistic movement beginning in the late eighteenth century and extending through the nineteenth. It stressed feelings, emotions, beauty, the sacred, fantasy, and the unusual as opposed to order and form. See also **modernity**.

Scientific Method (11)   According to Descartes, who took mathematics as his model, the scientific method is "nothing more or less than pure thought confronting the conditions of its own truth." Francis Bacon and Isaac Newton, however, argued that the scientific method entailed disciplined observation and experimental verification. See also **research cycle**, **positivist**, **objective knowledge**, **experimental verification**.

Secondary Socialization (10)   **Socialization** processes that take place after the basic structure of self-identity has emerged in primary socialization. Secondary socialization involves learning a variety of complex social interactions and institutions. It is a lifelong process of adaptation to new circumstances.

Semiology (8)   A "science of signs" proposed by Ferdinand de Saussure. The study of how language is meaningful, through an analysis of **signs** (the conventional association of sound or visual images with mental images). See also **concepts**.

Sensationalism (6)   A theory of human learning popular in the eighteenth century. Sensationalists argued that human beings acquire ideas, beliefs, and knowledge through sensory experience. Because of the influence of this philosophy, feral children became an object of much interest when it was thought that a study of such children could reveal the extent to which human existence was affected by sense experience alone, devoid of culture and language.

Settings (13)   In Goffman's sociology, the situations, spaces, or props necessary for a credible performance by a social actor (e.g., a doctor's office; a professor's classroom). See also **personal front**, **front stage**, **back stage**.

Sexual Orientation (15)   A tendency to be attracted to one sex as opposed to another. In Western societies, **homosexuality** (attraction to the same sex) has been negatively sanctioned while heterosexuality (attraction to the opposite sex) has been treated as normal or desirable. See also **bio-power**.

Sceptical Postmodernists (13)   Thinkers who react negatively to both modernity and to postmodernism, focusing on what they see as the

477

latter's fragmentation, disintegration, and meaninglessness. See also **affirmative postmodernists**.

Social Actors (14)   In the sociology of Marx, actual or potential social forces, such as **class.** Social actors are not individuals but rather define individuals and impel them into political action as part of a larger force.

Social Change (3)   A counter to the idea of **social reproduction**. The idea of social change encompasses all the processes by which change, innovation, and discontinuity happen in societies over time.

Social Constructionist Perspective (1)   A perspective that treats human knowledge as the product of human social activity. Objects of knowledge do not simply exist; they are meaningful insofar as they are constructed within a culture. A basic insight to be found in the work of Karl Marx, G.H. Mead, Peter Berger, Dorothy Smith and the later work of Emile Durkheim. See also **relativist, critical, critical thinking, metaphor, ideology, myth**.

Social Control (17)   A perspective on social life that focuses on the ways in which order is maintained and demands are controlled by those in authority or **power**.

Social Gender (15)   Cultural and social expectations, values, and beliefs built around sexual differences, and made meaningful within a particular framework. Social gender encompasses both **gender roles** (normative behavioural expectations) and **gender identity** (a gendered sense of self).

Social Inequality (14)   A concept used to describe how certain attributes thought to be desirable or valuable (wealth, prestige, occupation, knowledge, life chances) are unevenly distributed among individuals, families, communities, racial groups, genders, or age groups. See also **stratification, class, status, exploitation model of inequality, status attainment model of stratification**.

Socialization (6)   The process of becoming a member of **society**, of becoming a social being (gaining a self or an identity), or of learning **social roles**. Socialization takes place in stages,

(e.g., **primary socialization** and **secondary socialization**).

Socializers (10)   Socializers mediate between the **objective social structure** and the individual who is being inducted into it. Socializers present selected aspects of this world to those they help socialize, based on their own biographical circumstances. See also **agents of socialization, socialization, primary socialization, secondary socialization**.

Social Learning Theory (16)   A theory that views **gender identity** and **gender roles** as the product of learning rather than of genetics or physiology.

Social Norms (3)   A set of rules governing social interaction. Social norms can be prescriptive (they can tell us what to do) or proscriptive (they can forbid us to do certain things). Sumner distinguished between two types of norms: **folkways** and **mores**. See also **nomos/nomi**.

Social Physiology (12)   A term used by Auguste Comte to describe the guiding principles by which a new, **industrial society** should be organized. He argued that these principles should be established scientifically by an examination of the laws of social progress.

Social Relations of Production (12)   In Marxist sociology, the social relations between individuals in terms of how production is carried out; specifically, the social relations through which control over the **productive forces** is established and maintained. In their legal form, the social relations of production take the form of property laws.

Social Reproduction (3, 6)   A term designating those processes by which societies maintain continuity over time and social patterns, cultural traditions, and institutions. The process of social reproduction depends on the continuity of rules governing social interaction, and thus on the transmission of **social norms** and **ideologies** through **socialization**.

Social Roles (3)   Expected patterns of behaviour attached to particular **social statuses**. A number of different roles attached to the same status is called a **role set**. Social roles are governed by **norms** that dictate not only the actions we might take but also appropriate attitudes, beliefs, and emotions. The term social role (a **metaphorical concept**) is borrowed from the language of the theatre and entails the idea that we follow norms in social interaction in a manner analogous to the ways in which actors follow scripts.

Social Status (3)   The recognized position that a person occupies within a society or a social situation. A status has a number of rights, obligations, and expectations, which are widely acknowledged by members of a given society or social situation. Social status is often associated with prestige. See also **social norms**, **status**.

Social Structure (3)   The patterning of social interaction, governed by **norms**. This patterning takes on the appearance of a structure, especially from a **macrosociological** perspective. Social interactions are neither random nor totally unique to the participants, but ordered, patterned, regular, relatively predictable, and stable. See also **norms**, **social reproduction**.

Society (3)   The object of sociological study, society entails the existence of patterned social relations and of shared **norms**, values, and beliefs. Society is best thought of not as made up of individuals but as made up of relationships within which individuals are defined in terms of social **categories**. A society can be defined as a broad grouping of people who live together and who have developed, through interacting with one another, common interests, institutions, and collective activities.

Sociobiology (4)   A perspective on human culture and social organization based on two fundamental assumptions: that predispositions toward certain kinds of behaviours are transmitted genetically and that Darwin's theory of evolution is essentially correct. See also **parental investment**.

Sociology (1)   The study of all human social experience, whether the chance encounter of two human individuals, the outcome of a highly structured social group, or the result of a worldwide social phenomenon. In the broadest sense, sociology is an interpretation of or commentary on the social experiences that sociologists share with members of the wider society. See also **society**.

Stage Theories (11)   A product of Enlightenment and post-Enlightenment thinking. Stage theories were part of a new outlook on humanity and world history informed by the idea of progress. See also **taken for granted**.

Standard Deviation (9)   A term coined by Karl Pearson to designate a measure of the scatter of observations around their mean. See also **normal curve**, **statistics**.

Standpoint Epistemology (9)   An approach to knowledge and research that argues that the point of view of the researchers and the researched is shaped by their social positioning and material activities. Thus knowledge generated by research is itself shaped by the standpoint from which it is done. Standpoint epistemology involves the claim that less powerful members of a society have the potential for a more complete view of social reality than the powerful because their perspective is not limited by the need to justify or protect a privileged position. See also **relativist**.

Statistical Correlations (8)   In **positivist** sociology, **statistics** are often used to demonstrate or predict patterns of social behaviour or to hypothesize about their causes. But statistical analysis cannot give invariable cause-effect relations. The most that social scientists using this approach can hope for is to show that certain things tend to occur together or are distributed in the same way. Such correlations might point to a possible causal factor, but they do not prove its existence.

Statistics (12)   In sociology, the establishment of quantitative rates for different types of human behaviour, and the use of such numbers to establish **statistical correlations**. Émile Durkheim pioneered statistics in sociology by comparing suicide rates for different societies, genders, and religious groups. Statistical analysis also involves the use of **normal curves** or **standard deviations** to establish the existence of statistical norms from averages.

Status (14)   In the sociology of Max Weber, a system of **stratification** distinct from **class**. Weber argued that status, as well as class, affected an individual's ability to exercise **power** over others. Where class was defined in terms of wealth,

479

property, or income, status was defined in terms of honour and prestige. Status and class often overlap. See also **social status**.

Status Attainment Model of Stratification (14) A model of stratification that explains inequality in terms of individual achievement. Deviations from the expected norm of achievement may be explained either in terms of personal characteristics (a nonsociological explanation) or in terms of obstacles to individual achievement such as race, gender, sexual orientation, or ethnicity. See also **exploitation models of inequality**.

Stratification (14) The division of society into distinct or separate groups, which are ranked hierarchically in terms of power, wealth, property, or prestige. Weber contended that **class** and **status** were two separate dimensions of the process of stratification.

Structural-Functionalism (13) An approach to sociology focusing on the discovery and analysis of social systems. The basic **metaphor** underlying structural–functionalist sociology is that society is a large-scale living organism made up of a number of different but interrelated **social structures** or social institutions. These must function together for the survival of the whole social organism. See also **positivist**.

Superego (7) In Freudian psychology, that part of the psyche that internalizes demands from outside the individual to restrain the gratification of impulses and that judges the **ego** in terms of its ability to restrain the **id** in the interests of social conformity. The primary model for the superego, according to Freud, is the child's parents, but the superego later incorporates more generalized social commands and expectations. See also **reality principle**.

Symbolic Interactionism (7, 13) A style of sociology that emerged out of the Chicago School of sociology and that came to be associated with the work of Erving Goffman. Symbolic interactionism holds that human beings act toward things on the basis of the meanings that the things have for them, that these meanings are the product of social interaction, and that they are modified and handled through an interpretive process used by each individual in dealing with the **signs** and symbolic matter each

encounters. See also **generalized other**, **looking-glass self**.

Systemic Racism (18) Systemic forms of discrimination, evaluation, or ranking based on a conception of "race." Systemic racism refers to the existence of cultural attitudes, ideologies, and philosophies supporting social structures and economic arrangements that systematically disadvantage or degrade people deemed to be of different races.

Taken-for-Granted (1) The process of giving meaning to the world on the basis of unexamined assumptions. A noncritical approach to social explanation simply accepts cultural assumptions and established social practices as given without bothering to question or examine them.

Third World (18) A term widely used in the West to refer to nations and societies that are seen as underdeveloped, poor, technologically backward, or in need of assistance. The term contrasts to First World (developed Western countries) and Second World (what used to be the Communist bloc countries). The term "Third World" has been criticized for embodying ethnocentric assumptions about the countries and societies it is supposed to designate and for lumping quite different societies together under a single label.

Totemism (4) As defined by Levi-Strauss, "a belief system in which the members of a social group feel a mystical relationship of some sort with some natural category, usually an animal category." Members of a social group will often claim descent from their totem.

Transformationism (16) A perspective on the relation between cultural and biological factors in human existence that rejects as futile the nature/nurture debate and questions about whether genetic or cultural factors determine human behaviour. As developed by Ruth Hubbard, transformationism focuses on the complex interplay of physiological and cultural factors.

Transsexuals (15) A term used to describe persons who consistently adopt behaviour and appearances characteristic of the other sex,

480

thereby appearing to be a member of that sex. See also **transvestite.** In some other cultures transsexuals occupy accepted **social statuses**.

Transvestites (15)   Persons who regularly dress in clothing culturally associated with the opposite sex. This term is often used to single out such persons as deviant from a norm of sexual identity; in some cultures, however, transvestitism is an accepted social practice. See also **transsexuals**.

Unintended Socialization (10)   Socialization that takes place despite or alongside a **socializer's** intent. For example, a parent may give a child a verbal message about a prescribed behaviour but unwittingly contradict that message by her own actions. See **intended socialization**.

Value Systems (2)   Organized complexes of values in terms of which objects encountered in social life and objects of scientific study are interpreted. While individuals may arrange or select their own values to an extent, generally most of the values we accept are systematically organized by the culture of which we are members.

Variation (5)   A concept central to Darwin's theory of evolution. Darwin postulated that important variations occur not only between species, but within a species. Individual members of a species may vary in physical size, proportion, or characteristics. Some of these variations, if they aid an individual's ability to survive and adapt, can become characteristic of the species by being transmitted genetically to more offspring than the less-adaptive characteristics.

Verstehen (12)   A German word meaning "understanding" and, as used by Max Weber, usually translated as "interpretive understanding." Weber argued that a positivist approach to sociology, while useful to a limited degree, is insufficient to a full understanding of social life.

BIBLIOGRAPHY

■■■

Abberley, Paul. 1987. "The Concept of Oppression and the Development of a Social Theory of Disability." *Disability, Handicap and Society* 2, 1.

Abbott, Pamela, and Claire Wallace. 1990. *An Introduction to Sociology: Feminist Perspectives.* London: Routledge.

Abella, Irving. 1989. *A Coat of Many Colours: Two Centuries of Jewish Life in Canada.* Toronto: Lester and Orpen Dennys.

Abella, Irving, and Harold Troper. 1982. *None is Too Many: Canada and the Jews in Europe, 1933–1948.* Toronto: Lester and Orpen Dennys.

Abrams, Philip. 1972. "The Sense of the Past and the Origins of Sociology." In *Past and Present.* Vol. 55: 18–32.

Alberta. 1991. *Justice on Trial.* Edmonton: Task Force on the Criminal Justice System and Its Impact on the Indian and Métis People of Alberta.

Alexander, Jeffrey C. 1987. *Twenty Lectures: Sociological Theory Since World War II.* New York: Columbia University Press.

Allen, Prudence. 1985. *The Concept of Woman: The Aristotelian Revolution 750 BC–AD 1250.* Montreal: Eden Press.

Althusser, Louis. 1969. *For Marx.* Harmondsworth, England: Penguin Books.

Anderson, Karen. 1993. *Chain Her by One Foot: The Subjugation of Native Women in Seventeenth Century New France.* New York: Routledge.

Anderson, N. 1923. *The Hobo: The Sociology of the Homeless Man.* Chicago: University of Chicago Press.

Antill, J.K. "Parents' Beliefs and Values About Sex Roles, Sex Differences, and Sexuality: Their Sources and Implications." In *Sex and Gender,* edited by P. Shaver and C. Hendrick. Newbury Park, Calif.: Sage.

Ariès, Philippe. 1981. *The Hour of Our Death.* New York: Knopf.

Armstrong, Pat, and Hugh Armstrong. 1991. *Health Care as a Business: The Legacy of Free Trade.* Ottawa: Canadian Centre for Policy Alternatives.

Armstrong, Pat, and Hugh Armstrong. 1993. *The Double Ghetto: Canadian Women and Their Segregated Work.* Toronto: McClelland & Stewart.

Aron, Raymond. 1965. *Main Currents in Sociological Thought,* translated by Richard Howard and Helen Weaver. New York: Basic Books.

Aron, Raymond. 1967. *The Industrial Society: Three Essays on Ideology and Development.* New York: Praeger.

Aronowitz, Stanley. 1988. *Science as Power: Discourse and Ideology in Modern Society.* Minneapolis: University of Minnesota Press.

Ashley, David, and Michael Orenstein. 1990. *Sociological Theory: Classical Statements.* Boston: Allyn and Bacon.

Ashley, Richard, and R.B.J. Walker. 1990. "Speaking the Language of Exile: Dissident Thought in International Studies." *International Studies Quarterly* 34, 3: 259–68.

Ashmore, Malcolm. 1989. *The Reflective Thesis.* Chicago: University of Chicago Press.

Ashmore, Nels. 1989. *Health and Efficiency: A Sociology of Health Economics.* Philadelphia: Open University Press.

Astell, Mary. [1730] 1970. *Some Reflections upon Marriage.* New York: Source Book Press.

Bailey, B.L. 1988. *From Front Porch to Backseat: Courtship in Twentieth-Century America.* Baltimore: Johns Hopkins University Press.

Bandura, A., and R.H. Walters. 1963. *Social Learning and Personality Development.* New York: Holt, Rinehart and Winston.

Bannerji, Himani. 1993. "Returning the Gaze: An Introduction." In *Returning the Gaze: Essays on Racism, Feminism and Politics,* edited by Himani Bannerji. Toronto: Sister Vision.

Bannister, Robert C. 1987. *Sociology and Scientism: The American Quest for Objectivity, 1880-1940.* Chapel Hill: University of North Carolina Press.

Banton, Michael. 1987. *Racial Theories.* Cambridge: Cambridge University Press.

Banton, Michael, and Jonathan Harwood. 1975. *The Race Concept.* New York: Praeger.

Barlow, John Perry. *Edupage* (December 1993) with quotes from the *New York Times* (December 26, 1993).

Barrett, Edward, ed. 1988. *Text, ConText, and HyperText: Writing With and for the Computer.* Cambridge: MIT Press.

Barrett, Edward. 1992. *Sociomedia: Multimedia, Hypermedia, and the Social Construction of Knowledge.* Cambridge: MIT Press.

Barry, H., M.K. Bacon, and I.L. Child. 1957. "A Cross-Cultural Survey of Some Sex Differences in Socialization." *Journal of Abnormal and Social Psychology* 55: 327–32.

Basow, Susan A. 1992. *Gender: Stereotypes and Roles,* third edition. Pacific Grove, Calif.: Brooks/Cole Publishing Company.

Bataille, Georges. 1986. Cited in "Introduction." In *Deconstruction in Context: Literature and Philosophy,* edited by Mark C. Taylor. Chicago: University of Chicago Press.

Baudrillard, Jean. 1983. *Les stratégies fatales.* Paris: Bernard Gasset.

Bauman, Zygmut. 1987. *Legislators and Interpreters: On Modernity, Postmodernity and Intellectuals.* Ithaca, N.Y.: Cornell University Press.

Bauman, Zygmut. 1992. *Intimations of Postmodernity.* London: Routledge.

Beauchamp, Tom L., and James F. Childress. 1989. *Principles of Biomedical Ethics,* third edition. New York: Oxford University Press.

de Beauvoir, Simone. 1953. *The Second Sex.* New York: Knopf.

Becker, Carl Lotus. 1932. *The Heavenly City of the Eighteenth-Century Philosophers.* New Haven: Yale University Press.

Becker, Ernest. 1973. *The Denial of Death.* New York: Free Press.

Belson, W. 1978. *Television Violence and the Adolescent Boy.* Hampshire, England: Saxon House.

Bem, Sandra Lipsitz. 1981. "Gender Schema Theory: A Cognitive Account of Sex-Typing." *Psychological Review* 88, 4 (July): 354–64.

Bem, Sandra Lipsitz. 1989. "Genital Knowledge and Gender Constancy in Preschool Children." *Child Development* 60: 649–62.

Bem, Sandra Lipsitz. 1993. *The Lenses of Gender: Transforming the Debate on Sexual Inequality.* New Haven: Yale University Press.

Benedikt, Michael (ed.). 1992. *Cyberspace: First Steps.* Cambridge: MIT Press.

Benjamin, Jessica. 1988. *The Bonds of Love: Psychoanalysis, Feminism, and the Problem of Domination.* New York: Pantheon.

Berger, Peter. 1963. *Invitation to Sociology.* Garden City, N.J.: Doubleday.

Berger, Peter, and Thomas Luckmann. 1966. *The Social Construction of Reality.* Garden City, N.Y.: Doubleday.

Berlin, Isaiah. 1976. *Vico and Herder: Two Studies in the History of Ideas.* New York: Viking Press.

Berman, Marshall. 1982. *All That Is Solid Melts into Air: The Experience of Modernity.* New York: Penguin Books.

Bernard, Jessie. 1982. *The Future of Marriage.* New Haven: Yale University Press.

Bernard, Luther L. 1919. "The Objective Viewpoint in Sociology." *American Journal of Sociology* 25: 298–325.

Best, Steven, and Douglas Kellner. 1991. *Postmodern Theory: Critical Interrogations.* New York: Guilford Press.

Bettelheim, Bruno. 1967. *The Empty Fortress: Infantile Autism and the Birth of the Self.* New York: Free Press.

Billig, Michael. 1987. *Arguing and Thinking: A Rhetorical Approach to Social Psychology.* Cambridge: Cambridge University Press.

Birdsell, J.B. 1972. *Human Evolution: An Introduction to the New Physical Anthropology.* Chicago: Rand McNally.

Black, M. 1962. *Models and Metaphors: Studies in Language and Philosophy.* Philadelphia: University of Pennsylvania Press.

Block, J.H. 1978. "Another Look at Sex Differentiation in the Socialization Behaviours of Mothers and Fathers." In *The Psychology of Women,* edited by Julie A. Sherman and Florence L. Denmark. New York: Psychological Dimensions.

Blumer, Herbert. 1969. *Symbolic Interactionism: Perspective and Method.* Englewood Cliffs, N.J.: Prentice-Hall.

Boas, Franz. [1911] 1961. *The Mind of Primitive Man.* New York: Macmillan.

Boas, Franz. 1940. *Race, Language and Culture.* New York: Free Press.

Boldt, Menno. 1993. *Surviving as Indians: The Challenge of Self-Government.* Toronto: University of Toronto Press.

Borges, Jorge L. 1966. *Other Inquisitions.* New York: Washington Square Press.

Bourdieu, Pierre. 1984. *Distinction: A Social Critique of the Judgement of Taste.* London: Routledge & Kegan Paul.

Bourdieu, Pierre. 1987. "What Makes a Social Class?" *Berkeley Journal of Sociology* 22: 1–18.

Bowlby, John. 1960. *Maternal Care and Mental Health: A Report Prepared on Behalf of the World Health Organization as a Contribution to the United Nations Programme for the Welfare of Homeless Children,* second edition. Geneva: World Health Organization.

Bowlby, John. 1965. *Child Care and the Growth of Love,* second edition. Baltimore: Penguin Books.

Bowler, Peter J. 1986. *Theories of Human Evolution: A Century of Debate, 1844-1944.* Baltimore: Johns Hopkins University Press.

Brannigan, August. 1984. *Crimes, Courts and Corrections.* Toronto: Holt, Rinehart and Winston.

Brantlinger, Patrick. [1941] 1983. *Bread & Circuses: Theories of Mass Culture as Social Decay.* Ithaca, N.Y.: Cornell University Press.

Bredo, Eric, and Walter Feinberg (eds.). 1982. *Knowledge and Values in Social and Educational Research.* Philadelphia: Temple University Press.

Brettell, Caroline B., and Carolyn F. Sargent (eds.). 1993. *Gender in Cross-Cultural Perspective.* Englewood Cliffs, N.J.: Prentice-Hall.

Briggs, Jean. 1970. *Never in Anger.* Cambridge: Harvard University Press.

Brisenden, Simon. 1987. "A Response to Physical Disability in 1986 and Beyond: A Report of the Royal College of Physicians." *Disability, Handicap and Society* 2, 2: 175–82.

Brown, Jane, and Laurie Schulze. 1990. "The Effects of Race, Gender and Fandom on Audience Interpretations of Madonna's Music Videos." *Journal of Communication* 40, 2 (Spring): 88–102.

Brown, L. David, and Rajesh Tandon. 1983. "Ideology and Political Economy in Inquiry: Action Research and Participatory Research." *Journal of Applied Behavioral Science* 19, 3: 277–94.

Brubaker, R. 1985. "Rethinking Classical Theory." *Theory and Society* 14: 745–73.

Bruner, Jerome S. *Acts of Meaning.* Cambridge: Harvard University Press.

Brym, Robert, and Rhonda Lenton. 1991. "The Distribution of Anti-Semitism in Canada in 1984." *Canadian Journal of Sociology* 16, 4: 411–17.

Brym, Robert, and Rhonda Lenton. 1992. "Anti-Semitism in Quebec: Reply to Langlois." *Canadian Journal of Sociology* 17, 2: 179–83.

Burkitt, Ian. 1991. *Social Selves: Theories of the Social Formation of Personality.* London: Sage Publications.

Burr, Chandler. 1993. "Homosexuality and Biology." *Atlantic Monthly* (March).

Buxton, David. 1990. *From the Avengers to Miami Vice.* Manchester: Manchester University Press.

Caldicott, Helen. 1984. *Missile Envy: The Arms Race and Nuclear War.* New York: William Morrow.

Cancian, Francesca M. 1987. *Love in America: Gender and Self-Development.* Cambridge: Cambridge University Press.

Candland, Douglas. 1993. *Feral Children and Clever Animals.* New York: Oxford University Press.

Cannon, W.B. 1942. "Voodoo Death." *American Anthropologist* 44, 2 (April–June).

Carey, S. 1985. *Conceptual Change in Childhood.* Cambridge: MIT/Bradford Press.

Carpenter, Edward. 1896. *Love's Coming of Age.* Manchester: Labour Press.

Carr, Edward Hallett. [1961] 1965. *What Is History?* New York: Knopf.

Carroll, Michael P. 1989. "Culture." In *Introduction to Sociology: A Canadian Focus,* third edition. Edited by James J. Teevan. Scarborough: Prentice-Hall.

Carter, D.B., and L.A. McCloskey. 1983–1984. "Peers and the Maintenance of Sex-Typed Behaviour: The Development of Children's Conceptions of Cross-Gender Behaviour in Their Peers." *Social Cognition* 2: 294–314.

485

Castro-Magana, Mariano, Moris Angulo, and Platon J. Collipp. 1984. "Management of the Child with Ambiguous Genitalia." *Medical Aspects of Human Sexuality* 18 (April): 172–88.

Cate, Rodney M., and Sally A. Lloyd. 1992. *Courtship*. Newbury Park, Calif.: Sage Publications.

Cheney, Dorothy, Robert Seyforth, and Barbara Smuts. 1986. "Social Relationships and Social Cognition." *Science* 234 (December 12): 1361–66.

Child, V. Gordon. 1956. *Man Makes Himself*. London: Watts.

Chodorow, Nancy. 1978. *The Reproduction of Mothering: Psychoanalysis and the Sociology of Gender*. Berkeley: University of California Press.

Clark, Susan, and Andrew S. Harvey. 1976. "The Sexual Division of Labour: The Use of Time." *Atlantis* 2, 1 (Fall): 46–65.

Clement, Wallace. 1975. *The Canadian Corporate Elite: An Analysis of Economic Power*. Toronto: McClelland & Stewart.

Cleverly, John, and D.C. Phillips. 1986. *Visions of Childhood: Influential Models from Locke to Spock*. New York: Teachers College Press.

Clifford, James. 1988. *The Predicament of Culture*. Cambridge: Cambridge University Press.

Coleman, William. 1964. *George Cuvier, Zoologist: A Study in the History of Evolution Theory*. Cambridge: Harvard University Press.

Collins, Randall. 1988. *Theoretical Sociology*. San Diego: Harcourt Brace Jovanovich.

Comstock, G. and E. Strasburger. 1990. "Deceptive Appearances: Television Violence and Aggressive Behaviour." *Journal of Adolescent Health Care* 11, 1: 31–44.

Comte, A. 1970. *Introduction to Positive Philosophy*, translated and edited by F. Ferré. Indianapolis: Bobbs-Merrill.

Condillac, Étienne Bonnot de. 1930. *Treatise on the Sensations*, translated by Geraldine Carr. Los Angeles: University of Southern California.

Condorcet, Jean, and Antoine-Nicolas de Caritat, Marquis de. 1955. *Sketch for a Historical Picture of the Progress of the Human Mind*. New York: Noonday Press.

Cook, Judith A., and Mary Margaret Fonow. 1990. "Knowledge and Women's Interests: Issues of Epistemology and Methodology in Feminist Sociological Research." In *Feminist Research Methods: Exemplary Readings in the Social Sciences*, edited by Joyce McCarl Nielsen. Boulder: Westview Press.

Coontz, S. 1988. *The Social Origins of Private Life: A History of American Families, 1600-1900*. New York: Verson.

Copernicus, Nicolaus. [1543] 1976. *On the Revolutions of the Heavenly Spheres*. New York: Barnes & Noble.

Count, Earl W. (ed.). 1950. *This Is Race: An Anthology Selected from the International Literature on the Races of Man*. New York: Henry Schwanan.

Craib, Ian. 1984. *Modern Social Theory from Parsons to Habermas*. Brighton: Harvester Press.

Crichton, Michael. 1990. *Jurassic Park*. New York: Knopf.

Crompton, Rosemary. 1993. *Class and Stratification: An Introduction to Current Debates*. Cambridge: Polity Press.

Cullen, F., W. Maakestadt, and G. Cavender. 1987. *Corporate Crime Under Attack: The Ford Pinto Case and Beyond*. Cincinnati: Anderson.

Curtiss, Susan. 1977. *Genie: A Psycholinguistic Study of a Modern-Day "Wild Child."* New York: Academic Press.

Curtus, J.P. 1968. *Anglo-Saxons and Celts: A Study of Anti-Irish Prejudice in Victorian England.* Bridgeport, Conn.: University of Bridgeport.

Cuvier, Baron Georges von. 1817. *Le règne animal distribué d'après son organisation: pour servir de base à l'histoire naturelle des animaux et d'introduction à l'anatomie comparée.* Paris: Deterville.

Dahrendorf, Ralf. 1964. "Recent Changes in the Class Structure of European Societies." *Daedalus* 93: 225–70.

Darroch, Vivian, and Ronald J. Silvers. 1982. *Interpretive Human Studies: An Introduction to Phenomenological Research.* Washington, D.C.: University Press of America.

Darwin, Charles. 1871. *Descent of Man,* 2 volumes. London: J. Murray.

Darwin, Charles. [1871] 1981. *The Descent of Man.* Princeton, N.J.: Princeton University Press.

Darwin, Charles. [1859] 1968. *The Origin of Species.* Harmondsworth, England: Penguin.

Daubney, D. (Chairman). 1988. *Taking Responsibility: Report of the Standing Committee on Justice and Solicitor General on Aspects of Corrections.* Ottawa: Supply and Services Canada.

Davidson, Iain, and William Noble. 1989. "The Archaeology of Depiction and Language." *Current Anthropology* 30: 125–56.

Davis, Kingsley. 1949. "Final Note on a Case of Extreme Isolation." In *Sociological Analysis,* edited by Logan Wilson and William Kolb. New York: Harcourt Brace and World.

Davis, Kingsley. 1965. *Human Society.* New York: Macmillan.

Davis, K., and W.E. Moore. [1945] 1964. "Some Principles of Stratification." Reprinted in *Sociological Theory,* edited by L.A. Coser and B. Rosenberg. London: Collier–Macmillan.

DeJong, Gerben. 1979. "Independent Living: From Social Movement to Analytic Paradigm." *Archives of Physical Medicine and Rehabilitation* 60, 10 (October): 435–46.

Deleuze, Gilles. 1983. *Nietzsche and Philosophy,* translated by Hugh Tomlinson. New York: Columbia University Press.

Demo, David, and Michael Hughes. 1990. "Socialization and Racial Identity Among Black Americans." *Social Psychology Quarterly* 53 (December): 364–74.

Derrida, Jacques. 1967. *Writing and Difference.* Chicago: University of Chicago Press.

Descartes, René. [1641] 1993. *Meditations on First Philosophy.* New York: Routledge.

Dewhurst, Christopher J., and Ronald R. Gordon. 1969. *The Intersexual Disorders.* London: Baillière, Tindall and Cassell.

Diamond, Jared. 1992. "Turning a Man." *Discover* (June).

Diamond, Sondra. 1981. "Growing up with Parents of a Handicapped Child: A Handicapped Person's Perspective." In *Understanding and Working with Parents of Children with Special Needs,* edited by James L. Paul. New York: Holt, Rinehart and Winston.

Dixon, R.M.W. 1982. *Where Have All the Adjectives Gone?* Berlin: Walter de Grayter.

Dobzhansky, T. 1962. *Mankind Evolving: The Evolution of the Human Species.* New Haven: Yale University Press.

Donaldson, Margaret. 1979. *Children's Minds.* New York: Norton.

Donzelot, Jacques. 1979. *The Policing of Families.* New York: Pantheon Books.

Doran, Kevin. 1989. *What Is a Person? The Concept and the Implications for Ethics.* Lewiston, N.Y.: E. Mellen Press.

Douglas, Mary. 1984. *Purity and Danger: An Analysis of the Concepts of Pollution and Taboo.* London: Routledge.

Dreyfus, Hubert L., and Paul Rabinow. 1982. *Michel Foucault, Beyond Structuralism and Hermeneutics.* Chicago: University of Chicago Press.

Duffy, Ann, and Nancy Mandell. 1994. "The Widening Gap: Social Inequality and Poverty." In *Canadian Society: Understanding and Surviving in the 1990s,* edited by Dan Glenday and Ann Duffy. Toronto: McClelland & Stewart.

Durant, John. 1981. "The Myth of Human Evolution." *New Universities Quarterly.* 35: 425–38.

Durkheim, Émile. [1895] 1964. *The Rules of Sociological Method,* eighth edition. Translated by Sarah A. Solovay and John H. Mueller and edited by George E.G. Catlin. New York: Free Press.

Durkheim, Émile. [1895] 1982. *The Rules of Sociological Method and Selected Texts on Sociology and Its Method,* edited by Steven Lukes. New York: Free Press.

Durkheim, Émile. [1897] 1951. *Suicide: A Study in Sociology.* Glencoe, Ill.: Free Press.

Durkheim, Émile. [1912] 1965. *The Elementary Forms of Religious Life.* New York: Free Press.

Durkheim, Émile. [1951] 1966. *Suicide: A Study in Sociology,* translated by John Spaulding and George Simpson. New York: Free Press.

Dyer, Gwynne. 1985. *War.* New York: Crown.

Eccles, J.S. 1989. "Bringing Young Women to Maths and Science." In *Gender and Thought: Psychological Perspectives,* edited by M. Crawford and M. Gentry. New York: Springer-Verlag.

Economic Council of Canada. 1992. *The New Face of Poverty: Income Security Needs of Canadian Families.* Ottawa: Ministry of Supply and Services.

Edelman, Murray J. 1988. *Constructing the Political Spectacle.* Chicago: University of Chicago Press.

Edgell, Stephen. 1993. *Class.* London: Routledge.

Edgerton, Robert. 1967. *The Cloak of Competence: Stigma in the Lives of the Mentally Retarded.* Berkeley: University of California Press.

Ehrenreich, Barbara. 1983. *The Hearts of Men: American Dreams and the Flight from Commitment.* New York: Anchor Press.

Ehrenreich, Barbara, and Deirdre English. 1989. *For Her Own Good: One Hundred and Fifty Years of Experts' Advice to Women.* New York: Doubleday.

Eichenwald, Kurt. 1987. "Grown-Ups Gather at the Comic Book Stand." *New York Times* (September 30).

Eichler, Margrit. 1987. "And the Work Never Ends: Feminist Contributions." In *Gender Roles: Doing What Comes Naturally?* edited by E.D. Salamon and B.W. Robinson. Toronto: Methuen.

Ekmon, G., et al. 1984. "The International Language of Gestures." *Psychology Today* (May).

Elias, Norbert. 1978. *The Civilizing Process.* New York: Urizen Books.

Elliott, Jean-Leonard, and Augie Fleras. 1992. *Unequal Relations: An Introduction to Race and Ethnic Dynamics in Canada.* Scarborough: Prentice-Hall.

Ellis, Godfrey, and Larry Petersen. 1992. "Socialization Values and Parental Control Techniques: A Cross-Cultural Analysis of Child-Rearing." *Journal of Comparative Family Studies* 23, 1 (Spring): 39–54.

Elmer-Dewitt, Philip. 1994. "Battle for the Soul of the Internet." *Time* (July 25): 40–46.

Ember, C. 1973. "Feminine Task Assignment and the Social Behaviour of Boys." *Ethos* I: 424–39.

Employment and Immigration Canada. 1985. "Trends in the Employment Opportunities of Women in Canada, 1930–1980." *Equity in Employment: A Royal Commission Report,* volume 2. Ottawa: Supply and Services.

Epstein, Cynthia Fuchs. 1988. *Deceptive Distinctions: Sex, Gender and the Social Order.* New Haven: Yale University Press.

Etienne, Mona, and Eleanor Leacock. 1980. *Women and Colonization: Anthropological Perspectives.* New York: Praeger.

Eyer, Diane E. 1992. *Mother-Infant Bonding: A Scientific Fiction.* New Haven: Yale University Press.

Fader, Edward. 1955. *Comic Book Regulation.* Berkeley: Bureau of Public Administration.

Fagot, B.I., R. Hagan, M.D. Leinbach, and S. Kronsberg. 1985. "Differential Reactions to Assertive and Communicative Acts of Toddler Boys and Girls." *Child Development* 56: 1499–1505.

Fausto-Sterling, Anne. 1985. *Myths of Gender: Biological Theories About Women and Men.* New York: Basic Books.

Fausto-Sterling, Anne. 1993. "The Five Sexes." *The Sciences* (March/April): 20–21.

Featherstone, Mike. 1988. *Postmodernism: A Theory, Culture and Society.* Special Issue. London: Sage.

Febvre, L., and H.J. Martin. 1976. *The Coming of the Book.* London: New Left Books.

Fedigan, Linda Marie. 1982. *Primate Paradigms: Sex Roles and Social Bonds.* Montreal: Eden Press.

Feguson, Adam. 1971. *An Essay on the History of Civil Society.* New York: Garland.

Feyerabend, Paul. 1993. *Against Method: Outline of an Anarchistic Theory of Knowledge,* third edition. London: Verso.

Fiske, John. 1989. *Reading the Popular.* Boston: Urwin and Hyman.

Flax, Jane. 1990. *Thinking Fragments: Psychoanalysis, Feminism and Postmodernism in the Contemporary West.* Berkeley: University of California Press.

Forcese, Dennis. 1975. *The Canadian Class Structure.* Toronto: McGraw-Hill Ryerson.

Foucault, Michel. 1970. *The Order of Things: An Archaeology of the Human Sciences.* New York: Vintage Books.

Foucault, Michel. 1973. *The Birth of the Clinic: An Archaeology of Medical Perception.* New York: Vintage Books.

Foucault, Michel. 1977. "Nietzsche, Genealogy, History." In *Language, Counter-Memory, Practice: Selected Essays and Interviews,* edited by Donald F. Bouchard, translated by Donald E. Bouchard and Sherry Simon. Ithaca, N.Y.: Cornell University Press.

Foucault, Michel. 1979. *Discipline and Punish: The Birth of the Prison.* Translated by Alan Sheridan. New York: Vintage/Random House.

Foucault, Michel. 1980. *The History of Sexuality,* volume 1. Translated by Robert Hurley. New York: Viking.

489

Foucault, Michel. 1982. "The Subject and Power." In *Michel Foucault: Beyond Structuralism and Hermeneutics,* edited by Hubert Dreyfus and Paul Rabinow. Chicago: University of Chicago Press.

Foucault, Michel. 1984. "What Is Enlightenment?" In *The Foucault Reader*, edited by Paul Rabinow. New York: Pantheon.

Frank, Lisa, and Paul Smith. 1993. "Introduction: How to Use Your New Madonna." In *Madonna,* edited by Lisa Frank and Paul Smith. Pittsburgh: Cleiss Press.

Fraser, Nancy. 1989. *Unruly Practices: Power, Discourse and Gender in Contemporary Social Theory.* Cambridge: Polity Press.

Freedman, J.L. 1984. "Effect of Television Violence on Aggressiveness." *Psychological Bulletin* 96: 227–46.

Freedman, J.L. 1986. "Television Violence and Aggression: A Rejoinder." *Psychological Bulletin* 100: 372–78.

Freeman, Derek. 1983. *Margaret Mead and Samoa: The Making and Unmaking of an Anthropological Myth.* Cambridge: Harvard University Press.

French, Marilyn. 1985. *Beyond Power: On Women, Men, and Morals.* New York: Summit Books.

Freud, Sigmund. [1923] 1962. *The Ego and the Id.* New York: W.W. Norton.

Freud, Sigmund. [1930] 1963. *Civilization and Its Discontents*, translated and edited by James Strachey. London: Hogarth Press.

Freud, Sigmund. [1933] 1989. *New Introductory Lectures on Psychoanalysis.* New York: W.W. Norton.

Frideres, James. 1991. "From the Bottom Up: Institutional Structures and the Indian People." In *Social Issues and Contradictions in Canadian Society*, edited by B. Singh Bolaria. Toronto: Harcourt Brace Jovanovich.

Frisby, David, and Derek Sayers. 1986. *Society.* New York: Routledge, Chapman and Hall.

Gadamer, Hans-Georg. 1986. *Truth and Method.* New York: Crossroad.

Galen. 1968. *On the Usefulness of the Parts of the Body.* Ithaca, N.Y.: Cornell University Press.

Galen. 1978–84. *On the Doctrines of Hippocrates and Plato*, 3 volumes. Translated with commentary by Phillip Delacy. Berlin: Akademie-Verlag.

Galgan, Gerald J. 1982. *The Logic of Modernity.* New York: New York University Press.

Galton, Francis. 1869. *Hereditary Genius: An Inquiry into Its Laws and Consequences.* London: Macmillan.

Galton, Francis. 1883. *Inquiries into Human Faculty.* London: Dent.

Game, Ann. 1991. *Undoing the Social: Towards a Deconstructive Sociology.* Toronto: University of Toronto Press.

Gannagé, Charlene. 1986. *Double Day, Double Bind.* Toronto: Women's Press.

Garfinkel, Harold. 1967. *Studies in Ethnomethodology.* Englewood Cliffs, N.J.: Prentice-Hall.

Gay, Peter. 1966. *The Enlightenment, an Interpretation: The Rise of Modern Paganism.* New York: Knopf.

Gay, Peter. 1989. *Freud: A Life for Our Time.* New York: Doubleday Anchor.

Geertz, Clifford. 1984. *Local Knowledge.* New York: Basic Books.

Gelman, R., and C.R. Gallistel. 1978. *The Child's Understanding of Numbers.* Cambridge: Harvard University Press.

Gerth, Hans Heinrich, and C.W. Mills (eds.). 1946. *From Max Weber: Essays in Sociology,* translated and with an introduction by H.H. Gerth and C.W. Mills. New York: Oxford University Press.

Gerth, Hans Heinrich, and C.W. Mills. [1954] 1964. *Character and Social Structure: The Psychology of Social Institutions.* New York: Harcourt, Brace & World.

Gibson, William. 1984. *Neuromancer.* New York: Ace Books.

Giddens, Anthony. 1991. *Introduction to Sociology.* New York: W.W. Norton & Company.

Giddens, A., and D. Held (eds.). 1982. *Classes, Power and Conflict.* Macmillan: London.

Gitlin, Tod. 1989. "Post Modernism: Roots and Politics." *Dissent* (Winter): 100–108.

Godelier, Maurice. 1981. "The Origins of Male Domination." *New Left Review* 127 (May-June).

Godelier, Maurice. 1986. *The Making of Great Men: Male Domination and Power Among the New Guinea Baruya,* translated by Rupert Swyer. New York: Cambridge University Press.

Goffman, Erving. 1959. *The Presentation of Self in Everyday Life.* Garden City, N.Y.: Anchor.

Goffman, Erving. 1961. *Asylums: Essays in the Social Situation of Mental Patients and Other Inmates.* New York: Anchor Books.

Goffman, Erving. 1963. *Stigma: Notes on the Management of Spoiled Identity.* Englewood Cliffs, N.J.: Prentice-Hall.

Goffman, Erving. 1978. "Stigma and Social Identity." In *Social Deviance,* second edition, edited by Robert A. Farrell and Victoria Lynn Swigert. Philadelphia: J.B. Lippincott.

Goldberg, David Theo. 1993. *Racist Culture: Philosophy and the Politics of Meaning.* Oxford: Blackwell.

Goldberg, Gertrude Schaffner. 1990. "Canada: Bordering on the Feminization of Poverty." In *The Feminization of Poverty: Only in America?* edited by Gertrude Schaffner Goldberg and Eleanor Kremen. New York: Praeger.

Goldman, R.J., and J.D.G. Goldman. 1982. *Children's Sexual Thinking.* London: Routledge & Kegan Paul.

Goode, David. 1984. "Socially Produced Identities, Intimacy, and the Problem of Competence Among the Retarded." In *Special Education and Social Interests,* edited by Ian Barton and Sally Tomlinson. London: Croom Helm.

Goodman, Nelson. 1978. *Ways of Worldmaking.* Indianapolis: Hackett Press.

Gordon, Robert. 1980. "Research on IQ, Race, and Delinquency: Taboo or Not Taboo?" In *Taboos in Criminology,* edited by Edward Sagarin. Beverly Hills: Sage Publications.

Gordon, Robert. 1987. "SES versus IZ in the Race-IZ-Delinquency Model." In *International Journal of Sociology and Social Policy* 7, 3: 30–96.

Gossett, T.F. 1965. *Race: The History of an Idea in America.* New York: Schocken Books.

Gottesman, I.I. 1968. "Biogenetics of Race and Class." In *Social Class, Race and Psychological Development,* edited by M. Deutsch, I. Katz, and A.R. Jensen. New York: Holt, Rinehart and Winston.

Gould, Stephen Jay. 1981. *The Mismeasure of Man.* New York: W.W. Norton.

Gould, Stephen Jay. 1983. "Bound by the Great Chain." *Natural History* (November): 20–24.

Gould, Stephen Jay. 1991. "The Birth of the Two-Sex World." *New York Review of Books* 38, 11 (June 13): 11–13.

Gouldner, Alvin. 1971. *The Coming Crisis of Western Sociology.* London: Heinemann.

Gramsci, Antonio. 1971. *Selections from the Prison Notebooks.* New York: International Publishers.

Greenwood, Davydd J. 1984. *The Taming of Evolution: The Persistence of Nonevolutionary Views in the Study of Humans.* Ithaca, N.Y.: Cornell University Press.

Groce, Nora E. 1985. *Everyone Here Spoke Sign Language: Hereditary Deafness on Martha's Vineyard.* Cambridge: Harvard University Press.

Grosz, Elizabeth. 1991. "Drive." In *Feminism and Psychoanalysis: A Critical Dictionary,* edited by Elizabeth Wright. Cambridge, Mass.: Blackwell Publishers.

Grunwald, Lisa. 1993. "Babies Are Smarter Than We Think." *Life* (July).

Guo, Jin. 1992. *Voices of Chinese Canadian Women.* Toronto: Women's Press.

Habermas, Jürgen. 1970. *Toward a Rational Society: Student Protest, Science and Politics.* Boston: Beacon Press.

Habermas, Jürgen. 1971. *Knowledge and Human Interest,* translated by Jeremy J. Shapiro. Boston: Beacon Press.

Hacking, Ian. 1983. *Representing and Intervening: Introductory Topics in the Philosophy of Natural Science.* Cambridge: Cambridge University Press.

Hahn, Harlan. 1993. "Can Disability Be Beautiful?" In *Perspectives on Disability,* second edition, edited by Mark Nagler. Palo Alto: Health Markets Research.

Hale-Benson, Janice. 1982. *Black Children, Their Roots, Culture, and Learning Styles.* Provo, Utah: Brigham Young University Press.

Hall, Budd. 1984. "Research, Commitment and Action: The Role of Participatory Research." *International Review of Education* 30, 3: 289–99.

Hall, Stuart. 1982. "The Rediscovery of 'Ideology': Return of the Repressed in Media Studies." In *Culture, Society, and the Media,* edited by Michael Curveitch, Tony Bennett, James Curran, and Janet Woolacott. London: Methuen.

Hall, Stuart. 1986. "Gramsci's Relevance for the Study of Race and Ethnicity." In *Journal of Communication Inquiry* 10, 2: 5–27.

Hall, Stuart. 1992. "Cultural Studies and Its Theoretical Legacies." In *Cultural Studies,* edited by Lawrence Grossberg, Gary Nelson, and Paula Treichler, 277–85. New York: Routledge.

Hampson, G., and J.L. Hampson. "Hermaphroditism: Recommendations Concerning Assignment of Sex, Change of Sex and Psychological Management." *Bulletin of the Johns Hopkins Hospital* 97: 284–300.

Hampson, Norman. 1982. *The Enlightenment.* Harmondsworth, England: Penguin.

Hanson, Allan. 1989. "The Making of the Maori: Culture, Invention, and Its Logic." *American Anthropologist* 91: 890–902.

Harasim, Linda. 1993. "Networlds: Networks as Social Space." In *Global Networks: Computers and International Communication,* edited by Linda Harasim. Cambridge: MIT Press.

Haraway, Donna Jeanne. 1981. "In the Beginning Was the Word: The Genesis of Biological Theory." In *Signs: Journal of Women in Culture and Society* 6, 3: 469–81.

Haraway, Donna Jeanne. 1989. *Primate Visions: Gender, Race and Nature in the World of Modern Science.* New York: Routledge.

Haraway, Donna Jeanne. 1991. *Simians, Cyborgs and Women: The Reinvention of Nature.* London: Free Association Books.

492

Harcourt, Alexander. 1988. "Alliances in Contests and Social Intelligence." In *Social Expertise and the Evolution of Intellect,* edited by R. Byrne and A. Whitten. Oxford: Oxford University Press.

Harding, Sandra G. 1986. *The Science Question in Feminism.* Ithaca, N.Y.: Cornell University Press.

Harlow, Harry. 1958. *Biological and Biochemical Bases of Behavior.* Madison: University of Wisconsin Press.

Harlow, Harry, and Margaret Kuenne. 1974. "Social Deprivation in Monkeys." In *Readings in Psychology Today,* edited by James B. Maas. Del Mar, Calif.: CRM Books.

Harmon, Willis. 1988. "The Postmodern Heresy: Consciousness as Causal." In *The Reenchantment of Science: Postmodern Proposals,* edited by D.R. Griffin. Albany: State University of New York Press.

Harms, John B. 1992. "Critical Theory and Teaching Sociology: Critique in the Classroom." In *Free Inquiry in Creative Sociology* 20, 2 (November): 179–88.

Harris, Marvin. 1974. *Cows, Pigs, Wars & Witches: The Riddles of Culture.* New York: Random House.

Hartley, Keith, and Tod Sandler (eds.). 1990. *The Economics of Defence Spending: An International Survey.* Routledge: London.

Hartsock, Nancy. 1983. "The Feminist Standpoint: Developing the Ground for a Specifically Feminist Historical Materialism." In *Discovering Reality,* edited by Sandra Harding and Merrill B. Hintikka, 283–310. Dordrecht, Holland: D. Reidel Publishing Co.

Hazelrigg, Lawrence E. 1989. *Social Science and the Challenge of Relativism,* 2 volumes. Tallahassee: Florida State University Press.

Hearn, Frank. 1985. *Reason and Freedom in Sociological Thought.* Boston: Allen & Unwin.

Hekma, Gert. "A Female Soul in a Male Body: Sexual Inversion as Gender Inversion in Nineteenth-Century Sexology." In *Third Sex, Third Gender,* edited by Gilbert Herdt, 213–39. New York: Zone Books.

Hekman, Susan J. 1986. *Hermeneutics and the Sociology of Knowledge.* Notre Dame, Ind.: University of Notre Dame Press.

Hendrick, Susan, and Clyde Hendrick. 1992. *Romantic Love.* Newbury Park: Sage Publications.

Hennigan, K.M., M.L. Del Rosario, L. Heath, T.D. Cook, J.D. Wharton, and B. Calder. 1982. "Impact of the Introduction of Television on Crime in the United States: Empirical Findings and Theoretical Implications." *Journal of Personality and Social Psychology* 42: 461–77.

Herdt, Gilbert. 1987. *The Sambia: Ritual and Gender in New Guinea.* New York: Holt, Rinehart and Winston.

Herdt, Gilbert. 1993. "Sexual Repression, Social Control, and Gender Hierarchy in Sambia Culture." In *Sex and Gender Hierarchies,* edited by Barbara Diane Miller. Cambridge University Press.

Herdt, Gilbert. 1994(a). "Introduction: Third Sexes and Third Genders." In *Third Sex, Third Gender,* edited by Gilbert Herdt. New York: Zone Books.

Herdt, Gilbert. 1994(b). "Mistaken Sex: Culture, Biology and the Third Sex in New Guinea." In *Third Sex, Third Gender,* edited by Gilbert Herdt, 419–45. New York: Zone Books.

Heritage, John. 1984. *Garfinkel and Ethnomethodology*. Cambridge and New York: Polity Press.

Hertz, Friedrich. 1928. *Race and Civilization*. London: Kegan Paul, Trench, Trubner & Co.

Hill, Kim. 1993. "On Why Male Foragers Hunt and Share Food." *Current Anthropology* 34 (December): 701–10.

Hill, Willard W. 1935. "The Status of the Hermaphrodite and Transvestite in Navaho Culture." *American Anthropologist* 37.

Himmelfarb, Gertrude. 1968. *Darwin and the Darwinian Revolution*. New York: W.W. Norton.

Hirschfeld, Magnus. 1938. *Racism*. London: Gollancz.

Hirst, Paul Q., and Penny Woolley. 1981. *Social Relations and Human Attributes*. London and New York: Tavistock Publications.

Hodge, Robert, and Gunther Kress. 1988. *Social Semiotics*. Ithaca, N.Y.: Cornell University Press.

hooks, bell. 1993. "Power to the Pussy: We Don't Wanna Be Dicks in Drag." In *Madonnarama*, edited by Lisa Frank and Paul Smith. Pittsburgh: Cleis Press.

Hopkins, Gerald. 1989. *Education* 109, 3 (Spring): 352–57.

Horkheimer, Max, and Theodor Adorno. 1972. *The Dialectic of Enlightenment*. New York: Seabury.

Howell, Nancy. 1979. *Demography of the Dobe !Kung*. New York: Academic Press.

Hoyningen-Huene, Paul. 1993. *Restructuring Scientific Revolutions: Thomas S. Kuhn's Philosophy of Science*. Chicago: University of Chicago Press.

Hubbard, Ruth. 1990. *The Politics of Women's Biology*. New Brunswick: Rutgers University Press.

Huesmann, K.M., K. Lagerspetz, and L.D. Eron. 1984. "Intervening Variables in the TV Violence-Aggression Relation: Evidence from Two Countries." *Developmental Psychology* 20: 746–75.

Humphrey, Nicholas. 1986. *The Inner Eye*. London: Faber and Faber.

Husserl, Edmund. 1970. *Crisis of European Sciences and Transcendental Phenomenology: An Introduction to Phenomenological Philosophy*. Evanston, Ill.: Northwestern University Press.

Huston, A.C. 1983. "Sex-Typing." In *Handbook of Child Psychology*, edited by P.H. Mussen. New York: Wiley.

Imperato-McGinley, Julliane, et al. 1974. "Steroid 5-alpha Reductase Deficiency in Man: An Inherited Form of Male Pseudohermaphroditism." *Science* 186.

Imperato-McGinley, Julliane, et al. 1979. "Androgens and the Evolution of Male-Gender Identity Among Male Pseudohermaphrodites with 5-alpha Reductase Deficiency." *New England Journal of Medicine* 300.

Jaggar, Alison M. 1983. *Feminist Politics and Human Nature*. Totowa, N.J.: Rowman and Allanheld.

James, C.L.R. 1963. *The Black Jacobins: Toussaint L'Ouverture and the San Domingo Revolution,* second edition. New York: Vintage Books.

Jensen, A.R. 1969. "How Much Can We Boost IQ and Scholastic Achievements?" *Harvard Educational Review* 33: 1–123.

Joas, Hans. 1985. *G.H. Mead: A Contemporary Re-Examination of His Thought.* Cambridge: Polity Press.

Jolly, Alison. 1985. "The Evolution of Primate Behaviour." *American Scientist* 73: 230–39.

Katcher, A. 1955. "The Discrimination of Sex Differences by Young Children." *Journal of Genetic Psychology* 87: 131–43.

Keat, Russell. 1979. "Positivism and Statistics in Social Science." In *Demystifying Social Statistics,* edited by John Irvine, Ian Miles, and Jeff Evans. London: Pluto Press.

Keesing, R.M. 1981. *Cultural Anthropology: A Contemporary Perspective.* CBS College Publishing.

Keil, F.C. 1989. *Concepts, Kinds, and Cognitive Development.* Cambridge: MIT/Bradford Press.

Keller, Fox. 1993. "Fractured Images of Science, Language, and Power: A Postmodern Optic or Just Bad Eyesight?" In *Knowledges: Historical and Critical Studies in Disciplinarity*, edited by Ellen Messer-Davidow, David R. Shumway, and David J. Sylvan. Charlottsville, Va.: University Press of Virginia.

Kessler, Suzanne J. 1990. "The Medical Construction of Gender: Case Management of Intersexed Infants." *Signs* 16, 1: 5.

Kettle, Martin. 1993 "Television and Violence." *Guardian Weekly.* London (May 14).

King, Patricia M., and Karen Strohm Kitchener. 1994. *Developing Reflective Judgement: Understanding and Promoting Intellectual Growth and Critical Thinking in Adolescents and Adults.* San Francisco: Jossey-Bass Publishers.

Kinsey, Alfred Charles. 1948. *Sexual Behaviour in the Human Male.* Philadelphia: W.B. Saunders.

Kirby, Sandra, and Kate McKenna. 1989. *Experience, Research, Social Change: Methods from the Margins.* Toronto: Garamond Press.

Kirkham, Maurice. 1993. "Two-Year Follow-Up of Skills Training for the Mothers of Children with Disabilities." *American Journal of Mental Retardation* 97, 5: 509–20.

Kluckhohn, Clyde. 1949. *Mirror for Man.* New York: McGraw-Hill.

Knutilla, Murray. 1993. *Sociology Revisited.* Toronto: McClelland & Stewart.

Kohlberg, Lawrence. 1966. "A Cognitive-Developmental Analysis of Children's Sex-Role Concepts and Attitudes." In *The Development of Sex Differences*, edited by Eleanor Maccoby. Stanford: Stanford University Press.

Kohn, Melvin L. 1951. "Social Class and Parental Values." *The American Journal of Sociology* 64, 4 (January): 337–51.

Kohn, Melvin L. 1969. *Class and Conformity: A Study in Values.* Homewood, Ill.: Dorsey Press.

Kohn, Melvin, L. 1979. "The Effects of Social Class on Parental Values and Practices." In *The American Family: Dying or Developing?* edited by D. Reiss and H. Hoffman. New York: Plenum.

Kohn, Melvin, and Carmi Schooler. 1982. "Job Conditions and Personality: A Longitudinal Assessment of Their Reciprocal Effects." *American Journal of Sociology* 87, 6 (May): 1257–83.

Konner, Melvin, and Carol Worthman. 1980. "Nursing Frequency, Gonadal Function, and Birth Spacing Among !Kung Hunter-Gatherers." *Science* 207: 788–90.

Kroeber, Alfred Louis. [1917] 1952. *The Nature of Culture.* Chicago: University of Chicago Press.

Kroker, Arthur. 1993. "Codes of Privilege." In *Mondo 2000* 11: 62–63.

Kühl, Stefan. 1994. *The Nazi Connection: Eugenics, American Racism, and German National Socialism*. New York: Oxford University Press.

Kuhn, Thomas. 1962. *The Structure of Scientific Revolutions*. Chicago: University of Chicago Press.

Kuhn, Thomas. 1970. *The Structure of Scientific Revolutions*, second edition. Chicago: University of Chicago Press.

La Prairie, C. 1987. "Native Women and Crime in Canada: A Theoretical Model." In *To Few to Count: Canadian Women in Conflict with the Law,* edited by E. Adelberg and C. Currie. Vancouver: Press Gang.

Lakoff, George. 1987. *Women, Fire and Dangerous Things: What Categories Reveal About the Mind*. Chicago: University of Chicago Press.

Lakoff, George, and Mark Johnson. 1980. *Metaphors We Live By*. Chicago: University of Chicago Press.

Laitmann, J.T. 1983. "The Anatomy of Human Speech." *Natural History* (August): 20–27.

Landau, Misia. 1987. "Paradise Lost: The Theme of Terrestriality in Human Evolution." In *The Rhetoric of the Human Sciences*, edited by John S. Nelson, Allan Megill, and Donald N. McClosky, 111–24. Madison: University of Wisconsin Press.

Lapatpí, Pablo. 1988. "Participatory Research? A New Research Paradigm?" *Alberta Journal of Education Research* 34, 3: 310–19.

Laqueur, Thomas. 1990. *Making Sex: Body and Gender from the Greeks to Freud*. Cambridge: Harvard University Press.

Laqueur, Thomas, and Catherine Gallagher (eds.). 1987. *The Making of the Modern Body: Sexuality and Society in the Nineteenth Century*. Berkeley: University of California Press.

Lasker, G.W. 1973. *Physical Anthropology*. New York: Holt, Rinehart and Winston.

Latour, Bruno. 1988. *The Pasteurization of France*. Cambridge: Harvard University Press.

Latour, Bruno, and Steve Woolgar. 1979. *Laboratory Life: The Social Construction of Scientific Facts*. Beverly Hills: Sage Publications.

Leacock, Eleanor. 1993. "Women in Samoan History: A Further Critique of Derek Freeman." In *Sex and Gender Hierarchies,* edited by Barbara Diane Miller. Cambridge University Press.

Lebow, Richard Ned. 1976. *White Britain and Black Ireland: The Influence of Stereotypes on Colonial Policy*. Philadelphia: Institute for the Study of Human Issues.

Lee, Laurie. 1965. *Cider with Rosie*. London: Chatto & Windus.

Lee, May. 1993. "Finding the Way Home through Issues of Gender, Race and Class." In *Returning the Gaze*, edited by Himani Bannerji. Toronto: Sister Vision.

Leiderman, P.H. 1981. "Human Mother-Infant Bonding: Is There a Sensitive Phase? In *Behavioral Development: The Bielefeld Interdisciplinary Project,* edited by K. Immelmann, G.W. Barlow, L. Petrinovich, and M. Main. Cambridge University Press.

Leifer, A.D., P.H. Leiderman, C.R. Barnett, and J.A. Williams. 1972. "Effects of Mother-Infant Separation on Maternal Attachment Behaviour." *Child Development* 43: 1203–18.

Lengermann, Patricia Madoo, and Ruth A. Wallace. 1985. *Gender in America: Social Control and Social Change*. Englewood Cliffs, N.J.: Prentice-Hall.

Lévi-Strauss, Claude. 1963. *Totemism*. Boston: Beacon Press.

Lévi-Strauss, Claude. 1969. *The Elementary Structures of Kinship.* London: Eyre and Spottiswoode.

Levin, S.M., J. Balistrieri, and M. Schukit. 1972. "The Development of Sexual Discrimination in Children." *Journal of Child Psychology and Psychiatry* 13: 47–53.

Levy, Steven. 1984. *Hackers.* Garden City, N.Y. Anchor Press/Doubleday.

Lewin, Roger. 1988. *Bones of Contention: Controversies in the Search for Human Origins.* New York: Simon and Schuster.

Lewin, Roger. 1993. *Human Evolution: An Illustrated Introduction,* third edition. Boston: Blackwell Scientific Publications.

Lewis, Oscar. 1966. *La Vida: A Puerto Rican Family in the Culture of Poverty—San Juan and New York.* New York: Random House.

Lifton, Robert J. 1986. *The Nazi Doctors: Medical Killing and the Psychology of Genocide.* New York: Basic Books.

Lincoln, Abraham. 1894. *Complete Works,* edited by John G. Nicolay and John Hay. New York: The Century Company.

Lincoln, Yvonna, and Egon Guba. 1985. *Naturalistic Inquiry.* Beverly Hills: Sage Publications.

Littlefield, Alice, Leonard Lieberman, and Larry Reynolds. 1982. "Redefining Race: The Potential Demise of a Concept in Physical Anthropology." *Current Anthropology* 23, 6: 641–56.

Lloyd, Genevieve. 1984. *The Men of Reason: "Male" and "Female" in Western Philsophy.* London: Methuen.

Locke, John. [1690] 1979. *An Essay Concerning Human Understanding.* New York: Oxford University Press.

Locke, John. [1693] 1979. *Treatise of Civil Government* and *A Letter Concerning Toleration.* New York: Irvington.

Locke, John. [1693] 1989. *Some Thoughts Concerning Education.* New York: Oxford University Press.

Lord, Albert Bates. 1960. *The Singer of Tales.* Cambridge: Harvard University Press.

Lovejoy, Arthur. 1936. *The Great Chain of Being.* Cambridge: Harvard University Press.

Lovejoy, Owen. 1981. "The Origins of Man." *Science* 211: 341–50.

Lowe, Graham. 1989. *Women, Paid/Unpaid Work and Stress: New Direction for Research.* Ottawa: Canadian Advisory Council on the Status of Women.

Lukes, Steven. 1985. *Emile Durkheim: His Life and Work: A Historical and Critical Study.* Stanford: Stanford University Press.

Lynn, D.B. 1969. *Parental and Sex Role Identification: A Theoretical Formulation.* Berkeley: McCutchan.

Lyotard, Jean-François. 1984. *The Postmodern Condition: A Report on Knowledge.* Translation from the French by Geoff Bennington and Brian Massumi. Minneapolis: University of Minnesota Press.

Lyotard, Jean-François. 1994. *The Postmodern Condition.* Minneapolis: University of Minnesota Press.

Maccoby, Eleanor. 1980. *Social Development: Psychological Growth and the Parent-Child Relationship.* New York: Harcourt Brace Jovanovich.

Maccoby, Eleanor, and Carol Jacklin. 1974. *The Psychology of Sex Differences*. Stanford: Stanford University Press.

MacMurchy, Helen. 1908. *Report upon the Care of the Feeble-Minded in Ontario*. Toronto: L.K. Cameron.

Madonna. 1985. *Madonna: Close up and Personal*. London: Rock Photo Publications.

Malinowski, Bronislaw. [1925] 1954. *Magic, Science and Religion*. Garden City, N.Y.: Doubleday.

Malson, Lucien. 1964. *Les enfants sauvages: mythe et réalité*. Paris: Union generale d'éditions.

Marx, Karl. 1961. *Economic and Philosophic Manuscripts of 1844*. Moscow: Foreign Languages Publishing House.

Marx, Karl. 1967. *Capital: A Critique of Political Economy*, 3 volumes, facsimiles. Edited by Friedrich Engels. New York: International Publishers.

Marx, Karl. 1971. *The Grundisse*, first American edition. New York: Harper & Row.

Marx, Karl. [1859] 1971. *A Contribution to the Critique of Political Economy*. London: Lawrence & Wishart.

Marx, Karl, and Friedrich Engels. 1962(a). "Preface to *A Contribution to the Critique of Political Economy*." In *Selected Works*, volume 1. Moscow: Foreign Languages Publishing House.

Marx, Karl, and Friedrich Engels. [1848] 1962(b). *The Manifesto of the Communist Party*. Moscow: Progress Publishers.

Marx, Karl, and Friedrich Engels. 1985. *Communist Manifesto*, translated by Samuel Moore. Harmondsworth, England: Penguin Books.

Mathews, B. 1985. *Multiple Sclerosis: The Facts*, second edition. Oxford: Oxford University Press.

Mazlish, Bruce. 1993. *A New Science: The Breakdown of Connections and the Birth of Sociology*. Philadelphia: Pennsylvania State University Press.

McAllister, Matthew Paul. 1990. "Cultural Argument and Organizational Constraint in the Comic Book Industry." *Journal of Communication* 40, 1 (Winter): 57–65.

McCormick, Thelma. 1993. "TV and the Child Savers: Bad Habits and the Boob Tube." *The Canadian Forum* (November): 20–22.

McCormick, Thelma. 1994. "Codes, Ratings and Rights," unpublished ms.

McLuhan, Marshall. 1964. *Understanding Media: The Extensions of Man*. New York: New American Library.

McMullan, J. 1992. *Beyond the Limits of the Law: Corporate Crime and Law and Order*. Halifax: Fernwood Publishing.

McNall, Scott, Rhonda Levine, and Rick Fantasia (eds.). 1991. *Bringing Class Back In: Contemporary and Historical Perspectives*. Boulder: Westview Press.

Mead, George Herbert. [1934] 1967. *Mind, Self, and Society : From the Standpoint of a Social Behaviorist*. Chicago: University of Chicago Press.

Mead, Margaret. [1928] 1959. *Coming of Age in Samoa: A Psychological Study of Primitive Youth for Western Civilization*. New York: New American Library.

Mead, Margaret. 1961. "Cultural Determinants of Sexual Behaviour." In *Sex and Internal Secretions*, edited by William C. Young. Baltimore: Williams & Wilkins.

Mead, Margaret. [1935] 1963. *Sex and Temperament in Three Primitive Societies*. New York: William Morrow.

Meehan, Eileen. 1991. In *The Many Lives of the Batman: Critical Approaches to a Superhero and His Media,* edited by Roberta Pearson and William Uricchio. New York: Routledge.

Meissner, Martin, Elizabeth Humphreys, Scott Meis, and William Scheu. 1975. "No Exit for Wives: Sexual Division of Labour and the Culmination of Household Demands." *Canadian Review of Sociology and Anthropology* 12, 4, Part 1 (November).

Merton, Robert K. 1968. *Social Theory and Social Structure.* New York: Free Press.

Messner, Steven. 1986. "Television Violence and Violent Crime: An Aggregate Analysis." *Social Problems* 33, 3 (February): 218–35.

Michelson, William. 1989. "Divergent Convergence: The Daily Routines of Employed Spouses as a Public Affairs Agenda." In *Life Spaces,* edited by Caroline Andrew and Beth Morre Milroy. Vancouver: University of British Columbia Press.

Midgley, Mary. 1992. *Science as Salvation: A Modern Myth and Its Meaning.* London: Routledge.

Mies, Maria. 1983. "Toward a Methodology for Feminist Research." In *Theories of Women's Studies,* edited by G. Bowles and R. Dueilli Klein. London: Routledge & Kegan Paul.

Miller, Frank. 1986. *Batman: The Dark Knight Returns.* New York: D.C. Comics.

Miller, J. Hillis. 1981. "The Disarticulation of the Self in Nietzche." In *The Monist* 64 (April): 247–61.

Millett, Kate. 1970. *Sexual Politics.* Garden City, N.Y.: Doubleday.

Mills, C. Wright. 1959. *The Sociological Imagination.* New York: Oxford University Press.

Miner, Horace. 1956. "Body Image Among the Nacirema." *American Anthropologist* 58: 503–7.

Mischel, W. 1966. "A Social Learning View of Sex Differences in Behaviour." In *The Development of Sex Differences,* edited by Eleanor Maccoby. Stanford: Stanford University Press.

Money, John. 1974. "Psychological Consideration of Sex Assignment in Intersexuality." *Clinics in Plastic Surgery* 1, (April).

Money, John. 1988. *Gay, Straight, and In-between.* New York: Oxford University Press.

Money, John, and Anke Ehrhardt. 1972. *Man and Woman, Boy and Girl.* Baltimore: Johns Hopkins University Press.

Money, John, J.G. Hampson, and J.L. Hampson. 1955. "Hermaphroditism: Recommendations Concerning Assignment of Sex, Change of Sex and Psychological Management." *Bulletin of the Johns Hopkins Hospital* 97: 284–300.

Montesquieu, Charles de Secondat, Baron de. [1748] 1989. *The Spirit of the Laws.* Cambridge: Cambridge University Press.

Moore, Alan, and Brian Bollard. 1988. *The Killing Joke.* New York: D.C. Comics.

Morely, David. 1980. *The "Nationwide" Audience: Structure and Decoding.* London: British Film Institute.

Morely, David. 1981. "The Nationwide Audience: A Critical Postscript." *Screen Education* 39: 3–14.

Mussen, P.H. (ed.). 1983. *Handbook of Child Psychology.* New York: Wiley.

Myers, B.J. 1984. "Mother-Infant Bonding: The Status of this Critical-Period Hypothesis." *Developmental Review* 4: 240–74.

Nachbar, Jack, and Kevin Lause. 1992. *Popular Culture: An Introductory Text.* Bowling Green, Ohio: Bowling Green State University Popular Press.

Nation, Joseph. E. (ed.). 1992. *The De-escalation of Nuclear Crises.* London: Macmillan.

National Council of Welfare. 1990. *Women and Poverty Revisited.* Ottawa: Ministry of Supply and Services.

Nel, M., and A.K. Roychoudhurdy. 1972. *"Gene Differences Between Caucasian, Negro and Japanese Populations."* Science 177, 4: 434–35.

Newton, Isaac, Sir. 1953. *Newton's Philosophy of Nature: Selections from His Writings.* New York: Hafner Publications.

Nielsen, Joyce McCarl (ed.). 1990. *Feminist Research Methods: Exemplary Readings in the Social Sciences.* Boulder: Westview Press.

Nisbet, Robert. 1966. *The Sociological Tradition.* New York: Basic Books.

Nordenfelt, Lennart. 1992. *On the Notions of Disability and Handicap.* Monograph. Sweden: University of Linköping.

Nott, J.C., and G.R. Gliddon. 1854. *Types of Mankind.* Philadelphia: Lippincott, Grambo and Company.

Oakely, Anne. 1982. *Subject Women.* London: Fontana.

Oakley, Kenneth Page. 1966. *The Problem of Man's Antiquity: An Historical Survey.* New York: Johnson Reprint Corp.

Oliver, Michael. 1988. "The Political Context of Education Decision Making: The Case of Special Needs." In *The Politics of Special Needs,* edited by L. Barton. London: Falmer.

Oliver, Michael. 1990. *The Politics of Disablement.* London: Macmillan.

Ornstein, Michael, and Tony Haddad. 1991. *About Time: Analysis of a 1986 Survey of Canadians.* North York: Institute for Social Research, York University.

Outlaw, Lucius. 1990. "Toward a Critical Theory of 'Race'." In *The Anatomy of Racism,* edited by David Theo Goldberg. Minneapolis: University of Minnesota Press.

Padden, Carol, and Tom Humphries. 1988. *Deaf in America: Voices from a Culture.* Cambridge: Harvard University Press.

Papert, Seymor. 1980. *Mindstorms: Children, Computers, and Powerful Ideas.* New York: Basic Books.

Park, Peter. 1988. "Something I Would Like to Forget." *The Language of Pain.* Toronto: Roeher Institute.

Parkin, Frank. 1979. *Marxism and Class Theory: A Bourgeois Critique.* London: Tavistock.

Parkin, Frank. 1982. *Max Weber.* New York: Tavistock Publications.

Parsons, Patrick. 1991. "Batman and His Audience: The Dialectic of Culture." In *The Many Lives of the Batman: Critical Approaches to a Superhero and His Media,* edited by Roberta Pearson and William Uricchio. New York: Routledge.

Parsons, Talcott. 1951. *The Social System.* Glencoe, Ill.: Free Press.

Parsons, Talcott. 1955. "The American Family: Its Relations to Personality and to the Social Structure." In *Family, Socialization and Interaction Processes,* edited by Talcott Parsons and Robert F. Bales. Glencoe, Ill.: Free Press.

Parsons, Talcott. 1964. "Introduction" to *The Theory of Social and Economic Organization,* by Max Weber. Translated by A.M. Henderson and Talcott Parsons. Boston: Beacon Press.

Paul, Richard. 1990. *Critical Thinking: What Every Person Needs to Survive in a Rapidly Changing World.* Rohnert Park, Calif.: Sonoma State University.

Pearl, Raymond. 1908. "Breeding Better Men." *Worlds Work* 15.

Pearson, Roberta, and William Uricchio. 1991. *The Many Lives of the Batman: Critical Approaches to a Superhero and His Media.* New York: Routledge.

Pearson, Roger. 1991. *Race, Intelligence and Bias in Academe.* Washington: Scott-Townsend.

Pilbeam, David. 1980. "Current Arguments on Early Man." In *Major Trends in Human Evolution,* edited by L.K. Konigson. New York: Pergamon Press.

Plotnikoff, David. 1994. "Why Men Are Hogging the Digital Highway." *The Toronto Star* (August 24): E–4.

Polanyi, Karl. 1966. *Dahomey and the Slave Trade.* Seattle: Washington University Press.

Polkinghorne, Donald. 1988. *Narrative Knowing and the Human Sciences.* University of New York Press.

Popper, Karl R. [1902] 1961. *The Logic of Scientific Discovery.* Translation prepared by the author with the assistance of Julius Freed and Ian Freed. New York: Basic Books.

Popper, Karl R. 1969. *Conjectures and Refutations: The Growth of Scientific Knowledge,* third edition. London: Routledge & Kegan Paul.

Porter, John. 1965. *The Vertical Mosaic: An Analysis of Social Class and Power in Canada.* Toronto: University of Toronto Press.

Porter, Theodore. 1986. *The Rise of Statistical Thinking.* Princeton: Princeton University Press.

Poster, Mark. 1990. *The Mode of Information: Poststructuralism and Social Context.* Chicago: University of Chicago Press.

Postman, Neil. 1992. *Technopoly: The Surrender of Culture to Technology.* New York: Knopf.

Poulantzas, Nicos. 1975. *Classes in Contemporary Capitalism.* London: New Left Books.

Powell, Thomas. 1992. *The Persistence of Racism in America.* Lanham, Md.: University Press of America.

Quittner, Josh. 1994. "Johnny Manhattan Meets the Furry Muchers." *Wired* 2 (March): 92–97, 138.

Radway, Janice. 1984. *Reading the Romance.* Chapel Hill: University of North Carolina Press.

Reasons, C., L. Ross, and C. Patterson. 1991. "Your Money or Your Life: Workers' Health in Canada." *The Social Basis of Law,* second edition, edited by E. Comack and S. Brickey. Toronto: Garamond.

Rex, John. 1970. *Race Relations in Sociological Theory.* New York: Schocken Books.

Rheingold, Howard. 1991. *Virtual Reality.* New York: Summit Books.

Rheingold, Howard. 1993(a). "A Slice of Life in My Virtual Community." In *Global Networks: Computers and International Communication,* edited by Linda Harasim. Cambridge: MIT Press.

Rheingold, Howard. 1993(b). *The Virtual Community: Homesteading on the Electronic Frontier.* Reading, Mass.: Addison-Wesley.

Rich, Adrienne. 1976. *Of Woman Born: Motherhood as Experience and Institution.* New York: Norton.

Richards, Graham. 1987. *Human Evolution: An Introduction for the Behavioural Sciences.* London: Routledge & Kegan Paul.

Richardson, L.W. 1981. The *Dynamics of Sex and Gender.* Boston: Houghton Mifflin.

Ricoeur, P. 1970. *Freud and Philosophy: An Essay on Interpretation.* New Haven: Yale University Press.

Riel, Margaret. 1993. "Global Education through Learning Circles." In *Global Networks: Computers and International Communication,* edited by Linda Harasim. Cambridge: MIT Press.

Ritzer, George. 1992. *Sociological Theory,* third edition. New York: McGraw-Hill.

Roediger, David. 1994. *Towards the Abolition of Whiteness.* London: Verso.

Romm, Norma R.A. 1991. *The Methodologies of Positivism and Marxism: A Sociological Debate.* Basingstoke: Macmillan.

Rorty, Richard. 1991. *Objectivity, Relativism, and Truth.* Cambridge: Cambridge University Press.

Roscoe, Will. 1987. "Bibliography of Berdache and Alternative Gender Roles Among North American Indians." *Journal of Homosexuality* 14: 3–4.

Roscoe, Will. 1994. "How to Become a Berdache: Toward a Unified Analysis of Gender Diversity." In *Third Sex; Third Gender,* edited by Gilbert Herdt. New York: Zone Books.

Rosenau, Pauline Marie. 1992. *Post-Modernism and the Social Sciences: Insights, Inroads and Intrusions.* Princeton, N.J.: Princeton University Press.

Rosenblatt, J.S. 1967. "Non-hormonal Basis of Maternal Behaviour in the Rat." *Science* 156: 1512–13.

Rosenblatt, J.S., and H.I. Siegel. 1981. "Factors Governing the Onset and Maintenance of Maternal Behaviour Among Nonprimate Animals: The Role of Hormonal and Nonhormonal Factors." In *Parental Care in Mammals,* edited by D.J. Gubernick and P.H. Klopfer. New York: Plenum.

Ross, Andrew. 1993. *"This Bridge Called My Pussy."* In *Madonnarama,* edited by Lisa Frank and Paul Smith. Pittsburgh: Cleis Press.

Rousseau, Jean-Jacques. [1962] 1974. *Emile.* London: Dent.

Roychoudhury, A.K. *Human Polymorphic Genes: World Distribution.* New York: Oxford University Press.

Rubin, J.Z., F.J. Provenzano, and Z. Luria. 1974. "The Eye of the Beholder: Parents' Views on Sex of Newborns." *American Journal of Orthopsychiatry* 44: 512–19.

Rudé, George. 1959. *The Crowd in the French Revolution.* London: Oxford University Press.

Rushton, Philippe. 1988. "Race Differences in Behaviour: A Review and Evolutionary Analysis." In *Personality and Individual Differences* 9: 1009–24.

Rymer, Russ. 1992. *New Yorker* (April 13): 41–81.

Russell, Susan. 1989. "From Disability to Handicap: An Inevitable Response to Social Constraints?" *Canadian Review of Sociology & Anthropology* 26, 2: 276–93.

Ryan, Michael. 1988. "Postmodern Politics." In *Theory, Culture, and Society* 5, 2-3: 559–76.

Ryave, A. Lincoln, and James N. Schenkein. 1972. "Notes on the Art of Walking." In *Ethnomethodology: Selected Readings,* edited by R. Turner, 265–75. Harmondsworth, England: Penguin.

Sadker, Myra P., and David M. Sadker. 1988. *Teachers, Schools, and Society.* New York: Random House.

Saint-Simon, Henri, Comte de. 1975. *Henri Saint-Simon (1970-1825): Selected Writings on Science, Industry, and Social Organization,* translated and edited by Keith Taylor. London: Croom Helm.

Salmon, E.D., and B.W. Robinson. 1987. "Doing What Comes Naturally? Theories on the

Acquisition of Gender." In *Gender Roles: Doing What Comes Naturally*, edited by E.D. Salmon and B.W. Robinson. Toronto: Methuen.

Samuelson, Les. 1994. "Crime as a Social Problem: From Definition to Reality." In *Power and Resistance: Critical Thinking About Canadian Social Issues,* edited by Les Samuelson. Halifax: Fernwood Publishing.

Santrack, John W. 1983. *Life-Span Development.* Dubuque, Iowa: William C. Brown.

Saussure, Ferdinand de. [1916] 1964. *Course in General Linguistics.* London: P. Owen.

Savage, Mike. 1992. *Property, Bureaucracy and Culture: Middle-Class Formation in Contemporary Britain.* London: Routledge.

Scarr, Sandra. 1984. *Mother Care, Other Care.* New York: Basic Books.

Scheerenberger, R.C. 1983. *The History of Mental Retardation.* Baltimore: Paul H. Brooks.

Scherpe, Klaus. 1986–87. "Dramatization and De-dramatization of 'The End': The Apocalyptic Consciousness of Modernity and Post-Modernity." In *Cultural Critique,* No. 5 (Winter): 95–129.

Schiebinger, Londa. 1989. *The Mind Has No Sex? Women in the Origins of Modern Science.* Cambridge: Harvard University Press.

Schroyer, Trent. 1973. *The Critique of Domination: The Origins and Development of Critical Theory.* New York: G. Braziller.

Schumacher, Sally, and James H. McMillan. 1993. *Research in Education,* third edition. New York: HarperCollins.

Schutz, Alfred. 1967. *The Phenomenology of the Social World,* translated by George Walsh and Frederick Lehnert. Evanston, Ill.: Northwestern University Press.

Scott, R. 1969. *The Making of Blind Men.* New York: Russell Sage Foundation.

Shanklin, Eugenia. 1994. *Anthropology and Race.* Belmont, Calif.: Wadsworth Publishing Company.

Shapiro, Joseph P. 1993. *No Pity: People With Disabilities Forging a New Civil Rights Movement.* Toronto: Times Books/Random House.

Shattuck, Roger. 1980. *The Forbidden Experiment: The Story of the Wild Boy of Aveyron.* New York: Farrar, Straus and Giroux.

Shaver, P., and C. Hendrick (eds.). *Sex and Gender.* Newbury Park, Calif.: Sage Publications.

Sheets-Johnstone, Maxine. 1990. *The Roots of Thinking.* Philadelphia: Temple University Press.

Shibley-Hyde, J. 1985. *Half the Human Experience,* second edition, Toronto: D.C. Heath.

Shkilnyk, Anastasia. 1985. *A Poison Stronger Than Love.* New Haven: Yale University Press.

Shotter, John. 1993. *Cultural Politics of Everyday Life: Social Constructionism, Rhetoric and Knowing of the Third Kind.* Toronto: University of Toronto Press.

Simmons, H. 1982. *From Asylum to Welfare.* Toronto: National Institute of Mental Retardation.

Simon, Robin, Donna Eder, and Cathy Evans. 1992. "The Development of Feeling Norms Underlying Romantic Love Among Adolescent Females." *Social Psychology Quarterly* 55 (March): 29–46.

Sinclair, Peter R., and Lawrence F. Felt. 1992. "Separate Worlds: Gender and Domestic Labour in an Isolated Fishing Region." *Canadian Review of Sociology and Anthropology* 29, 1 (February): 55–71.

Singer, I. 1987. *The Nature of Love,* volume 3 of *The Modern World.* Chicago: University of Chicago Press.

503

Singh, J.A.L., and R.M. Zinng, 1939. *Wolf-Children and Feral Men*. New York: Harper.

Smedely, Audrey. 1993. *Race in North America: Origin and Evolution of a World View*. Boulder: Westview Press.

Smith, Charles Hamilton. 1848. *The Natural History of the Human Species*. Edinburgh: W.H. Lizars.

Smith, Dorothy. 1979. "A Peculiar Eclipse: Women's Exclusion from Men's Culture." In *Women's Studies International Quarterly* 1: 281–95.

Smith, Dorothy. 1990. *The Conceptual Practices of Power: A Feminist Sociology of Knowledge*. Toronto: University of Toronto Press.

Smith, Paul. 1988. *Discerning the Subject*. Minneapolis: University of Minnesota Press.

Snider, Laureen. 1993. *Bad Business: Corporate Crime in Canada*. Toronto: Nelson.

Spelman, Elizabeth V. 1990. *Inessential Woman: Problems of Exclusion in Feminist Thought*. London: Women's Press.

Spence, Janet T. 1984. "Masculinity, Femininity, and Gender-Related Traits: A Conceptual Analysis and Critique of Current Research." *Progress in Experimental Personality Research* 13: 84.

Spencer, Metta. 1992. *Foundations of Modern Sociology*. Scarborough: Prentice-Hall Canada.

Spiegelberg, Herbert. 1982. *The Phenomenological Movement,* third edition. Netherlands: Martinus Nijhoff.

Spier, Leslie. 1959. "Some Central Elements in the Legacy." *American Anthropological Association Memoirs* 61, 89.

Steinbacher, R., and F. Gilroy. 1990. "Sex Selection Technology: A Prediction of Its Use and Effect." *Journal of Psychology* 124: 283–88.

Steinbacher, R., and H.B. Holmes 1987. "Sex Choice: Survival and Sisterhood. In *Man-Made Women: How New Reproductive Technologies Affect Women,* edited by G. Corea et al. Bloomington: Indiana University Press.

Stern, Daniel N. 1977. *The First Relationship: Mother and Infant*. Cambridge: Harvard University Press.

Stern, Daniel N. 1985. *The Interpersonal World of the Infant: A View from Psychoanalysis and Developmental Psychology*. New York: Basic Books.

Stevens, S. 1991. "Aboriginal People and the Canadian Justice System." In *Criminal Justice: Sentencing Issues and Reform,* edited by L. Samuelson and B. Schissel. Toronto: Garamond.

Stocking, George W. 1968. *Race, Culture and Evolution: Essays in the History of Evolution*. New York: Free Press.

Stone, Allucquere Rosanne. 1992. "Will the Real Body Please Stand Up? Boundary Stories About Virtual Cultures." In *Cyberspace: First Steps,* edited by Michael Benedikt. Cambridge: MIT Press.

Stone, Deborah. 1984. *The Disabled State*. New York: Macmillan.

Sullivan, Edmund. 1984. *A Critical Psychology: Interpretation of the Personal World*. New York: Plenum Press.

Sumner, William Graham. 1907. *Folkways: A Study of the Sociological Importance of Usages, Manners, Customs, Mores and Morals*. Boston: Ginn.

Swidler, Ann. 1980. "Love and Adulthood in American Culture." In *Themes of Work and Love in Adulthood,* edited by Neil Smelser and Erik Erikson, 120–47. Cambridge: Harvard University Press.

Swingewood, Alan. 1984. *A Short History of Sociological Thought*. London: Macmillan.

Talaska, Richard A. (ed). 1992. *Critical Reasoning in Contemporary Culture*. Albany: State University of New York Press.

Tanner, Nancy M. 1981. *On Becoming Human*. Cambridge: Cambridge University Press.

Tanner, Nancy M., and Adrienne Zihlman. 1976. "Women in Evolution, Part I: Innovation and Selection in Human Origins." *Signs* 1, 3: 585–608.

Task Force on Aboriginal Peoples in Federal Corrections. 1988. *Final Report*. Ottawa: Minister of Supply and Services.

Taylor, Steven J., and Robert Bogdan. 1984. *Introduction to Qualitative Research Methods: The Search for Meaning*. New York: John Wiley & Sons.

Tepperman, Lorne, and R. Jack Richardson. 1986. *An Introduction to the Social World*. Toronto: McGraw-Hill Ryerson.

Terman, L.M. 1938. *Psychological Factors in Marital Happiness*. New York: McGraw-Hill.

Thomas, David. 1992. "Old Rituals for New Space: Rites of Passage and William Gibson's Cultural Model of Cyberspace." In *Cyberspace: First Steps*, edited by Michael Benedikt. Cambridge: MIT Press.

Thomas, W.I. [1923] 1967. *The Unadjusted Girl*. New York: Harper & Row.

Thomas, W.I., and Florian Znaniecki. 1958. *The Polish Peasant in Europe and America*. New York: Dover Publications.

Thompson, E.P. 1963. *The Making of the English Working Class*. London: V. Gollancz.

Thompson, S.K., and P.M. Bentler. 1971. "The Priority of Cues in Sex Discrimination by Children and Adults." *Developmental Psychology* 5: 181–85.

Tobias, P.V. 1970. "Brain-size, Grey Matter and Race – Fact or Fiction?" *American Journal of Physical Anthropology* 32: 325–84.

Todorov, Tzvetan. 1993. *On Human Diversity*. Cambridge: Harvard University Press.

Traweek, Sharon. 1988. *Beamtimes and LifeTimes: The World of High Energy Physics*. Cambridge: Harvard University Press.

Trevarthen, Colin. 1977. "Descriptive Analyses of Infant Communicative Behavior." In *Studies in Mother-Infant Interaction*, edited by H.R. Schaffer. London: Academic Press.

Trevarthen, Colin. 1980. "The Foundation of Intersubjectivity: Development of Interpersonal and Cooperative Understanding in Infants." In *The Social Foundation of Language and Thought: Essays in Honor of Jerome Bruner*, edited by M. Bullova. New York: Cambridge University Press.

Tumin, Melvin. 1970. *Readings on Social Stratification*. Englewood Cliffs, N.J.: Prentice-Hall.

Turkle, Sherry. 1984. *The Second Self: Computers and the Human Spirit*. New York: Simon and Schuster.

Tylor, E.B. [1871] 1903. *Primitive Culture: Researches into the Development of Mythology, Philosophy, Religion, Language, Art, and Custom*. London: J. Murray.

Tylor, E.B. [1881] 1946. *Anthropology*. London: Watts.

UNESCO Statement on Race and Racial Prejudice. 1967. Reprinted in *Race, Science and Society*, edited by Leo Kuper. Paris: The UNESCO Press, 1975.

Valverde, Mariana. 1991. *The Age of Light, Soap, and Water*. Toronto: McClelland & Stewart.

Van der Meer, Theo. 1994. "Sodomy and the Pursuit of a Third Sex in the Early Modern Period." In *Third Sex, Third Gender*, edited by Gilbert Herdt. New York: Zone Books.

Vanek, J. 1994. "Time Spent in Housework." *Scientific American* 231, 5 (November): 116–20.

505

Vanier, Jean. 1971. *Eruption to Hope.* Toronto: Griffin House.

Vattimo, Gianni. 1988. *End of Modernity: Nihilism and Hermeneutics in Postmodern Culture,* translated by Jon R. Snyder. Baltimore: Johns Hopkins University Press.

Verdun-Jones, S., and G. Muirhead. 1982. "The Native in the Criminal Justice System: Canadian Research." In *The Canadian Criminal Justice System,* edited by C.L. Boydell and I. Connidis. Toronto: Holt, Rinehart and Winston.

Vico, Giambattista. [1744] 1948. *The New Science of Giambattista Vico,* unabridged translation of the third edition. Ithaca, N.Y.: Cornell University Press.

Visser, Margaret. 1986. *Much Depends on Dinner: The Extraordinary History and Mythology, Allure and Obsessions, Perils and Taboos of an Ordinary Meal.* Toronto: McClelland & Stewart.

Vogt, Carl. 1864. *Lectures on Man.* London: n.p.

Vygotsky, L.S. 1978. *Mind and Society: The Development of Higher Psychological Processes.* Cambridge: Harvard University Press.

Walby, Sylvia. 1990. *Theorizing Patriarchy.* Oxford: Basil Blackwell.

Walker, Helen Mary. 1929. *Studies in the History of Statistical Method, with Special Reference to Certain Educational Problems.* Baltimore: Williams and Wilkins.

Waller, W. 1937. "The Rating and Dating Complex." In *American Sociological Review* 2: 727–34.

Waller, W. 1951. *The Family: A Dynamic Interpretation.* New York: Dryden.

Washburn, Sherwood, 1978. "Human Behavior and the Behavior of Other Animals." *American Psychologist* 33: 405–18.

Washburn, Sherwood, and Virginia Avis. 1958. "The Evolution of Human Behavior." In *Behavior and Evolution,* edited by Anne Roe and George Gaylord Simpson. New Haven: Yale University Press.

Washburn, Sherwood, and David Hamburg. 1965. "The Implications of Primate Research." In *Primate Behaviour,* edited by I. de Vore. New York: Holt, Rinehart and Winston.

Watson, John Broadus. [1925] 1970. *Behaviorism.* New York: W.W. Norton.

Weber, Max. 1949. "'Objectivity' in Social Science and Social Policy." In *The Methodology of the Social Sciences,* translated and edited by Edward A. Shils and Henry A. Finch. New York: Free Press of Glencoe.

Weber, Max. 1964. *The Theory of Social and Economic Organization,* first American edition. Translated by A.M. Henderson and Talcott Parsons. New York: Free Press.

Weber, Max. 1968. *Economy and Society: An Outline Of Interpretive Sociology,* edited by Guenther Roth and Claus Wittich, and translated by Ephraim Fischoff et al. New York: Bedminster Press.

Weber, Max. 1978. *Economy and Society: An Outline of Interpretive Sociology,* edited by Guenther Roth and Claus Wittich. Berkeley: University of California Press.

Wechsler, David. 1949. Wechsler Intelligence Scale for Children. New York: The Psychological Incorporation.

Weeks, Jeffery. 1985. *Sexuality and Its Discontents.* Boston: Routledge & Kegan Paul.

Weiss, D., et al (eds.). 1976. *The World Encyclopedia of Comics.* New York: Chelsea House Publishers.

Wertham, Fredric. 1949. *The Show of Violence.* Garden City, N.Y.: Doubleday.

Wertham, Fredric. 1954. *Seduction of the Innocent.* Port Washington, N.Y.: Kennikat Press.

Westfall, Richard S. 1993. *The Life of Isaac Newton*. Cambridge: Cambridge University Press.

Westman, Robert. 1975. *The Copernican Achievement*. Berkeley: University of California Press.

Wheeler, William M. [1939] 1966. *Essays in Philosophical Biology*. Cambridge: Harvard University Press.

Whiteford, Michael, and John Friedl. 1992. *The Human Portrait: Introduction to Cultural Anthropology*. Englewood Cliffs, N.J.: Prentice-Hall.

Whiting, B.B., and C.P. Edwards. 1988. *Children of Different Worlds: The Formation of Social Behaviour*. Cambridge: Harvard University Press.

Wilkinson, Derek. 1993. "Change in Household Division of Labour Following Unemployment in Elliot Lake." Paper presented at Learned Societies meetings, CSAA, Charlottetown, PEI, 1992, and cited in Armstrong and Armstrong, 1993, 79.

Williams, Raymond. 1976. *Keywords: A Vocabulary of Culture and Society*. New York: Oxford University Press.

Willis, Paul E. 1977. *Learning to Labor: How Working Class Kids Get Working Class Jobs*. New York: Columbia University Press.

Wilson, Edward O. 1975. *Sociobiology: The New Synthesis*. Cambridge: Belknap Press of Harvard University Press.

Wilson, Edward O., and George F. Oster. 1978. *Caste and Ecology in the Social Insects*. Princeton, N.J.: Princeton University Press.

Wilson, Logan, and William Kolb. 1949. *Sociological Analysis: An Introductory Text and Case Book*. New York: Harcourt Brace.

Wirth, Lewis. 1928. *The Ghetto*. Chicago: University of Chicago Press.

Wollstonecraft, Mary. [1792] 1985. *A Vindication of the Rights of Women*. London: Dent.

Wood, Ellen Meiksins. 1986. *The Retreat from Class: A New "True" Socialism*. London: Verso.

Woodill, G. 1994. "The Social Semiotics of Disability." In *Disability Is Not Measles: New Research Paradigms on Disability*, edited by M. Rioux and M. Bach. Toronto: G.A. Roeher Institute.

Worsley, Peter. 1982. *Marx and Marxism*. London: Tavistock Publications.

Wright, Erik Olin. 1994. *Interrogating Inequality: Essays on Class Analysis, Socialism, and Marxism*. New York: Verso.

Wynne, G. 1990. "Leisure, Lifestyle and the Construction of Social Position." In *Leisure Studies* 9: 21–34D.

Yanagisako, Sylvia J., and Jane F. Collier. 1990. "The Mode of Reproduction in Anthropology." In *Theoretical Perspectives on Sexual Difference*, edited by Deborah Rhode. New Haven: Yale University Press.

York, Geoffrey. 1990. *The Dispossessed: Life and Death in Native Canada*. Toronto: Little, Brown and Company.

Zeitlin, Irving. 1984. *The Social Condition of Humanity*. Cambridge: Oxford University Press.

Zeitlin, Irving M., and Robert Brym. 1991. *The Social Condition of Humanity*, Canadian edition. Toronto: Oxford University Press.

Zola, Irving Kenneth. 1993. "Self, Identity and the Naming Question: Reflections on the Language of Disability." In *Perspectives on Disability*, second edition, edited by Mark Nagler. Palo Alto: Health Markets Research.

507

INDEX
∎∎∎

517

COPYRIGHT ACKNOWLEDGMENTS
■ ■ ■

519

PHOTO CREDITS
■ ■ ■

Chapter 11 The Granger Collection, New York, 216, 218; Culver Pictures, 221, 223; The Granger Collection, New York, 228, 230; The Bettmann Archive, 233.

Chapter 12 The Bettmann Archive, 240, 241 (t. and b.), 250, 253, 254, 263.

Chapter 13 The Bettmann Archive, 277, 278; (Chicago Art Institute)/ Visual Arts Library, 280; Dick Hemingway: Photographs, 283; Earl Dotter, 295.

Chapter 14 The Bettmann Archive, 306; Provincial Archives of Manitoba/N12299, 308; The Bettmann Archive, 312; The Granger Collection, New York, 314, 323.

Chapter 15 The Bettmann Archive, 329, 331; Cytogenetic Laboratory, Oshawa General Hospital, 336; The Bettmann Archive, 347, 351.

Chapter 16 The Bettmann Archive, 360; Earl Dotter, 362; The Bettmann Archive, 369; Craig/Robertson/Canada Wide, 372.

Chapter 17 The Kobal Collection, 382; The Bettmann Archive, 384, 390; Canada Wide, 395; Earl Dotter, 400.

Chapter 18 Zoran Milich, 404; The Bettmann Archive, 413, 416; W. Phillips/Canapress, 424; The Bettmann Archive, 427.

Chapter 19 Erin Mills Town Centre, 435; NBC-TV (The Kobal Collection), 440; Warner Brothers (The Kobal Collection), 443; The Bettmann Archive, 447.

Chapter 20 M. McKee, photo #02SS73649, 455; Dick Hemingway: Photographs, 458; Compuserve, 463; MaryAnn Nilsson, 465.

To the owner of this book

We hope that you have enjoyed *Sociology: A Critical Introduction,* and we would like to know as much about your experiences with this text as you would care to offer. Only through your comments and those of others can we learn how to make this a better text for future readers.

School _____ Your instructor's name _____

Course _____ Was the text required? _____ Recommended? _____

1. What did you like the most about *Sociology: A Critical Introduction?*

_____

_____

_____

2. How useful was this text for your course?

_____

_____

_____

3. Do you have any recommendations for ways to improve the next edition of this text?

_____

_____

_____

4. In the space below or in a separate letter, please write any other comments you have about the book. (For example, please feel free to comment on reading level, writing style, terminology, design features, and learning aids.)

_____

_____

_____

_____

Optional

Your name _____ Date _____

May Nelson Canada quote you, either in promotion for *Sociology: A Critical Introduction* or in future publishing ventures?

Yes _____   No _____

Thanks!

FOLD HERE

MAIL ⮞ POSTE

Canada Post Corporation / Société canadienne des postes

Postage paid
if mailed in Canada

Port payé
si posté au Canada

Business Reply

Réponse d'affaires

0107077099 **01**

TAPE SHUT

TAPE SHUT

Nelson

0107077099-M1K5G4-BR01

Nelson Canada
College Editorial Department
1120 Birchmount Rd.
Scarborough, ON M1K 9Z9

PLEASE TAPE SHUT. DO NOT STAPLE.